RABBINIC LITERATURE
AND
GOSPEL TEACHINGS

THE LIBRARY

OF

BIBLICAL STUDIES

Edited by

Harry M. Orlinsky

RABBINIC LITERATURE
AND
GOSPEL TEACHINGS

BY

C. G. MONTEFIORE
HON. D.LITT. (OXFORD), HON. D.D. (MANCHESTER)

PROLEGOMENON BY
EUGENE MIHALY

KTAV PUBLISHING HOUSE, Inc.

NEW YORK

1970

FIRST PUBLISHED 1930

NEW MATTER
© COPYRIGHT 1970
KTAV PUBLISHING HOUSE, INC.

226
M76N
73118
Jan., 1971

SBN 87068-088-9

MANUFACTURED IN THE UNITED STATES OF AMERICA
LIBRARY OF CONGRESS CATALOG CARD NO. 68-19731

TABLE OF CONTENTS

PROLEGOMENON vii

PREFACE xxvii

INTRODUCTION xxxv

MATTHEW 1

LUKE 342

APPENDIX I. On Faith. By H. Loewe 377

APPENDIX II. On 'Acting Cleverly.' By H. Loewe 380

APPENDIX III. On Repentance 390

INDEX I. Rabbinic Passages cited or referred to 423

INDEX II. Subjects dealt with 437

PROLEGOMENON

I

Rabbinic Literature and Gospel Teachings is intended, Montefiore repeatedly informs the reader, to deal with rabbinic parallels to the Gospels.[1] Soon after the revised edition of his *Commentary to the Synoptic Gospels* appeared (1927), he wrote to a friend:

> "My new idea is a volume on parallel passages—not, I think the classical—Greek, Hellenistic and Roman ones, but the rabbinic ones only. The material is there, collected for me,[2] but it has not in my opinion, ever yet been properly or fairly used whether by Jew or Christian. Both, in my opinion, use it imperfectly though of course in opposite ways of depreciation and appreciation."[3]

The present volume is, according to Montefiore, a "sort of supplement" to his Commentary and provides the rabbinic parallels largely omitted in the earlier work.[4]

Despite Montefiore's avowed intention, however, this book is only incidentally and in a most limited sense a study of rabbinic parallels. It is essentially not a new work, but rather a new arrangement of material that had appeared in several previously published volumes.

In 1923, seven years before the publication of the present work, Montefiore wrote:

> "I have finished the proofs of my book now [*The Old Testa-*

ment and After] . . . I fear you may think me rather a poor, sad squirrel in a cage always treading the same narrow ground.[5] I am too elderly and uninformed to go elsewhere, I fear . . . I only write because of my peculiar point of view. . . . This is my last book, I think, except new editions which, if I did, the Gospel[6] and the Hibberts[7] might keep me going to the end."[8]

Four years later he wrote in the same vein:

"I have had some nice letters about the Gospels.[9] I ought to prepare for a 3rd edition I suppose, and correct all the mistakes and fill up all the gaps . . . I am not much fit for anything else."[10]

Montefiore wrote little that was really new in the twenties or thirties[11]; mostly, he reworked and elaborated on his earlier publications.[12] Thus his *Rabbinic Literature and Gospel Teachings* is largely a revision of an earlier work—a reorganized and somewhat expanded version of several chapters of his *Old Testament and After*[13] which are, in turn, expansions of two chapters of his previously published *Liberal Judaism and Hellenism*.[14] In their original form, the chapters were entitled "Liberal Judaism and the New Testament" and "Liberal Judaism and Rabbinical Literature." The focus of the two volumes was ". . . the contributions actual or possible of the Rabbinic Literature and of the New Testament to the building up of Liberal Judaism . . ."[15] This purpose remains essentially unchanged in the present work, despite the restructuring of the material,[16] the added rabbinic citations, and the new title. *Rabbinic Literature and Gospel Teachings* is primarily a restatement, in new form, of Montefiore's view of Liberal Judaism—the central theme of his numerous books and essays and the cause to which he devoted much of his life.[17]

Montefiore was convinced that his liberal religious stance enabled him to treat the classic sources of Judaism and Christianity as no one before him had done. "My only merit is my detached position (and this is original)," he wrote. "Nobody has ever written about the Gospels as I do. . . . It is all the point of view. I was very pleased by a letter I had from an American

Christian . . . He said: 'The *historic* point of view (of yours) is your liberal-Jewish point of view!' "[18]

He was, however, only dimly aware that along with liberating him from the traditional prejudices, both Christian and Jewish, his religious position could also distort his perspective and, even more so, would insinuate itself as the hidden agenda of every discussion and analysis. Montefiore does caution that though he attempts to be as "objective, detached and impartial" as he can, he is aware that he "can only imperfectly succeed" for he looks "at both the Gospel and the Rabbinic material through the spectacles of Liberal Judaism."[19] But this confession is largely ceremonial. It is intended to disarm the reader by acknowledging a universal human frailty. "All of us wear spectacles of one sort or another," he continues. "It is only a question how deep is their particular colour. I have, I hope, overcome the old Jewish difficulty of admitting that there is anything in the Gospels which is both excellent and new. . . ."[20] Nevertheless, I am sure that my spectacles are coloured to *some* extent by Liberal-Jewish prepossessions."[21]

Montefiore's "peculiar point of view," as he termed it,[22] represents, especially in the present volume, considerably more than mere coloring. His continual judgments on the relative merit of New Testament and rabbinic teachings, his criteria for and definition of "true parallels," his approach to the dating of rabbinic passages and toward establishing the "authenticity" of statements attributed to Jesus, as well as much of the contents of the volume—what he included and, more significantly, what he omitted —they are all consequences of and reflect Montefiore's conception of Liberal Judaism.

In an otherwise laudatory review, R. Travers Herford criticizes Montefiore for writing "from the point of view of Liberal Judaism" and for including only "those elements . . . which are of interest and importance at the present day. . . . A student who really wants to know how the case stands in regard to the 'parallels' between the Rabbinic and Gospel teachings, may fairly remark that he does not want to be told about Liberal Judaism and is not directly concerned to know what does or does not interest Dr. Montefiore." Herford concludes with the reassurance that "the student who reads this book will soon adjust himself to this special feature and will be grateful to the author for the abundant treasure which is offered him."[23]

It is doubtful whether "this special feature" may be as readily identified or that adjustment to it is as simple as Herford suggests. To appreciate the pervasiveness of Montefiore's personal viewpoint and the extent to which his religious position affected his approach to almost every subject requires a familiarity with his background and a close reading of his extensive writings on the various aspects of Liberal Judaism.[24] There is no doubt, however, about the "abundant treasure" of which Herford writes. The reissue of this long out-of-print volume makes readily available to students of Rabbinic and New Testament Literature a wealth of talmudic and midrashic material, learned analyses, in the light of extant scholarly literature, of many of the "religious and ethical" teachings of the Gospels and the Rabbis, as well as a valuable corrective of Strack-Billerbeck[25] and of the view of Rabbinic Judaism prevalent among Christian scholars of the nineteenth and early twentieth centuries.[26]

II

Montefiore's background and early environment shaped his profoundest loyalties and engendered many of the tensions and conflicts which, throughout his life, he struggled to resolve. He was of the fifth generation of Montefiores in England. His grandmother was a Rothschild. The Goldsmids (the maternal side of his family) and the Montefiores were among the most illustrious and affluent Jewish families in England. His mother, "a woman of strong character and rigid opinions, unswerving in her devotion to the Jewish faith both in its spirit and in its observance. . . . was the dominant influence in the home. . . . She had her children carefully instructed in Hebrew, supervised their daily devotions. . . . and regularly accompanied her children to religious services in the synagogue."[27]

The Reverend David W. Marks, minister of the family's synagogue on Upper Berkeley Street,[28] guided Claude Montefiore's early Jewish education and deeply influenced his religious development. "I have no doubt," he wrote when already in his late seventies, "that the roots of my belief *are* through Mr. Marks in the deep racial tradition. A man often and often rebels against his tradition and is *really* deeply influenced by it all the same."[29] A few years later (1935) he refers again to the teacher of his youth:

> "Some of the liturgy (of the Day of Atonement) affected me deeply when I thought of Germany . . . I read a good deal in the Hebrew. . . . The Berkeley Street liturgy is very fine and I can hear Mr. Marks' voice as if he were in the room, and I hear the choir too. I suppose I heard them forty-five years running."[30]

Yet, though the Montefiore home was "very Jewish in teaching, observance and atmosphere, very few Jews, except their relations, ever came to the house."[31] "Our environment was . . . purely English," Montefiore wrote much later.[32] After his sister, Charlotte, married a non-Jew—"a terrible, almost unbelievable blow to her mother"—he remarked, "My dear mother was very inconsistent in allowing so many Christian young men and women to stay in the house so frequently and for long periods."[33]

Up to the age of seventeen, the future Sir Philip Magnus was responsible for Montefiore's general education. Later, Arnold Page, the future Dean of Peterborough became his tutor and he was followed by Mr. Glazerbrook, the future headmaster of Clifton who, like Page, eventually became a Church dignitary. In 1878, following in his brother's footsteps, Claude Montefiore entered Balliol College, Oxford, and came under the influence of Benjamin Jowett who made a lasting impression on the young student. "Jowett's liberal views of the Christian religion affected his (Montefiore's) own line of thought," Lucy Cohen writes. "In his earlier sermons and writings there were few passages without a quotation from 'the Master'. . . His letters are full of references to Jowett . . ."[34]

Typical of Jowett's religious attitude is a letter he wrote to Montefiore on the occasion of his sister's marriage:

> ". . . I think it quite right that the wall of distinction between

Jew and Christian should be broken down. Has it not lasted long enough? In idea it has already broken down, for all intelligent persons are agreed that in the sight of God there is no distinction of race or caste, or circumcision or of uncircumcision . . . it would be vain and unpopular and impossible to get rid of distinctive customs which may have their use. But it would also be wrong to do violence to natural affection. . . . It seems to me that Jewish society in England is too narrow to allow of Jews only marrying within limits of their own community . . ."[35]

Jowett's advice and guidance, during Montefiore's years at Oxford and later, influenced not only his ideas and attitudes but the very choice and direction of his life's work. A number of Jowett's letters read like outlines of Montefiore's subsequent career. After the death of Nathaniel Montefiore, Claude's father, the Master of Balliol wrote to his former student:

". . . I cannot advise you for or against the ministry,[36] but I would certainly advise you to lead an ideal life, by which I mean a life not passed in the ordinary pleasure and pursuits of mankind; but in something higher, the study of your own people and their literature and the means of improving and elevating them. No life will make you as happy as that."[37]

A few years later Jowett focused Montefiore's attention on a problem with which he was to grapple much of his life:

"The difficulty of Reformers is how to attach themselves rightly to the old. In some imaginary dawn of liberty they cut the cord and find themselves helpless and isolated. The Jewish problem is not really different from that of other religions; they all belong to a former age. . . . The power of any man to do good in the Christian or Jewish Church depends upon his reconcilement of these elements."[38]

The publication of the Hibbert Lectures, which Montefiore gave at Jowett's invitation, was the occasion for another letter which, in retrospect, appears to be a concise summary of the objectives Montefiore persistently pursued:

". . . It appears to me that there is good work to be done in Judaism; Christianity has gone forward; ought not Judaism to make similar progress from the letter to the spirit, from the national to the historical ideal? The Jews need not renounce the religion of their fathers, but they ought not to fall short of the highest, whether gathered from the teaching of Jesus or from Greek philosophy.

"Did you ever think of devoting yourself to the Jewish race as the task of your life, first as a student. . . . Secondly, by endeavoring to raise the manner and ways of their teachers and educators. . . . I should never attempt to convert a person from one form of religion to another. But I think all persons are greatly the better for having a universal form of religion as well as a National and particular one."[39]

Another personality who profoundly affected Montefiore's intellectual development was the eminent rabbinic scholar, Solomon Schechter. After concluding his studies at Oxford, Montefiore spent a year at the *Hochschule für die Wissenschaft des Judentums* in Berlin, where Schechter was his tutor in Rabbinics. Montefiore persuaded Schechter to return to London with him to continue his tutorship. This relationship, which lasted well over a decade, left a permanent imprint on Montefiore's scholarly endeavors. It was largely through Schechter's influence that Montefiore came to appreciate the crucial importance of Rabbinic Judaism, its centrality in Jewish life. His lifelong preoccupation with Rabbinic Literature—from his first volume, *The Hibbert Lectures,* to the last, *The Rabbinic Anthology*—his conception of the Law and of its place in Judaism, his view that Rabbinic Judaism represents, to a degree, "progressive revelation," "continuous inspiration" and the "principle of development"[40] of which Liberal Judaism was the offspring—they were all due, in no small measure, to Schechter's teaching and inspiration.[41]

It was inevitable, because of the vast difference in their temperament, background, and outlook, that these two remarkable men would eventually part ways. "In the same year that Claude Montefiore founded in England the Jewish Religious Union (for the Advancement of Liberal Judaism) which was to introduce radical reform of the traditional synagogue service and of the religious relations of Jews and Christians," Solomon Schechter accepted the presidency of the Jewish Theological Seminary of America "to initiate what came to be called Conservative Judaism."[42] Montefiore would continue to associate himself and to collaborate with outstanding rabbinic scholars: Israel Abrahams (to whom the present volume is dedicated, the successor to Schechter as Reader in Rabbinics and Talmudic Literature at Cambridge)[43] and, after his death, Herbert Loewe (represented in this volume by numerous notes and two Appendices).[44] Schechter's influence was to remain, however, a permanent factor in Montefiore's scholarly work.

III

These various elements of Montefiore's background and education—his profound attachment to the faith of his fathers, its rituals and ceremonies, his wholehearted loyalty to his country, his pride in being English, the continuous contact with liberal Christian scholars and social friends, the influence of Rabbis and eminent Talmudists—all of these shaped his philosophy of Judaism and his conception of the role of the Jew in the Western World where he enjoyed the fruits of civil and political emancipation.

"The vast majority of men and women of England are Christians, of one shade or another. . . . The English Jews form, or seek to form, with this great majority a single nation, united in all things except in religion.

"But this very exception might under certain conceivable circumstances, cause a difference so acute and wide that it would be impossible for the Jew to find himself one with his neighbors. . . . For (under special circumstances) it would not only be speculative ideas about God and the unseen world which would divide them: it would be different conceptions of morality, different moral and spiritual ideals, different goals of social endeavor.

"Such incompatibility . . . however, is not the case as regards Judaism and Christianity. . . . The Jews and Christians can and do form one nation, one people, one political community, united by common ideals, affections, aims, united in the equal service of one and the same motherland. England can be and is 'Mother England' to the Jew no less than to the Christian."[46]

It is in the light of this central concern, many times reiterated throughout his writings, that we gain a clearer understanding of Montefiore's limiting himself in *Rabbinic Literature and Gospel Teachings* "entirely to the religious and ethical teaching of the Rabbis and the Gospels" and to matters that "have living value for us today." All else is "entirely excluded."[47] Montefiore's real interest is to demonstrate that the moral and spiritual ideals of Judaism and Christianity are not incompatible, that a Jew is and can be English. If Montefiore's purpose were an exposition of rabbinic parallels or an objective view of the religion of the Rabbis, he would not have omitted from his volume those areas to which most of Rabbinic Literature is devoted.

Montefiore's lack of interest in dating rabbinic passages or in determining whether a statement attributed to Jesus in the Gospels is genuine or of a later date is similarly motivated. "For *me* the question of dates is of very little importance," he writes; "... I take the Rabbinic literature as a whole and I ask: What was its ethical and religious product ... whatever their date, they are for my purpose, genuine and interesting parallels. As Jesus taught a particular doctrine so also did subsequent Rabbis teach it. As the Gospel religion comprises such and such a doctrine so does Rabbinic religion comprise it. ... Its value and interest are largely independent of its date."[48] In commenting on Matthew v. 43-48, Montefiore repeats: "For my own part, I am not greatly interested in dates, and I observe that Strack-Billerbeck in quoting all the *bad* passages, do not seem to mind that *they* are all later than A.D. 29. To me, the interesting thing is, Did the Rabbinic religion *on its own lines* rise to the conception of active benevolence (= love, for that is what Jesus meant by love) . . ."[49]

Montefiore was well aware that the Judaism of the Rabbis was not static, that it represented variety, change, and development. "Rabbinic Literature . . . contains the record of the men who lived from the first century to the sixth or seventh. . . . Six hundred years or more separate the earliest of these Rabbis (with their views and utterances) from the latest. Six hundred years!

Wycliffe on the one hand, and Dean Inge on the other."[50] He refers again and again to the historic circumstances which conditioned and gave rise to specific rabbinic attitudes and doctrines.[51] "No doubt another and most valuable enquiry would be . . . to trace the history of Rabbinic doctrine from, say, A.D. 30 to A.D. 500. But as such an enquiry would be beyond my power, so it is also outside the scope of the present limited work."[52] The difficulty of the enterprise was undoubtedly a factor,[53] but the primary reason was the underlying *tendenz* of the volume. Montefiore was not concerned with "parallels" in the sense of illuminating passages in Matthew and Luke (the scope of the volume), nor even in "parallels of meaning,"[54] which would have required dating and stratification of rabbinic material. His concern was to demonstrate that Judaism and Christianity shared, by and large, the same spiritual and ethical goals. To achieve this purpose, both the New Testament and Rabbinic Literature may be treated as if they were unities.

Montefiore did not, of course, feel bound by the totality of Rabbinic Judaism. He is frequently very critical of the teachings and of the attitudes of the Rabbis. "How could men come to imagine such absurdities and solemnly to write them down," he complains; ". . . I feel about the Gospel teaching that though there are things in it which I dislike and disbelieve . . . yet, somehow, there is never anything which is absurd. . . . It had been a disadvantage to Judaism to have for generations as its second sacred book (the Talmud) . . . one which is so long and so composite, so unedited . . . and unexpurgated, so full of 'high and low,' so completely in 'undress'. . ." (pp. 352 f.). He objects to the Rabbis' particularism (pp. 42, 209), to their casuistry (p. 184), their naiveté (p. 169), to the Rabbinic doctrine of 'measure for measure' (p. 145) and much else.[55] "If only they could have been made to go through a careful course of Greek philosophy, how immensely they would have gained! Paul's soteriology may be one-sided but it is profound; theirs is more many-sided but it is slight" (p. 175). In another context, he writes: "The Rabbinic study of the Law seems to us today both strange and undesirable. Much of it was casuistic; much of it narrowing; much of it trifling; much of it an appalling waste

of time and brain. Some of the Rabbinic laudations of various
ritualistic prescriptions of the Law are to us positively distaste-
ful . . ."[56]

Yet, despite these harsh criticisms, the dominant attitude
toward the Rabbis in Montefiore's writings is positive, even
laudatory. "The religion of the Rabbis is more balanced, more
comprehensive (than the religion of the Beatitudes); it lays
stress on the outward as well as the inward; it lays stress on the
institutional, on the legal; it lays immense stress on knowledge,
holding it to be no less important than humility and pity and
love . . . a religion which produced and fed the souls of martyrs—how can we speak of it as wanting in passion and in
intensity?" (p. 2); ". . . it is really a remarkable thing how
often the Rabbis rose above the level of their texts, or rather,
perhaps, how often they made the higher things in the Bible
correct the lower things, or how often they both adopted the
Bible teaching and yet, of their own impulse transcended it"
(p. 294). "There are some points in which Rabbinism is more
modern than any part or teacher of the Old Testament, not only
in time, but also in idea. It is occasionally much more modern than its Christian contemporaries or than any Christian
teachers up to a comparatively modern era. There are some
points in which we are nearer to Rabbinic Judaism than we are
to Isaiah. . . . In some things our views are its views . . ."[57]

In the early period of Reform Judaism in Germany, the conflict with Orthodoxy assumed a "Karaite" form: the authority
of the Bible was accepted but the authority of the Rabbinic
additions and interpretations, of the Oral Law, was denied.
Montefiore strongly opposed this tendency: "This was a very
unfortunate attitude, and was liable to lead either to an even
worse stagnancy and fossilisation than the stagnancy and fossilisation of existing orthodoxy, or to a hopeless identification of
Reform and Liberalism with a few useful externalities and external changes."[58]

Montefiore's criticism is not restricted to Rabbinic Judaism.
He does not hesitate to reject doctrines or utterances whatever
their source, be it the Old Testament, The Gospels, or the
Rabbis, if they fall below the level of his conception of religion—

his vision of Liberal Judaism. Similarly, wherever he finds his religious ideal expressed, he rejoices over it and lauds it. His criterion is Liberal Judaism. The theoretical justification is Progressive Revelation. "We take our stand upon the doctrine of continuous and progressive revelation. We find no difficulty in the hypothesis that certain elements of our faith today are later than the latest portion of the Hebrew Bible, and that we owe them partly to the Rabbinical period, partly to still later ages, and partly to our own time."[59] The freedom of Liberal Judaism enables the Jew to claim the revealed truth wherever it is found— no less in the Gospels[60] than in Hebrew Scriptures. Both the standard for evaluating the Christian or Jewish sources and Montefiore's purpose in making comparisons and judgments was Liberal Judaism and its corollary, the actual and possible role of the Jew in the contemporary society.

Throughout his life, Montefiore opposed every manifestation of Jewish Nationalism. "I have been brought up," he writes, "with the conviction (for my mother was filled with these ideas) that the Jews are a "religious community," and nothing more, and the newer ideals, "Zionism . . . leave[s] me cold."[61] Repeatedly he complained that "Zionism has put the clock back." "I find in the middle-class Jews, when not corrupted by Zionism, curious resemblances . . . to middle-class Christians, and many of them have Christian friends who don't look upon them as other than people like themselves. . . . Of course, that is what Liberal Judaism is there for, to *stop the rot* and to offer a religion which is not Zionist and is not orthodox and irrational and uncritical . . ."[62] "They (the Jews) would have become . . . more and more "like" the others. . . . But anti-Semitism on the one hand and Jewish nationalism (its product) on the other, destroyed it all."[63] "All has been interrupted by Zionism and Nationalism and Anti-Semitism. . . . Whether the good old tendency will come back in force, or whether Jewish nationalism will spread and ruin us all, I don't know."[64]

To Montefiore, Zionism was an attitude of despair to which he could not and would not submit. "It is easy, I admit, for an English Jew who lives in comfort, liberty and toleration . . . to put forward the specious plea that he does not think so basely of human nature; it is easy for such a one to combat the doctrine of despair. [He refers to Herzl who "became a nationalist through despair" and because of his belief that anti-Semitism was inevitable.] I admit that; I feel that. And yet I must combat this doctrine of despair, however much I lay myself open to the charge of indifference, or to the charge of clinging to outworn ideals of the emancipation era . . ."[65]

In a moving reminiscence of his meeting with Herzl, which Montefiore wrote in 1935, at the age of seventy-seven, he describes the growth of Zionism and its consequences. He concludes: ". . . you see before you a disillusioned, sad and embittered old man. But yet, not a hopeless old man, for he still believes in God. He refuses to bow the knee to the fashionable Zionist Baal. He refuses to succumb to Jewish nationalism, on the one hand, or to Gentile Anti-Semitism, on the other, even though these powerful forces so powerfully react upon, and stimulate, one another. He is an extremist, a die-hard, a fanatic, if you will, but he has not lost faith . . ."[66] Montefiore's response to, his evaluations of Zionism or the teachings of Jesus, the Rabbis, or the Bible are all of a piece—they are all expositions of his view of Liberal Judaism.

The judgment that Montefiore was a radical assimilationist, in its most negative sense, or even Zangwill's description of him as a "queer mixture, half Jew and half Christian"[67] are grievous errors and very unfair. Montefiore's commitment to Judaism was profound. He responded to the challenges of his time with honesty and integrity. Subsequent events proved his optimism and his lofty idealism to be naive and even tragic. But that is our anguish. The Messiah, it would seem, rather than being at hand —as Montefiore hoped—has never been more distant.

In response to a suggestion that the Jews had already accomplished their work and should eventually merge, he wrote: "The Jews, please God, will never be absorbed. God has chosen them for a religious purpose in the History of the World, and till this earth is filled with the knowledge of the One God—the God of Israel—the Jews will be his witness. I should collapse morally and *spiritually* if I did not believe that . . . I do still mean *chosen*, not choosing. I still believe in 'chosen.' If there is a

divine purpose in history, then I, C. G. M., and my fellow
Liberals *are chosen*. And in their degree all Jews are chosen,
though some refuse to serve."[68]

Montefiore was opposed to mixed marriages "for purely religious reasons." "If they contract mixed marriages, they must
inevitably die out and disappear. But that would be fatal. . . .
There is here nothing of racial distinctiveness or of national pride.
The reason is purely religious reason."[69] Similarly, he insisted
that the Bible of the Jews and Judaism "must continue to be
the Hebrew Bible and the Hebrew Bible only." This, despite the
argument "that our doctrine of inspiration is different now from
what it used to be, that we no longer suppose that only the Hebrew prophets . . . were inspired, but that if Jesus said anything
which was good, new and true . . . the Divine Spirit rested also
upon him . . ."[70]

He also advocated the retention of the rite of circumcision
because of his concern for the unity of the Jewish group. "Liberal Jewish Congregations do well, I think, in temporarily retaining this unattractive rite for infants. . . . The reason for this
retention is not religious and it is not hygienic . . . the rite may
justifiably be temporarily retained for reasons of a social and
juridical order . . . it is not desirable that any Liberal Jew
should be under disqualification or stigma in the eyes of their
orthodox brethren. That might lead to difficulties in the case of a
contemplated marriage between a 'Liberal' Jew and an 'Orthodox' Jewess."[71]

Much could be said about the advances in the study of Rabbinic texts since Montefiore's day—the gradual appearance of
"scientific" editions of the more important basic texts, the new
concordances and other aids, the heightened interest in and
deeper appreciation of rituals, symbols, and myths, the growing
tendency to apply methods of form criticism to Rabbinic Literature, the emergence of a revised concept of first-century Judaism,
one that is more complex and varied. This essay might also have
included a detailed investigation of the rare mistranslations or
misinterpretations of a Rabbinic passage, or of Montefiore's conception of parallels, or of his basic methodology which is esssen-

tially no different from that of Strack-Billerbeck whom he constantly criticizes. The present volume is, however, not to be judged in the framework of Rabbinic or New Testament scholarship. It is a work primarily dedicated to the exposition of Liberal Judaism.

Cincinnati, Ohio   EUGENE MIHALY
August, 1970   Professor of Rabbinic Literature
                                       and Homiletics
                                    Hebrew Union College—
                                       Jewish Institute of Religion

NOTES

1. *Rabbinic Literature and Gospel Teachings,* Preface and Introduction, pp. vii ff.

2. He refers here primarily to H. Strack and P. Billerbeck, *Kommentar zum neuen Testament aus Talmud und Midrash* (München, C. H. Beck, 1922-28). Cf. Montefiore, *op. cit.,* pp. xv and xix f.

3. Lucy Cohen, *Some Recollections of Claude Goldsmid Montefiore 1858-1938* (London, Faber and Faber, 1940), p. 170.

4. Montefiore, *op. cit.,* pp. vii and xv.

5. The subject matter of *The Old Testament and After* (London, Macmillan and Co., 1923) was treated by Montefiore in a number of his earlier writings. But, more specifically, this volume is an expanded version of an earlier work, *Liberal Judaism and Hellenism and Other Essays* (London, Macmillan and Co., 1918).

6. The first edition of his *Synoptic Gospels* appeared in 1909 and the revised edition in 1927. (The revised edition was reprinted in this series by Ktav in 1968, with a Prolegomenon by Lou H. Silberman.)

7. *Lectures on the Origin and Growth of Religion as Illustrated by the Religion of the Ancient Hebrews.* The Hibbert Lectures (London, Williams & Norgate, 1892).

8. Lucy Cohen, *op. cit.,* p. 102.

9. The revised edition of his *Synoptic Gospels* (London, Macmillan & Co., 1927).

10. Lucy Cohen, *op. cit.,* p. 171.

11. The possible exception is his *Rabbinic Anthology* (London, 1938), compiled in association with H. Loewe.

12. F. C. Burkitt published a partial bibliography of Montefiore's writings in *Speculum Religionis* (Oxford, Clarendon Press, 1929), pp. 15 ff. A full bibliography by V. G. Simmons is included in Lucy Cohen, *op. cit.,* pp. 267 ff.

13. "The Advance of the New Testament" and "The Advance in Rabbinic Literature," Chapters II and III, pp. 201-468.

14. Chapters II and III, pp. 77-182. Cf. *The Old Testament and After,* p. viii.

15. *Ibid.,* p. 548. Cf. *Liberal Judaism and Hellenism,* p. 284.

16. He apparently decided to organize the rabbinic material in the form of parallels to the Gospels after reading Strack-Billerbeck's *Kommentar.* The new element in the present work is the almost continuous critique of Strack-Billerbeck. Earlier, though he cited rabbinic parallels on occasion (in the *Synoptic Gospels,* etc.), he expressed reservations about such comparisons. See, *The Old Testament and After,* p. 449, and *Some Elements of the Religious Teaching of Jesus, According to the Synoptic Gospels* (London, Macmillan & Co., 1910), pp. 10 f.

17. *Liberal Judaism* (London, Macmillan & Co., 1903) and *Outlines of Liberal Judaism* (London, Macmillan & Co., 1923), in addition to the volumes mentioned in the text, as well as most of his lectures, essays, and sermons, are specifically addressed to aspects of Liberal Judaism. It is, however, the underlying theme of practically everything he wrote. Montefiore was also the founder and the guiding spirit of The Religious Union for the Advancement of Liberal Judaism; cf. Lily H. Montagu, "The Jewish Religious Union and its Beginnings," *Papers for Jewish People,* No. XXVII, 1927.

18. L. Cohen, *op. cit.,* p. 200.

19. *Rabbinic Literature and Gospel Teachings,* p. xix.

20. See Gerald Friedlander, *The Jewish Sources of the Sermon on the Mount* (London, G. Routledge, 1911); reissued by Ktav in 1969, with a Prolegomenon by S. Zeitlin.

21. *Loc. cit.*

22. *The Synoptic Gospels,* p. ix. Cf. Lou H. Silberman's Prolegomenon to *The Synoptic Gospels* (New York, Ktav, 1968), p. 15, and the letter quoted above, note 8.

23. *The Hibbert Journal* XXIX (1930-31), pp. 190 f.

24. W. D. Davies, *Paul and Rabbinic Judaism* (London, 1965), for example, takes as his point of departure Montefiore's view of Rabbinic Judaism (*Judaism and St. Paul,* London, M. Goschen, 1914) without appreciating, apparently, this *tendenz* in Montefiore's concept of early Palestinian Judaism. Note that the second part of *Judaism and St. Paul* is devoted to the use that the Liberal Jew can make of St. Paul.

25. Michael Guttmann writes in "Die Wissenschaftliche Talmudpflege der neueren Zeit," *Monatsschrift für Geschichte und Wissenschaft des Judentums,* LXXV (1931), p. 16: "Die Bedeuting dieses Buches (*Rabbinic Literature and Gospel Teachings*) liegt in seiner kritisch gerichteten Bezogenheit zu Strack-Billerbecks monumentalen *Kommentar* . . . Montefiore ist jedoch der erste der das Werk als ganzes unter die Lupe himmt und die Vergleichungen von Punkt zu Punkt durchprüft. . . ."

Samuel Sandmel, *The First Christian Century in Judaism and Christianity* (N.Y., Oxford, 1968), p. 100, writes: "Is it not tragic that much of Claude G. Montefiore, *Rabbinic Literature and Gospel Teachings* is devoted to the subjectivity (that is, the bias) of interpreters. . . ?" See, however, his "Parallelomania," *Journal of Biblical Literature,* LXXXI (1962), pp. 8 ff., where he offers his own, cogent, four-point criticism (not too different from that of Montefiore) of Strack-Billerbeck.

26. Cf. G. F. Moore, "Christian Writers on Judaism," *Harvard Theol. Review,* XIV (1921), and Morton S. Enslin, Prolegomenon to Abrahams, *Studies in Pharisaism and the Gospels* (N.Y., Ktav reissue, 1967), pp. vii ff.

27. L. Cohen, *op. cit.,* pp. 28 f.

28. The Reform Synagogue of British Jews which had existed for over half a century was traditional in its liturgy and ritual. Its "Reform" consisted primarily of some external changes and its decorum. The English equivalent of American Reform Judaism is Liberal Judaism, founded by Claude Montefiore.

29. L. Cohen, *op. cit.,* p. 208.

30. *Ibid.*, p. 223.

31. *Ibid.*, p. 31.

32. *Ibid.*, p. 230.

33. *Ibid.*, p. 31. Montefiore was opposed to mixed marriage. He did, however, arrange for his sister to be married by a Rabbi in Germany. Montefiore's second wife was not a born Jewess, but she adopted his faith. Nevertheless, he waited until after his mother's death to marry (*ibid.*, p. 72).

34. *Ibid.*, pp. 42 f.

35. *Ibid.*, pp. 35 f.

36. Claude Montefiore went to Oxford with the intention of becoming a Rabbi, "but his biblical studies in Germany and probably his association with men of very liberal thought at Oxford, made it impossible for him to follow the calling of an Orthodox Rabbi." (L. Cohen, *op. cit.*, p. 45.)

37. *Ibid.*, p. 47. Montefiore addresses himself to this problem in *Liberal Judaism and Hellenism*, pp. 65 ff.

38. *Ibid.*, p. 57.

39. *Ibid.*, p. 59.

40. *Ibid.*, pp. 63 f., 172. See *The Old Testament and After*, pp. 5 and 552. See, however, pp. 580 ff.

41. Montefiore expressed his indebtedness to Schechter in the Preface to the Hibbert Lectures, p. x: "To Mr. Schechter I owe more than I can adequately express here. . . ."

42. Norman Bentwich, "Claude Montefiore and his Tutor in Rabbinics," *The Sixth Montefiore Memorial Lecture* (Univ. of Southampton, 1966), pp. 9 f.
The entire essay is devoted to the Schechter-Montefiore relationship.

43. See Montefiore's acknowledgement of his debt to Abrahams and Loewe in his Preface to the *Synoptic Gospels* and in the Preface to *Rabbinic Literature and Gospel Teachings*. (London, Macmillan & Co., 1930).

44. Samuel Sandmel, *A Jewish Understanding of the New Testament* (Cincinnati, Hebrew Union College Press, 1956, p. xiv), very aptly remarks: "These partnerships were amazing affairs, in that neither subservience nor tyranny dictated the results of any difference of opinion; but both Abrahams and Loewe were cited constantly in Montefiore's writings in refutation of viewpoints which Montefiore expresses. The uniqueness of this relationship is the more discernible in the case of the collaboration with Loewe . . . a staunch Orthodox Jew. . . ."

45. L. Cohen, *op. cit.*, p. 56.

46. *Outlines of Liberal Judaism*, (London, Macmillan & Co., 1903, pp. 299 ff.) and "Assimilation: Good and Bad," *Papers for Jewish People*, 1914, No. IX.

47. Pp. xv, xix, xx. Note that over half of the book is devoted to the Sermon on the Mount. Cf. pp. 48, 309, 322, 357 f., 380, and particularly, *The Old Testament and After*, p. 430.

48. *Rabbinic Literature and Gospel Teachings*, pp. xvi f. Cf. pp. 300, 357, 368 and *The Old Testament and After*, pp. 293 ff.

49. *Ibid.*, pp. 71 f.

50. *The Old Testament and After*, p. 293.

51. See, for example, *Rabbinic Literature and Gospel Teachings*, pp. 70, 210; *The Old Testament and After*, pp. 366, 455. Note, however, pp. 294 f. and Michael Guttmann, *op. cit.* (n. 25, above), p. 247.

52. *Rabbinic Literature and Gospel Teachings*, p. xvii.

53. See *A Rabbinic Anthology*, Excursus IV, "The Dating of Rabbinic Material," pp. 709 ff.

54. See Morton Smith, *Tannaitic Parallels to the Gospels* (*Journal of Biblical Literature Monograph Series VI*, 1951), pp. 46 ff.

55. See, pp. 5, 21, 131, 183 f., and *passim*.

56. *The Old Testament and After*, p. 371. See Israel Abraham's lengthy note in refutation (p. 372). Much of his "distaste" was due to a Victorian prudery evident in his evaluation of and attitude toward aspects of Rabbinic Literature. See, for example, *Rabbinic Literature and Gospel Teachings*, pp. 43, 117, 278.

57. *Liberal Judaism and Hellenism*, p. 146. See the entire chapter on the relationship of Liberal Judaism and the Rabbis.

58. *The Old Testament and After*, p. 552. Cf. the references in n. 40, above.

59. *Liberal Judaism and Hellenism*, pp. 63 f. Cf. "Progressive Revelation," *Papers for Jewish People*, 1914, No. VIII.

60. See "Do Liberal Jews Teach Christianity?" *Papers for Jewish People*, 1924, No. XXV and *Some Elements of The Religious Teaching of Jesus*, *op. cit.*

61. L. Cohen, *op. cit.*, p. 78. Cf. "Liberal Judaism and Jewish Nationalism," *Papers for Jewish People*, 1917, No. XVI.

62. *Ibid.*, p. 105.

63. *Ibid.*, p. 245.

64. *Ibid.*, pp. 138 f.

65. *Outlines of Liberal Judaism*, p. 308.

66. L. Cohen, *op. cit.*, p. 227.

67. *Ibid.*, p. 189.

68. *Ibid.*, p. 218.

69. *Outlines of Liberal Judaism*, p. 298.

70. *Ibid.*, p. 333. Cf. *Liberal Judaism and Hellenism*, p. 90. His secretary reports that "entirely for his own interest—not to be published during his life-time, he went through the New Testament picking out bits which would be suitable for reading out at Sabbath services in Synagogue, if that time *ever* came when such readings would not do more harm than good." (L. Cohen, *op. cit.*, p. 110, note.)

71. *Liberal Judaism and Hellenism*, p. 69.

PREFACE

I HAVE explained the nature and object of this book in a short Introduction, and I need not, therefore, anticipate here what I have said there. A good deal of the Rabbinic material, here translated, and illustrative, in one way or another, of the Gospel teachings, has, I believe, not been hitherto available in English, and I hope that, for this reason, as well as, perhaps, for some others, my book may be of a little use and interest to English students both of the Gospels and of Rabbinic literature. It is somewhat difficult for one who, like myself, stands in a rather detached position both from the Gospels and the Rabbis, not occasionally to give the impression of writing in a sort of condescending way about either. A dear Jewish friend has sometimes accused me of doing this as regards the Old Testament. I would like to say that the impression, though very understandable, is, nevertheless, inaccurate. Though I may often have had to criticize all three—O.T., Gospels, and Rabbis—that does not mean that I do not feel a deep admiration for all of them : it does not exclude a feeling of true humility towards all three. The impression I allude to arises because I try to follow the spirit of Jowett's teaching, when he said : ' The facts of an ancient or religious history are amongst the most important of all facts, but they are frequently uncertain, and we only learn the true lesson which is to be gathered from them when we place ourselves above them.' I try to ' place myself above my documents,' whether they be the Gospels, the O.T., or the Rabbinic literature, but to place myself above the documents does not mean to look upon them, or to deal with them, condescendingly. The two things can be, at all events, quite different in one's own mind.

In the Preface to my Commentary upon the Synoptic Gospels, to which this book is a supplement, I expressed my deep indebtedness to my dear friend, colleague, and teacher, Dr. Israel Abrahams. Even before the second edition of the Commentary was published,

b

Dr. Abrahams had passed away. The present work is dedicated to his memory. I have been greatly fortunate in obtaining unstinted and invaluable help in its compilation from Mr. Herbert Loewe, of St. Catharine's College, Cambridge, and Exeter College, Oxford, Lecturer in Rabbinic Hebrew, University of Oxford. He has given as much care and thought to my book as if it had been his own. We have discussed a number of problems together, and he has aided me in the translation of very many Rabbinical passages. I am all the more grateful to Mr. Loewe for his constant help, because he and I do not always look at the subject from the same point of view or in exactly the same way. He does not by any means always agree with me in my estimates and judgments, whether of the Rabbis or of the Gospels. Needless, therefore, to add that he is not in the smallest degree responsible for any statement made, or for any opinion expressed, in the book except for direct contributions given under his own name. For these contributions I am specially grateful, and I am sure that my readers will also welcome them warmly : they show where, in judgment and opinion, I may have been one-sided, and how (as in most things) there is ' another side to the matter ' which should not be overlooked.

In one other point of a totally different kind I have insisted on going my own way, though I know that that way is unscholarly and wrong. It is in the English spelling of Hebrew names and words. I cannot bring myself to write Aqiba. I insist on Akiba, and, generally, on always using the familiar ' k ' where I ought to put ' q.' The rule that ' k ' should only be used for one Hebrew letter, and that ' q ' should be used for another, I venture to ignore. Nor can I bring myself to put dots under any English letters. I, therefore, insist on writing ' Chisda ' and not ' Ḥisda,' whatever the consequences. Mr. Loewe is dreadfully shocked. I fancy that he does not half so much mind any divergent and heretical views about Jesus and the Rabbis which I may happen to hold as he minds my obstinacy about the spelling of Hebrew names and words. He thinks me, I fear, a terrible *Am ha-Aretz*. I have made him a few concessions. Thus I have written *Kawwanah*, though I do not like it at all. It looks to me ugly and pedantic. Also *Rea'*, though the funny comma at the top of the ' a ' looks to me very queer and fantastic. Still I hope that *Kawwanah* and *Rea'* may comfort him a little.

I must make my last prefatory word one of apology. There is, I fear, a good deal of repetition in my book. This is partly due to its composition having been unduly dragged out, but partly also to its nature. It is not a book which will be read through continuously and consecutively, but students will, I hope, make use of it sometimes in relation to the particular verses and sections of the Gospels which it attempts to illustrate. It seemed better to make these illustrations fairly complete in each case, and not to refer the reader to two or three other places in which the same subject crops up, and is dealt with, again. To avoid such references, whether forwards or backwards, the same Rabbinic passages have often been quoted more than once, and the same sort of comments made upon them. For the compilation of the Index of Subjects, and for very great help in relation to Index I., I am deeply indebted to my old friend, Mrs. M'Arthur.

C. G. M.

May 1930.

LIST OF BOOKS

Quoted frequently by Abbreviations

STRACK (HERMANN) and BILLERBECK (PAUL). *Kommentar zum neuen Testament aus Talmud and Midrasch.* 4 vols. 1922–1928. Quoted as 'S.B.' or as 'B.'

ABRAHAMS (I.). *Studies in Pharisaism and the Gospels.* First Series, 1917; Second Series, 1924. Quoted as 'Studies I. or II.'

Annotated edition of the *Authorized Daily Prayer Book.* By ISRAEL ABRAHAMS. 1914. Now issued separately under title, *A Companion to the Authorized Daily Prayer Book.* Revised edition, 1920. Quoted as 'Annotated edition of P.B.' or as 'Companion.'

The Prayer Book itself, *The Authorized Daily Prayer Book of the United Hebrew Congregations of the British Empire,* with a new translation by the late Rev. S. SINGER, 14th edition, London, Eyre and Spottiswoode, 1929, is quoted as 'P.B.' or as 'Singer's Prayer Book.'

MOORE (G. F.). *Judaism in the First Centuries of the Christian Era.* 2 vols. 1927. Quoted as 'Moore.'

GUTTMANN (M.). *Das Judentum und seine Umwelt.* Vol. I. 1927. Quoted as 'Guttmann.'

KOHLER (K.). *The Origins of the Synagogue and the Church.* 1929. Quoted as 'Kohler.'

KITTEL (GERHARD). *Die Probleme des palästinischen Spätjudentums und das Urchristentum.* 1926. Quoted as 'Kittel.'

KLOSTERMANN (ERICH). *Das Matthäusevangelium.* 2nd edition. 1927. Quoted as 'Klostermann.'

SEVENSTER (GERHARD). *Ethiek en Eschatologie in de synoptische Evangelien.* 1929. Quoted as 'Sevenster.'

BÜCHLER (ADOLPH). *Types of Jewich-Palestinian Piety from* 70 B.C.E. *to* 70 C.E. 1922. Quoted as ' Types.'

BÜCHLER (ADOLPH). *Studies in Sin and Atonement in the Rabbinic Literature of the First Century.* 1928. Quoted as ' Sins.'

The Babylonian Talmud : Tractate Berakot. Translated by the Rev. A. Cohen. 1921. Quoted as ' Cohen.'

The Treatise Ta'anit of the Babylonian Talmud. Edited and translated by HENRY MALTER. 1928. Quoted as ' Malter.'

WINDISCH (H.). *Der Sinn der Bergpredigt.* 1929. Quoted as ' Windisch.'

ZIEGLER (J.). *Die sittliche Welt des Judentums.* Zweiter Teil : Vom Abschluss des Kanons bis Saadja. 1928. Quoted as ' Ziegler.'

For list of editions of Rabbinic books used see beginning of Index I.

INTRODUCTION

THE present book is intended as a sort of supplement to my *Commentary on the Synoptic Gospels*, to which I am often obliged to refer (second edition, 1927). In that Commentary I gave very few parallels to the religious and ethical teaching in the Gospels which can be gathered from the Rabbinical literature. Here the omission, to some extent at any rate, is supplied. In this brief introduction I want to explain the limitations of the book and its point of view.

I cannot claim credit for learning. Though some of the Rabbinical passages quoted come from my own reading, and though all, or almost all of them, have been directly translated from the original (while in doubtful or difficult cases I have had the immense advantage of Mr. Herbert Loewe's help and revision), yet far the greater number of the citations can be found in, and were indeed taken from, Strack-Billerbeck's magnificent collection. In fact, Strack-Billerbeck and Moore together would probably contain all that I have here quoted, with a great deal more. It is, perhaps, ' the great deal more ' which, together with my special point of view, may constitute the justification for the present venture. Strack-Billerbeck's volume on Matthew runs to 1055 closely printed pages, and the section in Volume II. which deals with Mark and Luke comprises 301—a total of 1356 pages. Moreover, in the big fourth volume, the salient excursuses come to many hundred pages more. It is to be feared that the scale of the book precludes the knowledge or the use of it from general readers. I do not suppose that my own modest work could have been written at all had not Strack-Billerbeck paved the way for it. But its comparative brevity may make it of use to those who would find Strack-Billerbeck too voluminous. I limit myself entirely to the religious and ethical teaching of the Gospels and of the Rabbis. All other matters—antiquarian, historical, even social and economic subjects—are entirely excluded. I freely allow that this means that I omit much which is interesting, and even much which any " Rabbinic commentary " on the Gospels ought to include ; but, at any rate, the omissions shorten the book.

I have to admit that the " parallels " are not allowed to speak for themselves, for I have added a certain amount of commentary. I discuss questions such as the following : How far are the parallels *true* parallels, and how far are they, perhaps, alike in form, but alien in spirit ? How far is the teaching in any particular passage representative or exceptional ? Again, how far are Rabbinic parallels to this or that particular saying or teaching of Jesus meagre or adequate ? How far does the Gospel teaching go beyond Rabbinic teaching in any particular point of doctrine— " beyond " in greatness, distinction, or originality ? How far is any particular Gospel doctrine off the Rabbinic line or characteristically Rabbinic ? Or, how far, while not *characteristically* Rabbinic, is it yet not antagonistic or opposed to Rabbinic teaching, but complementary to it ? How far does the particular Gospel doctrine carry forward and develop Rabbinic teaching to a still higher point of intensity and universality ? These are the kinds of questions which I have sought to discuss and to answer. Some of these questions, or, perhaps, all of them, have, doubtless, been often discussed and answered both by Jewish and Christian writers. But I venture to think that my line of approach to them is a little unusual. I am, I fancy, rather less concerned than most Jewish writers either to bring Rabbinic teaching on the religious and ethical topics touched on in the Gospels to the exact level of the teaching of Jesus, or to depreciate the teaching of Jesus when it appears (to Christian writers) to rise above the Rabbinic level. On the other hand, whereas a main interest for most Christian writers is to vindicate, so far as they can, the originality of Jesus, and, for that purpose, the question of dates is for them a matter of the utmost importance, for *me* the question of dates is of very little importance at all. I am not concerned to deny the originality of Jesus in that, so far as we know, he was, let us say, the first to enunciate a particular doctrine, even though all parallels from the existing Rabbinic literature are later in date than A.D. 30. What interests me is something quite different. I take the Rabbinic literature as a whole, and I ask : What was its ethical and religious product ? If some Rabbinic parallels to a given Gospel saying are all, let us suppose, from the third century A.D., I do not mind that, so long as they seem genuine and characteristic products of the Rabbinic spirit, and do not run counter to the general line of subsequent Rabbinic and Jewish doctrine. By that I do not mean that there must be *no* Rabbinic sayings which are opposed to such parallels (for the Rabbinic religion does not form a harmonious and consistent whole), but I mean that the parallels must be on *general* Rabbinic lines, and that they must not ever have been regarded as unusual, un-Jewish, paradoxical, or false. Then, whatever their date, they are, for my purpose, genuine and interesting parallels. As Jesus taught a particular doctrine, so also did subsequent Rabbis teach it. As the Gospel religion comprises such and such a doctrine, so does Rabbinic religion comprise it. On the other hand, we may find that some Rabbinic parallels, whatever, or however early, their date, are really exceptional, and do not become a regular or an essential part of Rabbinic religion, or that what contradicts them is more preponderating than what agrees with them. A given parallel to a Gospel saying may be much later than Jesus: from the point of view of chronology, the originality of Jesus is completely vindicated. That vindication having been secured, the interest of the Christian writer in the Rabbinic ' parallel ' usually ceases. For *his* purpose the parallel is of no value. He has bowled it over ; he has knocked it down. To me, and for *my* purpose, if it is a true parallel, in the sense of being characteristic and 'on the line,' its value and interest are largely independent of its date. No doubt another and most valuable enquiry would be (when things are ready for it) to trace the history of Rabbinic doctrine from, say, A.D. 30 to A.D. 500. But as such an enquiry would be beyond my power, so it is also outside the scope of the present limited work. I also assume (what I believe to be the truth) that, except in a few polemical directions, Gospel teaching had no influence upon Rabbinic teaching, and that therefore a late Rabbinic ' parallel ' to a given doctrine or saying ascribed to Jesus is a true parallel in the sense that it is a true and native development or product, not borrowed from, or influenced by, the Gospels.

It will, therefore, be observed that my present book is not by any means intended as an answer to the two questions : (1) What is the *total* value (as well as the originality) of the teachings of Jesus regarded as a whole? and (2) What is the *total* value (as well as the originality) of the teachings of the Rabbis? It may provide a little material for such a reply, but it does not pretend to do more. The value (with the originality) of the teachings in the Synoptic Gospels regarded as a whole depends partly upon considerations which are here entirely neglected. It depends partly upon their form, their artistry, their brevity, their concentration, upon their *comparative* homogeneity and consistency, upon what they do *not* include as well as upon what they do, upon their attribution to *one* great teacher. Moreover, they have to be considered, and to some extent they have to be appraised, in relation to the life and the personality of that teacher—to his character and his claims. Nothing of all this is here considered at all. Hence there is some amount of unfairness in my discussions and conclusions. It is quite reasonable to say, ' Though you are not out to discuss or assess the originality and worth of the teachings of Jesus regarded as a whole, yet indirectly, you necessarily, to some extent, do both, and the general result, because of your omissions, is inaccurate. It does not put the total teaching of Jesus in its right perspective, and it is, therefore, unfair.' I agree. But hardly less, and even, in some respects, more, may the book be regarded as unfair to the Rabbis. For I follow the Gospels chapter by chapter, verse by verse. I give parallels to Gospel teaching. But the teaching of the Rabbis touches on, and deals with, many topics which the Gospels altogether omit, and indeed much of the Rabbinic strength, and many of the Rabbinic excellences, in ethical and religious matters, deal with subjects which are not found in the Gospels at all, and which are, therefore, quite unrepresented here. For the truer picture of Rabbinic religion and of Rabbinic ethics *as a whole* one must go to Moore. Indeed I recognize that, when his book was published, I ought, perhaps, to have abandoned any further carrying forward of my own. For even on the subjects which I *do* touch upon and illustrate by quotations, if a reader were conscientiously to look up all Moore's references, he would mostly find more than he gets with me. But as I am unfair both to Jesus and to the Rabbis (though in different ways and for different reasons), perhaps the one unfairness may be allowed to compensate for, and to cancel, the other.

Let me, then, repeat: in each particular saying in the Gospels, or as regards each particular doctrine, I ask, (1) Is the teaching familiarly Rabbinic and virtually the same as what we often and commonly find in Rabbinic literature (and it may be this, even if there is no exact verbal parallel)? or (2) Is the teaching Rabbinic at bottom, but does it carry forward, intensify, generalize, and enlarge the teaching of the Rabbis ? Or (3) Is the teaching unusual among the Rabbis, but yet in no way opposed to Rabbinic religion at its best ? Or (4) Does it carry forward, intensify, generalize, and enlarge this unusual teaching ? Or (5) Is it off the Rabbinic line, opposed to the prevailing Rabbinic doctrine, and even to the very spirit of Rabbinic religion ? In the first four cases, the teaching can without difficulty be fitted on to Rabbinic doctrine and *a fortiori* to Judaism. Only in the last case can it not be so fitted on—not at least to Rabbinic religion, and *possibly* not to any form of Judaism. Whether such teaching as may be included under (5) is in itself good or bad, desirable to-day or undesirable, is again a quite different question, which falls outside the purview of my book. Another point which I can afford to neglect is the question of authenticity. For my present purpose it makes little or no difference whether a given saying was, or was not, spoken by Jesus. It is enough for me that it is in the Gospels as we have them now. Its greatness (if it is great) is not impaired, even its meaning is not necessarily changed, whether Jesus did not utter it or whether he did.

Though I try throughout to be as ' objective,' detached, and impartial as I can, I am well aware that I can only very imperfectly succeed in this endeavour. I look at both the Gospel and the Rabbinic material through the spectacles of Liberal Judaism. All of us wear spectacles of one sort or another. It is only a question how deep is their particular colour. I have, I hope, overcome the old Jewish difficulty of admitting that there is anything in the Gospels which is both excellent and new, and here I seem to differ from some Liberal Jewish writers who, in knowledge, rank high above me. Nevertheless, I am sure that my spectacles are coloured to *some* extent by Liberal-Jewish prepossessions, and therefore, in my occasional quarrels with Strack - Billerbeck and other Christian writers, they may be more in the right than my spectacles enable me to see and to believe. As I have once more mentioned Strack-Billerbeck—or, as I, more justly, should say, Billerbeck without the Strack, for *he* is the real author of these splendid volumes— I might fitly add that I do not always begin my cited Rabbinic passages where *he* begins them, or end where he ends them. Though, as I have said, where my Rabbinic quotations are taken from him, I have almost invariably translated from the original, and not from the German, this does not imply that his renderings are inexact. On the contrary: they are almost always correct, and this is not only my opinion, but that of Mr. Loewe (a far more competent judge) as well. And the accuracy of his references is remarkable. In the very large number which I have had to verify, I have hardly ever found the slightest error.

Whereas, in the Commentary, I naturally began with Mark, and went on to Matthew and Luke, here I begin with Matthew. And just as Billerbeck gives 1055 pages to Matthew, and only 301 to Mark and Luke, so that part of my book which deals with Matthew is by far the longest part of the whole. Mark I neglect altogether, and the pages devoted to Luke are but few. Moreover, in the Matthew section, the three chapters of the Sermon on the Mount take up more space than all the rest of Matthew put together. The reasons for these disproportions are obvious, and need not be enlarged upon. Matthew and Luke between them contain pretty well all the ethical and religious teaching which is found in Mark, and what is common to Matthew and Luke and what is peculiar to Matthew, when added together, are much larger in amount than what is peculiar to Luke.

Throughout my book there is, I fear, a good deal of caprice in the passages chosen for comment and illustration, as in those which have been neglected. Some of the things which Jesus is reported to have said may rightly be regarded as falling within the sphere of ' religious teaching,' and yet I have omitted them. I must admit that I have done so on no better principles than that they do not happen to interest *me*, or that they do not seem to have any living value for us to-day. Others would naturally make a different selection even on these very principles. The omitted passages relate chiefly to the teaching about what will befall men after death, or to the nature of the resurrection and of the Last Judgment. Of such matters Jesus and the Rabbis were equally ignorant, and the views of both the one and the other seem far removed from our own. Again, how far Rabbinic society, or how far the Jews, lived up to the level, or lived in accordance with the spirit and the letter, of the teaching contained in my quotations is a separate question

on which I have not touched at all. Here we have the ideals, or
the religious and moral precepts, which the Rabbinic teachers put
before themselves and their auditors, just as in the Gospels we
have the ideals and the precepts which Jesus put before his disciples
and the Jewish people at large. In what degree the ideals were
realized, and the precepts fulfilled, is another matter. For it is a
matter of dispute whether the degree in which an ideal is fulfilled
or fulfillable should affect our judgment as to its excellence and
value. In one respect, indeed, the nature of much (by no means
all) of the Rabbinic literature puts the Rabbis at some disadvantage
when we compare their utterances with those of Jesus. For whereas
Jesus is always speaking as a teacher and a prophet, Rabbinic
literature often reproduces the Rabbis talking, as it were, among
themselves, and without intending to be observed. In other words,
by no means all of what we hear from them is taken from sermons
or is deliberate teaching. Some things are casual remarks or discussions, when we catch the Rabbis off their guard. Perhaps it may
be argued that their characters or beliefs come out more truly and
exactly in such remarks and discussions than in their formal and
deliberate teaching. But I sometimes think that it is rather hard
lines on them when some of their casual utterances are compared with
the public teachings of Jesus at his highest and best. On the other
hand, I wish that I could have found space and opportunity for
quoting more Rabbinic stories about particular Rabbis or their disciples. For often these stories seem to throw more light upon the
true nature of Rabbinic religion—upon its peculiar character and
fragrance and idealism—than many of their more deliberate and
copy-book maxims and adages. I may be able, though this is
doubtful, with the help of a trained Rabbinic scholar, to publish
later on a selection of some of the most interesting and characteristic
of these stories. Sometimes the stories are not easy to translate
word for word, because our standards of taste, and those of eastern
Rabbis sixteen or seventeen hundred years ago, are not the same.
But it is a fact that these very stories almost always do high honour
to Rabbinic conceptions of morality.

As my book is intended only to deal with *Rabbinic* parallels to
Gospel teaching, I have entirely omitted all references to the
apocalyptic literature. The parallels (or the contrasts) from *that*
quarter are much better known and are easily discoverable. More-

over, the main apocalyptic literature itself is now ready to everybody's hand in Dr. Charles' great collection. A similar corpus of
translations of *Rabbinic* literature is not likely to be available for a
very long time! Hence one more justification, as it seems to me,
of the present attempt.

MATTHEW

v. 3–12. Apart from all questions as to the original form of the Beatitudes, and apart again from questions as to the parallels which may be found in Rabbinic literature for each verse taken separately, we have to consider the Beatitudes as a whole—as we have them *now*; and more especially as we have them in Matthew, for there is little doubt that the effect which they produce in Matthew is much greater than the effect produced by the shorter form of them in Luke (vi. 20–23). The Beatitudes in the mass are more than each Beatitude taken separately; and the Matthean additions, if such they are—' in spirit,' ' after righteousness,' ' the pitiful,' ' the pure in heart ' and ' the peacemakers '—add greatly to the beauty and solemnity of the whole. There is a certain glow and passion about the whole passage which are unique : there is a certain religious character and *ethos* about it which are marked and distinctive. The Beatitudes as a whole are not entirely Rabbinic, though we may find parallels to each statement taken individually. They may fairly be considered as new in spite of the parallels. The religion or the religious ideal which the Beatitudes teach or imply is one-sided ; it may be criticized ; it may need supplementing in more ways than one ; but it is certainly great. And if a good deal of the ten verses is due to the editor, or to a filling-in of what was originally said by Jesus, that does not much matter. We may say (1) that these fillings-in are according to the spirit of Jesus ; (2) that they show, what several bits in the prophets show also, that the compilers and editors, working upon a fine tradition, could also be inspired. It is a false argument to say : ' This passage or sentence is so fine, it must have been said by Isaiah or by Jesus.' The compiler *could* rise to great heights of inspiration because Isaiah and Jesus had lived and taught before him. If it be asked in *what* the impression left by the Beatitudes in Matthew is peculiar, and in *what* it appears different from anything which we may construct as the Rabbinic religion, or as the spirit of the Rabbinic religion, it would be very hard, I think, to put impression and difference into words. But I am not prepared to say that this proves that the difference must be imaginary and that the impression is illusive. I suppose one part of the impression is a feeling as if religion were concentrated and expressed in a certain condition of soul, which manifests itself in gentleness and pity and love and patient endurance of wrong ; in a certain peacefulness, which is also capable of heroism ; in a certain glow and enthusiasm, which produce a peculiar and indomitable happiness. This is the religion of the Beatitudes or their religious ideal ; all else falls away,—all that is external, institutional ; all that is civic and political ; all that has to do with beauty and art and knowledge ; all that makes for the careful and orderly and gradual removal of evils by intelligent legislation ; all conceptions of ' progress.' And yet the Beatitudes seem to teach the one thing which is more needful than any of these, which goes both before them and after them. The difference between this religion and the religion of the Rabbis is also difficult to express in words. The religion of the Rabbis is more balanced, more comprehensive ; it lays stress on the outward as well as the inward ; it lays stress on the institutional, on the legal ; it lays immense stress on knowledge, or, rather, on a peculiar kind of knowledge, holding it to be no less important than humility and pity and love. Yet, if it is more comprehensive than the religion of the Beatitudes, it seems also somewhat less concentrated, intense, and passionate. And yet a religion which produced and fed the souls of the martyrs—how can we speak of it as wanting in passion and in intensity ? We must, perhaps, be content to chronicle a difference, and leave it at that. It may be that the happiness of suffering for a cause seems more emphasized in the Beatitudes than in any passage of the Rabbinic literature except in the story of Akiba's martyrdom. And, perhaps, we may say that it is of spiritual and moral profit to us to have certain religious ideals put before us with intensity and one-sidedness : let each ideal be represented by itself and flashed before us with the utmost light. All-roundness and comprehensiveness cannot be expressed with equal intensity : we cannot take all in at once, and balance prevents enthusiasm.

Mr. Loewe observes : ' Your view that the Beatitudes as a

whole are not entirely Rabbinic is, I think, quite fair. Two
points occur to me. First, the Beatitudes seem biblical, rather
than Rabbinic. They go straight back to Hannah's song, or to the
Suffering Servant, or to the " meek " of the Psalms. Now in comparing N.T. with Rabbinics, the O.T. is often left out of account, as
being a common possession, and hence negligible in this connection.
This, I think, is wrong. The O.T. belongs to the Jewish side, and
just because the O.T. words were so deeply impressed in the hearts
of Rabbis and people, we sometimes find gaps that seem strange in
Rabbinic teaching. The fact is that a Rabbi did not deem it
necessary to repeat or enlarge upon a theme when a Bible verse
was already a motto to everyone on the subject. The N.T. was
chiefly addressed to pagans, and the audience would not be familiar
with the Old Testament, as a Jewish audience would have been.
Secondly, as to the two forms in which the Beatitudes are preserved :
the shorter form strikes one as the more original, but the growth
of additions is typically Rabbinic. Over and over again do we
find a paragraph of Midrash in which, after a Bible verse has been
expounded and applied to certain circumstances, the next sentence
records a slight variation, and the next yet another, and so on,
each by a different teacher. One feels that the mental effort involved in making these insignificant changes is so slight, and the
result is so puny, that the inclusion of all the variants is wearisome.
But these variants are nothing but recensions of the sayings of one
teacher, repeated by his disciples, altered, slightly or greatly, in the
lapse of time, and finally collected and put side by side by the author
or editor of the Midrash.'

3. There is not, perhaps, much for me to add beyond what I
have said in the Commentary and beyond the suggestions and
references in Dr. Abrahams' essay on the *Am ha-Aretz*. I feel pretty
sure that he is right in thinking that S.B. are wrong in identifying
the poor in spirit with the *Amme ha-Aretz*. The poor in spirit are
not necessarily the same as the ὄχλοι of ix. 36, who were ἐσκυλμένοι
καὶ ἐριμμένοι, 'harassed and prostrate.' Nor are they necessarily
the same as the νήπιοι of xi. 25, though, perhaps, they are to be
co-ordinated more with the second class than with the first. But
S.B. believe that 'the poor in spirit' *do* mean that broad stratum
of 'geringe und verachtete Leute' (unimportant and despised folk)

among the Jewish people, known as the *Amme ha-Aretz*, and regarded
by the Rabbis with disdain and hatred. (*Cp.* John vii. 49.) It
makes, they say, no material difference if Luke calls these people
simply 'the poor,' while Matthew calls them 'the poor in spirit.'
The same people are meant; only that Luke looks rather to their
outward condition, Matthew to their inward quality. Yet S.B.
appear to contradict themselves in the very next sentence, for they
say : 'the *Amme ha-Aretz* were by no means always people who were
wanting in earthly goods; there were rich people among them;
but what characterized them all was a certain poverty of a spiritual
kind. They were ignorant of the interpretation which the Scribes
and Rabbis gave to the Law, and they did not venture to ascribe
to themselves the power and the happiness of ordering and ruling
their lives according to Rabbinic injunctions. Thus they were
constantly experiencing the disdain and contempt of those who
strictly observed the Law. No wonder that they became a prey
to pessimism and regarded themselves as a *massa perditionis.*'
(' Sie kannten weder in genügendem Masse die Auslegung, die die
pharisäischen Schriftgelehrten dem Gesetz zuteil werden liessen,
noch trauten sie sich die Kraft und die Freudigkeit zu, ihr religiöses
Leben nach den Satzungen der Rabbinen erfolgreich zu ordnen und
zu regeln. Dabei erfuhren sie täglich aufs neue, wie sie von den
Gesetzesstrengen verachtet und vermieden wurden; was Wunder
also, wenn sie schliesslich eine Beute des Pessimismus wurden, und
sich selber als eine *massa perditionis* vorkamen ? ') This conception
of the *Amme ha-Aretz* is woven out of fragile and shaky material.
There is no adequate evidence that the *Amme ha-Aretz*, whoever they
were, were gloomy, unhappy, pessimistic, or that they thought of
themselves as doomed to perdition. Nor, again, is there any clear
evidence that they constituted a ' broad stratum,' a ' breite Schicht,'
of the whole population. On the contrary; the *Amme ha-Aretz*
and the Rabbis cordially disliked each other; but the people
regarded the Rabbis with great respect as their religious leaders
and teachers. How then can the *Amme ha-Aretz* be identified with
the ' broad stratum ' of the population, as if, on the one hand, you
had the great majority of the people, and on the other, a small
religious aristocracy ? Again, if there were many well-to-do folk
among the *Amme ha-Aretz*, how can Luke and Matthew refer to the
same persons ?

On the whole, it is more likely that Jesus was referring to real poverty, but that the addition was in so far justifiable as, in the Psalms, and doubtless in the ideas and in the terminology to which the Psalms gave vogue, poverty and humility, wealth and pride, were supposed by many to go together. It is true that there is a separate Beatitude for the meek (οἱ πραεῖς). Nevertheless, it may be doubted whether much difference is intended between the πτωχοὶ τῷ πνεύματι and the πραεῖς. If so, was there a real difference between the constant Rabbinic exaltation of humility and the Matthean exaltation of the poor in spirit ? S.B. think that there was. The humility which the poor in spirit possess is a humility which knows itself to be incapable of its own power to please God, and therefore expects, and prays for, the blessedness of the Kingdom of God to come exclusively from God's grace. It is a ' Demut, die im Bewusstsein der menschlichen Untüchtigkeit, Gott zu gefallen, die Seligkeit des Himmelreiches ausschliesslich von der Gnade Gottes erhofft und erbetet.' [1] But this is too Pauline and Lutheran a conception to be ascribed to Jesus. He was possessed by no such tremendous oppositions, such violent and yawning differences, between human will and divine grace. On the other hand, we may with propriety allow that the Rabbinic humility is one which could well consort with any amount of ' knowledge,' and indeed was regarded as the peculiar virtue of the truly learned. To the Rabbis, ignorance was rather associated with haughtiness than with humility. Whereas to Jesus there was no such association. We may, indeed, go so far as to say that he looked for the humble, the poor in spirit, among the ignorant rather than among the learned, and he associated pride with knowledge rather than with ignorance. I should imagine that both he and the Rabbis were somewhat prejudiced— they in favour of learning and of the association of humility with learning, and he in favour of ignorance and of the association of humility with ignorance. In reality, humility can go with both.

In Sabbath 33 a *ad fin.* three different diseases are stated to be the signs of three different sins : thus, dropsy points to unchastity, jaundice to causeless hate, quinsy to slander, while poverty is the sign of haughtiness. Whether the Rabbis or any Rabbi could really

---

[1] ' It is a humility which, realizing man's incapacity of himself to please God, hopes and prays for the blessedness of the Kingdom of God exclusively from the Divine Grace.'

have believed in such nonsense as quinsy being the sign or the
punishment of slander seems doubtful. But, perhaps, they were
more serious in joining haughtiness with poverty. In Sanhedrin 24 a
(*cp.* Kiddushin 49 b) it is said that the poverty meant is poverty in
the knowledge of the Law. Elsewhere (Nedarim 41 a) we are told,
'No one is poor except the man who is poor in knowledge. If he
has knowledge, he has all ; if he has none, what has he ? ' And
this aphorism is quoted many times. S.B. cite, as typical of the
Rabbinic attitude, sayings of a third-century Rabbi Elazar who
declared that it is forbidden to show compassion to a man without
knowledge ; that if a man gives bread to anyone who has no knowledge, sufferings will befall him ; that the man without knowledge
will go into banishment (Sanhedrin 92 a). The story of Rabbi (*i.e.*
R. Judah, the 'Prince') who grieved that, in a time of famine, he had
given from his store to an *Am ha-Aretz* will be quoted later on (Baba
Batra 8 a).[1] R. Elazar (Kethuboth 111 b) went so far as to deny any
hope of resurrection to the *Amme ha-Aretz*. R. Yochanan objected to
this, and R. Elazar thereupon so far modified his opinion as to
suggest that if an *Am ha-Aretz* married his daughters to disciples of
the wise, or if he looked after their business for them, and let them
benefit from his possessions, he might escape so tragic a doom.
We therefore see that the exclusion of the *Amme ha-Aretz* from the
life to come was, at all events, a subject of discussion, and Elbogen
is not justified in saying that such a view 'liegt der pharisäischen
Auffassung völlig fern. Sie unterscheidet wohl Gute und Böse, nicht
aber Gelehrte und Ungelehrte' (*Jewish Studies in memory of Israel
Abrahams*, New York, 1927, p. 140).[2] Rabbi said (Baba Batra 8 a)
that punishments come to the world only because of the *Amme
ha-Aretz*. Yet whether we may assume with S.B. that the man
without knowledge is always the *Am ha-Aretz* seems to me doubtful.
How far, again, the sayings are always seriously meant is also
doubtful. The same Rabbi Elazar is reported to have said of
the *Am ha-Aretz* that one might pierce him through (*i.e.* murder
him) even on a Day of Atonement which fell on a Saturday.
It is obvious from the next sentence in the Hebrew that this

---

[1] See p. 255.
[2] 'Such a view is quite alien to the Pharisaic point of view in this regard
which discriminates between the Good and the Bad, but not between the Learned
and the Unlearned.'

is only a paradox or a bitter joke. The saying occurs in the famous page of Pesachim (49 b) which contains most of the well-known fierce attacks upon the *Am ha-Aretz*, and tells of the bitter hatred between them and the Rabbis. ' The hatred of the *Amme ha-Aretz* for the *Talmide Chachamim* (the learned class) is greater than the hatred of the gentiles against Israel, and the hatred of their wives exceeds theirs.' While it is clear that R. Elazar's saying must be taken with many grains of salt, it is no less clear that there *were* certain people against whom the Rabbi felt bitterly, and who felt bitterly against the Rabbis, but anybody who reads Dr. Abrahams' essay with care will perceive how slight the evidence is for any identification of the *Amme ha-Aretz* with a broad stratum of the whole population in the first century. The big, mournful class of pessimists—religious outcasts, despairing of their own salvation, despised by the learned and more or less despising themselves —appears to be a figment of S.B.'s and other Christian theologians' vivid imagination. And if the *Amme ha-Aretz* are to be regarded as equivalent to the great mass of unlearned persons, why should there be any doubt expressed as to who the *Am ha-Aretz* actually is ? And yet we know that this very question is actually asked. ' Who is an *Am ha-Aretz* ? Whoever does not eat his non-holy food in a condition of ritual purity. Whoever does not properly tithe his fruits. Whoever does not read the *Shema* morning and evening. Whoever does not lay *tefillin*. Whoever has no *zizith* on his garment. Whoever has no *mezuzah* on his door. Whoever has sons, and does not rear them to the study of the Torah. Whoever, though he has studied Torah and Mishnah, has not ministered to the disciples of the wise.' These definitions vary from a very high to a very low demand, and show the uncertainty which prevailed or which came to prevail upon the subject (Berachoth 47 b; Sotah 22 a).

Again, that the Rabbis no less than Jesus genuinely admired humility; that they regarded pride and arrogance as hateful sins, and humility as an adorable virtue, is unquestionable. The passages which S.B. have the honesty to quote show all this very plainly. ' A humble mind and a lowly spirit are the tokens of the disciples of Abraham.' (Aboth v. 22. That Balaam = Jesus, as S.B. allege, is far from certain.) ' The Torah is maintained only among the humble ' (perhaps ' firmly established ' would be better than ' maintained ') (מתקיימת) (Tanchuma, *Ki Tabo*, 24 b). R. Joshua b. Levi held that humility was

the greatest of the virtues (Abodah Zarah 20 b). It is said that arrogance is equivalent to idolatry (Sotah 4 b) ; much more against
arrogance is found in Sotah 5 a and b. ' Of the arrogant God says :
he and I cannot dwell together in the world.' ' The Shechinah laments
over the arrogant.' ' Of the humble the Scripture declares that he is
regarded as if he had offered every sacrifice in the Law.' ' Who will
inherit the life to come ? He who is humble, and constantly studies
the Law, and does not claim credit for himself ' (Sanhedrin 88 b).
R. Joshua ben Levi put humility even above saintliness (חסידות),
for the Good Tidings which the prophet is to announce are sent,
not to the saints, but to the humble (Abodah Zarah 20 b). It would
be wearisome to quote more passages. Many more are given in Ziegler,
pp. 61, 63, and many about haughtiness on pp. 269–273 (cp. also
Moore, II. 273–275). I have not found any passages which definitely
say that an unlearned, but humble, person is acceptable to God, or
that a humble person, even if unlearned, is acceptable, yet one has
the impression that the majority of the Rabbis in every generation
did not despise unlearned piety, if it was not deliberately neglectful
of the Law. Let an artisan say a small modicum of prayer, let him
observe the ordinary elements of the ceremonial Law, and there is
no reason to believe that such a one would have been despised, or
regarded as an *Am ha-Aretz* in the objectionable sense of the word.
On the other hand, it is doubtful whether any Rabbi could have
regarded such a one as ideally qualified for heaven. The Rabbi
would not have said, ' Happy are the poor in spirit,' just *because* they
are ignorant of the Law ; he would not have said that just *because*
they were ignorant would they enter the Kingdom of Heaven. It
is certain that he would often have held that a man of virtue, or one
who displayed some special virtue, would, *in spite of ignorance*, enter
the Kingdom. But knowledge was an excellent qualification ; not
an impediment. The first of the Rabbinic Beatitudes might be,
' Happy are the humble.' But the second would be, ' Happy are the
wise,' or ' Happy are they who study the Law, for theirs is the
Kingdom of Heaven.' And instead of seeing any discrepancy
between the second and first Beatitudes, the Rabbis would have said
that they must go together. The second virtue could not attain
the goal without the first, though I do not think the Rabbis would
have refused to acknowledge that there might be cases in which you
could find the first without the second.

Whether the *Amme ha-Aretz* was as much a phenomenon of, say, A.D. 30 as of A.D. 100 or 130 is disputed. Dr. Abrahams appeared to think not (Vol. II. p. 657). S.B., relying to some extent perhaps on N.T. evidence, think ' yes.' In a well-known passage at the end of the Mishnah Sotah (ix. 15) we hear a great deal about deterioration. ' With the death of Rabbi X. this virtue, with the death of Rabbi Y that virtue, ended,' and so on. It also says that after the destruction of the Temple, ' the wise equal (are no better than) the teachers of children, the teachers equal the synagogue beadles (חזנא), and the beadles equal the *Amme ha-Aretz*, while the *Amme ha-Aretz* degenerate more and more ' (אזלא ודלדלה). One wonders whether there was any truth in this gloomy utterance.

Sometimes one feels as if the *Amme ha-Aretz* were used in a more restricted and technical sense, and sometimes in a more general sense. Who were the *Amme ha-Aretz*, for instance, ' attending ' whose ' houses of assembly ' ' puts a man,' like ' morning sleep and mid-day wine and children's talk,' ' out of the world ' ? (Aboth iii. 14). In Hillel's famous saying (Aboth ii. 6) the *Am ha-Aretz* seems rather to be a man with a particular character than to represent the whole broad unlearned class. For the empty-headed man (or boorish man), and the shamefaced man, and the passionate man, and the very business-engaged man, with whom he is associated, are people of a particular character rather than sections of the population. It is also noticeable that the *Am ha-Aretz* is said not to be capable of becoming a *Chasid* ; now the *Chasid* means a man of high piety : as if we said : no fool can be a saint. It would not follow that he could not be a very decent-living fellow. And, perhaps, Hillel meant no more. Certainly the boor is worse than the *Am ha-Aretz*, for he cannot be a sin-fearing man, as we might say that no really coarse-minded man can avoid falling into sin. With Hillel's saying goes naturally the saying about the four characters : The *Am ha-Aretz* says, What is mine is thine, what is thine is mine. Such a person seems to be a muddler and stupid ; he is not wicked. The wicked is he who says, What is thine is mine, and what is mine is mine ; and whereas the average man says, What is mine is mine, and what is thine is thine, the *Chasid* says, What is mine is thine, and what is thine is thine. Here, again, we see that the *Chasid* is the man who reaches a very high degree of goodness and self-sacrifice : the *Am ha-Aretz* falls below the average rather by folly than by obliquity,

and anyway he is better than the wicked. Resh Lakish compared
Israel to a vine : the stems are the householders (בעלי בתים), the
clusters are the 'disciples of the wise,' the leaves are the *Amme ha-
Aretz*, the dry suckers are the empty ones (apparently those who have
no discipline or morals). And the Palestine saying was, ' Let the
grapes pray for the leaves, for without leaves there would be no
grapes ' (Chullin 92 a). Here, again, the *Am ha-Aretz* does not equal
the sinner. He does not take the lowest place. On the other hand,
one sees how liable the Rabbis were to fall into pride, or, at all events,
how they must have needed the utmost self-control not to become
' proud.' For they honestly believed that they and their like were
the élite of the people, the grapes of the entire vineyard. Such a
belief must have been a great moral danger. Fancy if all the Dons
of Oxford and Cambridge, or all the Professors at the Universities,
really thought that they were the grapes of the national vineyard !
The Rabbinic exhortations to humility may have been needed.
Perhaps the Rabbis knew where their own shoes pinched. So it was
possible for the *Am ha-Aretz* and the disciples of the wise to fall into
the same sin of haughtiness and even of slander. It is said, ' What
is the remedy for slander, or how is a man not to succumb to the
temptation of uttering slander? If he be a disciple of the wise, let
him occupy himself with the Law ; if he be an *Am ha-Aretz*, let him
humble himself ' (ואם עם הארץ הוא ישפיל דעתו) (Arachin 15 b). In
such passages and in others it would seem as if the *Am ha-Aretz* is
simply to be identified (as S.B. always maintain) with the ignorant
—with the man who does not ' study.' So, too, when in Aboth R.
Nathan xvi. (32 b), it says, ' Let not a man accustom himself to say :
Love the wise, hate the disciples ; love the disciples, hate the
Amme ha-Aretz ; but let him love all, except the Heretics and the
Apostates and the Informers ; even as David said, Do I not hate
them that hate Thee ? ' And in that page in Pesachim already
alluded to (49 b), where R. Akiba speaks of his bitter hatred of the
' wise,' when he was still an *Am ha-Aretz*, before he began to
study, it seems still more clearly implied that the *Am ha-Aretz*
must be identified with the unlearned people at large. For it is
urged, Let a man sell all that he has and marry the daughter of a
disciple of the wise, for if he die, or have to emigrate, he may be
assured that his children will become disciples of the wise. But let
him not marry the daughter of the *Am ha-Aretz*, for if he die, or has

to emigrate, he may be assured that his sons will become *Amme ha-Aretz* (do.). . . . The Rabbis say: Let a man marry the daughter of a disciple of the wise ; if he cannot find one, let him marry the daughter of one of the great men of his generation ; if he cannot find one, then the daughter of a president of a synagogue ; if he cannot find her, then the daughter of the collectors of charity funds for the poor ; if he cannot find her, then the daughter of a teacher of children. But let him not marry the daughters of the *Amme ha-Aretz*, for they are loathsome, and their children are abominations, and of them Scripture says (Deut. xxvii. 21), Cursed be he that lies with any manner of beast ' (Pesachim 49 a *ad fin.*). In this appalling utterance the *Am ha-Aretz* is, inferentially, anybody who is not a learned man, a man of importance, a synagogue official, a distributor of communal charity, or a teacher. And yet we have so much evidence that the people were on the side of their Rabbis, and that the Rabbis sprang from, and were attached to, the people. Surely a thick mist still hangs over the thorny and lugubrious subject of the *Am ha-Aretz*.

Mr. Loewe writes : ' *Am ha-Aretz* is a very elastic term, and it often means " cad " rather than " fool." The last passage you cite is typical.[1] The scriptural verse shows that it refers to men with unrestrained sexual appetites, in other words, to men far removed from godliness, the last people whom Jesus would have called " blessed." Ignorance of the Law does not mean merely unletteredness, it means ignorance of decency, and even defiant ignorance, ignorance which refuses to amend. Who would wish to give his daughter to such a man ? The force of Akiba's reminiscences of his unregenerate days lies just in this. This *Am ha-Aretz* hated the Rabbi with the hatred of the souteneur for the Parson. That the *Am ha-Aretz* was lax in tithes, etc., is simply *pars pro toto* ; many of them were lax also in morals, and it was these who incurred the hatred of the Rabbis, and reciprocated it. But they were surely not " blessed." These immoral persons were doubtless found among all classes, not excluding the poor.[2] But that the poorer classes

---

[1] ' It should be supplemented by R. Meir's saying, on the same page : " He who gives his daughter in marriage to an *Am ha-Aretz* does as though he delivered her bound to a lion, who treads down and devours without shame." '

[2] ' No special stratum of society is implied. The same page in Pesachim describes the *Am ha-Aretz* as a man whose word is unreliable, who is unfit to be a guardian of an orphan or to be trusted with charity funds.'

also included simple pious believers is certain. I do not believe
that the " poor " or " meek " in the Beatitudes are the *Amme
ha-Aretz*. The meek are just the meek, and no others, in the
Beatitudes as in the Psalms. Overweening pride and its opposite
are the theme of many a psalm; why assume that Jesus meant
anything else ?

' The perversion of the use of *Am ha-Aretz* (I mean the idea that
it means " unlettered " and not " cad ") can be paralleled by the
biblical term " *Nabal.*" The " *Nabal* " is translated " fool " in the A.V.,
but modern scholarship has shown the inadequacy of this translation.
A distinguished scholar of my acquaintance used always to translate
" *Nebalah* " by " an outrage on public decency," and this rendering
may be illustrated by its use in Genesis (of the rape of Dinah), and
elsewhere. The *Am ha-Aretz* was usually a " *Nabal.*" See the
usage in 1 Sam. xv. 25; 2 Sam. iii. 33, xiii. 13; Isaiah xxxii.
5, 6. Notice Deut. xxxii. 6, where " *Nabal* " is contrasted with
" *Chacham* " (wise). This is significant, for it shows the beginning
of the association of goodness with knowledge, but " *Nabal* " still
means " cad," even here. Doubtless there were Rabbis who were
" learning proud." Here and there a man may have been un-
charitable, just as a parson may denounce those who stay away
from church, and may overestimate his profession. But wholesale
condemnations of the Rabbis are futile and false.'

I may add here an interesting quotation from the Sifre 27 a.
The close connection between the Biblical words עָנָו, ' humble,'
' meek,' and עָנִי, ' poor,' is well known. In Numbers xii. 3 Moses
is spoken of as ' exceedingly humble ' (עָנָו). The Sifre, however,
interprets the word to include, as it were, both poverty and humility.
It says : ' Poor, *i.e.* humble in his spirit ' (בְדַעְתּו). If an objector
were to argue that the text means poor in body (*i.e.* weak), the Sifre
rebuts this from a fanciful interpretation of Numbers xxi. 34,
according to which Moses himself slew with his own hands both
Sihon and Og ! If, on the other hand, it were suggested that the
text means poor in wealth, another fanciful interpretation of two
other Biblical passages proves that Moses was very rich. Hence
עָנָו (humble, poor) must mean ' poor in spirit.' (The passage is
translated and explained in ' Midrash Sifre on Numbers,' translated
by the Rev. P. P. Levertoff, S.P.C.K., 1926, p. 81.)

The student should read with great care Moore's short chapter concerning the '*Amme ha-Aretz*' in *Judaism*, Vol. ii. pp. 156–161. He seems to accept the view that they are the ' ignorant and negligent masses ' as opposed to those who were ' instructed in their religion, and scrupulous in the performance of its obligations.' This division of the population ' appears in the utterances of teachers of the first century as something universally understood, but its consequences were more fully developed in the schools of the second century in Galilee, where the scholars who migrated thither after the war under Hadrian probably found both in town and country a population which knew less about the traditional Law than the corresponding class in Judaea, and was more negligent in the observance of the law they knew.' ' The Jews in Galilee seem previously to have run more to a militant patriotism than to punctiliousness in their religious obligations. In Babylonia the "*Am ha-Aretz*" question does not appear to have had anything like the same importance.' ' The religious leaders tried to instruct the peasantry in the somewhat complicated laws of tithing and the like, and to induce them to fulfil the requirements. From a man who was recognized as "a tither" the scrupulous could buy without being under the necessity of tithing over again for themselves, and it would only be natural that they should do their marketing with him. Later, one who has undertaken to observe the regulations about these matters was certified as "trustworthy" (*ne'man*). The punctilious Jews, on their side, formed a voluntary association, the members of which pledged themselves in the presence of three associates to observe strictly the laws regarding uncleanness and the precautions by which they were surrounded, as well as those noted in the preceding paragraphs. The specific obligations assumed are thus enumerated : The Associate shall not give *Terumah* or tithes to (a priest or levite who is) an "*Am ha-Aretz*"; perform his purifications in the presence of a man of this class ; be the guest of one, or entertain one in his house, unless he leave his outer garment outside ; he shall not sell him of the products of the soil either "dry" (grain and the like) or "moist" (garden vegetables or fruits), or buy from him any but "dry" things (which are not liable to contract uncleanness by contact), etc. He should not travel in company with one of the class, visit him, study the Law in his presence, and much more to the like effect. The " people of the land " were not to be summoned as witnesses, nor their testimony admitted ; no secret

was to be entrusted to them ; one of them might not be appointed
guardian of an orphan, or custodian of the poor rates, etc. Marriage
between the classes was condemned in terms of abhorrence. Admission to the association was open to men of the common people on
the same conditions as to the educated class, with provision for
the instruction of the former in the obligations he assumed in a
probationary period. It was, in fact, one of the means by which
conscientious Jews tried to secure a more general knowledge of the
Law and regard for it. It may be suspected that the animosity
which many of the teachers of the second century express in most
emphatic language towards the " people of the land " was provoked
by the fact that few of them responded to this uplifting enterprise ;
the majority remained wilfully in their ignorance and negligence.'
Moore, who, throughout his book, presents the religion of the Rabbis
in the most favourable light, though always with the fullest knowledge of the sources, does not conceal the moral and religious dangers
which the division of a whole community into (religiously) Instructed
and (religiously) Ignorant involved. He says : ' The splitting of
society on such lines involves greater evils than the reciprocal antipathy of classes, however ugly the feeling and the expression of it
may be, and the worst effect of it is upon those of whom better
things are justly expected. The educated had the common pride
of learning in double measure because it was religious learning.
It was impossible to obey the divine laws without knowledge of the
Law, written and traditional. Hillel had put it in a word, "No
ignorant man (*Am ha-Aretz*) is religious." They were no less proud
of the pains they took to keep the laws in all their refinements,
and particularly, as we have seen above, those about which common men were most careless. They were led in this way to lay
special stress on articles in the laws which, from one point of view,
seem of the smallest religious significance—the taxation of agricultural produce for the support of a hereditary clergy that after the
destruction of the temple no longer had any sacerdotal functions,
and the various kinds of uncleanness which, detached from their
relation to participation in the cultus, were extended to social intercourse. The large development of these sides of the law long ante-
dates the Christian era, and preoccupation with such things is the
only notion many have of Pharisaism. So far as that is concerned,
the Pharisee or Schoolman would have replied: God gave these laws

for reasons sufficient to Himself ; it is not for men to set them aside as antiquated or unimportant. In the application of them many cases arise which require a definite ruling and a practice in conformity to it. You may think them small commandments by the side of those whose obligation the reason and conscience of all men recognize ; but fidelity to the revealed will of God is not a small matter, and the crucial test of it is precisely solicitude about keeping the commandments whose obligation is solely positive—God has commanded thus and so. It is, as has been repeatedly remarked, the unimpeachable logic of revealed religion. The effect of such a situation as we have been considering goes farther than this putting of all obligations in principle on the same plane. In all sects, and in every *ecclesiola in ecclesia,* it is the peculiarities in doctrine, observance, or piety, that are uppermost in the minds of the members ; what they have in common with the great body is no doubt taken for granted, but, so to speak, lies in the sectarian subconsciousness. Worse than this displacement of values by emphasis on the differential peculiarities is the self-complacency of the members of such a party or association and the self-righteousness that comes of believing that their peculiarities of doctrine or practice make them singularly well-pleasing to God. With this goes censoriousness towards outsiders, which often presumes to voice the disapprobation of God. The Pharisees and the Associates, who seem to have numbered among them in the second century most of the learned and their disciples, conspicuously illustrate these faults. It is not without detriment to himself that a man cherishes the consciousness of being superior to his fellows, and the injury to his character is not least when he has the best reason for his opinion.'

It would seem to emerge (1) that the Rabbis of Babylonia were less liable to the dangers connected with the *Am ha-Aretz* than those of Palestine ; (2) that after the second century the whole question became less acute ; (3) that even the Rabbis of Palestine of the first and second century were aware of the perils because of the constant and emphatic stress which they laid upon humility ; and (4) that it was much more the passionate desire to fulfil the Law to its very utmost which brought the whole opposition to the *Am ha-Aretz* about than any supercilious looking down upon ignorance as such. The Law is the source of all the best and noblest points in the Rabbinic religion and of all its weaknesses.

4. This verse is based on Isaiah lx. 2, and the mourners are meant quite generally. It is to my mind certain that S.B. are wrong when they interpret the mourners to mean ' die geistig Armen, die ihre Unzulänglichkeit vor Gott erkannt haben, und über diese, nachdem die Nähe des Himmelreichs verkündigt ist, Busstrauer empfinden.' [1] I presume that the implication of the verse is that God will be their consoler or comforter. Even so, already in the Old Testament, God is the supreme comforter. And the Rabbis were not slow to notice and bring together the two lovely O.T. verses about God, that he comforts and has pity like a father and a mother (Psalm ciii. 13 ; Isaiah lxvi. 13 ; Pesikta 139 a *fin.*). There is nothing in the verse which is off the Rabbinic line, unless it be the tendency to associate happiness with earthly mourning, as if, before the New Aeon, there was of necessity sorrow and mourning for the righteous and the repentant, and as if the more you ' mourn ' in this Aeon or world, the more you shall be comforted and rejoice in another. Though we may find parallels to this view in the Rabbinic literature, it is not in accordance with the predominating, or, at all events, with the conquering, strand. This Aeon and world are God's, as well as the New Aeon and the world to come. And happiness in this world is (*a*) possible and (*b*) desirable for the righteous, and not merely the portion of the careless and the wicked. How was it possible, and how and why was it desirable ? The Rabbinic answer would be, Through the. Law, its study and its observance ; through the Law, which sanctified, and gave sanction and decency to, the legitimate pleasures of sense, and which threw around them, and connected with them, many ceremonial observances, the keeping and practice of which gave happiness, and also increased the joy of these very pleasures themselves. Thus, *e.g.*, a Sabbath meal (Friday evening) was a pleasure in itself. It was sanctified by the Law. It was made additionally happy by the Grace which was said before and after it. In this attitude to material joys, and in its intensification of them through the Law, lies (as it seems to me) a real difference between Jesus and the Rabbis, or shall we more rightly say, between developed Rabbinic Judaism and developed orthodox Christianity ?

---

[1] 'The poor in spirit who, recognizing their own insufficiency before God, penitently deplore it when the near advent of the Kingdom has been proclaimed to them.'

5. The happiness of the Meek. The verse is perhaps an editorial addition easily made up from Ps. xxxvii. 11. We cannot properly distinguish, as S.B. would like to do, between *Demut* and *Sanftmut*, as if a special kind of humility were spoken of in 3, and a special sort of forbearance and meekness, in opposition to quick temper and irascibility, were alluded to in 5. S.B. admit that the words ענוה and ענותנות mean both *Sanftmut* und *Demut*, and that to the humble there stand opposed, not merely קפדן the hot-tempered, but also גס רוח the haughty. Meanwhile, both as regards pride and as regards hot-temperedness, the Rabbinic attitude is the same. And so as to the praise both of *Demut* and of *Sanftmut*, humility and gentleness (forbearance, meekness, etc.). S.B. quote all the familiar stories about Hillel, but I need not repeat them here. They are *too* familiar ! Quaint and rather illustrative of Rabbinic hospitality is the saying S.B. quote from Aboth R. Nathan vii. (17 b) : ' When a man is gentle, and his family is gentle, if a poor man stands at the door, and says, Is your father within ? they reply, Yes, enter. Then hardly has he entered, before the table is prepared, and he comes in, and eats, and blesses God. When they are hot-tempered, they reply, No, and they rebuke him, and drive him away with an outcry.'

6. I am still inclined to hold by what I said in my notes on this verse. I am sure that S.B. exaggerate when they say : ' Die vierte Seligpreisung handelt von solchen, welche wissen, dass sie aus eigner Kraft keine Gerechtigkeit aufzubringen vermögen, die vor Gott gilt, und doch nach dieser Gerechtigkeit Verlangen tragen.'[1] Such sharp antitheses, and such Pauline, or Lutheran, distinctions, were foreign to the teaching of Jesus, or even to the man who edited Matthew or compiled the Sermon on the Mount. So far as Jesus is concerned, I am still inclined to think that Luke's version is more authentic than Matthew's, and that Luke referred to material or literal hunger, just as he referred to material or literal poverty and to material or literal weeping. But taking the verse in Matthew as it stands, and ignoring the question whether Jesus spoke it or not, it does not mean what S.B. suppose it to mean. There is no

---

[1] ' The fourth Beatitude speaks of those persons who know that of their own power they cannot produce any righteousness which counts before God, and yet long to possess such righteousness.'

sharp antithesis between the righteousness which man can achieve, or rather, cannot achieve, by his own unaided efforts, and the righteousness which is imparted to him, or which is granted to him, through his faith, by the grace of God. Neither Jesus nor the compiler of Matthew ever makes this antithesis or teaches on these lines. Either the verse means simply, 'Those who try hard to be good shall be well rewarded in the New Aeon or in the world to come' (this seems to me the simplest interpretation); or, one may suppose the verse to mean that those who yearn to be regarded as righteous by God shall, by their happy lot in the new era, be shown that God does recognize them as such, and so they will be satisfied and happy. Meanwhile, in neither sense, in neither interpretation, can the verse be regarded (as S.B. regard it) as off the Rabbinic line. Just as S.B. assign to Jesus the sentiments of Paul or even of Luther, so do they assign to the Rabbis a sharp, consistent, and theoretic opposition to those sentiments, which is also inaccurate. It is quite true that the Rabbis were strong upholders and teachers of the Freedom of the Will and of Human Responsibility. It is also true that they did believe that man by his own powers could become either righteous or sinful: that we can justly blame the sinner and praise the righteous, even as everybody thinks to-day about all persons who are not morally degenerate or mentally half-witted. They did hold very strongly that a man may rightly accuse himself of yielding to temptation, or may rightly be pleased with himself (up to a point!) that he successfully resisted a temptation, if it was a very strong one. But this is by no means the whole truth. For if he resisted the temptation, the Rabbi would also say, 'Thank God who has helped me to resist the temptation,' and he might even go further and say, 'Thine only be the glory; thine only be the praise.' There was a pleasant inconsistency: the evil I do is all my own; the good I do is partly due to God. And the Jew prayed daily, 'Lead me not into temptation.' All was fluid; no theory existed: man is free, but God helps the righteous. And if man is free to sin and to do good, the Rabbis also recognized certain psychological facts. The more you sin, the more you are likely to sin; the more you do well, the more you are likely to do well. Both righteousness and sin become easier and easier, even of themselves, without bringing God in at all. And yet the facts are *also* put religiously by saying that heaven abets the righteous and gives opportunity to the sinner. Again, the Rabbis constantly speak of the perfectly righteous man, and of the completed or perfect sinner (even as Aristotle speaks of the ἀκόλαστος and the δίκαιος). But the same men could also speak of human righteousness as nothing in comparison with the righteousness of God. And because it is nothing, therefore man has no claim upon God for reward, even though he may hope to receive it, and even though he believes that God will undoubtedly reward the righteous. I would refer to Dr. Abrahams' remarks in the Annotated Edition of the *Authorized Daily Prayer Book* (p. xxi) which I shall quote in full later on.[1] ' Not because of our righteous acts do we lay our supplications before thee, but because of thine abundant mercies. What are we ? What is our piety ? What our righteousness ? ' Such was the prayer which, from a very early period, the Rabbinic Jew said every morning of his life.

Hence, if I am right, S.B. go too far when they say : ' Die alte Synagoge weiss nichts von der Unfähigkeit des Menschen, sich aus eigner Kraft eine vollgültige Gerechtigkeit vor Gott zu erwerben. Im Gegenteil, ihr soteriologisches System ruht ganz auf der Anschauung, dass der Mensch durch keine Gemeinsünde und keine Gemeinschuld infolge Adams Fall erblich belastet sei, vielmehr die volle sittliche Freiheit besitze, sich für das Gute zu entscheiden und den göttlichen Geboten nachzuleben, und so die Gerechtigkeit zu erlangen, die vor Gottes Richterstuhl besteht. Bei so grundverschiedenen Anschauungen des Christentums und des Judentums über die sittliche Anlage des Menschen ist es ein vergebliches Bemühen, innerhalb der rabbinischen Literatur nach Parallelen zur vierten Seligpreisung zu suchen.'[2] It is true that the Rabbis did not hold or teach in a definite, theoretic, or dogmatic way any doctrine about original or inherited sin, due to the ' fall of Adam.' Neverthe-

---

[1] P. 361.

[2] ' The synagogue in olden days knew nothing of man's incapacity of his own power to acquire a complete and adequate righteousness before God. On the contrary, its soteriology depends entirely upon the view that man is not hereditarily burdened by any generic sin and generic guilt because of Adam's fall. Man possesses complete moral freedom to choose the good and to live in accordance with the divine Commands, and so to acquire the righteousness which can stand firm before the judgment-seat of God. In the face of such fundamental difference of view between Christianity and Judaism as regards man's moral nature, it is a waste of time to look for parallels in Rabbinic literature to the fourth Beatitude.'

less, their doctrine of the *Yetzer ha-Ra*, inherent in every human
being, made them, for practical purposes, agree with Solomon
(I Kings viii. 46) that there is no man who does not sin. And it
cannot be said with truth that they held that there was no incapacity
on man's part by his own unaided power to acquire a *complete*
(*vollgültige*) righteousness (*Gerechtigkeit*), or justification, in the
sight of God. Even the Patriarchs are not *usually* regarded, even
Moses himself is not usually regarded, as sinless. Nor would they,
I think, have been ready to admit that the righteousness of the
Patriarchs and of Moses had been entirely achieved *aus eigener
Kraft*, by their own unaided power. S.B. allow that if one uses
Matt. v. 6 to suggest the thought that God helps those who seek to
fulfil his will, then the Rabbinic literature offers 'parallels' for such
a conception. (Some of the quotations they give may be used on
a subsequent occasion, *e.g.* on xiii. 12.) For example : ' He who
would purify himself, they (*i.e.* God) assist.' (באַ ליטהר מסייעים אותו)
(Sabbath 104 a and par.). ' They cause a man to walk in the way in
which he wants to walk.' בדרך שאדם רוצה לילך בה מוליכין אותו
(Makkoth 10 b). Just before this passage, Psalm xxv. 8, ' The
Lord instructs sinners in the [right] way,' is quoted, and it is
said of God, ' If he teaches the way to sinners, how much more to
the righteous.' Sometimes the Rabbis seem to assume that a man
may be sinless. Thus ' R. Yochanan said, When the majority of a
man's years have passed without sin, he will never sin ' (Yoma
38 b). But I do not suppose that R. Yochanan meant this saying
to be taken too literally. It might be that he was referring not to
sin in general, but to particular sins, as we might say, ' If a man has
not become addicted to drink and betting at sixty, he will never commit these sins.' ' In the school of Shela it was taught that when
the opportunity for sin comes the first and the second time, and is
resisted, the man will never sin ' (*ib.*). But the conception of God's
part in human virtue is never absent for long. ' If a man comes
to defile himself, " they " open the doors for him, but him who
comes to purify himself, they help. In the school of R. Ishmael
it was taught, It is as when a man sells naphtha and balm: when
a purchaser for naphtha comes, the shopman says, Measure it
out for yourself; but to one who asks for balm he says, Wait till I
help you measure, *so that we may each become perfumed.*' Here
it may be observed that God allows a man to sin, but does not aid

him : in goodness he helps him. But not only does he help him : the mystical idea is that God is made more beautiful or more beatific by man's righteousness. ' Do not defile yourselves,' say the Rabbis, ' lest you become unclean. If a man defiles himself a little, " they " defile him much ; if he defiles himself below, they defile him above ; if he defiles himself in this world, they defile him in the world to come. If a man sanctify himself a little, they sanctify him much ; if he sanctify himself below, they sanctify him above ; if he sanctify himself in this world, they sanctify him in the world to come ' (Yoma 38 b, 39 a). These passages are more emphatic about sin. Where we should say (as elsewhere the Rabbis also said), ' Sin brings sin ; if a man gets drunk seven times, he will get drunk seventy times,' the Rabbis here ascribed the awful issues of sin to the more direct agency of God.

Though S.B. exaggerate in the contrast which they draw between the attitude of Jesus towards ' righteousness ' and its acquisition and the attitude of the Rabbis, we have also to recognize that the Rabbinic legalism *did* sometimes lead to a certain view about righteousness and sin which we could not imagine Jesus wholly sharing. Jesus seems to understand the inwardness of character better than the Rabbis. It is true that, roughly speaking, a man's character is expressed in his deeds, and that we can justly say or infer that if we observe a man doing a series of sinful or righteous acts, he is a sinner or a righteous person. But the man is more than his acts, and even other than his acts. The Rabbis seem to judge too much from acts. It is true that they take account of intentions which, from reasons outside a man's power, did not become acts, as when they say that such intentions, if good, are reckoned unto the man as if they had become acts, but if bad, they are not so reckoned. Such is God's mercy. Yet even here the emphasis is on the acts. And this emphasis leads to a strange externalism. If a man's good deeds, at any given moment, exceed his bad deeds by one, he may be classed among the righteous ; if his bad deeds exceed his good deeds by one, he may be classed among the sinners. Thus his ' salvation ' may depend on whether, at the moment of death, his good deeds are in excess of his evil deeds by one. How far this clumsy method of reckoning, this superficial and external way of looking at human goodness and sinfulness, were really seriously meant, it is impossible to say. A well-known passage in Kiddushin 40 b, top, runs thus :

' The Rabbis say, Let a man always regard himself as if he were half
guilty and half meritorious ; then if he fulfils one commandment,
happy is he, for he has made his scale incline on the side of
merit; if he commit one sin, woe to him, for he has made his
scale incline towards guilt. R. Elazar said, The world is judged
by the majority (*i.e.* of its inhabitants), and the individual is judged
by the majority (*i.e.* of his acts). If he has fulfilled one command,
happy is he, for he has inclined his own scale and that of the
world to the side of merit' (and the contrary as above). We cannot
conceive Jesus saying anything like this, but the passage is not by
any means uncharacteristic of the Rabbis. Doubtless, some sins
were worse than others ; doubtless, some good deeds were better,
or counted more, than others ; doubtless, too, ' God demands the
heart ' ; there is much to be quoted (as usual) on the other side ; but
there *was* a tendency to regard the whole affair of life as if it were a
case of a schoolboy's marks. So many good deeds ; so many good
marks : so many sins ; so many bad marks. Subtract the number
of good marks from the number of bad marks, or *vice versa*, and the
good or bad remainder tells you if the man is, on the whole, good or
bad, and even if he will go to heaven or to hell. It is hardly necessary to say how unsatisfactory all this is, and how unlike the spirit
of the teaching of Jesus. Nevertheless, the full complexity of human
character was probably not realized or understood even by Jesus
himself. Many a Rabbi or Pharisee whom *he* would have condemned, God, in all probability, judged very differently. Men are
inconsistent without being necessarily insincere. A great teacher
has said : ' It is but a shallow haste which concludeth insincerity
from what outsiders call inconsistency—putting a dead mechanism
of " ifs " and " therefores " for the living myriad of hidden suckers
whereby the belief and the conduct are wrought into mutual sustain-
ment.' George Eliot writes this fine sentence as an introduction
to a chapter which deals with Mr. Bulstrode, whom one might have
regarded like the Pharisee in the parable : yet he was, though a
sinner, something better than the technical Pharisee ; so, too, many
a Pharisee, who may have seemed to Jesus like the Pharisee of his
parable, may in God's eyes (*i.e.* truly) have been far better. On the
other hand, the Tax Collector in the parable may have been judged
more truly by Jesus than the Rabbis would have judged him. And
a hunger and thirst after righteousness may consort with ignor-

ance and commonplace, and perhaps even with much stumbling and many failures. So true is it for us all to recall the Rabbinic maxim, ' Judge every one on the side of merit.' Finally, let it be noted that there is something extraordinarily moving and noble in the words ' who hunger and thirst after righteousness.' They seem to possess a touch of genius and inspiration, and yet they are so perfectly simple. For something of a verbal parallel one may quote : ' R. Tanchum b. Hanilai said, He who hungers—makes himself hungry—for the words of the Law in this world, God will satisfy him in the world to come ' (Sanhedrin 100 a). Did the original compiler of the Sermon mean to speak of persons who suffer hunger and thirst in the service and pursuit of righteousness (*i.e.* acting righteously and doing righteous deeds), rather than of those who have a hunger (*i.e.* a longing) for righteousness itself ? The Talmudic Rabbi clearly meant the former, and I imagine that the second part of his adage meant that, in recompense for a man's sufferings in the cause of the Law on earth, he should enjoy felicity in heaven. In the Beatitude, if the second sense is correct, as the wording would indicate, the second part of the verse might mean that in the next world the hungerers shall know what righteousness is still more completely. Yet the more probable view seems to be that the second half only means that they will obtain the heavenly felicities. Loisy, in his commentary, thought that the ' satisfaction ' meant both. ' Ils seront sanctifiés en même temps que glorifiés.'

7. A characteristically Rabbinic sentiment on which no time need be wasted. ' He who has compassion upon men, upon him God has compassion. And upon him who has no compassion upon men, God has no compassion' (Sabbath 151 b). The word for ' men ' it might be noted is *beriyyoth*, ' creatures '—a broad word, including both non-Jews and Jews. It is needless to multiply examples. They add nothing. Jesus says here what lots of Rabbis said in all ages. ' So long as you have pity on men, God will have pity on you' (Sifre 93 b *ad fin.*).

8. What does pure in heart mean in this verse ? The expression occurs in Psalms xxiv. 4 and lxxiii. 1, while the ' clean heart ' occurs in Psalm li. 12. Klostermann says that καθαροὶ τῇ καρδίᾳ ' meint neben 6 wohl nicht die völlige Reinheit von Sünde, sondern

die Aufrichtigkeit.'[1] He notes that in lxxiii. 1 the LXX render ἀγαθὸς ὁ θεὸς τοῖς εὐθέσι τῇ καρδίᾳ (though in xxiv. 4 they have καθαρός, and so too in li. 12). If it does mean *Aufrichtigkeit* (sincerity), Psalm xi. 7, ' the upright shall see his face,' would be the source of the verse in both its parts. It is interesting, as an illustration of Rabbinic theology, to quote some passages given by S.B. about the pure soul. They must not, I think, be taken too dogmatically. For it could also be shown how it was taught that man is born with two inclinations (*yetzers*), and that the evil *yetzer* or inclination is impure or unclean, so that man starts his earthly career with a certain poison or uncleanness in him from the very beginning. The Rabbis, quoting Ecc. xii. 7, say, 'Give it (*i.e.* the soul) back to God in purity, even as he gave it to you in purity ' (Sabbath 152 b). R. Yochanan, quoting Deut. xxviii. 6, said, ' May thy going out of the world be as thy coming into it : as thy coming in was without sin, so let thy going out be without sin ' (Baba Mezia 107 a). More elaborate is the passage in Lev. R., *Metzora* xviii. 1 *fin.*, on xv. 1, which deals with Ecc. xii. 7 and 1 Sam. xxv. 29. ' The matter is as if a strict (learned, *chaber*) priest were to give a loaf from the *Terumah* to an *Am ha-Aretz* priest, and were to say to him, I am pure, and my house is pure, and the loaf which I have given you is pure (clean) ; if you give it back to me as I have given it to you, well and good ; if not, I shall throw it away (זורקה) before thy face. So God says, I am pure, and my dwelling is pure, and my servants are pure, and the soul (*neshamah*) which I gave thee is pure ; if you return it to me as I gave it to you, well and good ; if not, I shall throw it down before thy face.' It is odd that S.B. do not quote here the prayer in Berachoth 60 b, ' My God, the soul which thou hast given me is pure,' for this prayer found its way into the Prayer Book, and is said every morning by every orthodox Jew. Perhaps, therefore, the idea that the soul starts pure without any inherited or innate sin was more usual and prevailing than any other. But this is a digression from which I must return.

Mr. Loewe writes : ' Traces of the conception of " original sin " crop up now and then : thus, " there is no generation that has not an ounce of sin from the Golden Calf " (Jer. Taanith iv. 7, 68 c, top and elsewhere). But perhaps the Rabbis saw the danger in the

---

[1] 'Pure in heart, taken in connection with verse 6, probably means, not complete absence of sin, but sincerity.'

logical consequences of the idea, and dropped it. It is remarkable how Jewish theology, owing to its lack of system, was able, as it were, to dabble in ideas without getting into trouble. So original sin is not quite unknown, but it is not allowed to upset the Jewish scheme of salvation by man's own efforts, helped by the divine mercy and grace.'

The phrase ' to see God ' could be used in many senses, and S.B. give many examples of such different usages. Klostermann rightly says that in the Beatitudes ' seeing God ' is used eschatologically. It refers to the ' eschatologisches Schauen von Angesicht zu Angesicht' ('the eschatological vision of face to face'). How far the Rabbis and Jesus believed that the righteous in another world or state would really *see* God, or, at least, see the light-radiance which actually and physically encompassed God, it is hard to say. To us such ideas seem remote and strange, but in spite of sayings about the ubiquity of God, they were by no means so strange as one might suppose to ancient Jews and Christians. Perhaps a semi-philosophic writer, like the author of Psalm cxxxix., might have advanced beyond such ideas, but I do not think that either Jesus or many Rabbis had advanced beyond them. I think Jesus *probably* believed that God *had* some physical substance, and that he lived in a particular bit of space, and that one could be near him spacially, and perceive the radiance which enveloped him. S.B. quote Rabbinic passages about seeing the Shechinah in the hours of death and in the intermediate (more spiritual) state between death and the resurrection, about seeing God after the resurrection, and even about seeing him in ' the days of the Messiah.' Whether these different divisions of time can be so accurately arranged—whether, I mean, it is possible to refer all the salient passages so accurately to the different periods —seems to me doubtful ; but, however this may be, I do not propose to quote any of these passages, as they have now lost their interest and value. Matt. v. 8 is on Rabbinic lines. S.B. try indeed to establish its originality in the following way. They say that there is no passage in Rabbinic literature in which seeing God is made conditional on purity of heart. ' Des Schauens Gottes dürfen sich versichert halten die Rechtschaffenen (Midrash, Psalm xi. (6), verse 7, 51 a), die, welche daherkommen in der Kraft ihrer Torakenntnis und ihrer guten Werke, die Schrift- und Mischnalehrer, die die Kinder treulich unterrichten (Pesikta 179 b), ferner wer fleissig

Synagoge und Lehrhaus besucht (Berachoth 64 a), wer den Armen Almosen spendet (Baba Batra 10 b), auch wer bedacht ist auf die Beobachtung des Schaufädengebotes (Menachoth 43 b). Es zeigt sich auch hier, wie Jesu Blick nicht an einer einzelnen Tugend, an einer einzelnen Leistung der Menschen hangen bleibt, sondern immer auf das Zentrum, auf das Herz des Menschen schaut; darum die reinen Herzens sind, die werden Gott schauen. Jesu Wort am nächsten kommt der Ausspruch des R. Menasya (um 300), der das Schauen der Schechinah dem in Aussicht stellt, der seine Augen nicht an Schändlichen weidet; denn das Verschliessen der Augen vor allem Garstigen setzt am ehesten das reine Herz voraus (Leviticus Rabba, אחרי מות, xxiii. 13 *fin.*, on xviii. 3). Ferner der Ausspruch des R. Pinchas (um 360), der den für würdig erklärt, das Angesicht der Schechinah zu schauen, dessen böser Trieb sich hat umwandeln lassen in das neue fleischerne Herz' [1] (Pesikta Rabbathi i. 2 a).'

S.B.'s praise of Jesus in this place is, I think, well merited, but I doubt whether much can be made of the chance that no Rabbinic passage happens to connect purity of heart with seeing God. And we have already heard how Klostermann thinks that καθαρὸς τῇ καρδίᾳ means *Aufrichtigkeit* (uprightness, sincerity); if so, the pure in heart would equal the *Rechtschaffenen*, the Upright, the *Yesharim*. On the other hand, that Jesus looks to the centre, to the heart, is very true. But did not the Rabbis also say that God looks to or demands the heart ? (Sanhedrin 106 b.)

Mr. Loewe writes : ' The phrase " to see God " was always altered by the Masorites to the passive, even when the sentence was wrested and grammar strained. They anticipated our objection to the use

---

[1] 'The upright (Psalm xi. 6) may hold themselves assured that they will see God; these are they who may walk confidently in the strength of their knowledge of the Law, and in the strength of their good works; so too the teachers of Bible and Mishnah who instruct the children faithfully, they who regularly attend the Synagogue and Houses of Study, they who give alms to the poor, and they who are diligent in the observance of the command of the Fringes. Here, as elsewhere, we may observe how the mind of Jesus is never directed to any one particular virtue or performance, but always looks for the centre, straight at man's heart; therefore they who are pure in HEART shall see God. Nearest to his saying is the utterance of R. Menasya that he who sees something foul (דבר ערוה), and does not let his eyes rest on it with pleasure (ואינו זן עיניו ממנה) is worthy to receive the vision of the Shechinah, for shutting the eyes against the sight of impurity may best of all offer the presumption of a pure heart. And next to that, the saying of R. Pinchas that every man who has made his *yetzer* as flesh in this world is worthy to see the Shechinah in the world to come.'

of such a phrase as "seeing God" literally. See Lauterbach's essay on the "Real Presence," in the Day of Atonement service, in the year-book of the Central Conference of American Rabbis for 1927.'

9. There is nothing novel in this Beatitude, even though (as in 8) S.B. say, 'Eine Stelle, in der die Friedfertigen oder die Frieden-stifter durch die Bezeichnung Gottes Kinder belohnt würden, ist uns in der rabbinischen Literatur nicht bekannt.'[1] There has been a doubt whether εἰρηνοποιός means here peaceably inclined, ready himself to make peace, conciliatory (cp. Psalm xxxii. 15, Matt. v. 23, Mark ix. 50), or a maker of peace, a man who produces peace, and allays dissension, between others. I observe that whereas the old edition of Preuschen's Lexicon opted for the first view, the new edition unhesitatingly adopts the second view. And as the word is used in the second sense by Dion Cassius and Plutarch, the new edition is probably right. Either interpretation would be Rabbinic, as a glance at S.B. is enough to show. The little tractate (Perek Shalom) on Peace, together with other Rabbinic laudations of peace, was translated by Wuensche in Vol. IV. of his *Aus Israels Lehrhallen*, 1909. The number of passages which deal with peace is so large that it is difficult to choose out two or three which are specially striking. The first one quoted in S.B. is very familiar. R. Yochanan ben Zakkai said, in reference to Deut. xxvii. 6, 'If in regard to stones, which cannot hear or see or talk, just because they are the stones of an altar which is to make peace between Israel and their Father in heaven, it is said, ye shall lift up no iron tool upon them, how much more shall no punishment befall him who makes peace between two men or between a man and his wife, or between two towns, or nations, or families, or governments' (Mechilta on Exodus xx. 25, 74 a). Endless sayings begin, 'Great is peace, for' (*e.g.* 'for even idolators, if they are at peace with one another, Satan cannot touch,' 'for God has ended his blessings with peace,' 'for it is the portion of the just,' 'for God's name is peace,' 'for it is equal to the whole creation,' and so on). 'R. Elazar said, Great is peace, for the prophets implanted upon the lips of all the creatures no word but peace (*i.e.* each man is to greet his neighbour with the word '*Shalom*,'

---

[1] 'We know of no Rabbinic passage in which the peace-loving or the makers of peace are rewarded by being called the children of God.'

'peace.' *Cp.* the whole of the long passage in Sifre 12 b, 13 a ; Levertoff, Midrash Sifre on Numbers, pp. 35–38). 'Aaron loved peace, and
pursued peace, and made peace between man and his fellow' (Sanhedrin 6 b). Hence, 'Be of the disciples of Aaron who loved peace,'
etc. (Aboth i. 12, one of Hillel's favourite sayings). Two of the stories
which S.B. quote are rather long-winded, but yet characteristic.
One depends upon Numbers v. 23–26, where, in the description of
the strange 'ordeal' rite, to which the woman suspected of adultery
had to submit, it is said that certain curses which contained the
Holy Name of God (Yahweh) were written on some material, which
was then dissolved in the water that the woman had to drink. In
the long praise of peace in Numbers Rabba vi. it is said that peace
must be great indeed, because for its sake (to restore peace between
a man and his wife) the holy name of God may be rubbed away and
dissolved in water. That quaint idea reappears in the story. Rabbi
Meir used to give every Friday evening a public sermon or exposition
of Scripture in a certain synagogue. A certain woman used to go
and hear him. One evening his sermon was very long, and when
the woman returned, the lamp had gone out. Her husband asked
her where she had been. She told him. He said, Never shall you
enter this house till you have spat in the eye of the preacher. R.
Meir saw what had happened through the Holy Spirit, and pretended
that he was suffering in his eyes. He announced : Any woman who
knows how to whisper a spell against pains in the eyes, let her come
and whisper it. The neighbours said to the woman, The time has
come when you can return to your house. Pretend that you are
going to whisper a spell, and then spit in his eyes. She went to
R. Meir, who said to her, Can you whisper a spell ? From nervous-
ness, she said, No. He said, Spit seven times into my eyes ; that
will heal them. She did so, and he said, Go and tell your husband :
You told me to spit once, and I have spat seven times. Then his
disciples said to R. Meir, Should the Law be thus made contemptible ?
If you had told us, we would have sent for the man and lashed him
with rods till he had made it up with his wife. Rabbi Meir replied,
Shall it not be with the honour of R. Meir as with the honour of his
Maker ? If the holy name may be washed away in water in order
to make peace between a man and his wife, how much more is this
true of the honour of R. Meir?' (Jer. Sotah i. 4, 16d; told with variants
in Lev. R., יצ, IX. 9, on vii. 12). The other story is connected with

a Midrashic interpretation of Psalm l. 23. ' R. Yannai was taking a walk, and he saw a man very neatly dressed (as a student). Rabbi Yannai said to him, Will the Rabbi be pleased to be our guest ? He said, Yes. So R. Yannai took him to his house. He gave him food and drink ; then he tested him in Scripture, but he found nothing, and so in Mishnah, Haggadah, and Talmud, and the man knew nothing. Then he said, Take (the cup), and say the blessing. The man said, Let Yannai say the blessing in his own house. R. Yannai said, Can you repeat what I say to you ? He said, Yes. Then say, rejoined Yannai, A dog has eaten Yannai's bread. The man jumped up and seized Yannai, and said, Would you withhold from me my inheritance ? Yannai said, How is thine inheritance with me ? He said, Once I passed a school and I heard the voices of the children say, The Law which Moses commanded us is the inheritance of the congregation of Jacob : they did not say, Congregation of Yannai. Then R. Yannai said, What merit have you (what meritorious deed have you done) that you should eat at my table ? The man said, I never heard an unkind word, and returned it to its speaker, and I never saw two men quarrelling without making peace between them. Then R. Yannai said, You have so much good breeding (*derech eretz*, a most characteristic and most important Rabbinic expression and virtue, equivalent to culture, good manners, decency, good taste, good breeding), and I called you a dog ! And to that man he applied Psalm l. 23, וְשָׂם דֶּרֶךְ אַרְאֶנּוּ בְּיֵשַׁע אֱלֹהִים.' The ' way ' is interpreted to mean *Derech eretz*. (Leviticus R., צו, ix. 3, on vii. 11.) Referring to Mal. ii. 6, ' He turned away many from iniquity,' it is said that if Aaron was on the road, and met a bad man he greeted him (*lit.* : ' gave him peace ' ; *i.e.* said *Shalom* to you, Peace be with you). The next day if that man wanted to commit a sin, he said, ' Woe is me, how could I then lift up my eyes, and look at Aaron ? I should be ashamed before him, for he gave me the greeting of Peace ' ; and so he refrained from sin. And, if two men had quarrelled, Aaron went and sat near one and said, See what thy neighbour says : he is tearing his heart and rending his garments, and saying, Woe is me, how shall I lift up my eyes, and look on my neighbour : I am ashamed because of him, for I have sinned against him : and he sat with him till he had removed hatred from his heart. Then he went, and did and said the same thing to the other man. So when these two men met, they em-

braced and kissed each other. (Aboth R. Nathan xii. 24 b.) Aaron
acted (proleptically !) on the advice of Rabbi, who said, ' All lies
are forbidden, but to make peace between man and his fellow it
is even allowed to lie' (Perek Shalom). R. Simeon ben Gamaliel
said, ' On three things the world stands, on justice, on truth and
on peace. R. Muna said, The three are one, for where there is
justice, there is truth, and where there is peace, there is justice'
(do.). R. Simeon b. Yochai said, ' All blessings are contained in
peace.' ' He who loves peace, pursues peace, gives the greeting of
peace, and returns it, shall inherit the life of this world and the life
of the world to come' (do.). But it is needless to multiply passages
further.

10–12. In these three Beatitudes is there anything novel or off
the Rabbinic line ? I think it may perhaps be said that the Rabbis
were hardly inclined to say : ' Happy are you when you suffer and
are in pain.' But, then, whether *ashre* means, or whether Jesus
intended the word to mean, ' happy ' in any but a very spiritual
sense may be doubted. He hardly meant ' in a condition of, or
experiencing, joyful sensations.' We must, however, note that
R. Joshua b. Levi said, ' He who rejoices in the chastisement (or
sufferings, יסורין) which befall him in this world, brings salvation
(or deliverance) to the world' (Taanith 8 a). Yet we may, perhaps,
say that, following on the lines laid down in these Beatitudes, some
Christians developed a certain passion for, and exultation in, martyrdom. That was not the Jewish line. The Jews were ready to undergo
martyrdom, and did undergo it, and I suppose the number of Jews
who have died voluntarily for their religion is, if not absolutely, yet
relatively, even greater than the number of Christians who have so
died. Yet I think that they and their teachers would always have
said that martyrdom was a sad necessity, not something to be welcomed or exulted in. We may, however, note that the reason why
Jesus bids the disciples ' exult ' (though I do not believe that Jesus
actually *said* 10–12 ; see my Commentary), or the reason why he
said that the persecuted were ' happy,' was because of what was
going to happen to them afterwards. It was (whether the Lutheran
theologians like it or no) because of the *reward* which God had prepared for, and would give to, them, *after* they had endured the persecution and the martyrdom. The exceeding great reward which

was to come was huge and permanent enough to make the temporary
pain well worth while—it was even enough to make it reasonable
to call those who suffered this temporary pain ' happy,' and to bid
them rejoice over it and because of it.   This conviction of special
reward for the persecuted and the martyrs is thoroughly Rabbinic,
though neither Jesus nor the Rabbis asked their disciples to endure
persecution bravely *for the sake of* the reward.   One must be faithful
for the cause, *lishmah* : in this they were both agreed ; but the reward would come all the same, and the assurance that it *would* come,
while not the motive for fidelity, could yet justly strengthen the
sufferer in bravely submitting to his pangs.   And the Rabbis do
allude to joy even in suffering.   ' Love God with all thy soul ;
that is, even when he takes thy soul' (*i.e.* thy life).   Simeon ben
Azzai said, ' Love him to the last breath ' (עד מיצוי הנפש) (Bacher,
Agada der Tannaiten, Vol. I. p. 418, n. 2).   ' Love him with all thy
might ; that is, with every measure which he metes out to you,
whether the measure of good or the measure of retribution ' (פורענות).
' A man should rejoice more over the chastisements which befall
him than over the good, for if he receives good all his life, his sins
are not forgiven him.   How are they forgiven him ?   By sufferings '
(chastisements יסורין).   ' Beloved are sufferings before God, for the
glory of God rests on those upon whom sufferings come.   Love God
with all thy soul : like Isaac who bound *himself* upon the altar.'
Isaac was the prototype of the martyrs.   (Sifre 73 a, b.   *Cp.* Mechilta
72 b, 73 a.)   In the Mishnah—the sheer law-book—we find the same
thought : ' Love him with all thy might [*m'odecha*] ; *i.e.* with whatever measure [*middah*] he metes out to thee, do thou return him
thanks ' (Berachoth ix. 5).   (*Cp.* Moore II. pp. 252–254 ; Bacher
ib. p. 321, n. 2.)   Moore rightly says about the Sifre passage : ' If
one remembers that several of those who made these statements
about sufferings were men who had witnessed the catastrophe of
their people in the war under Hadrian, or lived in the misery of
the generation following, one will then feel a deeper pathos in their
eulogies of suffering and in their gratitude to God in it and for
it.   Out of the same situation comes the saying of R. Simeon b.
Gamaliel : ' We also cherish (מחבבין) afflictions, but they are so
many that time would fail to record them ' (Sab. 13 b).   The beautiful Rabbinic term ' chastisements of love ' is spoken of elsewhere
(p. 220).   R. Huna, quoting Isaiah liii. 10, said, ' Every one in whom

God delights he crushes with sufferings,' but he added that the
scriptural verse showed that this is only true when a man receives the sufferings 'voluntarily (לדעת) and in love' (Berachoth 5 a).
When R. Akiba was martyred, the story ran that in the height
of his agony, he realized that the hour had come for saying the
Shema, and he said it and laughed for joy.   When he was asked
by Turnus Rufus why he did so, he replied because, now at
last, he could show that he loved God (not only as he had been
able to do before, with all his heart and might, but also) with all
his soul (i.e. with his life, by giving up his life for God's sake
and for the love of Him).   Now Akiba's martyrdom is the most
famous of all the Rabbinic martyrdoms, and this story how Akiba
laughed for joy in the midst of his torments became exceedingly
familiar, and must have had immense influence on all the martyrdoms of the future.   Again, that one sentence in Sabbath 88 b (and
par.) is quoted so often that it too must have had its effect: 'Of
them who are oppressed and do not oppress, who are reviled and
who do not (in reply) revile, who act only from love (to God), and
rejoice in their sufferings, the Scripture says: They who love Him
are like the sun when it rises in its might.'   The most amazing
saying, I always think, is that of R. Joshua b. Levi, who said (Sabbath
88 b), 'What means the verse, My beloved is unto me as a bundle
of myrrh that lies between my breasts ?   The congregation of
Israel speaks before God and says, Lord of the world, though my
Beloved oppresses me and makes my life bitter, yet shall he dwell
between my breasts.'

     That God is ever on the side of the persecuted and against the
persecutors is a Rabbinic commonplace.   Among the birds none is
more pursued (persecuted, attacked) than the dove ; and the dove
is the only bird offered upon the altar (Baba Kamma 93 a).   The
Midrash plays with the unintelligible second half of Ecc. iii. 15, and
it says: ' God always seeks (i.e. looks after) the persecuted.   If one
righteous man persecutes another, God seeks the persecuted, and
so if a wicked man persecutes a righteous man, or a wicked man
persecutes a wicked man, and even if a righteous man persecutes
a wicked man—God always seeks the persecuted.   God always demands the blood of the persecuted from the persecutors.   So with
the offerings.   The ox is pursued (persecuted) by the lion, the goat
by the panther, the lamb by the wolf : ye shall not offer from the

persecutors, but from the persecuted' (Lev. R., אמור, xxvii. 5, on xxii. 27).

S.B. give very fully and fairly the Rabbinic rules and views about martyrdom : when it was right to undergo it, when it was right, and within what limits it was permissible, to break the Law for the sake of continuing to live, and when death must be chosen instead of life. But these passages, though intensely interesting, do not concern us here. The reward of martyrdom is exceedingly great. 'Where they stand' (in the heavenly world) 'none others may stand' (Pesachim 50 a). More especially is the full beatitude of the life to come the lot of the great martyrs of the days of Trajan and Hadrian (Tanchuma B. iv. *Tabo* 24 a), 'All good is stored up for them' (כל טובה צפונה להם) (Pesachim 50 a, Baba Batra 10 b). 'None can stand in the compartment of the slain for the Kingdom.'

11. To this verse S.B. give a long catena of passages with the Rabbinic views about slander. (The evil or wicked Tongue, as they call it.) These passages are interesting enough in themselves, but hardly in point here. The Rabbis lay immense emphasis upon the iniquity of slander, which they put on a par with the very gravest sins. (*Cp.* Ziegler II. pp. 293–295.) In one passage (Jer. Peah i. 15 d, as the reverse of the famous saying about the good deeds which are rewarded in this world and the next) we are told that there are four sins which are punished in this world, but of which the capital (*i.e.* the chief) punishment is reserved for the world to come—Murder, Idolatry, Incest, and Slander. 'He who disseminates slander is as if he denied God. God says, I and the slanderer cannot live together in the world.' Slander, it is said, kills three—'the man who utters it, the man who receives it, and the man of whom it is told' (Arachin 15 b). (*Cp.* Moore II. p. 150.) These sayings and many others indicate how the Rabbis felt about this (perhaps specially Oriental ?) sin. I need not quote more. It is noteworthy (and it is nice of S.B. to notice it) that the Rabbis recommend the endurance of vilification in silence. 'He who hears his curse (מי ששומע קללתו ושותק) in silence is called a *Chasid* (pious)' (Midrash Psalms xvi. (11), verse 10, 62 a). 'He who hears his curse in silence, even though he could stop it (כל מי ששומע קללתו ושותק וספיקה בידו למחות) is called an ally (נעשה שותף) of God, for the nations revile him, and he keeps silence' (do. lxxxvi. (1), verse 1, 186 b). S.B. remark : 'Eine

ausdrückliche Seligpreisung unschuldig Verleumdeten ist uns in der
rabbinischen Literatur nicht begegnet.'[1] Nevertheless, no more than
the other Beatitudes is it off the Rabbinic line. The originality of
the Beatitudes consists partly in the grouping and choice ; partly
in the stress on present happiness. *Cp.* what I have said on p. 44
(Vol. II.) of the Commentary, which I think is fairly accurate. Mr.
Loewe writes : ' A good many Rabbinic passages about slander
have, I think, special reference to the *Delatores* (informers) ; *e.g.*
slander, whispered at Rome, slays a man at the other end of the
world ' (Eccles. Rabb. on x. 11).

12. The reward may be ' already, as it were, existent and prepared with God in heaven ' (Commentary, Vol. II. p. 39), but I do
not now think that it is accurate to say that ' the reward will not be
enjoyed in heaven, but upon the regenerated earth in the Messianic
age.' Jesus, or the writer, speaks quite *generally* about the ' life to
come,' the ' world to be.' ' Great is your reward,' and ' great will
be your reward,' is quite Rabbinic. The reward is not in proportion
to the merit. It far exceeds it. The proverb that as man measures
(= does), so do they (= God) measure (*i.e.* do) to him is not wholly
accurate even for Rabbinic theology. For God's rewards are conceived on a much more generous scale. The beatitudes of the life to
come cannot really be compared with earthly good deeds. Playing
on Psalm lxviii. 21, it is said that if a man gives his handful to the
poor on earth, God will give him *his* handful in the world to come.
But God's handful is utterly incommensurate with man's handful.
(See the odd passage in Sanhedrin 100 a, duly cited by S.B.)
Since the above was written the admirable book by Professor
Hans Windisch on *Der Sinn der Bergpredigt* has appeared (1929).
It is, I think, the most impartial and objective work upon anything
to do with Jesus and the Gospels by any German Protestant theologian that I have ever come across. Windisch quite rightly points
out a certain difference in tone and point of view—perhaps even in
soteriology ? (p. 81)—between the beatitudes and the demands or
injunctions which follow them. ' The Beatitudes appear to contradict the demands. In the former the Kingdom is promised to the
poor in spirit ; in the latter to those who do God's will. Thus

[1] ' A definite beatification of those who are unjustly slandered we have not
met in Rabbinic literature.'

there are many ways which lead to God, and the consciousness of
poverty (*i.e.* of spiritual humility), the consciousness of not as yet
having fulfilled the divine commands, is at least a station upon the
right way (pp. 136, 137). Here we have a truly evangelical or
Christian note : God is going to *give* us something, us who are unworthy of it, but who long for it and need it ' (pp. 137-139).

13-16. There is little to say in relation to these four verses.
S.B. are learned about salt, but it is needless to quote the passages.
(' As the salt cleanses meat, so chastisements purify the sins of
man,' Berachoth 5 a.) As to light, we may note that of Israel it
is said : ' Even as the dove brought light to the world, so do thou,
Israel, bring light to the world ' (Midrash Canticles, i. § 3, 3 on i.
3 ; i. § 15, 4 on i. 15) ; the Law and the Temple are also called
lights of the world, and so too were some few distinguished Rabbis.
For 16 *cp.* the passage in Yoma 86 a : ' The name of heaven (God)
is to become beloved through you ; if a man reads Scripture, studies
the Law and ministers unto the Wise, and bears himself graciously
in his dealings with his fellow men, people say of him, Happy his
father and teacher who taught him the Law, woe to those who have
not learnt the Law ; see how seemly are that man's ways, how
upright his deeds : but if a man has studied the Law, etc., but is
not honest and gracious in his dealings with his fellow men, then
people say : woe to him who has learnt the Law, woe to his father
and teacher who taught him, see how crooked are his deeds, how
ugly his ways.' ' If the Israelites do God's will, then his name is
magnified in the world ; if they do not do his will, then his name is,
if one may say so, profaned ' (Mechilta on Exodus xv. 2, 37 b).
To glorify God is the equivalent in this passage of the sanctification
or hallowing of God, which, as Moore says, is ' the supreme principle
and motive of moral conduct in Judaism.' For the use of the word
' glorify ' (δοξάζω) *cp.* Matt. ix. 8, xv. 31 ; Mark ii. 12 ; Luke ii. 20,
v. 25, 26, vii. 16, xiii. 13, xvii. 15, xviii. 43, xxiii. 47. But in
several of these passages ' glorify ' means, I think, little more than
' praise.' It is noteworthy that ἁγιάζω, the more direct equivalent
of ' sanctify,' is only found once in the Synoptic Gospels, namely,
in the Lord's Prayer, Matt. vi. 9 ; Luke xi. 2. With the Rabbis the
sanctification of God is a much more prominent and fundamental
idea. And we may observe with them a curious sort of see-saw.

God, as it were, needs man for the full sanctification of his Kingship and divinity ; he even needs man, as it were, for himself ; and yet he does *not* need man ; he is holy, he is divine in himself. Moore quotes a famous passage in the Sifra (86 c) as containing the answer to the question how, if God's holiness is his nature, men can make him holy. ' Ye shall be holy, for I the Lord your God am holy ' (Lev. xix. 2). 'As much as to say, If you make yourselves holy, I impute it to you as if you hallowed me ; and if you do not make yourselves holy, I impute it to you as though you did not hallow me. Can the meaning be, If ye make me holy, then I am made holy, and if not, I am not made holy ? The Scripture says, For I am holy —I abide in my holiness, whether ye hallow me or not ' (נקדשתי אני). Nevertheless, sometimes the daring thought of the Rabbis goes further. ' Ye are my witnesses,' says the Prophet in God's name : ' that is, *when* ye are my witnesses, I am God, and when ye are not my witnesses, I am, as it were (כביכול), not God ' (Pesikta 102 b). R. Simeon b. Yochai, to whom this saying is attributed, also used the metaphor of two ships lashed together, over which is built a palace. Loosen the ships, and the palace disappears ; so does God's heavenly palace depend upon the unity of Israel in fulfilling God's will. 'So it says : "Unto thee, O Lord, do I left up my eyes, O thou that sittest in the heavens "; otherwise (אלמלא) God would not be sitting in the heavens.' Yet he also quoted Exodus xv. 2 (' This is my God and I will make him lovely '), and he said, ' When I praise him, he is lovely, and when I do not praise him, he is, so to speak, lovely in himself ' (כשאני מודה לו הוא נאה וכשאין אני מודה לו כביכול) בשמו הוא נאה) (Sifre 144 a ; Moore ii. p. 104 ; and Bacher, *Agada der Tannaiten*, ii. p. 140, n. 1). The Rabbis were no philosophers ; yet at times they touch upon profound theological problems, and make profound theological remarks. The mind of Jesus was very simple ; he does not deal with these deeper problems.

Dr. Abrahams has a very good note on the ' Light of the World ' in Studies ii. pp. 15 and 16, supplementing and expanding S.B., and for the salt business *cp. Studies* ii. p. 183, where he points out that in Bechoroth 8 b the saying, ' Salt, if it has lost its savour, wherewith shall it be salted,' ' corresponds exactly with the reading in Matthew.'

17–20. In this section there is no direct teaching such as it is my purpose to illustrate from Rabbinic literature, so as to note whether the teaching is on or off the Rabbinic line. I have nothing to add to what I have said in my Commentary, Vol. II. pp. 46–55, nor do I desire to withdraw or modify anything that I said there. The quotations in S.B. are interesting, but, from my special point of view, need not be introduced here. It is unnecessary to emphasize or illustrate the Rabbinic appreciation of the Law. 'Turn it and turn it over again,' said Ben Bag Bag, 'for everything is in it' Aboth v. 25). The Law is compared with water because it is life-giving ; water cleanses ; so the words of the Law lead men from the evil way to the good way ; as water is given freely, so are the words of the Law given freely; as water is beyond price (אין להם דמים), so the words of the Law are beyond price. The words of the Law are like wine ; they rejoice the heart; as wine grows better by keeping, so the words of the Law become better as a man grows older. (Sifre 84 a.) And so on. The Law would retain its general value and validity for ever, as the most precious of God's creations. ' No letter of the Torah shall ever be made void' (ואות אחת ממך אינה בטלה לעולם) (Tanchuma, *Vaera*, 68 b). It may indeed be that, in the Messianic era, or in the world of the Resurrection, if sin and all evil disappear, there will be no need of many ordinances of the Law; they will thus become obsolete ; but the value, the pre-eminence, of the Torah itself, and as a whole, are eternal. S.B. are right enough here. For the words ' till all be fulfilled ' S.B. bring no parallels, and their meaning is very uncertain. Verse 19 remains a very odd and curious saying to have been put in the mouth of Jesus. It almost goes beyond what we can find among the utterances of the Rabbis. For the 'least' commands would, to the Rabbis, include some (by no means all) of the ceremonial commands. They *would* have regarded 'Thou shalt do no murder' as more important than 'A garment of mixed stuff of divers sorts shall not come upon thee.' Of this matter there may be something to say hereafter. It was indeed a 'moral' command which the Rabbis quote (Jer. Kiddushin i. 61 b) as the ' least ' of the positive commandments, but, perhaps, they rather meant the easiest to fulfil, not the smallest in worth or importance. It is the commandment in Deut. xxii. 6. 7, and they point out that to this ' least ' command the Law appends the same reward as to the greatest command (Exodus xx. 12). So Ben Azzai (Aboth iv. 2) said, ' Run to do even a slight precept, and flee from transgression : for precept draws precept in its train, and transgression, transgression ; for the recompense of a precept is a precept, and the recompense of a transgression is a transgression.' And Rabbi (Aboth ii. 1) said, ' Be heedful of a light precept as of a grave one, for thou knowest not the grant of reward for each precept.' But even S.B. quote no parallel for the thought that he who fulfils and teaches the smallest precepts shall be called great (or greatest : cp. ' least ') in the Kingdom of Heaven. This is Rabbinism with a vengeance ! One sometimes wonders whether the words of Jesus have not been altered, and did not originally run something like this : ' Ye have heard that it was said to the men of old time, Whoever abrogates one of the smallest commands in the Law shall be called least in the Kingdom of heaven, and whoever does and teaches them shall be called greatest in the Kingdom of heaven, but I say unto you that unless,' etc. And, then, out of this antithesis what we now read in 17–19 may have been evolved.

It is not wholly clear as regards 20 what Jesus means. Does he mean that the Scribes and Pharisees did not fulfil the Law which they professed to honour and obey ? If 20 looks back to 18, 19, that is what the verse would seem to mean. In that case it is an attack upon the morality of the Scribes and Pharisees, similar to the attack in xxiii. If, on the other hand, 20 looks forward, then it may mean that the righteousness, i.e. the limited fulfilment of the Law, practised and realized by the Scribes and Pharisees, is inadequate to secure admission into the Kingdom. A higher sort of righteousness is required. In either case we cannot accept the words as a just estimate of the moral condition of the Scribes and Pharisees of the period, or as a just estimate of the mercy of God. Heaven forbid that he should act upon the narrow and uncompassionate conceptions of the tests for entry into salvation which even the best of his human children in olden days devised.

21–22. There is no real advance from Rabbinic teaching in these verses. Anger was just as much denounced by the Rabbis as by Jesus. The many quotations in S.B. prove this clearly. ' By the angry man even the Schechinah itself is not esteemed' (Nedarim 22 b). ' The angry man loses his learning ' (Pesachim 66 b). And so on. ' All the divisions of hell rule over the angry man ' (Nedarim 22 a). ‏כל הכועס כל מיני גיהנם שולטין בו‎.

The use of the words *Rayka* and fool seems to have been tolerably frequent. I am inclined to think that there must have been a fair amount of basis for Jesus's reprobation. I rather wonder that S.B. did not attempt to score a point here. Even the Rabbis were apparently not averse from calling their antagonists or people who annoyed them *rayka* or *shoteh*. Thus there is the very odd story of R. Yochanan, who called a disciple, or, according to another reading, a heretic, who had mocked at something which he (R. Yochanan) had said, *Rayka*. The story is doubtless a legend, because it goes on to tell how R. Yochanan looked at the man, and he became a heap of bones. Nevertheless, it shows that it was not thought by any means inconceivable that R. Yochanan would have said *Rayka* to a man who had displeased him. (Baba Batra 75 a.) Then there is the charming story of R. Simon b. Elazar of Migdal Geder, who called the ugly man *Rayka*. The story is so pretty and so characteristic that it deserves to be quoted, though it is totally irrelevant. The Rabbi rode on his ass, and was very joyous and lifted up in spirit, because he had just come from the house of his teacher, and had learnt much Torah. He met a very ugly man, who greeted him. The Rabbi did not return the greeting, but said, ' You *Rayka*, how ugly you are ; are all the men of your town as ugly as you ? ' Then the man said, ' I do not know ; go and tell the Master who created me how ugly is the creature whom he created.' Then the Rabbi jumps down from his ass and begs to be forgiven of his sin. The story goes on to tell how at last the ugly man forgave him. (Taanith 20 a *fin.*, 20 b *init.*). *Shoteh* seems to have been the usual word for ' fool.' S.B. quote a passage in which even the famous R. Yochanan b. Zakkai calls certain antagonists ' fools ' (Menachoth 65 a).

On the other hand, the Rabbis speak very strongly against what they call oppression in words (אונאה בדברים) (insults, putting to shame, etc.), which they consider as worse than oppression (cheating) with money. (Baba Mezia 58 b.) The sin of *onaah* (insult) is as heavy as that of robbery or idolatry. (Do. 59 a.) Of those who go down to Gehenna and do not return (*i.e.* whose punishment is eternal) there are three classes—the adulterer, he who puts his neighbours to shame openly, and he who gives his neighbour an insulting name. (והמכנה שם רע לחבירו) (*ib.*). It would appear, then, that to use words like *Rayka* and *Shoteh* was an acknowledged sin, from

which the Rabbis were by no means free. The Talmud, written in
undress, reveals the sins of the Rabbis no less than their virtues.
Perhaps, however, the Rabbis would have said that it was no sin
to call heretics and mockers ' fools,' just as Jesus, perhaps, held it
no sin to call his own antagonists 'vipers and children of hell.' I fear
that in the matter of antagonists, such as the Jewish Christians
on the one hand, and the opposing Rabbis on the other, there is
not much to choose between the Rabbis and Jesus.

Mr. Loewe observes that *Shoteh* is a milder expression than
Rayka. Sometimes it is used good-humouredly and half-jokingly, as
we might say, ' You donkey, don't you see ? ' etc.

23–26. Not much need be said as to these verses. The allusion
which I make (Vol. II. p. 61 *fin.*) to D. H. Müller's pamphlet, *Die
Bergpredigt im Lichte der Strophentheorie* (1908, p. 13), may be
supplemented by giving the Rabbinic references on which Müller
relies. They are Sifra (28 a) on Lev. v. 23–25, Baba Kamma 110 a
[Mishnah ix. *fin.*], and Tosefta Baba Kamma x. 18, p. 368. The
teaching as regards reconcilement is on Rabbinic lines. It is well
known how insistent the Rabbis were on the duty of reconcilement.
Sins against his neighbour cannot be forgiven or atoned for by the
Day of Atonement unless a man has first been reconciled to his
neighbour. Such is the teaching of the Mishnah (Yoma viii. 9).
And a man who has been insulted in public had the right to demand
that the insulter should beg his pardon, and ask to be reconciled,
in the presence of those before whom he had insulted him. The
Pesikta passage (163 b) quoted by S.B. is pretty. ' It is a common
custom, said R. Elazar, that if a man has insulted his neighbour
in public, and after a time wants to be reconciled with him, the
other would say, You insulted me in public, and now you want to
make it up with me in private ; go, bring those men before whom
you insulted me, and then I will be reconciled to you. But God is
not so ; a man reviles and blasphemes him in the open street, and
God says, Repent in private, and I will receive you.' I like also
the quaint story about Raba and the poor man, who was supported
by the community, and came to Raba for a meal. Raba (fourth
century) asked him what he usually had for his fare. The man
replied fatted chicken and old wine. But do you not, said Raba,
feel worried that you are a burden to the community ? Do I eat

what is theirs, said the man ? I eat what is God's. (Psalm cxlv. 15.) While they talked, Raba's sister came to see him, whom he had not seen for thirteen years. She brought him a present of a fatted chicken and some old wine. That is a token, thought Raba. I apologize, said he to the poor man. 'Come and eat' (Kethuboth 67 b).

27, 28. The sayings about adultery contain nothing new or off the Rabbinic line. On the general subject of the intercourse of man and woman with each other, the views of the Rabbis are oriental. To talk to a woman, to look at a woman, indeed to have anything to do with a woman, was regarded as dangerous and objectionable. It may be questioned whether the Rabbis approved the free way in which Jesus (and he a bachelor) apparently mixed with women, but it must be admitted that we hear nothing of any criticism of his conduct on this count. More than once the saying occurs that there is an adultery of the eye or with the eye, as well as an adultery of the body or with the body. (Pesikta R. 124 b.) Adultery is forbidden, ' both with the eye and in the heart' (Mechilta R. Simeon p. iii : S.B. *ad loc.*). Resh Lakish, alluding to Job xxiv. 15, said, ' The verse is intended to indicate that one can commit adultery with the eye as well as with the body ' (Lev. R. xxiii. 12 on xviii. 3). ' God is long-suffering towards all sins except towards unchastity ' (זנות) (Lev. R. xxiii. 9 on xviii. 3). Balaam is supposed to have suggested to the Moabites to corrupt the Israelites through causing them to be unchaste with Moabite women. (Numbers xxv. 1 and xxxi. 16.) He said, ' The God of this people hates unchastity ' (זמה). (Sifre on Numbers xxxi. 16, 59 b *fin.*) (*Cp.* Kohler, *Origins*, p. 116 and p. 286, nn. 28 and 29.) ' He who looks at a woman with desire is as one who has criminal intercourse with her ' (Kalla, foot of col. 1 in ed. Vienna, 1868). The story in Sanhedrin 75 a (quoted in S.B. p. 300) is worth reading. A man conceived an illegitimate longing for a certain woman, and the doctor said that if his desire were not gratified, or partially gratified, he could not be cured. But the Rabbis said, ' Then let him die.' ' Evil thoughts ' (*i.e.* lustful thoughts) ' are even worse than lustful deeds ' (Yoma 29 a).

For the last passage *cp.* Sevenster, p. 141, n. 3. I believe that the Dutch scholar and the authorities he quotes are wrong, whereas Abrahams, Studies ii. 205, and Moore ii. 271, are right. The saying

means *morally* worse, and the word קשה does not compel us to
render, ' Evil *thoughts* are more injurious (to the constitution) even
than the hurtful *deed*.' Moore, among other passages, alludes to
Niddah 13 b *init*. ' R. Ammi says, He who gives himself up to sen-
sual thoughts (מביא עצמו לידי הרהור) is not allowed to draw near
to the divine presence, the מחיצה of the Holy One.' I am glad to say
that Mr. Loewe agrees with me as to the meaning of Yoma 29 a.

Kittel seems to make a blunder here. He says : 'Es ist wahr,
dass der Talmud sehr bedenkliche Laxheiten kennt : dass Gott nur
die gute Absicht zur Tat hinzurechne, die böse Absicht aber nicht,
und noch sehr viel schlimmere Dinge.'[1] What Kittel says about
the Deed and the Intention rests upon a misapprehension. The
Talmud means that God is so merciful that he does not punish an
evil intention which is prevented from being translated into action,
while he rewards the good intention which is so prevented. (Kiddushin 40 a. In Jer. Peah i. 16 b, top, the wording would rather seem
to mean that, in the case of the good action, the intention is rewarded
as well as the deed, while, in the case of the evil action, the intention
by itself is not punished). There is no suggestion that evil intentions
do not matter or are not sinful. On the contrary, so far as sinfulness is concerned, evil thoughts or intentions are as bad as, or worse
than, evil deeds. On the other hand, the Rabbis may (in Jer. Peah)
be blamed for their particularism, because with the heathen God
punishes the evil intention not followed by deed, and ignores the
good intention also not followed by deed. As regards ' the much
worse things,' some of them fall under the rubric of particularism.
It is, *e.g.*, not adultery to have intercourse with the wife of a heathen,
for he is not your ' neighbour.' But while that is the Law, it does not
follow that such unchastity was regarded as permitted. There are
sins which the Law cannot touch, but which are none the less sinful.
God will punish them, though man cannot. As to the others, which
concern the relations of Israelite men and women with each other,
the *sehr viel schlimmere Dinge* are substantiated by only three
examples out of the huge mass of Rabbinic material. It is doubtful
whether Kittel knows of any more examples, though his wording is
calculated to give the impression that such examples exist. He

---

[1] 'It is true that the Talmud contains very serious laxities; *e.g.* that God
only reckons the good intention on to the deed, but not the bad intention, and
many other very much worse things as well.'

says, ' Ferner ist etwa zu erinnern an,' and then follow the Three.
In view of the great importance of Kittel's book, of his own distinguished scholarship, and of his general desire, and even struggle,
to try to be fair, it is well worth while to examine the three instances
with care. One of them comes to very little ; one has been misunderstood ; one remains obscure. The first, Nedarim 20 b (not
20 a, as in Kittel), cannot easily be dealt with fully in a book intended
for general reading, but this fact is not to the discredit of the Rabbis.
It is due partly to difference in standards of taste as to what can
and cannot be spoken about in public, partly to the fact that the
Rabbinical literature deals with all the circumstances of life, with
all virtues and delicacies, and, where needful, with all sins and *indelicacies*. In the passage in question, Kittel complains of the
unbefriedigende Auskunft (the unsatisfactory, or unpleasing, reply)
given by two Rabbis to two women who asked for protection,
and the influence of their authority, in an ugly matrimonial trouble.
Now, it is rather striking that the passage occurs in connection with
a rather remarkable instance of Rabbinic delicacy. Certain ideals
(if one may use the word) or desiderata are laid down on the subject
of marital intercourse. I cannot quote these regulations or desiderata,
but anyone who chooses to look up the passage, even in Goldschmidt's translation, will see that I am speaking the truth. On
the other hand, these regulations (which touch the conduct of the
two husbands) are not ' law.' They are not the *Halachah*. The
women who came to Rabbi and Rab came to them in their capacity
as judges. The Rabbis' reply is brief, and we need not suppose that
the entire conversation between them has been preserved. The
Rabbis say, ' We are powerless ; your husbands have indeed acted
towards you improperly, but, legally, you are in these matters in
the power of your husbands, and it is impossible for us to interfere.'
The wording as given is abrupt. But the meaning and intention
are what I have indicated. It can therefore hardly be regarded
as a fair example of *noch sehr viel schlimmere Dinge*. The second
example is from Sanhedrin 11 a. Here, rightly understood, the
passage stands to the credit, rather than to the discredit, of Rabbi
Meir. But it needs an introduction to understand it. According
to Rabbinic law, cohabitation was held to constitute marriage. It
was not the desirable way of contracting a marriage ; that was by
the rite of *Kiddushin* and *Kethubah*, et cetera ; but, nevertheless,

if a man and woman lived together, they were assumed to be legally married, and their children were legitimate. (In Scotland, any acknowledgment of marriage, even without witnesses, followed by intercourse, or again, intercourse followed by a promise of marriage, constitutes an irregular marriage, which, under certain circumstances, may be held to be valid.) Now we are told, 'A woman once entered R. Meir's lecture room and said to him, Rabbi, one of you has married me by cohabitation (intercourse ביאה). R. Meir stood up and wrote her a bill of divorce (*get*), and gave it her. Whereupon they all rose up and did the same.' Kittel speaks of 'die wenig erfreuliche Art, in der R. Meir eine von einem seiner Schüler geschändete Frau abspeist.'[1] I have discussed this story (as well as the other two) with Mr. Loewe, and he tells me that one of two things must have happened. One of R. Meir's students had seduced the woman, and she did not know who he was, or did not know his name : or he had lived with her, and left her without divorcing her, so that she was a 'deserted' wife, who could not marry again. R. Meir sought to help her, but he also wished not to make the culprit publicly known. He was legally bound to recognize the 'marriage' as legal. Therefore he himself gives her a divorce, and his example is followed by all the others. One of these bills of divorce was obviously genuine, and so the woman was freed, but the culprit was not put to open shame. [Immediately before this story comes the famous tale about the garlic. 'It happened that Rabbi (R. Judah the Prince) entered his lecture room and smelt garlic : so he said, Let him who has eaten garlic (שום) leave the room. Then R. Chiya stood up and went out. Whereupon they all got up and went out.'] Again, we can hardly, in justice, call the second example a case of *noch sehr viel schlimmere Dinge*.

The third example is more difficult, and, on the face of it, it deserves, perhaps, even more than the comparatively mild way in which Kittel speaks of it. ('Die keineswegs von allen als harmlos verstandene Eintagsehe von Rab und von R. Nachman, Yebamoth 37 b, Yoma 18 b.')[2] It is told of Rab that when he came to Ardeshir (near Ctesiphon) he

---

[1] 'The disagreeable way in which R. Meir dismisses the woman who had been seduced by one of his own pupils.'

[2] 'The one-day marriage of Rab and R. Nachman by no means regarded by all as harmless.' This means, I suppose, that many commentators and interpreters are unable to explain away the 'one-day' marriage as morally innocuous, and as not meaning a real and consummated marriage.

used to proclaim, ' What woman wishes to marry me for a day ? '
(מאן הויא ליומא). When R. Nachman came to Shekanzib, he used to
make the same proclamation. These statements are extraordinary,
nor can they be fully explained, and their painful and apparently
immoral character cannot be entirely removed. From Kittel's
point of view, and with his object, they constitute the best of his
three instances. Mr. Loewe is of opinion that they are ' rhetorical,
and do not represent actual facts.' They occur in a difficult and
technical discussion about certain rulings of R. Eliezer b. Jacob.
These rulings were directed against polygamy, and declare (1) that
a man must not maintain households in different towns, as this might
lead to incest on the part of his children ; and (2) that a man must
not marry a woman with the intention of divorcing her. The statements about Rab and R. Nachman are related as being in opposition
to R. Eliezer's rulings. They are challenged on purely technical
grounds : their obvious immorality is not alluded to. But is it
conceivable that no word would have been said about this ? The
technical objections, and the various explanations of, and interpretations given to, the statements would take too long to state,
and *much* too long to explain, but they all seem to smack of a certain
unreality—of the lecture-room and of legal casuistry (not wholly
delectable and wholesome, but yet very different from direct
immorality) rather than of life. Mr. Loewe adds : ' The stories
regarded as facts are inherently improbable because of the person-
alities of Rab and R. Nachman b. Jacob. In Kiddushin 41 a Rab
says (in discussing marriage by proxy) " a man should not marry a
woman till he has seen her, lest he should see in her something unseemly, and she seem hideous to him, whereas the Law says, Thou
shalt love thy neighbour as thyself." Now if the statement in
Sanhedrin were true, would it not have been flung in his face in
Kiddushin ? Moreover, Rab, of all people, could not be accused of
indulging his passions. His family life is too well known. Curiously
enough he was married to a wife who treated him badly. Yet he
said (Baba Mezia 59 a), " A man must be scrupulous not to pain his
wife, because women are easily moved to tears, and therefore to
grieve them is the more culpable." In spite of the petty annoyances
which he suffered at the hands of his wife (Yeb. 63 a), and which
perhaps made him say, " Any evil rather than a bad wife " (Sabb.
11 a), he was honoured for his strict and holy life. (*Cp.* the odd

story, Chagigah 5 a.)   He cannot have been a hypocrite.   It is
equally hard to believe this of R. Nachman b. Jacob, who married
the daughter of the exilarch and had a happy home life.'   Thus we
may, upon the whole, acquit the Rabbis and the Talmud of *noch
viel schlimmere Dinge*.   If, from the immense Rabbinic literature,
so frank and undress and unworked up as it is, nothing worse on
the side of sexual baseness can be alleged than these three stories,
the verdict must be in the Rabbis' favour.

29, 30.   I now think that I was wrong in suggesting that in *this*
passage there is a ' distinct ascetic tinge.'   Even if such a tinge is to
be found in other passages (*e.g.* Matt. xix. 11, 12), I doubt whether
more is intended here than a hyperbolic warning against the smallest
yielding to illegitimate desire.   The hand is hardly in place here,
but it is brought in because of the eye.   Numbers xv. 39 is often
quoted and applied by the Rabbis.   ' Eye and heart are the two
go-betweens (mediators) (סרסורי) of sin.   So (Prov. xxiii. 26) God
says, If thou give me thy heart and thine eyes, then I know that
thou art mine' (Jer. Berachoth i. § viii. 3 c, and *cp.* Numbers R.
xvii. 6).   ' Do not stumble through thine eyes : all stumbling
comes through the eyes ' (שאין מכשול אלא בעינים) (Derech Eretz
Zuta i.).   The two remarkable passages quoted by Fiebig, and given
by me on p. 65 (Vol. II.) of the Commentary, are also quoted by S.B.
' In the first passage, and in the Mishnah passage on which it is
based (Niddah 13 a), the punishment of having the hand cut off is
to be the penalty of a man who is guilty of certain unclean acts.
When R. Tarphon is asked whether, under certain circumstances,
where life might be in danger, such an act might not be justifiable,
he replies, " It is better that a man's body should burst rather than
that he should go down into the pit " (*i.e.* Gehenna or Hell).'   The
expressions are, I should suppose, metaphorical.   In spite of Deut.
xxv. 12, there was, I presume, no question of a man's hand being
actually cut off for any of the offences suggested.   Besides, how
could they be known ?   The sayings and phrases, therefore, show
how vivid and strong oriental hyperbole could be.   On the whole,
therefore, there is little reason to believe that 29, 30 contain anything
which might not have been said by a Rabbi.

31, 32.   In these verses the originality of Jesus is made manifest.

So far, in the Sermon on the Mount, we have found nothing which goes beyond Rabbinic religion and Rabbinic morality, or which greatly differs from them. Here we do. The attitude of Jesus towards women is very striking. He breaks through oriental limitations in more directions than one. For (1) he associates with, and is much looked after by, women in a manner which was unusual; (2) he is more strict about divorce; (3) he is also more merciful and compassionate. He is a great champion of womanhood. And in this combination of freedom and pity, as well as in his strict attitude to divorce, he makes a new departure of enormous significance and importance. If he had done no more than this, he might justly be regarded as one of the great teachers of the world.

Mr. Loewe, generously anxious to champion the Rabbis, and to weaken any difference between their teaching and that of Jesus, if the teaching of Jesus appears superior to theirs, asks this question : ' If Jesus's association with women was so novel, what about " widows " houses ? (Mark xii. 40.) You cannot have it both ways. If the Rabbis never spoke to women, how could they have influenced them to such an extent as to get their property ? We often hear of women—including Roman matrons—asking Rabbis questions. It is true that we have sayings like, " A man should not walk four paces behind a (strange) woman," but such a prohibition related to casual meetings. As to divorce, if Jesus was strict about divorce, so was Shammai. If he was tender, so was Hillel. How was he then, in a quite new and special way, the champion of women ? '

It is needless for me to repeat what I have said upon the subject in the Commentary. The long pages of S.B. about the regulations and laws about divorce are full, and (I believe) accurate. Noteworthy (and to the credit of the Rabbis) are certain provisions, according to which, in certain special cases, a woman, on her side, could *compel* her husband to divorce her. There are a *few* stock passages which S.B. are fair enough to quote (p. 320) against divorce, especially against divorcing a first wife, the wife of one's youth. ' If a man divorces his first wife, even the very altar weeps ' (Gittin 90 b), said R. Elazar (A.D. 270) ; and R. Yochanan went so far as to say, ' Hateful is divorce.' But it would not appear that such passages are numerous, though it is rather nice that Tractate Gittin (on

Divorce) ends with this saying of R. Elazar and the quotation from Malachi ii. 13, 14. It was permitted to marry a divorced woman, but such marriages were looked upon as not likely to turn out well. S.B. give the passages in question. They are in the right as against the Dutch Jewish scholar and apologist, Tal. It is noteworthy that the one man whom a woman, divorced for adultery, might *not* marry was the co-respondent. Kittel (p. 101) also quotes a sentence from Pirke R. Eliezer xxxiv. (p. 254 in Mr. Friedländer's translation) : ' When a woman is divorced from her husband, her voice goes forth from one end of the world to another, but the voice is inaudible.'

33–37. The section about oaths and swearing is not of any great interest for us to-day. But it is clear from the Rabbinic literature that constant swearing, even in such lesser forms as ' by thy life ' was a fault to which the Jewish people, right through the Rabbinic period, were very liable. ' By thy life ' is even frequently put into the mouth of God. The Rabbis are often reported to use oaths. *Cp.* Kittel, p. 97. Thus R. Tarphon often said, ' May I lose my sons if I should not have done, or if I did not hear, so and so ' (אפקח בני. See Levy under פקח) (Sabbath 116 a, etc., and Baba Mezia 85 a with the queer story). Judah b. Tabbai says : ' May I not see the comfort (*i.e.* the Messianic redemption) of Israel if I did not do so and so' (Makkoth 5 b with the touching story attached). Yet the Rabbis condemn idle swearing severely. They say that even to ' swear upon the truth ' is unseemly. אמרו רבותינו אפילו על האמת אינו יפה לאדם להשבע (Tanchuma, *Vayikra,* 136 a). ' Our Rabbis have taught, Let no Israelite be hasty (פרוץ) in vows or in laughter or in deceiving another by an oath, saying it was no oath. In a certain district there were 2000 cities, and they were all destroyed because of a true, but idle, oath. For one said to the other, I swear I will go to such and such a place to eat and drink. And they went, and so their oath was fulfilled, but they all perished.' The Rabbis also condemn useless swearing. To use any form of oath in such an assertion as, ' That is an olive tree ' is an idle oath, however true it is that the tree is an olive tree. (Pesikta R. 112 b– 113 a.) A queer story is told of the evil effects of idle swearing, like ' May I bury my son if I did so and so.' ' A woman went to her neighbour's house to roll the dough. She had fastened two denars in the seam of her bonnet. They fell down and were rolled into the dough. When she returned, she looked for the denars and could not find them. She went back and said to her neighbour, Give me the two denars which fell down in your house. The neighbour said, I know nothing of them ; may I bury my son if I know about them. She buried her son. When they returned from the burial, she heard a voice saying, Had she not known about the denars, she would not have buried her son. She said, May I bury my other son if I know about them. And she buried him. They came to comfort her : at the meal a loaf was cut, and the two denars were found in it. So do they say : Be you guilty or innocent, do not swear ' (Jer. Shebuoth vi. § 6, 37 a). The third commandment is interpreted to mean a true, but idle, oath. זו היא שבועת אמת שהיא של שוא (Pesikta R. 112 b). Deut. x. 20 is used rather cleverly. ' God says to Israel, You are not to think that it is permitted to you to swear by my name ; even truthfully you are not permitted to swear by my name ; unless it be that you fear God and serve him and cleave to him, then only may you (also) swear by my name. . . . Be careful with vows, and not hasty with them, for he who is hasty with vows will end by false swearing (מועל בשבועות), and he who swears falsely, denies me, and will never be forgiven ' (Tanchuma B. I. *Mattoth* 79 a). To illustrate Matt. v. 36, S.B. quote a passage from Sanhedrin Mishnah iii. 2 in which ' by the life of thy head ' occurs as a swear formula in a vow, and a passage in Leviticus R., *Metzora* xix. 2, on xv. 25, where the impossibility is alluded to of all the peoples of the world making the wing of a single raven white. The ' yea, yea ' Rabbinic parallel occurs several times. ' Let your nay and yea be both *zedek* ' (righteous, accurate) (Baba Mezia 49 a). R. Huna said, ' The yea of the righteous is a yea ; their no is a no ' (Ruth R. vii. § 6, on iii. 18). ' Yes, yes ' and ' no, no ' may be regarded as equivalent to oaths. R. Elazar said, ' Yea is an oath, and nay is an oath ' ; Raba said, ' But only then if yea and nay are said twice ' (Shebuoth 36 a). The Israelites answered, ' Yea, yea ' and ' nay, nay ' to the commands at Sinai. (Yes, we will do this ; no, we will not do that.) (Mechilta on Exodus xx. 1, 2 ; 66 a.) A man may not be liable legally in certain cases of not absolutely scrupulous honesty, but ' though not liable in a human court, he is liable in the heavenly court (חייב בדיני שמים). If a man has given a salesman the money for produce (פירות), but has not actually taken the stuff into his hands or possession, he can legally draw back

E

from the transaction, but it is said that he who exacted retribution of the generation of the flood and the generation of the Dispersion (at the tower of Babel), will exact it of the man who does not stand by his word' (שאינו עומד בדיבורו) (Mishnah Baba Mezia iv. 2). (Moore ii. p. 140.) One must not say one thing with the mouth and another thing in the heart. (Baba Mezia 49 a.) I do not think that the 'unbedingte Wahrhaftigkeit im Reden ' (' unqualified truthfulness in speech ') which Jesus demanded was not *also* demanded, and was not also regarded as part of the moral ideal, by the Rabbis. Here even the impartial Windisch seems to me not quite accurate (p. 48 *fin.*, 49 *init.*). (*Cp.* Moore ii. 189, who gives several good passages.) On the other hand, so far as Jesus means : Never swear ; do not say more than Yes and No ; merely ' affirm,' he goes beyond the Rabbis. There is no Rabbinical ordinance or injunction *never* to ' swear ' or to take an oath. Here Sevenster, pp. 155–157, is right.

38–42. I am inclined to think that in the question as to the relation of these verses to Rabbinic teaching, both Jewish and Christian commentators often go wrong. The Jewish critic usually objects to these verses and to their doctrine. In many passages of the Sermon he is at pains to adduce Rabbinic parallels, and to argue that the teaching of Jesus is on all-fours with the teaching of the Rabbis. Here, however, he usually takes the other line. Here he assumes a contrast, and because there is a contrast, the new teaching of Jesus is unsatisfactory or bad. The saying, ' Resist not wickedness ' is taken at its face value and pressed. It is regarded as if it meant that no force is to be used in relation to *all* kinds of evil by whomever and whenever committed. It is regarded as meant to imply the wrongness of armies, of policemen, of law courts, of prisons, etc., and then it is easy to show that if the injunction were literally obeyed, society would collapse and become impossible. Again, from one definite point of view, to resist evil is a holy and righteous duty. 'Αντιστῆναι τῷ πονηρῷ is one of the motives of social well-doing and progress. To fight evil in all its many and complicated forms, to recognize it before the multitude recognize it, or before a ruling class recognizes it—is not this the mark of the prophet and the reformer ? On all that side of the matter Jesus never looked. He never thought about it. Even if the evil is personalized and embodied in a bad man or in bad men, it may

still be a holy duty to resist their wickedness and to fight them.
In the last resort, physical resistance may be justifiable enough.
There might even perhaps be cases where the offended might
justifiably fight the offender, over and above the cases of resist-
ance to violence and robbery. One remembers Browning's poem
'Before,' and the noble lines :

> Ah, ' forgive ' you bid him ?　While God's champion lives,
> Wrong shall be resisted : dead, why, he forgives.
> But you must not end my friend ere you begin him ;
> Evil stands not crowned on earth, while breath is in him.

But of such possibilities as Browning, in the wealth of his imagination, conjures up, Jesus was not thinking, and could not think.
The Christian commentator, on the other hand, too often compares
the teaching with lower conceptions, or immature legal ordinances,
in the Pentateuch, or with the *general* doctrine of tit for tat. Or the
teaching is compared either with some purely legal paragraphs in
the Mishnah or with some of the lower and grosser passages in
the Talmud. For, from the Talmudic sea you can fish out what
suits your purpose, and yet it does not follow that the ' bad ' product
of your dredging is really characteristic of Rabbinic teaching as a
whole. It is assumed that the *spirit* of the teaching of verses 38–42
is entirely opposed to, and different from, the teaching of the Rabbis ;
that the *spirit* of 38–42 is new and Christian ; that the opposite
spirit is old and ' Jewish.' Both these Jewish and Christian ways
of looking at the section are, to my thinking, inaccurate and unhistoric. Both are instinct with the manner of the apologist. Or,
if it is the Jew who is the apologist, then the Christian is the
thick-and-thin admirer, who delights in foils. Neither attitude
beseems the critical historian.

What I have said in the Commentary (II. pp. 69–76) seems to
me pretty right, but I feel more strongly than I did then that Jesus
is thinking of the recipient of an injury rather than of the man who
does the wrong. I agree with Klostermann : ' Der Jünger soll, um
seiner Jüngerschaft willen, so weit von jedem Gedanken an Vergel-
tung frei sein, dass er vielmehr sofort das Gleiche noch einmal zu
dulden bereit ist.' [1] Neither Matthew nor Jesus, on the other hand,

---

[1] ' The disciple, because of his discipleship. is to be so removed from every
thought of retaliation that he is ever ready at once to endure the same sort of
wrong over again.'

would, I suppose, have regarded the *teaching* in 39–42 as inconsistent with the *action* in xxi. 12.   Jesus is thinking of private injuries, not of public justice or public wrong-doing, or, indeed, of wrong-doing at all, except in so far as wrong-doing affects particular persons. He is thus concerned not so much about the wrong-doing as it affects the wrong-doer, but as to what is to be the sufferer's right attitude concerning it.   And so much is the receiver, and not the doer, of the wrong thought of that it does not seem incongruous to Jesus, or, perhaps rather, to Matthew, to add 42 to 38–41, though in 42 no evil is spoken of at all.   Jesus teaches an excess in virtue, an excess in forbearance, an excess in forgiveness, an excess in gentleness, an excess in giving and yielding.   He *does*—and here there *is* originality —very often oppose the principle of measure for measure, and it is against this principle that he is speaking here.   Virtue, the full virtue of a disciple, is an excess, a full devotion, an overflowing measure ; even Aristotle, who laid down the doctrine of virtue being a mean, had also to point out that this very mean is itself, in some sense, an excess (διὰ τὸ τὸ μέσον εἶναί πως ἄκρον).   So too ' virtue, if regarded in its essence or theoretical conception, is a mean state, but, if regarded from the point of view of the highest good, it is an extreme ' (Διὸ κατὰ μὲν τὴν οὐσίαν καὶ τὸν λόγον τὸν τί ἦν εἶναι λέγοντα μεσότης ἐστὶν ἡ ἀρετή, κατὰ δὲ τὸ ἄριστον καὶ τὸ εὖ ἀκρότης.—*Nicomachaean Ethics*, ii. 6).   But it will not do to maintain that Jesus' spirit of forbearance, of gentleness, of goodness, of charity, is wholly opposed to the teaching of the Rabbis.   It is the same spirit which inspired the best teaching of the Rabbis, carried to an extreme ; couched in vivid and hyperbolic language, expressed with intense earnestness, enthusiasm, and conviction, as central features of the teaching as a whole.   The Rabbis taught that a man must be forbearing ; that he must not stand upon his rights ; that not to reply to reviling and insult was the highest virtue ; that to give freely was a duty.   Jesus teaches the same things with burning passion, and as part of a rounded whole of self-sacrifice and devotion.

But the Rabbis are cooler and calmer.   They see other aspects of the relation between offender and offended, other aspects of the whole question.   Suppose a man is about to murder you : would Jesus have said that you need not defend yourself ?   The Rabbis do not hesitate to say that you may anticipate the man's evil-

doing by killing him yourself. And I am not inclined to say that
they are wrong. ' One is not to say or think, I shall be guilty of
his blood, but one is to kill him at once' (Midrash Psalms lvi.,
vi. verse 1, 147 b). The proverb is approved of : ' kill him before
he kills thee.' אל תעמוד : אל תאמר אתחייב אני בדמו : ואל תמלך
בלבך : אלא הרגהו מיד :. To act thus is even regarded as an
injunction of the Law (Sanhedrin 72 a, בא להורגך השכם להורגו ;
Berachoth 58 a, 62 b). One can hardly conceive Jesus saying such
a thing, and yet are we to blame the Rabbis for their realism ?
I hardly think so. In spite of their many crotchets and absurdities, there is often a healthy and breezy common sense about
the Rabbis which is very refreshing. And one also feels that if
they are sincere in their crotchets and absurdities, they are no
less sincere in their common sense, and again, if they are sincere
in their common sense, they are no less sincere in their high
idealisms.

S.B. consider that we may rightly compare with 39 the common
Rabbinic phrase, מעביר על מדותיו, ' He passes over his rights.'
He is gracious and yielding. The same idea is expressed by the
phrase, אינו עומד על מדותיו, ' he does not stand upon his rights.'
Levy and S.B. quote the same passages. ' He who is yielding—
who ignores a slight or a wrong—has all his sins forgiven him '
(Yoma 23 a). Rabbi Akiba's prayer for rain was answered,
while R. Eliezer's prayer was not answered, according to a heavenly
voice, not because Akiba was greater than Eliezer, but because
Eliezer was not forbearing and Akiba was forbearing (Taanith 25 b).
But I do not imagine that this forbearance went as far to the
Rabbis as the μὴ ἀντιστῆναι τῷ πονηρῷ inculcated by Jesus.
Yet it was in the same direction. The virtue which Jesus demanded
from his disciples was the ' forbearance ' of the Rabbis carried to
an extreme, auf die Spitze getrieben, as the Germans say.

The proverbs which S.B. quote about the donkey are, as they
themselves observe, of no great significance. ' The Rabbis have
a saying, If your fellows call you an ass, put the saddle on your
shoulders' (Baba Kamma 92 a), and ' As people say, If some one
says, Your ears are asses' ears, give no heed ; if two say it, get you
a halter' (Genesis R., לך לך, xlv. 7, on xvi. 9). But there may be
something else hinted at here than mere forbearance.

The famous passage in Sabbath 88 b has already been given.

It is not, however, without significance that the prayer of Mar b. Rabina was partially taken up into the liturgy, and is now said (silently) at the end of the Amidah. The words are well worth quoting: ' O my God, guard my tongue from evil and my lips from speaking guile ; to such as curse me let my soul be dumb, yea, let my soul be unto all as the dust.' It is true that there follows upon these words the prayer, ' If any design evil against me, speedily make their counsel of none effect, and frustrate their designs.' But is there any objection to an honest prayer of this kind ? Both parts of the prayer are equally simple and sincere. And it should be noted that the Rabbi does not pray for the destruction of his enemies, but only for the frustration of their designs (Berachoth 17 a, *Authorized Prayer Book*, p. 54, with Dr. Abrahams' note on p. lxx.). This prayer seems to me to stand on an equal footing with the idealism of Jesus. It is a true exemplification of ' resist not evil.'

The legal enactments, provisions, and discussions in the Mishnah and the Gemara about injuries and blows must not be compared with the teaching of the Sermon on the Mount, any more than one would compare the clauses of any other civil or criminal code book with that Sermon. On the other hand, it seems to me to the credit of the Mishnah (and a part of its *Eigenart*) that so many ethical or religious remarks are mixed up with its legal provisos. For example : ' Even if a man has paid compensation for an injury, he is not forgiven (by God) for his wrong until he has asked pardon from the man to whom he did the injury ' (Baba Kamma Mishnah, viii. 7, 92 a). And the Tosefta adds the following, which is really rather remarkable, coming as it does in a purely legal context. ' If a man has received an injury, and if the wrong-doer has not asked his forgiveness, he must nevertheless ask (God) to show him pity.' [Then follow the Biblical examples and proofs.] ' R. Gamaliel quoted Deut. xiii. 17 (" That the Lord may show thee mercy and have compassion upon thee "), and said, Let this be a sign in thy hand that whenever thou art compassionate, the Compassionate One will have compassion upon thee.'

It seems to me as if all these passages, taken together, show that there is really no antithesis between the spirit of the Sermon (in this section 38–42) and the spirit of the Rabbis. Naturally, for just comparison, one must choose the best sayings one can find, and it is legitimate to do this so long as it is justifiable to hold that these best sayings really *do* represent the prevailing line of the Rabbinic teaching, and that it is fair to assess that teaching by *them* rather than by any outburst of hatred or anger which can be fished up elsewhere from the Talmudic deep. Just so it is fair to assess the teaching of Jesus rather from the Sermon than from ' vipers and children of hell ' and ' depart from me, ye accursed, into the everlasting fire.' Both Rabbis and Jesus are inconsistent, but we will judge them from their higher, and not from their lower, utterances, so long as these higher utterances are not unusual and exceptional. That seems fair to both.

Windisch is very interesting on ' Resist not evil ' (pp. 14, 15, 56, 148, 156). He doubts whether I am right in thinking that the injunction has anything to do with the urgency of the time, the imminence of the New Aeon. (My Commentary, Vol. ii. p. 71 *fin.*) He says : ' Der Radikalismus der Sprüche erklärt sich hinreichend aus der Tendenz, Vergeltungstrieb, Gegenwehr, Rachedurst bis auf die letzte Wurzel auszutilgen.'[1] He then shows with what one-sidedness this is done (p. 14). Later on he points out what our modern attitude towards these injunctions should be and can be. I entirely agree with him. For us (not according to the literal meaning of the original speaker, but *for us*) the demands of the Sermon are ' keine imperativischen Gebote, keine wörtlich uns bindende Vorschriften, sondern individuell bedingte Ausprägungen einer heiligen Gesinnung, deren Wesen es ist, dass sie unter anderen Voraussetzungen zu ganz anderen Ausprägungen gelangen kann. Wir werden also, z.B. wenn wir geschlagen, beleidigt, in unserem Besitze geschädigt werden, von den uns zur Verfügung stehenden Rechtsmitteln Gebrauch machen, um Wiederholungen vorzubeugen, aber doch dabei uns bemühen, jedes Gefühl von Rachgier und Vergeltungssucht in uns zu bekämpfen. Wir werden dann nicht sagen, dass wir das Gebot so erfüllen, wie Jesus es gemeint habe, denn was Jesus gemeint hat, ist die wörtliche Erfüllung ; aber wir werden sagen dürfen, dass wir der Gesinnung, auf die er abzielte, auch in unserer Haltung Ausdruck geben können und wollen ' (p. 148).[2] And he is also right in saying that we justly criticize the

---

[1] ' The radicalism of the sayings is adequately explained by the desire to eradicate the instinct of retaliation and of resistance and the thirst for revenge to the very last root.'

[2] ' The demands of the Sermon are not definite commands ; they are not enactments binding us to their letter, but they are individualized and conditioned

words of the Sermon in so far as we point out that they are not
capable of literal fulfilment (*wörtlich ausführbar*). Yet this criticism
is not the end of the matter. The Sermon will continue to criticize
us. ' Wir haben uns auch vor der Kritik zu beugen, die die Bergpredigt trotz allem Widerstande, den wir leisten, an uns übt und
mit der sie uns niederschlägt' (p. 156).[1] I think that this is excellent.

42. This verse is certainly in strict accordance with Rabbinic
ordinances. And it may be added that the Rabbis have nothing
to fear from the closest inspection of their laws and regulations
about the poor. The combination of fullest charity, considerate
delicacy, and (occasionally) robust common sense is highly remarkable. It is interesting to note that while in the Mishnah (Peah i. 1)
the doing of lovingkindnesses (גמילות חסדים) is said to be one of the
five things for which no measure is laid down in the Torah, and
while the Rabbis emphasize this ruling in the case of the higher
charity—personal service, as we may call the ' doing of loving-
kindnesses '—they hold that for almsgiving there *should* be a limit.
That is one reason—there are many others—why charity in the
higher sense is for them so much greater a thing than almsgiving.
As to the latter, they held that the maximum a man should give away
was a fifth of his income. The Gemara of the Jerusalem Talmud
cites the saying in the Mishnah about there being no limit or measure
for charity, and continues : ' This is said for the body (בגופו), but
for money (ממונו) there *is* a limit. It is reported that at Usha the
Rabbis decided that a man should give a fifth of his possessions for
good works (in charity למצוה). If this means, said a Rabbi, a fifth
of his *whole* possessions, then in five years he would have nothing

---

exemplifications of a holy frame of mind, the essential nature of which is that,
under different presuppositions, it could result in quite different exemplifications.
Therefore if, for example, we are beaten, or insulted, or injured as to our property,
we shall make use of the legal means of redress which are available to us, in order
to prevent repetitions, but nevertheless we shall take great care to fight down
and quell within us every feeling of revenge and every desire of retaliation. We
shall not, indeed, then say that we have fulfilled the command as Jesus meant it
to be fulfilled, for what Jesus meant was a literal fulfilment, but yet we shall
be entitled to say that we can, and we intend to, express in our conduct the disposition of mind of which he was thinking and at which he aimed.'

[1] ' We must humble ourselves before the accusation which the Sermon, in
spite of all the resistance which we make to it, brings to bear upon us, and with
which it knocks us down.'

left. It was replied, The first year a fifth of the capital, afterwards
a fifth of the revenue.' (I do not find that this arrangment was
seriously meant or actually carried out. Anyway, it is intended as
a maximum levy by oneself upon oneself.) R. Yoshebab, we are
told, gave all his possessions to the poor. R. Gamaliel sent to him
to say : ' Do you not know that the Rabbis have ordered that a
man should not give more than a fifth ? ' (Jer. Peah 15 b). Elsewhere
the same rule is mentioned thus : ' In Usha they ordered that he
who desires to give profusely (המבזבז) shall not give more than a
fifth, lest he too come to need (the help of his fellow) creatures.
(But when a certain Rabbi gave away at his death half his
capital, it was said that the Usha rule did not apply to what
a man chose to do at his death.) (Kethuboth 50 a, 67 b.)
Though it is not entirely relevant, it might, nevertheless, be
desirable to give a few sentences from the passage of the Sifre 98 a
fin., 98 b *init.*, which is cited in full by S.B. It is supposed to be a
sort of commentary on, or further legal amplification of, Deut. xv.
7–11. ' There are people who are pained (or who cause pain)
whether they give or no. Be thou not so : harden not thy heart.
There are people who give, and then draw back : be thou not so :
if thou hast opened thine hand four times, thou must do so a hundred
times. " Thou shalt surely lend him," etc. : first they give to him,
and afterwards they take a pledge from him : so said R. Judah :
but the wise say, Tell him to bring a pledge so as *to quiet his mind.*
" According to his need " : you are not commanded to make him
rich : " what he wants " ; even if it be a horse or a slave, as Hillel
once gave a poor man of good family (who had come down in the
world) a horse and a slave. And once in Galilee they gave a man a
litra of fowl flesh a day. " What he wants " : " he " includes his
wife. " Beware," etc. : be careful that thou withhold not pity,
for he who withholds pity from his fellow is likened by Scripture
to an idolator, and he casts off from him the yoke of heaven.' ' A
pledge to quiet his mind.' Is not this charmingly delicate ? Not
less so is Kethuboth 67 b. To him who has nothing, and refuses to
let himself be maintained, one must lend on pledge, and afterwards
one must give it him. And he who has something, but from miserliness will not nourish himself, must be maintained, and after his
death one must get it back from his property. So said R. Judah.
The wise say, One need not bother oneself about him. He who has

nothing, and will not be maintained, let him be offered relief first
on loan, and then as gift. So said R. Meir. The wise said first as
gift, then as loan. He who has, and will not maintain himself (from
miserliness), let him be given sustenance as gift, and afterwards let
them demand it back (*i.e.*, it is explained, after his death). R. Simeon
said, The latter man need not be considered, but as to him who has
nothing and refuses to receive, let him be asked first to give a pledge
and then to take, so that his self-respect may be raised. How
delicate the words and ideas are ! (1) כדי להפיס דעתו, to appease,
to quiet his mind. (2) כדי שתזוח דעתו עליו, to raise his mind,
to bring back his self-respect.

More about public and private charity in Rabbinic times can be
read in Moore II. pp. 162–179, and in the long excursus in S.B.'s
Vol. IV., *Die altjüdische Privatwohltätigkeit* and *Die altjüdischen
Liebeswerke* (pp. 536–610). Even as giving to the poor is obligatory
' according to the measure of his need and to the ability of the
giver,' so also is it obligatory to lend to a would-be borrower.
In the words of the Mechilta (96 a) it is חובה, a duty, obligation,
and not merely permissive. R. Ishmael, using the words in Deuteronomy xv. 8, said, ' If a man of good family come and is ashamed
(to ask for alms), "open" to him with words, saying, My son, perhaps
you need a loan. Hence the saying, Alms are given as a loan '
(Midrash Tannaim, ed. Hoffmann, p. 82). ' R. Jonah said, It does
not say in the Psalms (xli. 1), Happy is he who gives to the poor,
but, Happy is he who has consideration for the poor ; therefore take
great thought how to give him charity aright (היאך לזכות עמו).
R. Jonah, if he saw a son of a great man who had become impover-
ished, and was ashamed to ask for relief, went to him and said, As I
have heard that an inheritance has been left to you overseas, take
this article of value, and when you realize your inheritance, you can
repay me. But after he had actually handed it over, he said, I give
it you as a gift ' (Leviticus R. xxxiv. 1 on xxv. 39). But it will
be found that, insistent as the Rabbis were on the duty of giving
and lending—and giving and lending with delicacy and grace—they
were also keen about *wise* giving. Some of their sayings could be
mottoes for the C.O.S. to-day. Striking is the remark of the Sifra on
Leviticus xxv. 35 : ' If thy brother be waxen poor, thou shalt not suffer
him to fall. He is like a load resting on a wall ; one man can then
hold it and prevent it falling (or keep it in its place), but if it has

fallen to the ground, five men cannot raise (or set) it up again '
(109 b). (Moore II. p. 178.)

43-48. We now reach the central and most famous section of
the whole Sermon. About no section are Christian commentators
and theologians more sensitive. In none are they more anxious
to prove and maintain the absolute originality of Jesus. The
originality has to be maintained (a) as against the O.T., (b) as
against the Rabbis. Thus several things have to be asserted,
some of which are more dubious than others. (1) The word
רע in the O.T. means exclusively fellow-Jew, and so it means
fellow-Jew, fellow-national in Leviticus xix. 18. (2) In the
interpretation of Leviticus xix. 18 by the Rabbis, the meaning
is always, and consciously always, limited : the love is limited to
the fellow-Israelite. (3) ' Enemy ' in Matthew v. 43 includes both
private enemy and public enemy, i.e. all non-Israelites, all the
nations. (4) Ger, in the O.T. means not stranger, or non-Israelite,
but only the resident alien. (5) Ger to the Rabbis means only the
full and complete proselyte. (6) As enemy in Matt. v. 43 means
both private enemy and public enemy, i.e. includes all non-Israelites,
Romans, etc., Jesus in vv. 43-48 consciously and designedly taught
universal love—love for all men, whether Jews or non-Jews, whether
believers or unbelievers, whether friends or enemies, whether
Pharisees or disciples. (7) Neighbour, chaber, and beriyyoth,
creatures, in Rabbinic literature only mean fellow-Jew ; the non-
Israelite is never consciously and deliberately included. (8) The
Rabbis do not unequivocally teach the love of enemies even when
the enemies are Israelites.

Of these eight assertions, some, as I say, are much more dubious
than others.

Meanwhile, before I deal with them, I will add one or two
general remarks to what I have said in the Commentary, II. pp.
76-93.

Is there not a good deal of cant in much of what we read about
universal love, allgemeine Menschenliebe ? I admit that we ought
not to hate the men and women of ' other nations,' or ' other
nations ' as a whole. No doubt German hatred of England and
English people, or English hatred of Germans and Germany, is
wrong and was wrong. But in ordinary life, for ninety-nine persons

out of a hundred, when does *allgemeine Menschenliebe* come in ? What good does a sort of vague universal love or *allgemeine Menschenliebe*, a sort of copy-book love for all men, do ?   No doubt it is better than active hate, but it does not appear as if, for 999 persons out of a 1000, it is ever translated, or can be translated, into action. A really intense love for your own nationals which is constantly overflowing into, and expressing itself in, deeds seems to me worth any amount of sloppy and vague adulations and laudations of *allgemeine Menschenliebe*.   These have too often a Joseph Surface sort of look, and what becomes of them at a pinch ?   (*Cp.* Vol. II. p. 88 *fin.*)   Whereas the man who is constantly *practising* love towards his fellow-nationals gets his heart set in the direction of love, and such a one, when the pinch comes, or when the opportunity offers, is not at all unlikely to act according to his wont, even though the object is a foreigner.   When the needy one is actually before him, he will not enquire too closely into his origin or into the composition of his blood.   Somehow, I feel as if I would prefer a man who loved his fellow-nationals so truly that he was constantly doing loving deeds (but who did not profess to love the foreigner at all, or even said frankly that he ' hated ' all foreigners), to the man who constantly proclaims his love for all men without distinction of race or blood, but has never helped a foreigner in his life (and rarely seen one), and has infrequently done loving deeds to his own nationals.   The loving *deeds* and the *number* of them : that is the real test or point ; not copy-book sentiments and their range.

Coming now to the eight assertions, I think that the Christian commentators are right about (1).   In the O.T. *Rea'* usually means fellow-Israelite, fellow-national, and certainly means it in Leviticus xix. 18.   I would say the same about (4) and (5). *Ger* in the O.T. means, not foreigner or stranger (if stranger = foreigner) but ' resident alien.'   The foreigner is the *nochri*, not the *ger*.   To the Rabbis *ger* without qualification is the full and complete proselyte.   So in (1), (4), and (5) the Christians win easily. The matter is far less simple as regards (2), (3), (6), (7), and (8).

(Perhaps I ought to add that Mr. Loewe still tries to maintain that *ger* does not usually mean ' resident alien,' but ' sojourner ' or ' guest,' and that *rea'* in Lev. xix. 18 does not mean fellow-Jew only.   His arguments fail to convince me : they are, I think, prompted by the intense *desire* that *rea'* in this verse as in

16 should, in the mind of the original writer, have consciously and definitely meant everybody, and so included the non-Jew.)

It is difficult for the Christian commentators to have it both ways. If the Rabbis consciously and habitually taught that one must love one's fellow-Israelites, but that one need not love, and that indeed one might hate, the non-Jew ; if they taught the identification of the non-Jew with the enemy, then it is very strange that Jesus, who *ex hypothesi* is teaching a new doctrine—universal love, the love of all men without distinction of nationality—does not definitely tell his disciples either that neighbour is to include the non-Jew as well as the Jew, or that by enemy he means the national and public enemy, the idolater and the Roman, as well as the private, Jewish enemy. It is inadequate to say, ' He does so in Luke x. 30–37, in the parable of the Good Samaritan.' Even *if* that be true, why does he not do so *here*, at so crucial and important a stage in his teaching, when (1) misunderstanding was so entirely likely, and (2) definite and decided instruction was so eminently desirable ?

For the hypothesis is : the Rabbis definitely limit love to the Jew. Jesus is out definitely to teach a new doctrine, a startlingly new doctrine. For the first time in the whole history and life of Israel, he is going to teach universal love, to the non-Jew no less than to the Jew. Why, then, does he not say, ' You have heard men teach you that your neighbour is your fellow-Jew ; but I teach you that your neighbour is every man, be he non-Jew or Jew ' ? Or why does he not say : ' And by enemy I mean not only your Jewish enemy, but your Roman oppressor and all the nations and idolaters around you ' ? But not a word is said on these lines, whether in the Sermon on the Mount in Matthew or in the Sermon on the Plain in Luke. I have made a few remarks of the same sort in the Commentary, and I shall have something more to say in detail later on. But, speaking generally, it appears to me that the Christian contention in (3) and (6) cannot be maintained. Jesus in this section is not definitely thinking of the public enemy and of non-Jews. He is not thinking of non-Jews one way or the other. I do not mean that he is consciously and deliberately *excluding* them. I only mean that he is not consciously and deliberately *including* them. If a popular preacher delivers sermons in country villages on love and the love of neighbour and of enemies, he is not thinking about contrasts between Englishmen and foreigners or between Christians and

Mohammedans.   He is just thinking of the neighbours of the men
and women to whom he is talking, and of *their* friends and *their*
enemies.   So, too, was it with Jesus.   The Roman oppressor and
the idolater, the nations around, were not on this occasion before his
mind.   The 'enemy' and the neighbour are the personal enemies
of the people he is addressing—the people within their own horizon,
the people with whom they had to do.   It is true that he mentions the 'gentiles' (ἐθνικοί) in 47, but he does so merely casually
for the purpose of an illustration, just as he mentions the tax
collectors.   It is true that he mentions 'those who persecute you,'
but (whether we have here authentic words or no) the persecutors
in this passage are, in all probability, not Gentiles but Jews.   The
stress is laid on the difference between friend and enemy, not on
the difference between Jew and Gentile.   And yet if, on the one
hand, the *old* teaching about love was so deliberately particularistic,
and if, on the other hand, the *new* teaching about love was so
deliberately universal, the stress should have been laid upon the
difference between Jew and non-Jew.

I do not mean for a moment to imply that, when the occasion
arose, Jesus would not have urged his disciples, or would not have
urged his fellow-Jews, to show mercy and love to a needy Roman or
to a needy Greek.   Assuming both the authenticity of the Good
Samaritan parable, and that Halévy's hypothesis is false, Jesus, in
reply to the question, Who is my neighbour ? did, on that occasion,
definitely teach that your neighbour is the man in trouble, and that
the man in trouble is your neighbour, whatever his race or nationality.
All that I am concerned about is the meaning and the implication of
this section in the Sermon on the Mount.   And *about this section* I
contend that it does not consciously and designedly teach, in contrast
to current particularism, the universality of love, the love of all
men without restriction of race and nationality.   It contrasts, not
the love of Jew with the love of non-Jew, but the love of friend with
the love of enemy, the love of those who like you with the love of
those who hate you.   It assumes—whether rightly or wrongly is
another matter—defective teaching about the love of *enemies*, that
is the love of those who hate you.   It does not assume defective
teaching (even though such teaching may have existed) about the
love of the foreigner, the love of Romans or Greeks.   To anticipate
what I have still to say : I think Rabbinic teaching *was* defective

about the love of the foreigner and the idolater, and that Jesus might very well have said, ' You all consider your neighbour to be only your fellow-Jew, but I tell you that the neighbour whom you are to love includes all men, the Roman and the Greek and the Syrian no less than the Jew.' That would by no means have been needless teaching. All I contend is that in Matt. v. 43-48 Jesus does not happen to say this : he happens to say something different. Nor can it, I think, be urged that Jesus often leaves you to *infer* to what he is alluding. When he has something very definite to say, as, for instance, in his teaching about the Sabbath, he is clear and distinct enough. I may be mistaken, but I have the feeling that *if*, in this section, or on this occasion, he had really wanted to censure the particularism of the Jews and of Jewish teaching, and to inculcate (in contrast to this particularism) the love of all men, be their nationality what it may, he would not have hesitated to make his intention perfectly clear. When he wanted to be definite, he did not mince his words. ' Er hielt sich kein Blatt vor dem Munde.' There is, however, one difficulty in my contention, an objection to my argument, which must now be mentioned. Jesus says : ' You have heard that it was said, Thou shalt love thy neighbour and hate thine enemy.' To this statement, as we know, the Jewish critics reply that nowhere is it stated in the Law or in the O.T. that ' thou shalt hate thine enemy.' On the contrary, passages can be quoted to the opposite effect, if by ' loving,' ' doing good to ' is meant, and by ' hating ' ' doing evil.' But *these* passages certainly refer to the Israelite, not to the foreigner or the idolater. If, then, Jesus bids his disciples, in contradistinction to current teaching, or to the teaching of the Law and of the O.T., to love their enemies, he must be referring, not to the Israelite but to the foreigner.

The Jewish critic is obviously right when he says that there is no passage in the O.T. which says, ' Thou shalt hate thine enemy.' He is also obviously right when he refers to passages like Exodus xxiii. 4, 5, or Proverbs xxv. 21, xx. 22. Nevertheless, if one were to take the O.T. as a whole, I am not so sure that one can honestly say that its general teaching is very definite on the love of enemies, even of Israelite enemies. Still less can it be said that it is so when the enemies, though Israelite, are conceived to be the enemies of the ' pious ' party, to whom the speaker or writer belongs. For this view the Psalms bear witness, so that even, in the noblest of all the

Psalms, we get the familiar verses, ' Surely thou wilt slay the wicked, O God : depart from me, therefore, ye bloodthirsty men. Do I not hate them, O Lord, that hate thee ? I hate them with perfect hatred : I count them thine enemies.' Though the Psalmist makes the order : God's enemies, *therefore* mine, he was probably half deceived ; the order was equally, or even primarily, my enemies, *therefore* God's. And there is no reason to believe that the Psalmist is here alluding to foreigners. It is against such teaching that Jesus (who was, in my opinion, apt to forget the Sermon on the Mount in the heat of conflict, and to show little enough ' love ' to the ' vipers and children of hell,' with whose religious opinions he disagreed, and whose characters he disapproved of) may very well have protested in Matt. v. 43. And, in that case, the enemy would still be an Israelite and *not* the foreigner. My view would, I admit, satisfy neither Jew nor Christian, but, for that very reason, it is all the more likely to be true.

Since writing these words the remarkable, but very doubtfully epoch-making, work of R. Eisler has appeared. In it the view is maintained that, whereas, in v. 40, Jesus is thinking of his fellow-Jew, in 41 he passes on to urge a policy of non-resistance towards the Romans. With his wonderful knowledge of all sorts of writers, both German and foreign, Eisler quotes the late Miss Lily Dougall as the one person who, in his opinion, has adequately explained the verse (in an article, ' The Salvation of Nations,' *Hibbert Journal*, Vol. xx., Oct. 1921, p. 114 f. *Cp. The Lord of Thought*, by her and the late C. W. Emmet, 1922, p. 148 f.). She says : ' Consider the teaching of Jesus, as it struck his first hearers. Who were those who compelled the Galilean peasant to go a mile ? They were Roman soldiers, . . . any man of whom had the right to make one of a conquered race carry his traps for a certain distance. . . . Who were those who " used despitefully " the people ? Assuredly the arrogant officials, both high and low, of a dominant race rose before the mind's eye of every member of those Jewish crowds to whom Jesus preached. . . . The Jewish nation, weak and poor, but the prouder for that, was at this time vibrating with suppressed revolution. Judas of Galilee had headed a rising ; Pilate more recently had ruthlessly quelled in blood a riot in the very Temple ; Theudas was soon to head a rebellion. If to members of *Sinn Fein* in the spring of 1921 had been said, " Forgive your enemies, bless them that persecute you, do

good to them that despitefully use you," to whom would they have
supposed the words to refer ? Would not such preaching to them
mean the suggestion of a national policy ? ' (Eisler : *Iêsous basileus
ou basileusas*, Vol. II. pp. 212, 213). The explanation, adds Eisler,
is the more obvious, seeing that a very similar line of thought is
taken in a speech of King Agrippa made to the Jews, according
to Josephus, when they were resolved to revolt against the Romans.
' Nothing restrains blows so much as enduring them. The quiet
endurance of wrong on the part of the wronged causes the wrong-
doer to feel ashamed ' (*Jewish War*, II. 16. 4). According to this
argument Jesus, in the whole passage from 38 to 48, would have
had both Jews and Gentiles consciously and deliberately in his mind.
I am still not convinced, and I leave my own arguments as they
were written.

The points involved in (2), (7), and (8) are more difficult and
involved.

S.B. and others have, I think, shown that the Rabbis understood
Rea' in the Pentateuch to mean the Jew or Israelite only. The
Rea' excluded the non-Israelite. Mechilta, Sifre, Sifra are all clear
and definite on this point. It has, however, to be borne in mind
that the majority of the passages cited by S.B. and others are
specifically *legal* : the legal relations between Jew and Jew were
different from the legal relations between Jew and non-Jew. Yet
it does not follow that the legal and the moral relation are identical,
and the Rabbis were well aware that a given action, which constituted, according to Pentateuchal law, a tort or wrong between
Jew and Jew, and therefore did not constitute a legal wrong between Jew and foreigner, might, and often obviously did, constitute
a *moral* wrong between the Jew and the foreigner. Quaint is a
passage in Tana Eliyahu, Seder Rabba, Chap. xxvi. p. 140 : ' Let a
man keep himself far from stealing from, or cheating (etc., etc.),
anybody, whether Jew or Gentile: for he who steals, etc., from a
Gentile will end by stealing from a Jew.' (*Cp.* Guttmann, *Umwelt*,
p. 35, and the whole chapter about the *Nochri*, pp. 20–42.) Thus
Mechilta on Exodus xxi. 14 ('If a man come presumptuously
upon his neighbour to slay him with guile,' etc.) declares that
' neighbour' excludes ' others.' But a Rabbi asks in astonishment (80 b *init.*) : ' Before the giving of the Law we were warned
(ordered) not to shed blood : after the giving of the Law is there,

F

instead of an increasing, a lightening ? ' (in that one is allowed
to kill a non-Jew !). The answer is : ' He is free according to the
judgments of flesh and blood, but his judgment is given over unto
heaven.' Again, in the law of Exodus xxii. 8–9, the Mechilta says:
' to his neighbour,' not ' to others.' The Law only applies to the
Israelite (88 b). So in the Sifra, about the law Leviticus xx. 10
('he that commits adultery with his neighbour's wife '), it is not
adultery if a Jew commits unchastity with a non-Israelite's non-
Israelite wife. (Sifra 92 a, on Lev. xx. 10.) Nevertheless, such
non-adulterous unchastity was severly reprobated. It is a moral,
though not a legal, offence. In Sifre (97 b), about the enactment
of Deut. xv. 2, 3, the Rabbinic law agrees with the words of the
Pentateuch : ' neighbour and brother,' not ' others.' And so with
Deut. xix. 4 and xxiii. 25 (108 a and 121 b) ' neighbour ' is in each
case explained to mean fellow-Israelite. These examples are all of
a strictly legal character, and the remark of the Rabbi as regards the
first may be held, in some measure, to apply to all. But that
cannot be said as regards the painful passage in Sifra (89 b) on
Leviticus xix. 18. (*Cp.* my Commentary, Vol. II. p. 88). There,
after quoting the words לא תקום ולא תטור את בני עמך, it distinctly
says נוקם אתה ונוטר לאחרים. ' Against others you *may* be
revengeful or bear a grudge.' And the ' others,' here as elsewhere,
are the Gentiles, the non-Jews. I do not see how such a passage as
this can easily be got over. The curious thing is that these four
Hebrew words occur just before R. Akiba's saying that ' thou shalt
love thy neighbour as thyself ' is the greatest, or most inclusive,
rule (*Kelal*) in the Law, and Ben Azzai's remark that ' This is the
book of the generations of Adam ' is a greater *Kelal* (rule) than
that other, to both of which utterances I must subsequently recur.

There was, one may presume, during the Rabbinic period, little
love lost between Jew and Gentile, whether the Gentile was a heathen
or a Christian. How could it well be otherwise in those days of
oppression and cruelty ? The feelings of the ordinary Jew towards
those who persecuted him, or at best despised him, are reflected in
the Rabbinic literature, and even in the codes, but they are often
transcended. One gets this kind of thing : ' R. Ishmael said, If a
goi and a Jew come before you in a law suit, use Jewish law if it
would be favourable to the Jew, and say to the *goi*, Such is *our* law,
but use gentile law if it would be favourable to the Jew, and say to

the *goi*, Such is *your* law : and if neither method will help the Jew, a subterfuge is permissible (ואם לאו באין עליו בעקיפין). R. Akiba said, A subterfuge is forbidden, because of the sanctification of the Name.' Yet apparently R. Akiba permitted the subterfuge where no profanation of the Name could become known. (Baba Kamma 113 a.) *Cp.* Sifre 68 b with Kittel's translation and notes (p. 25). Again, a little farther on, in the same Talmudic tractate, we read, ' R. Simeon the Pious said, To rob a *goi* is forbidden, but one may keep what is found ' (*i.e.* one is not bound to restore to him his lost property which one has found). ' R. Pinchas b. Yair said, Where the sanctification of the Name comes in, one must restore what is lost ' (Baba Kamma 113 b). (Moore II. pp. 105, 109.) That is, no doubt, the prevailing motive. One must do what is just to the *goi*, not for his sake, but for God's sake. The glorification of Israel's God is the greatest duty of the Israelite's life. ' A just judgment of R. Jonathan drew from a Roman the exclamation, Blessed is the God of the Jews ' (Moore II. p. 105 ; Jer. Baba Batra ii. 14, 13 c). Such an exclamation, from such a source, was, from the Rabbinic point of view, one of the most excellent and desirable things that could possibly happen. So it is decreed in the Tosefta : ' He who steals from a *goi* is bound to make restitution to the *goi* ; it is worse to steal from a *goi* than to steal from a Jew, because of the profanation of the Name ' (Tosefta Baba Kamma x. 15). And as *beriyyoth*, creatures, certainly means everybody, whether Jew or Gentile, it is pleasant to find that in the prohibition of every form of deceit the word *beriyyoth* comes in.

' Everybody who steals the mind (*i.e.* deceives them) of the creatures is called a thief ' (Tosefta Baba Kamma vii. 8). The wording in the Talmud is still more emphatic. Samuel said, ' One must not steal the mind of the creatures, not even of a *goi* ' (Chullin 94 a). (Moore II. p. 189.) I wonder whether one would find in any mediaeval code any rule like : ' One must not deceive anyone, not even a heretic.' ' One must not rob a Jew because of the sanctification of Christ.' The Rabbis were well aware that all men, and not only the Jews, were created by God. Moore has noted that in the famous passage in Mishnah Sanhedrin (iv. 5) ' the words " of Israel " found in some editions are modern interpolations ' (I. p. 445). ' For this reason a single man was created : to teach that if one destroys a single person, the Scripture imputes it to him as if he had destroyed

the whole world, and if he saves the life of a single person, as though
he had saved the whole world.' But though all men were created
by God, not all were God's friends. Even as the enemies of the
Church were the enemies of God, so to the Rabbis Israel's foes
were also God's foes. ' He who hates Israel is as one who hates
God. . He who rises up against Israel is as one who rises up against
God ' (Sifre 22 b).

The truth is that the Rabbis are not entirely of one mind on the
matter of loving or hating the non-Jew. It would be unjust to sum
up the matter by saying that the Rabbis generally taught that it is
right or permissible to hate the Gentile. On the other hand, it would
be hardly less unfair to say that the Rabbis taught that the love
which was to be shown to the Jewish ' neighbour ' was to be extended
equally to all men, whatever their race or nationality or creed. One
can hardly quote any unequivocal utterance from the Rabbis which
goes as far as this. The question is mixed up with the other question (8) which I have, so far, kept apart from it. How far, and to
what degree, and to what extent, did the Rabbis urge the love of,
or loving conduct towards, ' enemies ' ? Deferring further discussion
of that question for the moment, we may take it that the Rabbis did
not get beyond the attitude of the author of the 139th Psalm. That
was the attitude of the early or the mediaeval Christian as well. *The
enemies of God*, those who hated God, were in the eyes of Rabbis and
early Christians, as in the eyes of the Psalmist, justifiably hateworthy. The Rabbis did not, I think, reach the stage of religious
development at which men realize that God, if he be all-good, can
have no enemies. I fear they believed that those who (as they held)
hated God were also hated by God. At any rate, they held that
those men who hated God should be hated by the Rabbis. Now,
who were the men who hated God ? God and Israel were knit together by the closest of ties. And to worship idols was (1) a sin and
(2) an action indicative of a hatred of the true God. Therefore
there was every human temptation to regard all idolaters with
hatred, because they hated God. Moreover, the idolaters with
whom Jews came into contact were usually oppressors and masters :
enemies of Israel no less than enemies of God. The natural human
feeling to hate one's nation's enemies was reinforced by religion.
Instead of being held in check by religion, it was sanctioned by
religion, for the enemies of Israel were doubly enemies of God : they

were the enemies of his beloved and chosen people, and they were idolaters. In some moods, every non-Israelite, every *goi*, every heathen, was regarded as a representative of these enemies and included in the hate of these enemies. In such moods every *goi* seemed an enemy, latent and potential, if not actual, and every such enemy seemed hateworthy. ' Do I not hate them that hate thee ? ' And every *goi* hated Israel, and hated Israel's God.

One can understand these moods, and even forgive them. Upon the whole, they were the result (1) of oppression and of persecution, (2) of the hate which is born of hate, (3) of a sacred Scripture *all* of which was regarded as good and true and inspired, and *many* passages in which showed and manifested this hate, proceeding from prophets and psalmists, and often ascribed to God himself. From the vast compass of the Rabbinical literature it is not difficult for S.B. and for others before them to choose out a number of passages which illustrate Rabbinic hatred of the non-Jew, of the heathen world, of the *goyim*, and of the *goi*. Indeed, from my own reading, I could increase the number, and I could quote passages, not given by S.B., which illustrate the intense particularism of the Rabbis, a particularism which often passes over into contempt and hatred of the ' nations.' On the whole, I think we must allow that this particularism is their more prevailing mood. But I need cite only a very few of S.B.'s, or of my own extra, passages in this place. Thus God is said to ' love only Israel of all the nations whom he has made ' (Deut. R., v. שופטים, xvi. 18, near end). ' God is in a special sense the God of Israel ; he is not the God of the nations, though he is the God of all who have come into the world.' אלהים אנכי לכל באי עולם ולא ייחדתי שמי אלא על עמי ישראל, אין אני נקרא אלהי אלא אלהי ישראל, אלהים אלהיך אני (Ruth R. Introd., towards end of § 1, on i. 1). So, in the Midrash on Canticles, the constant line is that God and Israel belong together : they are Lover and Beloved. The nations have no part in him. ' I am his, and he is mine ' (Canticles R. on vi. 1 *init.* and on ii. 16, and Mechilta 37 a). ' R. Simeon b. Yochai said, The best of the *goyim* kill ! The best among the serpents crush ! ' (Mechilta on Ex. xiv. 7, 27 a). In Winter and Wuensche's translation of the Mechilta (p. 87) there is a footnote to this passage as follows : ' Joel M. Gutachten über den Talmud, Breslau 1877, S. 26 : Jeder, der von talmudischer Redeweise eine Ahnung hat, weiss, dass das so viel

besagt, wie unser : den besten Ägypter soll der Kukuk holen.
Rohling wird dem R. Simeon nicht die bêtise zutrauen, hier eine
gesetzliche Bestimmung aussprechen, und dabei noch der heiligen
Schrift im Gesicht schlagen zu wollen, welche ja lehrt : Den Ägypter
sollst du nicht verabscheuen, denn du bist ein Fremder in seinem
Lande gewesen.' [1]

Mr. Loewe tries to get over the trouble in another manner. He
recalls the fact that there are many sayings constructed in the same
way, which were ' once obviously united.' If the saying about the
Egyptian is ' taken alone, it is abominable ; but link it up with the
others, and the sting goes. Thus " the best among the serpents
should have his head smashed ; the best among the physicians
should go to hell." Can one take the first saying (about the Egyptian)
very seriously in view of the last ? ' These exculpations are not
entirely satisfactory. I do not mean for a moment to imply that
R. Simeon b. Yochai would have acted upon his own order. But
the saying, taken in conjunction with so very many other sayings
of bitterness and disdain, shows that, in certain moods, any idea of
universal love to all men, Gentile and Jew, was very far from the
Rabbinic mind. And these moods were pretty frequent. Such
feelings as those expressed in Mid. Psalms ii. (7) verse 5, ' The Lord,
the Lord, merciful and gracious : but he is only gracious to the
Israelites ; to the nations who terrify Israel, he will come with anger
and wrath,' occur again and again. So, too, that God judges
Israelites with one measure ; the heathen with another (e.g. ib.
xxx. (4) on verse 1). The same R. Simeon b. Yochai (let us remember
that he had gone through the persecutions and slaughterings of the
Hadrianic revolt, so that his remarks may be equivalent to those
men in one army who had witnessed the brutalities of ·certain
officers and soldiers in another) observed : ' The graves of heathen
do not make Israelites unclean, for in Ezekiel xxxiv. 31 the Israelites
are called men, the nations cattle ' (Baba Mezia 114 b). It stands
as codified law in the Mishnah (Abodah Zarah ii. 1, 26 a) that an
Israelite woman may not act as midwife to a heathen, because she

---

[1] ' Anybody, who has the smallest knowledge of Rabbinic phraseology, must
be well aware that their words mean no more than our German : May the best
Egyptian go to the devil ! Even Rohling would hardly credit R. Simeon with the
folly of having here stated a legal ordinance, and, moreover, by doing so of violently
contradicting the Law which said : Thou shalt not abominate an Egyptian, for
thou wast a stranger in his land.'

would be bringing an extra idolater into the world. In the Gemara it states that shepherds [this is very curious] and heathen are not to be pushed into a pit (to die there), but they need not be pulled out of it; heretics, informers, and apostates may be pushed in and not pulled out (do. 26 b).

Such quotations, and similar ones which could be cited, make it needful for much caution to be exercised before one can too readily assume that in any Rabbinic utterance about the love of neighbour the non-Jew is designedly and consciously included. Still one must also observe caution on the other side. If, as regards any particular ordinance of the Pentateuchal Law, the Rabbis pretty well always interpreted the Biblical *Rea* (neighbour) to mean ' Israelite only,' it is no less clear that their word *chaber*, and still more their word *beriyyoth* (creatures), by no means always excluded, but, on the contrary, often included, the non-Jew, or, at the least, were intended to mean men in general. There were (*a*) a few Rabbis (conspicuously R. Joshua, as we shall hear more than once) who were more tender towards the heathen, and (*b*) there were moods and seasons and times in which the Rabbis were not specifically thinking of Israel's oppressors and rulers, or of the nations as contrasted with Israel, or of idolaters as contrasted with the worshippers of the one God, but in which they, more quietly, thought of all men just generically as the creatures of God, and of God as the Creator and the Feeder of *all*. And, in such moods and seasons, they were disposed to say, Despise not any man, or, even, Care for all men, and perhaps even, Love all men, with the exception (not of ' the nations ' but) of the three hated classes—the heretics, the informers, and the apostates.

Nor do S.B. find it in their hearts impossible to allow that even the Rabbis had some glimmerings of *allgemeine Menschenliebe*, or universal love. The only absolutely necessary thing for S.B. is to prove that these glimmerings were all later than Jesus. For the one essential thing is that the first person ' der die Menschheit gelehrt hat in jedem Menschen den Nächsten zu sehen (what about Buddha?), und deshalb jedem Menschen in Liebe zu begegnen,'[1] must be Jesus. *Per contra*, the Jewish authorities and apologists are all out to prove that Hillel anticipated Jesus by a generation. For my own part, I am not greatly interested in dates, and I observe that

---

[1] ' Who taught humanity to see a neighbour in every man, and so to encounter every man in love.'

S.B., in quoting all the *bad* passages, do not seem to mind much that *they* are all later than A.D. 29. To me the interesting thing is, Did the Rabbinic religion *on its own lines* rise to the conception of active benevolence (= love, for that is what Jesus meant by love) to the enemy and to all mankind ? If Jesus did so rise, 50, 100, 200 years before the Rabbis, I am perfectly ready to concede him the priority ; the matter is to me of minor importance, because the Rabbis assuredly did not learn any doctrine of love and of *allgemeine Menschenliebe* from reading the Gospels. They did not read them, and *if* they ever acquired *allgemeine Menschenliebe* [love of man] they learnt it as a development of their own Rabbinic religion. How, then, does it stand with Hillel ? Here S.B. seem to me to argue with a little less than their usual fairness. In the famous story about the heathen who asked to be taught the whole Law while he stood on one leg, Hillel said, ' What is hateful (displeasing) to you, do not to thy neighbour : That is the whole Law. The rest is but commentary : go and learn.' Now Hillel's version of the Golden Rule is the negative form. Therefore S.B. say (1) there is no universal love in it. It is negative, not active benevolence. As to this, something will be said elsewhere, and has already been said in the Commentary. Jewish scholars argue that the negative form is more ' fundamental ' than the positive form, or that the two forms meant the same thing, and that both depended upon, and were evolved from, the Law of Leviticus, ' Thou shalt love thy neighbour as thyself.' However this may be, S.B. go on to argue that by *chaber* Hillel still only meant ' fellow-Israelite.' ' Though the man addressed was a heathen who wanted to become a proselyte, it does not *therefore* follow that Hillel understood by *chaber*, not fellow-Jew, but fellow-man. Hillel's purpose is to tell the man what the *Law* teaches, and Lev. xix. 18 speaks not of fellow-man, but of fellow-Jew.' This is very dubious. After all, the man was a heathen, and it is very cumbersome and improbable if we have to argue that what Hillel meant was, ' When you *have become* a Jew, the whole Law that you will have to observe is to love your fellow-Jew.' It is surely more natural to suppose that Hillel meant something far more general : something which applied to the man as heathen no less than it would apply to him if he became a Jew. *Chaber* assuredly, therefore, means ' neighbour ' generally ; the heathen's neighbour no less than the Jew's neighbour ; *i.e.* virtually, every man. Moreover, Hillel had said something more : ' Be of the disciples of Aaron, loving peace and pursuing peace, loving " the creatures " (את־הבריות) and drawing them near (ומקרבן) to the Torah ' (Aboth i. 12). Of this sentence S.B. say, ' Über den Kreis der Volksgenossen und etwaiger Proselyten geht Hillel's Blick nicht hinaus.'[1] This is special pleading. ' The creatures ' must mean here mankind generally, and these we are to·love. They are to be brought near to the Law. It seems very doubtful if one can legitimately cheapen, and chip at, the saying by speaking of ' etwaige Proselyten,' occasional or casual or possible proselytes ! Travers Herford in his edition of Aboth says : ' *Beriyyoth* denotes all created beings, although usually human beings are thought of. But love is to have no narrower limit than the human race. There is to be no national or sectarian bias to universal good will. The natural desire of one who feels thus towards his fellow men is to " bring them nigh to the Torah," for this means to make them sharers in the fuller knowledge of God and more conscious of his blessings.' No doubt the distinguished Unitarian scholar is somewhat prejudiced in favour of the Rabbis. Still I think his interpretation of the saying is more likely than that of S.B. If we had in Matthew a saying such as ' Love peace, love " the creatures " and bring them nigh to God,' there is little doubt that we should have had paeans of praise from the Christian commentators, and that we should have been told, ' Here we have a direct and unequivocal preaching of universal love.'

On the other hand, directly the date is later than A.D. 30, S.B. become fair enough. (Pp. 358, 359.) I quoted Ben Azzai's statement in the Sifra that ' This is the book of the generations of Man (Adam) ' was an even greater principle (*Kelal*) than ' Thou shalt love thy neighbour as thyself.' Ben Azzai may have meant (1) to mark the distinction between Adam (man) and *Reaʿ* (fellow-national) ; or (2) he may have meant to indicate that the constant recognition of the divine image in man was an even more comprehensive basis for religion and morality than the command of loving thy neighbour as thyself. In any case it is clear that he drew attention to the bond (viz. the divine image) which unites all men together. (The verse, of which the opening words only are quoted, goes on to say, ' In the day when God created man, in the likeness

---

[1] ' Hillel's vision does not go beyond the circle of his fellow-nationals and of occasional proselytes.'

of God did He create him.') It is not without significance that in
Gen. R., בראשית, xxiv. 7 *ad fin.*, on v. 1 (see my Commentary, Vol.
I. p. vi), where Akiba and Ben Azzai's utterances are quoted in
the reverse order, it is added, ' Thou shalt not say : because I am
despised, so may my neighbour be despised with me, and because
I am cursed, so may my neighbour be cursed with me. If thou
actest so, said R. Tanchuma, know whom thou despisest, namely,
a being made in the image of God.' Here it seems very probable
that ' neighbour ' means any human being, and not merely a fellow-
Israelite. In Aboth iv. 3 Ben Azzai is reported to have said,
' Despise not any man, and carp not at any thing : for you find
no man who has not his hour, and no thing which has not its
place.' The interpretation which S.B. (p. 358, n. 3) give to this
adage is too narrow (' there is no man whom you may not need ').
Herford is, perhaps, almost too generous. ' Some take the saying
as a mere counsel of prudence, Beware of consequences, since a
seemingly trivial thing may lead to great results, for evil no less
than for good. One commentator even draws the lesson, Despise
no man, for the time may come when he will be able to do thee a
mischief. This is surely to place a harsh and cynical interpretation
upon Ben Azzai's words, which is in no way called for. The real
lesson appears to be this : Call no man and no thing contemptible ;
for in God's world there is not a man or a thing unneeded or useless.
Great and small alike, they have their part to play, and their set
time in which to fulfil their Maker's purpose. The lesson is thus
that of a living sympathy with all created beings, and even with
their Creator, and an insight born of that sympathy into the deep-
lying unity beneath the infinite variety of the world.'

Thus the evidence would seem to show that the Rabbis could
and did, in the abstract, and as a general religious doctrine, teach
that one must love, and do good to all the ' creatures,' all the children
of men, created by the One God. But directly they thought of men
in the concrete, directly men became split up into Jews and heathen,
or Jews and ' nations,' their purer religious doctrine was often
driven into the background. The natural and ' national ' man re-
asserted itself and assumed the dominating influence, and nationalist
hatreds (whether largely justified or no) then proceeded to get strong
reinforcement from religious considerations. Nationalist hatreds
could get support from the Scripture to any desired extent, and the

close relationship of Israel to God, so exquisitely conceived as it
was in many ways, and so productive of a vivid consciousness of
God's nearness and love, had, as its dark shadow accompanying
it, the exclusion of the 'nations' from God's care and providence
and compassion. 'He is mine; I am His. And inasmuch He is
mine and I am His—Lover and beloved—others are outside the
range and glory of that love.' Such would seem to have been the
feeling. The strength of the Rabbinic religion was too often its
weakness. We see the same limitations in respect of the views of
the Rabbis about the life to come. That too was, upon the whole
(not by all the Rabbis), regarded as a prerogative of Israel. Idolatry
was sin. The nations were idolaters. How, then, could sinners
inherit the eternal beatitudes? Many passages illustrate this
view. Thus, to quote some of S.B.'s instances, in reference
to the numbering of Israel, God is made to say, 'All the heaps
of nations do not belong to me, but only to the treasury and
to Gehinnom' (Pesikta R. 36 b). Again, the nations are reckoned
as stubble or as thorns which are burnt, or as straw which is scattered
before the wind (do. 35 b). God has suffered the nations to eat
creeping things and abominations, and to commit all unchastities,
because anyhow they are destined for hell. (לפי שהן לגיהנם
(Tanchuma B. x., *Shemini* 14 b).) 'If a man repents, God accepts
him. Everyone? No, Israel, but not another nation' (Pesikta 156a.,
ad fin.). The verse in Proverbs xiv. 34, 'Righteousness (= almsgiving, or charity) exalts a nation, but the lovingkindness of
the nations is sin' (so the Rabbis translate), is constantly quoted.
Their good deeds are sins (*cp.* Augustine's 'shining vices' of
the heathen), because they boast about them. So said R. Elazar.
Rabban Gamaliel, however, said that the meaning was that
the lovingkindness shown by the nations was their sin-offering.
But the majority of Rabbis did not hold the more tolerant view.
(In another version of the story it is R. Yochanan b. Zakkai who
held this opinion. But Bacher thinks that this is an error.) (Pesikta
12 b, Baba Batra 10 b, Midrash Proverbs on xiv. 34, 38 b, and
Bacher, Agada der Tannaiten, i. pp. 34, 35, ed. 2.) R. Joshua was
specially large-minded. He believed that the nations could produce
righteous exceptions, and that these would not remain in, or go to,
Gehinnom (= Hell), or be annihilated. So in the famous passage
in Tosefta Sanhedrin xiii. 2, p. 434, R. Eliezer said that the 'nations'

have no share in the life to come, for it says (Psalm ix. 17) ' the
wicked shall return to Sheol (= Gehinnom), even all the nations
that forget God.' But R. Joshua made the verse mean that it was
only those among the nations who forget God to whom this fate
befell. Those who do not forget him have a share in the life to
come. So, too, Sanhedrin 105 a. So in Midrash Proverbs xvii. 1,
42 b, ' What shall a man do, said R. Eliezer, to avoid Hell ? '
The reply was, Let him do good deeds. Then said R. Eliezer, If
that be so, the nations will do good deeds, and so escape Hell.
R. Joshua said, ' The words of the Law are given not to the dead,
but to the living.' (He implied by this rejoinder that the righteous
among the nations could and would by good deeds escape Hell.)
Nevertheless, it must be confessed that R. Gamaliel and R. Joshua's
views are exceptional, and it is doubtful whether even R. Joshua
could have conceived of an actual idolater, any more than of a
heretic, enjoying the future life. (It is those who do *not* forget God
who obtain that life.) In this he would, I believe, have shared the
view of most of the Church Fathers, and probably of most orthodox
Christians up till modern times, at least so far as the heretic was
concerned, and perhaps as regards the idolater as well. The Rabbis
had their qualms about the ultimate fate of the heathen, even though
they were Israel's enemies. Why was the Law only given to Israel ?
As Moore has well said, ' Did it consist with the justice of God that
the heathen of all generations should be doomed for not keeping a
law which neither they nor their fathers had ever known'? Some
such reflections, I conceive, gave rise to the persuasion that the Law
must have been revealed to the Gentiles also ; not alone the rudi-
mentary Law given to Adam and repeated to Noah, but the Law in
its Sinaitic completeness. From the conviction *a priori* that God
must have done something to the assertion that actually he did,
and then to the discovery in Scripture of proofs of the fact, is a
process too familiar in the history of religious thought to require
explanation or extenuation in the particular case. That the whole
Law was revealed at Sinai to all nations and offered to them for
their acceptance, but refused by all except Israel, is not, like many
of the things we have had occasion to note—like Abraham's expert-
ness in the study and practice of the twofold Law, for example—a
scholastic conceit or a play of homiletical subtlety ; it was the
teaching of both the great schools of the second century, the schools

of Ishmael and Akiba, and is therefore presumably part of the earlier common tradition from which they drew ; and it is repeated in many places with varying circumstantial details. The Law was given in the desert (Exod. xix. 1), given with all publicity in a place which no one had any claim to, lest, if it were given in the land of Israel, the Jews might deny to the Gentiles any part in it, or lest any nation in whose territory it was given might claim an exclusive right in it. It was given in the desert, in fire and in water, things which are free to all who are born into the world. It was revealed at Sinai, not in one language, but in four—Hebrew, Roman, Arabic, and Aramaic. The foreign languages here named—" Roman " being the language of Seir (Esau)—are those of peoples living, one might say, within hearing distance of the thunder tones of revelation at Sinai, and it is these three neighbouring peoples which, in the often-repeated story, refused the Law because it forbade the sins to which they were by heredity addicted, murder, adultery, and robbery. In Jewish computation, however, based on Genesis x., the nations of the world were seventy, and the notion that the Law was given to all nations takes the form of a revelation in seventy languages. Sometimes it is God's voice at Sinai that is heard in all seventy at once ; or Moses in the plains of Moab interpreted the Law in seventy languages ; or, again, the Law was inscribed on the stones of the altar on Mount Ebal (Josh. viii. 31 f), and the nations sent their scribes, who copied it in seventy different languages. Everywhere the nations refused to receive the Law thus offered to them ; Israel alone accepted it, and pledged obedience to it. God foreknew that the Gentiles would not receive it, but he offered it to them that they might have no ground to impugn his justice ; it is not his way to punish without such justification, he does not deal tyrannously with his creatures. That Israel alone among the nations has the true religion argues, therefore, no partiality or injustice in God ; it is because, while all the rest refused the revelation he made of his character and will, Israel joyfully received it and solemnly bound itself to live in conformity to it.' The Rabbinic sources are given in Moore's footnotes. The chief ones are Mechilta 62 a and Sifre 142 b. The Scripture proofs are very curious and fantastic. In Psalm lxxvii. 14, ' Thou hast declared thy strength among the peoples,' ' strength ' is the Torah. The nations refused the Law ; therefore God was wroth with them and sent them to Gehinnom.

' R. Abbahu said, If God knew that the nations would not accept the Law, why did he offer it to them ? (מפני מה יצא מה ידיהם). Because such is the character (מדותיו) of God. He does not punish until he has done his part towards his creatures (עד שיצא ידי בריותיו), and then he expels them from the world : because God does not deal tyrannically (במטרוניא) with his creatures' (Tanchuma B. iii. ve-zoth ha-Berachah 28 a ; Pesikta 200 a). This curious vacillation is seen also in the Rabbinic view about the ' nations ' and repentance. Sometimes, as Moore points out, God's forgiveness after repentance is distinctly stated to be the privilege of Israel, and not to apply to any other people (e.g. Pesikta 156 a, last line) ; sometimes Gentile repentance is said to have been desired by God in order that he might forgive. Thus God ordered Noah to build the ark publicly, that the people around him might notice it and be told what it was for, and so that they might repent ; he bade the men who built the tower of Babel repent that he might receive them. Even to the people of Sodom and Gomorrah God ' opened a door to repentance,' which, I suppose, means that he incited them to repent. Jonah's attempt to escape from God was ' prompted by a presentiment that the heathen were near repentance,' and is apparently regarded as an honouring of the Son (Israel), but a dishonouring of the Father (God). (The Ninevites' repentance would show up by contrast the unrepentance of Israel, and God would hold the Israelites guilty and punish them for their sins.) Thus Jonah did not want to make Israel guilty (שלא לחייב את ישראל). (Moore I. pp. 528, 529 ; Tanchuma B. Bereshit xxxvii. 13 a ; do. Noah xxviii. 28 b ; Gen. R. xlix. 6, 9, on xviii. 25 ; Mechilta 38 b, 39 a ; Mechilta I b ; Jer. Sanhedrin xi. 30 b.) It is the manner or characteristic of the righteous to put in a defence, not only for Israel, but also for the wicked, hoping that the wicked may repent, and, as it were, reminding God of the prophetic word, ' I delight not in the death of the wicked.' So Abraham put up a defence for the cities of the plain, hoping that they would repent. Abraham said to God that he could not exercise strict justice, and yet maintain the world. A little he must give way, or the world could not endure. God said to him : ' Thou lovest to justify my creatures and refusest to condemn them ' (a play of punctuation and words upon Psalm xlv. 8). (Tanchuma B. Vayera ix. 46 a, Genesis R. xlix. 9.) Really it is in accordance with God's most essential nature that he wishes to

spare the wicked so far as he can, and therefore desires them to repent.
When they are not disturbed by remembrance (or experience) of
dire persecution and oppression, the Rabbis feel that this quality
of God extends to all. ' R. Phineas bar Chama said, God does not
desire to condemn any of his creatures (לחייב כל בריה); he desires to
justify all his creatures.' (Tanchuma B. *Va'era* xi. 13 b ; Moore,
I. p. 391.) In a passage which can be read in its entirety in Moore
(I. p. 380) and in Bacher (*Agada der pal.: Amoräer*, I. p. 182) it
is said that, whereas it might be imagined that God could no longer
properly be called ' great and powerful ' (Deut. x. 17)—since ' the
heathen were ramping (מקרקרן) in his temple, and his children
were enslaved by them—it is, on the contrary (אדרבה), the very
culmination of his power (גבורת גבורתו) that he represses his passion
(יצרו) and is long-suffering towards the wicked ' (Yoma 69 b). An
average Rabbinic view about the ' nations ' is well indicated in the
following passage : ' R. Chanina, according to others, R. Simlai, taught:
In the time to come the Holy One will take a scroll of the Law . . . ,
and say, He who has busied himself with this, let him come and
receive his reward. Thereupon, all the peoples of the world
will come pell-mell (בערבוביא) before him. . . . God will say,
Do not come before me all mixed up, but let each nation and its
scribes come one by one. . . . First, then, will come before him
the Roman kingdom. . . . God will say to them : With what have
you occupied yourselves ? They will reply : Lord of the world,
we have made many roads and baths ; we have amassed much gold
and silver, and all this we have done for the sake of Israel, so that
they might occupy themselves with the Law. Then the Holy One
will answer : Fools, all you have done you did for yourselves ;
you made streets to put harlots in them, baths for your own pleasure ;
the silver and gold is mine (Haggai ii. 8). . . . Then the Romans
will go out (from God's presence) grieved at heart. Then the
Persians will come in. . . . God will ask them the same question.
They will reply, we built many bridges, we conquered many cities,
we waged many wars, and all this we did only for the sake of the
Israelites, so that they might occupy themselves with the Law.
God will reply, All that you did you only did for yourselves : you
built bridges to get tolls from them, you conquered cities to get
forced service from them. As for the wars, I waged them, for it
says, The Lord is a man of war. Is there a man among you who

can say "this," and "this" is only the Torah, as it says "This is the
Torah which Moses", etc., Deut. iv. 44. Then the Persians will go
out grieved at heart. . . . To the other nations God asks the same
question about the Law. They reply : Lord of the world, did you
give the Law to us, and did we refuse to receive it ? ' [It is also
suggested that they will say : Did we receive it and not observe it ?
Or, Did you work a threatening miracle before offering it to us as you
did to the children of Israel.] (The miracle is then described.) ' Then
God will say : Well, have you kept the seven (Noachide) commands
which you *did* receive ? ' [R. Joseph said, God saw that the Noachides
did not keep the seven commands, so he stood up and freed them
from them. But, if so—it is argued—they received a profit ! Would
the sinner be rewarded ? Mar, the son of Rabina, replied, This
shows that, even if they keep them, they receive no reward. But
can this be ? Did not R. Meir say, Even a heathen who occupies
himself with the Law is equal to the High Priest ? The meaning
is that they receive no reward, because, if they keep the commands,
it is as if they keep them without being *ordered* to keep them.
For R. Chanina said, Greater is he who does something because
he thereby fulfils a command than he who does it without being
commanded to do it.] ' They will then say : Have the Israelites
who received the Law kept it ? God will reply : I bear witness
that they have kept it. They will answer, Can a father bear witness
for his son ? ' (Then there follows a long argument which I omit.)
' Then the nations reply : Offer us the Law anew, and we will keep
it. Then God will reply, Fools ; he who has provided himself
before the Sabbath has wherewith to eat on Sabbath : but he who
has not so provided himself, of what shall he eat ? Yet even so,
there is a light command called *Sukkah* (booths) : go and fulfil it.
. . . They will then all go and erect a *sukkah* upon their roofs.
But God will cause the sun to wax hot upon them as at midsummer,
and they will trample on their *sukkahs* and run away.' [But did
you not say that God does not act tyrannically to his creatures ?
Well, even among the Israelites the sun is sometimes very hot at
the season of *Sukkah*, and causes them pain. But did not Raba
say, He who is in pain is free (dispensed) from (the law of) *sukkah* ?
Well, even if free, they should not have hurled the *sukkahs* away
from them.] ' Thereupon the Holy One will laugh at them, as it
is said, He who sits in the heaven will laugh (Ps. ii. 4). R. Isaac

said that the Holy One only laughs on this one day. . . . R. Jose
said, In the time to come the nations will all desire to become
proselytes. But will they be received ? For the teaching is that no
proselytes are received in the days of the Messiah. . . . They will
become proselytes of violence (גרים גרורים. *Cp.* Matt. xi. 12. On
this see F. C. Burkitt in *J. T. S.* xxx. Ap., 1929, No. 119, pp. 25
seq.); they will lay *Tephillin* on their heads and arms ; they will
add *Zizith* (fringes) to their garments and put *Mezuzot* on their
doorposts. When they see the war of Gog and Magog, they will
ask against whom they come, and when they are told, against the
Lord and his Anointed, they will smash the commands (*i.e.* the
Zizith, etc.), and run away. And the Holy One will sit and laugh
at them. It was about this that R. Isaac said that God only laughs
on this day. But R. Judah had said in the name of Rab, The
day has twelve hours ; during the first three God occupies himself
with (=studies) the Law ; during the next three he sits and judges
the whole world, and when he sees that the world has merited
destruction (שנתחייב עולם כלייה), he gets up from the seat
of judgment, and sits down on the seat of mercy ; in the next
three hours he sits and nourishes the whole world from the horned
buffalo to the eggs of the lice ; in the last three hours he sits and
plays with the Leviathan. R. Nachman ben Isaac said, *With*
his creatures he laughs (plays) each day ; *at* his creatures he laughs
only on that one day. . . . R. Chama b. Chanina pointed out a
contradiction between " wrath is not in me " (Isaiah xxvii. 4) and
" the Lord is full of wrath " (Nahum i. 2). That is no difficulty :
the one verse applies to the Israelites ; the other to the nations.
. . . R. Alexander said, " I will seek to destroy all the nations "
(Zech. xii. 9). . . . God says, I will search in their records ; if
they have merit (*Zechuth*), I will redeem them ; if not, I will destroy
them. Raba said, . . . God tells Israel, When I judge Israel, I
do not judge it as I judge the nations ; I punish Israel only as a
hen pecks at her food ' (*i.e.* bit by bit, or individually, here and
there). Again, it is said, ' Even if Israel only does a few commands
here and there, as a hen pecks in the dung, I will collect them to
a great sum.' (Abodah Zarah, 2 a *fin.*–3 b, 4 a). ' R. Ishmael said,
There is joy before God when those who provoke him perish from
the world ' (Sifre 37 a). The prevailing feeling of the Rabbis is
here, quaintly but clearly, set forth. Of its prevailing particularism

there can be no question. Yet flashes of universalism break and
shine through the darkness. We see throughout the burden of
Scripture, which was known only too well. It would, I think, be
accurate to say that the number of those who, being idolaters, die
'in their idolatry,' and then inherit the beatitudes of the life to
come, would be exceedingly small. The horror of idolatry, its
identification with the denial of God, and this denial with deliberate
sin, were too strong. A Rabbi said that 'idolatry is like a man
saying to his neighbour, Thou hast scooped out the dish and
lessened it.' And another said, 'It is like a man who has scooped
out the whole dish and left nothing in it' (Sifre 33 a). (This Mr.
Levertoff explains to mean that an idolater impairs, so to speak,
the Divine Nature itself, and makes, as it were, the Creator non-
existent. Midrash Sifre on Numbers, p. 100.) It is recorded that
R. Reuben spent a Sabbath in Tiberias, and a philosopher asked
him, 'Who is the most hateful man in the world? The Rabbi
answered, He who denies his Creator.' (And I suppose that, in the
opinion of R. Reuben, and of every other Rabbi, an idolater was a
man who denied his Creator.) He explained this assertion by
quoting the fifth, sixth, seventh, eighth, ninth, and tenth commandments (*i.e.* all the commandments relative to morality) and declaring that ' no man denies (כופר) (the obligation of) any one of these
commandments until he denies the Root (בעיקר) (*i.e.* God), and
conversely no man transgresses any one of them (הולך לדבר עבירה)
unless he also denies him who ordered them.' (Bacher appears to
hold that we may hold the last three Hebrew words in brackets,
taken in their context, to mean what I have conveyed by my translation.) (T. Shebuoth iii. 6, p. 450 ; Moore I. p. 467 ; Bacher, *Agada
der Tannaiten* II. p. 384.) Like the Rabbis, Jesus, apparently, also
thought that many more people would be excluded from the beatitudes of the world to come than would be included within them
(Matt. vii. 13, 14). A loveless and painful doctrine, which persisted,
I imagine, both among Jews and Christians for a long while. How
it could *also* have been believed that God was loving or love is a
mystery. The inconsistencies of the human mind are amazing. But
when we find noble people like Jesus and R. Akiba exhibiting these
inconsistencies, what wonder that lesser men exhibited them too.

In his very interesting and able work, *Das Judentum und seine
Umwelt* (Vol. I. 1927), Dr. M. Guttmann attempts to show that the

Rabbis judged much more favourably about the 'salvation' of the heathen than has been here suggested. As regards the *successors* of the Rabbis he seems to be right. He seems to prove his case that the growth of broader views was fairly rapid. The mediaeval Jewish writers were far more large-hearted, as it would seem, than the contemporary Christians. Guttmann is also well able to turn the tables upon Billerbeck (p. 297 *seq.*). He is easily able to show that any limitation of God's mercy is by no means a merely Jewish or Rabbinic vice. Here he wins. But as regards the Rabbinic literature I am doubtful. He quotes, doubtless, some pleasant passages about righteous men among the nations, about people who, though not Jews and not proselytes, were yet conspicuously 'good,' and about others who were not considered as idolaters, though they were 'heathens,' but I hardly think that Billerbeck is wrong when he calls all these cases 'exceptions.' The Rabbis were probably not much more or less tolerant than Jesus, or than the author of the fourth Gospel; their notions as to the *proportion* of heathen and Israelites who would be 'lost' and 'saved' doubtless differed, but in the gross I do not think that the percentages of lost and saved would have been very unlike. Jesus would have admitted more Gentiles among the saved and fewer Jews than the Rabbis, and for the author of the fourth Gospel the saved Gentiles would have been the majority. But for all three, Rabbis, Jesus, and 'John,' the 'lost' would, I should imagine, have largely outnumbered the 'saved.' The ideas of all three concerning toleration were very limited. The Rabbis did probably think that most of the heathen would be annihilated after death, or at the judgment, or that they would remain in hell. But Jews seemed to have emancipated themselves from this cheerless doctrine sooner than Christians. And the reason, I take it, is curious. Rabbinic intolerance is largely national. It depended upon a hatred of the oppressor. It was less theological and systematic than the Christian intolerance. Therefore it was more easily overcome. Theological narrowness is the most severe and comprehensive, if I may use such a bull, of all narrownesses. One of the 'nice' passages Guttmann quotes is, 'A man can become a righteous man, even if he be a heathen. He cannot become a Cohen or a Levite, for that depends upon birth : righteousness does not. Therefore God loves the righteous, for they become righteous of their own choice' (Midrash

Psalms cxlvi. (7), verse 8, 268 b, and Num. R. viii. 2). The Midrash notices that the nations are called 'righteous' in Ezekiel xxiii. 45 (Lev. R. v. 8 *ad fin.*). 'There are always thirty righteous men among the nations by whom the nations are preserved' (מתקיימים עליהם), Chullin 92 a). The idea is that the thirty make atonement for the others, and this idea is significant. 'God uses the good as instruments for good and the bad as instruments for bad, and this rule applies to the nations as well as to Israel' (Tana Eliyahu, Seder Rabba, Chap. xvi. p. 81, and Seder Zuta, Chap. vii. p. 184. Repentance is in the power of all, whether Israelite or heathen (Seder Rabba, Chap. xvii. p. 88). The T.E. is more universalistic in tone than any other old Rabbinic work, so far as I can make out). 'God does not delay the reward of those who do good deeds among the nations' (Jer. Peah i. 1, 15 c). But these and a few other passages in the T. Eliyahu, and elsewhere, can hardly balance the larger number of passages in which the unfortunate future of the nations in the next world is complacently, and even joyfully, alluded to. Nevertheless, caution is requisite. Dr. Coulton, in a chapter called 'The Mind of Mediaevalism' in Harmsworth's *History of the World*, says that one of the four main threads before Christ was 'Judaism, strong in its Monotheism, its abhorrence of idolatry and its social cohesion, but too often narrow and intolerant, conceiving Jehovah as a tribal god, friendly to Israel and unfriendly to the Gentile.' How far is this description fair ? Notice the little 'g.' This is clearly intended to indicate that Jehovah was still conceived as a tribal 'god,' in the same sense as we should say that Chemosh was the tribal 'god' of Moab. But if so, how can it be right to speak of Jewish monotheism ? I am not prepared to deny that the Rabbis were often intolerant, and that they conceived of God too often as friendly to Israel and unfriendly to the Gentile. But, nevertheless, he was not for them a tribal God ; he was the one and only God ; the creator of heaven and earth, the father of all men. His frequent partiality was, in truth, inconsistent with his nature, even as that nature was described and believed in by the Rabbis themselves. To call the God of Hillel or of R. Yochanan b. Zakkai a tribal 'god' is absurd. And even of the very Rabbis who make narrow and intolerant remarks— even of these it is inaccurate to assimilate *their* God with Chemosh. It would be no less inaccurate to call their God a tribal 'god,'

because of their not infrequent narrowness and intolerance, than
to call the God of the fourth Gospel a sectarian ' god ' because its
author excludes from salvation those who disbelieve in God's son.
The one epithet would be as improper as the other. Akiba's God
was not tribal, ' John's ' God was not sectarian ; but the vision
of both Akiba and John was sometimes blurred and dim ; they
did not perceive their own inconsistencies. Akiba did not see that
his God was intolerant, John did not see that *his* God was unloving.
But yet it would be inaccurate to deny that Akiba believed in a
universal God, and ' John ' in a God of love.

Now let me pass on to the more definite question of hating and
not hating, loving and not loving, the enemy. When Jesus bade
his disciples to love their enemies, he did not mean that they were
to feel for them the same kind of feelings as they had for their
wives, their children, and their parents, but that (a) they were to
eradicate the feeling of hatred and revenge from their hearts ; (b)
they were not merely not to curse the enemy, but to pray for the
enemy's conversion and welfare ; (c) they were to do him good when
opportunity offered. They were not even to hope that God would
punish their enemies, but, on the contrary, they were to pray for
the enemies' good : that meant, I suppose, that the enemies too
should cease to hate and to do evil, and that, without punishment
or misfortune, they should repent. I have put the matter in very
simple words, but it can hardly be gainsaid that this is the meaning.
Compare, then, Matt. v. 43-48 and Luke vi. 27-35 with the Rabbinical teaching, and what must be the verdict ? Let us keep the
question of the range of the enemy separate, for the two points
are often mixed up. I am not clear that Jesus was definitely enlarging the range, but as to the private enemy (the enemy of whom
you are not thinking about his race, or nationality, or religious
opinions) my verdict would be that Jesus unites himself with the
very best Rabbinic teaching of his own and of later times. It is,
perhaps, only in trenchantness and eager insistency that he goes
beyond it. There is a fire, a passion, an intensity, a broad and deep
positiveness, about these verses, which is new. Jesus suffers no
exceptions : the Jew may not say, ' Isaac is not only my enemy,
but he is a bad Jew ; therefore I legitimately hate him,' or ' I keep
silent before Joseph's curses ; God will avenge me,' or ' I keep silent,
but I do not forget ' ; his heart must be pure and purged of all

hatred and ill-will; he must wish only good to the evil-doer; he must seek his welfare, and do him good when he can; he must pray for him unto God. I do not deny that there are parallels to these injunctions scattered about in the vast Rabbinical literature, but they are nowhere collected together in so pregnant, comprehensive or vivid a form as in Matthew and Luke, and sometimes there are qualifications and reservations of them which cannot be wholly ignored. Why may we not give to Jesus—himself a Jew—his own glory, and to his teaching its own praise? Let me now seek to illustrate and defend my general conclusions in more detail. Most of what I quote is taken from S.B.

It is perhaps needless to say anything more about the form of Matt. v. 43. ' Thou shalt hate thine enemy ' occurs nowhere in the Pentateuch. Various explanations have been given of it. S.B. admit that the second portion of the verse cannot be substantiated from a source. ' Das Ganze (the whole verse) wird eine populäre Maxime sein, nach der der Durchschnittsisraelit in Jesu Tagen sein Verhalten gegen Freund und Feind eingerichtet hat.' [1] This is not very satisfactory, for the wording is so precisely similar to that of 38 or 27. And indeed no explanation is quite satisfactory. Perhaps there is something to be said for the explanation of Güdemann. His pamphlet on ' Nächstenliebe ' (Vienna, 1890) is ingenious, but his theses that Jesus deliberately alludes to Hillel, that his teaching to love the enemy was in full accordance with the higher Rabbinic teaching of his time, and that chaber, if not rea', always meant ' every man,' cannot be maintained. He ignores too many of the counter passages. It is doubtful (1) whether R. Akiba in saying that Lev. xix. 18 was the greatest Kelal in the Law (the most fundamental or inclusive principle) thereby meant that to him rea' signified every man, or (2) whether on this point there was no opposition or difference of opinion between him and Ben Azzai. (Cp. however, Abrahams, Studies I. p. 20.) We have always the double current in Rabbinic literature. When the Rabbis are not thinking of the nations as contrasted with Israel, they can magnify ' man ' and the value of every human soul to any extent. And yet at other times, when they were concerned with idolatry and felt

[1] ' The whole verse may be regarded as a popular maxim, according to which the average Israelite of the days in which Jesus lived ordered his conduct towards friend and foe.'

pessimistic, or when persecution was sore, they could believe that
most of the heathen would end in hell or annihilation. But they
could hardly have held these two beliefs simultaneously. Akiba
can say, ' Beloved is man, for he was created in the image of God, but
it was by a special love that it was made known to him that he was
created in the image of God.' And here ' man ' is, by what follows,
specifically distinguished from Israel. Yet the same Akiba is reported to have said, ' The nations say to Israel, Whither is thy
beloved (God) gone that we may seek him with thee ? But Israel
replies, Ye have no portion in him ; my beloved is mine, and I
am his ' (*i.e.* exclusively). The second saying may be as authentic
as the first, and the first as the second : Akiba was doubtless inconsistent, but it would be dangerous, with this inconsistency before
us, to assume that he meant by *rea‘* more than fellow-Israelite.
But, on the other hand, there may be more value in Güdemann's
view that we should understand Matt. v. 43 to mean, ' You have
heard that it was said, Thou shalt love thy neighbour, and so you
might suppose that you may hate your enemy (whom, as he *is* your
enemy, and so, *ex hypothesi*, hates you, you may consider *not* to
be your neighbour). Therefore I say to you,' etc.

We may ask (1) who were the Jews whom some Rabbis allowed
their disciples either not to love or to hate ; (2) how far was such
teaching controverted by other Rabbis ? In Aboth we have the saying
of R. Joshua, The evil eye, the evil *Yetzer*, and hatred of his fellow-
creatures, put a man out of the world. Here ' creatures ' means
men generally. In the Aboth R. Nathan (xvi. 32 b) the saying is
quoted and commented on thus (we have heard it before, but it
must be quoted again) : 'Let not a man accustom himself to say :
" Love the wise, and hate the disciples, love the disciples, but hate
the *amme ha-aretz*, but rather, love all, and hate (only) the Heretics,
the Apostates, and the Informers," as David says, " Do I not hate
them that hate thee ; I hate them with a complete hatred, they are
my enemies." But does it not say, " Thou shalt love thy neighbour
as thyself, I am the Lord " (that is, I have created him) ? Yes,
if he acts as thy people should act, then thou must love him, but
if he does not, then thou must (or needst) not love him. [Güdemann
draws a dubious distinction here between "not loving" and "hating."]
R. Simeon b. Elazar said, With a great oath was this word said,
Thou shalt love thy neighbour as thyself ; I, the Lord, have created

him ; if thou lovest him, I am trustworthy to give thee good reward :
and if not, I am a judge to punish thee.' Now as to the apostates,
the heretics, the informers, there is no conflicting passage in which it
says that these people are to be loved, and perhaps it would be too
much to expect. Again, there is no definite passage that I know
of where it says that the *goi*, the idolater, the persecutor, the
oppressor, is to be loved (*i.e.* prayed for, done good to). I have said
that Jesus is not thinking in this passage deliberately of the Gentiles.
He does not deliberately mean the antithesis : ' You were told to
love your fellow-Jews; I tell you to love the Gentiles, who are
your enemies.' If he had meant that, he would, I feel sure, have
expressed himself more clearly. But perhaps I may have stressed
private enemies too sharply and heavily. Jesus *may* have referred
also to sections of Jews who showed hostility to himself and his
teaching, or, just possibly, in his moral enthusiasm and intensity,
and in the purity and depth of his religious insight, he *may* have
meant enemies generally, whether they happen to be Jews or Gentiles,
private or public. Did he, perhaps, speak in the broadest and most
general terms, not thinking of any one set of people in particular ?
One wishes he had been more definite. I wonder if he could have
brought it over him to say, ' Love the Pharisees and Rabbis, if
they persecute you ; love the Romans when they oppress you.' I can
believe the second more readily than the first, because till the *end* of
his life Jesus suffered very little from the enmity of the Romans.

To return, however, to the Rabbis and their teachings. We may
ask how far does Rabbinic teaching approach to the command,
Love your enemies—that is, seek their welfare ; and how far is it
removed from such a command ; or what qualifications do we find
in Rabbinic teaching in regard to this subject ? And now the
nationality and quality of the enemies can be neglected. That
point has been dealt with already. We are now dealing specifically
with Question 8. (P. 59.)

Hatred, and especially causeless hatred, are often unsparingly
condemned. The famous adage in Aboth has already been quoted.
' The evil eye, says R. Joshua, the evil *Yetzer*, and hatred of his
fellow-creatures drive a man out of the world.' On this saying
Mr. Herford comments thus : The three things which ' drive a man
out of the world ' are ' only three synonyms for selfishness which
is by its very nature unsocial. The selfish man cuts himself off

from human intercourse and the sympathy of his fellows ; it is
not they but himself to whom is due his exclusion. The phrase
" to drive a man out of the world " does not refer to death, and still
less does it imply exclusion from the world to come, as Taylor by
his reference to I John iii. 15 seems to suggest. Some commentators
explain the plural " (they) drive him from the world " as referring
to the people whom he hates ; but the reference to his own selfish
nature is simpler and psychologically truer. The selfish man hates,
but only the selfish hate him in return. The punishment he receives
is what he makes for himself.' Why was the second temple destroyed
although men occupied themselves with the study of the Law and
with performing the commandments and deeds of lovingkindness ?
Because causeless hate existed : and thus it is shown that causeless
hate weighs as heavily (is as great a sin) as incest and murder and
idolatry (which caused the destruction of the sanctuary at Shiloh
and of the first temple) (Yoma 9 a). In Sifre 108 b, Deut. xix. 11
is commented on, and it is said, ' He who violates a light command
will ultimately violate a heavy one ; he who violates, Love thy
neighbour as thyself, will ultimately violate, Thou shalt not hate
thy brother in thy heart, and thou shalt not take vengeance nor
bear any grudge ; and even " he shall live with thee " (Lev. xxv. 35)
till at the end he will come to shedding blood.' In this passage
the commandment to love thy neighbour is considered light in the
sense of being comparatively easy to fulfil, because it is natural to
man to love. The absence of love leads to hate, and so finally
to murder. The same passage in the Sifra (89 b, on Lev. xix. 18),
from which I have quoted before on ' Love thy neighbour as thyself,'
and about Akiba's comment, and about the limitation to ' the children of thy people,' also deals in quaintest mode with vengeance and
grudge. ' If A asks B, " lend me your scythe," and B refuses, and
next day B says to A, " lend me your spade," and A replies, " I will
not, even as you refused to lend me your scythe," that is revenge
(which the Law forbids). If A says to B, " lend me your spade,"
and B refuses, and next day B says to A, " lend me your scythe,"
and A replies, " here it is ; I am not like you, who would not lend
me your spade "—that is bearing a grudge, which also is forbidden.'
' Man must love the creatures, and not hate them ; the generation
who were dispersed over the earth (Gen. xi. 1-9) loved one another,
and so God did not destroy them, but only scattered them ; but the

men of Sodom hated one another, and so God destroyed them both from this world and from the world to come ' (Aboth R. Nathan xii. 26 b).   I may add here a few extra sentences from Dr. Abrahams' essay on Man's Forgiveness (*Studies* i.).   ' We have in a late Midrash the splendid generalisation that :   Whoever hates any man is as one who hates Him who spake and the world was (*Pesikta Zutarta* on Numbers viii. *seq.*).   This prohibition applied to all men, even to Rome (see the strong rebuke in Eccles. *Rabba* on xi. 1 on the text Deut. xxiii. 8).   Even the command to remember Amalek was explained by one Rabbi to mean, Remember your own sins which led up to Amalek's assault :   " A king owned a vineyard, round which he built a fence.   He placed inside the fence a savage dog.   The king said, Should one come and break through the fence, the dog will bite him.   The king's own son came, and broke down the fence. The dog bit him.   Whenever the king wished to mention how his son had offended in the matter of the vineyard, he said to him : Remember what the dog did to you !   So, whenever God wishes to recall Israel's sin at Rephidim (Exod. xvii. 8), he says unto them : Remember what Amalek did to you" (Pesikta K. 27 a) ' (p. 160). A series of ' ancient personal prayers has been preserved in the Jerusalem Talmud (Berachoth iv. § 2, 7 d).   Thus we find, " May it be thy will, O Lord my God and God of my fathers, that hatred and envy of us enter not into the heart of man, nor hatred and envy of any man enter into our heart."   On the same page may be seen the student's prayer :   " May it be thy will, that I be not angered against my fellows, nor they against me."   Yet another prayer occurs in the same context :   " Bring us near to what thou lovest, keep us far from what thou hatest."   These beautiful petitions may be paralleled by that of Mar Zutra, who every night, on retiring to his couch, said, " Forgiveness be to all who have troubled me " שרי ליה לכל מאן דצערן), Megillah 28 a) (p. 161).   " I never went to bed," said another Rabbi, at the close of a long life, " with the curse of my fellow " (Megillah, *ib.*) ' (p. 165).

But such passages as these deal only with hatred generally.   How stands the matter as regards the hatred of the enemy and the love of the enemy ?   We may note from this special instance how much depended upon Scripture, and especially upon the Pentateuch. (The Pentateuchal moral commands were often widened or developed : they were very seldom indeed diminished or cheapened.)   Now in

the Pentateuch there is no general command on the subject of being
kind or good to enemies, but there is a specific command about one
particular case, namely the striking law of Exodus xxiii. 4, 5. It
is a remarkable fact that Deuteronomy, which usually improves
on the older Book of the Covenant (Exodus xxi.–xxiii.), in this
instance goes back upon it. For the enemy, the man who hates
you, of Exodus, becomes merely the ' brother ' in Deut. xxii. 1–4.
Nevertheless, the Rabbis have a good deal to say about Exodus
xxiii. 4, 5, and in spite of the usual casuistical discussions, the letter
of the Law is maintained. It is also pretty clear that the ' natural
man '—and there was a good deal of the ' natural man ' in the
Rabbis, which had both its strong and its weak side—found the law
of Exodus xxiii. a hard law. Yet it was not explained or whittled
away. In the Mechilta—the old commentary, half halachic, half
haggadic—on Exodus xxiii. 4, the question is raised whether the
enemy is a Jewish enemy or no. R. Josiah said that it was the non-
Jew, the *goi*, the idolater : the *goyim* are ever the enemies of Israel.
Thus, even in the case of an idolater, the law of Exodus xxiii. 4 must
be obeyed. G. Kittel observes : ' Das ist einmal ein Fall, in dem die
nationale Schranke wirklich klar, deutlich und prinzipiell durch-
brochen ist ' (p. 116).[1] R. Eliezer said the enemy was a proselyte who
returned to his evil tendency (לסורו). R. Isaak said the enemy was an
apostate Israelite (משומד). R. Nathan, however, said that he was
an ordinary Israelite. But it is asked how *can* an *Israelite* be thy
enemy ? ' Well, if he has struck your ear, or picked a quarrel with
you, he is your enemy for the time ' (לשעה) (99 a). The general
view was that the enemy *was* an Israelite. The Mechilta continues
with a good deal of legal distinctions and discussions, but it lays down
the rule that though the Law speaks of helping the enemy only to
*un*load his ass, one must also help him to *load* it. For unloading is
easier than loading : if, then, you are to help in unloading, how much
more in loading. (דבר הכתוב בהווה בקל ללמד ממנו את החמור) (99 b).
There is another long discussion on the subject in Baba Mezia, both
in the Mishnah and in the Gemara (32 a and b), about loading and
unloading, but in the Mishnah the ' enemy ' is not mentioned, and
in the Gemara the discussion is complicated by the introduction of
the point of view of cruelty to animals (צער בעלי חיים). There is

---

[1] ' Here for once is an instance in which national limitations are clearly, plainly,
and as a matter of principle, broken through.'

a good deal of dispute as to whether help is to be rendered if the owner of the ass or of its burden is a *goi*. The decision is that help *is* to be rendered ' because of enmity ' (*i.e.* to allay enmity). Here the motive is on a par with the rule that the poor and the rich of the *goyim* are to be helped, their sick visited and their dead buried, ' for the sake of peace '—a motive which the modern Jewish commentators try to turn into an equivalent of universal benevolence, and S.B. and other Christian commentators regard as a mere motive of policy. (*Klugheitsmassregel*) (Gittin 61 a, etc.) The truth lies in between. Mr. Loewe writes : ' *Klugheitsmassregel* ("rule of good policy") is a big and categorical assertion. I do not think it is justified, though I am not prepared to maintain that every act of kindness by a Jew to a gentile was disinterested. But if self-interest or national interest was the motive in every case, why are stories of unkindness recorded ? These are often cited as proofs of Jewish "misanthropy," but the argument is double-edged. Either the Jew behaved naturally, and was sometimes kind and sometimes unkind, like most human beings, or, if policy alone animated him, why were there ever open and deliberate unkind acts ? The juxtaposition of "kind" and "unkind" is sometimes very forcible ; *e.g.* the two contrary stories of kindness and unkindness to Romans in the hour of need, which follow in succession in Eccles. *Rabba* ("cast thy bread," etc., xi. 1, cited below, p. 347). In face of the second, one can hardly maintain that a calculated policy of ingratiation existed. *Nebeneinanderleben* (Kittel's term) is a more probable explanation. If there had been no social intercourse and resultant friendship and kindness, the bulk of the regulations in Abodah Zarah would have been unnecessary.' Kittel (p. 115) says of these laws, as of the ruling that one is to greet a heathen upon the public way (Gittin Mishnah v. 9 and 62 a) : ' Freilich ist ein Verhalten solcher Art nicht aus prinzipiellen Erwägungen entstanden, sondern aus der unmittelbaren Praxis des Nebeneinanderlebens. Das beweist der begründende Zusatz, den die genanten Anweisungen in Gittin regelmässig haben : "Um des Friedens willen." Immerhin mag derartiges eine Brücke gebildet haben, hinüber zu einer ruhigeren und humaneren Beurteilung auch des Volksfremden.' [1] And in truth it has ever been so. The Jews

---

[1] ' Conduct of this kind did not, however, come to pass as a matter of principle, but it arose from the immediate practical needs of living side by side. That this

have almost always liked, and wished to live at peace with, their neighbours, and to cultivate friendly relations with them. Hitlerists, Hackenkreuzler, anti-Semites, would not, *mutatis mutandis*, have been a Jewish phenomenon. It is further said, If there were two cases of need, to *unload* a friend's ass, and to *load* an enemy's ass, the enemy takes precedence. Why ? To crush the evil desire. (לכוף את יצרו) (32 b.) This means to quell the *Yetzer* of the man who is tempted to leave the enemy and his ass unaided and to turn first to the friend. In Sifre (115 a) the contrast between Exodus and Deuteronomy is duly noted, and it is explained that the law about the enemy was made only as against the *Yetzer*, *i.e.* in order to subdue the evil inclination. (Here clearly it is the evil inclination of the man who might be tempted to leave the enemy without assistance.) In the Tosefta, however, the object is distinctly stated to be to crush (*i.e.* change) the heart of the hater, the enemy. To do that, it is one's duty to help the enemy in unloading before helping the friend in loading. (כדי לשבור את לבו) (T. Baba Mezia, ii. 26, p. 375). The Tosefta declares that the 'hater' is an Israelite, but it adds that one must help the ass of a non-Jew no less than the ass of a Jew, unless it is laden with libation—wine, in which case one may not help it (for that would be aiding and abetting in idolatry, which, presumably, is a greater sin than cruelty to animals). Charming is the story quoted by S.B. about the two donkey drivers. They hate each other : the ass of the one falls beneath his burden ; the other sees it, but passes on. But then he remembers the law of Exodus xxiii. 4, and at once returns, and helps the other. That other says, Did X love me so much and I knew it not ? So they went to an inn and ate and drank and got to love each other. And it was the knowledge of the Law which the one possessed that brought about this peace and reconciliation. (Tanchuma B. i. *Mishpatim* 40 b ; Tanchuma *Mishpatim* 91 a ; Midrash Psalm xcix. (3), verse 4, 212 a.) In Yalkut Shimeoni on Proverbs xxiv. 17, § 961, end, we find the following : So God has commanded : 'If thou see the ass of him that hates thee, etc., and if thou meet thy neighbour's ox, etc., God has said, Thou art not grander than I.' How is this ? Israel would, indeed, have been right in reading the

---

is so is proved by the addition which these rules and regulations in Gittin regularly have : For the sake of peace. Nevertheless, these practical needs may have formed a bridge for a calmer and more humane judgment of the foreigner.'

(whole) Hallel Psalms all the seven days of Passover, as they do read
it on the seven days of Tabernacles. But on Passover they read it
on the first day only. Why is this ? Because, says God, ' when
the Egyptians who were my enemies were drowned in the sea, I
caused it to be written, Rejoice not when thy enemy falls.' (The
Hebrew is אין אתה טוב ממני. Mr. Loewe says : ' *Tob* may not
have been the original reading. If it is, the sense is difficult ; no equivalent seems quite natural, and all renderings seem a little forced.
(1) You are not more merciful than I. If I can forego, so ought you.
But, *ex hypothesi*, man *is* less merciful. Or, (2) You are not better,
i.e. of more consequence than I. If I can feel sorry for such people
as the Egyptians, you should not rejoice over the fallen enemy.
What we should expect is " more righteous," or " keener on justice."
Tob might imply the former, hardly the latter. I think " of more
consequence " is the least harsh rendering.') S.B. note as a curious
fact that little use appears to be made in the Midrash of Proverbs
xxiv. 17, 18, or of xxv. 21, 22. Indeed the second adage, when
alluded to at all, is usually treated allegorically and made to refer
to the evil inclination (*Yetzer ha-Ra*). But there is a fine interpretation of the last two verses, namely : ' R. Chanina b. Chanina
said, Even though the enemy has risen up early to kill thee, and he
comes hungry and thirsty to thy house, give him food and drink.
Read not *yeshalem*, God will repay, but *yashlimenu* (ישלמנו) God will
make him at peace with thee ' (49 b). (Quoted by Abrahams, *Studies*
I. p. 165, also by S.B. III. p. 302). In Midrash Psalms vii. (3), verse 1
(*ad fin.*), 32 b, David is censured for having sung a song over the fall of
Saul which was against the teaching of Proverbs xxiv. 17. God said
to David, ' Had your star been Saul's star (מזל), and his star yours, how
many people such as David would I have destroyed before him.' The
particularistic tendency of the Rabbis is frankly expressed in one of
the many stories about Haman and Mordecai. When Haman tells
Mordecai to mount the horse which the king had sent for him (Esther
vi. 11), the latter pretends to be weakened by fasting and unable to
do so. Thereupon Haman bends down, and Mordecai steps upon
him and so mounts the horse. In doing so he gives Haman a kick,
whereupon Haman quotes Proverbs xxiv. 17. But Mordecai replies, These words only apply to an Israelite, but as to you (the
heathen) it is written, ' Thine enemies shall submit themselves unto
thee, and thou shalt tread upon their high places ' (Megillah 16 a).

How far, however, S.B. are justified in saying that the next quotation
shows ' Wie es im gewöhnlichen Leben um die Beobachtung von
Sprüche xxiv. 17, 18 stand,' may be doubted.[1] I question whether
Raba's remark (he died about A.D. 350) must be taken so seriously.
' R. Ashe said, He who is ill should not disclose the fact on the first
day so as not to cause himself bad luck ; but after that he may disclose it. As when Raba fell ill, on the first day he did not disclose
it, but after that he said to his attendant, Go announce that Raba
is ill. Let him who loves me pray on my behalf, and let him that
hates me rejoice over my plight, for it is written, Rejoice not when
thine enemy falls, and let not thy heart be glad when he stumbles ;
lest the Lord see it and it displease Him and He turn away his wrath
from him.' The point here is in the humorous turn given to the
last words. If an enemy rejoices, God will turn away his wrath
from Raba, and he will recover, so that the prayers of his friends
and the rejoicings of his enemies will be equally beneficial to him.
It is rather absurd to treat such a passage in the solemn manner of
S.B. (Berachoth 55 b.) One of the most definite passages which
teach the duty of ' rewarding ' *good* for evil, and not merely of *not*
' rewarding ' evil for evil, is in Genesis R. נח xxxviii. 3 on xi. 1,
where R. Alexander enlarges the meaning of Proverbs xvii. 13 to
include this case. Therefore whoso ' rewards ' evil *instead of good*,
from his house too evil shall not depart. And he quotes Exodus
xxiii. 5. Again, we observe the immense force of a Pentateuchal
injunction. In Psalm xli. 10 we read : ' Have mercy upon me ;
raise me up that I may requite them (*i.e.* my enemies).' The
Midrash (*ad loc.* (8), 131 a) says : ' But, then, how about
Proverbs xx. 22 ? The meaning is, *I* will requite them with good
instead of evil, and *the Lord* will punish them '—a combination of
high and low, not (unfortunately) without many Scriptural justifica-
tions. Once more : the Scripture is both burden and inspiration.
It drags down and drives forward. The same thought is repeated in
a conversation between David and God in which David asks God
to punish his enemies—to requite them with evil—because he (David)
had prayed for them in their illness and covered himself with sackcloth, whereas they, when *he* was ill, had prayed for his death.

The more usual attitude which is commended and enjoined is
not active benevolence to the ' enemy,' and not prayer for his con-

---

[1] ' How it stood in ordinary life with the observance of Proverbs xxiv. 17, 18.'

version, but silence and submission. ' Happy he who listens (to curses) and does not reply' (Sanhedrin 7 a). For that line of teaching there are many parallels, some of which have already been quoted. ' Learn to receive suffering (את הצער) and forgive those who insult you (עלבונך)' (Aboth R. Nathan xli. 67 a). ' If thy neighbour has done thee much evil, let it be to thee small' (ib.). ' Belong ever to the persecuted rather than to the persecutors' (Baba Kamma 93 a), and so on. The one or two familiar stories in which Rabbis pray for the repentance and conversion of their enemies are well known and quite honestly repeated by S.B. They are prefaced by the stories in which Rabbis refrain from cursing or doing evil. Thus, ' In the neighbourhood of R. Joshua b. Levi there dwelt a heretic who caused him much vexation (in Berachot, " who plagued him with questions about the interpretations of the Scriptures "). He took a cock, and tied it to the foot of the bed. He thought : when the comb of the cock grows white, which is the hour when God is wrathful against the wicked, I will curse the heretic. But when the hour came, he was asleep. When he woke he thought, One learns from this [that I was asleep] that it is not seemly (אורח ארעא) to do thus (i.e. to curse), even as it is written, To punish is not good for the righteous (Midrashic translation of Proverbs xvii. 26), and it is written, " His tender mercies are over all his works." Even a heretic it is not fitting (to curse) (אפילו במיני לא איבעי ליה למימר הכי) (Sanhedrin 105 a ; Berachoth 7 a).' ' Mar Ukba sent to R. Elazar and said, There are some people who oppose me whom I could deliver up to the Government. What shall I do ? R. Elazar quoted Psalm xxxix. 1. Mar Ukba sent again and said, They vex me greatly, I cannot stand up against them ; but again R. Elazar replied by quoting Psalm xxxvii. 7, adding (by a pun), God will cause them to fall before you in heaps. Be early and late in the house of study, and they will perish of themselves' (Gittin 7 a). The last two stories are more positive. ' In the neighbourhood of R. Zera there lived some coarse (or bad) men ; but he drew near them (had some intercourse with them) (מקרב להו), so that they might repent; his colleagues, the Rabbis, were angry with him. When R. Zera died, the men said, Till now we had R. Zera who besought compassion for us : who will do so now ? They pondered upon this in their hearts (or they took this to heart) and repented' (Sanhedrin 37 a). S.B. put R. Zera's date at about 300. This story seems to me very

significant. How well the words הוה מקרב להו כי היכי דניהדרו
להו בתשובה (Sanhedrin 37 a) correspond with the conduct of Jesus
towards the tax collectors and the sinners. And the Rabbis are
angry with R. Zera (הוו קפדי רבנן), just as they were angry with
Jesus. Thus R. Zera is an exception, even like Beruria and like
Jesus. Still, Rabbinism *could* produce a R. Zera; it *could* produce a Beruria. 'In the neighbourhood of R. Meir there dwelt
some coarse (bad) men who caused him much vexation. Once
R. Meir prayed that they might die. But his wife Beruria drew
his attention to the close of Psalm civ. (verse 35), which she said
meant, not, Let *sinners* be destroyed out of the earth (חַטָּאִים), but
let *sins* (חֲטָאִים) be destroyed out of the earth, and then the wicked
will be no more! So do thou pray for them that they repent, and
they will be wicked no more. He did so, and they repented'
(Berachoth 10 a, Midrash Psalms civ. (27), verse 35, 224 b). It
must, moreover, be stated that the codified rule of the Tosefta is
that one must pray for him from whom one has suffered wrong.
'If A has injured B, B is bound to pray God to show compassion
upon A, even though A has not asked B for his forgiveness'
(Tos. Baba Kamma ix. 29, p. 365 *fin.*; Kittel, p. 119; Abrahams,
Studies I. p. 164). Kittel says very honestly: 'Es ist nicht zu
bestreiten, dass auch das ausserchristliche Judentum stellenweise
von jener höchsten sittlichen Höhe gewusst hat, die für uns in Jesu
Weisung gegeben ist: προσεύχεσθε περὶ τῶν ἐπηρεαζόντων ὑμᾶς.' [1]
But he does not tackle the question whether Jesus was ever recorded,
over and above the dubious instance of Luke xxiii. 34, to have
practised what he preached!

S.B. quote the 'good' passages about 'hating,' etc., very fairly;
they also, not unjustifiably, call attention to the 'bad' ones. It
cannot be denied that hatred of the unworthy and the bad is sometimes permitted or even enjoined. How could Psalm cxxxix. *fin.*
—that, to the Rabbis, Davidic and inspired utterance—be got over?
'He who is insolent (שיש בו עזות פנים) may be called wicked,
and it is permitted to hate him. So said R. Nachman b. Isaac'
(Taanith 7 b). One wonders how far the next passage (Yoma 23 a)
is seriously meant. R. Yochanan said in the name of R. Simon b.

---

[1] 'It cannot be denied that Judaism, standing outside Christianity, did here
and there also know of that highest moral idealism, which is for us contained in
the order of Jesus, Pray for those who ill-treat you.'

H

Yehozedek : ' a disciple of the wise who is not revengeful, and does
not bear a grudge like a serpent, is no (true) disciple of the wise.'
But then (it is objected) how about Lev. xix. 18 ? That only refers
to (insults and injuries in respect of) money matters. But does it
not also apply to personal insults ? (וצערא דגופיה לא.) And then
the famous saying of Sabbath 88 b, etc., is quoted. (' They who
are humiliated without humiliating, who hear revilings and make no
reply, who act from love and rejoice in their sufferings, are as the
sun when he goes forth in his might.') To this it is rejoined,
' Nevertheless, he may bear the insult in his heart ' (לעולם דנקיט
ליה בליביה). Again, it is objected that Raba said that he who does
not stand upon his rights is forgiven all his sins. To which the
reply is made, This applies to the man who, when the other seeks
to appease him, lets himself be appeased. And here the subject
is dropped. Thus the conclusion seems to stand : One may bear the
insult in one's heart. In a sense the next quotation is less objectionable because the ' hatred ' is not directed to the man who has done
a personal injury, but to an evil-doer generally. It is said that
God hates three persons : he who says one thing, and thinks another
in his heart ; one who could give evidence in another's favour, and
does not do so ; and one who, being alone, sees a bad deed of his
neighbour (הרואה דבר ערוה בחבירו), and gives unsupported evidence
against him. But though to do this is a sin, for it merely brings
the neighbour into evil repute, yet one may hate him. (The
solitary witness may hate the evil-doer, but he should hold his
tongue.) R. Nachman b. Isaac, It is even a command to hate him,
for it says, the fear of the Lord is to hate evil. (Pesachim 113 b.)
As regards the ' hate ' of the Rabbis towards the *Amme ha-Aretz*,
and *vice versa*, enough has been said already. Also about the
hatred of the heretic, the apostates, and the informers. A special
curse was formulated against these, together with a curse against
the Roman oppressors. One of the oldest versions was : ' For
the apostates let there be no hope, and may the insolent kingdom
be quickly overthrown in our days, and may the Nazarenes and
the Minim (Christians and Heretics) be destroyed in a moment ;
may they be blotted out of the book of the living, and may
they not be inscribed with the righteous : blessed art thou,
O Lord, who humblest the insolent.' The Nazarenes were the
Jewish-Christians. Non-Jewish, *i.e.* Gentile, Christians were not

nearly so much disliked as Jews who became Christians. The wording of this famous Nineteenth ' Benediction ' was changed repeatedly, partly by the mediaeval censors. See Abrahams, Notes to the *Authorised Prayer Book*, p. lxiv. In its present form, the ' benediction ' runs thus : ' And for slanderers let there be no hope, and let all wickedness perish as in a moment ; let all thine enemies be speedily cut off, and the dominion of arrogance do thou uproot and crush, cast down and humble speedily, in our days. Blessed art thou, O Lord, who breakest the enemies and humblest the arrogant ' (*Authorised Prayer Book*, ed. Singer, p. 48). (The texts and the Talmudic passages can conveniently be read in Strack's useful book, *Jesus, die Häretiker und die Christen*, 1910.) Mr. Loewe writes : ' Probably this was a " test passage," inserted to prevent a Jewish Christian from acting as Reader and inserting Christological formulas. It was forbidden to answer " Amen " after certain persons of doubtful orthodoxy unless one had heard *all* the benediction. For the " test passage " *cp.* Abrahams, *Pharisaism* II. p. 59 *fin.*, and for the general situation see *ib.* p. 57 *fin.*' [The ' hatred ' of some Palestinian Rabbis of the Babylonian Rabbis is, perhaps, regarded rather too solemnly by S.B. It is more like our impatient ' I cannot bear ' than ' I hate ' in the stricter sense. (Pesachim 113 b, Menachoth 100 a, and Yoma 9 b).] The passage from Tosefta Sabbath xiii. 5 (p. 129) is especially interesting. (S.B. p. 367, Strack, p. 62 ; text pp. 28, 29.) ' The margins, or unused portions of the rolls, and the books, of the heretics must not be saved (from a fire), but they must be allowed to be burnt where they are together with the names of God which are in them. R. Yose, the Galilean, said, On a week day one should cut out the names, and hide them and burn the rest. R. Tarphon said, I would sooner lose my sons than I would not, if these books fell into my hands, burn them and the names of God contained in them : truly, if I were pursued (by a man seeking to kill me) I would take refuge in a heathen temple, but I would not enter one of their houses (of prayer) : for the idolaters know not God and deny him ; but the *Minim* know him and deny him, and of them the word holds Isaiah, lvii. 8 : " And behind the doors and the posts hast thou set up thy remembrance : for thou hast discovered thyself to another than me, and art gone up ; thou hast enlarged thy bed, and made thee a covenant with them ; thou lovedst their bed where thou sawest it." R.

Ishmael said, If in order to make peace between a man and his wife, God has said that his holy name may be extinguished by water (Numbers v. 23), how much more must the books of the heretics, which cause enmity and hatred and quarrels between Israel and their Father in heaven, be destroyed. Concerning them it is written, Should not I hate them that hate thee ? ' The Gospels would, I imagine, have undoubtedly been included by the Rabbis among these heretical works. Here I may fitly quote some paragraphs from Dr. Abrahams' study on ' Man's Forgiveness.' ' Mr. Monte-fiore's lament that Jesus displayed animosity against the Pharisees has been resented by critics of his volumes. His comment, it has been said, is due to psychological misunderstanding. If this be so, ought not the same principle to apply to the Pharisaic animosity— such as it was—against sectarians ? If Jesus might with propriety assail the Pharisees with threats of dire retribution, the same measure must be meted out to them, when they are the assailants of those whom they thought wilfully blind to truth and open rebels against righteousness. In no age have the sects loved one another overmuch, and much as one may sigh at this display, among all creeds, of human nature red in tooth and claw, it is happily true that the consequences have not been entirely bad for the world. The prophet is almost necessarily a denunciator, and the sect must fight if it would maintain the cause. " The emulation of scholars increases wisdom " (B. Batra 21 a), and the same principle applies to sectarian differences. The Pharisees of the age of Jesus were no doubt good fighters against internal heresies, just as they were good fighters against the common enemy, Rome. But there was more of this a century before and a century after Jesus than in his actual age. For it is in fact found on examination that the Jewish ill-feeling against the " nations " is correlated to the ill-feeling of the "nations " against Israel. The Maccabean spirit of exclusiveness was roused by the Syrian plot against Judaism, just as the later Pharisaic exclusiveness was roused by the Roman assault on the religious life of Israel. And the same is true even of the apocalypses, with their tale of doom. All of them must be placed in their proper historical background if the picture is to be just. Undoubtedly, with the terrible experience of the Great War before our eyes, with the recollection of much said and written and done burnt into our minds, our world is better able to judge the past. And it is not necessary to appeal to our own immediate experience of the hour. One would not deduce the theory of brotherly love held by Dutch Christendom from the language of Boers regarding English during the South African War ; one would not entirely gauge the condition of Elizabethan Anglicanism in relation to the forgiving spirit by its language or actions regarding Spanish Catholics. Nor would one be just to Puritanism if one read a complete theory of its attitude towards the persecutors of the Church into Milton's fiery sonnet on the massacre by the Piedmontese :

> Avenge, O Lord, thy slaughtered saints, whose bones
> Lie scattered on the Alpine mountains cold !

National, sectarian, animosities, even humanitarian indignations against the cruel and the unrighteous, do indeed stand on a different plane to personal vindictiveness, and men sometimes do well to be angry.

' It is, however, not the case that the Pharisaic liturgy enshrines any vindictiveness against Christianity. This denial is obviously true of the first century, but it is also absolutely true of later centuries. As a Jewish heresy, early Christianity was the subject of antipathy, as an independent religion it was scarcely assailed at all. Paganism was another matter ; against idolatry the Synagogue waged war, and sometimes idolaters came in for their share of the attack, and were, in moments of stress, regarded as outside the pale of the brotherhood of man. But even then, it was internal heresy that was more bitterly resented, and the deliberate sinner, the man of immoral and heretical life within the fold, was far more the object of recrimination than any one who stood outside. Here, again, we have a fact of human nature, not of Pharisaic nature only, and it is a pity that the Pharisees are made to bear the burden which should be put on the shoulders of mankind.

' The Rabbinic sayings to the effect that it is permissible to " hate " the wicked within the fold, have no reference to personal wrongs. The offences which make " hatred " justifiable are invariably breaches of morality or of the law of God which should not be condoned until the offender had repented. The personal foe does not come into the category. The same page of the Talmud (*Pesachim* 113 b) which records the duty to show detestation of the adulterer records also that beloved of God is he who forgives wrongs personal to himself. " I believe it to be quite one of the crowning wickednesses of this age that we have starved and chilled our faculty of indignation " (Ruskin, Lectures on Art, 1870, p. 83; cp. Sir J. Stephen, *History of the Criminal Law of England*, 1883, Vol. I. p. 478).' (P. 158.)

It is, I think, rather unworthy of S.B. to make a big print citation from Jer. Megillah iii. § 2, 74 a, as if it were a trump card. In 2 Sam. xix. 6, Joab says to David: ' Thou hast shamed this day the faces of all thy servants, who this day have saved thy life, and the lives of thy sons and of thy daughters, and the lives of thy wives, and the lives of thy concubines ; in that thou lovest them that hate thee, and hatest them that love thee. For thou hast declared this day, that thou regardest neither princes nor servants : for this day I perceive, that if Absalom had lived, and all we had died this day, then it had pleased thee well.' The citation, ' Thou lovest them that hate thee and hatest them that love thee,' happens to be referred to in a purely legal question (which has not the smallest relation to loving or hating the enemy), in the following way : ' R. Jeremiah sent a letter (כתב) to R. Judah ' [with these words] ' to hate those who love you and to love those that hate you ' [reversing the order in Samuel]. Nothing more. Why, or for what purpose, or in what connection, R. Jeremiah made the quotation we are not informed. Nevertheless, S.B. (p. 368) say, ' Inhaltlich ist das Zitat als eine Rüge gemeint [a pure supposition] : nicht den Freund soll man hassen und den Feind lieben ; das umgekehrte Verhalten, weil allein der allgemeine Anschauung entsprechend, sei das Richtige : liebe deine Fremde, und hasse deine Feinde. Das ist dieselbe Maxime die wir Mt. v. 43 lesen.' [1] A mountain based upon a molehill ! S.B. have no justification for their statement. R. Jeremiah may have quoted the words as a mere joke, or for a hundred possible reasons, not one of which would justify S.B. in insinuating that the customary Rabbinic morality or maxim was ' Love your friends, hate your enemies.' But the accuracy of Jesus must be defended at almost any price !

And yet S.B. have a fairly good case for the originality of Jesus, though not for his verbal accuracy. Putting the passages from the

---

[1] ' The quotation, from the point of view of its meaning, is intended as a blame : one must not hate the friend and love the enemy ; the contrary disposition, because it alone corresponds with the general and accepted opinion, is the right one, namely : love your friends, and hate your enemies. And that is the very maxim which we find quoted in Mt. v. 43.'

Testaments of the Patriarchs on one side, we have nothing in Rabbinic literature up to A.D. 30 which is a full parallel to Luke vi. 27, 28, or Matt. v. 43–46. Nor can it fairly be said that we have a *full* parallel even after A.D. 30. But there *are* stories and sayings which partake of the same spirit, and the teaching or tendency of which is on the same lines. S.B. are not *entirely* wrong, but yet a *little* unfair and ungenerous when they say : ' Zur klaren positiven Formulierung eines allgemeinen Satzes, wie Liebet eure Feinde, hat Exodus xxiii. 4, 5 in der alten Synagoge nicht geführt. Man hielt sich auf der Linie der Negative : Freue dich nicht über das Unglück deines Feindes und vergilt nicht Böses mit Bösem ' (p. 368).[1] But I would not cavil with the view that Jesus is to be regarded as the first great Jewish teacher to frame such a sentence as : ' Love your enemies, do good to them who hate you, bless them that curse you, and pray for them who ill-treat you ' (Luke vi. 27, 28). Yet how much more telling his injunction would have been if we had had *a single story* about his doing good to, and praying for, a single Rabbi or Pharisee ! One grain of practice is worth a pound of theory. (Luke xxiii. 34 is of doubtful range and doubtful authenticity.) We *have* at all events from the Rabbis one or two tales of kindness shown to Romans in their hour of need (see p. 347). Thus, as regards the Jewish and Christian advocates, the impartial historian must declare that the truth probably lies somewhere between the two. Windisch is very fair in all that he says about Jesus and the love of the enemy. Especially noteworthy are his remarks about the question of Jesus's consistency, or the conflict between his conduct and his demand. ' Eine befriedigende Lösung ist von christlicher Seite noch nicht gegeben ' (p. 27).[2] Whether his own partial explanation on p. 74 *fin.* and 75 *init.* can wholly be accepted I am not sure. He says that one must not judge a prophet, full of justified indignation with hypocrisy, etc., as one judges an ordinary man. But if Jesus was so marvellously perfect and sinless as his adherents maintain, should he not have been *more* able than other men to exercise patience, self-control, and love ?

---

[1] ' The Rabbis (= the old Synagogue) were not led by Exodus xxiii. 4, 5 to a clear formulation of any general statement, such as, Love your enemies. They did not get beyond the negative : Do *not* rejoice over the misfortune of your enemy and do *not* requite evil with evil.'

[2] ' A satisfactory solution from a Christian authority has, so far, not been given.'

Should we not rightly demand *more* from him than from ordinary men, and not less ? Windisch, however, admits *ein unaufgelöster Rest* ('an unsolved residuum') between the invectives and the Sermon. (P. 75.)

I repeat that what one would have wished to find in the life-story of Jesus would be one single incident in which Jesus actually performed a loving deed to one of his Rabbinic antagonists or enemies. That would have been worth all the *injunctions* of the Sermon on the Mount about the love of enemies put together. Even if such a deed were only reported, and it were of dubious authenticity, how valuable it would be. 'Father, forgive them' is of dubious authenticity, but it is little the less beautiful and inspiring. Even though it refers only to the Roman soldiers and not to the Jews, it is, nevertheless, of high ethical import. 'The deed ! the deed !' as the poet has it. But no such deed is ascribed to Jesus in the Gospels. Towards his enemies, towards those who did not believe in him, whether individuals, groups, or cities (Matt. xi. 20–24), only denunciation and bitter words ! The injunctions are beautiful, but how much more beautiful would have been a *fulfilment* of those injunctions by Jesus himself. Dr. Haas writes in his excellent essay, ' We Christians dare not say that we *do* love our enemies, but, at least, we know that we *ought* to love them. We are ashamed that we do *not* love them. What is demanded of us is not something which is impossible. Der Meister hat's uns vorgelebt.'[1] But when and where ? Dr. Haas very wisely gives no reference. ('Idee und Ideal der Feindesliebe in der ausserchristlichen Welt,' 1927, p. 96.) On the other hand, with Haas's criticisms of Eschelbacher and other Jewish theologians (pp. 21–24) I am more or less in agreement. (See my *Gospels*, II. pp. 85–91.)

45. ὅπως γένησθε υἱοί. 'That ye may become sons.' The idea is that if they imitate God's ways and character, then they are legitimately to be called God's children, and if they do not so imitate, then they are not his children and have no right to be so called. Similar remarks are frequent among the Rabbis. The Israelites are God's sons or children. Some Rabbis say that they are called his sons, when they do his will, or obey his commands ;

[1] 'The Master was an example of it for us in his own life.'

when they refuse or transgress, they are not called his sons. Others say, in either case they are sons : children they were, children they remain. The salient passages are given by S.B. quite fairly (p. 371). Another suggestion is : children when they do God's will ; slaves when they transgress it. *Cp.* p. 114. Mr. Loewe writes : ' *Cp.* " This day the world was called into being, this day thou causest all the creatures of the universe to stand for judgment, either as children or as servants; if as children, have pity on us, as a father pitieth his children; and if as servants, on thee do our eyes wait, until thou be gracious to us" (Davis and Adler, *Service of the* *Synagogue*, London, 1922, p. 156, and Gaster, *Book of Prayer.* . . . New Year Vol., London, 1903, p. 121).'

The bidding to imitate God is an exceedingly familiar Rabbinic motive. The imitation of God forms the subject of one of Dr. Abrahams' finest studies (II. pp. 138-182). He quotes the noble Sifre passage (85 a): 'As God is called merciful and gracious, so do thou be merciful and gracious, offering gifts gratis to all ; as the Lord is called righteous and loving, so be thou righteous and loving.' S.B.'s quotations, even by themselves, are adequate as illustrations, and the very first is especially in point in relation to Matt. v. 43-47. ' R. Meir said, What does עבור " pass on " mean ? (Exodus xvii. 5). It means, " Be like me. As I requite good for evil, so do thou, as it says, Who is a God like unto thee that pardons iniquity and passes by transgression "' (Micah vii. 18). (Exodus R. xxvi. בשלח, on xvii. 8.) 'As he is merciful and gracious, so be thou merciful and gracious ' (Mechilta on Exodus xv. 2, 37 a, *et saep.*). Then there is the famous passage in which we are told that as God had clothed the naked, visited the sick, comforted the mourning, buried the dead, so do thou imitate him, or his ways, or his attributes, in all these actions. (Sotah 14 a.)

But this very injunction or appeal to imitate God led to unfortunate or doubtful consequences, because in the Scripture God is not described as merely showing mercy and goodness. He ' hated Esau ' ; he ' laughs ' at the nations ; he is ' full of wrath ' ; he ' takes vengeance on his enemies.' And so on. Are we to imitate him in these respects also ? There were one or two especial passages which are constantly brought up. Thus, in I Samuel ii. 25, it says כִּי־חָפֵץ יְיָ לַהֲמִיתָם, ' the Lord took pleasure in slaying them.' And in Proverbs xi. 10 it says, ' when the wicked perish there is rejoicing.' Does God then rejoice over the death of the wicked ? How about Ezekiel xviii. 32, ' I have no pleasure in the death of him that dies ' ? In one passage the contradiction is solved (as we shall hear on p. 264) by the view that in the death of the sinner that repents God has no pleasure, in the death of the sinner who does not repent he has pleasure. (Niddah 70 b.) Here it would seem as if God did rejoice at the death of the unrepentant sinner. On the other hand, elsewhere a Rabbi declares that God does not rejoice in the downfall (במפלתן) of the wicked. And then follows the well-known story of the angels beginning a paean of joy when the Egyptians were drowned, and God saying, The work of my hands are sunk in the sea and ye would sing before me ! Then another Rabbi declares, God does not himself rejoice, but he causes others to rejoice. (Sanhedrin 39 b ; Megillah 10 b.) It says in the Mishnah, So long as the wicked are in the world, there is fierceness of anger in the world (Deut. xiii. 18) ; when the wicked have perished, the fierceness of anger is stilled. (Sanhedrin xi. 6, end.) And the Gemara adds : ' If a wicked man comes into the world, fierceness of anger comes into the world (Prov. xviii. 3), and when a wicked man perishes from the world, good comes into the world, as it is said, when the wicked perish there is rejoicing.' Surely the Scripture was often a burden. Yet the Rabbis do sometimes attempt to overcome the burden. *Cp.* Abrahams, *Studies* II. pp. 151, 177 (where in line 6 from bottom for lxxxiv read xciv.). ' I, God, am master of envy ; envy is not master of me,' is a suggested explanation of the text ' I, the Lord thy God, am a jealous God ' (Mechilta 68 a on xx. 5). More fully the same fine thought is expressed in Midrash Psalms xciv. (1), verse 1, 209 a. ' Man's anger controls him, but God controls (כובש) his anger—he is *master* of his wrath (Nahum ii. 2) ; man's jealousy controls him, but God controls his jealousy.' Again, in the Mechilta it says, ' God with jealousy punishes idolatry (*i.e.* the idolaters), but in other matters he is gracious and pitiful.' (So too in Genesis R. xlix. 8.) The most curious passage on the whole subject is one which is found with slight variants both in the Midrash on Ecclesiastes on viii. 4 and in Genesis R. וירא lv. 3 on xxii. 1. The inconsistency of God's command with God's own practice is called in question. On the one hand, there is Leviticus xix. 18, ' Hate not, bear no grudge, do not revenge.' On the other (Nahum i. 2), ' The Lord

avenges, and bears a grudge.' 'R. Levi said, The matter is
like as if a master forbade his disciple to pervert judgment, or to
respect persons, whereas he himself did so.   Then the disciple
said, Master, is it permitted to thee, but forbidden to me ? So
the Israelites say to God, Thou hast written in thy Law, Thou shalt
not take vengeance or bear a grudge, but thou takest vengeance
and bearest a grudge. God replies, I do not bear a grudge against
Israel, as it is said, He will not always contend, neither will he bear
a grudge for ever (Psalm ciii. 9). But as regards the heathen, God
takes vengeance on his adversaries, and bears a grudge against
his enemies. And God says, I wrote in my Law, Thou shalt not
avenge or bear a grudge against the children of thy people, but
thou mayest take vengeance against the heathen, as it is said,
Avenge the children of Israel against the Midianites.' Here we have
indeed naked particularism, but yet, perhaps, not *wholly* unashamed.
As breathing a different spirit a passage in Midrash Psalms ciii. 9 (12)
(218 b) is worth quoting, especially if Mr. Loewe's view of its rendering here given is correct. 'God says, I contended with the generation of the deluge and with the generation of the tower of Babel,
and I conquered them, and I suffered loss in respect of them
(והפסדתי אותם) ; but when Moses conquered me [by securing pardon
for Israel], I got gain in my world. That is the meaning of the words,
He will not always chide, neither does he keep his anger for ever.'
Wherever the Rabbis show any compunction in their nationalism,
whenever they are tolerant and universalistic, I feel as if the spirit
of God was working within them.   For they were such passionate
patriots, and religion was so entirely fused with their nationalism,
strengthening it and backing it up, that it would seem that it must
have been inspiration and grace which could have brought about
a breaking down of their religious limitations.   Somehow the
universalist passages of the Rabbis seem to me all the more remarkable in view of their prevailing particularism.

To the passage about the sun and the rain there are closely
parallel passages in the Rabbinical literature, though they are all
much later than Jesus. As S.B. justly observe, the Rabbis could
take good note of the tender universalism of such a verse as Psalm
cxlv. 9, and it is worth remembering that this Psalm was given a
very special place in the liturgy, and to its constant recitation were
allotted special rewards. 'R. Joshua b. Nehemiah (A.D. 350) said,

Have you ever noticed that the rain fell on the field of A who was righteous, and not on the field of B who was wicked ? Or that the sun arose and shone upon Israel who was righteous, and not upon the wicked (the nations) ? God causes the sun to shine both upon Israel and upon the nations, for the Lord is good to all.' (The passage goes on to say that man is often kind to his slaves and cruel to his animals, and *vice versa*, but that God is merciful to both man and beast.) (Pesikta R. 195 a *fin.*–b.) The blessing of rain is even greater than the resurrection of the dead, for the resurrection only applies to the righteous, the rain affects the wicked as well. (Taanith 7 a.) God's special attribute is compassion. He gives of his pity to his creatures (that they may be pitiful to one another). If, in a year of drought, men are merciful to each other, then God will be full of mercy to them (Gen. R. נח xxxiii. 3 on viii. 1). Then came the question as to other passages in Scripture where God is said to be good only to the good, and explanations had to be forthcoming. 'In this world God is good to all ; in the next only to the good' (Midrash Psalms xxii. (3), verse 1, 91 a). Or, though he is good to all, he shows special concern for the righteous. (Sanhedrin 39 b.) In the passage, alluded to elsewhere, about R. Gamaliel waiting at table, God is said to feed and satisfy all men, and not only the righteous, but even also the idolaters. (Mechilta 59 a on Exodus xviii. 12.) As to the degree and nature of God's long-suffering, there were disputes. One painful interpretation, often maintained and alluded to, is that God is long-suffering to the wicked in this world in order that he may punish them the more in the world to come. He requites them their few *good* deeds in this world that he may requite all their *evil* deeds the more fully in the next world. It is also said that God is long-suffering in exacting punishment. But clearly the doctrine of God's pity, his long-sufferingness, his readiness to forgive, led to consequences which were dangerous. If it is God's *métier* to forgive, why should not man sin in comfort ? So it is said, God is indeed long-suffering, but he exacts his own. (The mills of God end by grinding small.) (*Cp.* the long discussion in Pesikta 161 b, and Bacher, *Agada der pal. Amoräer* I. p. 545, n. 3, with other references.) Quaint and touching is the story of Sanhedrin 111 a, foot, quoted by S.B. on p. 377. 'And Moses bowed down and worshipped. What did Moses see ? R. Chanina said, He saw (the attribute) Long-suffering :

the Rabbis say he saw Truth. In accordance with the former view
it is taught that when Moses went up the Mount he found God
sitting and writing " Long-suffering." Moses said to him : Long-
suffering to the righteous. God replied : Also to the wicked. Moses
said, May the wicked perish. God said, You shall see what you
have asked. When the Israelites sinned, God said, Did you not
say to me, Long-suffering only to the righteous ? Moses replied,
But did you not reply to me, Long-suffering also to the wicked ? '
One Rabbi said that the dual in the phrase אפים ארך (long-
suffering) means that God is long-suffering towards the wicked
as well as towards the righteous (Baba Kamma 50 b). On the
whole, we may justly say that the teaching of Jesus in vv. 45
and 48 is very fairly reflected in the *higher* teaching of the Rabbis.
That God punishes the wicked, that he sends many people to hell,
and either keeps them there or annihilates them, was teaching
common to both Jesus and the Rabbis, and it has been teaching
which millions of pious persons have believed to this day, and
which thousands still believe. But within these limits, and in
spite of the inconsistency, both Jesus and the Rabbis taught that
God was loving and merciful and ' good to all,' and they both
believed that, somehow or other, it was in his attribute of pity
and goodness, rather than in his attribute of severity and punishment, that his true nature was revealed and even contained. When
Jesus bade his disciples be perfect like God, when the Rabbis
bade their followers imitate, and follow in, his ways, they quite
forgot his severity, they did not remember those qualities in virtue
of which he would say, ' Depart from me, ye accursed, into the
everlasting fire ' ; they only thought of, and remembered, his
pity, his lovingkindness, his forgiveness. In these qualities, and
in these alone, man was to imitate him. This happy limitation was
common to them both. Only after writing these lines did I notice
Dr. Abrahams' remark that ' the whole Rabbinic literature might,
I believe, and at all events hope, be searched in vain for a single
instance of the sterner O.T. attributes of God being set up as a
model for man to copy ' (*Studies* II. p. 152). In view of the passages
quoted on verse 45 there is a bit of exaggeration here, but sub-
stantially it is true.

Windisch has some very just remarks on v. 48 on pp. 58, 59.
He also points out that vii. II is really opposed to v. 45, or, at all

events, involves a certain limitation of its complete possibility.
(P. 144 *fin.*, 145.)

46. It is needless for my purpose to collect Rabbinic opinions
and sayings about the tax-collectors : they are to be found in
S.B. and elsewhere.

47. As regards greetings, the bidding of Jesus is in accordance
with the practice of the best Rabbis, who did not stand upon their
dignity, but gave the greeting beforehand. It was said of R.
Yochanan b. Zakkai that no one ever anticipated him in greeting,
not even a heathen in the public street. (Berachoth 17 a.) Though
the rule was that the less learned must be the one to greet first
(*cp.* Berachoth i. § 1, 4 b), yet the maxim in Aboth is, ' R. Mattith-
yah ben Charash said, Be first in greeting every man ' (iv. 20).
The saying of Abbaye is pleasant: ' A man should always be cunning
(ערום) in the fear of God, and ever answer softly, and turn away
wrath, and increase peace with his brethren and his relations and
with all men, even with a heathen in the public street (*i.e.* in greeting), so that he may be beloved above and popular (נחמד) on
earth and acceptable to his fellow-creatures ' (Berachoth 17 a).
For much further information about greetings and salutations
see S.B.

48. As to ' perfect,' *cp.* Abrahams (*Studies* II. 151): ' With
this idea of holiness went the other idea expressed by the term
tamim, perfect, without blemish, whole-hearted God-wards. It is
at first sight tempting to hold that this is why Matthew (v. 48)
expresses the Imitation formula in the terms " Be ye perfect, even
as your heavenly Father is perfect." Such a formula would be a
not unnatural derivative from " Be ye holy, for I the Lord am holy."
Yet there is no verbal parallel in Rabbinic literature to Matthew's
form; it is original to him, and unique in the Synoptics. Luke's
version (vi. 36), "Be ye merciful as your Father is merciful," has,
on the other hand, many Pharisaic parallels, as we have seen. We
find in Midrashim, side by side with the text "Be thou perfect,"
texts like "as for God his way is perfect"; but the Midrash has no
thought there of Imitation, it only expounds that man may become
perfect by obedience to the perfect Law. Matthew's phrase remains

unparalleled. Though, however, he differs in wording from Luke, he intends much the same, except that the first Gospel's " perfection in love" as the aim of imitation is a fuller concept than the third Gospel's " perfection in mercy." ' But, the Rabbinic ideal of holiness as the quality in God which man is to imitate, is no less grand than Matthew's conception of ' perfection.' I again quote from Dr. Abrahams. ' What of the Divine Holiness ? Does it not stand for the supreme and unique hall-mark of Deity, the fence to his unapproachable Self ? Here, surely, imitation is impossible ; and if so, what becomes of the Imitation ideal ? But, as with the divine Uniqueness so with the divine holiness—there is the constant correlative, the derived holiness of Israel. Holiness means separateness, but it is a separateness in which man may have his reflected part. How the old idea of separateness clung to the term is seen from the comment of the Sifra (86 c) on Leviticus xix. 2. "Be ye holy—be ye *perushim* " (separated), " even as God is *parush* " (separated). And then, since separateness means aloofness from the foul, the unchaste, the cruel, the term "holiness " came to concentrate in itself the whole of the perfect life as Israel understood it ; life perfect ritually, morally, spiritually. The word *kadosh* grows ever richer in significance with the ages. Ritual cleanliness, dietary abstinences, communal separateness, detestation of the grosser indulgences and vices and moral licentiousness, the inspiration to purity of thought, action, and belief—in brief, the hallowing of life, and of the martyr's sacrifice of life for the hallowing of God—all these ideas, and more, accumulated round the Jewish conception of *kedushah* (holiness). "It is," as Dr. Kohler well says, " holiness which permeates the thoughts and motives of life, and hence it is the highest possible principle of ethics." And since the Pentateuch has chosen to put the Imitation formula in terms of holiness, it is therefore quite natural that the Jewish commentators should connect Leviticus xix. 2 with Genesis i. 26. The formula of Imitation is "Be ye holy, for I am holy " ; and, " created in the Image of God," man imitates God by stretching upwards towards the Holiness which resides in Him.'

vi. 1–4. As to the reproach in vi. 2, it is needless to add anything to what I have said in Vol. II. pp. 95, 96 of the Commentary. S.B. would like to prove that there was much ostentation and pride in the giving of alms among Jewish communities in the age of Jesus. Very possibly there was *some*; so there has been in every age, whether among Jews or Christians. Yet not only the ideal, but also the practice, of secret charity was very prevalent among the Rabbinic Jews, and the delicacy of practice was, perhaps, higher than it would be easy to match elsewhere. On this head the Jews have nothing to learn from Jesus, as indeed S.B., by their ample quotations, are honest enough to allow. And several stories could be added to their quotations, as of the Rabbi who gave alms in secret, but burnt his feet, and was rebuked by his wife (Kethuboth 67 b). It is said that the Egyptians ' sinned secretly, and God made them known publicly.' ' If, as regards the Attribute of Punishment, which is small, he who acts in secret is made known by God publicly, how much more, in regard to the Attribute of Goodness, which is great (will God make known deeds of goodness done secretly).' A very characteristic bit of Rabbinic theology and religion. (Sifre 35 a.) In the school (רבי) of R. Yannai the word ' evil ' in the sentence of Ecclesiastes—' God will bring every deed into judgment whether good or evil '—was interpreted to mean giving alms to the poor in public (בפרהסיא). Seeing some one who openly gave a coin to a poor man, R. Yannai said, ' It were better you had given him nothing than that you gave him something, and put him to shame' (וכספתיה) (Chagigah 5 a). ' He who gives alms in secret is greater than Moses ' (Baba Batra 9 b). This is said half jestingly, with a half-jesting proof from Proverbs xxi. 14 and Deut. ix. 19, but it shows how important this virtue was held to be. There is a kind of almsgiving which saves from unnatural or untimely death. And which is that ? When the recipient does not know from whom he gets it, and when the giver does not know to whom he gives it. (Baba Batra 10 b.) And this method is said to rule out the method of the two Rabbis, one of whom was wont (see the story in Kethuboth just alluded to) to help a poor man furtively, while the other used to throw money behind him and knew not who picked it up. (Baba Batra 10 b and Kethuboth 67 b.) There was a chamber in the Temple called the chamber of the silent (לשכת חשאים). Into this chamber sin-fearing people placed their gifts secretly, and the poor of good families were secretly sustained from these gifts. (Shekalim Mishnah v. 6.) These quotations are adequate to show that the ideal of secret almsgiving was

as much prized by the Rabbis as by Jesus. It may be noted that
Jesus here, as mostly, looks at the matter only from the point of
view of the agent. The Rabbis, very properly, thought much also
of the recipient.

The story of Abba is so characteristically Rabbinic that though
only a part of it is here in point, I must not spoil it by not giving it
in full. 'Abba the Bleeder received every day a greeting from the
heavenly academy while Abbaye received one every Friday, and
Raba every year on the eve of the Day of Atonement. Abbaye felt
discouraged on account of the greater distinction of Abba the Bleeder.
Abbaye was therefore told, "Thou canst not perform deeds like those
of Abba the Bleeder!" What were the deeds of Abba the Bleeder?
When he performed the operation (of bleeding), he had a separate
place for men and another for women. He had a garment ready in
which there were numerous slits, and when a woman came, he made
her put it on, so that he should not have to look upon her bare body.
Outside of his office he had a place (box) where his fees were to be
deposited. Whoever had money could put it in, but those who had
none could come in without feeling embarrassed. When he saw a
person who was in no position to pay, he would offer him some
money, saying to him: "Go, strengthen thyself." One day Abbaye
sent a pair of scholars to him to find out the truth about him. When
they came to his house, he gave them to eat and to drink and laid
cushions before them to sleep on. The next morning the scholars
took the cushions with them and brought them to the market-place.
Abbaye then sent for Abba, and the scholars requested him to
appraise the value of the cushions. Abba said, they are worth so
and so much. "But, perhaps, they are worth more?" the scholars
inquired. "This is what I paid for them," he replied. "Of what
did you suspect us?" the scholars asked. "I thought," he said,
"the gentlemen happened to be in need of money for some charitable
purpose and were ashamed to tell me." "Take them back now,"
they said. "No," he replied, "from that moment I diverted my
mind (from them), considering them consecrated to charity"'
(Taanith 21 b *ad fin*. Dr. Malter's version). (Pp. 157, 158.)

I do not here quote passages to show the use of 'our Father'
or 'Father' as a synonym for God, or as an invocation of God, in
Rabbinic literature. The curious can find a considerable number
quoted or referred to in Moore's *Judaism* (II. 203–211). It may be

I

admitted that the fatherly relationship of God to the individual was
often mediated by the dominating conception of God being Israel's
father and Israel being God's son.   One must, perhaps, not leave
unquoted the familiar saying in Aboth by R. Akiba (iii. 18): ' Beloved
is man in that he was created in the Image (*i.e.* of God).   Still greater
was the love shown to him in that it was made known to him that
he was so created.   Beloved are the Israelites in that they are called
sons of God.   Still greater is the love shown to them in that it was
made known to them that they were so called.'   One or two Rabbis
argued that Israel's sonship depends upon Israel's right-doing.
' R. Judah said, If you behave as sons, you are called sons, but if
you do not behave as sons, you are not called sons ; but R. Meir
said, In either case you are called sons,' proving his case, as usual, by
various Scriptural quotations. (Kiddushin 36 a.)   ' Hearken to thy
Father who is in heaven.   He deals with thee as with an only son
(if thou obeyest him), but, if not, he deals with thee as a slave.
When thou doest his will, he is thy Father, and thou art his son,
but if not, against thy will, and opposed to thy consent, he is thine
owner, and thou art his slave ' (Pesikta R. 132 b).   R. Meir said,
' Even if the Israelites are full of blemishes, they are yet called
sons' (alluding to the corrupt and difficult passage, Deut. xxxii.
5, 6, where God is called Israel's Father, and they are called
his sons).   ' Isaiah (i. 4) calls them sons who do corruptly.
If they are sons when they do corruptly, when they do *not* act
corruptly, how much more are they sons ! ' (Sifre 133 a *fin.* and
137 a).   ' R. Meir said, Beloved are Israel, for whether they do
God's will or no, they are called his sons ' (Midrash Tannaim,
p. 71.   Here the opposition between sons and slaves is not felt.
Both the angels and Israel, it is said, are called God's slaves and
God's sons).   As God is Israel's father, so is he the father of
every collection of Israelites, and of every individual Israelite.   God
is father, not as the creator of man, but because he has freely chosen
Israel to be His son, and Israel has accepted God as his father.   The
intensely intimate and close relation of God to Israel extends to his
relationship with every individual Israelite.   Nevertheless, there
was nothing in the language or in the terminology used by Jesus
which would have seemed novel to any Rabbinic Jew.

Windisch has some good and fair remarks about the motive of
reward (*Lohnmotiv*) which Jesus here employs. (Pp. 16, 17.)

5–8. Anyone who has read Abrahams' essays on ' Some Rabbinic Ideas on Prayer ' and on ' The Lord's Prayer ' in *Studies* II. pp. 72–108 will have to confess that the Rabbis have not much to learn upon this subject from the Sermon on the Mount. That there were ' hypocrites ' in the age of Jesus is very likely, and the need of the warning conveyed in 5, 6 was, most probably, real enough. But as Abrahams says : ' The real point of the Gospel reprobation is not against Pharisaic prayer, but against ostentatious prayer, and ostentation is neither a vice from which Pharisees were free, nor a vice of which they had a monopoly. As Dr. Oman truly says : " Most of what he (Jesus) says to the Scribes and Pharisees applies to the dangers of outward organized religion at all times." Or to quote that older Christian writer, Chrysostom, to whom one rarely turns without profit, " Here it is well to sigh aloud and to wail bitterly : for not only do we imitate the hypocrites, but we have even surpassed them." Pharisaism, because of its theory of Law, was more liable to the fault than less legalistic systems. But in the ultimate diagnosis the fault is not Pharisaic, it is a fault of human nature, which needs stern rebuke by the homilists of every age. Unfortunately insincerity is a hydra which to-day's denunciation cannot scotch for to-morrow ' (p. 103). On the other hand, his brief caution is also well worthy of remembrance. ' Some things which, observed by an outside critic, seem ostentatious, take another aspect when experienced by a devotee from within.' The disciples themselves watch Jesus praying ' in a certain place.' Did he desire to be observed ? (Luke xi. 1.) It does not follow because certain Rabbis loved to pray long in synagogue that they did it to be noticed.

The bidding of Jesus in 6 seems to imply a certain bias against public prayer or against praying in synagogue. Yet it is not likely that Jesus had any objection to all public prayer. We know that he did visit and use the synagogues. Perhaps he meant that private prayer should *always be* in private. The Rabbis would not have gone so far as that. The matter is complicated by the statutory prayers which the pious Jew was supposed to say twice or, later, thrice a day. As he had to say these prayers within or before certain fixed times, he had to say them wherever he might happen to be (with certain exceptions). Jesus, again, is not alluding to these statutory prayers : he is alluding, so it would seem, to certain special extra petitions, praises, communings, which an individual may feel inclined, or desirous, to put before God, incidentally and spontaneously, quite apart from, and over and above, the statutory prayers. Such prayers are to be a secret between man and God, and the less man is seen uttering them the better. That Jesus is specially thinking of petitions seems likely from verse 8. It would not be accurate to suppose that the Rabbis placed any bar upon private devotions being said elsewhere than in a synagogue. Nor are we, I imagine, to infer that Jesus means to order his disciples to pray only indoors, in their own rooms. The verse in Matthew is oddly reminiscent of Isaiah xxvi. 20 (εἴσελθε εἰς τὰ ταμεῖά σου, ἀπόκλεισον τὴν θύραν σου) and 2 Kings iv. 33 (καὶ εἰσῆλθεν Ἐλισαῖε εἰς τὸν οἶκον καὶ ἀπέκλεισεν τὴν θύραν κατὰ τῶν δύο ἑαυτῶν, καὶ προσεύξατο πρὸς κύριον). Jesus did not mean more than a warning against ostentation and publicity. He did not want to limit private prayer to the house. His own practice, so often alluded to in the Gospels, would make such a limitation inconceivable. Nor did the Rabbis desire to suggest that prayer should be limited to the synagogue, though doubtless there was a feeling that the synagogue was the most appropriate and fitting place. I suppose that the synagogues of old were like Roman Catholic churches—always open for private devotion and prayer. S.B. quote a passage from Berachoth (6 a): ' There is a teaching: Abba Benjamin said: A man's prayer is only heard [by God] when offered in a synagogue.' But this passage must undoubtedly be considered as a paradox or whimsical exaggeration. Dr. Cohen observes (p. 28) : ' The prayer referred to here is not private devotion, but the statutory service which is congregational in character.' The Rabbis seem to like the idea that a certain particular spot should be associated with prayer, as if this association of place with prayer helped a man to *feel* prayerful. ' R. Huna said, Whoever fixes a place for his prayer, has the God of Abraham for his help. R. Yochanan said, Whoever fixes a place for his prayer, his enemies fall beneath him' (Berachoth 6 b, 7 b). And the Rabbis laid immense stress upon public or communal worship, upon praying *with* the community, upon not separating oneself *from* the community or congregation, but of always joining with them in prayer. God is supposed to love to see his children praying *together*. Israel at study in the *Beth ha-Midrash*, Israel at prayer in the synagogues, fills him with joy. But the number of stories about prayer said on the public way, or in the market-place, or in other localities, and the

rules respecting the recitation or non-recitation of the statutory
prayers at certain particular spots, show that prayer was constantly
said outside the synagogue. Some of these stories and rules are given
in S.B. pp. 399 and 401. The pretty passage from Midrash Psalms
iv. 9, 23 b, and Pesikta 158 b, is also given. 'God says to Israel,
Pray in the synagogue of your city ; if you cannot, pray in the field ;
if you cannot, pray in your house ; if you cannot, pray on your bed ;
if you cannot, commune with your own heart upon your bed and be
still.' In the Jerusalem Talmud R. Yochanan's remark is given in
the form that man should have a place which is exclusively kept for
prayer (מיחד לתפילה). (So, too, he is to have his own special place
in the synagogue.) (Jer. Berachoth iv. § 4, 8 b.) Nevertheless, R.
Yochanan said that the man who prays in his house surrounds it with
a wall of iron. There is no contradiction. In the one case he is
alluding to private prayer, in the other to public prayer (with the
congregation) (v. § 1, 8 d). Thus though he who prays in the synagogue is as one who offers a pure sacrifice, and though in explanation
of the bidding 'seek God where he may be found,' it is said that
God is to be found in the synagogue and houses of study, we may
be sure that the Rabbis held that God was *also* to be found in the
fields or in a house. For workmen a good many convenient concessions were made to enable them to say the statutory prayers at
the fixed time. The recitation of the *Shema* was apparently allowed
somewhat greater freedom than the recitation of the statutory
Amidah prayer. Thus in the Mishnah the rule is laid down : 'Workmen may say the *Shema* on the top of a tree or on the top of scaffold-
ing, but they may not do so as regards the *Tefillah*' (Mishnah
Berachoth iv. 4). The Gemara adds : 'Workmen may say the
Tefillah on the top of an olive tree or fig tree ; but with all other
trees they must descend to the ground.' (The fig and olive are easy
trees, with many branches ; hence the workmen are not afraid of
tumbling down, and can pay attention to what they are saying.)
'The employer must come down to the ground from every tree,
because his mind is not settled.' (His time is his own ; therefore with
him the Law is stricter.) (Berachoth 16 a. See Dr. Cohen's translation.) In the Jerusalem Talmud (Berachoth, ii. 5, 5 a) the reason
of the exception in the case of the fig and the olive trees is said to
be that it is so fatiguing to get down from these trees. In Tosefta
Berachoth ii. § 7 (p. 4 *init.*) it says : A load carrier, even when the

burden is on his shoulders, may recite the *Shema*. But while he is
either putting on or taking off the load, he may not recite it, because
he cannot direct his heart (*i.e.* properly fix his attention upon the
prayer) (שאין לבו מכוון). The *Amidah* he may not say (literally he
may not pray) ' until he has taken off his load.' The words ' because
his heart cannot be rightly attuned ' (שאין לבו מכוון) show that the
fundamental prerequisite of prayer was never lost sight of. ' To
serve God with all your heart. What is a service in the heart ?
That is prayer ' (Sifre 80 a). (Moore gives an excellent account of
Rabbinic views about Prayer, II. pp. 212–235.)

The attack on hypocrites and the association of hypocrisy with
the Pharisees and the Rabbis are familiar notes in the Gospels.
The Rabbis denounce hypocrisy no less hotly than Jesus. Their
word for it is *Chanufa*. The root is found in the O.T. in many
places : the A.V. translates it by hypocrisy and hypocrites, but it
would seem that in the O.T. it means ' impiety,' ' wickedness.' In
Rabbinic Hebrew it includes both flattery and hypocrisy. Both are
deviations from truth. ' R. Elazar said, A man in whom is hypocrisy brings wrath upon the world, and his prayer is not heard.
He also said, A man in whom is hypocrisy the children in their
mother's womb curse. He also said, The hypocrites fall into
Gehinnom ' (Sotah 41 b). He also said, ' A congregation in which is
hypocrisy is loathsome.' (In oriental phrase it is מאוסה כנדה.) ' A
congregation in which is hypocrisy will go into captivity.' R.
Jeremiah said, ' Four classes of men do not receive the face of the
Shechinah : the mockers, the hypocrites, the liars, and the slanderers.'
(Sotah 42 b.) ' The hypocrites are supposed to know Bible and
Midrash, but they do not : they are covered with their praying
shawls and wear the tefillin. God says of them, I must punish
them, for it is said, Cursed be he who does the work of the Lord
deceitfully ' (Ecclesiastes R. on iv. 1 ; Kittel, p. 102, and Moore II.
pp. 191, 192). Commenting on Lev. xxvi. 3, ' To *do* them,' it is said,
' One learns to do ; one does not learn not to do : he who does not learn
to do, it were better for him that he had not been born ' (Sifra 110 c
ad fin. on Lev. xxvi. 3 ; *cp.* Lev. R., בחקותי, xxxv. 7 on xxvi. 3, and
Kittel, p. 103). Familiar is the saying, ' A disciple of the wise (*i.e.*
a man of learning) whose inside is not as his outside is no disciple
of the wise : he is an abomination ' (Yoma 72 b ; *cp.* Berachoth 28 a ;
Moore II. 191 ; Kittel, p. 103). Hypocrites must be exposed, because

of the desecration of the Name (which hypocrisy causes). (Yoma 86 b.) There were Rabbinical decrees as to certain things which ought not to be done in public, lest it would *seem* as if a command was being violated, though it really was not. Some Rabbis went further, and said that everything which the Rabbis had forbidden for the sake of appearances (מפני מראית העין) must not be done even in the strictest privacy. (Bezah 9 a; *cp.* Ziegler, II. p. 287.) Kittel (p. 102), naturally anxious to prove that such attacks as those in Matt. vi. are historically accurate, quotes from Esther R. i. 3, where it says that of ten portions of hypocrisy in the world, nine were in Jerusalem. How far such enumerations are deserving of much credence is doubtful. Still they may be said to show a popular view.

7. Dr. Abrahams has noted that though Jesus ascribes length of prayer to the heathen and not to the Rabbis, yet many theologians want to make this too a Rabbinic vice. (P. 102.) It was certainly not a fault of the public prayer in the age of Jesus, nor of such private prayers as have been preserved for us in the Talmudic literature. The well-known sayings of R. Eliezer who saw the destruction of the Temple are given honestly enough by S.B., as they are given by Abrahams and by every Jewish apologist. But familiar as they are, they must not be omitted here, because they show that the root idea of Matt. vi. 7 was also not unfamiliar to the Rabbis, who, however, looked at the matter in a somewhat larger way. Long prayers, like short prayers, have their justification. On Exodus xiv. 15 R. Eliezer said, God said to Moses, My children are in danger, the enemy is at their heels, and you stand and keep on praying (מרבה בתפילה). God said to Moses there is a time to prolong [prayer], and there is a time to cut it short. Thus, ' O God heal her ' (Numbers xii. 13) is an example of shortness ; and ' I worshipped before the Lord forty days and forty nights ' (Deut. ix. 18) is an example of length. (Mechilta 29 a.) In a subsequent passage on Exodus xv. 25 (45 b) it says : ' Hence we can gather that the prayer of the righteous is easily accepted ; also that the prayer of the righteous is short. It happened that a disciple in the presence of R. Eliezer made his benedictions short (קצר בברכותיו). The disciples said, Have you noticed X, how he shortened his benedictions, and they mocked him and said, That is a disciple who

shortens. R. Eliezer said, He did not shorten more than Moses, who said, " God, heal her ! " Another disciple lengthened his benedictions. When the disciples said, Do you notice how Y lengthens ? R. Eliezer said, He does not lengthen more than Moses, citing again the words in Deut. ix. 18. For there is a time to shorten and a time to lengthen.' In the Sifre R. Eliezer makes these rejoinders to disciples who ask him, What is the shortest or longest prayer a man should pray ? (28 b). Of R. Akiba we are told that when he prayed with the congregation, he was short ; 'when he prayed by himself, you could leave him on one side of the room and find him on the other because of his genuflexions and prostrations.' (Tosefta Berachoth iii. § 7, p. 6.) The story about R. Chanina is pleasing. ' A certain man went down to the Ark (to act as Precentor) in the presence of R. Chanina. He said (Cohen's translation of Berachoth 33 b, p. 226) : " O God, the great, the mighty, the revered, the glorious, the powerful, the feared, the strong, the courageous, the certain, the honoured." R. Chanina waited until he had finished. When he had finished, he said to him, Hast thou exhausted all the praises of thy Lord ? What is the use of all those adjectives ? The three which we do say (great, mighty, and revered), if Moses had not used them in the Torah, and if the men of the Great Assembly had not come and instituted them in the *Tefillah* (Prayer), we should not have been able to say ; and thou goest on saying all those ! A parable : It may be likened to a human king who possessed a million gold *denarii*, and people kept praising him as the possessor of a million *denarii* of silver ; is it not an insult to him ? ' ' It is forbidden to lengthen out (לספר, which Rashi glosses with בקביעות ברכה) the praise of the Holy One.' (It says in the Psalms : ' *Who can* recite the mighty deeds of the Lord, *who can* proclaim his praise ? ' (cvi. 2). Therefore only *he who can* may lengthen out and tell all his praise : but nobody can !) 'R. Yochanan said, He who enumerates (המספר) the praise of the Holy One more than is adequate (יותר מדאי) will be extirpated from the world.' And most ingeniously another Rabbi quoted the first three words of Psalm lxv., rendering them, 'For thee silence is praise' (לך דמיה תהלה). (Megillah 18 a.) ' Rab Huna stated that Rab said in the name of R. Meir : A man's words should always be few before the Holy One, as it is said in Eccles. v. 1, etc.' (do. 61 a). The practice of different Rabbis varied as regards short prayers and long, and the utterances of the same

Rabbi are, on the surface, not always consistent. And the claims and powers of prayer were sometimes contrasted with the claims and powers of the study of the Law. Thus length of prayer is sometimes said to be good and to obtain favour from God. In a long and odd passage in Jer. Berachoth iv., 7 b *ad fin.* (given by S.B.), R. Levi is credited with the saying that whoever is long in prayer is heard, or whoever increases his prayer is heard (כל המרבה בתפילה נענה). Elsewhere R. Levi appeared to give a contrary view. The solution suggested is, In the one case he referred to public prayer, in the other to the individual, but apparently in *this* passage the long prayer is held to be beneficial and good as regards public prayer, the short as regards the prayer of the individual. The same praise of long prayer is ascribed immediately after to R. Meir (based on 1 Sam. i. 12. Hannah prayed long and was ' heard '). Again (Berachoth 32 b), R. Chanina said, Whoever prolongs his prayer, his prayer will not return empty. (*Cp.* Berachoth 54 b *fin.*) To this it is objected that R. Yochanan said that he who prolongs his prayer and calculates on it (מעיין בה) will end in pain of heart. The solution of the difficulty is that it is only the long prayer ' with calculation ' which ends in pain and disappointment. (As to this ' calculation ' [or *Iyyun*] see Abrahams, pp. 78, 79, with the many interesting and delicate Rabbinic passages there quoted and referred to. I should like to quote them here too, but they are not strictly in point as regards length of prayer. *Cp.* also Moore, II. 235.) Raba noticed how R. Hamnuna prolonged his prayer. He said, Men neglect the eternal life and occupy themselves with the life of the hour. (He meant, More time for study of the Law, less time for prayer, which is a petition for matters connected with temporal things—a low view of prayer, apparently.) R. Hamnuna thought that there is a time for both, each for itself (לחוד). Once when R. Jeremiah and R. Zera were studying, and were late for their prayer, R. Jeremiah hurried. R. Zera quoted about him Prov. xxviii. 9, ' He that turns away his ear from hearing the Law, even his prayer is an abomination ' (Sabbath 10 a). One or two other passages commending lengthy prayers or continuance in prayer are cited by S.B. Thus : Yoma 29 a : ' Whenever the righteous make their prayer long, their prayer is heard.' Such sentences must be compared with Paul's ' Pray without ceasing,' or still more with Jesus himself when he ' spoke a parable unto them to show that they ought to pray continually (πάντοτε), and not to lose heart (ἐγκακεῖν).' So it was with R. Yochanan who said, 'Would that a man could pray all day ' (Berachoth 21 a). The saying of Jesus in Luke can be reconciled with the saying in Matthew, and even so the utterances of the Rabbis about long prayers or prolongation of prayer are not really inconsistent with their appreciation of short prayers. The differences between individual Rabbis, and even between the practice of Palestinian and Babylonian Rabbis, is alluded to in the quaint story of R. Chiya and R. Kahana. These two Rabbis meet and say their prayers. R. Chiya (of Palestine) finishes first, and sits down to wait till the other has finished, so as not to pass R. Kahana while he was praying. R. Kahana prolongs his prayer, and when he has done, R. Chiya says to him, Is it the custom with you thus to trouble your Rabbis ? (הכין אתון נהיגין גביכון מצערין רבריכון) (Jer. Rosh ha-Shanah ii. 6, 58 b). (The reply of R. Kahana would take us too far afield. It is, however, curious, and tends to make one believe that these old Rabbis lived in an ethical and religious world and atmosphere which, in its strength and weakness, in its beauty and delicacy, as well as in its occasional harshness and folly, it is almost impossible to reproduce or even accurately to appraise.)

In spite of their own material to the contrary, and in spite of the fact that Jesus makes no charge of πολυλογία against the Rabbis, S.B., like other Christian commentators, try to make the accusation apply to them also. But it can hardly be said that the attempt is successful. So far as the liturgy for the age of Jesus is concerned, the evidence points the other way. So far as the practice of the Rabbis was concerned, both in public prayer (where, in the age of Jesus, much interpolation, variety, and freedom were allowed) and in private prayers, we have seen that S.B.'s own quotations do not amount to more than this, that some Rabbis believed in the value of long or prolonged prayers or prayer either for the individual or the congregation, though not necessarily or usually for both. The only other evidence which S.B. bring forward is the old prayer ' True and firm ' (אמת ויציב). (Prayer Book, p. 42.) This prayer, which is very ancient, opens with an accumulation of sixteen adjectives. But there is good evidence that, in the age of Jesus, it opened with not more, or perhaps even with less, than six. (The Christian theologians who are so down upon Jewish apologists when they quote nice Rabbinic passages which are later than Jesus, cannot have it both ways. If there is to be ἀκριβεῖα on the one side, there must be ἀκριβεῖα on the other !) Moreover, the prayer in itself is by no means long. (*Cp.* Abrahams' *Annotations to Prayer Book*, p. lv ; Elbogen, *Gottesdienst*, pp. 22, 26, 514 ; and especially *J.Q.R.* x. 656.) Then the eight verbs in the second section of the *Kaddish* are mentioned. Here we do find eight verbs one after the other. ' Blessed, praised and glorified, exalted, extolled and honoured, magnified and lauded, be the name of the Holy One,' etc. The date of the prayer is uncertain ; uncertain whether it existed so early as A.D. 30, and uncertain, too, if it then existed, whether it existed in its present form. Still, as regards Rabbinic prayers in general, we may notice a certain evil tendency to needless amplification, to a loss of simplicity, to a piling up of verbs and adjectives. To that extent S.B.'s charge of πολυλογία for the Rabbinic period as a whole may be justified. De Sola Pool observes : ' The tendency towards piling up synonyms of praise existed ' comparatively early. He then gives some examples, and continues, ' to say nothing of Biblical examples,' such as Daniel iv. 34 or I Chron. xxix. II. ' The very maxim of R. Meir, Few should be the words man utters to God, of R. Yochanan, He who gives God immoderate praise destroys himself, and other similar sayings, must be understood as showing that the opposite tendency was prevalent, and against it they warn ' (The old Jewish Aramaic Prayer, the *Kaddish*, by David de Sola Pool, 1909, p. 56). And I suppose this is about the truth of it. Mr. Loewe writes : ' " Snowball " or cumulative prayers are characteristic of non-statutory portions of the liturgy, *e.g.* Selichoth (penitential prayers) and *Piyyutim* (hymns). They were the product usually of the precentor, and were artificial, to give him an opportunity of singing. They were alphabetical, because they were composed before printing was invented or common, and therefore arranged so as to assist the memory, when printed books were rare. (But this device was also employed for more " serious " prayers and formulas, *e.g.* the confession of sin, for similar reasons.) The stock examples are neither beautiful nor old. Most have been omitted in the modern orthodox prayer books. A few of the better ones remain ; *cp.* Davis and Adler's Atonement Volume (II.), pp. 68 foll. Their merit is simplicity, and they are retained for the sake of children. For parallels in the Roman Catholic liturgy, *cp.* the litany of the Virgin in the Benediction Service, which closely resembles some of the cumulative prayers in structure.' Finally, I hardly think that the praise given in a few well-known Talmudic passages to the pious men who continued long at their prayer has much relevancy with the subject under discussion. What Jesus, I imagine, objects to, is not the length of time devoted to communion with God, but the idea either that God needs elaborate explanation as to the exact needs of his children, or that long prayers are more likely to extract and extort a favourable reply—a granting of petitions—than short prayers. But the passages about the pious men of old have nothing to do with such volubility in petition. Mishnah Berachoth v. 1 states : ' One must not stand up to say the *Tefillah* except in a serious state of mind ' (אלא מתוך כובד ראש). (Dr. Cohen, p. 202, by this translation assumes that להתפלל means merely to say the statutory prayers in the synagogue. It may, however, have a more general meaning, and be rightly translated, as by Goldschmidt, simply ' to pray.' The German scholar renders the Hebrew מתוך כובד ראש ' with bowed head.')   ' The pious men of old used to wait an hour and then say the *Tefillah* (or " then pray ") in order to direct their heart (כדי שיכונו לבם) to their Father in heaven.' The Gemara observes (omitting all the Biblical references and proofs) : 'R. Joshua b. Levi said, A man should wait an hour after his prayer. And there is a teaching : A man should wait an hour before and an hour after his prayer. The Rabbis have taught : The pious men of old used to wait an hour, pray for an hour, and wait again an hour.' But if (the question is asked) they thus spent nine hours in prayer (since one has to pray three times a day), how was their study of the Law kept up (משתמרת), and how was their work [the work by which they got their livelihood] achieved ? The reply is : Since they were pious, their study was preserved (משתמרת), and their work was blessed. (Berachoth 32 b.) The parallel passage in Jer. Berachoth iv. § 1, 8 d, is closely similar. It says, however, more plainly, ' When did they occupy themselves with the study of the Law and when with their work ? ' R. Isaac b. Eliezer said, Because they were pious, a blessing was given to their study and to their work. Such passages as these need not be taken into account in relation to Matt. vi. 7. The pious men of old would not have been censured by Jesus for their long communion with God.

About *Kawwanah*, that fine and purely Rabbinic conception, in its relation to prayer and generally, something will be said further on.

8. ' Your Father knows your needs before you ask him.' Oddly enough this verse is overlooked by S.B. I cannot recall reading any exact Rabbinic parallel, but one of the short prayers suggested as suitable to be said in a place of danger, more especially in the form in which it is given in the Palestinian Talmud, seems to contain something of the same idea. ' The needs of thy people Israel are many, but their knowledge is small. May it be thy will, O Lord our God and the God of our fathers, to give to every person (creature) his need and to every body (גויה) what may be lacking to it. Blessed be the Lord who hast heard the voice of my supplications. Blessed are thou, O Lord, who hearkenest to prayer' (Jer. Berachoth iv. § 4, 8 b. In Berachoth 29 a the prayer is exclusively directed to each person's bodily wants and his maintenance : in the other version the ' needs ' (צרכים) may be more generally interpreted as equivalent to Matthew's ὧν χρείαν ἔχετε).

9. As to the wording of the Lord's Prayer, a few parallels in language or idea may be added here. ' Father in heaven.' I may mention a few of the passages which are enumerated by Moore II. pp. 201–211. ' If a man fulfils the Law, and does the will of his Father in heaven, he is like the creatures of the Above (*i.e.* the angels) ; if not, then he is like the creatures of the Below ' (Sifre 132 a *fin.*). It says in Proverbs xxiii. 15, ' My son, if thine heart be wise, my heart shall rejoice, even mine' (גם אני). R. Simeon b. Yochai said, ' Not only his earthly father rejoices, but also his Father who is in heaven, for by the words *Gam ani* we must understand to be included his Father who is in heaven ' (Sifre 84 b). The phrase is also used in a famous passage in the Mishnah Rosh ha-Shanah iii. 8 about the uplifted hands of Moses securing victory to the Israelites (Exodus xvii. 11), and about the serpent in Numbers xxi. 8, quoted on p. 204. So too : ' In evil days whom have we to lean upon ? Upon our Father who is in heaven ' (Sotah ix. 15). Some other passages quoted by Moore are cited by me in other connections. ' Our Father ' in the Jewish liturgy is frequent, and

more especially when joined with King in the phrase ' Our Father
and King.' So in the old *Amidah* prayers for repentance and
forgiveness (*Authorized Prayer Book*, p. 46): in the old prayer
beginning ' With abounding love ' (p. 39). So, again, pp. 53, 58,
and 69, and in the long series of invocations, each one beginning
with ' Our Father and King,' on p. 55, concerning which see the
article on *Abinu Malkenu* in the *Jewish Encyclopedia*, I. p. 65.
There are a large number of other instances of the use of ' Father
in heaven' given by Marmorstein, *The old Rabbinic Doctrine of
God* (1927, Vol. I. pp. 56–61), over and above those adduced by
Moore. The term is frequent from R. Yochanan b. Zakkai onwards,
who said, ' The stones of the altar are peacemakers between Israel
and their Father in heaven ' (Mechilta 74 a). Akiba seems to have
liked the phrase. ' Happy are ye Israelites. Who purifies you ?
Your Father in heaven.' Moses was ' worthy to become an inter-
mediary (שליח) between Israel and their Father in heaven' (Yoma
Mishnah viii. 9, 85 b and Sifra 112 c *fin.*). (*Cp.* also the discussion, and
the passages quoted, in Büchler, *Studies in Sin and Atonement*, pp.
77–81.) I may also quote Abrahams' *Companion to the Daily Prayer
Book* (1922): ' *Our Father who art in heaven* is not a common liturgical phrase when used vocatively. This (*i.e.* p. 9) is the only case
in which it is found in the P.B., though in the Sephardic rite there
is for the Penitential days a long litany, every line of which begins
Our Father who art in heaven. But the idea is common. *Cf.* P.B.
pages 69, 70 four times and page 76 (second line), *May it be the will
of our Father who is in heaven.* . . . In the Mishnah (Rosh ha-
Shanah iii. 8) occurs " when Israel looked on high and submitted
their heart to *their Father who is in heaven* they were healed "
(with reference to Numbers xxi. 8). The phrase occurs fairly frequently in the Talmud (*e.g.* Menachoth 110 a *init.*). So too in the
Ethics of the Fathers (Mishnah, Aboth, v. 23, P.B. page 203); " Be
strong as a leopard, light as an eagle, fleet as a hart, and strong as
a lion to do the will of *thy Father who is in Heaven.*" The vocative
use of " Our Father who art in heaven " becomes frequent in the
poetical additions to the liturgy in the middle ages ' (p. xxiii).
Mr. Loewe writes : ' It is, perhaps, noteworthy that *Maran
di-bi-shemaya*, " our Lord, who art in heaven," is not uncommon :
it occurs in Aramaic prayers which are old; *cp.* Singer,
p. 152, line 2 and end of next paragraph. [*N.B.*—Read מָרַן, not

מָרָן, and translate " our Lord " in each case.] (For מרן *cp.* I Cor.
xvi. 22, S.B. *in loc.*) Notice two old *Selichah* prayers (non-statutory
penitential prayers), also in Aramaic, and common both to the
Ashkenazic and Sephardic rites (with variants) : " Our Lord, who
art in heaven, thee do we supplicate as a slave supplicates his lord,
give us a heart for penitence, that we turn not empty-handed from
before Thee." The Ashkenazic rite has : " Our Lord, who art in
heaven, Thee do we supplicate, as a slave supplicates his lord ;
oppressed are we and dwelling in darkness ; bitter are our souls
by reason of troubles that are many ; strength is not with us to
appease Thee, our Lord ; do it (*i.e.* save us) for the sake of the
covenant which Thou didst make with our fathers." The second
verse of the Sephardic version runs : " Our Lord, who art in
heaven, Thee do we supplicate, as a captive supplicates his lord.
Captives are redeemed with silver, but Thy people Israel with
prayers and supplications. O lift up Thy right hand, and cause
thy redemption to spring forth [*cp. Kaddish*], O Thou, the hope
of the living and the dead ! " (Gaster, *Book of Prayer*, New Year
Volume, p. 19). The Ashkenazic version runs : " Our Lord,
who art in heaven, Thee do we supplicate, as a captive supplicates
his lord : captives are redeemed with silver, but Thy people
Israel with mercy and supplications. Grant us our request and
petition, that we turn not away empty-handed from Thee." '
Jesus may have used the briefer ' Father ' (*cp.* Luke xi. 9). But
Abba (Mark xiv. 36) should probably be rendered ' my Father '
(Dalman, *Worte Jesu*, I. 157 ; S.B. on Mark xiv. 36). ' My Father '
is also used by the Rabbis, but not frequently. Sifra on Lev. xx.
26 : ' R. Elazar b. Azariah said, One must not say, I have no wish
to eat pig's flesh, I have no wish to wear a garment of mixed stuff,
I have no wish to commit unchastity (לבוא על העריה) ; one
must say, I *do* wish these things, but what am I to do ? My Father
in heaven has so decreed ' (93 d). [The passage, it may be noted
incidentally, is curious and interesting. It has an obvious polemical
tendency and is intentionally paradoxical. The Rabbis can hardly
have meant it seriously that to desire to be unchaste, but to refrain
from unchastity because of the divine command, is a higher moral
condition than not even to *desire* to do evil. Aristotle would turn
in his grave at such an idea. The saying is probably a deliberate
defence of the legalistic position. So far from ' thou shalt not '

being a lower stage of religion, consciously to refrain from sin because of the commands of God is the highest stage : deliberate and conscious obedience to God's will is the highest to which man can attain.] R. Nathan said on Exodus xx. 6, 'They who love me, etc., are the Israelites who gave their lives for the commandments. Why wast thou brought out to be killed ? Because I circumcized some Israelites. And why wast thou brought forth to be burnt ? Because I read the Law. And why wast thou brought out to be crucified ? Because I ate unleavened bread. And why wast thou scourged ? Because I carried the lulab on Tabernacles. These wounds have caused me to be loved by my Father who is in heaven' (Mechilta 68 b). ' R. Zadok entered into the ruined Temple. He said, My Father in heaven, thou hast destroyed thy city, and burnt thy temple, and remainest calm and at peace. Then R. Zadok slept. Then he saw God mourning, and the angels of the service mourned behind him. He said, Have trust, O Jerusalem' (Tana Eliyahu, Seder Rabba, chapter xxviii. p. 149). In a long prayer beginning at the foot of p. III of the Tana Eliyahu, Seder Rabba (chapter xix.), the phrase 'my Father who is in heaven' occurs five times in rapid succession. Again, 'R. Gamaliel was on a ship in a storm. The disciples said, Master, pray for us. He said, Our God, have pity upon us ! His disciples said that he was worthy to use the singular pronoun, so he said, My God, have pity upon us.' (The source is given by Bacher, *Agada der Tannaiten*, I. p. 94, n. 2, ed. 2.) S.B. say that it is not by accident that the phrase ' my Father ' is comparatively rare, whereas ' our Father ' is common. There was a fear that to say ' my Father ' might seem, or become, familiar : it might be considered an infringement of the right reverence for God. In I. p. 410, S.B. speak of superstitious motives, but this is, I think, unfair. If it was said by Abaye in the fourth century, ' Always let a man unite himself with the community in his prayers' (Berachoth 29 b), this was not due to superstition ; nor, I think, is Rashi right in saying that the reason was because the man's prayer would more likely be granted. The reason was rather the dominant impulse that every Israelite should join with, and not separate himself from, the community. His prayers should, so far as possible, be prayers for what others could and would and did desire as well as himself. I cannot refrain from adding here the pretty story of Chanin ha-Nechba. ' He was the son of the daughter of Honi the circle-drawer. When the world needed rain, the Rabbis would send school children to him, who would pull him by the corners of his garments and say to him : " Father, Father ! Give us rain ! " Said Chanin : " Master of the world ! Do it for the sake of these, who do not distinguish between the Father who gives rain and a father who does not give rain." And rain came ' (Taanith 23 b ; Dr. Malter's translation, p. 175).

Perhaps it may be desirable that I should refer here to the Rev. A. Lukyn Williams' interesting article on ' " My Father " in Jewish Thought of the First Century ' in the *J. T. S.* of October 1929, pp. 42–47. Mr. Williams gives a very good summary of the facts, and shows that the phrase ' my Father ' occurs in the Rabbinic litera-ture seldom, whereas in Luke, and more especially in Matthew, it is recorded that Jesus used it very often. On the assumption that the records are accurate, and that Jesus really did frequently speak of God as ' my Father ' (as well as ' Father '), Mr. Williams holds that this usage means that Jesus had a consciousness of a more than merely human relation with God, ' reaching up to such connection with the divine as had, in fact, existed before He came into the world.' I can see no adequate evidence for this opinion. If. R. Nathan or R. Zadok or Rabbi Elazar could say ' my Father,' without any idea in their minds that they were semi-divine beings, why should not Jesus ? Is it not enough to assume that he felt God to be his divine Father with peculiar and passionate intensity ? I do not think that he separated himself from other men. For them, too, God was Father, and as Father they too were able to conceive him.

9. ' Hallowed (or sanctified) be thy name.' The *Kaddish* prayer begins in much the same way. ' Magnified and sanctified be his great name.' The meaning of the petition—for it is a petition —is the same to the Rabbis and to Jesus. By establishing his Kingship God will cause the complete sanctification of his name. He alone can and will bring the complete Kingship about at the end of the ordinary world era. Yet, even in this era, the Israelite by his sins or his virtues can increase or diminish God's sanctifica-tion. God's *full* sanctification and his *full* kingship will require that all men shall acknowledge his Unity and his Rule. The

Sanctification and Kingship are therefore necessarily universalistic. Of that universalistic hope an example can be given under the next clause. Though resting upon Pentateuchal ordinances and conceptions, the Sanctification of the Name was, in every sense, a peculiarly Rabbinic conception. Israel must give itself up to sanctify God's name. Only on that condition was Israel redeemed from Egypt (שתתמסרו עצמכם לקדש את שמי) (Sifra 99 d on Lev. xxii. 33). In fact, only to Jews was the Sanctification of the Name a direct motive for human conduct and for martyrdom. The sanctification was effected both by God and by Israel simultaneously, and if Israel sanctified God, so was God asked to sanctify his Name through Israel. A prayer as old as the *Kaddish* runs (P.B. p. 9 *init.*) : ' Sanctify thy name through them that sanctify it, yea, sanctify thy name throughout thy world, and through thy salvation let our horn be exalted and raised on high. Blessed art thou, O Lord, who sanctifiest thy name amongst the many.' The meaning of the opening words ' sanctify thy name through (על) them that sanctify it ' is a little doubtful. Mr. Singer has ' upon,' and S.B. translate ' because of '; but על can hardly mean ' because of ' or ' for the sake of,' and ' upon ' seems to make little or no sense. ' Through ' seems the best and most accurate rendering. For the idea of sanctifying and magnifying the name of God I may quote two further passages. ' May his great name be blessed. (To which the response is) For ever and ever ' (Sifre 132 b, *ki shem*, in which paragraph the phrase 'in order to sanctify God's great name ' repeatedly occurs). Again, in Ecc. R. on ix. 15, ' A little city ' (towards the end). ' When the senior man present in the synagogue sits and expounds, and when the people answer after him, " Amen, May his great name be blessed," even though there impend a list of punishments for a hundred years, God pardons all the sins.' So too, God spake to Israel : ' If you sanctify my name, I will sanctify my name through you (על ידיכם), even as Michael, Chananyah, and Azaryah did, for when all the nations of the world bowed down to the idol, they stood erect as palm trees. And God said, To-day I am exalted (=sanctified) through them (בהם) in the eyes of the nations ' (Sifra 86 b on Lev. xviii. 5). The Sanctification of the Name has been entrusted to Israel alone ; it is their privilege and duty in one ; not the privilege and duty of the ' nations.' And yet God's name will not be fully sanctified till all the nations of the world acknowledge his Godhead and his

Unity. S.B., pages 408–418, contain much interesting material about the Sanctification of the Name, but to quote more from them, or to quote other passages over and above those they give, would lead me too far afield.

10.   (a) ' Thy kingdom come ' ; or, perhaps better, ' thy kingship come.'

It is impossible to deal fully with the Rabbinic conceptions of the kingdom or kingship—God's rule and lordship—in this place. Just as in the Gospels, so in the Rabbinic literature, we can detect a double strain. The kingship is an eschatological conception, and the Rabbis pray for the coming or establishment of the kingship in its fullness at the end of the age. Nevertheless, the kingship is in a sense always existent and already here, for ' the Lord reigned, the Lord reigns, the Lord will reign, for ever and ever.' Israel accepts the ' yoke of the kingship,' for Israel, by its observance of God's will, and by the fulfilment of his commandments, acknowledges his kingship, and hastens on its more complete manifestation. And yet Israel prays : ' May his kingship be soon revealed and made visible to us.' The full universalism of the conception of the kingship is expressed in the ancient prayer : ' Our God and God of our fathers, reign thou in thy glory over the whole universe, and be exalted above all the earth in thine honour, and shine forth in the splendour and excellence of thy might upon all the inhabitants of thy world, that whatsoever hath been made may know that thou hast made it, and whatsoever hath been created may understand that thou hast created it, and whatsoever hath breath in its nostrils may say, the Lord God of Israel is King, and his dominion ruleth over all ' (P.B. p. 249). And in the second portion of the *Alenu* prayer : ' We therefore hope in thee, O Lord our God, that we may speedily behold the glory of thy might, when thou wilt remove the abominations from the earth, and the idols will be utterly cut off, when the world will be perfected under the kingdom of the Almighty, and all the children of flesh will call upon thy name, when thou wilt turn unto thyself all the wicked of the earth. Let all the inhabitants of the world perceive and know that unto thee every knee must bow, every tongue must swear. Before thee, O Lord our God, let them bow and fall ; and unto thy glorious name let them give honour ; let them all accept the yoke of thy kingdom, and do thou reign over them speedily, and for ever and ever. For the kingdom is thine, and to all eternity thou wilt reign in glory ; as it is written in thy Law, The Lord shall reign for ever and ever. And it is said, And the Lord shall be king over all the earth : in that day shall the Lord be One, and his name One ' (P.B. pp. 76, 77 ; and cp. Abrahams in *Companion*, pp. lxxxvi.–lxxxviii.). In the *Kaddish* we find : 'May he establish his kingdom during your life and during your days, and during the life of all the house of Israel, even speedily and at a near time, and say ye, Amen ' (p. 75). But it would be undesirable for me to say more now about the kingdom and the kingship. A little book upon the subject might be of value. It is too big and central a conception for discussion here. *Cp.* S.B. pp. 172–184 and an endless number of other passages in an endless number of other books. But nothing is finer and more illuminating for the Rabbinic conception of the kingship than Schechter, *Some Aspects of Rabbinic Theology*, pp. 64–115 (written in his best period).

10.   (b) ' Thy will be done, as in heaven so in earth.' I had said in the Commentary, ' There is no exact Rabbinic verbal parallel,' and this is borne out by S.B., and not really contradicted by Abrahams' *Studies* (II.), p. 100. The meaning is much the same as the former petition. When the kingdom in its fullness has arrived, when the kingship is universally acknowledged, when the Golden Age or New Era has come, then all men will do God's will upon earth even as now it is done in heaven.

11.   ' Give us this day our daily bread.' *Cp.* Proverbs xxx. 8 with the versions as given in S.B. The prayer I quoted before is, I observe, given in full by S.B. in this place, namely, the one in which the words occur, ' Give to every creature his needs and to every body what it requires.' Mechilta on Exodus xvi. 4, 47 b, about the manna is quaint. ' The portion of a day in its day : He who created the day, created too the sustenance for the day.' R. Elazar of Modin said, ' He who possesses what he can eat to-day and says, what shall I eat to-morrow ? is a man of little faith.' We may also compare the blessing on the years in the Eighteen Benedictions : ' Bless this year unto us, O Lord our God, together with every kind of the produce thereof, for our welfare ; give a blessing (give dew and rain for a blessing) upon the face of the earth : satisfy us with

thy goodness, and bless our year like other good years ; blessed art
thou, O Lord, who blessest the years ' (P.B. p. 47).

12. 'Forgive us our debts.' What I say on pp. 102, 103, Vol.
II., seems to me accurate. I still cannot think that Dr. Abrahams
is right. What can be more closely parallel than Sirach xxviii. 2 ?
' Forgive thy neighbour the wrong he has done thee, and then thy
sins will be pardoned when thou prayest. One man cherishes hatred
against another, and does he seek healing from the Lord ? He shows
no mercy to a man like himself, and does he make supplication for
his own sins ? Being flesh himself he nourishes wrath, who shall
atone for his sins ? ' I assume that 12 contains the same thought
as 14. ὡς, as Klostermann says, is ' begründend,' ' seeing that,'
nearly = because. ' Nicht, dass wir Gott dies (i.e. our forgiving
those who have done us an injury) als zwingenden Grund vorhalten,
sondern es ist praktisch die condicio sine qua non, aber die einzige,
für die Anbringung unserer Bitte um Vergebung.'[1] The forgiveness
prayer or blessing in the *Amidah* runs thus : ' Forgive us, O our
Father, for we have sinned; pardon us, O our King, for we have transgressed ; for thou dost pardon and forgive. Blessed art thou, O
Lord, who art gracious and dost abundantly forgive.' This prayer
is as old as, or older than, Jesus.

For sin as debt, cp. Büchler, *Studies in Sin*, p. 154, n. 1, and his
pretty quotation : ' What right have I to tell the Creditor not to
collect his debt ? ' (Jer. Taanith iv. § 4, 66 c); and cp. Moore, *Judaism*,
Vol. II. p. 95.

13. ' Lead us not into temptation.' The prayer (Talmudic ; cp.
Berachoth 60 b) as it now stands in the P.B., to which I allude on
p. 103, Vol. II., runs as follows : ' May it be thy will, O Lord our
God and God of our fathers, to make us familiar with thy Law, and
to make us cleave to thy commandments. O lead us not into sin,
or transgression, iniquity, temptation, or shame : let not the evil
inclination have sway over us : keep us far from a bad man and a
bad companion : make us cleave to the good inclination and to

---

[1] ' It is not that we put forward our forgiveness of those who have done us an
injury as the reason why God should be compelled to forgive us; but our forgiveness of our fellow-men is the condition, though the only condition, which
must, in actual life, precede our bringing any request for forgiveness before
God.'

good works : subdue our inclination so that it may submit itself unto thee ; and let us obtain this day, and every day, grace, favour and mercy in thine eyes, and in the eyes of all who behold us ; and bestow loving-kindnesses upon us. Blessed art thou, O Lord, who bestowest loving-kindnesses upon thy people Israel ' (P.B. p. 7).

' Deliver us from evil.' Many and various were the evils from which the Rabbinic prayers ask to be delivered. In the P.B., following on the prayer already given, we find (Berachoth 16 b) : ' May it be thy will, O Lord my God and God of my fathers, to deliver me this day, and every day, from arrogant men and from arrogance, from a bad man, from a bad companion, and from a bad neighbour, and from any mishap, and from the adversary that destroys ; from a hard judgment, and from a hard opponent, whether he be a son of the covenant or be not a son of the covenant.' (Here ' the adversary that destroys ' should be ' the Sa'tan, the destroyer,' or ' the Devil, the destroyer.' There is a prayer (Berachoth 17 a) which it is said that Mar b. Rabina used to add at the conclusion of his statutory prayer, part of which is found in the P.B. p. 54. ' O my God, guard my tongue from evil and my lips from speaking guile ; and to such as curse me let my soul be dumb, yea, let my soul be unto all as the dust. Open my heart to thy Law, and let my soul pursue thy commandments. And do thou deliver me from mishap (פגע רע), from the evil *yetzer*, and from an evil woman, and from all evil which breaks forth to come upon the world ' (מכל רעות המתרגשות לבא בעולם). All these various evils are simply and curtly summed up in the brief phrase ' deliver us from evil.'

13. The doxology is based upon 1 Chron. xxix. 11. ' Thine, O Lord, is the greatness and the power and the glory and the victory and the majesty, yea, thine is all that is in the heaven and in the earth ; thine is the kingdom, O Lord, and thou art exalted as head above all.' (These words occur in the daily liturgy of all rites, *e.g.* P.B. pp. 33, 44.) S.B. observe that the doxological application of the divine kingship was already customary during the existence of the second temple. At present, at the recitation of the Shema, after the invocation, ' Hear, O Israel, the Lord our God, the Lord is One,' the same words as used then are still repeated to-day. ' Blessed be the name of the glory of his Kingdom for ever and ever.' (Mr.

Singer renders, ' Blessed be the name of his glorious kingdom for ever and ever ' : on the meaning and history of this doxology, see the article by V. Aptowitzer, pp. 93-118, in the *Monatsschrift für Geschichte und Wissenschaft des Judentums* : 73. Jahrgang, 1929.

14, 15. The explanation of 12. The number of Rabbinic parallels is very large. ' When thou art compassionate, God will have compassion upon thee.' The context in which these words are placed makes it clear that what is referred to is the forgiveness of offences and wrongs. (Tosefta Baba Kamma ix. 29, p. 366.) (*Cp.* Sabbath 151 b, where the negative form is also found.) This is quite definite in Rosh ha-Shanah 17 a : 'Raba said, He who is forgiving, him they forgive all his transgressions. Whom does God forgive ? Him who overlooks the transgression (of others).' The Rabbis think no less of the case of the man who has done the wrong. His sin against God, which is implied in the sin against his neighbour, is not forgiven till he has sought forgiveness from his neighbour. In the long and interesting passage in Pesikta R. (165 a) and in Tanchuma B. xxx. (*Vayera* 52 a) on the subject, the famous sentence from Yoma is quoted that the Day of Atonement does not bring forgiveness of sins to any man till he has appeased, and sought pardon from, his neighbour whom he has wronged. But suppose that other refuses to forgive him, what then ? ' Let him take ten men and speak openly before them, and say, I wanted to be reconciled to him, but he refuses, whereas I have humbled myself before him. For if God sees that he has humbled himself, then He will forgive him his sins. For so long as a man stays in his stiffness (בזדונו) God does not forgive him.' (So Job was only forgiven when he forgave, and prayed for, his friends.) And then the passage goes on to play with Deut. xiii. 17 (Heb. 18) and to make the words mean : ' And the Lord will put mercy (into you) that He may be merciful to you. So R. Yose said, Let this be a sign to you, Whenever you have pity (*i.e.* forgive your neighbour), God forgives you.' Jesus seems always to think of the receiver, not of the doer, of the wrong. The Rabbis thought of both. (*Cp.* the passages from Megillah 28 a quoted on p. 90.) ' Rabbi Zutra said when he went to bed, Forgiven is everybody who did me an injury ' (שרי ליה לכל מאן דצערן). (Megillah 28 a.) In this matter of forgiveness the Gospel has nothing to teach the Talmud, so far as wrongs done to individuals by individuals are concerned. For different reasons the wrongs done to Israel by the national enemies of Israel stand outside the purview of both. Sevenster, in his section on forgiveness, attempts to make a large difference between the teaching of Jesus and of the Rabbis, but not very successfully. (Pp. 164, 165.)

Dr. Abrahams has said : ' Nothing is more remarkable than the extraordinary number of original individual prayers in the Talmud, and the faculty and process of ready improvisation for public as well as private worship have continued with copious flow to our own times in the synagogue, though the stream of such inspiration was more generous in the spacious times which preceded the age of printing. The latter invention did more than Pharisaism to give rigidity to Judaism. It is not possible to give by quotations any true impression of the vast mass of new prayers which entered the publicity of the synagogue liturgy or the privacy of the Jewish home during the first fourteen centuries of the Christian era ' (*Studies* ii. p. 86). It may be desirable to give some specimens of these Talmudic prayers over and above what have already been cited. Some of the best are found in Jer. Berachoth iv. § 2, 7 d. (A few of these have been quoted before on v. 43 on p. 90.) R. Pedath's prayer was : ' May it be thy will, O Lord my God and God of my fathers, that no hatred against any man come into our hearts, and no hatred against us come into the hearts of any man, and may none be jealous of us, and may we be not jealous of any ; and may thy Law be our labour all the days of our lives, and may our words be as supplications (תחנונים) before thee.' R. Chiya said, ' May our hearts be single (united) to fear thy name, keep us far from what thou hatest, and bring us near to what thou lovest, and deal charitably with us because of thy name.' R. Yannai's disciples were taught to say on awakening : ' Blessed art thou, O Lord, who quickenest the dead. May it be thy will, O Lord my God, to give me a good heart, a good *yetzer*, a good hope, a good name, a good eye, a good soul, a lowly soul, and a humble spirit ; may thy name not be profaned among (or through) us, and make us not a mockery in the mouth of men ; may our end not be cut off, nor our hope be a vexation, and may we not need the gifts of flesh and blood, and put not our sustenance into their hands, for their gifts are small, and the shame (which they inflict) is great ; and place our portion in thy Law, with those who do thy will ; build up thy house, thy sanctuary, thy city, thy temple, speedily in our days.' R. Chiya bar Abba was wont to pray : 'May it be thy will, O Lord our God and the God of our fathers, that thou put it into our hearts to perform a perfect repentance before thee, so that we be not ashamed before our fathers in the world to come.' R. Tanchuma prayed : 'May it be thy will, O Lord our God and God of our fathers, that thou break, and cause to cease, the yoke of the evil *yetzer* in our hearts, for thou hast created us to do thy will, and we are bound to do thy will : thou desirest it, and we are desirous, and what prevents ? The dough in the leaven (*i.e.* the evil *yetzer*). It is revealed and known before thee that we have not within us the strength to resist it : therefore may it be thy will to cause it to cease from us, and to crush it ; and then we will do thy will as our will with a perfect heart.' R. Yochanan was wont to pray : 'May it be thy will, O Lord our God and the God of our fathers, that thou grant to us (*lit.* cause to reside in our lot) love and brotherhood, peace and friendship, and prosper our end, and give us hope and posterity, and enlarge our borders among the disciples, and may we rejoice in our portion in Paradise, and cause us to acquire a good heart and a good companion ; and may we find each day the hope of our hearts, and may our souls have rest before thee to our good.'

In B. Berachoth there are also some interesting prayers. I quote Dr. Cohen's translation : 'R. Yochanan used to add at the conclusion of his prayer : May it be Thy will, O Lord our God, to glance at our shame and look upon our evil plight ; and do Thou clothe Thyself in Thy mercy, cover Thyself with Thy might, enfold Thyself with Thy piety and gird Thyself with Thy grace, and may Thy attribute of goodness and gentleness come before Thee.' 'Rab used to add at the conclusion of his prayer : May it be Thy will, O Lord our God, to grant us long life, a life of peace, a life of good, a life of blessing, a life of sustenance, a life of bodily vigour, a life marked by the fear of sin, a life free from shame and reproach, a life of prosperity and honour, a life in which the love of Torah and the fear of Heaven shall cleave to us, a life wherein Thou fulfillest all the desires of our heart for good' (16 b) (p. 108). The 'short' prayer of R. Eliezer is specially beautiful, 'Do Thy will in heaven above ; grant tranquillity of spirit to those that fear Thee below, and do that which is good in Thy sight. Blessed art Thou, O Lord, who hearkenest to prayer' (29 b).

16–18. Neither S.B. nor Abrahams give any direct parallel to these verses. But the Rabbis would, I have no doubt, have approved of their spirit, as Abrahams also suggests in his essay on 'Fasting' in *Studies* I. pp. 121–128. It is interesting that the Shulchan Aruch should declare : ' He who fasts, and makes a display of himself to others, to boast of his fasting, is punished for this.' Perhaps I might add that the Rabbis were, upon the whole, not very anxious to stimulate the practice of self-imposed fasting over and above the public fasts enjoined upon the whole community. It is true that R. Elazar said that he who fasts is called holy, for if the Nazarite is called holy because he abstains from wine, all the more so one who denies himself all the enjoyments of life. On the other hand, Samuel said, ' He that fasts is called a sinner, for the Scripture in one place inferentially calls him who abstains from the enjoyment of wine a sinner. Now if a person who denies himself only the enjoyment of wine is called a sinner, all the more so one who denies himself all the enjoyments of life.' This would be, I think, the more usual view. (Taanith 11 a, based on Dr. Malter's rendering.) The occasional ascetic touches in the Gospels are, speaking generally, off the Rabbinic line. Moore cites the saying of R. Isaac, ' Are not the things prohibited in the Law enough for you that you want to prohibit yourself other things ? ' A ' vow of abstinence is like an iron collar, such as is worn by prisoners, about a man's neck : one who imposes on himself such a vow ' is like a man ' who meets a detachment of soldiers (קסטורייא) with such a collar, and puts his own head into it.' Or he is like ' a man who drives a sword into his body ' (Jer. Nedarim i. 1, 41 b). By a fanciful interpretation of Numbers vi. 11 R. Elazar ha-Kappar Beribbi taught that a Nazarite had to bring a sin-offering because he put a painful restraint upon himself by not drinking wine (ציער עצמו על היין). And the Rabbi added that if he who refrained only from wine is called a sinner, how much more is he a sinner who painfully refrains from everything ' (המצער עצמו מכל דבר). (Nazir 19 a.) And then there is ' the often quoted saying of Rab ' : A man ' will have to give account on the judgment day of every good thing which he might have enjoyed and did not ' (literally, ' which his eyes saw and he did not eat '). (Jer. Kiddushin iv. 12, 66 d *fin.*; Moore II. p. 265.) On the other hand, Moore adds, ' Such statements, however frequent they may have been, must not be taken as the voice of an anti-ascetic "spirit of Judaism." They are expressions of personal temperament, circumstance, and surrounding, and not to be broadly generalized.' Still, I venture to think that they are rather on the Rabbinic line than off it. And it is exceedingly characteristic of Rabbinic Judaism that the conception of holiness is positive : the actions of the natural man must be hallowed. The details sometimes given may seem to our ears strange, but the conception, for example, of a man acting in a holy manner in the marriage-bed is fine and characteristic- ally Rabbinic (המקדש עצמו בשעת תשמיש). (Shebuoth 18 b.) Note- worthy is the saying, ' Hallow thyself in what is permitted thee, and sanctify thyself (even) in that which is (otherwise) permitted to thee ; in things permitted (generally) while some have regarded them as forbidden, thou art not allowed to treat them as permitted in the presence of those who take the stricter view ' (Sifre 95 b ; Moore II. p. 271).

19–21. ' Treasures in heaven.' The famous passage about King Monobaz (the proselyte ruler of Adiabene is, though a hack- neyed, yet a very complete parallel. It is repeated in several places. ' Monobaz distributed all his treasures to the poor in the year of trouble (famine). His brothers sent to him and said, Thy fathers gathered treasures, and added to those of *their* fathers, and thou hast dispersed yours and theirs. He said to them, My fathers gathered treasures for below, I have gathered treasures for above ; they stored treasures in a place over which the hand (of man) can rule, but I have stored treasures in a place over which the hand of man cannot rule ; my fathers collected treasures which bear no fruit (interest) ; I have gathered treasures which bear fruit ; my fathers gathered treasures of money (mammon) ; I have gathered treasures in souls ; my fathers gathered treasures for others, I have gathered treasures for myself ; my fathers gathered treasures in this world, I have gathered treasures for the world to come ' (Jer. Peah i. 1, 15 b, foot). The familiar passage in Aboth vi. 9 must also be alluded to. R. Yose ben Kisma, when asked by a certain man if he would come and dwell in the man's city on condition of receiving much wealth, replied that for all the wealth in the world he would not dwell anywhere but in a home of the Law ; ' in the hour of man's departure neither silver nor gold nor precious stones accompany him, but only Torah and good works.'

24. As to Rabbinic views about riches, see Matt. xix. 22, 23.
The trenchant saying is wonderfully striking and suggestive. Single-
minded devotion to God and righteousness and the kingdom is what
Jesus demands.   He is more antagonistic and hostile to wealth than
the Rabbis.   Does the Rabbinic prayer 'Unite our hearts to love
and fear thy name' (P.B. p. 40) mean 'make us single-minded'?
Dr. Abrahams (*Companion*, p. xlix.) says, 'In the *Ahabah* prayer,'
(P.B. p. 39, beginning 'with abounding love') there is a 'characteristic union of the practical and the ideal.   Israel entreats the merciful
Father, out of his very love for the fathers and the children, to
bestow a practical knowledge of his precepts and a power to perform
them.   There is also a yearning for an inward sense of God, that
each man's heart may be one and undivided in love and reverence.
(*Cf.* Psalm lxxxvi. 11.) Israel's mission is at once a life and a creed,
to obey the Law and proclaim the Unity, and Israel's salvation
consists in, or at least is conditioned by, fulfilment of that mission.
Another idea suggested by the words is this.   They breathe the hope
that the hearts of all Israel may be *united* in the love and fear of God,
so that minor differences may not lessen the solidarity of Israel in
its enthusiasm for the mission ' (p. l.).

25.   *Cp.* the passage about ' littleness of faith ' from the Mechilta
on Ex. xvi. 4 (47 b).   In the same passage it is also said : R. Simeon
b. Yochai declared that the Law was given only to the Manna eaters
to study.   Apparently the idea is that they had no worry, and were
not occupied by business cares.   A man sits and studies, and he
knows not whence he may eat and drink, and whence he may be
clothed.   That, it is meant, is the proper attitude of mind. (Yet,
just before, the remark of R. Joshua is given : If a man learns two
Halachah's in the morning and two in the evening, and occupies
himself with his trade all the day, ' they ' reckon it to him as if he
had fulfilled the whole Law.) Those who come next to the Manna
eaters are the *Terumah* eaters (*i.e.* the Priests : they too have not
to worry about their food).   The saying about the Manna eaters
and the *Terumah* eaters is repeated on Ex. xiii. 17.   It is preceded
by the following very curious words : ' God said to himself, If I
bring the Israelites straightway into the Promised Land, they will
occupy it at once, and each man will be busy with his field and his
vineyard, and they will neglect the Law (והן בטלים מן התורה) ; I

will bring them round by the wilderness after forty years, so that they eat manna and drink water, and the Law will be mixed up with (will become inseparable from) their bodies' (והתורה נבללת בגופן) (23 b). A passage from the Testament of Issachar (iv.) is well worth reading, but it would be out of place to quote it here. (In Charles' translation, pp. 105, 106, and in the Oxford edition of the *Apocrypha and Pseudepigrapha*, II. p. 326.) To the Rabbis the ideal life is the study of the Law. To Jesus it is something more broadly human, or something more purely 'moral.' But the conditions for the pursuit of the ideal are much the same. We may also compare the 48 qualifications for the acquisition of the Law. (Aboth vi. 6 ; P.B. p. 206.)

26. The usual parallel for this verse is the well-known end of the Mishnah of Kiddushin (iv. 14, 82 a). ' R. Meir said, Let a man always have his son taught a decent (respectable) and easy handicraft (or occupation), and pray to Him to whom riches and property belong, for there is no occupation from which poverty or riches may not come ; for neither wealth nor poverty come from the occupation, but all is according to desert (וכותו). R. Simeon b. Elazar said, Have you ever seen an animal or a bird which has an occupation (craft) ? Yet they are nourished without worry ; and they have been created only to serve me ; how much more should I, who have been created to serve my Maker, be nourished without worry. But I have corrupted my deeds, and I have impaired (injured) my sustenance.' In the Gemara (82 b) the words are given thus : ' R. Simeon b. Elazar said, In my life I never saw a stag as a dryer of figs, or a lion as a porter, or a fox as a merchant, yet are they all nourished without worry. If they who are created only to serve me are nourished without worry, how much ought I, who am created to serve my Maker, to be nourished without worry, but I have corrupted my ways, and so I have impaired my sustenance.' The conception seems the product of a very simple world ; there are no economic troubles ; only ethical ones. If we were all ' good,' we should all easily find enough to live on without any worry from our respective occupations. Jesus generalizes the idea, and in a sense purifies it. The notion of sin is absent. (*Cp.* Sevenster, p. 124.) He also makes it all the more difficult. For he appears to throw over, like R. Nehorai in the last words of the Mishnah, the idea of working for one's sustenance altogether. (*Cp.* my Com-

mentary, II. pp. 110, 111.)   R. Nehorai said, מניח אני כל אומנות
שבעולם ואיני מלמד את בני אלה תורה.   ' I put aside every occupation
in the world, and teach my son nothing but the Law.   For the
reward (interest) of it a man enjoys in this world, and the capital
remains for him in the world to come.   It is not so with all other
occupations.   If a man is sick and old or suffering, he cannot
practise his occupation, and he dies of hunger.   But the Law keeps
a man from all evil in his youth, and gives him hope and an assured
outlook (אחרית) in his old age.'

30.   In addition to the Mechilta passage, S.B. quote a saying in
Sotah 48 b : ' R. Eliezer the Great said, He who has bread in his
basket (פת בסלו) and says, What shall I eat to-morrow, belongs
to those who are little in faith ' (מקטני אמונה).

33.   ' R. Jonah said in the name of R. Zera : Whoever attends
to his personal affairs before offering his prayers is as though he had
created an idolatrous altar.   He was asked : Dost thou say " an
idolatrous altar " ?   He answered : No, I only mean it is prohibited ; and it is in accordance with the statement of Rab Iddi b.
Abin who said in the name of Rab Isaac b. Ashyan : It is forbidden
a man to attend to his personal affairs before offering his prayers ;
as it is said, " Righteousness shall go before him, and shall make his
footsteps a way " (Ps. lxxxv. 14).   Rab Iddi b. Abin also said in
the name of Rab Isaac b. Ashyan : Whoever prays and afterwards
goes on his way [to attend to his affairs], the Holy One, blessed be
He, attends to them for him, and He shall make his footsteps a way '
(Berachoth 14 a, in Dr. Cohen's translation, p. 90).   ' Our Rabbis have
taught : " And thou shalt gather in thy corn "—What has this
teaching to tell us ?   Since it is written, " This book of the law shall
not depart out of thy mouth [but thou shalt meditate therein day
and night] " (Josh. i. 8), it is possible to think that these words [are
to be understood] as they are written ; therefore there is a teaching
to say, " And thou shalt gather in thy corn," i.e. conduct at the
same time a worldly occupation.   These are the words of R. Ishmael.
R. Simeon b. Yochai says: Is it possible for a man to plough at the
time of ploughing, sow at seed time, reap at harvest time, thresh at
the time of threshing, and winnow at the time of wind—what is to
become of Torah ?   But when Israel perform the will of the All-

present, their work is done by others ; as it is said, " And strangers shall stand and feed your flocks," etc. (Is. lxi. 5) ; and at the time when Israel perform not the will of the All-present, their work has to be done by themselves ; as it is said, " And *thou* shalt gather in thy corn." Not that alone, but the work of others will be done by them ; as it is said, " And thou shalt serve thine enemy," etc. (Deut. xxviii. 48). Abbai said : Many acted in accord with the teaching of R. Ishmael, and it proved efficacious ; but he who acted in accord with R. Simeon b. Yochai did not find it so. Raba said to the Rabbis : I beg of you not to appear before me during the days of Nisan and Tishri, so that you may not be concerned about your maintenance the whole year. Rabbah b. Bar Hannah stated that R. Yochanan said in the name of R. Judah b. R. Ilai : Come and see that the later generations are not like the former generations. The former generations made their Torah their principal concern and their work only occasional, and both flourished in their hand ; whereas the later generations made their work their principal concern and their Torah only occasional, and neither flourished in their hand ' (do. 35 b, p. 237). In other words, the former generations sought first the kingdom of God and his righteousness and the other things were added unto them. The Rabbis express the same idea by different words. The Torah must come first. Yet the general line is according to R. Ishmael's saying : A man should not omit a ' worldly occupation ' altogether. For (a) no salary is to be taken, or gain made, from the study of the Law, and (b) men must all be independent. The less business, however, the better ! ' R. Meir said, Do little in business and be busy with the Law ' (Aboth iv. 12). ' Rabban Gamaliel said, An excellent thing is study of the Law combined with some worldly occupation, for the labour demanded by it makes sin to be forgotten. All study of the Law without work must in the end be futile and become the cause of sin ' (Aboth ii. 2). Quoting Solomon's prayer for wisdom and God's reply, it is rather nicely said in Pesikta R. (59 a) : ' All things are appendices to wisdom,' כל הדברים טפלים לחכמה. A *direct verbal* parallel to the bidding to ' seek first God's kingdom and his righteousness ' does not apparently exist, but the idea was familiar enough. Windisch argues that vi. 33 is not quite on all-fours with 25–32. The eschatological note of 33 is wanting in 25–32, which represent Jesus as a teacher of wisdom—of religious wisdom, *bien entendu*—and are not thinking of the end of the world. The two points of view can be combined, but are really distinct. (Pp. 17, 18.) He has some good remarks upon the differences between Jesus's position and our own in regard to these matters. (Pp. 148, 149, 153, 154.) There is a nice story in Taanith 21 a about R. Yochanan. ' Ilfa and R. Yochanan were greatly distressed by poverty, and therefore said to one another, Let us go into business and thus make true in our own lives the words (Deut. xv. 4) : " Howbeit there shall be no needy among you." They then went and sat down under a ruined wall. While eating, R. Yochanan overheard one angel saying to another, Let us throw down the wall upon them and kill them, for they are going to neglect the life everlasting and busy themselves with the life of the moment. The other angel, however, replied, Let them alone, for one of them has a great future before him. Said R. Yochanan to Ilfa : Did you hear anything ? Ilfa replied, No. R. Yochanan then said to himself, I must be the one with the great future before him ; I will therefore go back (to my studies) and make true of myself the words (Deut. xv. 11) : " For the poor shall never cease out of the land " ' (Dr. Malter's rendering). (For ' a great future before him ' it would be more literal to say ' the hour is favourable.' The words are קיימא ליה שעתא.)

34. Sanhedrin (100 b) quotes a similar adage from Sirach. It does not exist in the Sirach which we possess. ' Do not worry over to-morrow's evil, for you know not what to-day will bring forth. To-morrow perhaps you will not be (alive), and you would have worried for a world which would not be yours.' The equivalent of the second half of the verse is used by Moses against God, when God bids him tell the Israelites that he has been with them in the bondage of Egypt, and that he will be with them in the future bondage of the kingdoms. To which Moses replies : The woe of the hour is enough (דיה לצרה בשעתה). One trouble at a time ! (Berachoth 9 b.) (So S.B.) *Cp.* also Abrahams, *Studies* II. p. 209, and Sevenster, p. 126. He is right as regards the Sanhedrin quotation when he says : ' The advice is the same ; the spirit is not.'

vii. 1–5. There is nothing in these verses which is not entirely on Rabbinic lines. Indeed, the words about ' measure ' and 'meting' are much too Rabbinic! I mean that the doctrine of 'measure for measure' is emphasized too often and too much in the Rabbinic literature, and its truth and virtues are lauded too frequently and unreservedly. Jesus is more original when he attacks 'tit for tat' than when he accepts and uses it. Some Rabbis were so infatuated with the easy and inadequate doctrine of measure for measure that one of them dared to say that all God's measurements, *i.e.* his judgments, are on the principle of tit for tat (כל מדותיו של הקדוש מדה כנגד מדה). (Sanhedrin 90 a.) And another said, 'All measures will cease; but measure for measure will never cease.' 'At the very beginning of his creation of the world God saw that " they " would measure unto man according as he measured' (Genesis בראשית R. ix. 11 on ii. 1). And the Rabbis showed a Mikado-like ingenuity in proving how God made or makes the penalty fit the crime. The subject is unpleasant, and need not further be pursued here. The exaltation of measure for measure is, I suppose, one of the evil effects of Legalism.

Much more pleasant are the parallels to the other portion of the passage. 'Judge not.' The usual Rabbinic wording is rather 'judge favourably'; find kind and favourable explanations for a man's seemingly bad conduct rather than condemn him; 'be lenient in judging.' Thus Hillel said, 'Do not judge (*i.e.* condemn) a man till you yourself have come into his circumstances or situation' (Aboth ii. 5). And the still more famous and favourite adage is that of R. Joshua b. Perachyah: 'Judge every man in the scale of merit' (דן את־כל־אדם לכף זכות). (Aboth i. 6.) 'He who judges his neighbour favourably (לכף זכות) will be judged favourably (by God).' (Sabbath 127 a.) Then follow three stories where appearances speak against a man, but where observers find favourable explanations of his strange conduct, and these explanations turn out to be the true ones. One must always, therefore, try to interpret another's conduct in a good way; that is, judging him ' on the side of merit.' To judge on the side of merit ranks with early attendance at the house of study, visiting the sick, hospitality, devotion (עיון) in prayer, educating sons for the study of the Law, as one of the six things of which a man enjoys the interest in this world while the capital is reserved for him in the world to come. (Sabbath 127 a.) The things are elsewhere given differently. (*Cp.* Peah i. 1, quoted on p. 158 and on p. 318, and Kiddushin 39 b.)

L

The metaphor of the beam and the splinter is also found, and there are others of a corresponding nature. They are all given by S.B. ' Rabbi Tarphon doubted whether anyone in his generation could bear reproof. If a man said to his neighbour, Take away the splinter from your eye, the other would reply, Remove the beam from your eye ' (Arachin 16 b. *Cp.* Baba Batra 15 b). Jer. Taanith ii. 1, 65 a, foot : ' Remove the burrs from yourself before you remove them from others ' (נתקושש גרמך עד דלא נקושש חורנין). (It is a play on Zep. ii. 1.) So Sanhedrin 18 a, 19 a : ' Clean yourself, before you seek to clean others.' (*Cp.* Baba Mezia 107 b, foot ; Baba Batra 60 b.) The story in the last passage which ends with the adage is not given by S.B., but is very characteristic. ' R. Yannai had a tree the branches of which leant over the public way, and another man had a similar tree. Then the people came to the other man, and told him to remove it. He came to R. Yannai, who said to him, Go away now, but come again to-morrow. During the night the Rabbi had his own tree cut down. When the man came again, R. Yannai said, Cut down your tree. Then the man said, You have a similar tree. Then R. Yannai said, Go and look. If my tree is not cut down, do not cut yours down. Why did R. Yannai change his mind ? Before, he thought that the people liked the tree, because they could sit in its shade, but when he found that they disliked the trees, he cut his tree down. Why did he not say to the man, You cut yours down, and then I will cut mine down ? Because of a teaching of Resh Lakish who said, First clean yourself, and then clean others.'

R. Nathan said,' A blemish which you have yourself do not ascribe to your neighbour ' (מום שבך אל תאמר לחברך). (Baba Mezia 59 b.) ' He who pollutes another is polluted ; he never speaks praise-worthily ' (כל הפוסל פסול). (Kiddushin 70 a and b.)

6. S.B. quote rather an interesting parallel from Jer. Abodah Zarah ii. 8, 41 d, beg., based on a fanciful interpretation of Exodus xxi. 1. ' Even as a treasure must not be shown to everyone, so with the words of the Law : one must not go profoundly into them except in the presence of suitable people ' (אין לך רשות לשקע את עצמך בדברי תורה אלא לפני בני אדם כשירין).

7–11. On the subject of prayer Jesus spoke as the child of his age. Or we may say that he spoke on the lines of the Rabbis. Naturally, being what he was, a man of great religious power, fervour, and purity, he expressed the best current Rabbinic ideas with beauty and vividness. But anyone who reads the parallels which honest S.B. bring together for 7-11 can hardly say that Jesus goes much beyond what we find there, or says anything really new. Doubtless some of the rather trivial and foolish things which, among the mass of material about prayer, can be fished up out of the Rabbinic sea, are absent from 7-11, but on the other hand, the Rabbis have some touching sayings about God and prayer which are peculiar to themselves. A complete belief in the ' efficacy ' of prayer was common to both Jesus and the Rabbis. Any idea of the value of prayer as consisting merely in its effect upon the man who prays was equally far both from Jesus and the Rabbis. Both Jesus and Rabbis equally believed that prayer was heard and answered by God, and that it was what God *did* in reply to the prayer which constituted its essence and its success. The efficacy of prayer is due to God and to the action of God.

Perhaps it may be well to quote some of the ' nice ' passages given by S.B., and also a few others from my own reading which they do not appear to have included.

The idol is near, and is yet far. God is far (for is he not in the heaven of heavens ?), and yet he is near. For a man enters a synagogue, and stands behind a pillar, and prays in a whisper, and God hears his prayer, and so it is with all his creatures. ' Can there be a nearer God than this ? He is as near to his creatures as the ear to the mouth ' (Jer. Berachoth ix. § 1, 13 a). ' In every place where thou findest the impress (רושם) of the feet of a man, there am I before thee ' (Mechilta, 52 b ; Moore I. 371). God needs no intermediaries. A man need not be introduced to him by anybody else : no one need ' announce ' him to God. ' If a man is in distress, let him not call on Michael or Gabriel, but let him call direct on me, and I will hearken to him straightway ' (do.). ' Human beings can hardly hear two people talking at once, but God, if all the world calls to him at one time, hears their cry ' (Mechilta on Exodus xv. 11 ; 41 b). A man has a " Patron." If he worries him too much, the Patron is annoyed, but not so with God. ' A man who worries him he receives ' (Midrash Psalms iv. 3, 21 b). ' A man is annoyed by being worried by the requests of his friend, but with God, all the time a man puts his needs and requests before him, God loves him all the more ' (do.). ' Man makes distinctions between rich and poor : not so God. Before him all are equal. Women and slaves ; rich and poor ; in prayer all are equal before God ' (הכל שוין בתפלה לפני המקום). (Exodus R. בשלח xxi. on xiv. 15.) ' A man must purify his heart before he prays ' (do. בשלח xxii. on xiv. 31 *fin.*). ' If a man turns his heart in prayer, his prayers will be answered' (Midrash Psalms x. 16, 49 a). (כוון אדם לבו בתפלה יהא מבושר שנשמעה תפלתו.) ' Prayer is the service of the heart ' (Taanith 2 a). The whole passage from which these words are taken should be read in Malter's edition and rendering. ' Better is one hour of prayer than good works.' Not because of all his good works, but because of his prayer, was Moses supposed to have been allowed to view the promised land. (Sifre 71 b.) In the Mishnah of Berachoth iv. 4 R. Eliezer says that if a man makes his prayer a fixed task (קבע) his prayer is no supplication. The Gemara asks what *keba* means. The replies are suggestive. (1) If the prayer is a burden, (2) If the prayer is not said as if it were a supplication, (3) If a man does not add something new to his prayer. (Berachoth 29 b.) (4) If a prayer is read as if it were a letter or a legal document (איגרת). One Rabbi said, One should say something new every day. Rabbi Eliezer said a new prayer every day. R. Abbahu said a new bene- diction every day. (Jer. Berachot iv. 3, 8 a *fin.*) ' He who prays must direct his heart to heaven ' (Berachoth 31 a). ' Greater is prayer than good deeds and sacrifices ' (do. 32 b). ' Prayer like study, good deeds and worldly occupation, needs effort ' (חזוק) (do.). But it also needs humility. (' Man's prayer is not heard unless he makes his heart (soft) as flesh.' Sotah 5 a.) ' To thee shall all flesh come.' Why all flesh, and not all men ? ' To show that prayer is only then heard if a man makes his heart soft like flesh ' (Midrash Psalms lxv. (2), verse 3, 156 b). Nevertheless, as is implied in Luke xi. 8, importunity avails in prayer. *Chutzpah* (חוצפא) (shamelessness) helps even with God. Is there a father who ever hates his son ? (חוצפא אפילו כלפי שמיא). (Sanhedrin 105 a.) *Chutzpah* conquers badness ; how much more the goodness of the world (*i.e.* God). (Pesikta 161 a, and *cp.* Jer. Taanith 65 b.) ' God said to Moses, when Moses prayed to God that he might enter the promised land, Let it suffice thee ; speak no more unto me of this matter. Yet did Moses not cease to seek compassion from God.

How much less should the rest of mankind cease to keep on praying '
(Sifre 71 b). Yet the Rabbis realized that a prayer which asked for
something that was not desirable for a man to have, God would not
grant. Thus Solomon said to God, ' When an Israelite comes to
the Temple and prays for sons or for anything else, if it is fitting
(ראוי), give it to him ; if it is not fitting, do not give it him. But
if the foreigner comes, give him whatever he asks.' (This is elicited
from the wording in 1 Kings viii. 39–43.) The reason is that the
foreigner, if he does not get what he asks, will be angry, and say,
' I came from the ends of the earth to Solomon's temple, and I have
fared no better than in a heathen temple.' But if he gets what he asks
for, he will believe in God. But the Israelite, like the righteous Jacob,
even if God refused his request or chastized him, will not quarrel
with (לא קורא תגר אחר מדת הדין) the divine attribute of justice.
(Tanchuma B. *Toledoth* xiv. 67 b and parallels ; Moore II. p. 233.)
One must not take too seriously any passages in which the gates of
prayer are spoken of as not always open. Such phrases are only
used paradoxically in relation to something which is even greater than
prayer and includes it. For instance : ' The gates of prayer may be
locked, the gates of tears remain unlocked' (Berachoth 32 b). Or
' The gates of prayer are sometimes open and sometimes shut, but
the gates of compassion are never shut' (Midrash Psalms iv. 3,
22 a). ' Prayer is like a public bath, repentance like the sea. The
bath is sometimes open, sometimes shut ; the sea is always open.
So the gates of prayer are sometimes open and sometimes shut ;
the gates of repentance are always open. But others say the gates
of prayer are also always open ' (Lamentations Rabba on iii. 43, 44).
One should never be too tired to pray. ' God says : You are not
tired of doing your own business all day, but to pray before me you
are too tired.' (Introduction, § 10, Wuensche, p. 9). These quotations
are sufficient. I do not mean to imply that you cannot find some
disagreeable, particularistic things about prayer in the Rabbinic
literature, and some foolish or superstitious things, but, taken as
a whole, the Rabbinical teachings on this subject are fine and pure,
if also, like those of Jesus, simple and almost naïve in their absolute
faith in the power and omniscience of God.

11. The story of the man who, in a time of drought when a
fast had been proclaimed, which had not produced rain, and when

R. Tanchuma had urged everyone to do some good or merciful deed, saw, spoke with, and gave money to, his divorced wife, is referred to by S.B., with its touching close. Some informer tells the Rabbi how suspiciously the man has acted (one may not have any dealings with one's divorced wife). The man justifies himself : she was in sore distress. The Rabbi prays : 'If this man who is but flesh and blood and hard (*i.e.* as opposed to God), yet has given help to his divorced wife, to whom he was under no obligation, how much more shouldest thou, whose obligation it is to sustain us, have pity on the children of thy children, Abraham, Isaac and Jacob' (Lev. R., בהר, xxxiv. 14, towards the end, on xxv. 39).

12. As to the Golden Rule I have nothing to add to what I said in the Commentary ; the best words about it are those of Dr. Abrahams in *Studies*, who occupies a sane middle position between the Christian and the Jewish apologists. The famous story about Hillel and Shammai runs thus : 'A heathen came to Shammai, and said, I am prepared to be received as a proselyte on the condition that you teach me the whole law while I stand on one leg. Shammai drove him away with a foot-rule (אמת הבנין) which he had in his hand. He went to Hillel who received him as a proselyte. He said to him, What is hateful to yourself, do to no other : that is the whole Law, and the rest is commentary. Go and learn ' (דעלך סני לחברך לא תעביד). It is one of three similar stories of proselytes who, making silly conditions, are driven away by Shammai and accepted by Hillel. And all three exclaim : ' The wrath of Shammai would have driven us from the world, the gentleness of Hillel has brought us under the wings of the Divine Being.' קפדנותו של שמאי בקשה לטורדנו מן העולם ענוותנותו של הלל) (קרבנו תחת כנפי השכינה. (Sabbath 31 a.) S.B. honestly point out that the letter of Aristeas really contains a combination of the Rule both in its positive and negative form. (§ 207.) To the question of the king, τί ἐστι σοφίας διδαχή; the reply is, καθὼς οὐ βούλει σεαυτῷ τὰ κακὰ παρεῖναι, μέτοχος δὲ τῶν ἀγαθῶν ὑπάρχειν ἁπάντων, εἰ πράσσοις τοῦτο πρὸς τοὺς ὑποτεταγμένους καὶ τοὺς ἁμαρτάνοντας, εἰ τοὺς καλοὺς καὶ ἀγαθοὺς τῶν ἀνθρώπων ἐπιεικέστερον νουθετοῖς· καὶ γὰρ ὁ θεὸς τοὺς ἀνθρώπους ἅπαντας ἐπιεικείᾳ ἄγει.

S.B. also quote from Aboth and Aboth R. Nathan. ' R. Eliezer said, Let the honour of thy neighbour be as dear to thee as thine own. As a man has pleasure in his own honour, so let him have pleasure in the honour of his neighbour. As a man has pleasure in [the welfare of] his own family, so let a man have pleasure in the [welfare of] the family of his neighbour' (Aboth ii. 10, 11 and 15, and Aboth R. Nathan xv. 30 a (*init.*), xvi. 31 b (*init.*)).

Kittel, with his usual fairness, makes the following remarks about the positive and negative form of the Golden Rule. ' In Wirklichkeit dürfte fast alles, was man an Nüancierung empfinden zu müssen glaubte, moderne Reflexion sein. Für das Bewusstsein der Zeit Jesu waren beide Formen des Spruches kaum unterschieden. Dafür ist Beweis die Tatsache, dass im ältesten Christentum der Spruch promiskue überliefert worden ist' (p. 109). . . . ' Dem antiken Menschen liegt der Gedanke an einen Unterschied beider Formen völlig fern' (p. 110).[1] (*Cp.* Moore II. p. 87.) The reply to this on the Christian side would, I suppose, be that it is the gift of genius to speak words the full significance of which is revealed only in the future, and is not even consciously present to the mind of the speaker.

It may be noted that duty or morality can be summed up in other ways than by the Golden Rule. One might adduce R. Simeon b. Gamaliel's saying, ' By three things is the world preserved, by truth, by justice, by peace' (Aboth I. 18); or, again, ' What did the Law say to the Israelites ? Take upon you the yoke of the kingdom of heaven, and excel (הכריעו) one another in the fear of heaven and practise loving deeds towards one another ' (Sifre 138 b ; Moore II. pp. 86, 173, 174).

13, 14. The words in their mournful exclusiveness are plain enough. They can but mean that, according to Jesus, the large majority of the men and women then existing on the earth would walk along the path which led to destruction, and would reach their goal. There is no indication that they would ever be saved from, or be pulled out of, destruction, or that they would ever reach

---

[1] 'In reality almost everything which has been thought to exist in delicate difference between the negative and positive form is due to modern reflection on the subject. For the consciousness of the age of Jesus the two forms were scarcely distinguishable. The proof of that is that in the oldest Christian literature the two forms are recorded promiscuously. The idea of a difference between them was quite unapparent to the men of antiquity.'

'life'—namely, 'eternal life.' How this mournful doctrine can be reconciled with the doctrine of an all-powerful, all-wise, and all-beneficent God is a mystery. Directly the glaring inconsistency is perceived, there must be an end to either one doctrine or to the other. You cannot exculpate God by saying that such 'destruction' is man's own fault, or that it is the condition of moral freedom and of righteousness. For the God of Jesus was under no compulsion to have created the world at all, and he had foreknowledge. A God who deliberately created rational beings of whom he foreknew that they would end in ἀπώλεια, in destruction, seems to me doubtfully good. Even if ἀπώλεια means annihilation, the absolute extinction of all memory and consciousness and 'life,' at what an appalling cost do the few find bliss. If, however, ἀπώλεια meant to Jesus something more, *abiding* pain or punishment, then I see no excuse for God at all. And yet there is no doubt that there have been heaps of people who believed (whatever Jesus may have believed) that ἀπώλεια did and does mean abiding pain and punishment, and yet believed in a perfect and loving God! Poor human nature and its immense capacity of illogicality! I wonder if some are right in thinking that I, in my beliefs, am guilty of illogicality no smaller. I hope it may not be so.

As regards the Rabbis, were they, in this respect, better than Jesus? Hardly. The Rabbis too knew of the two ways, of which one led to Paradise, the other to Gehinnom, one the way of Life and one the way of Death. (Deut. xxx. 19.) We have the power to choose on which way we will elect to walk. The matter, they say, is like one 'who sits at a cross-way (פרשת דרכים), and before him lie two paths; the one is at the beginning smooth, but ends in thorns, and the other begins in thorns and ends plain and smooth' (Sifre 86 a; Moore I. p. 454). Moreover, the Rabbis thought that most pagans were bad people; their idolatry was their sin, and with idolatry usually went immorality and other wickedness. Also, they were usually oppressors of Israel, and so, on every count, the enemies of God. So far as the Jews were concerned, I fancy they believed that all Israel, barring the worst sinners, would, either at once after death, or after a purgatorial period, obtain the bliss of the world to come, and would, after the final 'resurrection of the dead,' enjoy everlasting life. Moreover, to the repentant sinner God is ever willing to show mercy.

Hence the number of excluded Israelites would be a small minority. But the number of included pagans (to say nothing of heretics, apostates, and informers) would also be a small minority. So if you take the total number of living men and women in any one generation, the percentage of the 'saved' to the Rabbis would probably have not been so very much greater than the percentage of the 'saved' to Jesus. It is a very painful subject.

Windisch points out that the pessimism of these verses is in contrast with the general spirit of the Sermon, which is optimistic. But the verses do not imply that the 'demands' are not fulfillable: they only state that they will not be fulfilled except by a very few. (P. 70.) (*Cp.* Luke xiii. 24.)

13. To the actual metaphor of the two ways there are several Rabbinic parallels. But I do not find any which are as cheerless as the metaphor in Matthew. It is nowhere, I think, said that those who choose the good way which ends in the eternal beatitudes are few, while those who choose the evil way which leads to perdition are many. Apart from the question of Israel's enemies, the outlook of the Rabbis was less sombre than the outlook of Jesus, if indeed Matt. vii. 13 justly represents his usual line.

15-20. For my purposes it is unnecessary to consider any parallels to these verses. The maxim, 'By their fruits ye shall know them,' would be quite in accordance with Rabbinic teaching. The test is the deed. Even study must be put on one side for a deed of kindness, just as to teach is greater than to learn. One Rabbi wanted a dead Rabbi to appear to him in a dream. They said, 'You are not worthy.' When he asked 'Why? Have I not learnt as much as he, and did I not travel as far in order to learn?' They replied, 'You travelled to learn; he travelled to teach' (Eccles. R. on ix. 10). The second half of Prov. xxix. 4 is said to refer to the wise man who is learned in Halachah, in Midrash, and Agadah. An orphan and a widow came before him, and asked him to plead their cause. He replied, 'I am occupied with the Mishnah; I have no leisure. Of him God says, I reckon it to thee as if thou hadst destroyed the world.' (Exodus R., משפטים, xxx. 13 on xxii. 1.)

21-23. Here, too, I need not seek for parallels. Profession of faith is not conclusive ; nor are exorcisms and miracles proof of true discipleship. Holy deeds are test and proof. That too would be approved by the Rabbis.

24–27. The emphasis upon deeds is continued and deepened by the concluding words and simile. The doctrine is still Rabbinic. It is prophetic doctrine, which both Judaism and Christianity have required and require to keep before them, and which both have often neglected. οὐ πᾶς ὁ λέγων μοι κύριε κύριε : these words may be enlarged in their scope to signify that credal orthodoxy is of much less consequence in God's eyes, and in the eyes of the noblest teachers of religion, than holy deeds. In the case of Judaism the antithesis would be far less between holy deeds and orthodoxy *in creed*, than between holy deeds and orthodoxy in ritual practice and outward conformity. It is not unnatural that this prophetic antithesis is not represented in the Rabbinical literature. As I have so often pointed out, if the inspired and perfect word of God tells you in one and the same breath to love your neighbour as yourself and not to wear a ' mixed ' garment, how can *you*, believing firmly in the binding character, divine origin, and consummate perfection of both laws, greatly distinguish between them ? How can you make any trenchant contrast between the moral and the ceremonial ? Just in the same way it was not (I fancy) till modern times, and till dogmas began to lose their hold, that the Christian antithesis could be made between the imitation of Christ in holy deeds and the belief in doctrines *about* Christ and his nature and about such complicated matters as the Atonement and the Trinity. The antithesis in the Gospel was not effectively continued and maintained. And would any believing Roman Catholic to-day say that it does not so much matter what you believe about the nature of the Christ so long as you imitate his life ? It is true that the end of chapter vii. 21–27 does not say, ' It does not matter whether you call Jesus Lord or not.' It only says that ' in addition to calling him Lord and hearkening to his words, you must do holy deeds.' Nevertheless, even with this limitation, the antithesis is sufficiently remarkable, and perhaps it is all the more remarkable if the seven verses are all, or are mainly, later than Jesus himself. The emphasis upon doing is undoubtedly one side of the *Jewish* element in Matthew. In the Rabbinic literature the antithesis is not between hearing and doing, but between 'study' and doing—between learning and doing. Considering the enormous stress which the Rabbis laid upon the study of the Law, it is remarkable that many of them thought that doing was still more important than learning; or, again, that if learning was more important than doing, this was only because it was primary, seeing that, without a basis of study, doing could hardly be maintained and continued. How could the Law be fulfilled if all were ignorant of it ? This does not seem unreasonable. S.B., who give all the salient passages, attempt to show that, while the earlier Rabbis undoubtedly held that doing was more important than learning, after the Hadrianic revolt, when for a time the study of the Law was so rigidly forbidden, the tide of opinion changed, and that henceforth learning was regarded as more important than doing. It is at least doubtful whether this distinction and difference can be maintained. They quote for the earlier period Aboth i. 17. Simeon, Rabban Gamaliel's son, said, ' Not learning, but doing, is the chief thing ' (עֲקָר). (This is a very famous sentence.) And iii. 11, ' R. Chanina, the son of Dosa, said, He in whom the fear of sin comes before wisdom, his wisdom shall endure ; but he in whom wisdom comes before the fear of sin, his wisdom shall not endure. He used to say, He whose works exceed his wisdom, his wisdom shall endure ; but he whose wisdom exceeds his works, his wisdom will not endure ' (P.B. p. 192 *ad fin.*, 193 *init.*). And, again (iii. 21, 22), R. Elazar, the son of Azariah, used to say, ' Where there is no wisdom, there is no fear of God. Where there is no fear of God, there is no wisdom. He whose wisdom exceeds his works, to what is he like ? To a tree whose branches are many but whose roots are few ; and the wind comes and plucks it up and overturns it upon its face, as it is said, And he shall be like a lonely juniper tree in the desert, and shall not see when good comes ; but shall inhabit the parched places in the wilderness, a salt land and not inhabited (Jer. xvii. 6). But he whose works exceed his wisdom, to what is he like ? To a tree whose branches are few, but whose roots are many, so that even if all the winds in the world come and blow upon it, it cannot be stirred from its waters ; and that spreads out its roots by the river, and shall not perceive when heat comes, but his leaf shall be green ; and shall not be troubled in the year of drought, neither shall cease from yielding fruit (Jer. xvii. 8) ' (P.B. p. 194). In

Aboth R. Nathan xxiv. (39 a) there are other similar metaphors put in the mouth of R. Elisha b. Abuyah. Always the moral is that he who has learnt much Torah, but has no good works, is not proof against temptation, or rather his knowledge is of slight avail. It is like a man who builds first with bricks and then with stones : the floods soon wash away his building. Or : a man who has both learning and good deeds is like chalk put upon stones : the rain cannot wash it from its place ; he who has learning and no good deeds is like chalk put upon bricks : even a little rain washes it all away. We may note that nothing is said of the man who has good deeds, but no learning, just as Jesus says nothing of the man who lives a holy life, but would refuse to call him Lord. We might, however, notice the last of the curious responses of R. Yochanan b. Zakkai. The wise man who is a sin fearer is like a craftsman who has the tools of his craft ready in his hand. The wise man who is not sin fearing is like a craftsman who has no tools. And, finally, the sin fearer who has no wisdom is like a man who has the tools, but is no craftsman. (He has the will, but does not know what he ought to do.) (Aboth R. Nathan xxii. 37 b *fin.* *Cp.* Exodus R. xl. R. Yochanan said, ' He who knows the Law, but does not according to the Law—it were better for him that he had never been born.' ' R. Hoshaya said, Everyone who knows, and has no fear of sin, has nothing. Every craftsman who has not his tools is no craftsman.') ' R. Elisha b. Abuyah said that a man who has learnt much Torah and has good deeds is like a horse which has reins (בלינום, χαλινός). The man who has the first, but not the second, is like a horse without reins : it soon throws the rider over its head.' (Aboth R. Nathan xxiv. 39 a.) On Leviticus xviii. 4 the Sifra 85 d has the words : ' Not learning is the leader : doing is the leader (to the blessings of the life to come)' (לא המשנה נגוד המעשה נגוד). *Cp.* a few extra passages given on Matt. xxiii. 3. ' Rabba b. R. Huna said, He who has knowledge of the Law, but no fear of God, is like a keeper of a treasury, who has the inner keys, but not the outer keys. He cannot enter.' (Sabbath 31 b, top.) Quaint is the passage in Leviticus R. xxv. about the man who has committed a sin for which the punishment is being ' cut off ' by God. What is he to do ? If he is wont to study either Bible or Mishnah, let him read twice as much as before each day ; but if not, let him become a head of a community or a collector of public alms (פרנס על הציבור וגבאי של

צדקה). For in Deut. xxvii. 26 the curse runs, not against him who does not learn the words of the Law, but against him who does not fulfil them ; if it said, A tree of life is the Law for him who studies it, then there would be no chance for him (survival, power of resistance, see Leviticus xxvi. 37) (לא היתה תקומה), but it says ' for them who take hold of it (*i.e.* do it). (Therefore good deeds will help his case.) It is recorded of R. Judah that when he was teaching his disciples, and a funeral or a marriage procession passed, he would interrupt his lecture to say, ' Doing goes before learning ' (the duty of following the dead to the grave, or of following the bridal procession, even goes before the study of the Law). (Jer. Chagigah i. § 7, 76 c.)

S.B. give several quotations which speak of learning as more important than doing, and it is a fact that the large majority of these are later in date than the majority of those which speak of doing as more important than learning. But not many of them appear to consider learning as more *important* than doing in any literal sense. There was, first of all, the view that learning is the condition of doing. Secondly there was, undoubtedly, I think, the view that learning or study (of the Law) was more *glorious* than doing. It was not for a moment meant that doing was not indispensable, or that a man's sins and frailties could, and would, and should, be condoned by God and men if only he were learned. The view was that the learned man must be good ; he must most certainly not transgress and do wrong. That is a *sine qua non*. But wisdom was even greater than practical goodness. Just as Aristotle thought that θεωρία was greater than πράξις, so some Rabbis thought that study was greater than doing. The subject-matter of wisdom is very limited : it is only Torah and all that Torah includes, but within that limit there is a distinctly intellectual element in the Rabbinic religion. The ideal is study, learning for its own sake, and there *is* a sense in which the study of the Law transcends its practice. To that extent S.B. are right. The good feeling of the Rabbis was always strong enough to make them realize that righteousness, and the love of God, and the love of neighbour, come first in the list of duties, but, nevertheless, breaking through, or co-ordinate with, this consciousness and conviction, was the passionate devotion to, or glorification of, the Law and its study. (And by Law all branches of sacred learning must be included : the whole Scripture and the interpretation of it : halachic and haggadic.) This was their very life : they *were* students ; they *were* theologians. How could they, with their beliefs about that Law and its divinity, not think that the study of it was not the greatest and holiest thing to which a man could devote his energies and his life ?

S.B. quote first of all the famous passage about R. Tarphon and R. Akiba and the Rabbis, how they sat in the upper chamber (בעלית) of the house of Nitza in Lydda, and the question was raised : Is study (תלמוד) greater, or doing ? R. Tarphon said : doing was greater. Akiba said : study was greater. Then they all said that study was greater for it led to doing (שהתלמוד מביא לידי מעשה) (Kiddushin 40 b). (' Faith leads to deed '.) On Exodus xv. 26 the Mechilta observes (46 a), 'If thou wilt diligently hearken.' The Hebrew is אם שמוע תשמע. R. Elazar b. Modin said, If it were only שמוע, one could imagine it were in your option to hear or not to hear. Therefore it says תשמע thou *shalt* hear, it is duty (חובה) and not option (רשות). ' Thou *shalt* hear.' That is the general principle in which all the Law is contained (זה הכלל שהתורה כלולה בו). (Hearing involves study.) But R. Jonathan said that the famous words in Joshua i. 8, ' Thou shalt meditate therein (the Law) day and night,' were not command or obligation (חובה), but blessing. They meant that because Joshua loved the words of the Law so much, therefore they should never depart out of his mouth. ' In the school of R. Ishmael it was taught that the words of the Law are not to be unto you an obligation, but, on the other hand, you are not free to dispense yourself from them ' (Menachoth 99 b ; Moore II. p. 240). ' R. Yose of Galilee said, Study is greater than doing ' (Sifre 79 b). Again, on the words ' That ye may learn them and observe to do them ' (Deut. v. 1) it is said, ' The Scripture shows here that doing depends upon learning, and not *vice versa* ; and we find that the punishment for not learning is heavier than that for not doing.' (I omit the fanciful proof.) (Sifre 79 a.) In the well-known saying already (p. 145) quoted (Mishnah Peah i. 1) about the good deeds of which the fruit is enjoyed in this world and the capital remains for the life to come, the study of the Law comes last, but ' it is equal to all the others ' (כנגד כולם). ' R. Yochanan said : The Law is greater than the commandments (המצות), for a commandment stands to the Law as a lamp to the sun ' (Midrash Psalms

xvii. 12, 66 b). But the story in Aboth R. Nathan xli., as given by S.B. (iii. p. 87), depends on a mistaken text or reading, and is not in point. (See Schechter's note 2 to version I on p. 65 b of his edition.) And the story about R. Abbahu cannot be used as S.B. (*ib.*) wish to use it. He sent his son to Tiberias to study : the son, it was reported, occupied his time in good works (burying the dead, visiting the sick, etc.). R. Abbahu sent to him to say 'Are there no graves in Caesarea that I sent you to Tiberias ? ' Quite a sensible message. As if a man sent his son to Oxford, and the son occupied himself with good works and neglected his studies. The father could justly complain. Moreover, the Rabbis in Caesarea said : What you, R. Abbahu, say is justified if there was anybody else to do the 'loving deeds,' but if there was not, then doing goes before study. (Jer. Chagigah i. § 7, 76 c.) Even as the punishment for not studying is greater than that for not doing, so too is the reward for study greater than the reward for doing. (Sifre 79 b.) No doubt one can find isolated sayings of this kind. Again, one Rabbi said : ' The whole world is not equal to one word of the Law.' Another said : ' [The doing of] all the *commandments* of the Torah is not equal to one *word* of the Torah ' (Jer. Peah i. 1, 15 d). As study precedes doing (קודם ל'), so judgment about study precedes judgment about doing. ' R. Hamnuna said, The beginning of judgment upon a man is for [his neglect of the study of] the words of the Law, and as the judgment upon study precedes that on doing, so its reward precedes the reward of doing.' (Kiddushin 40 b.) In spite of sayings such as these, the ethical sense of the Rabbis was always keen and strong and pure. Their general view is well summed up in Sifre 84 b. ' Why is it said, Ye shall diligently keep the commandments of the Lord your God—to do them ? (Deut. vi. 17, xi. 22). One might suppose : if a man guards (keeps) the words of the Law, he need not do them. Therefore it says, To do them. So you must do them. If a man learns the words of the Torah, he has fulfilled one command, if he learns and guards them, he has fulfilled two ; if he learns and guards and does them, there is no one greater than he ' (אין למעלה הימנו). Doubtless, as to other scholars, ' study ' was for *them* the chief duty and glory of life, and the 'Law' was the greatest of God's creations and gifts. But it is also true that the needs of the poor and the needy, and the demands of love (*chesed*), were always regarded as unconditionally imperative. They had to be fulfilled. And if they could not be fulfilled except at the cost of ' study,' I think that almost every Rabbi would have said that study must, for the time being, be postponed.

Every now and then, Windisch, in spite of his remarkable fairness, says things to which I must take exception. For instance, he remarks : ' So sehr das Prinzip der radikalen Hingabe auch schon im Gesetz betont war, so neu und so fremd war den Juden doch die konsequente Anwendung auf die Verhältnisse des konkreten Lebens ' (p. 108).[1] But for this statement he brings no evidence. And this is what we must always demand. Sweeping generalizations are easy to make ; but should they be made without the chapter and verse ? The ' demands ' about alms, forgiveness, lustful thoughts, truthfulness, prayer, at any rate, were neither new nor strange in their consistent application to the circumstances of practical life. And, indeed, Windisch's paeans about such points in the Sermon as God's forgiveness sometimes strike a Jewish reader as exceedingly odd. For *to Jews* all the teaching here is the most natural thing in the world. It is so essential a part of Judaism that they cannot inordinately praise any one teacher who enunciates it.

The summing up on p. 111 would need a long chapter for adequate discussion. Windisch says : ' Die Bergrede enhält viel Jüdisches, aber als Ganzes ist sie antijüdisch. Der Talmud befasst viel " Christliches," als Ganzes ist er antichristlich.'[2] The second sentence is truer than the first. The Talmud (it is curious how some sort of strange horror seems still to cling to the Talmud, though not to the Rabbinic literature as a whole. *Cp.* the odd attempt to differentiate between the Talmud and the other Rabbinic books on p. 98) is anti-Christian, if Christianity involves the belief in the Deity of Jesus, in the Atonement, and in the Trinity. It is anti-Christian also if Christianity involves the denial of the perpetual obligation upon Jews to observe the whole Law, both moral and ceremonial, or if it involves a denial of the plenary inspiration and divine perfection of the entire Law. Therefore there is much to be said for the view that the ' Talmud '—I should prefer to say Rabbinic Judaism—is

[1] ' Though the principle of unqualified devotion is emphasized in the Law, its consistent application to the conditions of concrete life was new and strange for the Jews.'

[2] ' The Sermon on the Mount contains much Jewish material, but as a whole it is anti-Jewish. The Talmud contains much that is " Christian," but as a whole it is anti-Christian.'

anti-Christian. But it is not anti-Christian if you mean by anti-Christian that there is any large and essential difference (apart from any question of the Law, and apart from any question about his own person and authority) between the religious and ethical teaching of Jesus and the best religious and ethical teaching of the Rabbis. And that is why the first statement that the Sermon as a whole is anti-Jewish is inaccurate. I have, I think, successfully shown that the spirit of the Sermon is Jewish—in full accordance with the highest teachings of the O.T. and of the Rabbis. We *must* avoid these tempting antitheses and contrasts. They are very rarely true.

The "Nachwert zur Bergpredigt " in S.B. (pp. 470–474) is interesting and honest, but vitiated by the contrast which the author seeks to make between the teaching of Jesus and the teaching of the Rabbis, and more especially between the *Gesetzesgerechtigkeit* of the Rabbis and the new righteousness of Jesus. That there *was* a difference in the attitude towards the Law between Jesus and the Rabbis is true. I have repeatedly called attention to it and to the inevitable conflict which ensued. Indeed, the antagonism of the Rabbis to Jesus, and their share in his death, were very largely due to this difference of opinion about the Law. Nevertheless, B. exaggerates. For he misinterprets the inner meaning of the Rabbinic legalism. As an orthodox Lutheran theologian, drenched by the doctrines of Paul, and passionately attached to them, it is hard for him fully to appreciate the Rabbinic point of view. Otherwise he could scarcely have called the ethical teaching of the Rabbis a mere *Aufputz* to their nomistic or legalistic *Lehrgebäude*. For the two form a whole, a unity : you cannot say where one begins and the other ends. The nomistic *Lehrgebäude* is itself ethical. If, indeed, the Law were an external body of rules given by a non-ethical and non-beloved, but exceedingly powerful and divine, authority, who, if you observe his law, would give you eternal sugar-plums, and, if you disobey it, would send you to eternal flames, then all that B. says would be true. Then the ethical teachings might be mere *Aufputz* to the nomistic *Lehrgebäude*. But if the authority is believed to be adorably good, loving, and merciful, and if it is immensely beloved, if to obey its rules is not merely duty, but also gratitude and joy and privilege, then the antithesis falls to the ground. And this is what the Law was. Doubtless God does send the high-

M

handed and unrepentant violator of the Law to hell; doubtless he
does give blissful and eternal sugar-plums to those who obey it:
but the better spirits among the Rabbis did not obey it for that
reason; they obeyed it because to do so was high joy and delightful
privilege and altogether adorable. This, on the one hand; on the
other hand, Jesus was no Paul. In spite of Matt. v. 20, he never
really taught, like Paul, a theoretic antagonism to the Law. *Cp.*
Fridrichsen in *Congrès d'Histoire du Christianisme*, I. p. 172: 'Nous
voyons qu'il n'est pas question, comme chez Paul, d'une justice
entièrement différente de la justice juive, et entièrement originale
par rapport à elle; il n'est question que d'une justice *meilleure*.
C'est évidemment le Judéo-christianisme qui parle ici. Ignorant
l'opposition de principe entre Christianisme et Judaïsme, il veut
être un Judaïsme supérieur, purifié, accompli.' It is just and true
when B. says: 'In demütigem Vertrauen auf die Gnade Gottes
sollen die Seinen alle Güter und Segnungen des Himmelreichs aus
der Hand ihres himmlischen Vaters hinnehmen, um dann in kind-
licher, dankbarer Gegenliebe Gott zu dienen und zu leben in auf-
richtiger Gottesfurcht und in rechtschaffener Nächstenliebe' (p.
473).[1]   But no Rabbi would have objected to such a statement.
'Those are my views too,' he would have said. 'For I too believe
in the grace (*Gnade*) of God; I too depend on it. Do I not repeat
every day the words: Not relying on our righteous acts do we lay
our supplications before thee, but relying on thine abundant mercies?'
The antithesis which B. constructs is a false antithesis.

In other respects, over against, *e.g.*, the exaggerations of a Tal,
B. is right enough. The teaching of Jesus is original both in what
it says, and in what it does not say: it is original in its bulk as
coming essentially from one man, or as constructed in his spirit;
it is original in certain definite enunciations and demands; it is
original in its combinations and as a whole; it is original in its
pronouncedly prophetic and anti-ceremonial utterances and spirit;
and if it is taken sentence by sentence (which is largely to destroy
it, for it must be considered as a whole), and confronted with
Rabbinic parallels, the priority in date is almost always on the side

---

[1] 'The disciples of Jesus are to receive all the blessings and felicities of the
kingdom of heaven from their heavenly Father, in humble reliance upon his
grace, in order that they may serve God in childlike, grateful and reciprocated
love, and live in the sincere fear of God and in the upright love of man.'

of Jesus. Nevertheless, the later Rabbinic parallels are genuine developments and products, and in no way borrowed from, or due to, the teaching of the Gospels. As is usual in such quarrels, the truth lies between Jewish exaggerations on the one hand, and Christian exaggerations upon the other.

Since the foregoing words were written, the fourth and concluding volume of S.B.'s monumental work has been issued (October 1928). The first of the twenty-nine excursuses of which it consists is a (comparatively) short one entitled, 'Zur Bergpredigt Jesu.' It is coloured by the dogmatic standpoint of the author (Billerbeck), and contains some questionable statements. Yet, as usual, with these statements is appended much valuable material from which the student (though hardly the casual reader) is put in a position to criticize the statements, and to form his own conclusions. Billerbeck's object is to stress the immense difference between the poor, verbal, legal ' righteousness ' of the Rabbis and the glorious, evangelical ' righteousness ' taught by Jesus. He also desires to contrast the soteriology of the Rabbis and the soteriology of Jesus. The old Jewish (i.e. Rabbinic) religion is, he says, a religion of redemption by oneself and one's own power ; it has no room for a redeemer and saviour who dies for the sins of the world. ('Die altjüdische Religion ist eine Religion völligster Selbsterlösung : für einen Erlöser-Heiland, der für die Sünde der Welt stirbt, hat sie keinen Raum' (IV. p. 6).) That sentence is largely true, especially the second part of it. But it is not wholly true ; it is not wholly true to say that the Rabbinic religion is one of 'völligster Selbsterlösung.' It is partially true, but not wholly true. It is not wholly true, just because the Rabbis never worked out a complete and consistent theological system. They were inconsistent, and being inconsistent, and not being conscious, or afraid, of inconsistency, they were able, at one and the same time, to maintain various religious propositions and positions which it would be difficult to harmonize completely with one another or to weld into a consistent whole. The result was not unhealthy. It may, indeed, be that living and practical religion depends upon the individual carrying within him, working upon, and believing in the truth of, unharmonized (and perhaps humanly unharmonizable) positions and doctrines.

Thus (to begin with), the Rabbis held, says Billerbeck, that the soul of man, not infected by original sin, is given to him by his creator pure and good. That is true. *Cp.* the passages which I have cited in Matt. v. 8, to which may be added the sentence in Pesikta 61 b, 'like a child of a year old who is free from all sin.' (*Cp.* Targum on 1 Sam. xiii. 1.)   Nevertheless, much which B., with his usual honesty, quotes in his excursus on the good and evil *Yetzer* considerably modifies the significance and inclusiveness of this asserted sinlessness of man when he starts upon his earthly career. For the evil *Yetzer* begins in man from his birth, or even at his conception, or, at all events, before the child leaves his mother's womb. (See the passages in B. iv. p. 470 c.)   The evil *Yetzer* is regarded as older than the good *Yetzer*.   'The good *Yetzer* is not united (מזדווג) with man till his thirteenth year' (*i.e.* till puberty, Ecclesiastes R. on iv. 13).   I suppose the idea is that you only become good by observing the Law, and that you do not observe the Law on your own responsibility till you are thirteen, when you become *Bar Mitzvah*, Son of the Commandment ; till then you receive neither reward nor punishment.   Again, 'The evil *Yetzer* is older than the good *Yetzer* by thirteen years' (Ecclesiastes R. on ix. 15).   Here it is also said that the good *Yetzer* is not found in all men, and that most men do not obey it.   As the evil *Yetzer* is more especially the source of all sexual incontinence and immorality (if also, from another point of view, the source and condition of legitimate and sanctified married life), it might be regarded, perhaps, as equivalent to the 'dirt' (זוהמא) which the Serpent injected into Eve, and which continued among her descendants.   But this 'dirt,' while it still continues among the heathen, has ceased among the Israelites since the giving of the Law at Sinai.   It is, therefore, not to be identified with the evil *Yetzer*, and is rather the propensity to unnatural lust or bestiality.   (Yebamoth 103 b ; Abodah Zarah 22 b ; and the translations in S.B. i. p. 138, iii. p. 71.)   The passage in Aboth R. Nathan, xvi. 31 b, is very curious.   (S.B. iii. p. 95.)   'The evil *Yetzer* is thirteen years older than the good *Yetzer*.   From the womb of his mother it grows up with a man and continues with him. If the wish to violate the Sabbath arises in him, nothing forbids him.   [I suppose the meaning is, as he is not supposed to be yet responsible for his actions, he is not pricked by conscience] ; even if he wishes to murder, nothing forbids him ; if he wishes to commit any sin, nothing forbids him.   After thirteen years the good *Yetzer* is born. Then if he begins to violate the Sabbath, it says to him, You fool (ריקה), Does it not say in the Law, He who violates the Sabbath shall be put to death ? If he would murder, it says, Fool, He who sheds the blood of man, by man shall his blood be shed. If he desires to commit impurity, it says, Fool, Adulterer and adulteress shall be put to death. If a man becomes heated with passion, and wants to commit a lustful deed, all his limbs hearken to him, because the evil *Yetzer* is king over all his 248 limbs, whereas the good *Yetzer* is like unto one who is fettered in prison.' ' The evil *Yetzer* is older than the good *Yetzer* by thirteen years. The good *Yetzer* is called poor (it is the "poor man" of Ecc. ix. 15) because ' (as the reading must almost certainly run) ' it is common to all mankind, but only a minority obey it ; yet those who do are saved ' (*i.e.* from the evil *Yetzer*) (Ecclesiastes R. on ix. 15). Neumark says that, though in the individual the evil *Yetzer* precedes the good *Yetzer*, yet ' an sich ist die Natur gut,' and the true priority must be assigned to the good *Yetzer*. As Aristotle would say, the evil *Yetzer* is first for us, but the good *Yetzer* is first by nature (φύσει). (Neumark, *Geschichte der jüdischen Philosophie des Mittelalters*, II. 2, p. 45, 1928.) But, however that may be, these passages about the evil *Yetzer*, all quoted by S.B., to which others could be added, show that the ' good soul ' with which we are endowed at birth, must be accepted with qualifications. What the relation of the good soul (*neshamah*) or spirit (*ruach*) to the evil *Yetzer* exactly is I cannot find. Clearly, however, self-redemption, the keeping of the Law, is no easy matter, nor does the doctrine of the evil *Yetzer* differ much from the ordinary interpretation of the English version of Jeremiah xvii. 9, ' The heart is deceitful above all things and desperately wicked ' (A.V. The R.V. has ' sick ' for ' wicked.' I notice that the Jewish American translation has ' exceeding weak ' אנוש). And the Rabbinic teaching about the *Yetzer* is all based upon the Pentateuchal saying, ' The imagination (*Yetzer*) of man's heart is evil from his youth ' (Genesis viii. 21). Can man, then, unaided from God, conquer this evil *Yetzer* which has accompanied him from his youth or his birth ?

Again, it is perfectly true that the freedom of the will, man's capacity to do right and to obey the commands of the Law, is strongly maintained by the Rabbis, even as it is emphasized by Sirach (xv. 11-20). We all know the saying in Berachoth 33 b,

'Everything is in God's hand except the fear of God.'   And no less
familiar is the saying (by Akiba) in Aboth, 'Everything is foreseen,
but free-will (רשות) is given' (iii. 15).   (Cp. also passages quoted
on Matt. x. 29.)   The number of quotations given by S.B. on Matt.
xix. 18 (i. pp. 814–816) is long and apparently very definite : e.g.
'If the evil Yetzer would licentiously excite you, drive it away with
words of the Law, and do not say, The Yetzer is not in my power,
for I (God) have said, It is entrusted to you (to conquer) and you
must rule over it' (Genesis iv. 7).   [Sound common sense : drive
away evil thoughts with good thoughts ; that is in our power.]
Again, passages occur in which it is implied, or even stated, that
one can live to old age without sinning at all, and that there have
been people who fulfilled the entire Law from A to Z. (Cp. the
passages from Yoma 38 b, quoted on p. 20).   The expression
צדיקים גמורים, 'completely or perfectly righteous people,' as also
'completely or perfectly wicked people,' occurs frequently.   Both
are spoken of as actual, living people.   R. Joseph describes the
former as the men who have kept or fulfilled the whole Law from
A to Z. (Sabbath 55 a.) (Cp. the odd argument about the perfectly
and imperfectly righteous in Abodah Zarah 4 a.)   Notorious
Zaddikim gemurim, perfectly righteous men, were various Biblical
heroes : Abraham, Isaac, Jacob, Elijah, Hezekiah, Moses, Aaron,
and a few others, though it was also maintained (in accordance
with the words of the Pentateuch) that Moses and Aaron had not
been sinless.   More important is it that certain actual Rabbis
claimed to have fulfilled all the commands of the Law, and so apparently to be without sin.   There is an odd tale, e.g., (S.B. 1.
pp. 148, 816), about R. Chanina b. Papa and his conversation
with the Angel of Death.   The story is too complicated, and would
need too many lengthy explanations, to be given in full, but in
the course of the conversation between the Rabbi and the angel,
the Rabbi asks the angel to bring a roll of the Torah, and to show
him if there be anything written therein which he had not fulfilled.
It must be noted (S.B. have omitted this) that something which has
happened to R. Chanina is held to happen to none except to him
who is unique in his generation (חד בדרא), or has only one other like
him. (Kethuboth 77 b.)   It is more indicative, perhaps, of what
S.B. are anxious to maintain that, in a simple, non-miraculous, and
not necessarily legendary, story about the sick-bed of R. Eliezer,

he asks R. Akiba, Is there anything in the Law which I have not observed? (כלום חיסרתי מן התורה) (as the reason why he was in pain). But S.B. might have added that Akiba replies, ' Master, you have yourself taught us that there is no man so righteous in the world who has done naught but good and has never sinned' (Sanhedrin 101 a).[1] Another odd story concerns an unnamed *Chasid* (very pious man) who had palpitation of the heart. (So Levy.) ' All the men of special learning (the אשכולות) from the days of Moses to the death of Joseph b. Yoeser of Zereda were without blemish. From then onwards they were not. But can this be ? We are taught : there was once a *chasid* who had heart palpitations. The doctors said, " The only remedy for him is that he should drink fresh warm milk in the morning." So they brought a goat, and bound it to the foot of his bed, and he drank its milk. His colleagues came to visit him, but when they saw the goat, they said, " Armed robbers are with him in the house : are we to go in and visit him ? " They sat down, and investigated (his deeds), and they found no guilt in him except having that goat. And when he came to die, he said, " I am conscious within me of no sin except as to that goat, because I acted against the words of my colleagues, for the wise have said, No goat must be kept in the land of Israel "' (Baba Kamma 80 a ; Temurah 15 b). (Cp. Büchler, *Types of Jewish Palestinian Piety*, p. 17, 41, n. 2.) It may be noted that curious details of their attitude towards sin and righteousness which we find even in the Rabbis of the first century, as well as of their naïveness and simplicity, are illustrated by many stories and quotations given in Dr. Büchler's book. I refer especially to pp. 73-81, and pp. 111-114. On the one hand, we hear of a child-like freedom from any consciousness of sin ; on the other, of the greatest anxiety, not only to avoid sin, but to offer sin-offerings for sins unwittingly committed. Thus ' in the early description of the popular Feast of Water-drawing, celebrated on the Temple Mount on the second night of Tabernacles,' we are told that ' the *Chasidim*,

---

[1] *Cp.* Büchler, *Sins*, p. 187 and n. 1. Dr. Büchler says, ' No other instance of a scholar occurs to my mind that thought himself free from sin, except R. Simeon b. Yohai in Sukkah 45 b ; Yer. Berakh. ix. 3, 13 d ; Gen. Rab. xxxv. 2, when he said, " I have seen that those worthy of the world to come are few ; if they are a thousand or a hundred, I and my son are of them ; if they are two, I and my son are of them. I can free the whole world from punishment from the day on which I was created till now, and if my son Eleazar is with me, then from the creation of the world till now, and if Yotham, the son of Uzziyyah, were with us, then from the creation of the world to eternity." '

the pious men, and the men of deed (apparently, doers of charity and lovingkindness), danced before the people with torches in their hands, and recited before them songs and praises. They said, Happy art thou, my youth, that thou didst not put to shame mine old age (they were the men of deed). Others said, Happy art thou, mine old age, that thou hast atoned for my youth (they were the repentant). Both groups said, Happy is he who sinned not, and to him who sinned may it be forgiven.' (Apparently the *Chasidim* are the repentant.) (Jer. Sukkah v. 3, 55 b; T. Sukkah iv. 2, p. 198. Also Mishnah Sukkah v. 4, and Sukkah 53 a; Büchler, *loc. cit.* pp. 79–81.) Again : ' Marauding bands approached the city of R. Levi b. Sisi. He took a scroll of the Law, and went on to the roof, and said, Lord of the World, if I have neglected (במלית) any word of this book of the Law, let them come up ; if not, let them go away. And it was so ' (*i.e.* they went away). (Jer. Taanith iii. § 7, 66 d.)

But R. Eliezer, on the other hand, said : ' One may every day and at any time, whenever one likes, bring voluntarily a trespass-offering brought for a doubtful sin ; it was called the guilt-offering of the pious men. It is said of Baba b. Buta that he voluntarily brought every day a guilt-offering for a doubtful sin, except on the day after the Day of Atonement, and that he said, By this Temple, I should bring one, if they allowed me to do so ; but they tell me to wait till I have come to a doubt.' (Keritoth vi. 3 ; T. Keritoth iv. 4, p. 566 ; Büchler, p. 73.) Again, R. Judah b. Ilai reports : ' The ancient pious men desired to bring a sin-offering, because God did not bring an offence into their hands ; what did they do ? They voluntarily made the vow of the Nazirite to God in order to become liable to bring a sin-offering.' (Nedarim 10 a; T. Nedarim i. 1, p. 276.) Dr. Büchler explains this to mean : ' These pious men were filled with the anxiety lest they might be committing sins and in need of atonement. The sin-offering prescribed in Lev. iv. 27 in the case of a transgression in error of a biblical prohibition required that the sinner should have later become conscious of having unwittingly committed a definite offence ; but the pious men, who in their strict care and watchfulness naturally did their utmost to avoid such a violation of the Law, could not satisfy that condition laid down for a sin-offering, and found no occasion for bringing such a sacrifice. Their desire for it suggests that, in their opinion, a sin-offering brought for one definite sin would, at the same time, atone for other offences which, on account of their uncertainty, had to remain without atonement by sacrifice. For that purpose they looked out for an act which implied no sin, but automatically provided an occasion for a sin-offering. . . . The sin-offering prescribed in Num. vi. 14 for the Nazirite at the conclusion of his temporary vow was not brought for any definite breach of the Law, but for an unknown, yet possible, levitical defilement and for other offences against the rules of the vow, and could therefore include in its atonement other trespasses of the same uncertainty. As the temporary vow of the Nazirite extended only over thirty days, the pious men could repeat the vow as often as they liked, bring the sin-offering every month, and thus satisfy their desire for regular atonement' (p. 77). We may also notice the view that minor sins are atoned for by physical suffering (as generating reflection and repentance). Thus the same R. Judah reports that 'the ancient pious men were chastised by a disease of the bowels for about twenty days before their death in order that it should purge everything, so that they might come pure to the world to come.' (Semachoth iii. *fin.* and Gen. R. lxii. 2 on xxv. 8.) According to Dr. Büchler this means that God sent the illness to the pious men in order to purge them by suffering of their few sins, so that their souls should arrive in heaven free from sin. No less odd and bizarre is the wish of R. Yose b. Chalafta to share the lot of those who died of diarrhoea, or the observation that it is a good sign for a man if he dies of diarrhoea, since most righteous men die of that disease! (Sabbath 118 b; Kethuboth 103 b; Büchler, p. 112.)

A few of these stories imply a certain naïve belief in the complete virtue of various heroes and Rabbis. They also show a certain not wholly pleasant self-confidence, and a child-like, or even childish, consciousness of virtue, on the part of a very few exceptional Rabbis. It may also be said that they exhibit the legalism of the Rabbinic religion in a not wholly pleasant light. Virtue, most strictly and definitely, consists in fulfilling, and in not violating, the commands, positive and negative, of the Code. These commands *can* be fulfilled; man has the power to fulfil them; by some few people they *have* been fulfilled, and (the worst point) a very few people believed and felt and said that they *had* fulfilled them. It was, doubtless, supposed that there were a few superlatively righteous people who did really observe the Law from A to Z. (Lamentations R. on ii. 1 (§ 3).) But all this is only one part of the full story; there are many qualifications to be made, and the dogmatic deductions which S.B. draw from all these odd, and sometimes unpleasing, sayings and stories are of doubtful validity. It cannot be fairly said, without many saving clauses, that the Rabbinic religion is one of complete self-redemption. The enormous mass of Israelites did *not*, in Rabbinic opinion, completely fulfil the Law, and so far as they did fulfil it, they did not fulfil it (in their own opinion) entirely from their own strength and by the power of their own free-wills. Nor would it be true to say of the vast majority of the Rabbis that they believed that they were sinless people who, so far as they were concerned, needed no Day of Atonement and no divine forgiveness. They did not believe this, I think, either about themselves or about one another. The first thing about the matter which one is inclined to say is that the liturgy is, perhaps, the truest index of the Rabbinic religion both in its strength and its weakness. If the liturgy includes such a passage as that on page 121 (*Authorized Daily Prayer Book*, ed. Singer), it is also noticeable that it never alludes to anything like sinlessness in adults. The soul is indeed pure (p. 5), but 'what are we?', 'what is our righteousness?' (p. 7). Man must always pray: 'Lead us not into sin; let not the evil *Yetzer* have sway over us; subdue our *Yetzer* so that it may submit itself unto thee' (p. 7). These are daily prayers. Daily too are the prayers: 'Cause us to return, O our Father, unto thy Law; draw us near, O our King, unto Thy service, and bring us back in perfect repentance unto Thy presence. Blessed art Thou, O Lord, who delightest in repentance.' 'Forgive us, O our Father, for we have sinned; pardon us, O our King, for we have transgressed, for Thou dost pardon and forgive; blessed art Thou, O Lord, who art gracious and dost abundantly forgive' (p. 46).

It may, perhaps, be questioned—I do not want to exaggerate the 'case' for the Rabbis—whether they had always an adequate, or an adequately passionate, sense of human unworthiness—a sense of the immensity of the difference between the ideal and the accomplishment. For it may be justly said that the better a man is, the more he should be conscious of the distance between him and the ideal; the nobler and the greater he is, the nobler and the greater becomes the ideal. The greatest saints have felt the most acutely their own unworthiness; that is, how far they

fall short of the Ideal. Did the Rabbis feel all this adequately ?
If the Ideal is a series of Laws, *could* they feel it ? In this
sense it may be that there *is* a higher righteousness than legal
righteousness, and that legal righteousness cannot adequately
generate a hunger and thirst for ideal righteousness, or make vivid
the contrast between the Ideal of Righteousness and human
unworthiness. The greatest are the humblest ; even though they
rejoice in their divine sonship and image. They are proud and
self-abased in one, filled with shame, and yet also filled with pride
in their kinship with the divine. I am not clear whether the Rabbis
had enough of this sense of the divine ideal, receding even as you
approach it—of the ideal becoming greater even as you become
more righteous, of love becoming more tremendous and exacting
and unattainable even as you become more loving. And if so, was
this lack (if it existed) due to their legalism, to the fact that the
ideal of righteousness was the execution of a series of laws ? I
throw out these doubts and hesitations : I do not feel competent
to solve them. But it may be that the fact that a few distinguished
Rabbis seem really to have believed that they had fulfilled all the
demands of the Law, and that they were therefore completely
righteous, shows that there was something lacking in the whole
Rabbinic conception of righteousness and in the legalism which was
the root of it. I do not feel wholly clear about this point.

Mr. Loewe calls my attention, as an illustration of the higher
teaching of the Rabbis, to the noble passage at the end of Berachoth.
' R. Chiya bar Ashi said in the name of Rab, The disciples of the
wise ' (but a less literal rendering such as ' the searchers after truth '
would be more accurate) ' have no rest either in this world or in
the world to come, as it is said, They go from strength to strength
until they appear before God in Zion ' (Zion here stands for heaven).

S.B. justly say that even the righteous, according to Rabbinic
doctrine, must never be confident of salvation : they quote the
familiar saying of Hillel : ' Trust not in thyself till the day of
thy death ' (Aboth ii. 5). The saying is quoted in Jer. Sabbath
i. 3 b *ad fin.*, and the following story is added. A certain *Chasid*
went so far as to modify Hillel's saying into ' Trust not in thyself
till thy old age.' Upon which a spirit came, [in the guise, it is understood, of a beautiful woman], and tempted him. But he soon
repented. The spirit said, ' Do not be distressed ; I am about to

vanish, but do you not put yourself above your fellows!' (Schwab,
Vol. IV. p. 15.) S.B. also quote the saying of R. Simeon b. Yochai:
'God does not unite his name with the righteous in their lifetime
(אין מיחד שמו על הצדיקים בחייהון), but only after their death. When
are they holy (saints, קדושים)? Only when they are buried in
the ground. Why is this? Because God has no faith that the evil
Yetzer will not lead them astray' (Tanchuma, *Toledoth*, 33 a). In
Berachot (29 a) quite incidentally, in the middle of a discussion
about something else, the question whether a righteous man may
fall into sin is alluded to. 'Abbaye said: We have a tradition that
a good man does not become bad. He does not? Behold it is
written, "But when the righteous turneth away from his righteousness and committeth iniquity" (Ezek. xviii. 24). That refers to a
man who was originally wicked; but the man who is originally
righteous does not. He does not? Behold there is a Mishnaic
teaching: "Trust not in thyself until the day of thy death"; and
Yochanan the High Priest held the office of High Priest for eighty
years and eventually became a Sadducee' (Cohen's translation, p.
190). I might note that close before this passage is the famous
story of R. Yochanan b. Zakkai's death-bed (28 b), which I have
quoted elsewhere (p. 227), and also (29 a) the short condensation
(מעין) of the eighteen benedictions of which the opening words run:
'Give us understanding, O Lord, our God, to know thy ways;
circumcise our hearts to fear thee, and forgive us so that we may be
redeemed.' The Rabbis are always more or less in the wrong, according to S.B.! If they allude to righteous persons whose salvation and beatitude are assured, they are accused of self-righteousness,
of overweening confidence in a purely human power of doing and
becoming good, in a false belief in self-redemption; if, on the
other hand, they bid their hearers and disciples never to rest ignobly
in their own righteousness, to be ever on the watch lest they fall
into temptation, never to cease striving towards moral perfection,
ever to regard 'salvation' as something to be striven for till the day
of death, then they are held to be in a state of irreligious fear, and
never to attain to a blissful certitude of salvation. Thus S.B. say:
'Romans v. 1 is one of the proof passages for Christian certitude of
salvation: as opposed to this certitude the lack of it is a most
notable characteristic of Rabbinic religion. It is a Rabbinic dogma
that there is no confidence for the righteous in this world, no certainty

as regards his salvation (*sein Heilsstand*) before God ' (iii. p. 218).
Then follow a number of illustrations, all of which seem to make a
fairly just balance with the other passages about the ' perfectly
righteous ' and the men who fulfilled the Law from A to Z. The
starting-point is the sentence in Genesis R., וישלח, lxxvi. 2 on xxxii.
7. ' There is no confidence (הבמחה) for the righteous in this world.'
Even David said, ' I am assured that thou, O God, wilt give a good
reward to the righteous in the world to come, only I know not
whether my portion will be among them or not ' (Berachoth 4 a).
Nevertheless, we are told that all Israelites will have a share in
the world to come, that even a bondswoman who lives in Palestine
will have a share in the world to come (Kethuboth III a), and of
those who perform this rite or that, or who execute this commandment or that, we often read that they will inherit the life to come.
(For example, He who recites Psalm cxlv. three time daily, he who
studies the Halachah, he who lives in Palestine, speaks Hebrew,
eats his fruits (פירותיו) in purity, repeats the Shema evening and
morning, brings up his sons to study the Law, says the blessing
over the wine at the outgoing of the Sabbath, are all said to be
sure of enjoying the beatitudes of the world to come). (S.B. iii.
pp. 7, 208, 209, 219–221, who give all the references.)

Mr. Loewe holds that these sayings really mean, not that the
mere performance of these particular commands or actions, etc.,
will ensure eternal felicity, but that the doing of them is calculated
to generate a habit which will avoid sin and make for righteousness.
They are disciplinary, and tend to make the doer of them holy, and
therefore likely to inherit the joys of heaven.

About these and other passages S.B. say that such utterances
are not to be regarded as protests against the general doctrine that
there can be no certitude of salvation (*Heilsgewissheit*) for the
righteous upon earth. Almost always (S.B. add) these sayings
relate to some unimportant or indifferent externality, and they were
probably coined in order to encourage the masses of the people to
observe certain special religious duties, or to warn them against
some definite (objectionable) tendencies of the age. To this it must
be observed (1) that, even if this be so, the duties referred to were
not, in the eyes of the Rabbis, mere indifferent externalities, and
(2) that ' eternal life ' is often connected with actions that even
S.B. could not consider mere ceremonial externalities, as, *e.g.*, in the

case of the famous jokesters who were praised by Elijah. But (3) the real trouble is to assign the correct weight to these Oriental hyperboles and exaggerations, and (4) to estimate correctly the real and prevailing attitude of mind which such various and inconsistent sayings as have been, and will be, cited in the course of these reflections upon S.B.'s excursus actually imply. My criticism upon them would not be that they show either too much confidence or too little. On the whole, they seem to indicate that the Rabbis felt (1) that it was man's duty to strive towards moral and religious perfection (*i.e.*, to them, the complete observance of the Divine Law), (2) that God had given man free-will and the power to fulfil the Law, but that, (3) because of the *Yetzer*, God had made it difficult for him to do so, and (4) that for the immense majority of Israelites a complete observance of the Law was impossible. Therefore, (5) both God's help in that observance must be always prayed for, and (6) man must always be on his guard against temptation and sin, while (7) God's grace and forgiveness (and his love for Israel !) would always be required. Moreover, to the Rabbis the Law represented an odd combination which it is almost impossible for an orthodox Lutheran to appreciate or even to understand. On the one hand, the Law *was*, as Paul said (though the Rabbis could and would never have said it or understood it), ' the strength of sin.' That is to say, goodness meant the keeping of the Law and sin meant its violation. The Law said, Thou shalt, and thou shalt not, and because the Israelite does not, and could not always, do, and refrain from doing, *all* that the Law ordains and forbids, therefore, in a certain sense, it is the Law which causes his sins. But (8)—and here is the amazing thing, so ignored by Paul, so impossible for any disciple of Paul to appreciate—the Law, if it causes the poison of sin, also supplies the medicine and the antidote ! Study the Law, meditate on the Law, love the Law, rejoice in the Law, and the Law will give you—such was the divine intention in giving it—the strength you require to fulfil it. The Law, being divine, is almost alive ! God fills the Law with his grace ; he makes the Law provide the medicine and the stimulus whereby the solicitations of the *Yetzer* are overcome. The theory rests upon a view of the Law which knowledge and criticism have, in my opinion, made impossible, but its nobility and efficacy, given the belief, cannot be gainsaid. My own criticism would lie in a different direction. It is that though, for practical purposes, the rather see-sawy doctrine of the Rabbis was healthy and adequate, it was somewhat too childish and too unsystematic. The Rabbis seem hardly to realize the enormous difficulty, complexity, and significance of the subjects with which they, so summarily, so casually, and so inconsistently deal. If only they could all have been made to go through a careful course of Greek philosophy, how immensely they would have gained! Paul's soteriology may be one-sided, but it is profound; theirs is more many-sided, but it is too slight. And the same defect I find in some modern Jewish students of the Rabbis at the present day. Great subjects like sin, atonement, salvation, forgiveness, need more than separate and disconnected sentences. They need, I should have thought, systematic disquisitions.

I will now, with S.B. for guide, add a few more quotations to those I have already given. When Samuel was 'called up' by the witch of Endor, he said, 'Why hast thou disquieted me'? The Midrash remarks, Samuel said, 'I was alarmed lest the Day of Judgment had come, and I was afraid.' If Samuel, the leader (רבן) of all the prophets, was afraid of the Day of Judgment, how much more should the rest of the sons of men be! (Tanch., *Emor*, 171 b.) (Would B. entirely repudiate the *Dies irae*? and 'quid sum miser tunc dicturus, quum vix justus sit securus?') *Per contra*, if a man keeps himself from a transgression three times, God keeps him away from it henceforward. So said one Rabbi; but another said, Only if he does not return to it. Apparently this very oddly worded qualification (which seems to be rather a direct negative than a qualification) means that God will *usually* keep him from further sin, or that God will keep him from further sin, unless he very strongly determines to embark upon sin, for the verse in Ecclesiastes is quoted: 'A triple cord is not easily broken.' It does not say (the passage goes on to remark) that the cord is *never* broken; it only says that it is not *easily* broken. If you press it *too* hard, it breaks (אין מטרחת עלוי מפסק הוא). (Jer. Peah i. 16 b.) We note how the Rabbis play about with the subject; how undogmatic they are, how unsystematic. We may note too how easily they pass from a theological way of looking at the matter ('God will keep a man from sin') to a psychological way of looking at it. A habit of virtue is likely to be formed if, *e.g.*, temptation occurs three times and is thrice resisted. 'R. Elazar bar Azariah said, Woe to us because

of the Day of Judgment, woe to us for the day of rebuke. . . . How
shall men be able to stand before God, who is judge and lord of
judgment, when he sits upon the throne of judgment and judges us
all ? ' (Genesis R., *Vayiggash*, xciii. 11 on xlv. 9 *ad fin.*). Nevertheless, the righteous are supposed to die in joyous expectation of the
beatitude of the world to come, for God reveals it to them before
they pass away. (Gen. R., *Chaye Sara*, lxii. 2 on xxv. 8.) The
identification of moral and religious perfection with fulfilling the
Law (here, I think, S.B. are not without a little justification in their
attacks) sometimes leads to a rather mechanical conception of goodness and badness. God keeps an account against every man; a man is
' good ' if the laws he has fulfilled are more numerous than the laws
he has broken ; if he has more good entries and marks against his
name than bad ones ; all is reckoned according to the amount of
the deed ; a hundred fulfilments against ninety-nine violations :
you are righteous ; a hundred violations against ninety-nine fulfilments : you are guilty. No doubt the weight, *i.e.* the gravity and
importance, of the particular laws which a man fulfils and violates
are also taken into ' account.' R. Akiba said, ' Everything is foreseen, yet freedom of choice is given ; and the world is judged by
grace, yet all is according to the amount of the work. He used to
say, Everything is given on pledge, and a net is spread for all the
living : the shop is open ; and the dealer gives credit ; and the
ledger lies open ; and the hand writes ; and whosoever wishes to
borrow may come and borrow ; but the collectors regularly make
their daily round, and exact payment from man whether he be
content or not ; and they have that whereon they can rely in their
demand ; and the judgment is a judgment of truth ; and everything is prepared for the feast ' (Aboth iii. 19–20 ; P.B. p. 194).
(Note, however, ' the world is judged by grace.') And R. Elazar
Hakkappar said, ' Everything is according to the reckoning '
(לפי החשבון). (Aboth iv. 29 ; P.B. p. 198.) The passage in Kiddushin 40 b (*init.*) is well known. It runs thus : ' The Rabbis teach :
Let a man always regard himself as half guilty (חייב) and half
meritorious (זכאי or " pure "). Then if he executes one (more)
command happy is he, for he has inclined himself to the side of
merit ; if he commit one (more) sin, woe to him, for he has inclined
himself to the side of guilt ; as it is said, a " sinner can destroy much
good " (Ecc. ix. 18) ; by the one sin which he has committed he has

destroyed much good from himself. R. Elazar b. R. Simon said,
The world is judged by the majority, and the individual is judged
by the majority (אחר רובו) ; if he does one commandment (a good
deed), happy is he, for he has inclined himself and all the world to
the side of merit ; if he commit one sin, woe to him, for he has
inclined himself and the world to the side of guilt.' This sounds
horribly mechanical, but I am not sure that things were anything
like as bad as they sound. The odd mixture of particularism and
legalism, on the one side, of true prophetic doctrine, of high appreciation of human repentance and divine compassion, on the
other side (without any notice of the dissonance), is well shown
in some passages in Pesikta R. (185 b and 186 a), which are also
quoted in S.B. (iii. pp. 202, 203). The simple Rabbinic doctrine
is given in the Midrash on the Psalms *ad loc.* ' If a man does complete repentance (תשובה שלימה), so that his heart is uprooted within
him (שלבו עקור עליו), God forgives him.' But, over and above
repentance, there is the Day of Atonement, and so we get these
passages in the Pesikta Rabbathi : ' Happy are the men to
whom God imputes not guilt. Who are these ? They are those
whose transgressions God forgives. They are the Israelites who
are made pure (meritorious, זכאין) on the Day of Atonement, who
specify (פרטים) all their sins, and God forgives them.' Again, ' He
who observes a self-pollution on the Day of Atonement, let him
wash himself in the usual way ; only let him wash himself in a
secret (צנוע or lonely) place, for nothing is more beloved by God
than humility (צניעות) (chastity, lowliness, purity), as it is said,
walk humbly before thy God. . . . And it says, On this day he
will make an atonement for you to clean you, from all your sins
shall he clean you. Dost thou say, So, too, he cleans another nation ?
No : he does thus to Israel only. He forgives Israel only.' ' On the
Day of Atonement, Satan comes to accuse Israel, and he enumerates their sins. He says, Lord of the World, there are adulterers
among the nations, and also in Israel ; there are thieves among the
nations, and also in Israel. God enumerates the merits (good deeds)
of Israel. He takes the handle of the scales, and weighs the merits
against the sins, and the two are equal in weight, and the scales
hang down equally. Then Satan goes to find (some more) iniquities,
and to put them in the pan of guilt so as to make it go down. What
does God do ? Before Satan returns, God takes the iniquities from

the pan and hides them under his purple. Satan returns, and finds
no iniquities there, as it is said, The iniquity of Israel shall be
sought for, and there is none. (Jeremiah l. 20.) Then Satan says,
Lord of the World, Thou hast taken away (= also forgiven) the
sin of thy people : wonderful ! ' S.B. quote these passages, but
they do not seem fully to realize that the mind which they disclose, the religion which they reveal, are by no means a merely
mechanical or outward mind and religion. The religion may be
something of a medley, even as so many of our minds and moods
are to-day ; it may be too simple and naïve ; but it is far from
meriting the harsh condemnation which S.B. mete out to it. The
attempt to make God's grace or compassion prevail over the
mechanical weighing of good deeds against bad frequently occurs.
The entire passage in Jer. Kiddushin 61 d from the citation of the
Mishnaic sentence, ' He who does one good deed,' etc., to the end
of Section 1, is very curious and worth reading. The French
translation of Schwab (Vol. ix. pp. 236–239) makes the intricate
reasoning fairly clear. Bits of the passage are given in various
places in S.B. For the world to come a majority of good deeds
makes a man inherit Paradise, a majority of sins makes a man
inherit Gehinnom. How, then, about him whose good and bad
deeds are equal ? One Rabbi said, ' God quickly tears away
(חוטף) one of the sins, so that the merits prevail.' Another said,
' Thine, O Lord, is mercy, for thou requitest a man according to his
work ; but if he has not (enough), then thou givest him from thine.
(ואין לית ליה את יהיב ליה מן דידך). God inclines towards mercy.'
S.B. add rather churlishly, ' God's mercy (Gnade) only comes into
play at the judgment in the case of the in-between men, whose
merits and sins are in equipoise.' But this is hardly fair. Such
sentences as the last two have a wider significance. The Rabbis
unconsciously struggle against the letter which, as casuists, they love,
and which, as legalists, they are bound to adore. Their *deepest*
thoughts rise above their mechanical dicta. We cannot imagine
Jesus saying such things as the Rabbis say about the ' majority '
of good deeds and bad, and the equipoise, and the extra ' one ' in
either pan of the scales. He could not have spoken such mechanical
trivialities, yet, on the other hand, the deeper thought of the Rabbis
is *not* alien to his own. In the famous passage in Rosh ha-Shanah
16 b, 17 a, it is probable that the ' in-between ' people are by no

means merely those who are *precisely* half good and half bad ; they
are rather the great mass of men who are neither *very* good or *very*
bad (גמורין). It is towards these that, according to the school
of Hillel, God is merciful. In the school of R. Ishmael it was said,
' God passes over sin by sin, for this is his nature.' (מעביר ראשון
ראשון וכך היא המדה). Raba, however, did apparently limit God's
mercy to the case of merit and guilt being equal. But these limiting
utterances do not appear to be as important as those which imply
that God will do much more than only be merciful to those whose
merits and sins, whose good deeds and bad deeds, precisely equal
one another. How often one comes across passages like these :
' Israel says, God of my righteousness ; it is thine to justify me ;
even if I have no merit (זכות), act towards me charitably ' (play
on צדקה and צדקני = justice, charity, justify). (Midrash Psalms
iv. 1, 20 b.) ' If we have merit, act with us accordingly, if not
act with charity and mercy ' (do. 2). Or, again, ' David said to
God, Some come before thee in the strength of the Law and of their
good deeds ; but I have no strength before thee ; I come as a
poor man who seeks charity (alms, charity, righteousness, צדקה),
even as it says, As for me, I shall behold thy face in righteousness '
(do. on xvii. 14, 67 b). I hope it is not prejudice if I feel that
in such a passage as this last, which, so far, I have not found in
S.B., the true genius of Rabbinism is more apparent than in the
mechanical and legalistic trivialities. (*Cp.* on Luke xvii. 7–10.)
Anyway, both sets of passages must be taken into account, and
not only the trivialities, in making up our final estimate of the
religion. (*Cp.* Midrash Psalms cxli. 1, 265 b, cxix. 123, 250 b. Also
Genesis R., שרה חיי, lx. 2 on xxiv. 12 *ad init.*, quoted on p. 363.) Very
significant is the famous passage in Tanchuma B. xvi., *Ki Tissa*, 58 b.
' Rabbi Yose b. Chalafta said, It does not say " Behold I am in this
place," but it says, " Behold there is a place by me ": (Ex. xxxiii.
21), that is, my place is non-essential to me, but I am essential to
my place. And it says, " I will cause *all* my goodness to pass
before thee " (Ex. xxxiii. 19) ; that is, my goodness is the attribute
of reward, but *all* my goodness includes also the attribute of justice '
(punishment. This is translated from an emended text). ' Then
God showed Moses all the treasuries of rewards laid up for the
righteous, and Moses said, Whose treasure store is this ? God said,
It is for those who give alms. And Moses said, And whose is this ?

It is for those who rear orphans. So he reviewed treasury after treasury, until Moses saw a big treasure store, and he asked God for whom it was laid up. And God said, If a man has, I give him of his own, and for him who has not I do it out of grace (or gratis), for it is said, I will be gracious to whom I will be gracious.' Man's free-will is limited in fact, though unlimited in theory. It is never too late to mend ; the power to repent is always there.

Per contra, the responsibility for sin is never removed. But the evil *Yetzer* is a sore burden and a heavy trial. It is true that the *Yetzer* grows by the encouragement which is given it. At first as thin as a spider's web, it becomes at last as thick as a cart rope. At first a passing guest, it becomes at last master of the house. On the one hand, God is represented as throwing the full responsibility, so to speak, upon man for his yielding to the solicitations of the *Yetzer* ; on the other hand, God is represented as repenting that he ever created the *Yetzer*, which presumably means that he feels that he has imposed upon man a struggle too sore for him, a burden too hard. And, from the human side, man is represented as complaining that God expects man to ' be good ' (*i.e.* to fulfil the commands of the Law), whereas it is God who, by creating the *Yetzer*, has made it almost impossible for man to execute all the divine behests. S.B.'s quotations in excursus 19 (pp. 466–483), as well as the quotations and references in Moore and in F. C. Porter's excellent essay (' The *Yetzer Hara* : a Study in the Jewish Doctrine of Sin,' in *Biblical and Semitic Studies from Yale University*, 1901), give the supporting material for all these statements. As to human responsibility, and man's duty and power to cope with and master the *Yetzer*, some passages have already been cited. It is constantly repeated : ' If you would say the *Yetzer* is not in my power, the reply is : It has been entrusted to you (Isaiah xxvi. 3), and it was written of old in the Law, Its desire is toward you (*i.e.* to enslave you), but you must rule over it ' (Gen. iv. 3). (Genesis R., בראשית, xxii. 6 on iv. 6.) There is a curious passage in Tanchuma, *Bereshith*, 4 b, which S.B. quote in full (iv. p. 469) : ' If you say, Why did God create the *Yetzer* ? Or, No man can keep himself (from the power of the *Yetzer*), the reply is : Why does a child of five, six, seven, eight or nine years not sin, but only at ten years and upwards ? He himself makes his *Yetzer* big. *You* make your *Yetzer bad*. Why did you, when you were a child, not sin ? But when you grew up, you sinned. There are many things in the world harder and bitterer than the *Yetzer*, such as lupin, mustard and capers, but by soaking them in water, etc., you know how to make them soft and sweet. If the bitter things which I have created you can make sweet to meet your own needs, how much more the *Yetzer* which has been delivered into your hand.' On the other side, that God is grieved or repents to have created the *Yetzer* is frequently stated. (Sukkah 52 b and many parallels.) Famous and familiar is the passage : ' Wretched is the yeast which its creator himself testifies to be evil. Wretched is the plant which the gardener himself calls bad. Wretched is the dough which the baker himself testifies to be evil ' (Gen. R., *Noah*, xxxiv. 10 on viii. 21). And no less well known is Berachoth 17 a, how a Rabbi was wont to add to the conclusion of his (statutory) prayer : ' Lord of the universe ! It is revealed and known before thee that it is our will to perform thy will ; but what stands in the way ? The leaven that is in the dough, and the servitude of the kingdoms. May it be thy will to deliver us from their hand, so that we may again perform the statutes of thy will with a perfect heart ' (Dr. Cohen's translation, p. 109). God says, ' If I had not created the evil *Yetzer* in man, he would not have rebelled against me. It is I who put the bad leaven in the dough ' (Gen. R., *Bereshith*, xxvii. 1 on vi. 6 ; Tanchuma B. iv., *Noah*, 15 b. The second passage makes God almost admit that he made a mistake, ' even as a man grieves when he has done evil.') Though the purpose of the *Yetzer* being created is often said to be that man may conquer it, and by the conquest win merit and reward, the Israelites, in one remarkable passage (S.B. iii. 112), far too long to quote, are represented as saying, We want neither the *Yetzer* nor the reward (the game is not worth the candle). I have already quoted the touching prayer of R. Tanchuma (Jer. Berachoth, iv. § 2, 7 d) : ' May it be thy will, O God, that thou shouldst break the yoke of the evil *Yetzer*, and remove it from our hearts. For thou hast created us to do thy will, and our duty it is to do thy will ; thou desirest it, and we desire it ; and what prevents ? The yeast in the dough. It is revealed and known before thee that there is no power in us to resist it (the *Yetzer*). May it be thy will, O God, that thou cause it to be quiet within us, and that thou subdue it within us, and we will do thy will as our will with a perfect heart.' Here we find Rabbi Tanchuma

asking God's help, and that was also the daily prayer of every Jew :
' Subdue our *Yetzer*,' which can only mean, *help us* to subdue our
Yetzer. But God has given the Israelite the means wherewith to
subdue it. The divine help is, as it were, made concrete, and lies
to the Israelite's hand. It is the study and the practice of the Law.
If the Law by saying, ' Thou shalt and thou shalt not,' stirs up the
Yetzer to resist and oppose God's will, it also affords the remedy.
The Law might say in the words of the supreme poet : ' So that
myself bring water to my stain.' This is the real soteriology of the
Rabbis : free-will, yes ; but also (1) God's compassion, both directly
and through the Day of Atonement, and then (2) the Law ! Turn
your thought toward God's holy word and will ; seek, when temptation comes, to do some command : study a page of the Torah, and
the *Yetzer* will be weakened and conquerable. The passages on
these lines are too numerous to quote. But they all tend to one
conclusion : ' The evil *Yetzer* has no power over against the Law,
and he who has the Law in his heart, over him the *Yetzer* has no
power ' (Midrash Psalms cxix. (7), verse 11, 246 b). If the evil
Yetzer meets you and attacks you, draw it into the house of study.
' Feed it with the bread of the Law ' (Mid. Psalms xxxiv. (2),
verse 23, 124 a). And so on and so on. Many more passages
are given in S.B. iv. 176, 477. Quite simple and trenchant is the
saying : ' God has created the evil *Yetzer*, but he has also created
the Law as a spice (against it) ' (תבלין). (Baba Batra 16 a.) Most important of all is the passage in Sifre 82 b (*cp.* Kiddushin 30 b) : ' The
words of the Law are likened to a medicine (סם) of life. Like a
king, who inflicted a big wound upon his son, and he put a plaster
(רטיה) upon his wound. He said, My son, so long as this plaster
is on your wound, eat and drink what you like, and wash in cold or
warm water, and you will suffer no harm. But if you remove it,
you will get a bad boil (נימי). So God says to the Israelites, I
created within you the evil *Yetzer*, but I created the Law as a drug
(תבלין). As long as you occupy yourselves with the Law, the
Yetzer will not rule over you. But if you do not occupy yourselves
with the Torah, then you will be delivered into the power of the
Yetzer, and all its activity will be against you.' That the Rabbis
did not mean that the *mere* occupation or study of the Law would
be a sort of outward charm may be gathered from a passage where
it says : ' Woe to the Disciples of the Wise who occupy themselves

with the Torah, but have no fear of God. Woe to him who has
no house, but makes a door for it. R. Joshua b. Levi said, Is his
intent pure (זכה) (be he worthy), the Law is made for him a medicine
of life : if it is not, it is made for him a medicine of death.' Or, as
Raba put it, ' For him who knows how to use it aright (אומן לה) it
is a drug of life; if he does not, it is for him a drug of death.' (Yoma
72 b.) Resh Lakish said, in reference to Psalm xix. 9, ' The word
of the Lord is pure (צרופה) : If his intent is pure, the Law purifies
him to life, if his intent is not pure, it purifies him to death ' (do.).
' If the scholar is worthy, the Torah will distil on him as dew, but
if he is not, it will drop on him as rain ' (*i.e.* the learning will harm
him, as a heavy rain harms the crop); ' if a man studies the Torah for
its own sake, it becomes to him an elixir (סם) of life ; if he studies
the Torah not for its own sake, it becomes to him a deadly poison '
(סם המות). (Taanith 7 a, in Dr. Malter's rendering, p. 40.) The Law
is the true antidote to the *Yetzer*, but the antidote must be rightly
used. Practice is the condition of right study. The finest medicine
falsely used can become a poison. Such is Rabbinic soteriology.
Can it rightly be so sharply opposed to the soteriology of Jesus ?
I hardly think so.

The real point of difference between B. and myself—where I
think B. does the Rabbis an injustice—is in refusing to allow that
what we may call the spiritual sayings and adages of the Rabbis are
any the less an indication of their complete and general point of view
than their outward minutiae and legal casuistry. The two formed a
whole—a strange whole, doubtless, to me as well as to B., but none the
less a whole. The spiritual sayings did not flow from their troubled
hearts as an attempted, but unsuccessful, corrective to the legalisms
and the casuistry, but quite naturally as an expression of their
actual feelings, and also with complete unconsciousness that these
utterances were inconsistent, or, at bottom, unharmonizable, with
the utmost ceremonial exactitude. R. Elazar said, ' Always let
a man test (ימוד) himself : if he can direct his heart (לכוין את לבן), let
him pray ; if he cannot, let him not pray ' (Berachoth 30 b). Yet
I suppose R. Elazar would have been shocked if a disciple had not
worshipped at the statutory times. ' God demands the heart '
(Sanhedrin 106 b)—a favourite and well-known Rabbinic saying—
but he demands also the outward deed. Nevertheless, the determining point is the *Kawwanah* (devotion) of the heart. *Kawwanah*

is, indeed, a remarkable term, and let us remember that this familiar word, and the idea which it expresses, are the creation of these legal Rabbis.

The Rabbinic conception of *Kawwanah* has a Biblical basis, but is an original development. It is one of the conceptions or creations by means of which the Rabbis attempted to prevent the obvious dangers of legalism. It should be taken in connection with the noble term *lishmah*, ' for its own sake,' or again in connection with the ideal that all the injunctions of the Law must be carried out *in* love or *from* love. The substantive *Kawwanah* (not found in the O.T.) is derived from the Biblical verb *kun*, and the conception starts from such Biblical passages as Job xi. 13, ' If thou direct thy heart '; or I Sam. vii. 3, ' If ye direct your hearts unto the Lord '; or 2 Ch. xxx. 19, ' May the Lord pardon everyone who directs his heart to seek God '; or Ezra vii. 10, ' Ezra had directed his heart to seek the law of the Lord.' To direct the heart or the mind (דעת) towards some end, or towards the deliberate execution of some command, became a very common Rabbinic term. Its general meaning is ' intention,' ' purpose.' Together with a fine ethical development of the idea (especially in the derived substantive), there went also a certain amount of casuistry. It is clear, and all Rabbis would agree in this, that to fulfil a command with the full intention of fulfilling it, keeping, as it were, one's mind fixed upon what one is doing, is much better than to fulfil it carelessly, in a casual sort of way, or letting one's mind wander. Nevertheless, from the strictly legal point of view, it can be argued that a command performed is a command performed. The question, therefore, arose : is *Kawwanah*, in its primary meaning of full and deliberate intention, *necessary* for the execution of a command ? Has a man fulfilled his obligation if he has, indeed, executed the command, but executed it without *Kawwanah*, without concentration, or deliberate intent ? Opinions were divided. Thus Raba said (Rosh ha-Shanah 28 a) that *Kawwanah* is not *necessary* (מצות אין צריכין כוונה). But the more general view seems to have been that even for sheer legal performance, *i.e.* for the needful minimum, intention was required. So T. Rosh ha-Shanah (iii. 6 *fin.*, p. 212) sums up and decides. ' All depends upon the intention of the heart ' (= mind). (אין הכל הולך אלא אחר כוונת הלב). So too in Erubin 95 b (*fin.*), 96 a (*init.*), in a long and highly casuistical debate about ' intention '

in connection with laying the Tefillin. So in the Mishnah Megillah
ii. 1, about reading the book of Esther on Purim. If a man copies
the scroll, or studies it or corrects it, he has only fulfilled his obligation
(יצא) if he intended thus to fulfil it (אם כיון לבו), but not otherwise.
Where the purely legal point of the *opus operatum* was not in
question, the minimum amount required for the bare, but yet legal,
performance—where, in other words, the moral aspect of the matter
was being taught, the Rabbis spoke with no uncertain voice. ' A
man ought to direct his eyes and heart and ears to the words of the
Law, as God says to Ezekiel about the temple (xliv. 5). If in the
case of a temple which can be seen by the eye and measured by the
hand, ears and eyes and heart must be directed (" collected " in the
religious sense) (מכוונים), how much more for the words of the Law,
which are as mountains which hang upon a hair ' (Sifre, 140 b).
The teaching that God reckons the honest intention to perform a
command, which a man is prevented from fulfilling by *force majeure*
or unavoidable accident, as equivalent to the enjoined action, is
indicative of the same point of view. (Berachoth 6 a ; Kiddushin
40 a.) (מחשבה כמעשה.) So too is the famous adage at the end of
a familiar passage : ' It was a favourite saying of the Rabbis of
Jabneh : I am a creature [of God], and my neighbour is also His
creature ; my work is in the city, and his in the field ; I rise early
to my work, and he rises early to his. As he cannot excel in my
work, so I cannot excel in his work. But perhaps thou sayest,
" I do great things and he small things ! " We have learnt that
[it matters not whether] one does much or little, if only he direct his
heart to Heaven ' (Berachoth 17 a, Dr. Cohen's translation, p. 111).
It was, perhaps, with the idea of fulfilling each command with due
reverence and *intention* that the order was coined, ' One should not
perform the commands in heaps ' (אין עושין מצות חבילות חבילות).
(Berachoth 49 a and par. *Cp.* Ziegler ii. p. 152.)

But it was in relation to prayer that the word *Kawwanah* was
most frequently used, and was most excellently developed. For
here it passed from meaning merely intention or purpose to meaning
devotion, or rather to meaning that frame of mind which in German
is called *Andacht*, and for which we in English have no exact equivalent. It is true that here too, as regards the statutory reading of the
Shema and of the Amidah, disputes arose, and casuistry found a
happy field as to *how much* of the Shema and of the Benedictions

required *Kawwanah*, and how much might legally be said without
it. (Berachoth 13 a and 13 b.)   But, here again, these discussions
refer only to legal minima.   The general ethical and religious view
is reflected in the saying : ' Prayer needs *Kawwanah* ' (Jer. Berachoth iv. 1, 7 a).   (תפילה צריכה כוונה.)   So too in the verbal form. 'He
who prays must direct his heart ' (T. Berachoth iii. 4, p. 6).   We
may also note the passage already quoted on xvi. 7 : ' The pious
men of old used to wait an hour, and then say the Tefillah, in order
to direct their heart to their Father in heaven ' (Mishnah Berachoth
v. 1).   Again, ' He who makes his voice heard during prayer is of
the small of faith.   Rab Huna said : This teaching applies only
to one who is able to direct his heart when whispering [the words
of prayer] ; but if he is unable to do so, he is permitted [to pray
aloud].   This holds good only of one praying alone ; but with a
congregation it would cause disturbance to others ' (Berachoth 24 b ;
Dr. Cohen's translation, p. 159).   ' If a man is riding on an ass
(and the time for prayer comes), if there is anyone who can hold his
ass, let him get off and pray ; but if not, let him remain on the ass
and pray.   Rabbi said: In either case let him remain on the ass and
pray ; the only important thing (ובלבד) is that his heart should
be directed ' (מכוון).   (T. Berachoth iii. 18, p. 8, top.)   This ruling
is repeated in Tanchuma in the form, ' Let him get off his ass and
pray ; but if he cannot get off, since his mind would not be
calm (מיושבת) within him because of his money which is on the ass,
or because he is afraid of gentiles or of robbers, then let him pray on
the ass.   For as Rabbi Yochanan said, He who prays must have his
mind calm within him ; then let him pray before God.   Abba Saul
said, If a man has directed his mind in prayer, he may be confident
that his prayer is heard.'   (Tanchuma, *Chaye Sarah, ad init.* p. 28 b).
It is a fine thing, when one comes to think of it, that in a regular
legal code like the Mishnah one should find the rule : ' Should a
man be reading in the Torah [the section of the Shema], and the
time of reciting the Shema arrived, if he directed his heart, he has
fulfilled his obligation ' (Berachoth ii. 1 ; Cohen, p. 82).   Because
it says in Deut. vi. 6, ' These words shall be upon thy heart,'
Akiba held that the whole section (vi. 4–9) even legally required
Kawwanah ; others held that *Kawwanah* was legally required only
up to the word ' heart,' or even only up to the word ' one.'   It
is also said, ' One who says the Tefillah must direct his heart to

each benediction; but if unable to do so to each one, he must at least direct his heart to one' (Berachoth 34 b). The Rabbis made concessions to the weakness of human nature. But their feeling and desire are contained in R. Meir's dictum : ' All depends upon the *Kawwanah* of the heart' (אחר כוונת הלב הן הן הדברים). (Megillah 20 a.) More generally, Rab said ' He whose mind (דעתו) is not calm (מיושבת עליו) should not pray.' ' R. Chanina was wont not to pray when he was irritated ' (רתח). (Erubin 65 a.) 'God said to the priests, Not because I *ordered* you to bless the people (Numbers vi. 24–27) are you to bless them with compulsion and in confusion, but you must bless them in devotion of heart (בכוונת הלב) so that the blessing may be fulfilled unto them' (Tanchuma, *Naso*, p. 197 a *ad fin.*). In the many stories about praying for rain in Taanith it is said in one place, ' Let us come together with minds directed, perhaps if the congregation breaks its heart, rain will come' (25 a) (ניתי ונכוין דעתין אפשר דתברי צבורא לביהו... ואתי מטרא). I may finally quote a pretty passage in Canticles R. (viii. § 11, 2 on viii. 13) which runs thus: ' When the Israelites are collected in their synagogues, and read the *Shema* with devotion (בכיוון הדעת), and harmoniously and with intelligence (בדעה), and with the same tones (accents, ומעם אחד), then God says to them, Thou that dwellest in the gardens, I and my family listen to thy voice ; but when Israel read the *Shema* with inattention (confusion) (בטירוף הדעת), and when they do not say the same words at the same time, but one is before, and the other behind, and when they show no devotion in the reading of the *Shema*, then the Holy Spirit laments and says, Flee away, my beloved, like the gazelle (*zebi*) ; that is, let the angelic hosts (*zeba*) retire within the highest heaven of heavens.' (There is a good essay on *Kawwanah* by Rabbi H. G. Enelow in *Studies in Jewish Literature*, issued in honour of Kaufmann Kohler, 1913, pp. 82–107. Dr. Enelow shows the fine development and use of the word and the conception in post-Talmudic Jewish literature.) I might just mention the frequent use of the phrase, ' I am here intent on ' doing such and such a command (הנני מכון), as, *e.g.*, in the late prayer on laying the Tefillin in Singer, *Prayer Book*, p. 15, or in the late prayer on taking the *Lulab*, where the Hebrew is in the passive form, הנני מוכן, *Service of the Synagogue*, *Tabernacles*, ed. Davis, p. 95.

' He who does not fulfil the Torah for its own sake, it were better for him that he had never been born' (Berachoth 17 a). Here we have that other great creation of the Rabbis, *lishmah*, 'for its own sake'—a phrase which, because, I suppose, of its exceeding commonness and simplicity, Levy left out of his great Dictionary, and it had to be added on in the little Supplement. And yet how remarkable it is, and how significant, and how native to the Rabbinic soil.   And again we see how oddly common sense mingles with the Rabbinic idealism.   To act *lishmah* is as different from acting without *lishmah* as chalk from cheese.   And yet how often do we have the remark that it is better to fulfil the Law without *lishmah* than not at all, because if we fulfil it often enough with a lower motive (*i.e.* without *lishmah*) we may end by fulfilling it from the one and only right motive (*lishmah*). That this is the one and only right motive is indicated, not only in the paradox of Berachoth 17 a, but also in the odd saying of R. Nachman b. Isaac, that a sin which is done *lishmah* is better than a command done not *lishmah*; that is, a sin with good intent is better than a command not done for its own sake.   This view the Gemara criticizes by the remark : ' Say they are equal, but not that the sin is superior.' (Nazir 23 b).   Certainly all the Rabbis would have agreed with R. Alexandri, who said, ' He who occupies himself with the Law for its own sake makes peace in the world below and in the heavens above ' (Sanhedrin 99 b).   And *lishmah* implies love, just as love implies *lishmah*. The man who acts from love acts *lishmah* and *vice versa*.   He cares for *doing* God's will and not, primarily, for the rewards of doing it.   (Abodah Zarah 19 a.)   Again, to act from love is to act for God's sake.   ' Execute the commands for the sake of their Creator, and speak of them for their own sake, and make them not a crown wherewith to exalt thyself, or an axe with which to dig ' (Nedarim 62 a).   The Law is a joy and a glory.   The words, ' This book of the Law shall not depart out of thy mouth, but thou shalt meditate thereon day and night,' are not a duty or a command ; they are a blessing. (Menachoth 99 b.)   That saying of R. Jonathan's occurs a few pages before the more familiar : ' It matters not whether your offering be much or little, so long as your heart is directed to heaven ' (do. 110 a).   We may compare the not less familiar story in Leviticus Rabba iii. 5 on Lev. ii. 1 : 'A woman once brought a handful of meal as an offering.   The priest despised

it. He said, What is that for an offering, what is there in it for
eating, what for a sacrifice ?　But in a dream it was said to the
priest, Despise her not ; but reckon it as if she had offered herself
as a sacrifice.' (כאלו נפשה הקריבה.)　Playing upon the verbal fact
that in Lev. ii. I the Hebrew word for " anyone " is *nefesh* (literally,
" soul," " life," " person "), the Midrash goes on to say : ' If in
regard to anyone who does *not* sacrifice himself, the word *nefesh*
is used, how much more fitly of one who *does*.'　In Ecclesiastes
R. on iv. 6 (*fin.*) it is said that God prefers one handful of free-will
offering of the poor to the heap of incense which is offered by the
high priest.　' What is the peculiarity of the meal offering that
the word *nefesh* is used in respect of it (in Lev. ii. I) ?　Who is wont
to bring a meal offering ?　The poor ?　I reckon it, says God, as
if he offered himself before me ' (Yalkut on Lev. ii. I, § 447).
These last three quotations are given by S.B. on Mark xii. 43.
' God says, An offering is only then *my* offering if you bring it
freely and with good intent (ברצון ובטובה) ; if you bring it by
compulsion (באונס), it is a mere burning, and it does me no honour.'
R. Isaac said that it is a matter of good breeding and propriety
(דרך ארץ) that he who executes a command should do it with a joyful heart. (Lev. R., *Behar*, xxxiv. 8 on xxv. 39.)　The piety of
the Rabbis and their simplicity are well shown in such a passage
as this : ' They who study the Law in order to puff themselves
up by it, and not for God's sake, and who hope for their reward in
this world, are the haughty doers of Psalm xxxi. 23.　They who
occupy themselves with the Torah for God's sake, and look for
their reward only in the world to come are those who "hope in the
Lord " of verse 24.' (Midrash Ps. xxxi. (9), verse 24, 121 a.)　Or
again : ' R. Nehemiah said, Even when we practise charity, we must
be ashamed, when we look upon our deeds.　At no moment can we
come (before God) with a strong arm (*i.e.* trusting to our merits
and deeds) unless in the time when we give our tenths.　And why
then ?　Because it says in Deut. xxvi. 12, Look down from thy
holy dwelling (in the passage about the tithing).'　There is a playful
element in all this, but also a vein of deep seriousness ; only one
must have the tact to discriminate between the playfulness and the
seriousness. (Exodus R., *Ki Tissa*, xli. on xxxi. I, 2 *init.*　Cp.
Fuerst's note to Wuensche's translation (p. 285), on p. 383.)　Moses,
the greatest of the prophets, approached God only with supplica-

tion. His prayer was supplication. (Deut. iii. 23.) Hence we may
learn that man can ask for grace only. (The Hebrew words for supplication and grace are practically the same.) אֵין לַבְּרִיָּה כְּלוּם אֵצֶל
בּוֹרְאוֹ. (Deut. R., *Va-et-channan*, ii. 1 on iii. 23.) Have not
those five simple Hebrew words—the creature has nothing (to claim)
before his Creator—quite a Pauline ring ? Nevertheless, a little
later on Moses can say, ' If I may enter the land by justice (דִּין)
(on my merits), let me do so ; if not, let me enter it through thy
grace (gratis). For God (Exodus xxxiii. 19) had said to Moses, As
for him who has any virtue to his credit with me, I will be merciful
to him, as for him who has nothing to his credit, towards him I will
be gracious ; with a free gift (gift of grace) will I deal with him.'
R. Yochanan, to whom these quaint remarks are attributed, meant
to imply that even if a man has something to his credit—some virtue
—yet even he has to rely on the divine mercy. Grace goes beyond
mercy, and comes into play when even mercy is inadequate ! Yet,
a little later on, justice (*i.e.* merit) is contrasted, not with grace,
but with mercy. We note how in these various sayings the doctrine
implied seems to be fluid and naïve. It is interesting that the not
wholly translatable word *Chesed* alternates with ' love.' Thus, while
in Nedarim 62 a we heard how all must be done in love, and how
in Sotah 31 a the love of God is exalted above the fear of God, in
Succah 49 b we have the contrast between a Torah of *Chesed* and a
Torah which is not of *Chesed*. The one is Torah *Lishmah*, the other
is Torah which is not *Lishmah*. (The saying is dependent on Prov.
xxxi. 26.)

S.B. give a list of passages which they speak of as the ' external
ornaments.' Most of them have already been quoted in other
connections. They give also the Sotah passage about fear and
love of God—love is greater than fear—and the Jer. Sotah (v., 7, 20 c)
parallel, that one must both fear God and love him, and the
happy Sifre remark (73 a, quoted again on Matt. x. 28) that everywhere else there is no love when there is fear, and *vice versa*,
except in relation to God. Again, ' Love God with all thy heart,
that is with both the good and the bad *Yetzer* : so that thy heart be
not divided in thy love ' (שֶׁלֹּא יִהְיֶה לִבְּךָ חָלוּק עַל הַמָּקוֹם)—a very
profound remark. ' With thy whole soul ' : even if he takes away
thy soul, even up to martyrdom. With every measure that he
metes to thee, be it of good, be it of chastisement, love him !

(73 a.) The whole long passage in the Sifre 73 a and 73 b is well worth reading. It ends with the pretty conceit that Isaac so loved God that he bound *himself* upon the altar, freely giving up to God his life. (*Cp.* on Matt. x. 28.) Now the point for me of all these passages is that they are bone of the Rabbinic bone and spirit of their spirit. They are neither more nor less bone of the Rabbis' bone than the legalisms and the outwardnesses. B's final judgment is that they are 'Kautelen,' and that they resemble 'Schmuck-und Zierstücken, die man äusserlich am nomistischen Lehrgebäude angebracht hat : sie hätten auch fehlen können : die nomistiche Soteriologie wäre von ihrem Fortfall unberührt geblieben.'[1] Here B.'s Lutheran prejudices seem to have led him astray. His words seem to me both inaccurate and unfair.

The famous term *lifnim mishurat haddin* is also an indication that the Rabbis knew what equity meant as against a mere verbal interpretation of the Law or of justice. Jerusalem was destroyed, says R. Yochanan, because men judged according to the letter of the Law. (Baba Mezia 30 b. *Cp.* 88 a *fin.*) Mechilta 59 b (*fin.*) on Exodus xviii. 20 runs: 'Make known to them the "way": that is the study of the Law; make known to them the work they must do, that is good deeds. Or: "the way," that is visiting the sick; "they should walk," that is the burial of the dead ; " therein," that is deeds of loving-kindness ; the "work," that is the letter of the Law (*shurat haddin*); " which they are to do," that is equity ' (*lifnim mishurat haddin*). It may be questioned whether even equity is an adequate translation of *lifnim mishurat haddin*. I am not sure that it does not include *all* going beyond the letter of the law, whether in legal matters, or in any other of the commands, say, of benevolence, charity, or loving-kindness, which the Law enjoins. All that fervour and excess in right-eousness, which were to characterize the disciples of Jesus (Mt. v. 20), might be regarded as the expression of the principle of *lifnim mishurat haddin*. Stories are told how various Rabbis acted or judged or ruled according to the principle of *lifnim mishurat haddin*; though again it has to be noted, I fear, that the equity according to which one Rabbi ruled was an equity for the Israelite only. (Baba Mezia 24 b.) But, any way, it shows that the principle of equity was known to

---

[1] 'These sayings are ornaments and decorations added on as mere appendages to the legal and doctrinal system : they could just as well be wanting ; the nomistic soteriology would not have been affected by their removal.'

the Rabbis.   B. does not notice (so far as I can see) another Rabbinic phrase which is not less significant.   It is *debar masur leleb* : ' a matter which is left to the heart.'   Thus it is improper to stare at the goods in a shop if one has no money with one, or no intention of buying.   (One raises vain expectations in the mind of the shopman.) Many other similar improprieties are mentioned.   To a repentant sinner one must not say : ' Think of your former actions ' : if a man is suffering from sickness or bereavement, one must not suggest to him (as Job's friends did) that it is due to sin.   All such indelicacies are ' matters given over to the heart,' and of such things it is said, ' And thou shalt fear the Lord thy God ' (Baba Mezia 58 b). One must not shut one's eyes when one sees an old man in order to avoid the trouble of getting up.   This too is a ' matter delivered to the heart ' (Kiddushin 32 b).   Here, too, we notice how the Rabbis, in spite of their legalisms and of their passion for the strict observance of the letter of the Law, yet could see and act and feel beyond the letter.   Nor, finally, is it quite fair when B. says : ' The Law ceased to serve ethical purposes, the fulfilment of the Law became an end in itself.'   The opposition is a false opposition. The fulfilment of the law *was* an end in itself : nevertheless, it was always believed that, even as the laws were given by a perfectly wise, perfectly good, and perfectly gracious Lawgiver (God), these laws were given to help man to be good, and for his moral profit as well as for his spiritual welfare and joy.   B. quotes, as proof of his assertion, certain passages which do not prove it—partly because they mean something different, partly because there are other passages to set them in their proper light.   He quotes the famous utterance of R. Yochanan ben Zakkai about the water of purification and the red cow.   Here was a rite about which men might scoff, or, again, it was a rite about which superstitious ideas could cling. The best that could be done, then, was to say with the Rabbi : the dead body does not really pollute ; the water does not really purify ; it is just a decree of the King of Kings ; and God says of his decrees : no man is entitled to transgress them.   (Pesikta 40 b.) This is a liberating saying.   It prevents superstition.   Better a ukase of a perfectly wise God than any superstitious idea about the physical effects of a corpse or of water.   The next quotation given by B. is the interesting passage in Berachoth 33 b which comments upon the Mishnah v. 3.   That section runs : ' Whoever says

[in his Tefillah] " To a bird's nest do thy mercies extend," or " For
the good be thy name remembered," or " We give thanks, we give
thanks," him do we silence.' Upon which the Gemara remarks ' It is
right that we silence him who says, "We give thanks, we give thanks,"
because he makes it appear as though there were two Powers ; and
likewise him who says, "For the good be thy name remembered,"
the inference being that for the good [may it be remembered], but
not for the bad ; and we have a Mishnaic teaching : A man is in
duty bound to utter a benediction for the bad even as he utters one
for the good. But why [do we silence him who says] " To a bird's
nest do thy mercies extend " ? Two Amoraim in the West differ,
viz. : R. Yose b. Abin and R. Yose b. Zebida : one said : Because
he causes jealousy between God's creatures ; the other said :
Because he makes the ordinances of the Holy One, blessed be He,
to be simply acts of mercy, whereas they are injunctions ' (Dr.
Cohen's translation, p. 225). Doubtless the meaning of the last few
words is that the laws ' must be obeyed without speculating about
their motives,' but it must be observed that the Mishnaic passage
is obscure ; it refers to the Law, Deut. xxii. 6, which seems always
to have struck the imagination of the Rabbis as a very odd enactment. In any case the saying of R. Yose must not be taken to mean
that God's laws had no purpose, and were simply motiveless and
haphazard injunctions. On the other hand, it is true that the idea
of the ukase had always to be preserved. If God is *ex hypothesi*
perfectly wise and good, we must obey his laws just as laws, and we
need not worry ourselves as to their hidden meanings. Such a view,
however, only relates to the ceremonial laws, not to the moral laws.
B. further calls attention to two remarkable passages in the Sifra.
The first, on Lev. xx. 26 (93 d), has already been quoted on Matt. vi.
9. It runs : ' A man must not say, I have no desire to eat pig, I
have no desire to have intercourse with a woman whom I may not
marry : but he must say, Yes, I would like to do these acts, but
what can I do ? My Father who is in heaven has forbidden them.'
(The paradoxical nature of the second example is obvious. It
is only chosen to arrest attention.) Only thus does he accept the
yoke of the Kingdom of God. But that in no wise made the Law
cease to serve ethical purposes. The Rabbinic point of view was
that man stands before the Law of the perfectly wise and perfectly
good God. His glory and his duty, his happiness and his obligation,

lie alike in fulfilling God's declared will. In this view there lies
nothing unethical. That the Rabbis were alive (1) to the distinction
between moral and ceremonial laws ; (2) to the criticisms made by
many heathens upon the queer ceremonial laws is shown by B.'s
second passage from the Sifra (on Lev. xviii. 4, 86 a). 'My "judgments" ye shall do: those are the words of the Law, which, had they
not been written down (there), would have had to be written down
(elsewhere), e.g. about theft and incest and idolatry and blasphemy
and murder. These things, if they had not been forbidden in the
Law (בדין), would have had to be written down (elsewhere) : "mine
ordinances " : these are the laws against which the evil Yetzer and
the nations raise objections, to wit, the prohibition to eat pig, or
to wear garments of linen and woollen mixed, or the law of
Chalitzah, or the leprosy laws, or the law of the Red Cow, or the law
of the scapegoat. Therefore it is said, I, the Lord, made decrees.
It is not permitted to you to raise objections to them' (אין את
רשאי להשיב עליהם). Here, again, no ethical exception can be taken
to the point of view. But the odd thing is that S.B. on Vol. iii.
pp. 397, 398, put in big print, immediately after these two passages,
another passage which represents the general and fundamental point
of view of the Rabbis with complete clearness. And it shows that
the two purposes were in their eyes identical. If the commands of
the Law are ends in themselves, they were also given for the very
purpose of making men better. Even the ceremonial commands,
which, when they were criticized either within or without the Jewish
pale, or when some doubt or heresy was suspected, put the backs of
the Rabbis up, and made them say, ' The laws are the ukases of the
perfect God, obey them and question not,' yet essentially had the
same object as the moral commands : their end was purification.
And this other passage has frequent parallels. ' All the ways of
God are perfect. What does it matter to God if you kill your cattle
the ritual way or not ? Do you profit him thereby or injure him
at all ? Or what does it matter to him if you eat what is pure
or eat what you find dead ? Behold, the laws were only given in
order to purify men through them' (Tanchuma, Shemini 149 b).
If so, surely we cannot say that the Law ceased to serve any
moral purpose, for this very passage and its parallels show most
clearly what is in the Rabbinic mind. Here, then, we may leave
the subject. The supposed ' cautions ' let me, however, repeat,

were not deliberately intended to weaken the observed ill-effects of legalism and letter worship. They are part and parcel of the religion of the Rabbis as a whole; a not fully harmonized religion to our modern minds, but harmonious to *them*. To them they are fully consistent with legalism, nor is the letter inconsistent with the spirit. S.B. speak of a higher and more perfect fulfilment of the Law than that which consists in the mere following of its letter. In one sense this is true, and, so far as it is true, the Rabbis realized it right enough. In another sense, it is not true. How can one do more than love God with ALL one's heart and ALL one's soul and with ALL one's might? And yet to love Him so is the mere fulfilment of the letter. B. supposes that the rejection of Jesus as Messiah implied the final moral and religious degradation of Israel. But it was not so. There are many pathways to the knowledge and the love of God. Moreover, the alleged sharp opposition between the soteriology of Jesus and the soteriology of the Rabbis has, I think, been shown to be uncritical. It is forced out of, and into, the texts. Historically, this sharp contrast cannot be maintained. Jesus was not so far from the Rabbis, nor were the Rabbis so far from Jesus. That is not to say that the legalism of the Rabbis would have been accepted by, or acceptable to, Jesus. It would not. But it does mean that, so far as God's grace and human effort and freedom of will and human weakness and human repentance and God's forgiveness are concerned, the Rabbis and Jesus were by no means poles asunder. As Windisch rightly says : ' Kein Gedanke dass die Bergpredigt dem Menschen die Unausführbarkeit der göttlichen Forderung vor Augen halten wolle : diese Absicht ist ihr ebenso fern wie der Thora' (*Z. N. W.* XIX. p. 178, n. 1).[1] G. Kittel indeed has recently said that ' Repentance in the religion of "works' (*Leistung*) and in the religion of "grace" (*Gnade*) are two different things' (*T. L. Z.*, 1928, p. 541). But he does not inform us in what the difference consists, or wherein lies the superiority of repentance in the religion of grace ! In truth the religion of the Rabbis cannot justly be described—here we·come to the same point over again—as a religion of works as *contrasted* with a religion of grace. It is a religion of both *Leistung* and *Gnade*,

---

[1] ' The Sermon on the Mount has no intention whatever of putting before us the impossibility of carrying out the divine commands; such a purpose is as foreign to the Sermon as to the Law.'

of works *and* grace.   For the works are never adequate without the
grace, though the grace may be given without the works.

Perhaps the full passage from S.B. ought to be translated, of
which only a sentence or two has, so far, been given. ' Simple as
the Rabbinic soteriological system was, simple too was the exegetical
and theological presupposition upon which it rested, namely, that
the literal (verbal, *buchstäblich*) fulfilment of the Law was adequate
in order to satisfy the divine Lawgiver. This fundamental presupposition was regarded as so obvious that it was not even debated.
It lies in the nature of any Code that it can only then be applied
when a deed falls under the wording of one of its paragraphs '
(iv. p. 13).   Hence B. shows how the Rabbis had to determine
exactly what constituted an offence against the Law, and so on.
Every sentence, every word, of the Law had to be explained ; one
enactment had to be compared with another, and all had to be
analysed, etc. ' The entire learned labours of the Rabbis turned on
the letter of the Law ; from the letter it is decided at what point
you become guilty, when any particular command has to be fulfilled ;
how much one has to do in order to fulfil it ; what deeds go beyond
what is required, when a violation of a Law is to be regarded as
voluntary or involuntary ; what punishments follow from what
transgressions ; how violations of the Law can be atoned for, and
so on.   The Halachah of the Mishnah is the codification of the Law
which was built upon the letter of the Pentateuchal Code.   The
Israelite's life was to be a legal life ; that is, it was to fulfil the
provisions of the Halachah whether it was a question of his moral and
religious duties towards God or of his relation to society and to his
fellow-Jews; in either case, and always, what the Jew did, and what
he was to avoid doing, was regulated entirely by the ordinances of
the Halachah.   Always and everywhere, both as regards positive
and negative commands, both for what the Jew had to do and to
avoid, it was the letter of the Law which determined the assessment
and the judgment of his actions.   He who had fulfilled the letter
of the Law had fulfilled the will of God.   Instructive in this
respect are those cases in which certain legal enactments are twisted
to one's own advantage on the basis of the letter of another legal
enactment.   That was called acting " cleverly or slyly." [1]   In such
cases there was an actual circumvention of an ordinance of the Law,

[1] About this matter see Mr. Loewe's interesting essay in the Appendix.

but as this circumvention was legalized by the letter of another legal enactment, it was regarded as permitted and justified. That such " clever " procedure is not specially ethical is clear, but it shows how the all-prevailing legalism of the Rabbis gradually lowered moral conduct to a level of a mere correctness towards the letter of the Law. The Law ceased to serve moral ends ; the fulfilment of the letter became an end in itself. That was the final result of the fundamental axiom that the fulfilment of the letter of the Law was completely coextensive with, and equivalent to, a fulfilment of the will of God. More thoughtful minds (*ernstere Gemüter*) could not help realizing that this axiom was bound to blunt the conscience, and to make moral action mechanical. So they sought for protective measures against the danger. As such are to be regarded :

' (1) The demand that in any fulfilment of a commandment of the Law " intention " (כונה) must not be wanting, *i.e.* the Israelite was to have the deliberate purpose in his mind to satisfy and fulfil the particular command before him. In this way *complete* thought-lessness or carelessness in the execution of the commandments was, at any rate, prevented.

' (2) The rule that the fulfilment of a positive command was invalid if it was brought about by the violation of a prohibition (or negative command).

' (3) The recognition of the principle that a forgiving and benevolent attitude (*das nachsichtige und wohlwollende Verhalten*) towards your fellow-men was better than a purely legal attitude according to the strict measure of the rigid letter of the Law.

' (4) A large number of sayings of learned Rabbis who seek, by emphasizing the true piety of the heart, to obtain a corrective against the debasing moral effects of a legal righteousness of works (" die in der Betonung der rechten Herzensfrömmigkeit ein Korrektiv suchen gegen die sittlich verflachende Werk- und Gesetzesgerechtig-keit "). But all these measures and sayings remained without con-siderable (*durchgreifenden*) effect. They did nothing to shake the conviction that the literal fulfilment of the Law satisfied the will of God, nor were they able to modify the soteriology of the synagogue which had been formed upon the basis of legal righteousness. These cautions and saving provisos resemble ornaments and decorations which were just externally fastened on to the legal building (*das nomistische Lehrgebäude*) ; they might as well have been wanting ; the legal soteriology would have been untouched by their disappearance.'

According to Billerbeck's theory, indeed according to his statements, the religious and ethical condition of the Jews from, let us say, A.D. 30 to A.D. 500 must have become worse and worse. The moral degradation produced by the Law must have deepened from generation to generation. But no evidence is produced by Billerbeck that such was the case. Professor Burkitt thinks that the purgations of Titus and Hadrian produced religious improvement. Yet the legal system was still more universal and more complete than before. It is a considerable omission that B. has nothing to say about Joy. Yet the joy of the commandments—the sheer delight in executing and fulfilling the divine commands, the sense of sonship and privilege and honour (which no doubt had its dangers on the side of particularism and pride), immensely mitigated the danger of mechanical observance. It was not a case of trying to dodge the laws, and to do as *little* as you could in order just to satisfy the letter of the Code ; it was a case of delighted doing as *much* as you could ; the more you did, the greater the joy, the greater the honour, the greater the love—no doubt also fused with all these, but *not* predominant, the greater the reward. And the very commands which were regarded as greatest and most glorious were the commands for which there was no exact verbal fulfilment. How are you verbally to fulfil the commands of honouring your parents, of visiting the sick, of showing lovingkindness to the poor, of loving your neighbour, of loving God ? They must be fulfilled ungrudgingly and not according to an exact letter and measurement, or they cannot be fulfilled at all. The legal righteousness of the Rabbis was, in frequent practice, an odd combination of minute 'ceremonial' and outward observances and of the most delicate lovingkindness and the sweetest piety. The combination is impossible to most of us to-day, but it existed and worked well among the Rabbis and among those who were influenced by their teaching and regarded them as their religious leaders.

A little further on B. says (IV. p. 19 *fin.*) : ' In the Sermon on the Mount Jesus mentions directly neither the soteriology of the Rabbis nor the presupposition upon which it rests : namely, the opinion that the literal or verbal fulfilment of the Law is enough

to satisfy the will and demand of the divine Legislator. And yet
he does actually attack both in the most decided way. But his
method of attack is of a peculiar kind ; he does not fight with words
against the old and the unusable, in order to destroy them, but he
substitutes constructively for them the New and the Better. And
then he leaves it to the conscience of his hearers to decide for themselves in full freedom, whether for the Old or for the New. First
of all, he opposes to the Pharisaic legal righteousness a higher and
better Righteousness without which nobody can enter the Kingdom
of God. He then clearly explains wherein this higher Righteousness consists. By various examples he shows how infinitely more
the demands which are included in God's commands imply—how
immensely they exceed—the verbal interpretation which the
Rabbis gave to these commands.' [And yet, in almost each instance,
the Rabbis interpreted the commands *precisely* as Jesus interpreted
them.] ' But if the verbal interpretation of the commands does
not do justice to the sense which God really intended his commands
to have, it follows that their verbal fulfilment cannot satisfy God's
will, or give, or secure, that righteousness, which counts as such
before God. In this way the basis was destroyed upon which the
soteriology of the Rabbis rested, and the legal system of the Pharisees was broken down and collapsed of itself. But Jesus does not
rest there. By the interpretation which he gives to the divine
commands, he seeks to bring to the consciousness of his hearers,
and to make them realize, that their own power is wholly insufficient
to fulfil the divine commands as they ought to be fulfilled according
to the divine will. That " poverty of spirit " of which the first
Beatitude speaks is to be evoked in the minds of his hearers, so that
the anxious question may be aroused in them, " Who then can be
saved ? " (Matt. xix. 25).' [A dubious juxtaposition of two distinct
and heterogeneous passages.] ' That hunger is to be awakened in
them which contains within itself the promise of its own satisfaction (Matt. v. 6), the hunger for the true righteousness, which
Jesus will give and ascribe to those (*die Jesus den beilegen wird*)
who follow his words in faith. Round them the storm may howl,
even the storms of the divine Judgment ; they will not fall. For
they have God's verdict upon their side. This is the point, where
every man has to decide for himself. For Jesus or against him.
The Jewish people as a whole decided against Jesus. His gentle

allurement and urgings were in vain. Other means seemed to be
required in order to loosen that close armour of self-righteousness
and legal righteousness which the Rabbis had laid around the
people. A Rabbi who lived early in the fourth century once said,
" The removal of the seal ring of Ahasuerus had greater results
than the 48 Prophets and the seven Prophetesses who prophesied
to Israel : for all these could not make Israel duly repent and
amend its ways, but the removal of the ring did so " (Megillah, 14 a).
By this saying R. Abba b. Kahana meant to teach that God's
punitive judgments were more efficacious in Israel than all the
preachings of the Prophets. And, indeed, when the punitive judgment of A.D. 70 fell upon the Jews, it seemed as if the fall of the
Jewish state would have also effected in many Pharisaic circles
the collapse of the proud structure of legal righteousness before
God. Then men began to realize their own powerlessness, and they
bethought them of God's grace. And yet this great judgment only
produced very partial and imperfect results (*wirkte nur Stückwerk*).
The moral courage which inspired Paul was wanting, the courage
to break *wholly* with the old self-righteousness, and to take refuge
exclusively in the grace of God. They stopped half-way : half grace
and half merit (*eigenes Verdienst*) was to produce salvation. And
what might have been expected ensued. The veil of Moses again
began to cover Israel's heart, perhaps even more firmly and more
thickly than before. Only when Israel shall be converted to the
Lord will the veil be taken away (2 Cor. iii. 16).' But, historically,
there is no reason to believe that the Rabbis thought more of
God's ' grace ' and of human ' weakness ' after 70 than before it,
or again, that they insisted more on man's responsibility and on
his capacity (within limits) to fulfil the Law before 70 than after
it. (The famous prayer, ' Not because of our righteous acts,'
which, with Dr. Abrahams' comments, I have quoted in another
connection, may, I understand, well have been composed before
the fall of Jerusalem.) The words *eigenes Verdienst* carry a
certain sting. But if for them we substitute human responsibility
or human effort, the half-way house seems religiously correct.
The *Stückwerk* then becomes more accurate. Man's effort, God's
help ; man's striving, God's grace. We ought and we can. But
though we ought, we cannot *wholly* : there God's mercy comes in
as well as his help. This seems to answer to our religious experi-

ence and to the facts of life. We cannot *prove* the 'grace' or the
'help.' We cannot quantitatively divide up any action into our
part and God's part. But we may none the less believe in both.
The *Stückwerk* seems right. It is *not* all God's grace. It *is* partly
man's own effort. And if man's efforts do, according to Rabbinic
doctrine, receive recognition at God's hands, if because his will is
free, he is justly punished and justly rewarded, yet, as Dr. Abrahams
points out, these very rewards are themselves 'grace.' 'Nothing
that man, with his small powers and finite opportunities, can do
constitutes a *claim* on the favour of the All-mighty and the Infinite.
Hence : Not because of (*i.e.* relying on) our righteous acts [which
are humanly righteous ; they are *not* unreal] do we lay our supplications before thee, but because of (or relying on) thine abundant
mercies.' Surely no ignoble position, no unworthy doctrine. But
that is not to say that the Pauline and Lutheran position and
doctrine in this matter—very different as it is— is not *also* noble
and worthy. If Billerbeck quotes Paul, I will quote him too.
'One star differeth from another star in glory.' Yet both are
glorious. 'There is one glory of the sun and another glory of the
moon.' Which has the greater glory we need not argue. Many
roadways lead to God. Both the 'righteousness' of the Rabbis
and the 'righteousness' of Jesus are excellent righteousnesses.
Each thought that the other was quite inadequate for the entering
into the Kingdom of Heaven. Yet surely here were Jesus and the
Rabbis equally in error. For both righteousnesses, honestly pursued,
are acceptable unto God.

viii. 10. In the teaching—both direct and implied—attributed
to Jesus on the subject of Faith, there seems something special,
but it would be hard to say exactly in what it consists. It is not
the same teaching as that of Paul. Still less is it that of Luther
and of the German Lutheran theologians. It is not opposed to
'works.' It is not faith in Jesus ; it is not faith in any doctrine.
It is essentially trust in God, confidence in his supreme goodness,
in his willingness, and even desire, to help the troubles, and to
answer the prayers of his human children. In order that he may
put this power and desire into practice, trust on the part of man
seems to be an indispensable prerequisite. It may be supposed
that the teaching of Jesus on the need of this prerequisite arose

out of what actually took place. *We* to-day should and could account for some of his experiences on purely scientific lines. The man who believed that Jesus could cure him was cured. The disciple who doubted whether he would be able to heal him he failed to heal. Faith was needed in the patient and in the healer (though this faith would not account for such a purely supernatural healing, if it be historic, as that of the Centurion's son). However this may be, the faith which Jesus himself possessed, and the faith which he demanded from others, and desired others to possess, was of a simple kind: it was, as I have said, trust in God's goodness and power. So far as it involved any trust in Jesus himself, it was trust that he was empowered by God to heal or to work miracles. It cannot be maintained that the Rabbis were not equally solicitous that men should have trust in God, that they should not believe whole-heartedly in his goodness and in his power. In the Mechilta we have a whole long section in which the value, the efficacy, and the greatness of faith (*emunah*) are set forth and belauded. This section is the 'commentary,' if one can call it so, on Exodus xiv. 31, 'And they believed in the Lord and in Moses, his servant,' where, as we might also notice, you get in the O.T. itself a concurrent 'faith' in God and in God's messenger or prophet. Nor did the Rabbis lack appreciation of, or fail to comment on, the famous saying in Genesis xv. 6 : 'And Abraham believed in the Lord, and the Lord accounted it to him for righteousness.' S.B. very naturally seek to depreciate the Rabbinic conception of faith, and to contrast it, to its disfavour, with the conception of Paul. They are obviously bound to press this difference to the utmost, for it is of the very essence of their creed. They argue that Rabbinic 'faith' shows a decline from the place and conception of faith in the Pseudepigrapha and in Philo. With the Rabbis 'faith' has become a mere *Leistung*, a good 'work,' on a par with other good works. It can claim merit, just like other good 'works.' It is no humble yearning ; no giving and craving of the soul, no passionate submission and longing and conviction, without any taint of claim or merit or virtue or achievement. And so on, and so on. We need not, however, here enter into the truth of these oppositions and contrasts, for the 'faith' taught by Paul is very different from the 'faith' taught by Jesus. The faith which Jesus taught, asked for, and possessed—trust in

God's power and goodness—was not essentially different from the faith (*emunah*) which is praised by the Rabbis. On the other hand, the *place* of faith in the teaching of Jesus seems somewhat different from the place of faith in the teaching of the Rabbis. In the teaching of Jesus faith seems more central than it is in the teaching of the Rabbis. In the teaching of Jesus, faith keeps constantly cropping up ; we can hardly say that it keeps constantly cropping up in the teaching of the Rabbis. Moreover, faith seems more central for another reason : it is the first virtue which is asked for, the fundamental prerequisite. ' Do not fear ; only have faith. Thy faith has saved thee. Be it done unto thee according to thy faith. " If thou canst," sayest thou ? All things are possible to him who has faith.' These sayings seem not only central to the teaching as a whole, but to strike a somewhat different note from anything spoken about ' faith ' in the Rabbinic literature. Nevertheless, the conception itself : trust in God, trust in God's power and goodness, is thoroughly Rabbinic, and the teaching, however pregnant and fresh, is not off the Rabbinic line. (It may be noted that the words πίστις [faith] and πιστεύειν [have faith, believe] do not occur in the Sermon on the Mount.) Whether the words used are faith or trust or hope, the meaning with the Rabbis is always much the same. The Biblical verbs *Kivvah* and *Yichal*, which occur so repeatedly in the Psalms, are translated in the English version by ' wait on ' and ' hope in.' They too mean trust. In the Synoptic Gospels the phrase to hope in God is not found : we have only ' believe ' and ' faith.' The Rabbinic terminology is more fluid. Thus, in Midrash Psalms xl. 1 (on ' I waited patiently for the Lord '), it is said : ' If you hope, and you are not delivered, hope and hope again. Do you say, How long shall we hope ? Was it not written of old, O Israel, hope in the Lord for evermore ' (Psalms cxxxi. 3).

Some of the Mechilta passages about Faith run thus : ' The faith with which Abraham believed in me was sufficient (worth enough) that I should cleave the waters of the Red Sea. The faith with which the Israelites believed in me (Exodus iv. 3) was sufficient that I should divide the waters of the Red Sea. For they did not say to Moses, How can we go up into the wilderness, seeing that we have no food for the journey, but they believed and followed Moses. (29 b, 30 a.) Great was the faith with which the Israelites believed (or trusted) in God, for as the reward for that faith the

Holy Spirit rested upon them, and they sang the song' (Ex.
xiv. 31, xv. 1). 'Abraham only inherited this world and the next
world by the merit (zechuth) of his faith in God. Anyone who
fulfils a single command in faith, is worthy that the Holy Spirit
should rest upon him. The Israelites were redeemed from Egypt
only as a reward of their faith' (Ex. iv. 31). By combining Isaiah
xxvi. 2 and Psalm cxviii. 20, the righteous are identified with the
men of faith. Quoting Psalm xcii. 4, it is said that the rejoicing
was 'the reward of the faith of our fathers which they showed here
in this world which is all night' (as compared with the next world).
Quoting Ex. xvii. 11, 'When Moses held up his hand Israel prevailed,' etc., and Numbers xxi. 8 ('Make thee a serpent and set it
upon a pole '), it is said : ' Did Moses' hands make Israel strong or
overcome Amalek ?   Can a snake kill and bring to life ?   No ; but
while Moses held up his hand, the Israelites looked at him and
believed in Him who had ordered Moses to do this, and so with the
serpent, and then (as a reward of their faith) God did wonders for
them or healed them.' [A characteristic Rabbinic explaining away
of a superstitious passage.]   In the Midrash to Psalm xxxi. (8),
verse 24, 120 b, ' The Lord preserves the faithful,' it says : ' These
are the Israelites who say, Blessed be the Lord who quickens the
dead, and they answer Amen in faith, for they believe with all
their strength that God will quicken the dead, though the resurrection of the dead has not yet come.   And they say, Blessed be
God who redeems Israel though Israel is not yet redeemed.   And
they say, Blessed be God who rebuilds Jerusalem, though Jerusalem
is not yet rebuilt.   God says : Israel is not yet redeemed, but is
again in servitude, yet they have faith that I shall redeem them
in a time to come.'   Playing with Genesis xxviii. 12 and Jeremiah
xxx. 10, it is said (in Leviticus Rabba, אמור, xxix. 2 on xxiii. 24),
God showed Jacob the princes of Babylon, Media, Greece, and Edom
(i.e. Rome) rising and falling.   'He said to Jacob, Thou too wilt
rise.   But Jacob was afraid, and said, Perhaps I shall also fall, like
them.   Then God said, Fear not, if thou fall, it shall not be for ever.
But he did not believe, and so he did not rise.   And God said to
him, If thou hadst believed, thou wouldst have risen and not fallen ;
but now as thou didst not believe, thy children will be enslaved
under these four kingdoms with tribute and taxes and levies and
imposts.'   R. Eliezer the Great said, 'He who has yet bread in his

basket and says, what shall I eat to-morrow, belongs to those who are small in faith.' 'R. Elazar said, What has caused it that the table of the righteous in the world to come is plundered ? Their smallness of faith (playing on Zech. iv. 10) because they did not believe in the Holy One' (Sotah 48 b). The conceptions of *Zechuth* and Faith are oddly mixed up in the passage (Exodus Rabba, בשלח, xxiii. 5 on xv. 1). 'R. Nehemiah said, The Israelites were accounted worthy (*zachu*) to sing the song at the Red Sea only through the merit (*Zechuth*) of their faith. R. Isaac said, They saw all those marvels that were done for them ; how should they not have had faith ? (there was no merit in their faith). R. Simeon b. Abba said, It was only because of Abraham's faith that the Israelites were accounted worthy (*zachu*) to sing the song.'

Mr. Loewe writes as follows : 'I have read, very carefully, one after another, all the passages which are to be found in the Gospels about faith, in order to test their cumulative effect. As to their grace and charm, there is nothing to be said : they speak for themselves. But you raise the question of novelty. There *is* a certain novelty about the passages, but it is not that, which to my mind at least, makes them attractive. They are, in fact, attractive in spite of that novelty. They reflect the same spirit of trust in God as one finds elsewhere ; you emphasize this. But the novelty consists of two departures—that is to say, in two ways I feel I am outside Rabbinic thought. The first is the importance attached to miracles. In the Gemara or Midrash, miracles take a secondary place. They are there, it is true, but they do not count so much. Either they point a moral in an almost natural way, *e.g.* if a man incurs a loss by doing a *Mitzvah*, God makes it up to him by allowing a red heifer to be born in his herd or by causing his harvests to be exceptionally good. Or, when miracles are frankly miraculous, I think they were related with the tongue in the cheek. Especially is this the case with the grotesque ones, *e.g.* the Sindbad tales recounted by Raba. But in very few cases do miracles seem to count for something. Onias, the circle-drawer, for example, is miracle pure and simple, but he comes into the scope of hagiology rather than Scripture. What I mean is that, on the Rabbinic side, miracles *don't* matter, in the Gospels they do. אין סומכין על הנס (we must not rely on a miracle) is far more typical than any of the contrary type of sayings. Because the Red

Sea was cleft for the Israelites by reason of faith, *we* must not expect the same. Miracles belong to the past ; they piled up miracles for bye-gone ages and gloried in them. For the present they said "we are not worthy that a miracle should be worked for us," and I do not think that this was uttered regretfully. The sort of miracle that might justifiably be expected was collective, not personal, *e.g.* freedom from Rome, coming of the Kingdom, Messiah, etc. Personal miracles were more of the type of expecting that if one had bread to-day, one would have some to-morrow. The Bible miracles do not concern us here : they were the common property of both sides.

'Now in the Gospel, faith and miracle seem inseparable. All these passages, more or less, link the two. Of course, the question arises how far are the miracles claimed for Jesus by a later age and projected backwards, and how far are they authentic. I feel that if you cut away miracles, what remains ? Where is your lesson on faith, on trust in God, amid the ordinary events and dangers of life ? A Jew can derive this lesson without the superstructure of the miraculous ; can the Christian do so ? Suppose he says (1) " I do not believe that Peter walked on the sea by faith," (2) " all that Jesus did in the way of faith-healing can be explained psychologically—why, then, do you ask *me* to have faith ? "

'My second point is that in nearly all of these passages faith means faith in Jesus.' (I do not agree : to Jesus at least, as *he* spoke them, they usually meant faith in God.—C. G. M.) 'The prophets were more impersonal, and the Rabbis most of all. Faith in God, not in His mouthpiece. "And they believed in the Lord and in Moses His Servant" is a case that shows this well. Superficially the same faith is claimed for both, but the whole conception of the life and work of Moses shows that two entirely different ideas of faith are meant. If Bar Kochba or Akiba had made such claims for themselves as Jesus made, what would be said ? When Muhammed does so, do we not consider that the axe exalts itself over Him that wields it ?

'Here, again, the question arises, how did Jesus describe these acts, how did he conceive of his mission, and how far have divine powers and divine claims been superadded by the Evangelists ? But again I feel that if the personal element is eliminated, the bulk of the teaching vanishes. For these two reasons : (1) the stress on the miraculous and its inextricable association with faith, (2) the emphasis on the personality of Jesus, I feel that the " novel " features are not of value to Jewish readers.'

11. It would take far too much space to write an essay on the Universalism and the Particularism of the Rabbis. Particularism and Universalism are hardly live issues for us now. We are all universalists. It may be doubted very much whether the attitude of Jesus himself towards the heathen differed much from that of the old prophets in their higher, more universalist, moments. We have to take into consideration *all* the passages which have to do with non-Jews, both the friendly and the unfriendly ones, and if we do so, I think that what I have just said will probably be the conclusion of impartial criticism. I admit that there are many doubts and difficulties on either side. The unfriendly passages, or some of them, may not be authentic; the friendly passages, or some of them, may not be authentic. The Samaritan passages, *e.g.*, are only in Luke, and as to the good Samaritan it is still (to my mind) an open question whether he is an original figure in the parable. There is no strong evidence that Jesus meant to include the ' heathen ' among the ' enemies ' whom we are to love. One has to remember what Jesus does *not* say as well as what he does. And if this canon works in one (anti-Rabbinic) direction, as Wellhausen urges in his famous and bitter apophthegm, it also works in another. How easy and how necessary to have said, ' Ye were told to hate the heathen and to love the Jew ; I tell you to love all men. Ye were told that neighbour only meant fellow-Jew ; I tell you it means the heathen as well.' But of all this, except in the dubious instance of the Good Samaritan, there is no clear indication at all.

On the whole, the Rabbis are frankly particularist. The ' pro-gentile ' passages are *comparatively* few in number. Even the passages in which some (usually awkward) justification is sought for the Rabbis' particularism, for their hatred of the Gentile oppressors, and for the hatred which God is usually represented as feeling towards them, are not very many. On the other hand, what has just been said must be strictly understood as referring to the passages in which the Rabbis definitely refer to the ' nations,' and mean by the nations either the actual peoples under whose subjection they lived, or definitely the ' idolaters.' When, in their

quieter moods, or perhaps in quieter seasons (in eras of less oppression, persecution, or tension) they thought of God and of his benefi-
cence and lovingkindness, they could use very universalist language.
Just as the Psalmist could say, ' The Lord is good to all, and his
mercies are over all his works,' so too could the Rabbis.   And
they did.   Nor were they any the less sincere when in such moods
they spoke of God's love for and towards ' all ' than when they
spoke with glee of the annihilation of the nations—the enemies of
Israel and of God—or of their punishment in Hell.   They are always
in undress and always sincere.   When they speak of God's un-
bounded love, they usually use the term ' creatures ' (בריות), and
by this term they certainly mean men generally, and are *not* thinking specifically of Israel.   For example : ' R. Elazar said in the
name of Abina, Whoso recites Psalm cxlv. thrice daily is assured
of the world to come.   Why ?   Is it because it is alphabetical ?
Then let a man rather recite Psalm cxix., which has an eightfold
alphabet.   No.   The reason is because it contains the verse, " Thou
openest thine hand, and satisfiest the desire of every living thing."
But, then, let a man say Psalm cxxxvi., which says, " He gives
food to all flesh."   No.   Psalm cxlv. is better, because it has two '
(Berachoth 4 b).   (Mr. Loewe takes ' two ' to mean two universalist
verses, 9 and 16).   It is as illegitimate to ignore such passages as
it is illegitimate to ignore the particularist passages about the
' nations.'   Both must be taken into account.   It is true to say
that when Israel and the nations are considered, and God's relation
to the one and to the other, the Rabbis are ' frankly particularist.'
God loves Israel with a peculiar, special, and passionate love.   He
has no such love for the nations.   For the most part he may be
said to dislike them.   On the other hand, when God's goodness is
spoken of without special thought either of Israel on the one hand,
or of the nations on the other, then the divine ' universalism '—
his love and his pity towards all his human creatures, and even
towards the animals—is strongly emphasized.   Dr. Marmorstein in
his book on *The Old Rabbinic Doctrine of God* (Part I. pp. 196–208),
quotes a number of passages of this description.   Even to the wicked
God is merciful and good.   ' God feeds and sustains all ' (Mechilta
38 a).   ' Just as God's love extends to human beings, so his mercy
is upon the cattle and birds' (Deut. R., *Ki Tetze*, vi. 1).   'God satisfies
all and even the wicked ' (Mechilta 59 a).   'God is the Father of

all beings ; God is the Father of the whole world.' ' God is good
to all and his mercy extends over all, for his nature is to be merciful.' ' God is good to all, and the greatest good is that his creatures
learn of him to be merciful to each other' (Genesis Rabba, נח,
xxxiii. 3 on viii. 1). ' To each creature is granted the desire of its
heart.' ' The world was created out of goodness ' (Midrash Tadshe
29). And so on. And Dr. Marmorstein gives the references to all
these and many more passages of a similar kind. But he says
nothing about the mass of passages which breathe a very different
spirit and tell a very different story. Yet this second class of
passage is even more numerous than the first class, and is quite as
characteristic. Both, as I have said, would have to be taken account
of in forming the complete picture.

One of the oddest examples of the mixture of Universalism and
Particularism which I have come across is the following. (The
Rabbis' minds must have been pulled both ways, and the result is
a funny muddle. As usual, it is the text of the Bible which helps to
cause the muddle.) ' A land which the Lord cares for' (Deut. xi. 12).
' Rabbi said, But does he only care for Palestine ? Does he not care for
all lands ? It is as if (כביכול) he only cared for Palestine, but as the
reward of his caring for it, he cares with it for all other lands.'
' The Guardian of Israel.' ' But is he only the Guardian of Israel ?
Does he not guard all ? (Job xii. 10.) It is, as it were, like this.
He guards Israel only, but as the reward of guarding them, he guards
all with them ' (Sifre 78 b).

Different again from both sets of passages are those which deal
with the question of proselytes, and with the conversion of the
heathen in the ' latter days.' Here there is a considerable degree
of universalism. And many passages could be quoted to show a
Rabbinic belief in the ingathering of a large number of heathen at
the coming of the Messianic age. Matthew viii. 11, 12 goes, however,
beyond this ; it is not certainly authentic. It speaks of the *exclusion* of Jews and the admission of Gentiles. (*Cp*. xxi. 43.) That is
definitely anti-Jewish, and naturally finds no parallel in Rabbinic
literature.

The large number of passages in S.B. illustrating Rabbinic
particularism (*e.g.* Vol. III. 81–83, 140–155 ; Vol. I. pp. 360–363) need
not be quoted here. They undoubtedly indicate a prevailing feeling.
The Rabbinic literature makes no attempt to disguise that feeling

P

or any other feeling. In its good points and in its bad points, it is entirely sincere. More especially did the horrors and agonies connected with Titus and Hadrian leave a deep mark upon the minds and hearts of the Rabbis. In the night of oppression and cruelty, from which the Jews were more or less always suffering, it was a relief to vent their feelings in this way. They were entirely powerless to vent them in any other. It was, moreover, an encouragement to the masses to remain firm in their faith to tell them that, in the Messianic age, or at the resurrection of the dead, and the final judgment, Israel would triumph for ever and its foes be annihilated. It was a comfort to insist that, in spite of all Israel's woes, God loved Israel with a peculiar and passionate love, and that he hated the ' nations ' —that they only enjoyed, and were allowed to enjoy, ' this world ' in order to be the more assuredly punished or destroyed in the world to come. We are far removed from those days. The particularism has disappeared for good. It seems needless here to recall it.

Though the great number of anti-Gentile passages are obviously not wholly unpleasing to S.B., and though they supply a nice foil for Pauline universalism, it cannot fairly be said that S.B. suppress the citation of passages on the other side ; the only thing that can be said is that S.B. somewhat unduly depreciate the force of these passages. They are also rather inclined to argue that Rabbinic particularism grew worse and worse, and that feelings in (say) 400 were more bitter than in 100. However this may be (and it is, I think, very dubious), the pro-Gentile passages are not omitted by S.B., just as the nice and generous passages about proselytes are given as well as the nasty ones. We are duly informed of the famous saying of R. Joshua (end of first century), who, as against R. Eliezer, declared that there *were* some good men among the *massa perditionis* of the Gentiles, and that these good men *would* share in the blessed life of the world to come. (Sanhedrin 105 a ; Tosefta Sanhedrin xiii. 2, p. 434 ; Bacher, *Agada der Tannaiten*, Vol. i., ed. 2, p. 134.) And it is, perhaps, implied (though not distinctly told) that this saying of R. Joshua became more and more the official opinion of the synagogue, so that Maimonides definitely lays down the statement that the righteous of all nations shall have a part in the blessedness of the world to come. It is a curious thing that Orthodox Judaism which, if we regard it as starting with the Rabbis, began with a prevailing particularism, developed into something near a satisfactory universalism. For conduct, morality—according to the official dogma of the mediaeval synagogue—enabled a man to obtain salvation whatever his creed (at all events if he was a Theist), whereas Christianity, which, if we regard it as starting with Paul, began with a prevailing universalism, developed into something near a disagreeable particularism. At all events, creed, not conduct, became the test for salvation, and the position of the unbeliever (let alone the heretic) became as dangerous and doubtful as the position of the Gentile in Rabbinic Judaism.

As I have already indicated, I do not think it needful to quote the passages in Rabbinic literature about proselytes. From the saying, in Pesachim 87 b, that the whole purpose of Israel's dispersion is the making of proselytes, to the saying of R. Chelbo that proselytes are to Israel what an eruption is to the body, every sort of opinion about them can be illustrated by quotations. (See as to the meaning of R. Chelbo's saying, Moore I. p. 346 *fin.*) And, doubtless, some attempt could be made to adjust these varying views chronologically, or by reference to the circumstances in which they were uttered. The generous sayings are, I think, more numerous, and represent the predominant view more faithfully, than the churlish and narrow sayings. I will just give one of the nice sayings of which I have always been fond. To understand it one must remember that the Biblical word *ger* (A. and R.V. ' stranger,' or, as the scholars say, ' resident alien ') has in Rabbinic the meaning of ' proselyte.' Thus the Biblical injunction, ' love ye the stranger,' is constantly interpreted by the Rabbis to mean, ' love ye the proselyte.' 'The Holy One loves the *Gerim* exceedingly. To what is the matter like ? To a king who had a lot of sheep and goats which went forth every morning to the pasture and returned in the evening to the stable. One day a stag joined the flock and grazed with the sheep, and returned with them. Then the shepherd said to the king : There is a stag which goes out with the sheep and grazes with them, and comes home with them. And the king loved the stag exceedingly. And he commanded the shepherd, saying : Give heed unto this stag, that no man beat it ; and when the sheep returned in the evening, he would order that the stag should have food and drink. Then the shepherds said to him, My Lord, thou hast many goats and sheep and kids, and thou givest us no directions about these, but about this stag thou givest us orders day by day.

Then the king replied : It is the custom of the sheep to graze in the pasture, but the stags dwell in the wilderness, and it is not their custom to come among men in the cultivated land. But to this stag who has come to us and lives with us, should we not be grateful that he has left the great wilderness, where many stags and gazelles feed, and has come to live among us ? It behoves us to be grateful. So too spake the Holy One : I owe great thanks to the stranger, in that he has left his family and his father's house, and has come to dwell amongst us ; therefore I order in the Law : Love ye the stranger ' (Midrash Psalms on Psalm cxlvi. 9). The same passage is found in Numbers R. viii. 1, 2. Here it has a good introduction. ' The proselytes are as radically important to God (עיקר) as the Israelites. A man (however much he might wish it) cannot become a Priest or a Levite, if he is not born one. But anyone, even a *goi*, can become righteous. And because such men of their own free will come to love God, therefore God loves them.' (*Cp.* Midrash Sifre on Numbers, tr. Levertoff, 1926, p. 4.) ' Who is greater, he who loves the King, or he whom the King loves ? Say : He whom the King loves, even as it says, God loves the *gerim* ' (*i.e.* to the Rabbis, not the ' resident alien ' or the ' stranger,' but the proselytes). (Mechilta, *Mishpatim*, xviii., ed. Horowitz and Rabin, p. 311.)

A similar variety of view could be found as regards Rabbinic views about the entry of the Gentiles into the Messianic age or into the Final Beatitudes. (*Cp.* Moore I. p. 323–353.) Some Rabbis would seem to have believed that ultimately nearly all the Gentiles would be permanently located in Hell or annihilated, while others believed that a very considerable number would be ' converted,' and share with Israel in Messianic and everlasting beatitudes. Moore cites the passage : ' In this world, through the efforts of the righteous (על ידי הצדיקים), individuals become proselytes, but in the Age to Come God himself will draw the righteous near, and bring them under the wings of the Shechinah, as it is said (Zeph. iii. 9), Then will I give the peoples a pure language that they may all call on the name of the Lord ' (Tanchuma B., *Vayera*, xxxviii. 54 b). This passage would seem to mean that God will induce great masses of men to become proselytes in the Messianic Age. It would be interesting to know what the Rabbis would have thought about a non-Jewish people who, nevertheless, were all Monotheists,

and worshipped no material representation or image of the Divine
Being. It was idolatry which provoked their particularism quite
as much as, and more than, their nationalistic feelings. It is stated
more than once that the mere rejection of idolatry is almost equivalent to being a Jew. ' He who rejects idolatry is as if he agreed to
the whole Torah ' (כל הכופר בעבודה זרה כמודה בכל התורה כולה).
(Sifre 32 a, 85 a.) So heavy (חמורה) is (the prohibition of) idolatry.
(Nedarim 25 a.) And yet a few lines before we are told that the
law of Fringes weighs as much as all the other commands in the
Law put together. How hard it is to know when the Rabbis are
in deadly earnest or not. In a well-known passage in Megillah
13 a R. Yochanan says that he who renounces idolatry is called a
Jew (יהודי). But, of a truth, all these opinions about the destruction or the conversion of the Gentiles in the Messianic Age have now
only a somewhat remote historical interest.

More interesting are the signs in Rabbinic literature of the heart-
searching which their particularism gave to its authors. It was in
one way very pleasant to believe that God hated the enemies and
oppressors of Israel, and that their power and prosperity and happiness were strictly limited to earth and to the pre-Messianic age.
But, after all, there was only one God. He had created everybody,
Gentile no less than Jew. He was said to be, and believed to be, just,
compassionate, loving. Was there not some discrepancy between
the two sets of propositions ? Many theories were, therefore,
devised. The Gentiles were wicked, they deserved their fate. The
Gentiles had deliberately turned away from the true God and worshipped false gods. Their false beliefs were in themselves sinful.
And so on. Again, the Law had been offered to the Gentiles, but they
had refused it. They would not accept its obligations ; therefore
it was just that they should not participate in those ultimate beatitudes which its faithful observance would—at long last—bring to
every humble observer. All these semi-explanations and excuses it
would take too long to illustrate by citation. It was a good thing
that these various views about the ultimate lot and fate of the
heathen world remained more or less fluid and undefined, so that it
was possible for the good exceptions to grow stronger, and ultimately
to become predominant. For R. Joshua's tolerant and exceptional
point of view—exceptional, I fancy, throughout the strictly Rabbinic period (say 100 B.C.–A.D. 500)—yet quietly grew in strength,

and became, as I have said, the codified doctrine of the mediaeval synagogue.

One of the oddest mixtures of universalism and particularism is a passage quoted by S.B. in illustration of Romans xi. 11. It says in Jeremiah xxx. 6, ' Why are all faces turned into paleness ? ' ' R. Yochanan said, These are the upper family (*i.e.* the angels) and the lower family (*i.e.* Israel) in the hour when God says, These (the Israelites) are the work of my hand, and those (the gentiles) are the work of my hands. How am I to destroy the latter for the sake of the former ? [The angels and Israel are alarmed at this compunction shown by God at the destruction of the Gentiles.] Rab Papa said, That is what the people say : If the ox falls at his work, the horse is put instead of him in his stall.' [This is explained to mean that, even when the ox is healed, it is hard to get rid of the horse. It would be hard for God, even when and if the Israelites adequately repent, to annihilate the Gentiles.] The favourite quotation of Jewish apologists is the story how God, when the angels sang their paeans of delight at the destruction of the Egyptians in the Red Sea, rebuked them, saying, ' My children lie drowned at the bottom of the sea, and you would sing before me in joy ' (Sanhedrin 39 b ; Megillah 10 b ; and *cp.* Ex. Rab. xxiii. on xv. 1 ; Mech. p. 34 b). Unfortunately the passages which could be quoted showing a very different tendency are much more numerous. Nevertheless, in the long run, and if we look back upon all that is past and gone, Rabbinic particularism did not so very much matter. It did not, I mean, so much matter to *Judaism*. For it was not part of the *essence* of the religion. The compassion or love of God *was* of the essence of the religion. It was easy to shed a bad particularism which was opposed to that essence. The somewhat casual and isolated Rabbinic dictum that ' the righteous of all nations should have a share in the world to come ' could easily be expanded, generalized, and deepened. A false particularism opposed to the dictum could easily be dropped. In no religion can universalism be purer than in modern Liberal Judaism, and so far as Matthew viii. 11, 12 is concerned, while the harsh second verse need not be used, the spirit of the first verse can be, and is, accepted to the very fullest possible degree.

To this note Mr. Loewe has made the following interesting observations : ' I quite agree with your point that Jewish scholars sometimes quite unfairly suppress unfriendly passages and sometimes argue merely from the friendly ones, as though these alone were typical. There can be no doubt that there were teachers whose point of view was unpleasantly particularist, but I would plead that (1) their teaching was but the reflection of their own individual outlook, and (2) that they may have uttered their remarks with reference to a particularly bad group of non-Jews. Thus the Conservative party in English politics has been the champion of the principle of liberty as much as the Liberal party, yet many Conservative—and Christian—speeches on the subject of aliens have been as bad as anything uttered 1900 years ago by particularist Jews. No doubt the Conservative speakers were confronted by aliens whose actions were as antipathetic to them as were those of heathens to the Rabbis who denounced them. The life of the average Provincial must have been very low. Quite apart from idolatry, the general morality must have been deplorable. When we read in the Mishna that it is not safe to stable a horse in a pagan inn because of the prevalence of bestiality, when we think of the arena, of the temples of Venus, of the Groves of Daphne, etc., what can be said of the Gentiles! We are too prone to take an Aurelius or a Cato as the typical Gentile. This may, to some extent, explain the anti-Gentile remarks. They are reflections, estimates, summings up of the present, not curses or wishes. But what about the future? Are the Rabbis anxious to ameliorate the low moral condition of the Gentiles? I wonder if the answer is this. The Rabbis hoped for the ingathering of the bulk of the Gentiles in the future, welcoming stray individuals, while Jesus hoped for wholesale conversions straightway? I think that the pro-Gentile passages must be assessed not merely quantitatively but qualitatively. Far more important than one cruel *obiter dictum*, than a dozen sarcastic, proud, exclusive, contemptuous anecdotes, is the effect of the liturgy. Now the liturgy is based on the doctrine of the Remnant, and the liturgical development from the Remnant to the Universe is clear and speedy. Take the tremendously important New Year prayer (*Amidah*) ובכן תן פחדך, where the redemption of "all thy works" is linked with that of Israel, and is made the *raison d'être* of Israel. Take the daily service, morning and evening, see how general is this parallelism, Israel's choice, Israel's mission; the same applies to the Grace after Meals and to the Blessings. The sum total of all this liturgical material is great and the effect lasting.

' I think the Rabbis took a political outlook : they saw that the world could not be changed so long as the Roman Empire lasted, and they realized their impotence against Rome. The Kingdom of God and the kingdom of pride could not co-exist. Hence the emphasis on the Remnant, to keep alive the ideals of God during the dark period. *Interim-ethik*, if you like, for a lengthy interim. It is not fair to blame Bar Kochba for trying to upset Roman Rule in order to leave Israel free for the Kingdom (for, had he been purely Imperialist, Aqiba would not have supported him), and, at the same time, to praise Jesus for trying to do the same thing by different means, *e.g.* peaceful penetration. The Rabbis took long views : Jesus emphasized the present ; he would have attacked Rome, as Prussia used the Bolshevists to capture Russia, by undermining idolatry from within and making it collapse, and he (or Paul) succeeded. Rome became Christian, but did the result tally with the hope, and was this disappointment accidental ? Was it not inevitable ? " He who believes will not be impetuous." Jesus, I think, was impetuous, the Rabbis were long-sighted. Hence he stressed the Gentiles, they, the Remnant. That there was much good and a little bad in both I feel sure. We could do well without the hostile passages in Midrash and in Gospels, and in fact we do ignore them. What I mean by all this is that, *au fond*, there was nothing very new in the Gospel teaching about Gentiles. It was sound, it was typical, it was Rabbinic. Moreover, one of the reasons why we have more anti-Gentile passages may be that comparatively little is known of the teaching of the missionary Rabbis. No doubt *their* message would have been more evangelical. The Rabbis in the homeland had another duty, to safeguard the Remnant, rather than to proselytize. Both duties go hand in hand, for the doctrine of the Remnant is useless without that of the ingathering of the Gentiles. But the man whose business it was to prevent his flock from being contaminated with Gentile sin was—for better or worse —less interested in converting the external sinner. Jesus, on the other hand, was more free in this respect because all his followers were presumably pure and spiritual, or else they would not have followed him, and he could be more certain of his small band than the Rabbis could of the masses. So he could tackle the bigger field with an easy mind. It would be an interesting experiment to analyse the pro- and contra-Gentile sayings, and classify them according to date and environment of the speaker. I feel that the contra-Gentile sayings were not deliberate, not intended to spread an anti-alien sentiment, but merely to stress the avoidance of Gentile sin. As you say, Judaism remained unaffected by them in practice. You cannot get away from such a definite statement as Gittin 61 a, " Gentile and Jewish poor must equally be supported, Gentile and Jewish sick visited, and Gentile and Jewish corpses buried." That is the outcome.'

13. It is not strictly within the chosen limits of my book, but I may, perhaps, be permitted to quote the story of R. Chanina b. Doza. ' It once happened that the son of R. Gamaliel was ill. He sent two disciples of the wise to R. Chanina to pray on his behalf. When he saw them, he ascended to an upper chamber, and prayed on his behalf. On descending, he said to them, Go, the fever has left him. They said to him : Are you a prophet ? He replied, I am no prophet nor a prophet's son ; but so is my tradition (מקובלני) : if my prayer is fluent in my mouth, I know that it is accepted ; if not, that it is rejected. They sat down and wrote and noted the time. When they came to R. Gamaliel, he said to them, By the Temple-Service ! You have neither understated nor overstated [the time]. But thus it happened ; at that very hour the fever left him, and he asked us for water to drink' (Berachoth 34 b, Dr. Cohen's translation).

15. The relation of Jesus to women seems unlike what would have been usual for a Rabbi. He seems to have definitely broken with orientalism in this particular. S.B. quote from Kiddushin 70 a : ' Samuel (circa A.D. 250) said, One must not be waited on by a woman. This was quoted by one Rabbi to another, when the latter suggested that his daughter should come in and serve them with drink. She is still young, said her father. To which the other replied : Samuel said, that it made no difference whether a woman is young or not : she must not wait on men.' S.B. might have added the rather pretty story in Kiddushin 81 b (fin.). ' R. Acha b. Abba visited his son-in-law, R. Chisda, and took his grand-daughter on his lap. The son-in-law said : Do you not know that

she is betrothed ? R. Acha said, You have transgressed a ruling
of Rab, for Rab said, A girl must not be betrothed till she is grown-
up (over 12), and till she can say, So and so pleases me. Then the
son-in-law said, You, too, have transgressed a ruling of Samuel,
who said that a man must not be waited on by a woman. R. Acha
said, I act according to another opinion of Samuel, for he said, All
in the name of heaven' (*i.e.* the intention, not the mere outward
deed, is the determining factor). But certainly the relations of
Jesus towards women, and of theirs towards him, seem to strike a
new note, and a higher note, and to be off the line of Rabbinic
tradition.

Mr. Loewe calls my attention to the fact that we hear of no
attack upon Jesus on the part of the Scribes and Rabbis because
of his consorting so much with, or being so much waited on by,
women. If what is indicated in viii. 15 had so much violated the
Jewish habits of the time, should we not have been told something
of some criticism of Jesus from the Rabbis in this regard ?

17. It will be better to speak about vicarious suffering on
another occasion. (xx. 28.) This verse may not suggest this doctrine.
See my note *ad loc.*

21. Discipleship such as Jesus demanded and inspired (a
following, not for study but for service—to help the Master in his
mission, to carry out his instructions and so on) was apparently a
new thing, at all events, something which did not fit in, or was not
on all-fours, with usual Rabbinic customs or with customary Rabbinic
phenomena.

As to the saying in 21 and 22, see my note. I think it is accurate.
S.B.'s quotations as to the duty of burying the dead, and as to its
place in Rabbinic ethics and 'duties,' are quite pertinent. And
their remark about the passage as a whole is also justified. 'Erwägt
man diese Anschauungen, die im jüdischen Volk über die Bestattung
eines Toten und noch dazu des eignen Vaters herrschten, dann wird
man sich den Eindruck vorstellen können, den Jesu Antwort gemacht
hat : Lass die Toten ihre Toten begraben—du aber folge mir nach.' [1]

---

[1] 'If we consider and weigh the opinions which were cherished by the Jewish
people about the burial of the dead, and still more about the burial of one's own
father, it is easy to imagine the impression which Jesus's reply must have
produced.'

My note is inadequate, inasmuch as I only speak of the reference to the man's father, whereas the actual deed which Jesus regards as secondary—burying the dead—is also a no less important, or rather, is the crucial, element in the story. For on the duty of burying the dead, and of taking part in funerals and burials, the Rabbis laid the very greatest stress.

22. If the ' dead ' means the spiritually dead in the first half of the sentence, the quotations in S.B. constitute a very fair parallel for similar use of the word among the Rabbis. In several passages the wicked are said to be ' dead while yet alive,' whereas the righteous are ' alive in their death.' As regards the righteous, this seems to mean no more than that the righteous will live again after their death. And so, perhaps, the saying about the wicked does not mean that the wicked are spiritually dead, but rather that they will not enjoy the beatitude of the life to come.

ix. 2, 3. We have, I suppose, to distinguish in Rabbinic theology between sufferings as such and punishments as such. There are many punishments (פרעניות) which are not sufferings. (Cp. the passage quoted in Marmorstein, The Old Rabbinic Doctrine of God, Part I. p. 188, from Mechilta 63 b : ' If you receive upon your-selves the chastisements with joy (God says to Israel), you will receive reward ; if you murmur against them, they will change into punishments. Therefore they received the chastisements with joy.') Thus it says in The Ethics of the Fathers (Authorized Daily Prayer Book, Singer's edition, p. 200), ' Seven kinds of punishment come into the world for seven important transgressions.' Such punish-ments are drought, pestilence, noxious beasts, etc. Sufferings (יסורין) which, to the Rabbis, seem usually to be bodily suffer-ings, stand in a category by themselves. And in spite of the saying of R. Ammi that there are no sufferings without sin, it was very generally held that there were. Again, sufferings purify, sufferings atone, and though it may be said that such purification and atone-ment can only be a purification from some fault, or an atonement for some transgression, yet, even so, they would not be regarded as punishments in the ordinary sense of the word. Even the righteous need purification, and all need atonement. Thus sufferings may be the sign not of serious sin, but of God's love. Punishments, such as pestilence, could not be so regarded. 'Chastisements of love' is a very common Rabbinic phrase. R. Joshua ben Levi (Genesis Rabba, מקץ, xcii. 1 *init.* on xliii. 14) said, 'All sufferings which prevent a man from studying the Law are sufferings of rebuke (תוכחת), whereas those which do not are sufferings of love'—a quaint distinction. The physical and the ethical are most oddly mixed up together in the conceptions of some Rabbis. I have already quoted some of the strange passages about diarrhoea and disease of the bowels given and discussed by Büchler in his *Types of Jewish Palestinian Piety*, and also in his *Sins*, pp. 328, 329, 340. It was said that 'three persons will not see the face of hell; those who suffer grinding poverty, those who suffer from the Government, and those who suffer from disease of the bowels.' (Erubin 41 b.) What seems meant is (1) that the disease is sufficiently severe to make it reasonable that a man should not suffer any more hereafter; (2) that the suffering actually makes a man less sinful, it purges his tendency to sin; (3) that the suffering is accepted or sent by God as an adequate punishment for sin, so that the man is pardoned because he has endured it; (4) that, somehow or other, the man as a whole is better and 'purer' if his body is 'purer,' and his body is purer if all decaying food and excrement are removed from it. These four ideas are not clearly separated, but flow into one another. At bottom the immense importance attached to fasting communion, or to fasting administration and partaking of the sacrament by the priest, on the part of many Christians, rests, I should imagine, upon the same mixture of the material and the spiritual. The body must be as 'pure' as possible when a holy act is being performed, and 'pure' means having as little decaying food, etc., inside you as possible. No doubt, these old ideas are at present greatly 'purified.'

The saying in the 'Ethics of the Fathers' (iv. 19) that 'it is not in our power to explain the prosperity of the wicked or the sufferings of the good' also, I think, reflects one 'Rabbinic' point of view.[1] Whether certain permanent bodily afflictions such as blindness, paralysis, or leprosy were more especially looked upon as due to sin, I do not know. In the story in Mark ii. 1–12, Matthew ix. 1–8,

---

[1] The meaning of the saying is not wholly clear, and the interpretation given is only one of many. See Mr. Travers Herford's excellent edition of Aboth (New York, 1928).

Jesus appears to accept this view. Whether he *really* did so is perhaps doubtful. For (*cp.* my note on Mark ii. 1–12, Vol. I. p. 43) this is the only story in the Synoptic Gospels in which the conception that a diseased person is a sinful person, or that disease is a punishment for previous sin, comes in. The story as it stands obviously implies that the cure of the disease must imply forgiveness of the sin. For if the sin were *not* forgiven, the man would not or could not be cured.

6. The power to forgive sins is only twice (here and in Luke vii. 47) attributed to Jesus in the Synoptics, for the other healings are not connected with sin. S.B. declare (and, I think, correctly) that such a power is never predicated of the Messiah in Rabbinic literature. If, in one passage, Messiah's tongue is said to be pardon and forgiveness, that phrase must be interpreted to refer to his mild judgments and to his gentleness, which will be ever ready to forget and ignore any wrong done to him. Meanwhile the connection of physical suffering with sin seems very deep-rooted in Judaism, and is hardly eradicated even to-day. Thus in the *Authorized Daily Prayer Book*, p. 316, the prayers ' to be said by a sick person ' combine supplication for restoration to health with a fairly lengthy confession of sin. The long prayer ' for a sick man dangerously ill ' in the Sephardic ritual includes the following : ' May God heal his wounds and sorrows, pardon all his sins, forgive all his transgressions and lengthen his days and his years.' And (as Mr. Loewe points out) the regular Rabbinic doctrine is that healing could only follow forgiveness (*i.e.* sin is assumed as the cause of sickness). That is why in the Amidah the prayer for forgiveness precedes the prayer for healing. (Megillah 17 b.) And R. Chiya definitely stated, ' The patient is not healed of his sickness until his sins are forgiven ' (Nedarim 41 a).

11, 12. Here we meet a new and gracious characteristic of Jesus, and to it there are no parallels in the Rabbinic literature. On the contrary, a respected Rabbi and teacher would have *avoided* eating or sitting at table with persons of ill-repute. Even to eat and sit at table with an *Am ha-Aretz*—with a man, let us say, who was doubtful as regards his observance of the law of tithing—was generally held to be improper, as S.B. show in their quotations. To eat with tax-collectors and 'sinners' (whoever these 'sinners' may actually have been) would have been regarded as still more improper or objectionable. That a teacher should go about and associate with such persons, and attempt to help them and ' cure ' them by familiar and friendly intercourse with them, was, I imagine, an unheard of procedure. That the physician of the soul should seek out the ' sick ' was a new phenomenon. According to the Rabbis, the visiting of the *bodily* sick was an obligation and a duty of the first order. But the seeking out of the *morally* sick was not put upon the same footing, nor, so far as we can gather, was it practised. Here Jesus appears to be ' original.' The great significance and importance of this new departure and its effects are obvious. There must have been among some Rabbis a tendency to aloofness. We rarely are allowed to get any criticism of the Rabbis, for the Rabbinic literature is compiled entirely by themselves. An occasional remark is all the more significant. Such is one definition of the ' Epicurus.' (See note on x. 32.) They are the men who say : ' What are the Rabbis to us ? *They learn for themselves and teach for themselves* ' (Sanhedrin 99 b).

Mr. Loewe adds the following : ' You will note that neither here nor in Mark nor in Luke is Jesus blamed after he has given his explanation. His presence was at first misunderstood ; he was assumed to be amusing himself with sinners and participating in their revelry. When he made it clear that he was there for a different purpose, his word was accepted, whereas, on your theory, there should have been a further reply, after verse 13, to the effect that sinners should be left alone. If you saw a divinity professor consorting with Newmarket bookmakers, or in the green-room of the ballet, you might think some explanation called for on his part. There is always the contrast between the itinerant evangelist with a roving commission and the parson with a cure of souls, who has a definite parish to look after. I am always reminded of the early Wesleyan preachers and always quoting them. But the C. of E. vicars of Wesley's day would have been justifiably angry if you had said of them that " the seeking out of the morally sick was neither required nor practised." I think the farthest that you can go is to say that Jesus was able, owing to his independent position, to be more free in going about in doubtful society, that he could spend more time in the slums, and that he could go here and there as he pleased. I am inclined to think this was a new move on his part, but I pause because it is such a gigantic statement to make without very definite evidence. But, speaking subject to correction, I feel that it will stand. I cannot at the moment recall cases of Rabbis who specialized in reclaiming the lowest sinners to the same extent. I think the Rabbis were more general in their methods; they addressed themselves to the whole, calling upon the people as a whole to repent, without having a special mission to particular classes. But I feel very doubtful even about this qualified sentence.'

The foregoing paragraphs would give a false impression if it were to be supposed that the Rabbis did not *actively* labour in the relief of suffering and distress. There is evidence for the existence of organizations for the performance of different kinds of ' deeds of lovingkindness,' such as visiting the sick and comforting the sorrowing (*Cp.* Kohler, *Origins of the Synagogue and the Church*, p. 132), and to these organizations Rabbis belonged. ' These are they who fear the Lord, who make a compact, and say, We will go and release the prisoners and redeem the captives' (Aboth R. Nathan, viii., 18 b). We are told of two ' pious men ' (presumably Rabbis) who heard of a girl being taken captive, and journeyed forth to set her free, and we are told of their adventures on the quest. We only get to know quite casually of their actions, because of the stories (*very* odd stories too) connected with them. (Aboth R. Nathan, viii., 19 a.) (Kohler, *ib.* p. 40.) Much went on, doubtless, of devoted and active goodness which found no chronicler. Note the following story. 'R. Joshua b. Chananya journeyed to a big city in the Roman Empire, where they said that a boy was imprisoned in the house of shame (*i.e.* he was to be used for unnatural purposes). He went there, and saw a boy with beautiful eyes and fair to look on and with curly, wavy hair, and he was standing there for purposes of unnatural lust. He stood at the door of the place to test the boy, and he spoke the verse in Isaiah, Who gave Jacob for a spoil and Israel to the robbers ? Then the boy answered and said, Was it not the Lord, he against whom we sinned ? When R. Joshua heard this, he exclaimed about him the verse (Lam. iv. 2) : " The precious sons in Zion, comparable to fine gold," etc., and his eyes poured with tears, and he said, I call heaven and earth to witness that for this boy a teaching post has been reserved in Israel, and I will not budge from

here till I have redeemed him with whatever money they fix for
him. And he did not budge till he had redeemed him for much
money, and after a little time he taught in a teaching post in Israel,
and his name was R. Ishmael b. Elisha' (Lamentations R. on iv. 1).
Kohler alludes to the story in Jer. Terumoth viii. 10, 46 b. ' If a
company of Israelites on a journey meet a band of heathen who say,
Deliver us up one of your number, and we will kill him ; if not, we
will kill you all, then they must all be killed, for no Israelite must be
delivered up to the heathen. But if they say, Deliver us up such a
one, mentioning him by name, then they may deliver him up. One
Rabbi said, Yes, but only if he has already committed an act for
which he is liable to be put to death. R. Yochanan, however, said,
Even without this restriction. Ula was sought for by the Government : he fled and took refuge at Lud with R. Joshua b. Levi.
They came and told the inhabitants that the place would be laid
waste unless he were given up. R. Joshua went and persuaded Ula
that he should let himself be delivered up. Now Elijah was in the
habit of appearing to R. Joshua, and he came no more. Then R.
Joshua fasted many days, and at last Elijah appeared. He said
to R. Joshua, Should I reveal myself to informers ? (delatores).
I only acted according to a teaching, said the Rabbi. Is that
a teaching for the pious, said Elijah ? ' (משנת החסידים). Kohler
quotes this story, together with the saying in Aboth, ' He who says
mine is thine and thine is also thine, is a true chasid,' to show that
there was a similar spirit of idealism afoot among the ' pious '
Rabbis to that which Jesus desired to evoke among his disciples :
' Except your righteousness exceed the righteousness of the Scribes
and Pharisees, ye shall not enter the kingdom of heaven.'

16, 17. As to these verses, it is hardly possible to ask for parallels.
Their meaning is somewhat dubious. Cp. my note on Mark ii. 21,
22. If they refer to new teaching and old institutions, or to the
incompatibility of combining new teaching with old, or of fitting
on the one to the other, it is obvious that there could be no real
parallels to them in the Rabbinic literature.

x. 5. It is not within the purpose of this book to deal with
matters such as the relations of the Rabbis with the Samaritans.
They can be studied in detail in S.B.

8. 'Give gratis.' The Rabbinic view as regards the teaching of the Law was precisely the same. For the teaching of children payment might be made and taken (in view of the loss of time incurred in doing what was really the parents' duty), but not for the regular teaching, in the academies and seminaries, of adults. The usual passages quoted by S.B. on pp. 562, 563 are quite clear and definite, and some of them may be repeated here. 'R. Zadok said, Make not of the Torah a crown wherewith to aggrandize thyself, nor a spade wherewith to dig. So also used Hillel to say, He who makes a worldly use of the crown of the Torah shall waste away. Hence thou mayest infer that whosoever desires a profit for himself from the words of the Torah is helping on his own destruction' (Aboth iv. 5). 'Take no payment for thy knowledge of the Torah, for God gave it gratis; so do thou' (Derech Eretz Zuta iv.). 'As Moses taught Israel gratis, so do thou' (Bechoroth 29 a). Isaiah lv. 1 is quoted to the same end : 'Ho, every one that thirsts, come to the waters, and he that has no money : come, buy and eat ; buy wine and milk without usury and without price.' The waters, the wine, the milk, are to the Rabbis all metaphors for the Torah. (Numbers R., במדבר, i. 7 on i. 3.) The charming story about R. Tarphon, given by S.B., is quoted also in my essay on *The Spirit of Judaism*. (*Beginnings*, Vol. I. p. 80.) 'One day, at the close of the fig harvest, he was walking in a garden, and he ate some figs that had been left behind. The custodians of the garden came up, caught him, and beat him unmercifully. Then Tarphon called out, and said who he was, whereupon they stopped and let him go. Yet all his days did he grieve, for he said, " Woe is me, for I have used the crown of the Law for my own profit." For the teaching ran : A man must not say, I will study, so as to be called a wise man, or Rabbi, or an elder, or to have a seat in the College, but he must study from love, the honour will come of itself' (Jer. Shebiith iv. § 2, 35 b ; Nedarim 62 a). R. Elazar (Eliezer) b. Sadok (first century), who, an older man than Tarphon, also saw the fall of Jerusalem, was wont to say, 'Do the words of the Law for the doing's sake, and speak of them for their own sake. Make them not a crown with which to exalt thyself, or a spud with which to weed' (Nedarim 62 a ; Aboth iv. 7).

10. 'The labourer is worthy of his food.' It would seem that

Q

many Rabbis, if they were poor, supported themselves, like Paul, by following some trade or handicraft. But it was also regarded as a great *Mitzvah* (privilege, good deed, honour) to support a Rabbi and pay for his sustenance. ' R. Eliezer b. Jacob said, He who receives a Rabbi in his house as his guest, and lets him have enjoyment from his (the owner's) possessions, the Scripture ascribes it to him as if he had offered the continual offerings ' (Berachoth 10 b). And R. Yochanan speaks as if it were a law or an obligation for the members of a Jewish community in a town to support a Rabbi (or a man of learning), just because such a one neglects his own affairs and occupies himself with the affairs of God. Nevertheless—the proviso is added—this rule only extends to giving him ' his bread.' I suppose this means that while the Rabbi is to be supported, his maintenance need not be on a luxurious scale. The quotation given by S.B., Tanchuma, *Ki Tissa*, 119 a, does not seem in point. It appears only to indicate that he who occupies himself in the study of the Law shall succeed and prosper and become rich : one of the paradoxes like ' He who begins the study of the Law in poverty shall end it in wealth.' One need not lay much stress upon such sayings.

25.   There is a similar saying in the Talmud (Berachoth 58 b), but it occurs in a different setting. The Master is God. The whole passage is worth quoting. ' Ulla and Rab Chisda were journeying along the road. When they reached the entrance of the house of Rab Chana b. Chanilai, Rab Chisda broke down and sighed. Ulla asked him, ' Why dost thou sigh ? For lo, Rab has said : A sigh breaks half the body of a man ; as it is said, " Sigh therefore, thou son of man, with the breaking of thy loins," etc. (Ezek. xxi. 11) ; and R. Yochanan has said : It even breaks the whole body ; as it is said, " And it shall be, when they say unto thee, Wherefore sighest thou ? that thou shalt say, Because of the tidings, for it cometh ; and every heart shall melt," ' etc. (*ibid*. v. 12). He answered him, ' How should I not sigh [on beholding] a house in which there were sixty cooks by day and sixty cooks by night, and they baked for each person what he desired. Nor did he ever take his hand away from his purse, thinking that perhaps there may come a poor man, the son of respectable people, and while he is reaching for his purse, he would be put to shame. Moreover, it had four doors

open to the four directions, and whoever entered hungry came out
sated. He used also to cast wheat and barley outside during the
years of drought, so that anybody who was ashamed to take it by
day came and took it by night. And now that it is fallen into
ruins, shall I not sigh ? Ulla said to him, Thus spake R. Yochanan :
From the day the Temple was destroyed, a decree was issued that
the houses of the righteous should be destroyed ; as it is said, " In
mine ears said the Lord of Hosts : Of a truth many houses shall
be desolate, even great and fair, without inhabitant " (Is. v. 9).
Also said R. Yochanan : The Holy One, blessed be he, will restore
them to habitation ; as it is said, " A Song of Ascents. They that
trust in the Lord are as Mount Zion " (Ps. cxxv. 1)—just as the
Holy One, blessed be he, will restore Mount Zion to habitation, so
will he restore the houses of the righteous to habitation. He perceived that his mind was still not at rest, so he said to him, It is
enough for the slave to be like his master ' (Dr. Cohen's translation, p. 384).

28. ' Fear him who can destroy both body and soul in hell,'
i.e. fear God. The sentiment is Rabbinic, but it would be totally
false to suppose that this is the only, or even the predominant
attitude of the Rabbis towards God, any more than it was the only
or predominant attitude of Jesus. The famous death-bed scene
of R. Yochanan b. Zakkai has been quoted too often, and far too
much stress has been laid upon it. It is given in S.B. p. 581, in
my *Old Testament and After*, p. 409, and in my ' Spirit of Judaism,'
Beginnings, p. 51. But perhaps I had better quote it again.
' When R. Yochanan b. Zakkai was ill, his disciples went in to visit
him. On beholding them, he began to weep. His disciples said
to him, O lamp of Israel, right - hand pillar, mighty hammer !
Wherefore dost thou weep ? He replied to them, If I was being
led into the presence of a human king who to-day is here and
to-morrow in the grave, who, if he were wrathful against me, his
anger would not be eternal, who, if he imprisoned me, the imprisonment would not be everlasting, who, if he condemned me to death,
the death would not be for ever, and whom I can appease with words
and bribe with money—even then I should weep ; but now, when
I am being led into the presence of the King of Kings, the Holy
One, blessed be he, who lives and endures for all eternity, who,

if he be wrathful against me his anger is eternal, who, if he
imprisoned me, the imprisonment would be everlasting, who, if
he condemned me to death, the death would be for ever, and whom
I cannot appease with words nor bribe with money—nay, more,
when before me lie two ways, one of the Garden of Eden and the
other of *Gehinnom*, and I know not in which I am to be led—shall
I not weep ? ' (Dr. Cohen's translation, p. 188, Berachot 28 b).
I do not think that Yochanan's weeping can be regarded as the
usual or characteristic attitude of the Rabbis upon their death-
beds, or that it was considered the correct and pious attitude.
On the whole, the doctrine that ' all Israelites (except a few very
grave sinners) shall have a share in the world to come ' tended to
make all Jews, whether Rabbis or no, comfortable and confident
at the near coming of death.   Moreover, that to love God is a better
and nobler attitude than to fear him the Rabbis were well aware :
to serve him from love is better than to serve him from fear.   There
are a number of passages to this effect.   One or two familiar ones
are : ' The Scripture has made a distinction between him who acts
from fear and him who acts from love.   The reward of him who
acts from love is double and quadruple.   Act from love, for there
is no love where there is fear, or fear where there is love, except
in relation to God. (*Cp.* Büchler, *Sins*, p. 160.)   Love God with all
thy soul—even when he takes thy soul (= life), even to the last
outpressing (מיצוי) of thy soul ;   even like Isaac who himself
bound himself upon the altar ' (Sifre 73 a and b). (Bacher, *Agada
der Tannaiten*, Vol. I. p. 418, n. 2.) ' Do you perchance say, I will
study to become rich, or to be called Rabbi, or to receive a reward ?
Therefore it says, Love your God.   All that you do, do only from
love ' (Sifre 80 a *init.*).   Then there is the passage in Mishnah
Sotah iv. 5 about Job serving God only from love, and the remarks
of the Gemara (30 b).   R. Meir said that God-fearing is said both
of Abraham and of Job, and in both cases the God-fearingness was
from love. (*Cp.* Büchler, *Sins*, p. 126.)   Thus fear, or rather, reverence,
is always to be present as well as love. ' Fear God and love God :
the Law says both ; act from both love and fear ; from love, for if
you would hate, no lover hates, and from fear, for if you would
kick, no fearer kicks ' (Jer. Sotah v. 7, 20 c). (*Cp.* Büchler, *Sins*, p.
164.) ' R. Judah b. Tema said, Be bold as a lion, quick as a stag, to
do the will of thy Father who is in heaven. . . . Love and fear God.

Rejoice, and yet fear, in the execution of his commandments'
(Aboth R. Nathan xli. 67 a). That sums up the Rabbinic view
in this matter of love and fear. On the whole, the Rabbis seem
to have taught that every Israelite who did not deliberately turn
his back upon the Law would undoubtedly be saved. He might be
purgatorially punished after death, but it would be for purification, and not eternally. (There is a very full treatment of love and
fear in Büchler, *Sins*, and a long statement concerning the various
views of different Rabbis about Job, and whether he served God
from love or from fear (pp. 122–189). A full collection of material
can be found in these pages, and much of it is given both in the
original and in a translation.)

29, 30. *Cp.* Luke xxi. 18. The doctrine of providence here
enunciated appears quite Rabbinic, and S.B.'s quotations are in
point—on, and not off, the Rabbinic line. The story about R.
Simeon b. Yochai (*circa* 150) affords even a verbal parallel, and
reappears a large number of times with slight variations. To escape
capture in the time of persecution under Hadrian he lived in a cave
for thirteen years. He then came out, and sat at the entrance of
the cave. He saw a man snaring birds. Before a bird was caught,
he heard a heavenly voice say ' Judgment,' but when he heard the
voice say ' Remission,' the bird escaped. So he said, ' If even a
bird is not captured without the will of God, how much less a man '
(Jer. Shebiit ix. § 1, 38 d ; Genesis Rabba, וישלח, lxxix. 6 on xxxiii.
18 ; Pesikta 88 b, etc.). ' R. Chanina said, No man hurts his finger
here below without their proclaiming it in regard to him above '
(*i.e.* unless it is so disposed for him by God : ' they ' as usual = God).
(Chullin 7 b.) ' God sits and feeds the world from the buffalo's
horns to the eggs of the louse ' (Sabbath 107 b). 'He gives bread
to all flesh ' it says in the Psalms (cxxxvi. 25) after speaking about
the Exodus, and Hillel said that the juxtaposition showed that God's
giving of bread was as great and wonderful as the cleaving of the
Red Sea and the Exodus from Egypt. As the Exodus needed
miracles, so the bread which a man puts into his mouth is a divine
miracle (Pesikta R. 152 a). Man's daily sustenance (פרנסה) is
God's work. (Gen. R. xx. 9 on iii. 17 ; Moore I. p. 379. Parallels
in Bacher, *Agada der pal.: Amoräer* I. pp. 179, 487 ; *cp.* also
Moore I. pp. 384, 385.) ' Even the keeper of the cistern is

appointed by heaven' (Baba Batra 91 b, and again in Berachoth 58 a). R. Chanina also said, in a constantly quoted passage, 'All is in the hand of heaven, except the fear of heaven' (Man's will is free). (Berachoth, 33 b.) In a very odd passage in Tanchuma, *Pekude*, 127 a it is described, in the queerest manner, how God decides beforehand about every one, at the earliest stage of formation, if ' he ' is to be a man or a woman, rich or poor, short or tall, weak or strong, ugly or beautiful, fat or thin, honoured or despised; and he also determines as to everything which is to befall the man. But whether he is to be righteous or wicked, God determines not, for that is left to his own will. (*Cp.* Sotah 2 a.) The parallel to the verse about the hair of the head given by S.B. is most odd. It comes to this : ' God said to Job, I have made many hairs on man's head, and for every hair I have made a little canal by which it is nourished. I distinguish between canal and canal ; should *I* not do justice ? ' (This all depends upon a pun between two Hebrew words of the same sound meaning ' storm ' and ' hair,' and on a playful interpretation of Job ix. 17 and xxxviii. 1.) (Baba Batra 16 a.) Still odder is the story in Tanchuma B. (*Tazria* viii. 18 a, b.) Here it is said that certain priests had to deal with certain cases of leprosy by an examination of the hair. One of these priests became poor, and wanted to go abroad : he, therefore, began to instruct his wife in the matter so that she might do the investigations in his absence. He told her of the ' canals,' and said, ' If these canals dry up, then a man has leprosy. To each hair its canal : if the canal dries up, the hair dries up. His wife said, If God has created a separate canal for every hair to drink from, shall not God appoint for you your sustenance, who art a man who has to give food to his children ? And she would not let him go abroad.' In these strange, quaint sayings and tales the Rabbis yet seem to teach much the same doctrine as Jesus.

37. *Cp.* my note *ad loc.* The saying, however justifiable or defendable, has an anti-Rabbinic ring. It is true that the honour of God is to be put before obedience to parents—so that if a father commands his son to violate an injunction of the Law, the son must disobey his father (Yebamoth 5 b)—but this seems different from what we read in 37.

A main characteristic of the teaching of Jesus is its absoluteness, and hence its paradoxicalness. This absoluteness must have led through the ages to strangely different results. It must have led to very many grand and noble actions ; to very many actions which, though grandly and nobly intended, produced undesirable results ; and also to many doubtful or even bad actions. Is this wholly to be wondered at ? The absolute, translated into finite action in a concrete world, must sometimes produce strange results. In the particular case under consideration, surely many girls have become nuns, or many boys monks, who would have done far better to look after their parents, and to do their various small duties in practical life. Many must have become missionaries who were ill suited for the life, and who made a mess of it. They would have done better to love God through loving their parents. For the Rabbis are right when they indicate that for *most* of us, though not, I admit, necessarily for all of us, it is in the ordinary duties and affections of life that the love of God can best and most dutifully be displayed.

38. *Cp.* Mark viii. 34 ; Luke ix. 23. These noble verses are not off the Rabbinic line. They express Rabbinic spirit and Rabbinic action. The martyrs show that this is so. For ' Jesus ' must be substituted ' God and his Law.' But the spirit remains the same. The Rabbis, reflecting upon past martyrdoms, and upon the great probability of future martyrdoms, lay down some rules for right conduct in such emergencies. These rules, though showing a certain prudence and common sense, are, nevertheless, not opposed to, but, on the contrary, are consistent with, the passionate words of Jesus. The line which the Rabbis take is this. Where the public Sanctification, or the open Profanation, of God's name is concerned, a man must be prepared to give his life. Where that is not in question, a man may rightly violate every injunction of the Law in order to save his life, with the exception of three. He may not commit any idolatrous act ; he may not commit an act of unchastity ; he may not murder. Thus if a Jew were (let us say) seized by a Roman, and the Roman mockingly said to him, ' Eat this bit of bacon, or die,' he may eat the pig. ' God's laws were given for life and not for death.' But if the Roman said, ' Eat this bit of bacon as a sign that you renounce Judaism,' or ' as a sign that you are ready to worship Jupiter,' then the Jew must die.

Or if he is bidden to eat the bacon at a time of religious persecution, then he must refuse and die. Moreover, a difference was made according as the bidding to violate the law occurred in private or in public. A public violation was a far worse thing than a private violation. Some said that a Jew must sooner die than openly violate the smallest injunction of the Law. Oddly enough, it was regarded as more obligatory to die if the demanded violation was to take place when other Israelites were present than if it took place when only heathen were present. All this is stated at length in Sanhedrin 74 a and b. As regards the violation of the Name in public, Kiddushin 40 a is worth consulting. A man had better commit a sin in private than publicly profane the name of God. The Jew, as God's witness, must never profane God's name by his open sin. In comparison with that, secret sin is less terrible. The relation between God and Israel is as the relation between husband and wife. ' The relation between Israel and God is primarily, it might even be said, a relation for themselves, just as the relation between a lover and his beloved, between husband and wife, is a relation between themselves and for themselves. The relation is a puzzle to the nations. What has your lover, they ask, above all other lovers that you are ever ready to be killed and slain for him, and that you love him even unto death ? The readiness for martyrdom, the unquenchable love of God, which no adversity and no suffering can drown or destroy, are quite as prominent, and quite as genuine, factors in the Rabbinic religion as the desire for reward. In the Rabbinic literature you have them both in undress. The one is just as simple and real as the other. What does " I am sick of love " mean ? What is the sickness ? It is not a bodily sickness, but the love of God, which is a sickness even unto death. Much appreciated and quoted were the words of the Psalter: " For thy sake are we killed all the day long." How far does the son love the Father ? So far that he gives his life for the Father's honour, even as the righteous did, the sons of the living God, who gave their lives for his unity; even as Shadrach, Meshach, and Abednego were willing to do, for they said, Even though God should not rescue us, thy god we will not serve. So they were ready to give their lives, not on the condition of being saved, but on the risk of being burnt, for love is stronger than death. The heroes and martyrs of the Hadrianic persecution, as twin sisters with God, gave their lives for the sanctification of the name. As the dove does not shrink when she is killed, so the Israelites did not shrink when they were slaughtered for the sanctification of the Name. Israel is called a stiff-necked nation. Three are insolent. Among animals it is the dog ; among birds it is the cock ; among the nations it is Israel. Yet this is not said in blame, but in praise ! Either Judaism or crucifixion ! It is impossible to question the passion or the purity of the Rabbinic love for God. It was not dependent on the prospect of reward in heaven, even though such reward was both expected and desired. It shines before us as a resplendent example. "Thou shalt love God with all thy heart." With both thy inclinations, says the Midrash, both with the good *Yetzer* and the evil one : a brief and profound remark. Thy heart must not be divided towards God. The whole man is to love him ; feelings, instincts, desires, all are to be used for, and directed towards, his love. "And with all thy soul " : even if he takes away thy soul (*i.e.* thy life) ; even if he demands that thou give up thy soul (in martyrdom). "With all thy might " is added because some men love their possessions more than their life, and some men love their life more than their possessions. With every measure that God metes out to you, must you love him, be it the measure of good or the measure of affliction ' (*Old Testament and After*, pp. 363, 364).[1] One Rabbi said, ' The words of the Law are only firm (or established) in that man who would die for their sake ' (Berachoth 63 b).

Mr. Loewe suggests to me that the various discussions on the matter, and the somewhat various opinions expressed as regards martyrdom, may reflect the varying conditions in certain periods. Perhaps in some places and times, some Rabbis were anxious to restrain the zeal for martyrdom ; in others, they may have wished to stimulate the zeal. That the absence of other Israelites constituted ' privacy,' and that the presence of many ' gentiles ' was not supposed to constitute ' publicity,' may have been precisely due to a desire, somehow or other, by some device or ingenious interpretation, to restrain the desire for martyrdom. A curious example of the combined idealism and realism of the Jewish mind seems to

[1] The sentences cited from my book depend on a number of Rabbinic passages, such as Canticles R. on i. 15, ii. 16, vi. 1 ; Exodus R., *Ki Tissa*, xlii. 9 on xxxii. 7 *ad fin.* ; Midrash Psalms ix. *fin.*, 46 a, xviii. (11), verse 7, 71 a ; xxviii. (2), 115 a ; lxviii. (8), verse 14, 159 a.

me the naïve remark of R. Chiya bar Abba, who said : ' If a man
say to you, give your life for the sanctification of the Name of God,
do you answer, I am ready to do so, only let me be beheaded right
away, and let it not be as in the Day of the Persecution (*i.e.* the days
of Hadrian) when they took iron globes, and made them red hot,
and put them under the arm pits, and put splinters under the
nails of the martyrs ' (Pesikta 87 a). The conclusion of the whole
matter is that Jewish teaching is here at one with the teaching of
Jesus, just as in practice the Jews have been ever ready to give their
lives in the cause and for the honour of God's unity and for the
sanctification of his holy name.

39. The famous verbal parallel to this great saying is in
Tamid 32 a. ' Alexander of Macedon asked the wise men of the
south, what shall a man do that he may live ? They answered, Let
him kill himself. And what should a man do that he may die ? They
answered, Let him keep himself alive.' *Cp.* also Aboth R. Nathan
xxxii. (2), 36 a. ' Rabbi Judah the Prince said : If thou hast done
his will as thy will, thou hast not done his will as his will ; and if
thou hast done his will as against thy will, then thou hast done his
will as his will ; if it be thy will that thou shouldst not die, die that
thou mayest not die ; if it be thy will that thou shouldst live, live
not, so that thou mayest live ; it is better for thee to die in this
world against thy will, than to die in the world to come.' The
probability seems to be that both Jesus and the wise men and R.
Judah all meant the same thing. He who from cowardice or sin
seeks to save his earthly life will lose the life to come : he who is
willing to lose his earthly life will gain the life to come and its
beatitudes. We may say, however, two things : (1) that this
teaching, as given in all the Gospels, occupies a more central place
there than similar teaching does in the Rabbinic literature ; (2)
that the saying in the Gospels was soon interpreted to mean (*cp.*
John xii. 25) that one must die to live, in a spiritual sense, as within
earthly life itself (die to the lower, live to the higher, etc.). In
that applied sense it has been of enormous influence, and is so still
to-day. In that applied sense I do not think that the parallels are
used in the Rabbinic literature.

40. Many of the passages in S.B. (i. 589-592) are salient and

illustrative. The Rabbis combined humility with an immense
appreciation of ' learning ' (that is, of learning in relation to the
Law). They both magnified their office and yet were individually
humble. Or rather, as Mr. Loewe suggests to me, they did not so
much magnify their office or their caste, as they magnified learning.
A student, a ' wise ' man, a learned man, a disciple, stood, they
held, in a special group—sharply separated from the ignorant. It
was a dangerous view, but yet it must, I think, be admitted that
they held it with a certain amount of good humour. In spite of
the *Am ha-Aretz* passages, the Rabbis learnt (was it only gradually ?)
not to despise a combination of goodness and ' ignorance,' and they
learnt to believe that such a combination was possible and not
infrequent. And their profound veneration for learning was quite
independent of what other profession the ' learned ' person followed.
Be he a tailor or a farmer, be he a mason or a carpenter, if he were
learned, or if he even studied at all, he had entered into a charmed
circle. If you could not study, the next best thing was to help
those who could and did. And so when Jesus said, ' He who receives
(shows hospitality to) you receives me,' that would be in complete
agreement with the views of the Rabbis, if for ' you ' we were to
put ' wise men ' or 'students ' or ' learned,' and for ' me ' we were
to put God. For the cause of study—the cause of the study of the
Law, the cause of learning—is the cause of God. Thus ' he who
shows hospitality to the " wise " or to the student (*Talmid chacham*,
a disciple of the wise, a man of learning, a student) is as if he brought
the first fruits of his produce unto God ' (Leviticus Rabba, בהר,
xxxiv. 8 on xxv. 39). ' He who greets the learned, is as if he greeted
God ' (מקבל פני שכינה). (Mechilta to Exodus xviii. 12, 59 a.)
[In looking up this passage my eye happened to fall upon what
immediately precedes it; it runs as follows : ' " And Aaron came
and all the elders of Israel to eat bread with Moses' father-in-law
before God." Whither had Moses gone ? Had not Moses gone before
to meet him ? ("And Moses went out to meet his father-in-law.")
This means that he stood and waited on them. Whence had he
learnt that ? From Abraham, our father. R. Isaac said, When
R. Gamaliel prepared a banquet for the wise, and they were at table
with him, R. Gamaliel stood and served them. They said, we are
not worthy that he should wait on (or serve) us. Then R. Joshua
said to them : Permit him to wait on us, for we find that a greater

than R. Gamaliel waited on the creatures (*i.e.* on men). They said, Who was this ? He said, Abraham, our father, the greatest in the world, who waited on the angels, but he thought they were men, Arabians, idolaters. How much more should R. Gamaliel wait on the wise who are studying the Law. R. Isaac said to them, We find that One who is even greater than Abraham and R. Gamaliel waits on the creatures (*i.e.* on men). They said, Who is this ? He said, The Shechinah, for in every hour the Shechinah provides sustenance for all the inhabitants of the world according to their need, and satisfies every living thing, and not only the pious and the righteous, but also the wicked and the idolaters. How much more then may R. Gamaliel wait on the wise and the students of the Law.' (The same story is found in Sifre 77 a.) One never knows where to have these old Rabbis. Hardly has one quoted one sentence one way than one finds another which says something very different !] ' R. Abin, the Levite, said, He who enjoys a meal at which a learned man is present is as one who enjoys the radiance of the Shechinah ' (Berachoth 64 a). Quaint and odd is the story about R. Yochanan in Kethuboth 111 b. ' R. Elazar said, The *Am ha-Aretz* will not rise up at the resurrection. R. Yochanan said to him, The Biblical verse on which you rely (Isaiah xxvi. 14) only means that idolaters shall not rise up. Well, then, replied Elazar, I will prove that the *Am ha-Aretz* do not rise up from Isaiah xxvi. 19 ; he who serves the light of the Law, him the light of the Law will quicken, and contrariwise. When R. Elazar saw that R. Yochanan was pained by this, he said to him, I have found healing for the *Am ha-Aretz* out of the Law, for it says, Ye who clave to the Lord your God are alive to-day. Can one cleave to the Shechinah ? Is not God a flaming fire ? (Deut. iv. 24.) But it means : He who marries his daughter to a learned man, looks after the learned man's business, and lets the learned profit (or get enjoyment) from his (the *Am ha-Aretz's*) property, him the Scripture regards as if he were cleaving to the Shechinah.' Certainly the Rabbinic world is an aristocracy of learning, but there is no desire to keep the aristocracy small. The larger the circle of the learned the better. Birth, wealth, priesthood—nothing is of importance compared with learning.

42. It would seem that there is no exact Rabbinic parallel-

ism for the use of 'little ones' as meaning 'disciples.' But the term *is* used to mean 'young,' or as yet imperfectly equipped, or imperfectly learned, students of the Law. (S.B. p. 592.)

xi. 25. It is only right that S.B. give no parallels (except one irrelevant, if amusing, story) to this verse. It is clear that what is here said and implied is in prevailing opposition to Rabbinic teaching. That for which Jesus praises God would have seemed, I feel pretty sure, to most of the Rabbis, a punishment and a disaster. The verse, whether authentic or not, shows Jesus in antagonism to the Rabbis, not merely on the score of some particular question (*e.g.* the observance of the Sabbath), but absolutely and altogether. The spirit of the one (according to this verse) is removed from the spirit of the other. Whereas learning and knowledge and study are the supreme excellences and divinest gifts of God to the one, they are here apparently depreciated and rejected by the other. The Kingdom is not for the wise and the learned ; it is for the simple and the ignorant. The opposition seems complete. Nevertheless, even here one must not exaggerate. When Elijah is reported to have told R. Berokah that the jokesters and the gaoler were going to inherit the life to come, a certain rebuke must be intended for the 'pride of learning' (Taanith 22 a). Or, at all events, the story must be meant to indicate that heaven and its beatitudes are by no means limited to the "wise." Part of the story of R. Berokah runs thus : ' R. Berokah of Chuza frequented the market of Lapet. One day Elijah appeared to him there, and R. Berokah asked him : Is there among the people of this market any one that is destined to share in the world to come ? Elijah replied, There is none. In the meantime a man drew nigh and Elijah said, This man is one who will share in the world to come. R. Berokah thereupon called to the man, but the latter did not heed the call, so R. Berokah went over to him and asked him what his occupation was. " I am a jailer," the man declared, " and I keep men and women separate. At night I place my bed between the men and the women, so that no wrong be committed." Then two other men appeared on the scene, and Elijah said to R. Berokah, " These two will also share in the world to come." R. Berokah then asked them, " What is your occupation ? " They replied, " We are merry-makers ; when we see a man who is downcast, we cheer him up ; also when we see two people quarrelling with one another, we endeavour to make peace between them " ' (Dr. Malter's rendering). Again, a page or so earlier in the same tractate (21 b) we read, ' An epidemic once broke out in Sura, but in the neighbourhood of Rab's residence the epidemic did not appear. The people thought that this was due to Rab's merits, but in a dream they were told that the miracle was too slight to be attributed to Rab's great merits, and that it happened because of the merits of a man who willingly lent hoe and shovel to a cemetery (for the digging of graves). A fire once broke out in Drokeret, but the neighbourhood of R. Huna was spared. The people thought that it was due to the merit of R. Huna, but they were told in a dream that R. Huna's merits were too great, and the sparing of his neighbourhood from fire too small a matter, to attribute it to him, and that it was due to the merits of a certain woman who used to heat her oven and place it at the disposal of her neighbours.' May we go so far as to say that, with the gradual disappearance of the *Am ha-Aretz* in the technical sense, the teaching of the Rabbis tended (1) in no wise to lessen the honour and preciousness of study and learning and wisdom, but (2) to become more definite in the direction of believing and teaching that simple, unlearned goodness was adequate for admission to heavenly bliss ?

Mr. Loewe suggests to me as parallels : (1) the remark in the Mechilta on Exodus xv. 1 (37 a, top), that the handmaidens by the shore of the Red Sea saw that which Ezekiel and the prophets did not see. (2) Exodus R. xxiii., *Beshallach*, on the same verse, ' R. Judah said, Who started the song of praise (מי אמר קילום) to God ? The babes, whom Pharaoh had wanted to cast into the river, for they recognized God.'

28–30. The inference usually drawn from these verses is that Jesus is contrasting his own ' yoke ' with that of the yoke of the Law. The one is light and delightful ; the other heavy and burdensome ; the one joyous, the other terrifying. Jesus is supposed (I imagine) to address (1) those who observed the Law and were weighed down by its burden, its detail, and its minutiae ; (2) those who had fallen out of the ranks, and for one reason or another did not, could not, or would not, obey the ' endless ' injunctions of the Law. Either class could be, I imagine, regarded as κοπιῶντες and πεφορτισμένοι ' weary and heavy laden.' See further my notes *ad. loc.* How far there then existed many persons who, *not* obeying the Law, were weary and heavy laden, it is *very* hard to say. The answer involves the whole complicated question of the *Am ha-Aretz*, of whom Dr. Abrahams gives the most impartial, and, perhaps, therefore, no very conclusive, information in his essay at the end of Vol. II. of my Commentary, pp. 647–669. So far as those who obeyed the Law are concerned, the evidence through the ages goes quite the other way. To them the Law was a delight and no burden, and in practice and life all this talk of ' *endless* ' injunctions and minutiae is largely a figment of Christian theologians. How could or can these theologians help themselves ? They only knew and know the Law from outside. How it really affected and affects life they knew and know not. Moreover, the Rabbis were not above making an occasional joke about the Law's many injunctions, as in the famous story which is given in the Midrash on Psalms (7 b on i. § 15), solemnly quoted by S.B. on Acts xv. 10 (ii. p. 728). The joke is put in the mouth of Korah, because he, as a mocker and a rebel, may fitly say these things. ' Korah mocked and said : There was a poor widow in my neighbourhood who had two daughters and a field. When she began to plough, Moses said, You must not plough with an ox and an ass together. When she began to sow, he said, You must not sow your field with mingled seed ; when she began to reap, and to make stacks of corn, he said, Take not the gleaning, or what you forget (Deut. xxiv. 19), or the corners (Lev. xix. 9); she began to thresh and he said, Give me the heave offering, the first tithe and the second tithe. She accepted the ordinance and gave them all to him. What did the poor woman then do ? She sold her field, and bought two sheep, to clothe herself from their fleece and to have profit from their young. When they bore their young, Aaron came and said, Give me the first born. So she accepted the decision and gave them to him. When the shearing time came, and she sheared them, Aaron came and said, Give me the first fruit of the fleece (Deut. xviii. 4). Then she thought, I cannot stand up against this man. I will slaughter the sheep and eat them. Then Aaron came again and said, Give me the shoulder and the two cheeks and the maw (Deut. xviii. 3). Then she said, Even when I have killed them, I am not safe from you. Behold, they shall be "devoted." Then Aaron said, In that case they belong to me entirely (Numb. xviii. 14). He took them, and went

away and left her weeping with her two daughters.' But the real
Rabbinic feeling is that the Law is a delight. The more laws, the
more honour to Israel : the more laws, the more grace of God.
So on Psalm cxix (41), verse 97, 249 b, David's love, and the
Israelites' love, of the Law are tenderly dwelt on. ' I have not
neglected thy Law, and because I have not neglected it, it has been
to me, not a burden but a song.' (As it says ' Thy statutes have
been my songs.') That the ' yoke ' of the Law drove away other
' cares ' is stated in one of the ' Sayings of the Fathers.' ' Whoso
receives upon himself the yoke of the Law, from him the yoke of
the earthly kingdom and the yoke of wordly care will be removed '
(Aboth iii. 6). ' R. Chananya said, He who puts the words of the
Law in his heart, from him they remove (*i.e.* God removes) many
(evil) thoughts, [the Law drives away all desire to sin], for it says,
the Law of the Lord is perfect, rejoicing the heart ; the commandment of the Lord is pure, enlightening the eyes ' (Aboth R. Nathan
xx. p. 35 b). As to ' rest ' and peace, the Law was always supposed
to lead to, and was identified with, peace. ' Great peace have they
who love Thy Law ' is a favourite Biblical quotation. (Psalm cxix.
165.) From another point of view R. Chiya said, ' The wise have
rest neither in this world nor in the world to come, as it says, They
go from strength to strength ' (Ps. lxxxiv. 8). In truth the same
satisfactions, the same joys, can be won by the disciples of Jesus
and by the disciples of the Law. The yoke of both is, in one sense,
hard, and may even require martyrdom : in another sense, it is
beautiful and easy, yielding peace and contentment and joy.

xii. 7. In spite of the fact that the Rabbis were more tied than
Jesus to the letter of the Law, and more rigidly bound to recognize
the obligation of fulfilling all its injunctions without cavil or hesita-
tion, they nevertheless appreciated the distinction between ' moral '
and ' ceremonial.' From one point of view, all the laws were the
gift, as well as the command, of God, and if the ceremonial laws
were binding only on Israel, that made them the more precious :
they were a special gift, a special sign of grace. Nevertheless, the
Rabbis had also (they were a funny mixture) a good deal of common
sense ; moreover, the teaching of the Prophets was by no means
lost upon them. They too used the quotation from Hosea which
Jesus uses here and in ix. 13. Yet I do not suppose they would have

used it in relation to any loosening of the very minute and elaborate laws about the observance of the Sabbath. For the minute observance of the Sabbath was regarded as of enormous importance. And, for the ordinary Jew of the Rabbinic period, I am inclined to think that these Sabbath laws were the only laws which caused any real trouble. The food laws, once known and provided for, gave little bother. They mainly concerned the women folk, and for the vast majority of Jews, who lived among themselves and within their own community, these food laws must have been matters of course, just as it is no difficulty to us not to eat horse, or as we should not think of having a mutton chop at our five o'clock tea. The *one* section of the ceremonial Law which caused some trouble was the observance of the Sabbath. And yet—note the customary paradox —the Sabbath was pre-eminently the day of delight and feasting, the day of joy and peace and sunshine, for all the harassed communities of Israel! ' Come, O bride, come, O bride ' ; how popular the song became in every household! ' Und der Hund wird aufs neu ein menschlich Wesen.' Heine's words are strictly true. How entirely is the Sabbath of the Rabbis and of all orthodox Jews misunderstood and caricatured by all those who look only at the legal minutiae of the Mishnah and the Talmud. So difficult is it for the members of one religion to understand the joys, the intimacies, the paradoxes and the realities, of another. But Jews should be warned by this truth as well as Christians. Their blunders in judgment are sometimes equally grotesque.

Meanwhile, as I have said, the Rabbis as well as Jesus could use Hosea to good purpose. And S.B. are quite fair in their quotations, which could easily be multiplied. ' R. Elazar said, Almsgiving is more important than all sacrifices, as it says, To do justice (= almsgiving) is more acceptable to God than sacrifice. (Proverbs xxi. 3.) Nevertheless, charity (*Gemiluth chesadim*, the doing of loving deeds) is greater than almsgiving.' And this view is quaintly elaborated. (Succah 49 b.) ' R. Simeon the Just said, The world is established on three things, on the Law, on the Sacrifices (the Temple Service), and on Charity.' How on charity, asks the Midrash ? Because it says, I desire love, and not sacrifices. (Hosea vi. 6.) The world was created at the beginning only by love. Then follows the well-known story how R. Yochanan b. Zakkai and R. Joshua took a walk and looked at the ruins of the Temple. ' R. Joshua said, Woe is us,

R

for the place where the sins of Israel were atoned for is laid waste.
R. Yochanan said, Do not grieve ; we have an atonement as powerful as the altar : that is charity, the doing of loving deeds ' (Aboth
R. Nathan iv. 11 a). In another passage it is even expressly stated
that in Hosea it says, not that love ' is as good as sacrifice,' but that
love ' is better than sacrifice.' And then follows a quaint justification of this assertion. (Deut. Rabba v., שופטים, on xvi. 18.) There
are other similar passages. It seems to me, therefore, quite clear
that Jesus in such a passage as Matt. xii. 7 is not only teaching
sound prophetic doctrine, but also sound Rabbinic doctrine : doubtless Rabbinic doctrine at its best, but Rabbinic doctrine none the
less, and not very unusual Rabbinic doctrine either. Jews, therefore, must be considered as justified when they say that in such a
passage as this Jesus has nothing fresh or out of the way to teach
them. They knew it already from the Prophets and from the
Rabbis. (With Mark vii. 15 the case is very different.) On the other
hand, one must not suppose that the Rabbis thought that the sacrifices
had ever been really unimportant or not the express will of God.
The letter of the Law forbade any such view. They longed and
prayed for a time when the Temple would be re-established, and
the sacrifices offered again. ' R. Isaac said, To study the laws about
the sin-offerings (as one cannot offer sin offerings any longer) is
as good as offering them.' Though Raba said, ' He who occupies
himself with the Law needs no offerings of any sort,' he would not
have meant that the sacrifices had ever been negligible. (Menachoth,
110 a.) The study of the sacrifices is equivalent to offering them.
(Pesikta 60 b.) Yet there was no more any *superstition* about the
sacrifices. ' Let no man say within himself, I will go and do ugly
and improper things (דברים מכוערים ושאינן ראויין), then I will
bring a bullock, which has a great deal of meat, and offer it as a
burnt offering upon the altar, and I shall obtain mercy with God ' (Lev.
R. ii. 12 *fin.* on ii. 2 ; Moore I. p. 505). Only repentance and amend-
ment secured forgiveness ; then the sacrifice could be great or small.
In fact, ' whether a man bring a large offering or a small one does
not matter, provided only he directs his mind intently to heaven '
(Menachoth 110 a). Very significant is the following : ' R. Simeon
b. Azzai said, Notice that in all the ordinances in the Law about
sacrifices, the terms God, or thy God, or Almighty or Zebaoth are
not employed, but only the Tetragrammaton (Yahweh, the Lord),

so as not to give an opening to the heretics to mock (לרדות), and notice that the words " sweet savour unto the Lord " are used in the case of an ox or a sheep or a bird, to show you that the big and the little sacrifice are equal before God, for before him is no eating or drinking, but he has ordained, and we must do his will.' Then Psalm l. 12, 13 is quoted, and it is asked, ' Why did God bid us offer sacrifices to him ? Just to execute his will ' (Sifre 54 a). The ordinances of God must be obeyed. Whatever they happen to be, the Israelite finds his joy in fulfilling God's commands : why God ordered them is God's affair, and not man's. ' I have decreed a decree. It is not permitted to man to transgress it ' (Pesikta 40 b ; Numbers R. xix. 1). ' I have made a decree, and ordained a statute : man is not to criticize it ' (אין להרהר אחריה). (Midrash Psalms ix. 1, 40 b.) This reflection often comes in in regard to the strange and curious law about the Red Cow and its ashes. (Numbers xix. 2-19.) Even Moses asked, ' Is *that* a purification ? God replied, Moses, I have made a decree, no creature may transgress my decree ' (אין בריה לעבור על גזירתי). (Ecclesiastes R. on viii. 1.)

12. I have indicated the general point of view in my notes. To save life, whether one's own life or the life of another, the Sabbath may be violated. ' It is right to violate one Sabbath in order that many may be observed.' ' The laws were given that men should live by them, not that men should die by them.' This was the general and widely prevailing Rabbinic view. Moreover, as regards illness, and when it might justly be said that there was danger to life, the Rabbis were inclined to make considerable concessions, though doubtless, in all such matters there was opportunity for much legal and dialectical casuistry, so delightful and interesting to them, so dull and trifling to us. It is very doubtful to me whether, in practical life, they or anybody else would have paid any attention to all this solemn casuistry or fooling.

But the words of Jesus go further than the saving of life. Even in Mark we have not only the words ψυχὴν σῶσαι ἢ ἀκοκτεῖναι, but also ἀγαθὸν ποιῆσαι ἢ κακοποιῆσαι (to do good or to do evil), and in Matthew we find nothing but καλῶς ποιεῖν, to do good. That would have been much too wide an extension or application of the Rabbinic principle for the Rabbis to have accepted. If a person had ' a withered hand,' there was no danger to life. He could quite well wait till the Sabbath was over. It is true that certain minor infringements of the Sabbath might be permitted in sickness. Thus one might put out a light on the Sabbath to help a sick man to go to sleep. But unrestricted permission to 'heal' on Sabbath would not have been permitted : even miraculous healings on the Sabbath would not, I think, have been looked upon with favour. As to the care of the animals mentioned in verse 11, the Rabbis appear to have permitted that they should be extracted from a ditch or cistern on the Sabbath, though the passages given in S.B. show that if the animal could be made comfortable and given food, it might, in certain circumstances, have been considered more proper for it to remain where it was till the Sunday. But, probably, practical life solved such matters without casuistical distinctions. In any case, the Rabbis would have held that if the animal was in actual pain, the Sabbath might be violated, for cruelty to animals (צער בעלי חיים) was strictly forbidden in the Pentateuch, and the violation of some Rabbinical application or development of the Sabbath Law was less grave than the violation of a Pentateuchal injunction (Sabbath 128 b). Jesus, one notices, gets hold at once of the right principle, and pays no heed to legal subtleties. Both he and the Rabbis use and cite the maxim, ' The Sabbath was made for you, you were not made for the Sabbath ' (Mechilta on Exodus xxxi. 14, 104 a *init.*), but only Jesus (Mark ii. 27) drives the maxim home. For the Rabbis S.B. justly say that the ' Grundsatz hat nicht allgemeine Gültigkeit, sondern besagt nur, dass der Sabbat lediglich zur Rettung eines Menschenlebens entweiht werden dürfe ' [1] (ii. p. 5). Jesus goes at once to the root and heart of the matter. Moreover, to the Rabbis (this must be allowed) the Sabbath was a more adorable, divine thing than it was to Jesus : in spite of the maxim, it was more, if I may put it so, a sort of living, separate entity. (*Cp.* Abrahams, *Studies* I. p. 129–135, a luminous analysis of the whole subject.)

32. As regards severity, Jesus and the Rabbis seem about on a par. On the whole, it may, I think, be said that the general view, which maintained itself and became codified, was that the Israelites who would never receive forgiveness in the next world were only

[1] ' The maxim has no universal validity; it merely means that the Sabbath may be desecrated in order to save a human life.'

those who denied the divinity of the Law, or who denied God, or who deliberately abandoned Judaism. All other sins could be atoned for by repentance or by restitution, or by the Day of Atonement, or by a combination of these. Or, again, they could be atoned for by death; or they would be forgiven by some temporary purgatorial punishment after death. It is true that it says in Aboth R. Nathan xxxix. *init.* (p. 58 b), ' For five classes of persons there is no forgiveness : he who constantly repents (and then sins again); he who sins repeatedly (or who sins much) ; he who sins in a pious generation ; he who sins with the intention of repenting ; he who profanes the name of God.' But other utterances contradict this one. Thus, for instance, as regards the Profanation of the Name, it says in Yoma 86 a that repentance and the Day of Atonement and sufferings—all three—only leave the question in suspense ; but death atones. In the next page of Yoma (86 b) it is said by one Rabbi that God forgives a man who has committed a sin [the same sin] once, twice, thrice, but if he commits it for the fourth time, God does not forgive him. Nevertheless, in other places we hear that the gates of repentance are never closed. Who could possibly have been a worse sinner than Manasseh ? He was a wicked idolater ; he shed innocent blood ; yet, as the Rabbis observe, he repented and was forgiven. I verily believe that, even for the sins next to be mentioned, if an Israelite repented and declared his error, and returned to ' right belief,' the Rabbis would have held that he would be forgiven by God. (All that I have quoted refers only to Israelites.) In the famous eleventh section of Mishnah Sanhedrin it is said, ' The following have no share in the life to come : He who says that the Torah teaches no resurrection of the dead ; he who denies that the Torah is from God ; and " Epicurus " (*i.e.* probably the Atheist, the Denier of God, the Arch-Heretic). R. Akiba said, He also who reads the external books (probably some Christian gospel or heretical writings), and he who whispers over a wound and repeats Exodus xvi. 26 (*i.e.* uses magic). Abba Saul said, He too who says the Tetragrammaton (Yahweh) out loud.' In the Gemara many rather trivial explanations of ' the Epicurus ' are given ; thus it is suggested that ' the Epicurus ' is the man who despises (or mocks at) the learned. Or it is he who says, ' What use are the Rabbis to us ? They learn for themselves and teach for themselves.' As regards the man who says that the Law is not from heaven, the sentence ' For he has despised the word of the Lord ' (Numbers xv. 31) is quoted. Some include under it those who speak insultingly of (or who make false interpretations in) the Torah ; others those who (artificially) violate the Abrahamic covenant. One Rabbi, Elazar of Modin, said, ' He who profanes the holy offerings, despises the festivals, breaks the Abrahamic covenant, makes false interpretations of the Law, puts his fellow-man to shame openly—even if he is learned, or even if he does good works, shall have no share in the life to come ' (Aboth iii. 15). And another Rabbi said, Even though he says the whole Law is from God with the exception of one verse which Moses wrote without God having told it to him, or with the exception of a variation in spelling, or an argument *a fortiori*, or of an argument by analogy, he too has despised the word of the Lord, and has no share in the life to come. Yet it may be doubted whether if such a one repented and retracted, he would not have been regarded by *these very same Rabbis* as forgiven by God. Incidentally, one may notice the extraordinary importance attached by the Rabbis to ' putting another to shame openly.' The other excluding sins are religious, and deal with matters of *belief*, and even ' good works ' cannot counteract their deadly issues. Yet among these religious sins and unbeliefs one ethical offence is illogically introduced : putting a fellow-man to shame openly.

Mr. Loewe sends me the following note : ' We always have to remember that the Rabbis had the difficult task of working out a system and administering it. They had to be practical, and it is easy both to call system casuistry and for system actually to become casuistry. Jesus, on the other hand, was not faced with practical responsibilities. He could speak with the freedom of a leader in opposition. It was easy enough for him to let off the adulterous wife without seeming to condone adultery. But could he do so if he were charged with the duty of upholding public morality ? So with regard to repentance. The Rabbis aimed (1) at keeping the door open as widely as possible ; (2) at enforcing respect for law and order also. The idea of an unforgivable sin seems abhorrent : they solved the problem by retaining the hypothetically unforgivable sin and by finding excuses or extenuating circumstances for the unforgiven sinner, so that in fact he was forgiven.'

36. For this verse S.B. give the necessary parallels, *e.g.* 'Even the words of no importance—casual utterances spoken by man—even his idle talk with his wife, are written upon his tablet, and are read out to him on his death bed' (Lev. Rabba, אמור, xxvi. 7 on xxi. 1). 'Keep thy tongue from idle words lest thy throat thirst (in Hell)' (Yoma 77 a *fin.* *Cp.* Jeremiah ii. 25).

39. I see no adequate evidence that the Jews in the age of Jesus or the Rabbis suffered from *Wundersucht*, an exaggerated or unseemly desire for miracles and signs. Nor do I see any evidence that Jesus was specially averse to miracles, or that he was lifted high above his contemporaries by his dislike of signs and miracles and his refusal to work them. His refusal to give a sign in this story (of which xvi. 1 is, I suppose, only a variant) is not due to his dislike of signs in the abstract, but to his view (whether justified or not) of the wickedness of his own generation. To a good generation a sign might be given ; to an evil generation no sign will be given. The various Rabbinic quotations given by S.B. do not show any violent passion for signs. No doubt a man who gave himself out as a prophet, and substantiated his claim by miracle, would, in the eyes of the Rabbis, have been worth more than a man who did not effect such a substantiation, though it is doubtful whether he would have been listened to, if he had attacked the Law, however great his miracles. Thus R. Yochanan is reported to have said, 'If a prophet tells you to transgress the words of the Law, listen to him ; but if he tells you to commit idolatry, do not listen to him, even if he made the sun stand still in the sky' (Sanhedrin 90 a), and perhaps the first part of the saying is intended almost playfully as a foil and introduction to the second. Generally, the sayings about miracles show a more or less common-sense attitude from people who believed in their occurrence, and while not specially anxious to secure them, and while not unaware that they might be improperly used, nevertheless held that, when all is said and done, miracles do, *prima facie*, show some supernatural power on the part of those who perform them, and *may* therefore show the will and purpose of God. The most famous story about miracles is perhaps the well-known tale in Baba Mezia 59 b. On a certain occasion R. Eliezer (*circa* A.D. 90) used all possible arguments to substantiate his opinion, but the Rabbis did not accept it. He

said, ' If I am right, may this carob tree move a hundred yards from
its place. It did so. . . . They said, From a tree no proof can be
brought. Then he said, May the canal prove it. The water of
the canal flowed backwards. They said, Water cannot prove anything. Then he said, May the walls of this house of study prove it.
Then the walls of the house bent inwards as if they were about to
fall. R. Joshua rebuked the walls and said to them, If the learned
dispute about the *Halachah* (the rule, the Law), what has that to do
with you ? So, to honour R. Joshua, the walls did not fall down,
but to honour R. Eliezer they did not become straight again.
Then R. Eliezer said, If I am right, let the heavens prove it. Then
a heavenly voice said, What have you against R. Eliezer ? The
Halachah is always with him (as he thinks). Then R. Joshua got
up and said, It is not in heaven. (Deut. xxx. 12.) What did he
mean by this ? R. Jeremiah said, The Law was given us from
Sinai. We pay no attention to a heavenly voice. For already
from Sinai the Law said, By a majority you are to decide. (Exodus
xxiii. 2.) R. Nathan met Elijah and asked him what God did in
that hour. Elijah replied, He laughed and said, My children have
conquered me ! ' The story has a certain characteristically Rabbinic flavour and charm. It shows a remarkable religious independence—the very opposite of *Wundersucht.*

Mr. Loewe sends me the following note : ' This point strikes
me. If Jews of the first century were so keen on miracles, why has
this keenness left no trace in the liturgy and been without influence
on ritual ? What relics of *Wundersucht* can we find in the prayer-
book or in ceremonial ? There were certainly a few curious
customs, *Minhagim,* that prevailed here and there and vanished.
But a *Minhag* is not *Din* (law). They were mostly the outcome of
the so-called practical Cabbala, accretions to mysticism, but they
were neither official nor universal, and when they became at all
common, they were condemned. The *Shinnui hash-Shem* (change
of name *in extremis*) was certainly as old as the Talmud, but it was
sporadic and optional : it was not necessarily superstitious in origin,
though it degenerated. A good instance of thaumaturgy is the
skiomancy on the seventh night of Tabernacles, *i.e.* the forecasting,
by means of the shadow cast by the *lulab* or palm branch, what
destiny the opening year held in store. Leusden's *Philologus* contains an interesting illustration of this practice. Similar examples

are the cures, etc., alleged to be wrought by the secret of the
ineffable Name. But all these operations belong as little to Judaism
as alchemy does to Christianity. In the whole range of the liturgy
I can think only of two post-Biblical miracles. The former occurs
in the well-known Ashkenazic Hanuca hymn *Ma'oz Tsur* (Singer,
p. 275, "The legend that when the Priests re-entered the Temple
they found only one small flask of consecrated oil, and this lasted
for eight days until new oil could be provided for the Cande-
labrum," p. cciv). The latter is the inclusion of Onias the
circle-drawer in the list of those for whom miracles had been performed, "May He who heard Onias in the circle, hear us." This
occurs in a hymn attributed to Hai, the last Gaon, A.D. 1017. It is
to be found in the Sephardic liturgy for the Day of Atonement.[1]
Miracles were limited to the Bible, and these do not come into
question here. Jesus and the Rabbis probably held similar views
about them. But if a love for miracles had been specifically Jewish,
where are the results ? When did the miracles cease ? We know
well enough when they ceased in Christianity, but nothing in extent or importance comparable to the Reformation attack on shrines
and wonder-working relics is known in Judaism.'

50. The story, striking as it is, has no Rabbinic ring. It would
be impossible to imagine R. Tarphon saying it of *his* mother. See
the story about him in ' Spirit of Judaism ' (*Beginnings*, Vol. I. p. 80).
' One Sabbath day his mother's sandals split and broke, and as she
could not mend them, she had to walk across the courtyard barefoot.
So R. Tarphon kept stretching his hands under her feet, so that she
might walk over them all the way.' (The story is most intelligently
told in Jer. Kiddushin i. 61 b. *Cp.* Jer. Peah i. 15 c ; Bacher, *Agada
der Tannaiten*, p. 344, n. 11.). I have said nothing about Matt. xv.
4–6 in its place. The sayings about the honour and reverence
which should be paid to father and mother in the Rabbinical
literature are endless. The reference to the matter in Kittel (p.
106) is not very generous and not very fair. It is true that there
are legal discussions as to whether, if a father bids his son disobey
a Biblical command, he should be obeyed, or if the father tells him
to do something which involves the infraction of a command, the
son should obey him. The terms of these discussions show clearly

[1] Gaster, Atonement volume, p. 12.

how painful such a possible conflict of duties was to the mind of the
Rabbis. The passage in Kiddushin 32 a which Kittel quotes does
not show any real lack of filial affection. ' R. Elazar b. Mattya
said, If my father were to say to me, Give me some water to drink,
and I had at that moment a command to fulfil, then I should omit
the honour due to a father, and fulfil the command. R. Isi b.
Judah said, If the command can be executed by others, let it
be done by others, and let the son fulfil the honour due to a father.
The *Halachah* is as R. Isi said.' Immediately before this passage
is one in which a son is reported as having corrected his father in an
interpretation of a passage in the Law. ' R. Judah said, Speak
not thus to thy father, for it is said, If a father makes a mistake in
the words of the Law, let not the son say, Father, you have made a
mistake, but let him say, Father, in the Law it is written thus. But
(it is replied) would not even such a reply pain the father ? Rather
let the son say, In the Law we find the following verse.' A little
before we are told, ' When R. Joseph heard the footsteps of his
mother, he said, I must stand up before the Shechinah who is coming ' (31 b). ' R. Abimi was asked by his father for a tumbler of
water. When he brought it, the father was asleep. He bent over
him and stood there till his father woke up' (31 b). I may also quote
from Moore : ' Among all the commandments, the "weightiest of
the weighty " is filial piety. In Exod. xx. 12 the father is named
first, in Lev. xix. 3 the mother, showing that both parents are
equally to be honoured and revered. Dear to God is the honouring
of father and mother, for the Scripture employs the same expressions
about honouring, revering, cursing parents, as about honouring,
revering, or cursing Himself, thus, according to a hermeneutic rule,
equating the things themselves. Simeon ben Yochai said, Great is
the honouring of father and mother, for God makes more of it than
of honouring himself.' This is proved because it says, ' Honour the
Lord with thy substance ' (*i.e.* by paying tithes, giving to the poor,
etc., etc.). Hence, if you are very poor, you have not to ' honour '
God ; you have not the wherewithal. But when it comes to
honouring father and mother, whether you are poor or no, you
must honour them, even if you have to beg your living from door
to door. ' When a man honours his father and mother, God says,
I impute it to them, as if *I* were dwelling among them, and they
honoured *me*. When a man does despite to his father and his

mother, God says, I have done well not to dwell among them, for
if I dwelt among them, they would do despite to me.' 'The Talmud
has a collection of anecdotes illustrating the length—and the extrava-
gances—to which filial piety could go. Some of them are told of
eminent scholars, such as the story of R. Tarphon and his mother
[quoted above]; but the model son who best showed how far a
man could go in honouring father and mother was Dama ben
Netina, a heathen of high rank in Ashkelon' (Moore II. pp. 131–133;
Mechilta 70 a; Jer. Peah i. 1, 15 c; Kiddushin 31 a). A pretty nuance
is added by R. Eliezer. 'God knew that a human being honours
his mother more than his father' ('honour' seems here to equal
'love'), 'because she soothes him (שדלתו) with words; therefore
father is put before mother in Ex. xx. 12; God knew that a man
reverences his father more than his mother, because his father
teaches him Torah; therefore mother is put before father in Lev.
xix. 3' (Mechilta 70 a and Kiddushin 31 a). The story of Dama b.
Netina is as follows. One of the precious stones of the High Priest's
breastplate had to be replaced, and it was reported that Dama had
a stone such as was required. Some Jews went to him, and he
agreed to sell the stone for a hundred dinars. He went to fetch
the stone, but his father was asleep, holding, or sitting on, the
purse which contained the key of the box in which the stone was.
Dama went back, and said he could not, after all, sell the stone.
They offered him two hundred, and even up to a thousand dinars,
but in vain. Soon after, his father woke up, Dama took the stone,
ran after the Jews, and gave it them. When they wanted to
give him the thousand dinars, he refused to take more than the
hundred, for he said, Can I sell to you for money the honour which
I owe to my father? I will not make any profit from the honour
which I paid to my father' (אנא מזבין לכון איקרא דאבהתי
בפריטין איני נהנה מכבוד אבותי כולם). (Jer. Peah i. 1, 15 c; Kiddushin
31 a.) I should think that upon the whole the fifth commandment had been more persistently and beautifully obeyed
by Jews than by any other religious community. When Jesus
says, 'He who loves father or mother more than me is not
worthy of me,' he may be saying something that has its meaning
and its justification. But the saying has always a painful sound
to Jewish ears, in spite of Deut. xxxiii. 9. It is probable that the
saying, in spite of the sorrow of their parents, has made many women

become nuns, and made many men go as missionaries to distant lands. That may sometimes have been right, but it is doubtful whether Rabbinically trained Jewish sons and daughters would have thought that any such pain to parents could be religiously and ethically right. The force of the fifth commandment was so enormous.

xiii. The Rabbis, who made such large use of parables, were alive to their value as a method of teaching and for the purpose of vivid illustration. Jesus undoubtedly used his parables to illustrate and explain, not to darken or keep concealed, his meaning. In Hebrew *Mashal* means proverb as well as parable, and thus Solomon is regarded as the great author and originator of the *Mashal*, who by that means elucidated and made plain the words of the Torah. Before his time nobody properly understood the Torah; after him all could understand. So the Rabbis say, ' Let not the *Mashal* be despicable in thine eyes, for through the *Mashal* a man can understand the words of the Law ' (Canticles R. i. § 1, 8 on i. 1).

12. The fundamental idea of this verse is not unfamiliar to the Rabbis, where it is more usually directed to the acquisition of knowledge. Thus Hillel said, ' He who does not increase his knowledge decreases it ' (Aboth i. 13). More generally, we have : ' If a man hearkens to one commandment, they (= God) cause him to hearken to many commandments ; if a man forgets one commandment, they cause him to forget many commandments.' ' If a man desires to hearken at once, they cause him to hearken even subsequently ; if a man forgets at once, they cause him to forget subsequently. [For the text and translation *cp.* Bacher, *Agada der Tannaiten*, Vol. I., ed. 2, p. 412, n. 4.] If a man hearkens with his free will, they cause him to hearken even against, *i.e.* without, his will ; if he forgets with his free will, they cause him to forget even against his will.' [Initial] free-will is given [for the meaning *cp.* Bacher, *ibid.*]. (Mechilta 46 a, b on Exodus xv. 26.) (*Cp.* Moore I. 456.) ' Not as with men is the method of God. With men a full vessel receives no more : an empty vessel gets filled. With God, the full is filled : the empty is not filled. If you have heard, you will continue to hear ; if you have not heard, you will not hear (subsequently). If you have heard the old, you will

also hear the new; if you have turned your heart away, you will
hear no more' (Berachoth 40 a).

31. Mr. Loewe writes: 'Mustard, as a symbol, occurs in the Midrash, but it is used as a symbol of something small, not of something
that grows very quickly. So, in Ber. 31 a, a microscopic drop of blood
is said to have been no bigger than a mustard seed. In Leviticus
Rabbah, אמור, xxxi. § 9 on xxiv. 2, a saying of Isaac b. Zera is
quoted in which the sinking sun is said to disappear as "a spot
of blood as (small as) a mustard (seed)." Interesting is the parable
in Canticles R. vi. § 1 on vi. 11 (" To the nut garden I went down ").
It is ascribed to R. Levi (ii., third century ?). He says: "In a
sack full of nuts you can put ever so many (sesame or poppy ?)
seeds and ever so many mustard seeds, and the nuts will hold them.
Thus ever so many proselytes may come unto Israel and be in-
corporated, as it is said, 'Who can count the dust of Jacob ? ' "
(See variants in Pesikta Rabb. 42 b : this, and other parables on
nuts are discussed by A. Feldman, *Parables and Similes of the Rabbis,
Agricultural and Pastoral*, Camb., 1924, p. 179.) On the other hand,
עיסה, dough, is a metaphor of evil. So far from being used as a
simile for the incorporation of Gentiles in a good sense, it is used,
on the contrary, of degeneracy and the mixing of descent, *e.g.*
Kiddushin, 69 b.

'Great stress is laid by the Rabbis on the conception of the
Kingdom of Heaven, but it finds expression differently. One must
look for parallels in thought, not in form. Thus, every blessing
must contain a definite reference to the Kingdom : the wording
must include " King of the universe " (Ber. 12 a). One of the three
main portions of the Additional Service for the New Year is called
Malchoyoth, or "declaration of the Kingdom," and consists of ten
Scriptural verses emphasizing this idea. (See Singer, pp. 247–249,
and Abrahams' Notes, p. cxcviii.) The " Kingdom " forms the
keynote of the Kaddish (*ib.* 75 and lxxxv.), *i.e.* " May He establish
his Kingdom speedily." Finally, the recital of the first paragraph
of the *Shema* was called " taking upon oneself the yoke of the
Kingdom," and a response " Blessed be his glorious Kingdom, etc."
(*ib.* 40 and li.) was inserted. On this formula see V. Aptowitzer,
pp. 93 *seq.*, *Monatsschrift f. Gesch. u. Wissenschaft d. Jud.*, March-
April 1929.'

45. We may compare the story which S.B. use in relation to xix. 21. 'R. Yochanan walked from Tiberias towards Sepphoris and leant on R. Chiya b. Abba's arm. They passed a field. He said : That field belonged to me, but I sold it so as to occupy myself with the Law. They passed an olive garden. He said the same. They passed a vineyard : he said the same. Then R. Chiya wept and said, What have you left yourself for your old age ? He replied, Does what I have done seem foolish (נקלה) in thine eyes ? I have sold what was created in seven days, but I have acquired what was given in forty days' (Canticles R. viii. on viii. 7 and many parallel passages). The Torah was to the Rabbis the pearl of great price. It contained, as it were, the Kingdom of God within itself. By studying and serving the Torah, by practising it and fulfilling its laws, the Israelite both accepted and took upon himself the glad yoke of the Kingdom ; he widened the range of the Kingdom, and in the eschatological sense he brought the advent of the Kingdom nearer.

xv. 11, 20. I have dealt with this passage at great length in my Commentary in the notes on Mark vii., and I need not repeat here what I have there said. There are no true parallels to quote. Jesus speaks here like a new Amos or Isaiah. It is one of the two or three most original and novel sayings in the Gospels, though it is only an application, we might say, of a principle laid down by the prophets, or it is only a principle which runs on all-fours with theirs. We might raise the question : how far could the Rabbis appreciate the prophets ? When we remember that the Law is posterior to the prophets (' coming in between '), and when we remember that, to the Rabbis, the Law (and here I mean by the Law the Pentateuchal code or codes) was all Mosaic, homogeneous, perfect, authoritative and divine, the wonder is, not that the Rabbis appreciated the prophets so little, but that they appreciated them so much. Yet we have seen that they could follow Hosea when he said, ' I desire love rather than sacrifices.' But here Jesus goes further. The principle which he enunciates would, as applied to sacrifices, not merely say, ' Love is better than sacrifices,' but ' sacrifices are needless.' The Rabbis were clearly not in a position to say that. If the principle of xv. 11 is valid, no food makes a man unclean ; the only uncleanness that counts, the only ' holiness ' that counts, are moral cleanness and moral holiness. If this be so, the Jews are not made more holy by observing any food laws, and they would not be made less holy by disregarding them. But the Pentateuchal law says precisely the reverse. In the heat of conflict, and in the ardour of his ethical enthusiasm, Jesus probably did not realize the implications, the *Tragweite*, of his own saying ; but the Rabbis never lost the sharpness of their wits, or the coolness of their heads. They could see whither the principle led, and they could not do other than reject a principle which had such revolutionary and heretical implications.

27. The parallel given in S.B. as regards the dog has more than a verbal interest. It shows the weakness and narrowness of the Rabbinic position : it also shows its beauty. ' Rabbi opened his granary (or storehouse) in a year of famine. He said, Let those who know Scripture, Mishnah, Talmud, Halachah or Haggadah enter. But let not the *Amme ha-Aretz* enter. Then R. Jonathan pressed forward and entered and said, Rabbi, feed me. Have you read the Scripture, said Rabbi. No. Have you read the Mishnah ? No. Then how can I feed you ? Feed me like a dog or a raven (*i.e.* from the bits which fall to the ground). Then he fed him. But when he went out, Rabbi was grieved and said, Woe is me that I have given my bread to an *Am ha-Aretz*. Then his son said to him, Perhaps it was R. Jonathan who never is willing to get any profit (or enjoyment) from the honour of the Law. They investigated, and found that it was so. Then Rabbi said, Let all enter. Rabbi acted according to his view that no punishment (from God) comes upon the world except on account of the *Amme ha-Aretz* ' (Baba Batra 8 a).

XVI. 18. The passage quoted in Moore I. p. 538, about Abraham is interesting. ' As a king who dug in several places for a foundation (תמליום) for his palace. But he came upon morasses and bogs (בצם של מים). At last he struck rock (פטרא), and he said, Here will I build, so he laid the foundation and built. So God, when he sought to create the world, examined the generations of Enosh and of the flood, and said, How can I create the world when these wicked people will rise up and provoke me to anger ? When he saw Abraham, who was to arise, he said, Now I have found a rock on

which to build and establish the world. Therefore he called Abraham
a rock ' (Isaiah li. 1).   (Yalkut § 766 on Numbers xxiii. 9.)   ' For
Abraham's sake both this world and the world to come were created '
(Tanchuma B., *Chaye Sarah*, vi. 60 a).

23.   There are passages in the Gospels to which, from the
nature of the case, there can be no direct parallels, but which, nevertheless, contain high ethical or religious teaching. This is because
such teaching is indirect and implied. It is not direct. One can
neither ask for parallels nor fitly seek to find contrasts.

26.   The passages given in S.B. pp. 749, 750 are not parallels
in any reasonable sense, though many of them are very interesting
in themselves, and show some fine perceptions. In particular, they
show, as S.B. say, the Rabbinic appreciation of the immense value
of every human soul (*der unendliche Wert eines Menschenlebens*).
The idea at the bottom of 26—that no amount of money or earthly
prosperity is worth while if purchased at the risk of losing the
immortal beatitudes of the world to come—would be entirely in
accordance with the views of the Rabbis, just as for them the
knowledge of the Law outweighed every other human good.   It
may, perhaps, though not strictly ' in order,' because not constitut-
ing a parallel, be desirable to quote the remarkable and very famous
and familiar section of the Mishnah Sanhedrin iv. 5. ' One man
only was created at the beginning to teach you that he who destroys
one soul is regarded as if he had destroyed the whole world, and he
who preserves one soul (life) is regarded as if he had preserved the
whole world.'   Then follow other reasons. Finally, it is added,
' Therefore every individual must say, For my sake was the whole
world created.'   There is a parallel passage in Aboth R. Nathan
xxxi. 46 a, which ends with the words, ' Hence thou canst learn
that one man weighs as much (is as important) as the whole creation.'
    The Rabbis were also able to perceive that a man must not
claim material benefit from his devotion to the Law or from his
righteousness. ' R. Levi said, From all which men do in *Mitzvot*
and *Maasim Tobim* (commandments and good works) it is enough
(it is adequate reward) that God lets the sun shine ' (Ecclesiastes
i. 5. The saying of R. Levi is in connection with Ecclesiastes i. 3).
' The Rabbis say, It is enough that God will renew their face like

the ball of the sun' (Judges v. 31). 'R. Yudan said, Under the sun man may get no reward (profit), but he will above the sun.' This pregnant saying of R. Yudan as well as the saying of the Rabbis must refer to the beatitudes of the world to come. (Leviticus Rabba, אמור, xxviii. I *ad init.* on xxiii. 10.) The usual view of the Rabbis would be that fidelity to, and study of, the Law ought to, and will, in normal circumstances, bring prosperity on earth as well as beatitude in 'heaven.'

xviii. I. It would seem that the question as to precedence and ranks in the world to come or in heaven was occasionally debated among the Rabbis. Thus, in Pesikta Kahana 180 a (Wuensche, p. 263), one Rabbi gives the precedence to those who were pre-eminent in Torah and in good works, another to the teachers of Mishnah and Torah who teach children truthfully. These shall sit at God's right hand. In Midrash Psalms mention is made of the seven classes of the just who shall 'receive the face of the Shechinah.' Of these seven, the highest is the class of the upright, for it says, 'The upright shall see his face' (Mid. Psalms xi. (6) on verse 7, 51 a ; *cp.* Pesachim 50 a). Elsewhere it is said that though there are degrees (מעלות) among the righteous in the world to come, there is among them no jealousy. For as with the stars, the light of one star is not like the light of another, and yet there is among them no hatred, jealousy, or strife, so is it with the righteous. Among them, too, there will be no hatred, jealousy, or strife (תחרות). (Sifre 83 a.) It is argued that the completely righteous have a place above the penitent and also, contrariwise, that the penitent stand above the completely righteous. (Berachoth 34 b.) The martyrs of Lydda had nothing before them in their division of heaven. (Ecclesiastes R. on ix. 10, אין לפנים ממחיצתם מחיצתם.) In another Midrash it is said that, 'The division of the righteous will be next to the angels of the service' (Deut. R. i. on i. I *fin.*).

3, 4. An infant is stated by the Rabbis to be without sin ; but I do not find any parallel given, nor have I noticed any, for the child as the symbol of humility and *Anspruchlosigkeit.* On the other hand, so far as humility is concerned, the Rabbinic teaching is the same as that of Jesus. This has already been observed in the notes on Matthew v. 3, 19. 'He who makes himself small in this world for the sake of the Torah will be great in the world to come ; he who makes himself a slave in this world for the sake of the Torah shall be free in the world to come' (Baba Mezia 85 b). This is the regular line. Pride, conceit, worldly ambition, etc., are inconsistent with study and learning ; they are also inconsistent with righteousness and the knowledge and the 'presence' of God. The Rabbis, as we have seen, manage mostly to combine personal humility with pride of their class, or rather with pride of learning. At all events, if we cannot see into their long-dead hearts, we may, at least, say that they combined the utmost appreciation of humility, the utmost denunciation of conceit, with a perfectly unabashed and avowed pride in learning, with high praise of knowledge, and a sincere depreciation of ignorance.

5. *Cp.* x. 40. The child is here supposed to be 'symbolical of lowly, humble and insignificant believers or would-be believers' (My Commentary, II. p. 247). Service rendered to the most insignificant of God's human creatures is direct service rendered to God. *Cp.* xxv. 40. It may, I think, be justly said that this emphasis upon the service of the insignificant and the small as equivalent to the service of God, and as specially beloved in his sight, is more characteristic of Jesus than of the Rabbis. Nevertheless, none more than they pressed the duty of lovingkindness to the poor and the needy. To them the true imitation of God is imitating him in his goodness and mercy. 'As God is called compassionate and gracious, so be thou compassionate and gracious, and give freely unto all. As God is called righteous and loving, so be thou righteous and loving' (Sifre 85 a). The difference between Rabbis and Gospel is rather one of language than of substance. At the same time, we have to admit that the finest benevolence to the Rabbis was help rendered to needy scholars ; and here the learned are, as it were, pleading for their own class.

As regards children in the literal sense, *cp.* Megillah 13 a, ' As for him who brings up an orphan boy and girl in his house the Scripture reckons it to him as if he had begotten them.' To the quotation on verse 4 may be added the quaint remarks about Joktan. (Genesis x. 25.) Why was he called Joktan ? ' Because he made himself and his affairs small. And for that merit he was the ancestor of (משפחות י"ג להעמיד וזכה) thirteen families. If a small man who makes his affairs small has this reward, how much more shall a great man have who makes his affairs small ! ' (Genesis R., *Noah*, xxxvii. *ad fin.* on x. 26).

6. The hyperbole of this verse is quite in accordance with Rabbinic phraseology. Thus R. Simeon ben Yochai said, ' It were better for a man that he threw himself into a fiery furnace than that he should openly put his neighbour to shame ' (Kethuboth 67 b).

7. The idea of, and the term, stumbling-blocks are also known to the Rabbis. The Rabbinic word for the term is תקלה. R. Nechunyah b. ha-Kanah, when he entered the house of study, used to pray that no stumbling-block should happen to anyone through him (*i.e.* that he should give no false decision or pronouncement). (Berachoth Mishnah iv. 2 and 28 b.) ' Why should the Law order that the animal with which a man has sinned (Lev. xx. 15, 16) should be killed ? What sin has the animal committed ? It is killed because it was a stumbling-block (occasion for sin). ' If of trees used for idolatry the Law says, " burn them," because they caused men to sin, how much more worthy is he of death who has caused another to stray from the ways of life to the ways of death ' (Sanhedrin 55 a). Generally, the Rabbis' view was that he who causes others to sin is worse than he who sins himself. Jeroboam was the arch-sinner because he sinned himself, and caused others— all Israel—to sin.

12. S.B. give no close parallel for the ninety-nine and the one. The parallel in the story they quote from Gen. R., ויישלח, lxxxvi. 6 on xxxix. 2 is only verbal. It would have been better, I think, to quote the pretty story about Moses from Exodus R. ii., וארא, on iii. 1. ' While Moses was feeding the sheep of his father-in-law in the wilderness, a young kid ran away : Moses followed it until it reached a ravine, where it found a well to drink from. When Moses got up to it, he said, I did not know that you ran away because you were thirsty. Now you must be weary. He took the kid on his shoulders and carried it back. Then God said, Because you have shown pity in leading back one of a flock belonging to a man, you shall lead *my* flock, Israel.' S.B. do, however, refer to this story on xxv. 21.

13. As regards the general doctrine of repentance in Rabbinical literature I have written at length in the *J. Q. R.* (1904, Vol. XVI. pp. 209–257). The Rabbinic teaching about repentance is perhaps the brightest jewel in the Rabbinic crown, and all that I have said on the subject in my Commentary (*e.g.* II. p. 249) seems to me fully justified. Nothing that Jesus says about it beats, or goes beyond, what the Rabbis say about it. In fact, the Rabbinic teachings about repentance are far more fully worked out (though doubtless with a certain amount of 'legal' admixture and casuistry) than the teachings of Jesus on the same subject. And the legal admixture and casuistry partly raise problems of ethical delicacy and difficulty which it is proper and reasonable to discuss, partly are of a playful character, and partly seek to bring needful theories in regard to the Day of Atonement into harmony with the deeper prophetic doctrine. I say 'needful' theories, because we have to remember that every word of the Pentateuch is for the Rabbis perfect and divine, so that the declaration in Leviticus xvi. 30 must be no less true and no less divine than (*e.g.*) Psalm li. 17. Even with the legal admixture and casuistry of which I have spoken, the Rabbinic doctrine about repentance is sound and lofty, pure and wholesome. But the passages concerning it are so numerous and so important that it is hardly possible to give a selection which would adequately represent the whole. I have therefore reprinted the larger part of my article on Repentance in the *J. Q. R.* as an appendix. *Cp.* also S.B. I. 785 ; 162–172 ; II. 210–212.

As regards the *particular* point suggested by Matt. xviii. 12, the sayings quoted by S.B. from Berachoth 34 b (in Vol. I. 785, 37 b should be 34 b) and Sanhedrin 99 a offer a parallel which is very fairly complete. One Rabbi declares (*cp.* on xviii. 1) that where the repentant stand the righteous (who have not sinned) do not stand ; another Rabbi declares that the 'completely righteous' occupy a still higher place. Each disputant justifies his view by a fanciful interpretation of Isaiah lvii. 19. But really one extra saying as to the superior position of the repentant does not add much to that general laudation of repentance, to that most delicate appreciation of the repentant, and to that most tender regard for their feelings, which are characteristic of Rabbinic teaching. There was nothing particularly 'daring' about Matt. xviii. 13. No Rabbi would have been astonished by it. It was quite on Rabbinic lines, and in accordance with Rabbinic teaching. Doubtless, some other Rabbi could and would have playfully retorted by a text which would prove the opposite, but that would not have meant that he, too, did not appreciate God's love for, and delight in, the repentant sinner. It is not to the point for S.B. to say in their solemn manner (seeking to cheapen, and chip off, the value of the saying) : 'The opinion of R. Abbahu (that the repentant occupy a higher place [in heaven] than the righteous who have not sinned) was probably never generally recognised.' There is no proof of this one way or the other. It was a paradox, just as the saying of Jesus is a paradox; both mean the same thing, and have the same object : to accentuate the sovereign beauty and efficacy of repentance, and God's love for, and delight in, the repentant sinner. And this was quite as much Rabbinic doctrine as it was the doctrine of Jesus.

14. In this verse Jesus is referring not to children, but to 'humble believers,' the 'little ones' of the community, but not the 'little ones' in age. (Whether such a reference proves that the verse is later than Jesus does not here concern us.) The quotations in S.B. do not therefore appear to apply.

It would be very difficult to answer the question : which teaches, on the whole, a more forgiving conception of God—the Jesus of the Synoptic Gospels or the Rabbis. We have a number of exquisite and tender sayings such as Matt. xviii. 14, but these are counterbalanced by Matt. xxv. 41–46 and similar passages, where 'aeonian' and painful hell is declared to be the lot of the wicked. We have also such a hard and gloomy utterance as that in Matt. vii. 13, 14, which seems to teach that those who perish shall be far more numerous than those who shall be saved. We have a cruel denunciation and threat, such as Matt. xi. 20–24. But it has also to be recognized that the main strain of Synoptic teaching is (a) sound as regards the purely ethical tests for salvation or destruction, as the case may be ; (b) of a less nationalist tendency than that of the Rabbis; (c) less burdened by verses in the O.T. of a low ethical quality; and (d) more definitely solicitous (as here) for the 'little ones,' or the 'simple.' The new particularism of creed has hardly begun to rear its ugly head in the Synoptic Gospels. The Rabbis were more 'nationalist' than Jesus : their hostility to the idolater and the alien (who for them mean so largely and often the oppressors and the ' Romans ') was more intense and more constant. As regards sinners *in* Israel, so long as these were not anti-Rabbinic ' enemies,' the Rabbis were, I should think, no less eager for their repentance than Jesus, though they did not, like him, seek them out and try actively to convert them to righteousness. The O.T. burden was, however, very grave for them. It reinforced the hatreds and animosities of the natural man. Jesus did not, I should imagine, know the O.T. in the same wonderful way that they did. Nor did he regard it in the same way. He had present in his consciousness and memory only those verses which had specially struck him, or which chimed in with his own teaching. He was more independent and inspired. The Rabbis knew the whole O.T. too painfully well, and to them, unfortunately, all statements about God in the O.T. were almost equally true. Thus, if God is said to ' hate ' Edom, if he is said to ' laugh at ' the wicked, all of whom he will at the last ' destroy ' (and we know that there are many similar passages), all these sayings must somehow be true—just as true as the loving and beautiful and tender sayings, and they all came in most conveniently, and were all most ' handy,' when nationalist and particularist animosities craved Biblical sanction. On the whole, the Rabbis come out of this great difficulty fairly well; but if both Jesus and they equally believe in hell and its eternity (and I see no difference here), there is, sometimes, in the Rabbinic conception, more zest attributed to God in the destruction of enemies who are both his enemies and Israel's. The question is often asked, Does God rejoice at the destruction or discomfiture of the wicked ? The more usual answer is that he does not. Thus Mechilta 34 b on Exodus xv. 1, with quaint proofs from 2 Ch. xx. 21, 22 : ' God does not rejoice over the destruction of the wicked.' In Deut. xxviii. 63 God is said to rejoice at the destruction even of the wicked in Israel. This is, however, doubted, and in Megillah 10 b we have the famous saying how God rebuked the angels when they began a hymn of praise at the destruction of the Egyptians in the Red Sea. ' My children are drowned in the sea, and ye would sing a paean of praise ? ' It is, however, suggested that though he does not rejoice himself, he causes others to rejoice. (Sanhedrin 39 b and par.) Proverb xi. 10 is continually quoted : ' When the wicked perish, there is shouting (*i.e.* rejoicing).' Certain passages in the Song in Deuteronomy must have stimulated the desire for revenge (*e.g.* 41, 42). Thus R. Ishmael, being asked the question, replied that there *was* rejoicing before God (= God rejoices) when those who provoke him perish from the world. (Sifre, p. 37*a*.) When God judges (*i.e.* condemns) the nations, there is rejoicing before him; when he judges Israel there is, as it were, repentance (*i.e.* God grieves. Sifre 139 a on Deut. xxxii. 36). ' Überwiegend,' say S.B., very honestly, ' ist jedoch in Übereinstimmung mit Ezechiel xviii. 32, xxxiii. 11, die Meinung dahin gegangen, dass Gott keine Freude am Untergang der Gottlosen habe ' (iii. p. 497).[1] I am not sure, however, whether that would be equally true when the fate of the nations is concerned. The odd see-saw in the mind of the Rabbis might be illustrated by a citation from the last paragraph of the Midrash on Psalm civ. ' R. Judah said (on verse 35, " Let the sinners be consumed out of the earth and may the wicked be no more "), Let the sinners become perfect (*i.e.* sinless), a play upon the Hebrew words for " consumed " and " perfect," and the wicked will be no more ; *i.e.* in that hour they will no longer be wicked. R. Nehemiah said, May wickednesses cease, and the wicked be no more ; *i.e.* in that hour they will no longer be wicked.' R. Meir had a heretic in his neighbourhood who annoyed him as regards the Scripture. He prayed that he might die. His wife Beruria said to him, ' Are you thinking of the verse, Let the wicked be no more ? We should read : Sins, not sinners. [A small difference in punctuation.] Let the sins cease, and the wicked will be no more. He prayed for him (the heretic) that he should turn and repent. R. Samuel b. Isaac said, In this world every wicked man is judged by himself (separately), but in the world to come all the sinners will be judged and annihilated at once and together, as it is said, The sinners will be consumed out of the earth and the wicked will be no more. R. Simeon bar Abba said : From the beginning of the Book till this Psalm inclusive there are 104 psalms, and in none of them occurs the word Hallelujah. But when the sinners are destroyed from the earth, and the wicked are no more, then we find, Bless the Lord, O my soul, Hallelujah. And what is the reason ? When the wicked perish, there is rejoicing ' (Prov. xi. 10).

So, too, we read, among a number of apparently contradictory

---

[1] ' In accordance with Ezekiel xviii. 32, xxxiii. 11, the predominant opinion came to be that God has no pleasure in the destruction of the wicked.'

sentences in Scripture which it is sought to reconcile, 'Ez. xviii. 32, God has no pleasure in the death of him that dies (*i.e.* the sinner): but 1 Sam. ii. 25 states, "God had pleasure in killing them" (Midrashic rendering). The one passage refers to those who repent; the other to those who do not repent' (Niddah 70 b. *Cp.* Sifre 12 b). Then there is the famous passage in the Mishnah of Sanhedrin. When a criminal is going to his execution, the Shechinah says, 'How heavy is my head, how heavy is my arm. If God suffers so much for the blood of the wicked, how much more for the blood of the righteous' (vi. 5). God first told Balaam not to go with the messengers; but as he wanted to go with them, he let him go, and said, 'You wicked one, I have no pleasure in the destruction of the wicked, but since you wish to go with the men in order to perish from the world, go!' (Numbers Rabba, בלק, xx. 12 on xxii. 20–22). A pleasant passage—and by no means uncharacteristic—is the following from Tanchuma, *Vayera*, 24 a, foot (S.B. III. p. 775); R. Pinchas b. Chama (*circa* 360) said, 'God has no pleasure in condemning any man' (*beriyyah*, creature, quite a general word, which includes both Jews and Gentiles). Then Ez. xviii. 32, Psalm v. 5, and Ez. xxxiii. 11 are quoted. In what has he pleasure? In declaring his 'creatures' righteous. (Isaiah xlii. 21.) 'When his creatures sin and provoke him, and he is angry, what does he do? He seeks for them an advocate, who may find for them a merit, and he makes a a way for the advocate, as Abraham made intercession for the Sodomites.'

The conclusion of the matter would seem to be that Matt. xviii. 14 is not off the Rabbinic line. It is in accordance with Rabbinic teaching at its best, and can hardly be said to go beyond it.

15. There are many Rabbinic parallels about Reproof (*Zurechtweisung*) which are duly given in S.B. The Rabbis set great store, and put much stress, on Reproof, but they also realized its difficulties. It is dealt with both ethically, and also sometimes half legally, half casuistically, in the Rabbinic manner, yet with no evil intent or harm. Sometimes, too, we find in connection with it some of the usual Rabbinic paradoxes and exaggerations. S.B., not understanding this, or taking playful exaggerations or casuistic enjoyments too seriously, and never *quite* averse to criticizing the Rabbis adversely, where, as they think, they honestly *can*, make

some solemn remarks on the subject which are hardly accurate. One must decide when the Rabbis are in deadly earnest, and when they are not ; when they are to be taken at the foot of the letter, and when they are not. To do this requires knowledge, flair, and complete impartiality. S.B. have the first ; they are occasionally wanting in the third ; and do not possess *quite* enough of the second. I quote some of their citations, ' If you have companions, of whom some reprove you and others praise, love him who reproves, hate him who praises, for the former brings you to the life of the world to come, the latter removes you from the world ' (Aboth R. Nathan, xxix. 44 a). ' Rabbi said, Which is the right way that a man should choose ? Let him love reproof. So long as there is reproof in the world, quiet of mind comes to the world and prosperity and peace.' R. Jonathan said, ' He who reproves his fellow for the sake of heaven (*i.e.* with pure intent) has his portion with God (זוכה לחלקו של הקדוש ברוך הוא), and God draws over him a thread of love ' (Tamid 28 a). One Rabbi said, ' Jerusalem was destroyed only because none reproved his fellow. R. Tarphon, who witnessed the destruction, said that there was none in his generation who knew how to give reproof rightly (*i.e.* without putting his fellow to shame), or how rightly to receive it. If one said to another Take away the splinter from your eye, he replied, Take away the beam from your own eye.' (In the version of this saying by R. Tarphon in the Sifre 64 a it is added that R. Yochanan said, I call Heaven and earth to witness that R. Akiba was censured (נתקרקר) because of me five times before R. Gamaliel in Yabneh, because I complained about him, and he (R. Gamaliel) censured him. And I know that his love for me increased, so that the word of Scripture in Proverbs ix. 8 was fulfilled. But a little further on, 65 b, it is said that a man should only be reproved shortly before his death, and that for four reasons—so as not to have to reprove him again and again ; so that he should not feel shame in the presence of the reprover, whenever he should happen to see him ; so that he should feel nothing in his heart against the reprover ; and so that the reprover should part from him in peace, for reproof then brings him unto peace.) ' The Rabbis have taught, It says (Lev. xix. 17) Thou shalt not hate thy brother in thine heart. You might think that you must only not hit or beat or curse him. Therefore it says " in thine heart." Even in your heart you must

harbour no hatred. How do we know that he who sees anything
disgraceful in his neighbour must reprove him ? Because it says
(Lev. xix. 17), Thou shalt surely reprove him.' And because of
the verb occurring in the Hebrew idiom twice, it is inferred that if
he does not receive the reproof, it must be repeated. 'One might
think that one must continue to reprove him, even if he is ashamed
(or put to shame), therefore it says, Thou shalt not incur sin
because of him.' (Putting a man to shame before others is one of
the greatest of all sins according to the Rabbis.) The Rabbis spoke
of a reproof which was done for God's sake, and a reproof which
had some lower aim or intention. 'R. Judah b. Simeon was asked,
Reproof for its own sake (in purity, *lishmah*), and humility not
for its own sake (which, therefore, does not reprove for fear, *e.g.*
of not causing enmity or annoyance) ; which is greater ? He
replied, You would allow that humility for its own sake is greater.
For it has been said that humility (for its own sake) is the greatest
of all the virtues. And humility not for its own sake is greater
(than reproof). For Rab said, Let a man occupy himself ever with
the Torah and the Commandments, even not for their own sake,
because from the second (less good) motive he may come to the
first (the pure motive, "for its own sake "). Which is the reproof
for its own sake and the humility not for its own sake ? It is like
that of R. Huna and like that of R. Chiya bar Rab. They sat
before Samuel (who died about 254), and R. Chiya said to Samuel,
you see how R. Huna pains me. Then R. Huna determined that
he would not pain him any more. When R. Chiya went away,
R. Huna said to Samuel, Thus and thus had R. Chiya done before.
Then Samuel said, Why did you not tell him of it in his presence
(to his face) ? R. Huna replied, Far be it from me that the son of
Rab should be put to shame through me!' Thus R. Huna acted
from a humility which was not for its own sake in not putting
R. Chiya to shame in the presence of Samuel, and this secondary
humility was, nevertheless, superior to a reproof which, though
for its own sake, would have put R. Chiya to open shame (Arachin
16 b). This very fairly tenable view hardly justifies the severe
remark of S.B.: 'Mit diesem Grundsatz konnte natürlich die
Unterlassung jeder Zurechtweisung gerechftertigt werden ' (Vol. i.
p. 790).[1]

---

[1] ' By this principle the omission of every reproof could obviously be justified.'

20. The mystic presence of Jesus among his faithful flock is paralleled by the mystic presence of the Shechinah, that is, of God, among those who occupy themselves with the study of the Law. ' If two sit together and exchange words of Torah, the divine presence abides with them, and even when a single individual occupies himself with the Torah, the Shechinah rests upon him ' (Aboth iii. 7). ' Why is God called *Makom* (Place) ? Because in every place where the righteous are, God is there also ' (Exodus xx. 24). (Midrash Psalms xc. (10), verse 1, 196 a.) To such ideas there are many parallels. The profound remarks of R. Yose b. Chalafta and of R. Isaac are not in point here, but because they occur in the same paragraph in the Midrash, I may as well drag them in, even if irrelevantly. ' R. Isaac said, We should not know if God were the dwelling of the world, or if the world were the dwelling of God, but Psalm xc. 1 shows that the world is God's dwelling (*i.e.* God pervades, or is omnipresent in, the world, but is not co-extensive with, or exhausted by, it.). R. Yose said, We should not know if the world were an appendage to God, or God an appendage (מפילה) to the world, but Ex. xxxiii. 21 (" There is a place by me ") shows that the world is only an appendage to God. He is the place of his world : the world is not his place.'

21. As to 35 see Matt. v. 24 and vi. 14. As to 21 it may be argued that Jesus demands a more repeated and unlimited forgiveness from man to man than do the Rabbis. R. Yose b. Chanina said, ' Let him who asks his fellow for forgiveness do so three times and not more.' (There follows a fanciful Biblical proof.) A little farther on the next page of the Talmud (Yoma 87 a and b) we are told a quaint story about two Rabbis, of whom one (very unjustly, we should say) had been annoyed by the other. It seems that Rab was reading a passage from the Bible out loud, when he was interrupted by the entry of Rabbi X. He began again. Rabbi Y came in ; he began again ; Rabbi Z came in ; he began again. Then a fourth Rabbi (R. Chanina) came in, and Rab did *not* begin again. R. Chanina was annoyed. Then Rab went on thirteen successive evenings of the Day of Atonement to ask for forgiveness, but R. Chanina was not appeased. Why did Rab act thus in spite of what R. Yose had taught ? Well, Rab thought differently. Why did R. Chanina act as he did, for had not Raba taught, ' He

who does not stand upon his rights is forgiven all his sins ? ' Then
follows a very absurd reason.   R. Chanina had dreamt of Rab
that he was hung on a palm tree, and as the tradition is that if you
see in a dream that a man is hung on a palm tree, he will become
head of a seminary, he concluded that Rab would become the head
of the seminary of which he, R. Chanina, was head, and that he
(R. Chanina) would die.   Therefore he refused to be appeased, so
that Rab might go away and teach the Law in Babylon and the
dream might not be fulfilled.

In these odd sayings and stories we hardly know what is jest
and what is serious, what is fact and what is fiction.   That a man
must forgive his neighbour before he can expect forgiveness from
God was fixed Rabbinic doctrine.   Whether it was to be taken as
equally rigid doctrine that a man was only to *ask* for forgiveness
three times may, however, be doubted.   Moreover, the case of *repeated* offence is not discussed, so far as I see, one way or the other.
What is discussed is repeated requests for forgiveness for the *same*
offence.   And we see by Rab's action that the view of R. Chanina
was not regarded as authoritative.   (*Cp.* Abraham, *Studies* I.
chapter xx.)   I suppose R. Chanina thought that the cruelty and
wickedness of him who had suffered the offence in not forgiving
the offended, even when he had thrice begged him to forgive, justified
the offender in not asking him a fourth time for forgiveness.

23–35.   The moral of the parable is thoroughly Rabbinic.   There
is nothing new about it.   The mercy of God in forgiving those who
have sinned against him is constantly insisted on.   The passages
which S.B. quote on 33 (p. 800) are very strong, but not exceptional
or in any way off the line.   ' There is no man,' runs one of these
passages, ' who is not God's debtor, but God is gracious and pitiful
and forgives previous sins.   It is like a man who borrowed money
and forgot to pay it back.   After a time he came to the creditor
and said, I know that I owe you money.   The other replied : Why
remind me of the old debt ?   It has long ago vanished from my mind.
So with God.   Men sin against him ; he sees that they do not
repent, [and that they go on sinning; yet if at last they repent],
he remits them their previous sins, and if they come before him in
repentance, and mention the previous sins, he says, Remember
not your previous sins.   If a man repents, even if he has committed

many sins, they are reckoned (by God) to him as if they were
merits.' (Exodus R. xxxi., משפטים, on xxii. 25 *ad init.*)

35. The corresponding teaching from the point of view of the
sinner is taught in the reply of R. Yose the priest to Valeria the
proselyte, who asked for an explanation of the apparent discrepancy
between Deut. x. 17, ' God regardeth not persons,' and Numb. vi.
26, ' The Lord lift up his countenance upon thee '—a discrepancy
not perceivable in an English rendering. A man borrows money
from another, and in the king's presence swears by the life of the
king that he will repay by a certain date. When he cannot pay, he
asks the king's forgiveness, who replies, The insult to me is forgiven
you ; now go and ask your neighbour for *his* forgiveness. God
forgives sins against himself ; but the injured neighbour's forgiveness must be sought as well. *Cp.* Matt. vi. 14.

xix. 1–12. For divorce see Matt. v. 31. There is no parallel
for 12. The saying is undoubtedly off the Rabbinic line, and the
famous story of Ben Azzai, who remained unmarried because, as
he said, he was so occupied with the Law that he had no time for
anything else (' My soul clings to the Law; let the world be
maintained by others ') is no good parallel. Ben Azzai's attitude
and remark are quite exceptional. And Ben Azzai himself taught
(wherefore R. Elazar b. Azariah accused him of inconsistency
between doctrine and practice) that he who does not fulfil his duty
in marriage is regarded as if he had diminished the divine image.
(Yebamoth 63 b.)

It may be added that there are indications that some Rabbis
regarded abstention from marital intercourse as an indication of
holiness. On this point *cp.* Büchler's *Types*, p. 50 *seq.* The
Rabbis, in their queer exegesis and fancy, assumed that Noah
and his sons, while in the ark, lived apart from their wives.
After normal relations could be resumed, Noah maintained his
abstention, about which a Rabbi observes, he ' continued in holiness ' (בקדושה, Gen. R., *Noah*, xxxv. 1 on ix. 8). And in a very
odd passage in Sabbath 87 a it is said that Moses gave up all intercourse with his wife. He argued thus : ' God bade the Israelites
keep away from their wives before he gave the revelation on Mount
Sinai. God spake to *them* for once only, for a short time and on a

fixed occasion ; how much more must I keep [always] away from
my wife, to whom God speaks at any time, and without fixing the
occasion.' Thus religion may, as it were, demand sexual abstinence
on great or adequate occasions.

13. The Rabbis also speak very highly and admiringly of children, though, characteristically enough, they usually think of them
as school children. One Rabbi interprets the verse, 'Touch not mine
anointed and do my prophets no harm,' by saying that the prophets
are the students of the Law (the wise, the *Talmide Chachamim*),
while the anointed are the school children. 'Rabbi said, The world
is maintained only by the breath of the school children.' Said
Rabbi X to Rabbi Y, ' What about your breath and mine ? ' The
other replied, ' The breath of one who has sin cannot be compared
with the breath of one who has no sin.' Among a number of ethical
reasons given for the destruction of Jerusalem, one is that the children
were kept away from school. ' Rabbi said, The school children must
not be kept from (or interrupted in) their work even for the building
of the Temple. A city in which there are no school children should
be destroyed or excommunicated' (Sabbath 119 b). It is also said
that the children of the poor and of the *Am ha-Aretz* must not be
neglected, for from them Torah may proceed. To teach the sons
of an *Am ha-Aretz* Torah is peculiarly gratifying to God, as drawing
the precious out of the vile! (Nedarim 81 a ; Sanhedrin 96 a ;
Baba Mezia 85 a, in the midst of the oddest stories imaginable.)
It is rather interesting, though not pertinent, to note that the
Nedarim passage adds : ' Why do learned fathers not usually have
learned sons ? ' Some very curious replies are given. (1) That the
Law may not become their inheritance (*i.e.* there must not be a
learned caste). (2) That they may not exalt themselves over the
community (or congregation). (3) Because they *do* exalt themselves
over the community. (4) Because they call people (the common
people, the unlearned) donkeys. (5) Because they do not say the
blessing over the Torah before they begin their study. Perhaps
the nicest things about children are the two passages from the
Midrash given by S.B. on p. 781 : ' See how dear the children are
to God. The Sanhedrin went into exile, but the Shechinah did not go
with them ; the priests went into exile, but the Shechinah did not
go with them, but when the children went into exile, the Shechinah

went with them.' 'One Rabbi said, 'If a child in its reading
says Mose for Moses or Ron for Aaron, God says, Even its stam-
mering I love. So too if a child jumps over the name of God, God
says, Even his jumps I love. Or if he puts his thumb on the name
of God, God says, His thumb on me I love. [I note that in these
passages the child is spoken of as such; not the school child.]
(Lamentations R. on i. 6; Canticles R. ii. § 4, on ii. 4; Numbers R.,
במדבר, ii. 3 on ii. 2.)

20. S.B. bring two charges against the Rabbinic religion, or,
as I ought more correctly to say, against the religious teachings
and opinions of the Rabbis. On the one hand, the Rabbis have
no *Heilsgewissheit*. 'Der Mangel jeder Heilsgewissheit erscheint
als ein hervorstechendes Merkmal der altjüdischen Religion'
(III. p. 218).[1] About this supposed fault I have said a few words
elsewhere. On the other hand, they believed that a man by
his own unaided power could perform all the commands of the
Law from A to Z. 'Dass der Mensch die Fähigkeit besitze, die
Gebote Gottes restlos zu erfüllen, stand den rabbinischen Gelehrten
so fest, dass sie allen Ernstes von Leuten redeten, die die ganze
Tora von A-Z gehalten hatten.'[2] As to 'man's own power'
I have also spoken elsewhere. S.B. are hardly accurate. The
Rabbis do not, as we have seen, neglect God's help, or regard it
as superfluous. Yet they do consider man's will as free, even though
the *Yetzer ha Ra*, if man once begins to yield to its solicitations,
can make that will a slave. If man tries, God aids. Man *must*
and *can* try. That seems to be their simple doctrine in a nutshell.
But as to the statement that there were men who had fulfilled the
Law from A to Z a few words may be added. S.B. quote this curious
passage. 'R. Acha b. Chanina said : God said to Gabriel (Ezekiel
ix. 4), Go and mark a *Tau* (תו) of ink upon the foreheads of the
righteous so that the angel of destruction may have no power over
them, and so too upon the foreheads of the wicked, that the angel
may have power over them. Then the Attribute of Justice said to
God, How do the one differ from the other ? God replied, The first

---

[1] 'The lack of any assurance of salvation is a conspicuous feature of the old
Jewish (= Rabbinic) religion.'
[2] 'That man possesses the power to fulfil *all* the commands of God was so
sure and convinced a belief to the Rabbis that in all seriousness they spoke of
people who had observed the whole Torah from A to Z.'

are completely righteous (צדיקים גמורים); the others are completely wicked. The Attribute said, The first could have rebuked
(prevented, מחה) those others : and they did not do so (ולא מיחו).
God replied, I know that they would not have accepted reproof.
The Attribute of Justice said, Though *you* may know it, did they
know it ? ' [This last part of the quotation is omitted by S.B. It
means that some responsibility rests upon the righteous for the
sins of the wicked.] And it is said : ' The aged, the young, the virgin,
infants and women, shall ye slay for the destroyer, but to none shall
ye draw nigh that hath the mark upon him, and with my sanctuary
shall ye begin ' (Ezek. ix. 6). It continues ' And they began with
the elders that were before the house (*ib.* 7).' With regard to this
R. Joseph taught : Read not ' my sanctuary ' (*mikdashi*) but ' my
consecrated ones ' (*mekuddashai*) : these are the men who have
fulfilled all the Torah from *Alef* to *Tau* (beginning to end). And
it says (*ib.* ix. 2) : ' And behold, six men came from the
way of the upper gate, which faces the north, each with
weapon in hand. And in their midst was a man clothed in
linen and with a scribe's ink-horn at his loins, and they came
and stood before the bronze altar.' ' The Holy One, blessed be
he, spake to them, Begin from the place where they (*sc.* the
Levites) were wont to sing songs to me. Who were these six
men ? R. Chisda says : Wrath, anger, fury, destruction, breaking,
and wasting. Why should a *Tau* have been chosen as the sign ?
Because *Tau* can stand for *Tihyeh* (thou shalt live) and *Tamuth*
(thou shalt die). Samuel said : *Tau* stands for *Tammah* (it has
come to an end) : the merits of the patriarchs are exhausted. R.
Yochanan said : *Tau* stands for *Tachon* (may it find compassion) :
may the merits of the patriarchs find compassion. Resh Lakish
said : *Tau* is the last letter of the seal of the Almighty, for, as R.
Chanina has said, the seal of the Almighty is *Emeth* [*i.e.* Truth,
spelt *Alef, Mem, Tau*, the first, middle, and last consonants of the
Hebrew alphabet]. R. Samuel b. Nachmani said : these are the
men who observed the whole Torah from *Alef* to *Tau*.' [Note the
juxtaposition of Torah, *Emeth* and perfection : the implication is
that the completely righteous are those who, by keeping the Law
most closely, approximate to the divine nature.] (Sabbath 55 a.)
The explanation of ' completely righteous ' is found elsewhere. Who
were these people ? S.B. go on to point out that the Patriarchs,

Moses, Aaron, Samuel, Elijah, Hezekiah are sometimes spoken of as completely righteous and as having kept the whole Law. (*Cp.* p. 166.) It was even said that four persons died only because of the serpent's counsel (*i.e.* on account of the general doom then inflicted upon all mankind, not because of their own sins). These four are Benjamin, Jesse (David's father), Amram (the father of Moses), Kilab (David's son). (Sabbath 55 b.) But these sayings are of no dogmatic importance, and can be outweighed by others in which it is said that even Moses, Aaron, David and all the other great ones were not sinless. Yet the theoretical possibility of saintly people who have never known sin was allowed. S.B. quote the well-known saying, ' R. Simeon b. Chalafta said, All the blessings and consolations which the prophets have perceived (in their visions) are for the penitent, but as for him who has never tasted (טעם) sin in his life, Eye has not seen what is prepared for him' (Isaiah lxiv. 3; Ecclesiastes R. on i. 8 *fin.*). With regard to actual Rabbis who thought themselves sinless, something has already been said. Stories like the following make, it must be admitted, an odd, and not altogether pleasant, impression. ' When R. Yochanan was dying, he requested that he should be buried neither in white clothes nor in black, so that if he stood (at the resurrection) among the righteous, he should not feel ashamed, and if among the wicked, he should not be put to shame. R. Joshua, on the other hand, asked to be buried in white clothes, seeing that he was not ashamed because of his deeds to come before the presence of his creator' (Genesis R., xcvi. 5 on xlvii. 29). In Jer. Kilaim ix. 4 (32 b) it is R. Judah who asks for garments which should be neither white nor black, and when the bystanders, in astonishment at R. Joshua's request, say, ' Are you better than your master ? he replies, Need I be ashamed of my deeds ? ' Nevertheless, the many stories about the Rabbis are rather indicative of a certain naïve simplicity than of serious conceit or of dogmatic conviction that many people were sinless. One is indeed often amazed at the loose way in which the Rabbis use language. There was a quaint idea among them that at the New Year God held a sort of divine assize, and made judgment decrees over individuals and nations lasting for a year. It is said, ' If, at the beginning of the year, the Israelites are wicked, and little rain is decreed for them, and if they then become good (ויחזרו), it is not possible to add (to the rain), because the decree has been decreed, but God sends the rain upon

T

the land at seasons when the land needs it most. Conversely, if the Israelites, at the beginning of the year, are perfectly righteous (צדיקים גמורים), and ample rain is decreed for them, and they become wicked (חזרו) towards the end of the year, it is not possible to diminish the rain, because the decree has been decreed, but God sends the rain at seasons when it is not needed (and sends it) upon deserts and seas' (Sifre 78 b). How intensely hard it is to enter fully into the minds and feelings of men whose conceptions of the divine rule and of much else were so different from our own! Nevertheless, the usual idea was that no man is free of sin, that all men require constant watchfulness and self-control, and the grace and forgiveness of God. There were very few men, I should say, who, in the opinion of the Rabbis, did not need the Day of Atonement with its call to repentance, and this need would apply to themselves as well as to others.

21–23. S.B. collect at this place a very large number of passages dealing with the Rabbinic estimate of poverty and riches. The Rabbis looked at wealth and poverty from a more realistic and common-sense point of view than Jesus. In this matter they were less paradoxical, or, if you will, less idealistic, than he. In their own environment, and in the Jewish society of their times, they saw that there were good rich men and bad rich men, good poor men and bad poor men. Among themselves and in their own body, there were learned Rabbis who were rich, and learned Rabbis who were poor. The Law and its study could go, and did go, with both. Whereas the Psalmists appear to have had a bias against the rich (and in this point Jesus appears to follow them)—as if the pious were almost all poor, and as if the rich were almost all oppressors and wicked—the Rabbis take a different, and, I should imagine, a more accurate line. Riches have their temptations. They involve many moral dangers, and a modest competency is more likely to secure a decent, honest, good and God-fearing life than great wealth, yet riches *can* be well and nobly used. They are an opportunity, and a man *can* rise above their temptations : a rich man *can* be humble and learned, as well as charitable and generous. The thing *can* be done, though it may not be easy. Such seems to be the Rabbinic line. Moreover, besides this common-sense estimate of riches, the Rabbis, it must be admitted, shared with their fellows a very considerable dislike of poverty. In spite of the fact that one could be poor and yet learned (and that many Rabbis had actually shown that one could attain to great learning from the midst of great poverty), yet poverty was a hard discipline, and, to speak frankly, a burden and an evil. It is true that ignorance was a greater evil than poverty, and knowledge a greater good than riches—and in this estimate the Rabbis were absolutely sincere—but yet poverty *was*, in spite of its moral dangers, an evil and not a good, and an adequate competence *was* a good and not an evil. For one thing, the Rabbis, with all their exaltation of almsgiving and charity, had yet a horror of losing their financial independence. This horror is reflected in the well-known words of the 'grace after meals' in *The Authorized Daily Prayer Book*, where it says, 'We beseech thee, O Lord our God, let us not be in need of the gifts of men or of their loans, but, only of thy helping hand,' etc. (Singer's *Prayer Book*, p. 281). (*The Sephardic Prayer Book* has this extra invocation : ' May the All-merciful grant us sustenance with honour, and not with contempt ; lawfully, and not by forbidden means; in ease, and not with trouble' (Ed. Gaster, 1901, Vol. I. p. 61).) In one of the prayers of the High Priest upon the Day of Atonement he was wont to say, ' May thy people Israel never be in need of supporting one another or of assistance from another people ' (Taanit 24 b). And there were other degradations, often connected with poverty, of which the Rabbis were acutely conscious. But, in spite of these feelings, the Rabbis possessed a middle point of view. There was no vulgarity about them. A more learned man who was poor was always held by them in higher honour than a less learned man who was rich. Again, in relation to the advice for perfection given to the rich young man, it may, I think, be said that the Rabbis, while appreciating, and sometimes practising, an idealism of the kind recommended, yet, on the whole, preferred a more sober sort of charity. Riches were to be used year by year in almsgiving, but not to be given away all at once. They constituted a prolonged responsibility. Moreover, while almsgiving is greatly praised, the Rabbis showed a good deal of a wise C.O.S. spirit. They knew something of the evils of indiscriminate almsgiving, and they objected to the professional beggar. Care and thought and time must be associated with ' giving.' Here, as in several other instances, if it is difficult to combine common sense with high idealism, it does not follow that we do not need both. There is a place for the teaching of Jesus, and there is a place for the teaching of the Rabbis, in this matter of riches and almsgiving. There is some truth in both, even though the harmony between them may be hard to find.

The thirty-first section of Exodus R. (xxxi. *Mishpatim* on אם כסף xxii. 25), parts of which are quoted in S.B., is worth reading as a whole. It contains a great deal of the Rabbinic teaching and point of view on the subject. It is all spun, as it were, out of Exodus xxii. 25–27. ' Poverty,' it is said, ' is the heaviest of all evils in the world. All other evils in one scale of the balance, and poverty on the other scale : the scales are even.' ' All other evils in one scale : poverty in the other ; poverty would outweigh them all.' ' Four people are likened to the dead : The poor, the leprous, the blind, he who has no children ' (Nedarim 64 b). ' He who hopes for the table of others (*i.e.* depends for his sustenance on the bounty of others)— for him the world is darkness. So said Rab. R. Chisda said, His life is no life. The Rabbis say : Three lives are no lives : He who looks for the table of others, he who is ruled by his wife, he whose body is overcome by sufferings' (Bezah 32 b). ' Three things drive a man out of his mind : (1) Gentiles, (2) an evil spirit, (3) crushing poverty. What follows ? One must pray to God that through his pity one may be spared from them. Three will not see Hell : (1) They who suffer from crushing poverty, (2) they who suffer from pains of the intestines, (3) they who are persecuted by the heathen power (or who have many creditors). Some add (4) they who have a bad wife (*i.e.* they are already punished for their sins in this world). What follows ? One must receive these evils in love (*i.e.* in pious resignation towards God).' (Erubin 41 b.)

Parallel to some extent with the view of Aristotle, who thought that a certain amount of wealth or of τὰ ἐκτὸς ἀγαθά was necessary for complete happiness or for the most perfect life, the Rabbis tended to hold that a certain amount of riches was requisite for the man who is to be regarded as both inwardly and outwardly in complete harmony and most fully endowed. The well-known passage in Aboth vi. 8 (with its parallels) is in general accordance with Rabbinic sentiment. ' Beauty, strength, riches, honour, wisdom, old age, children, are comely to the righteous and comely to the world.' One cannot imagine Jesus saying this ; but it is not exceptional for the Rabbis. Always, however, the Torah comes first, as it also says in Aboth (iv. 11), 'He who fulfils the Torah in poverty shall in the end fulfil it in wealth, and he who neglects it in wealth shall in the end neglect it in poverty.' It is remarkable that it should be said, 'All the prophets were rich.' 'The Shechinah rests only upon one who is wise, strong, rich, and tall' (Sabbath 92 a). [Note the curious emphasis here on height and in Aboth on beauty ; the resting of the Shechinah means inspiration, the spirit of pro- phecy.] Jesus could not have said this, but it is not to be regarded as off the Rabbinic line. Again, 'God lets his Shechinah rest only on one who is strong, rich, wise, and humble' (Nedarim 38 a). Yet riches are a testing discipline no less than poverty. God tests the rich whether he will give adequate alms, and the poor whether he will endure his suffering (*i.e.* his poverty) without murmuring. The men of Sodom were very rich and prosperous. 'But they did not trust in the shadow of their Creator, but in the multitude of their wealth, for wealth thrusts aside its owners from the fear of heaven' (Pirke R. Eliezer xxv., Friedlander's translation, p. 181). With the strong tendency to dwell on rewards and punishments, and on the external, as well as the internal, results of righteousness and wickedness, which is as characteristic of the Rabbis as of the O.T. teachers, it is added that the rich who is niggardly and stingy will ultimately lose his wealth, while the poor will receive a double portion in the world to come (Exodus R. xxxi. § 3 on xxii. 25, etc.). From the words used in the whole passage, the stress seems to be laid upon the world to come for the rich as well as for the poor. The Rabbis show a tendency to wish to believe that even in this world the bad rich man will lose his wealth, and the good poor man will gain wealth (or at all events, cease from being poor), but they knew, and they sometimes say, that this is not so, and that the bad rich man often continues rich, and the good poor man continues poor, till they die. But for them the solution and explanation are easy enough. (How different for the O.T. teacher!) The bad rich man is punished in Hell ; the good poor man enjoys the beatitudes of the life to come. And no facts contradict this view, because there are no facts to appeal to one way or the other. Though the Rabbis, seeing that there are rich and poor men in almost every occupation or profession, sometimes say that all depends on a man's moral worth (his *Zechuth*) (*e.g.* Mishnah Kiddushin iv. 14, 82 a), yet they also admit that there are strange chops and changes. They often speak of the wheel of circumstances; God turns it as he will, making the poor (or his son) rich and the rich (or his son) poor. A man should pray that he may not suffer this reversal; yet if poverty does not befall him, it will befall his son, and if not his son, his grandson, for there is a turning-wheel in the world. (Sabbath 151 a.) Sometimes, indeed, the view of the Psalmists, which, I fancy, was more or less the view of Jesus, finds an echo; e.g. (Exodus R., מִשְׁפָּטִים, xxxi. 5 on אִם כֶּסֶף xxii. 24). In this world the wicked are rich, and enjoy quiet and peace, and the righteous are poor, but when God will open for the righteous the treasures of the (heavenly) Eden, the wicked, who have lived through usury and interest, will bite their flesh with their teeth, and they will say, Would that we had toiled and carried on our shoulders, or been servants, then it had been better for us. The Israelites say to God, Who is thy people? He answers, The poor. God protects only the poor.' The cautious moderation of Sirach is also to be found in the Rabbinical literature ; as riches have their great moral dangers, and as poverty is a sore evil, the best thing is a moderate amount of wealth ; not too much and not too little. S.B. quote Gittin 70 a. Eight things are good in moderation ; bad in excess ; of these, riches is one. And, always, knowledge is held to be better than riches. The constantly quoted saying : ' Have you knowledge, what do you lack ? Have you no knowledge, what have you ? ' was meant sincerely. ' Thy teaching and thy statutes are better unto me than thousands of gold and silver.' This opinion of the Psalmist (cxix.) was also the opinion of the Rabbis. ' For gold and silver take a man out of both this world and the world to come, but the Torah brings a man to the life of the world to come '—a pretty strong utterance about the dangers of wealth and of money. (Sifre 39 b, last line.) Again, one must not ignore familiar sayings, such as : ' Who is rich ? He who is contented with his lot ' (Aboth iv. 1, with its parallels). (R. Tarphon gives a quantitative reply ; R. Akiba says he who has a good wife ; R. Yose gives a highly peculiar reply, which is hardly quotable in this place. (Sabbath 25 b.) We also find the view that a man cannot have it, as it were, both ways ; great prosperity on earth and great felicity beyond the grave. This idea may be mixed up with the other idea that to lay up treasure in heaven does not consort with laying up treasure on earth (the idea of Matt. vi. 19 and of xix. 23), but it is not identical with that other. It is illus-

trated by the following two stories, and there are others like them.
' There was once a disciple of R. Simeon b. Yochai who went to
India, and he came back laden (? with merchandise). When his
fellow-disciples saw the gain which he had made, they felt chagrin.
What did Rabbi Simeon do ? He took his disciples, and went with
them into a valley, and he said, Valley, valley, be filled with golden
coins. And it was filled. Then he said to his disciples : Let each
take his portion, yea, take all ye will, but know that he who takes it
takes (off) his reward in the life to come.' ' Once it happened to
R. Simeon b. Chalafta that on the morning before the evening of
Passover he had not money to buy anything for his household.
His wife said to him, We have not even a penny with which to keep
the Passover. When her neighbours cooked, and she had nothing
to cook, she took a vessel, and filled it with water, and kindled a
fire beneath it, for she was ashamed that she had nothing to cook.
When R. Simeon saw what she did, he went outside the city, and
prayed, and a sort of a hand appeared and gave him a jewel ; he
took it and showed it, but nobody could tell him its value. Then
he pawned it, and received for it a gold piece, and changed the gold
piece into small coins, and bought meat and wine and vegetables,
and brought them all back to his house. He said to his wife, Here
we have wherewith to eat. She said, Whence did you get all these
things ? Perhaps you have worried (troubled, הטרחת) your
Creator ? He refused to tell her. She said to him, I swear that I
will not use anything of them until you tell me whence they came.
When he saw that she worried him, he told her the whole story.
Then she said, You have received of what was appointed to you
in the world to come, and your table will be much poorer (פגום)
than that of your colleagues. Go, therefore, and pray, and return
the jewel to him who gave it you. At the end of the festival he went
to restore what he had taken, and he paid what he had received
for the jewel, and he took it and went outside the city and prayed,
and a sort of hand appeared and took it back from him' (Mid.
Psalms xcii. (8). (In the parallel story in Exodus R. lii. 3 and Ruth
R. ii. on chapter i. verse 17, for Passover eve we have Sabbath eve.)

Poverty, as we have seen, is regarded as a testing or ' temptation.' It is also sometimes regarded as a punishment for sin. One
of the worst and weakest points in Rabbinic theology is the
tendency to link particular physical evils with certain sins. (*Cp.*

the passage in Sabbath Mishnah ii. 6, which still defames the
orthodox Jewish prayer book. See Singer, p. 121.) Thus, the sign of
unchastity is dropsy (*i.e.* dropsy is the punishment of unchastity),
jaundice of causeless hate, quinsy of slander, poverty of pride.
(Sabbath 33 a). More frequently, hardness of heart, uncharitable-
ness to the poor, is said to lead to poverty as its punishment, which,
on the Mikado's principle of making the punishment fit the crime,
seems more reasonable. Elsewhere it is said that poverty is necessary or useful for Israel, so that they may repent, or so that they
wax not fat and kick. Famous is the saying of Akiba: 'Poverty
suits the daughter of Jacob as a red trapping on the neck of a
white horse.' R. Acha said, 'When the Israelites have to eat the
carob tree, then (only) do they repent' (Pesikta Kahana 117 a).
The poor who study the Law are richly rewarded after death by
God. 'Why are they poor in this world ? So that they may not
occupy themselves with vain things and forget the Torah, for one
must neglect one's business and occupy oneself in the Torah, for the
Torah goes before everything' (Midrash Psalms v. (3), verse 1, 26 a).
So it is said that the poor, the rich, and the wicked (here equivalent
to the rake) come to the judgment. They ask the poor man why he
had not occupied himself with the Law. If he says, I was poor,
and I was busy in getting my livelihood, they say, Were you poorer
than Hillel ? (For they tell of Hillel that he used to gain by work
a stater a day, and half of it he gave to the porter at the House of
Study, and half he used for his own maintenance and that of his
family. One day he had earned nothing, and the porter would not
let him in. So he climbed up, and sat by the edge of the window
on the roof, so that he might hear the words of the living God from
the mouth of Shemayah and Abtalion. And it happened that it
was a Friday in winter, and the snow from the sky fell upon him.
At the break of dawn, Shemayah said to Abtalion, My brother,
usually it is light ; to-day it is dark ; perhaps the day is cloudy.
They looked up, and saw the shape of a man against the window,
and they found three cubits of snow upon him. They took off the
snow, and washed him, and anointed him, and put him by the fire,
for they said, He is worthy that the Sabbath be profaned for his
sake.) They ask the rich man, Why did you not occupy yourself
with the Law ? If he says, I was rich, and I was busy with my
possessions, they say, Were you richer than R. Elazar ? (For

they say of R. Elazar b. Charsom that his father left him a thousand cities on the land and a thousand ships on the sea. Every day he took a sack of meal upon his shoulder, and went from city to city to study the Law. Once his own slaves found him and made him do forced service (אנגריא). Then he said to them, I beseech you, set me free, that I may go and study the Law. They said, By the life of R. Elazar B. Charsom, we will not let you go. For he never saw them in his life, but was always, day and night, studying the Torah.) They ask the rake, Why did you not occupy yourself with the Torah ? If he answers, I was beautiful, and I was pressed by my *Yetzer*, they say, Were you more beautiful than Joseph ? (For the wife of Potiphar sought daily to persuade him with words [משדלתו] ; she put on fresh garments by day and by night; she said to him, Yield to me. He refused. She said, I will put you in prison. He said, The Lord sets free the prisoners. She said, I will crush you. He said, The Lord lifts up the bowed. She said, I will blind you. He said, The Lord opens the eyes of the blind. Then she offered him a thousand talents of silver, that he might yield to her, to sleep with her and to be with her, but he would not yield ; he would not sleep with her in this world so as not to have to be with her in the world to come.) Thus Hillel accuses the poor, R. Eleazar the rich, and Joseph the rakes ' (Yoma 35 b).

On the whole, then, we may say that the Rabbis took a less extreme view of the danger and undesirability of riches than Jesus, and that they were more keenly alive to the possible degradation, and to the inevitable burdens and evils, of grinding poverty. It may next be asked whether they show any tendencies similar to the teaching indicated in verse 21. The Rabbis would appear to teach that wealth is a trust to be used wisely, and for the benefit of society at large, but that it is not right or needful or beneficial (to society) that a man should, by one sudden act, make himself poor instead of rich, and give all his riches away to the indigent and needy. Moreover, Jesus in 21 is not laying down a general rule, nor is he looking at the matter in an all-round sort of way, or from the point of view of society. He is thinking of the man's character or soul, and of that alone. Economic and social questions (in our sense of the word ' social') do not concern him. They never concerned him. His interests lay elsewhere. And he believed that the end of the old-world order was very near at hand. At such a time it is obvious that the only really important thing is the 'salvation' of the individual. 'Society' is about to break up altogether. Again, Jesus is thinking of the individual case; of this particular rich man, and what would be best and finest and most testing and most 'costing' and 'costly' for *him*. We cannot, therefore, rightly compare (or contrast) the advice given to this *particular* man with the *general* injunctions or recommendations of the Rabbis, or with their general opinions as regards the right use of riches.

The contrast made between 'keeping the commandments' and being or seeking to become, τέλειος, or perfect, is certainly not a contrast which could have been put in this form by the Rabbis. To them there could be nothing more perfect than a perfect keeping of the commandments. Mark's version has not this antithesis. The Rabbis could not, I imagine, have said ἕν σε ὑστερεῖ. Nevertheless, the Rabbis were perfectly well aware of (a) an extra legal excellence, a virtue which went beyond the mere letter of the Law (see *Old Testament and After* on the striking phrase *lifnim mishurat haddin*, pp. 434, 435; see also p. 191 in this book), just as (b) they were aware of a difference in the motives of virtue and law-observance, *i.e.* whether it were 'fear' or 'love,' desire of reward or 'for its own sake,' *lishmah*.

Moreover, there are some passages which show that the Rabbis realized that the full love of God or the love of the Torah might well require a sacrifice of riches. Just where the shoe pinches, there must the sacrifice be made. ' This is the way that is becoming for the study of the Torah: a morsel of bread with salt thou must eat, and water by measure thou must drink, thou must sleep upon the ground, and live a life of trouble, the while thou toilest in the Torah. If thou doest thus, Happy shalt thou be, and it shall be well with thee (Ps. cxxviii. 2); happy shalt thou be in this world, and it shall be well with thee in the world to come ' (Aboth vi. 4). There is a famous and very well known passage in Berachoth (61 b) in which R. Eliezer asks, 'If it says in the Shema Thou shalt love God with all thy soul, why does it also say with all thy might' (which R. Eliezer takes to mean 'possessions '), and *vice versa*. The answer is that for those who love their body (= life) more than their money, it says 'with all thy soul' (= life), while for those who love their money more than their body, it says 'with all thy might.' There is a curious remark in Sotah 12 a, according to which the righteous, just because they know how many sins may be connected with money, and how important it is to preserve independence and self-respect, are said to 'love' their money more than their bodies. There are stories, some of which are quoted by S.B., of Rabbis giving away all, or most of, their possessions. R. Yochanan it is said, sold (and then presumably gave away the proceeds of) his landed property that he might the better and more wholly devote himself to the Torah. His disciple wept that he had left himself nothing for his old age. He replied, 'I have sold what was created in six days, and thereby acquired what was given in forty days (*i.e.* the Law).' (Pesikta Kahana 178 b.) The moral of the story of the man who sold all his possessions and gave them to the poor (Leviticus Rabba xxxvii. 2 on xxvii. 2) is vitiated by the ending, in which he gets all his wealth back again, and gets his brother's wealth (the stingy man) in addition (who is killed with all his children in a flood).

Rather quaint and pretty is the story in Taanith 24 a. 'The collectors of charity funds used to hide themselves whenever they saw R. Elazar of the village of Bartota, because he was in the habit of giving them everything he happened to possess. One day he was going to the market in order to buy a wedding outfit for his daughter, when the collectors espied him and tried to hide themselves. Elazar, however, followed them and said : 'I adjure you to tell me for what purpose you are collecting ? For a marriage between an orphaned boy and an orphaned girl, they replied. By the service of the Temple ! they have precedence over my daughter, exclaimed he, and putting together all that he had, he gave it to them, except one *zuz* that remained in his possession. For this he bought wheat and deposited it in the granary. Thereupon his wife enquired of her daughter what her father had brought her. All that he brought he took up to the granary, the daughter replied. The wife then went up to the granary and found it full of wheat, to the extent that it came through the door hinges. When Elazar returned from the *Bet ha-Midrash*, she said to him, Come and see what thy Friend (God) has done for thee ! Said he : By the service of the Temple ! this wheat shall be sacred property, and thy share in it shall not be more than that of any among the poor of Israel' (Dr. Malter's translation, pp. 179, 180). No less interesting is the story in the same tractate, 20 b, of R. Huna. ' Every Friday toward evening R. Huna would send a servant to the market who would buy up all the vegetables left over with the gardeners and throw them into the river. Why did he not rather give them to the poor ? Because they would sometimes rely on these gifts and fail to provide themselves for the Sabbath. Why did he not throw it to the animals ? He was of the opinion that food proper for human beings should not be given to animals. Why did he buy them at all ? Because if he had not done so, it would lead the gardeners to sin in the future (by failing to provide the community with vegetables)' (Dr. Malter's translation, p. 148). R. Huna did not give the vegetables to the poor, because he did not want to prevent them from fulfilling a holy duty of buying food for the Sabbath. In other words, he thought of the recipients : he did not want to weaken their independence and to make them rely too exclusively upon charity.

The parallel given by S.B. in the brief order of Rabba b. Abbahu, who told some would-be proselytes, ' Go and sell all that you have, and then become proselytes' (Abodah Zarah 64 a) is purely verbal. It relates to a legal point about idols and idolatry, and has no real relation to the subject under discussion.

Looking back over the whole series of quotations (and S.B. give a great many more), it would seem as if the Rabbis were alive both to the solid advantages and to the moral dangers of wealth or of ' possessions.' Any idea of a fundamental change in the economic arrangements of society was foreign to them. If they sometimes wondered why some people should be so poor, and others should be so rich, they gave to this difference a purely religious explanation. Both riches and poverty were a discipline : the one had to be borne well ; the other to be used well. If all men were ' comfortably off ' there would be no opportunity for such right endurance, on the one hand, or for constant exercise of charity and almsgiving, upon the other. And if the rich are often not charitable, but wicked, and if the poor are often not duly and adequately supported by the rich, then the only explanation can be that, in the next world, the one will be greatly punished, thus enjoying only a brief temporary felicity, and the others will be greatly rewarded, thus suffering only a temporary misfortune.

So far as 'giving' is concerned, the Rabbis, in this unlike Jesus, looked at the matter from the point of view of the recipient as well as of the donor. To give away everything to the poor might not be desirable, even for the sake of the poor. Yet they were not insensible to the idealism of 'All for the Highest.' Their Highest was the study of the Torah : sacred knowledge. 'If you will be perfect,' they might have said (I think) : 'Give up your lucrative profession—or live in poverty—and study the Law.' In a sense they too, as far as they could or did admit that not all people *could* study the Law, would have recognized a double morality. The perfect thing was to give up anything for study. The less perfect thing was to live a good life without study and to help those who do study. In this way too you would surely get to heaven. To Jesus the Highest was very different. It was (for the Old Order was rapidly approaching its term) the Salvation of the Soul. Yet are we not to say, with rather facile and cheap criticism, that his Highest was a self-regarding Highest. For to Jesus the salvation of the soul implied the practice of lovingkindness and charity. Whether Matt. xxv. 34–40 was spoken by Jesus or no, it is entirely in his spirit, and in it we see how, according to Jesus, salvation is to be won. On the other hand, we need not depreciate the 'Highest' of the Rabbis. The study of the Law also involved the practice of lovingkindness and charity, for the Rabbis insisted that practice and study must always go together, and an essential portion of the Law's requirements was justice and lovingkindness towards man and piety and love towards God. Nevertheless, I venture to think that there *was* a certain touch of narrowness about *either* 'Highest,' and that both were susceptible of more than one kind of degradation and caricature. These I need not here particularize or draw out. Our Highest to-day seems to me wider and more comprehensive than the Highest whether of Jesus or of the Rabbis. It includes study or knowledge, it includes 'social service,' it includes self-realization or the salvation of the soul. It is a more conscious harmony of all of these, and, perhaps, even of more.

xx. 1–16. Of the great parable of the Labourers in the Vineyard I have spoken at some length in my Commentary (Vol. II. pp. 273–275, ed. 2). I do not think that I have praised it unduly. What have we to say about it from the Rabbinic point of view ? It must,

I think, be said that while the teaching of the parable is not *wholly* without its parallels in the Rabbinic literature, the opposite doctrine of measure for measure is more prominent with the Rabbis than with Jesus, and the doctrine represented by the parable is more prominent with Jesus than with the Rabbis. Jesus is by no means ignorant of the doctrine of measure for measure. He makes use of it. ' According to your works, so shall you be rewarded or punished ' is by no means an unknown or unused teaching. But the balance is better kept by him than by the Rabbis. Nor do we find with him any examples of ' such punishments for such and such sins,' as we get among the Rabbis, of which the passage still kept and used in *The Authorized Daily Prayer Book* is so ugly an example. (Singer's *Prayer Book*, p. 121.) Neither Jesus nor the Rabbis, it might be observed, see any difficulty in God appointing final or perpetual punishments for finite and definite sins. It does not strike them, as it strikes us to-day, that to annihilate a person altogether, or to give him perpetual punishment for a finite and temporal sin, is unjust. To this difficulty Jesus and the Rabbis are equally blind. On the other hand, the Rabbis are willing to allow that God rewards more than man deserves : for finite virtues man receives heavenly and everlasting bliss. Again, the Rabbis recognize that in relation to the greatness of the ' reward '—the joys of the life to come—man may be said to contribute practically nothing. What is human righteousness ? All depends upon, all is given by, the mercy and the grace of God. God's goodness supplies man's insufficiencies. Or the merits of the fathers are so abundant that they too eke out what is wanting in their descendants.

Meanwhile, the complaint made by the labourers in the vineyard is very similar to the astonishment of Rabbi at the immediate reward vouchsafed to the repentant R. Eliezer b. Durdaya or the Roman executioner of R. Chananya b. Teradyon. ' Some obtain the Kingdom in an hour, while others hardly reach it after a life-time.' An hour's repentance produces the same result as a life-time spent in the study and fulfilment of the Law.

There is a most interesting passage in Tanchuma, *Ki Tissa*, 110 a, of which only a few words are given in S.B. p. 833. Here the case is put of one man dying at forty and another at eighty. Both were righteous and studious. It would not be just, however, that the second should have a greater reward in heaven than the first. Each

did his best, and it was not the first man's fault that he died at forty.
The reward of Samuel was no less than that of Moses, though one
died at 120, and the other at fifty-two. This is fancifully proved
by Psalm xcix. 6. 'So began R. Tanchuma b. Abba to expound:
Sweet is the sleep of a labouring man, whether he eat little or much;
but the abundance of the rich will not suffer him to sleep (Eccles.
v. 12). They said to Solomon, Had anyone but you said this verse
we should have laughed at him; you, of whom it is written, And
he was wiser than all men (1 Kings iv. 31), can *you* say, Sweet
is the sleep of a labouring man, whether he eat little or much?
Not thus is the matter, for if anyone hungers and eats a trifle, his
sleep departs from him, but if he eats much, sweet is his sleep.
He said to them, I am speaking only of the righteous and those who
labour in the Torah. How so? Take a man whose whole life is
thirty years. From ten years upwards he labours in the Torah and
in the *Mitzvoth*, and dies at the age of thirty. Then consider another
of eighty years, who likewise from the age of ten upwards labours
in the Torah and in the *Mitzvoth* until his death. Are you going
to say that, seeing that the former laboured in the Torah for twenty
years only and the latter for seventy years, therefore will God
apportion a greater reward to the latter? Therefore I say, Whether
it be much or whether it be little that he eat. For the twenty
years man might say before God, Hadst thou not removed me
from the world half-way through my life, I should have prolonged
my years and increased Torah and *Mitzvoth*. Therefore I say,
Whether much or little, for the rewards of each are equal.'
'Thou mayest know,' said R. Chanina, 'that Moses served Israel
in Egypt and in the wilderness for forty years, and that he lived for
120 years, while all the days of Samuel's life were only fifty-two
years. He bore the burdens and troubles of Israel. And the
Scripture counts them as one, for it says, Moses and Aaron among
his priests and Samuel among them that called on his name.
So you see, Sweet is the sleep.' Then the passage goes on to
give the following illustration. 'A king hired workmen to work for
him. While they were working, he took one of them (away from
his work) and walked with him. In the evening the workpeople
came to receive their wages, and that workman with them. The
king could not have said to him, You have only worked two hours;
take in proportion to your work, for the workman could reply,

Had you not walked with me, my wages would have been greater. God is the king.   The workmen are they who labour in the Law. They who so labour for ten or twenty or thirty years could say, Hadst thou not taken me away (by death), I should have laboured longer.   Hence, the rewards of all must be equal.'   The illustration is not so cogent as the parable in Matthew, for it still seems to imply that the particular cases are exceptional.   It was not the man's fault that he could not work longer.   Death hindered his service. Where A *could* have worked as long as B and did not, A should not receive the same reward as B.   In the Gospel parable it is implied that though A might have been able to have begun working as soon as B and did not, yet his labour in the shorter time during which he did work may, as God sees things, and as God rewards, and according to *God's* conceptions of equity, produce for A the same reward as is given to B.   The Tanchuma passage does not go so far as this ; yet it is on the same lines.   In the Gospel parable it is not stated whether the labourers who worked for a shorter time, having met the master of the vineyard at a later hour, were at all in fault through having come later, or whether they were, in this respect, wholly guiltless.   As this is left vague, it seems to show that the point on which the Tanchuma passage lays all the stress (namely, that it was in no wise the *fault* of the labourers if they worked for a shorter period) was regarded by Jesus as immaterial.   What he laid stress on was that the heavenly reward was not allotted by strict measure for measure, and not strictly according to desert.   God's justice is a higher justice than man's, and works in a different way. Perhaps he meant also to indicate that, whether the labourers having arrived later was in any way their own fault or not, they had, at all events, done their best during the hours in which they *did* work. And perhaps too he meant to indicate that, generally speaking, there were no elaborate gradations according to degrees of ' desert ' in ' heaven.'   For ' heaven ' is altogether beyond desert.   And there is more equality in heaven than on earth.   But that the life to come and its beatitudes are not awarded according to strict rule and measure of tit for tat is the main burden of the parable.   And the Tanchuma passage, though not going to the same lengths as the parable, is nevertheless a most interesting parallel to it.

Perhaps, however, the best parallel to the Gospel parable is a passage from Deuteronomy R. (*Ki Tetze* vi. 1 on xxii. 6).   ' R. Abin bar Kahana said, Thou shalt not sit and weigh the commands of the Law. Thou art not to say, Because there is a greater reward for this command, I will do it, and because there is only a small reward for that command, I will not do it. What has God done ? He has not revealed to the creatures (*i.e.* to men) the particular reward for each particular command, in order that they might do all the commands in integrity (בתום). The matter is like a king who hired labourers, and brought them into his garden ; he hid, and did not reveal, what was the reward of (working in) the garden, so that they might not neglect that part of the work for which the reward was small, and go and do that part for which the reward was great. In the evening he summoned them all, and said, Under which tree did you work ? The first answered, Under this one. The king said, That is a pepper tree ; its reward is one gold piece. He said to the next, Under which tree did you work ? He said, Under that one. The king said, It is a white flower tree, its reward is half a gold piece. He asked a third, Under which tree did you work ? He said, Under this one. The king replied, That is an olive tree ; its reward is 200 zuzim. The labourers said to him, Ought you not to have told us the tree under which the reward was greatest ? The king replied, If I had done that, how could all of my garden have been tilled ? Even so, God has not revealed the reward of the commandments, except of two—one heaviest of the heavy, the other lightest of the light, viz. Exodus xx. 12, Honour thy father and thy mother, and Deut. xxii. 7, Thou shalt let the mother bird go ; for both the reward is the same, namely, long life.' The chief point of all this lies in the last words. The reward of the two commands, so unequal in value, is nevertheless the same. At all events, therefore, God's justice is not according to strict measure. It is a higher justice than the justice of tit for tat. Thus the teaching of Jesus in the great parable of Matt. xx. was not teaching which was wholly unknown to, or never preached by, any Rabbi. We hear a form of it in the passage which has just been quoted.

The same remark about the equal reward for two such strangely different commands as the bird's nest and the honouring of parents occurs frequently. Thus Proverbs v. 6 is quoted, ' That thou weigh not the path of life ; her paths move, thou canst not know them.' This was said so that you should not weigh the commands of the

U

Law, and find out which command has the greatest reward, and do that one : therefore the paths of the law are mobile (ממולטלין). It is like a king who had a garden, and brought workmen into it, but he did not tell them the reward for each planting, for if he had, they would have done only the planting for which the reward was greater, and the work of the garden would have been half done and half neglected. So God did not reveal the reward of the commands, so that the Israelites should not consider which command had a big reward and fulfil it, and the Law would have been half fulfilled and half neglected (בטלה). That is why the wise men said, Be as eager about a light command as about a heavy command, for thou knowest not the rewards of the commands. Thus God moves about (טלטל) the rewards of the commands in this world, so that the Israelites may consider them and accomplish them all sincerely (משלם). 'And when God' [I suppose in the world to come] 'gives them their rewards, he gives them a reward for their faith and a reward for their deeds, and he reveals to them the meaning and interpretation of the commands' (טעמן ופירושן). (Midrash Psalms ix. (3), verse 1, 41 a, foot.) So, again (Tanchuma, *Ki Tetze*, 19 b). 'It is like a king who sent workmen into his field to plant, and he did not tell them the reward of their planting. In the evening he gave to all the workmen one gold piece. Then the workmen wondered and said, To him who has only planted one small tree a gold piece has been given ; to us who planted many, how much more should be given. If the reward for the " bird " command is length of days, the rewards for commands the doing of which may involve loss and trouble and risk of life (החיות נפשו) should be much greater. Therefore God did not make known the reward for those who execute the commands of the Law, so that the Israelites might do them of their own will (מעצמן), so as to increase their reward, even as we have been taught, Be not as slaves who serve their master with the object of getting a reward.' In this last passage we must notice the odd naïveness and mixture. The object of keeping the exact amount of reward for each command dark is precisely to increase the amount of the rewards, and *yet* we are told in the same breath, Do not serve for reward. The reward assuredly will come, and it will be all the greater if and because you do not think of it—if you fulfil the commands willingly, for their own sake, for the love of them.

All these passages and some others are honestly given in the interesting excursus on the parable of the Labourers in the Vineyard in S.B. Vol. IV. pp. 484–500. The dogmatic bias of the author, however, is as much apparent in this excursus as in the one on the Sermon on the Mount. To Billerbeck, as an orthodox Lutheran Christian, nothing is more horrible in religion, and more false, than any notion of merited reward. God *does* give rewards; yet are all rewards rewards of grace, and none are rewards of merit. No reward from God is, as it were, the payment of something due by God to man. God *owes* man nothing; man can claim nothing from God. Whatever God gives, he gives by grace, and as a free and undeserved gift. It is man's duty to serve God, but he must not serve him through desire of reward. The consciousness of God's mercy and grace must make him all the more eager to serve God. Towards, and in relation to, God there is no such thing as merit. ' For merit lives from man to man, And not from man, O Lord, to thee.' Tennyson's words exactly express the Lutheran doctrine.

There is little doubt, I think, that we to-day largely share this doctrine and this point of view. We should, I think, agree that, so far as there can be such a thing as reward at all, it must be of grace, and not of debt or claim. I suppose that we even go farther. The whole idea of reward, whether of debt or grace, has become vague and shadowy, and it tends to disappear altogether. If there are rewards as from God, we tend to regard them as the necessary product of the act, as internal rather than external. It is true that on earth adversity is often conjoined with righteousness, and we should all admit that an eternal conjunction of righteousness and misery would be irrational and undivine. In that sense, beatitude must ultimately attend upon, and be conjoined with, righteousness. But, even so, we hardly regard this ultimate, essential conjunction of bliss with righteousness as in the nature of a reward, but rather as the removal of those earthly conditions which prevent such a conjunction.

The mediaeval Jewish philosopher Maimonides (1135–1204) in his Siraj, the Arabic commentary on the Mishnah, has a famous section about Rewards and Punishments and the Future Life. I may quote some paragraphs from Yellin and Abrahams' little-known booklet on Maimonides, published in 1903. ' " Every Israelite has a share in the world to come," runs a Mishnah in

Tractate Sanhedrin. But who is an " Israelite," and what is the
" life to come " ? These questions suggested to Maimonides the
desirability of examining current conceptions of immortality, and
forced upon him the duty of formulating the ultimate doctrines,
belief in which made the Israelite. The essay in which Maimonides
attempts to solve these problems is unquestionably the most significant section of the *Siraj*. He opens with the lament that many
take a material view of eternal bliss, conceiving it as a Garden of
Eden, where flow rivers of wine and spiced oils ; and men, free
from toil, inhabit houses built of precious stones, and recline on
silken couches. Hell to them is equally materialized, as a place
of burning fires and bodily torments. Others, again, attach their
hopes of bliss to the conception of an approaching Messianic Age,
in which men will be as kings, living eternally, gigantic in stature,
provided by a bountiful earth with garments ready woven and
meats ready baked. A third class rest their hopes on the Resurrection, believing that a man will be in a happy state if, after his
death, he live again with his dear ones and household, eating and
drinking, but never again dying. Yet others hold that the good
derived from obedience to the divine law consists in earthly happiness, and that earthly misery and " captivity " result from disobedience. A fifth class, a very numerous section, combine all
these ideals, holding as their ideal that Messiah will come, and will
quicken the dead ; that they will enter the Garden of Eden, and
eat there and drink, healthy throughout eternity. All of these
base their views, in part successfully, on Scripture and Tradition,
but they succeed by interpreting literally texts that need to be
explained as figures. The real marvel and mystery, the whole
conception of a future world, they do not attempt to examine.
They rather ask, " How will the dead arise ?—naked or clothed ?
attired in the embroidered shrouds in which they were interred,
or dressed in simple garments to cover their flesh ? " As to the
coming of the Messiah, they are concerned with such questions as,
" Will all men, rich and poor, be equal then ? Or will one be strong
and another weak ? " Now a wise teacher attracts the child by
nuts, and figs, and honey ; for the child cannot appreciate the
real purpose of his studies. As the pupil grows older, the reward
must change, and the nuts having palled, the teacher must charm
with fine shoes and dainty apparel. Later he will offer more sub-

stantial bribes, such as money; later still he will say, Study to become a *dayan*, to win men's respect, that the people may rise before thee as they do before such and such a one. But can a man of character and intellect be satisfied with this ? Is the end of wisdom to be found except in wisdom itself ? Shall men learn except to win truth, or obey the Law for any motive except obedience ? Man must study the Law simply to know it, seeking truth for truth's own sake, and knowing in order to perform. It is unlawful to say, I will follow the good to win reward, and eschew the evil to escape punishment. Maimonides is very forcible in maintaining this view, and cites with affectionate approval the saying of " that perfect man, who reached the truth of things," Antigonus of Socho, whose utterance has ever since been the keynote of the higher Judaism : " Be not like servants who minister to their master upon the condition of receiving a reward ; but be like servants who minister to their master without the condition of receiving a reward." Maimonides follows this up by several apt quotations in which Rabbinical sages inculcated " service from motives of love towards God," especially the famous comment of R. Eleazar on the text, " In His commandments he delights exceedingly," " In His commandments, not in the rewards for them, he delights," and the equally famous saying in the *Sifre*, " All that you do must be done for pure love of the Lord." What then of the offers of reward and threats of punishment ?

'Maimonides answers by the· theory which he subsequently developed in explanation of the Sacrifices. A concession was necessary to the average man, who is incapable of such pure devotion, but needs a specific stimulus, just as the schoolboy does from his teacher ; but the concession was a means to an end, the end being the attainment of such a spiritual exaltation in which the love of good will be the sole stimulus to good, and the ideal will be realized in a perfect knowledge of the divine truth. Let men, said the Rabbi, serve God at first for reward ; they will end by serving Him without any such motive. Thus the concession is educational. But Maimonides carries the argument farther. The material rewards prescribed in Scripture were aids to virtue rather than payment for it. When a man is sick, hungry, thirsty, or at war, he cannot obey the ordinances of God. The object of reward for obedience is not that the land shall be fat, and men live long and healthily, but that these blessings shall help them to perform the law, while the penalties of disobedience are penalties only in this that man by his very sin is rendered incapable of serving God. " If " (Maimonides puts this into God's mouth) " thou performest part of a single ordinance from love and desire, I will help thee to perform all ordinances, and will ward off all obstructive ill; but if thou leavest one thing undone from motives of contempt, I will bring on thee consequences which will prevent thee from obeying the whole law." Now it may be that Paradise will give to the righteous all that men dream of delight, and more ; and Gehenna may be a fiery torture for the wicked. The days of the Messiah will fulfil all that the prophets have prophesied, and Israel will regain the sovereignty and return to their land. But our hope in the Messiah is not made up of dreams of wealth or hopes of Eden —a dream of bliss to spur us to righteousness. Eternal bliss consists in perfect spiritual communion with God. He who desires to serve God from love must not serve to win the future world, but he does the right and eschews the wrong because he is man, and owes it to his manhood to perfect himself ; and this effort brings him to the type of perfect man, whose soul shall live in that state which befits it, viz., in the world to come ' (pp. 60-65).

As we moderns look at the whole matter, the Rabbis could not look at it. The Bible prevented them. For the Bible undoubtedly speaks of reward in the frankest and simplest way ; moreover, it does occasionally say, ' Do this, or fulfil that, divine command, in order that you may obtain such and such a reward.' When we remember that every word of the Bible, and especially of the Pentateuch, was regarded as perfectly good and perfectly wise and perfectly inspired, it is really a remarkable thing how often the Rabbis rose above the level of their texts, or rather, perhaps, how often they made the higher things in the Bible correct the lower things, or how often they both adopted the Bible teaching, and yet, of their own impulse, transcended it. Nevertheless, this did not always happen. Sometimes the higher and lower things in the Bible, all regarded as true and inspired, made them, the Rabbis, inculcate contradictory teachings, and they did not harmonize them, or harmonized them very imperfectly. And we may even go farther, and say that they sometimes systematized and worsened the Bible teaching, though at other times they corrected and transcended it. Thus we have, I think, to admit that the naïve Bible teaching about rewards is, in some respects, coarsened and systematized by the Rabbis. In addition to the doctrine of rewards, the Rabbis invented the corresponding, and logically connected, doctrine of Merits (*Zechuth*). What I have so far said seems to me to be corroborated by Dr. Marmorstein's wonderfully learned book, *The Doctrine of Merits in Old Rabbinical Literature* (1920), and corroborated the more because Dr. Marmorstein himself seems to have no knowledge of any religious objection to the doctrine of Merits, and so writes about it quite simply and naïvely. Thus in his excellent introduction, by way of giving the net results of the various, and not always consistent, Rabbinic ideas upon the subject, he says : ' Man has power to acquire merits. . . . By performing the commandments man is entitled to a reward.' Again, ' The laws and observances were given to man for man to obtain merits ' (p. 15 *fin.*, p. 16). ' *Entitled*,' observe, to reward. Man, *has*, therefore, a claim. And yet the very opposite of such a doctrine, as *both* Marmorstein and Billerbeck show, was *also* taught by the Rabbis.

We may, indeed, say of their teaching :

(1) Man does, as a matter of fact, garner or acquire merits ; he, as it were, can collect tickets on which, or through which, he obtains reward. But we may no less say (as we have already heard in the remarks upon the Sermon on the Mount) :

(2) *Man* has *no* claim upon God. This view meets us not infrequently, though hardly so frequently as (1).

(3) All God's rewards are due to his goodness, his mercy, his grace : or, again, they are, as it were, the necessary conditions of his glory. For his own sake he pardons and rewards. Or—for the teaching of the Rabbis is for *Jewish* listeners and pupils—he pardons and rewards for the sake of Israel and for the honour of the Torah ; for the bliss of Israel, and what one might call the higher success of the Torah, are intimately bound up with the glory of God. And if the individual Israelites of whom Israel is composed are not in ultimate bliss, the divine purposes are not fulfilled, and the divine Torah is not glorified and vindicated.

Again, it adds to God's honour and praise when he shows grace and does good to man in disaccord with man's deserts. Thus man may even ask for disproportionate reward. The following little

passage from Midrash Psalms xxvi. 2–4, 109 a is thoroughly Rabbinic
in its quaint simplicity and frankness. ' Solomon said to God
(I Kings viii. 57), If a king hires good workmen, who do their work
well, and the king gives them their hire (reward), what praise
(שבח) has the king ? When is he praised ? When he hires lazy
workmen, and gives *them* their full hire (משלם). So too our
fathers wrought and received good reward : what goodness (on God's
part) was there in that seeing that they wrought and took (their
reward) ? But we are lazy workers; yet do thou give us good
reward. That would be *great* goodness ! '

(1) and (2) are, essentially, contradictory to one another : yet
we may, perhaps, semi-harmonize them thus. Man acquires merit
by the grace of God. There is no magic or compulsion about it.
It is an arrangement or a plan which God in his goodness has
devised. Securing the tickets or the merits, on which man draws
reward, purifies him. And unless he is purified, he does not get the
tickets. In order that getting the tickets (securing the merit) may
purify him, he must get the tickets in a pure way, for the sake of
the commands, out of love for God. It almost comes to this, that
if you fulfil the commands merely and solely in order to pile up
merit, you will not get the merit and, therefore, the reward. But it
never *quite* comes to this. About the efficacy of the Day of Atonement we are told : ' He who says, I will sin, and the Day of Atonement will secure me forgiveness, for him the Day of Atonement
secures no forgiveness ' ; but I do not think that anywhere is it said,
He who says ' I will fulfil the commands in order to gain merit
and reward will gain no merit and no reward.' On the contrary,
it is deliberately stated that the whole object of the Law is that
man *may* gain merit through fulfilling its commandments, and he
who seeks to gain such merit is not reprobated but praised. It is
only side by side with this teaching, but not as cancelling it, that
you find the teaching that all the commandments must be fulfilled
from love or for their own sake. And if it says (as we have so often
heard) that it is even good to fulfil the laws *not* for their own sake,
because from fulfilling them *not* for their own sake you may come
in the end, and be drawn on in the end, to fulfil them *for* their
own sake, it never, I think, definitely gives as an example of fulfilling them *not* for their own sake to fulfil them in order to gain
merit.

The theory of *Zechuth* (merit) seems partly bettered, and partly worsened, by the vicarious nature of much *Zechuth* (by the theory of imputed merit). It appears to be bettered, first, because it is a fine idea that one may be kept from sin because one may injure one's children (or even one's parents!). Secondly, it prevents conceit, for you may believe that, not your own little merits (your few little tickets) will win you salvation and bliss, but rather the big merits (the many large tickets) of the Righteous, the Saints, the Martyrs, the Patriarchs, Israel as a whole, or the Law as a whole. It could be worsened (as we may read in Marmorstein, and as the Rabbis themselves realized, protesting sometimes against the idea) by the notion that a man need not worry, because the merits of the Patriarchs or Israel or the Saints will pull him through.

Mr. Loewe says: ' Transmitted *Zechuth* practically means, for the Rabbis, the heredity of acquired characteristics, about which psychologists are so much exercised to-day, and which they seem inclined to accept. The Rabbis were empiricists, not scientists, and they observed that a man could teach his son to avoid drunkenness, that drunkards tended to beget children who had a hard struggle to overcome the drink craving. If you are a drunkard, you disgrace your parents, and so lessen *Zechuth*. Conversely, the good which a man does need not be interred with his bones; it may be transmitted. Secondly, *Zechuth* has a *nuance* which must not be forgotten; it often means the feeling of inward happiness which is the result of duty done. This is sometimes called *Simchah shel Mitzvah*, the joy of the command.'

What the net, or even the average, ethical and religious result of the doctrine of *Zechuth* and of Reward may have been it is indeed difficult to say. It is unlikely to have been so bad as Billerbeck hints that it was. It is unlikely to have been so excellent as Marmorstein so constantly suggests. Some danger must have resided in the immense power for gaining *Zechuth* which was associated with the commands. For the more the commands are, as it were, manifested and made actual and real by the doing of them, the more they will benefit the doers of them, those who, as it were, make the potential actual. The effect must have tended to be regarded as automatic, an effluence flowing inevitably from the deed. The *opus operatum*, with all its evils, was always lurking round the corner. It was so fatally easy to believe in its efficacy, and, in a sense, so very difficult *not* to believe in it. Nevertheless, it is remarkable how much we find which mitigated the danger, and ran counter to any lower teaching. If the Rabbis devised the doctrine of *Zechuth*, they no less devised the doctrine of *lishmah*. The one is as much their creation as the other. And they also elaborated the Biblical teaching about Love. They urged that Love (*i.e.* the love of God and of his Law) should, in the last resort, be the only, or the ultimate, motive for all man's doings, and perhaps it was a perception of such dangers as I have indicated which led R. Bannayah to say, ' If you do not fulfil the words of the Law for their own sake, they will kill you ' (Sifre 131 b *ad fin.*; S.B. iv. p. 496). Or, again, ' As for him who does not fulfil the Law for its own sake, it were better he had never been created ' (Berachoth 17 a). So too the Law must never be used for worldly profit or worldly reputation, and so degraded and profaned. Hillel said, ' Everyone who makes a profit of the words of the Law is helping on his own destruction ' (Aboth iv. 5). ' Do the words of the Law for the doing of them ' (Sifre 84 b ; Moore II. p. 97 ; Bacher, *Agada der Tannaiten*, I. p. 48, nn. 2 and 3).

There is a fine passage in Professor Curtis's essay on the Parable of the Labourers, published in the *Festgabe für Adolf Jülicher zum 70. Geburtstag* (1927), which puts the teaching of the parable very lucidly before our eyes. ' God is the Great Employer of souls. Spiritual life is His vineyard. Short or long, man's allotted span is a day. At sunset comes the reckoning. The award is that eternal life on which the Teacher had just before been dwelling. Can you divide eternal life, the peace of God that passeth understanding, heaven, into fractions, fewer or more of which can be doled out in reward of the varying merit of earthly life ? . . . If He is the Great Employer, He pays His willing workers not by time nor by piece-rate, but according to their spirit of service and His spirit of grace. There is no market-place in heaven ; let there be none in religion, earth's foretaste of heaven. Think more of opportunity, less of reward. Eternal life cannot be reckoned as any servant's due, as any saint's earnings. Rejoice when others are called, though their hour comes later in the day than yours. Least and greatest, last and first, forget these distinctions while you press on to life's end and goal. . . . The Searcher of hearts can judge as no human master can. His estimate of a man's life in His service takes account of more than the hours of toil and the worker's completed output ' (p. 67).

25-28. The doctrine of service and of the humility of service was a notable feature in the teaching of Jesus. It was also a comparatively new feature. There are no complete parallels to the doctrine in the Rabbinic literature, so far as I am aware and have been able to probe the matter.[1] For Jesus means something more than the dialectical question whether a king, a prince, or a learned man may yield precedence, or renounce the particular honour which is due to him, on a particular occasion. He means more than such a small point as serving or pouring out wine at a banquet, though such action might be the occasion or the illustration of his teaching. He meant the service of a life-time ; the lowly or devoted service of others. He meant spending oneself for the sake of the lowliest, in the manner, for example, of St. Francis. Such a conception was a new thing, a new teaching. And of its gigantic importance and effects in history it is needless here to speak. The long passage from Kiddushin 32 b, part of which is cited in S.B., is therefore no real parallel. It is true that R. Joshua allows R. Gamaliel, who was a ' Nasi ' (prince), to pour out wine and hand it to him and R. Eliezer and the others at a banquet. The example of Abraham, a greater than R. Gamaliel, is cited. He ' served ' the angels, thinking them to be mere Arabians and idolaters. Finally R. Zadok says, ' How long will you forget the honour due to God, and occupy yourselves with the honour due to man ? God makes the wind blow, the rain fall, the earth produce, and provides the Table for one and all ; why should not R. Gamaliel stand up and pour out wine for us ? ' But this ' parallel ' passage, if it can be called so, goes a very little way. The second quotation from Horayoth 10 a (ad fin.) is somewhat more in point. There we read how R. Gamaliel thought of appointing two Rabbis to be the heads of a certain congregation. They only came at his second summons. He said to them, ' You thought I was going to offer you rule (serarah) ? (And so in humility they wanted to evade the honour.) It is service that I am giving you (Abduth),' and he quotes 1 Kings xii. 7 ("If thou wilt be a

[1] I do not by any means overlook or underestimate the great religious or ethical value of the passage from Sotah 14 a (or of its parallels) quoted on p. 105.

servant unto this people this day "). Here the idea that rule, or leadership, means service, a certain bondage, is clearly brought out. So again in Taanit 10 b, where the passage depends upon a possible difference between a student and a " man of distinction " (יחיד). The " man of distinction " is he who is worthy (or fit) to be appointed head (פרנס) of a community. Now R. Meir and the Rabbis said, Not everyone who wants to act as a *Yachid* may do so ; though all students may. R. Yose said, Everyone may do so, and deserves to be well thought of for wishing to do so, for to do so brings him no glory (שבח) but only suffering (צער). (To be a leader is to suffer.) Another view (R. Simeon b. Gamaliel) was that when to act as leader would bring him glory, he may not so act ; when it would bring him suffering, he may ! (*Cp.* Dr. Malter's rendering.) Judges must regard themselves as the servants of the community. So too the officers of a Rabbinical college (who were by reason of their office also judges). When R. Gamaliel appointed R. Yochanan b. Nuri and R. Eleazar b. Chisma to be officers, and the disciples did not pay them due regard (לא הרגישו בהם), they, in dudgeon, sat down among the disciples (instead of in the seats appointed for officers). When R. Gamaliel entered the college, and saw them, he said, ' You have let the community know that you seek to exercise rule (לעשות שררות) over the community. Before (your appointment) you were independent (הייתם ברשות עצמיכם), but from henceforward you are servants of, and subjected to, the community ' (עבדים ומשועבדים לצבור). (Sifre 68 b.) (Bacher, *Agada der Tannaiten*, p. 366, n. 3.)

28. λύτρον. The conception of vicarious suffering and death was known to the Rabbis, but whether it was spoken of by them so early as, say, A.D. 30 seems more doubtful. But I am not here concerned with dates. I am interested only in the fact that in the course of the development of the Rabbinic religion the conception made its appearance and was taught. The illustrative passages are given very fully by S.B. in Vol. II. pp. 279–282 ; Vol. IV. pp. 771, 1045, 1049; Vol. III. p. 261, and I have little else to do than to make a selection from them. The dominant idea, very frequently repeated, is that the death of the righteous has atoning power (*i.e.* it atones, or helps to atone, for the sins of the community as a whole). Thus the question is asked, Why is the death of Miriam

mentioned immediately after the passage about the Red Heifer ?
The reply is that as the Red Heifer makes atonement, so too
does the death of the righteous. As the clothes of the priest
make atonement, so does the death of the righteous. (Numbers xx.
28.) (Moed Katon, 28 a.) Again as the Day of Atonement atones,
so, too, does the death of the righteous. (Leviticus R., *Achare
Moth*, xx. § 12 *ad fin.* on xvi. 1.) When it is said that the blood of the
Israelites who are slain by the ' nations ' is their atonement (כפרה)
for the world to come (*i.e.* atones for sins and so secures felicity
in the life to come), it is not quite clear if it is meant that their
death is an atonement for their own sins or for the sins of the
people as a whole. (Sifre 140 a *ad fin.*) (*Cp.* the well-known
passages in 4 Maccabees i. 11, vi. 28, f. xvii. 20 *seq.*) It is said that
at a time when righteous men exist they are ' taken ' (נתפסים) for
the generation (*i.e.* to atone for the sins of their contemporaries) ;
where there are no righteous, school-children are ' taken.' (' Taken '
means that they die.) (Sabbath 33 b.) There is a remarkable
passage in Midrash Psalms (Moore, *Judaism*, I. p. 548) : ' When
God sought to give the Torah to Israel, he said, Give me sureties
that you will keep the Law. They offered the Patriarchs as surety.
But God said that these are in debt to him, he must have sureties
who owe him nothing. Who are these ? said they. He replied,
The children. Then they brought the children who were in
their mothers' womb, and at the breasts of their mothers, and
these fruits of their bodies (כרים) stood there like crystal (in
purity), and they looked at God from the wombs of their mothers
and spoke with him. God said to them, Will you be sureties for
your fathers, that if I give them the Law, they will keep it, and if
they do not (will you agree), that you should be taken (נתפסים)
instead of them ? Then they said, Yes' (Midrash Psalms viii. 3, 38 b).
It is also said that the Sanctuary was a pledge (play on two Hebrew
words of the same sound), for, when the Israelites deserve destruction, the Sanctuary will be pledged in their stead. ' Then Moses
asked God, But will there not be a time when they will not have a
sanctuary ? Then, replied God, I will take (נוטל) from them one
righteous man and make him a pawn, and so, through him, make
atonement for their sins.' (Here again, I suppose, that ' take '
means that the righteous man will prematurely die.) (Exodus
R., *Terumah*, xxxv. § 4.) In a highly curious passage it is said

that God told Abraham that if his descendants sinned, then God would take a great man among them, a man who could be an atonement for their sins, and could say to the Attribute of Justice, ' Enough.' Such a man God would take as a pledge in their stead (אני נוטלו וממשכנו בעדם). (Canticles R.i. § 4, 3 on i. 14.) That the death of the great man is here meant seems fairly clear from the parallel in Gen. R. xliv. 5 on xv. 1. In these passages the vicarious death is involuntary. But it is also said that some great men of Israel's past were ready to die for Israel's sake, e.g. Moses and David. (Of Moses, cp. Berachoth 32 a. שמסר עצמו למיתה עליהם.) It is said that Jonah ran away only to destroy himself in the sea, and that the Patriarchs and the Prophets were ready to give their lives for the sake of Israel. (Mechilta, Bo, 2 a. Cp. Sotah 14 a.) David said, ' Let thy hand be upon me and my father's house ' (2 Sam. xxiv. 17). This means that he wished to suffer death so that Israel might live. At the judgment day the willingness of Isaac to be sacrificed will be regarded as an expiation for Israel's sins. See the story in Sabbath 89 b given in Moore 1. p. 540. It is very curious how the ' atonement ' wrought by Phineas in the story (Numbers xxv. 13) is made expiatory in a new sense by the Rabbis. ' He exposed his soul unto death (Isaiah liii. 12) ; and this readiness to die made atonement, and even to the present time he has not ceased (לא זז), but he stands and makes atonement till the resurrection of the dead ' (Sifre 48 b, Levertoff p. 143 ; Moore 1. p. 540). It was not, so it would appear, his slaying of the Israelite and the Midianite woman which wrought the atonement, but the peril of his life to which the act exposed him. Moses asked to be blotted out of the book which God had written if God would not forgive the Israelites' sin. But the Rabbis seem to regard this request of Moses as equivalent to a readiness to die for the sake of gaining Israel's forgiveness from God. (Sotah 14 a.) This readiness of Moses to die for his people would undoubtedly be a case of a ransom ; they sinned, and he was ready (as the Rabbis held) to die in their stead. Sufferings atone for sin, even as death atones, and that they have this vicarious or substitutionary effect is one of the reasons why they can be called ' beloved.' It is stated that when Isaiah said, ' Here am I, send me ' (Isaiah vi. 8), God replied, ' Isaiah, my children are troublesome (טרחנין) and disobedient (סרבין). If you will agree to let yourself be reviled and ill-used by my

children, then go on in my sending of you : but if not, then go not.'
Isaiah said, 'I go on that very condition, namely, that I give my
back to the smiters, and my cheeks to those who pluck off the hair
(Isaiah l. 6), and I am not even worthy to go in thy sending to
thy children.' Then God said, 'Thou lovest righteousness, that
is, thou lovest to justify my children, and thou hatest wickedness, that is, thou hatest to hold them guilty, therefore God has
anointed thee above thy fellows' (Psalms xlv. 7). (Leviticus R.,
Tsav, x. § 1, *init.* on viii. 1, 2; Pesikta 125 b; Moore II. 550, 551.)
Quaint are the stories about R. Judah the Prince (Rabbi) and
R. Elazar b. Simeon.   The former was one day immersed in a
lecture when a calf ran up to him for protection, and mooed, as if
to say, Save me. But R. Judah said, ' What can I do for you ?
You were created to be killed.' For this callousness Rabbi was
afflicted with toothache for thirteen years. In all these thirteen
years the story went that no pregnant woman died and none had a
miscarriage. At the end of the thirteen years, Rabbi was angry
with R. Chiya. One day Elijah came down in the form of R. Chiya,
and laid his hand on Rabbi's tooth, and he was immediately healed.
The next day R. Chiya came to see him, and said, How is your tooth?
Rabbi said, Since you came yesterday and laid your hand on it,
I am cured. Then R. Chiya said, Woe to the pregnant women in
Israel. It was not I who touched your tooth. Then Rabbi knew
that it was Elijah, and from that time he showed great respect to
R. Chiya. (Genesis R., *Vayechi*, xcvi. 5 on xlvii. 29 *fin.* and Jer.
Kilaim ix. § 4, 32 b.) In this legend it is to be noted that Rabbi's
toothache is a punishment; yet he is so great and good a man that his
sufferings atone for other people's sins. No woman who, because of
some sin she had committed, would have died in childbirth or had a
miscarriage, did so die or suffer. The story about R. Elazar is too
long and complicated to quote, but the point which concerns us
here is that the Rabbi had an uneasy conscience that he had not
dealt quite fairly or justly in regard to certain judicial decisions
about Jewish malefactors in which he had acted on behalf of the
government. In consequence he inflicted upon himself certain severe
bodily sufferings, and of these the Talmud observes that they were
superior to (more excellent than, עדיפי) the sufferings of Rabbi.
For *his* were inflicted upon him by God, whereas the sufferings of
R. Elazar were self-inflicted ; in the words of the Talmud, ' they

came from love and went from love.' And this expression again is
due to a detail in the story according to which R. Elazar's sufferings
were inflicted at night, whereas in the morning, by certain food
which his wife gave him to eat, he was healed. 'So at the evening
he said to his sufferings, Come, my brothers and friends (אחיי
ורעיי בואו); in the morning he said to them, Go away,' so that
they might not disturb his study of the Law.' R. Elazar's pains
were also of atoning efficacy; during the years through which they
lasted, no man died prematurely. (Baba Mezia 83 b–85 a.) Even
the suffering which comes to a man of distinguished piety through
the death of a child could be regarded as having atoning power,
as in the story of R. Chiya b. Abba. His child died, and R. Judah
b. Nachman in a visit of condolence quoted Deut. xxxii. 19. The
quotation, we are told, was not intended, as one might think, to
give pain. On the contrary, R. Judah meant, 'You are worthy
to be taken because of the generation' (חשיב את לאתפוסי אדרא).
The use of the word תפש seems due to the death of the child.
(Kethuboth 8 b.) In this last citation the sufferings, though voluntarily accepted out of love (of God), are not, however, undergone
for the sake of others, though God so arranged things that they
acted to the advantage of others. The conception of being or
acting as an atonement for others was, however, so well known that,
as S.B. points out, the phrase 'May I be an atonement for so and
so' became also not infrequent. Thus Rabbi Ishmael, in saying
something about the colour of Israelite leprosy, remarks, 'The children of Israel—may I be their atonement—have the colour of,' etc.
(Dr. Hoffmann comments thus: 'Aus Liebe zu seinem Volke ge-
braucht der Rabbi hier dieser Redeweise, da er von einem Aussatz
der Israeliten spricht'; and the meaning is, I will [I would like to]
take the sufferings which may have been decreed against them upon
myself, in order to obtain for them atonement and forgiveness.)[1]
(Mishnah Negaim ii. 1.) Resh Lakish, in another legal discussion,
said, 'I am ready to be the atonement for R. Chiya and his sons'
(Sukkah 20 a). The formal character of the phrase is shown by the
use which is to be made of it by the 'people' who, on a given
occasion, are to say to the High Priest, 'We will be thy atonement'
(Mishnah Sanhedrin ii. 1). The most interesting of the passages

---

[1] 'The Rabbi uses this expression out of love for his people, because he is
speaking of a leprosy of the Israelites.'

quoted by Levy and S.B. is perhaps that in which we have an early instance (in a Baraita) of the conception of the dead in their purgatorial period being beneficially affected by the prayers, or the sufferings, of the living. A son is to honour his father among other things by saying, 'Behold, I will be the atonement for his death-bed' (כפרת משכבו). He is to say this for twelve months after his father's death, because the idea was that the purgatorial period in Gehenna would only last twelve months at longest. By his readiness to accept sufferings in lieu of his father the son could shorten the purgatorial period. (S.B. Vol. IV. p. 1045.) (Kiddushin 31 b.)

The precise force or bearing of the word λύτρον is a matter for a commentary on the Gospels, not for a book like this one. Here I look upon it in its wider aspect, not specifically and narrowly as 'ransom,' but in the sense in which it may be regarded as more equivalent to a substitutionary and vicarious sacrifice. The Hebrew כופר, ransom, which is often rendered by λύτρον in the LXX, is closely connected, both etymologically and in sense, with sacrificial and atoning conceptions. It is therefore sufficient for my purpose to have indicated that the Rabbis were not unfamiliar with the idea of losing your life, whether voluntarily or involuntarily, for the sake and the benefit of others.

The next question which Matt. xx. 28 raises is in relation to the Messiah. Any idea of his *death* as an atonement or as a 'ransom' was unknown to the Rabbis, but to his sufferings—and even to his sufferings for the sake of his people—there are occasional allusions. (The passages in which these allusions occur are a good deal later than A.D. 30.) The conception arose that the Messiah already existed from the Creation in heaven, and also that he had been born as man long ago, but had been kept hidden away (on account of Israel's sins ?): his public manifestation as Messiah was still to come. In this hidden life he had to endure many sufferings for Israel's sake. Thus it is said that 'Sufferings are divided into three portions, of which one part has been allocated to all the generations of the world, and one part to the age of the Persecutions (Hadrian), and one part to the Messiah, as it is written, He was wounded for our transgressions' (Midrash Samuel xix. 29 b, ed. Buber, 1925). The same verse from Isaiah is referred to the sufferings of the Messiah in Ruth R. on ii. 14, 'Dip thy morsel in the vinegar : those are the sufferings of the Messiah, as it says, He was

pierced for our iniquities ' (Midrash Ruth v. § 6 on ii. 14). Again,
' Our teachers have said, His name shall be the Leprous One of
the house of Rabbi (perhaps in reference to Rabbi's sufferings
for the thirteen years), even as it says, Surely he bore our sickness
and carried our pains : yet we esteemed him as one stricken with
leprosy, and smitten of God' (Sanhedrin 98 b) (חיוורא דבי רבי).
A more familiar passage in the same tractate runs thus : ' R.
Joshua b. Levi met Elijah at the mouth of the cave of R. Simeon
b. Yochai. He said to Elijah, Shall I enter the life to come ? Elijah
replied, If it so please the Master (= God). Then he asked him,
When will the Messiah come ? Elijah replied, Go and ask him.
But where is he ? At the gate of Rome. And what is his mark ?
(How shall I recognize him ?) He sits among the wretched who
are laden with sicknesses [sores and wounds are meant, and it is
implied that he too has sores and wounds] ; all the others uncover
all their wounds, and then bind them all up again, but he uncovers
and 'binds up each one separately, for he thinks, Lest I be summoned
and should be detained. So Rabbi Joshua went and said to him,
Peace be with thee, Master and Rabbi. He replied, Peace be with
thee, son of Levi. He said, When is the Master coming ? He
replied, To-day. Then R. Joshua returned to Elijah, who said,
What did he say to you ? He replied, Peace be with thee, son
of Levi. Elijah said, Then he assured to you (אבטחך) and to
your father (a place in) the world to come. The Rabbi said, He
spoke falsely to me, for he said he would come to-day, and he has
not come. Then Elijah said, He meant To-day, if ye hearken to
my voice ' (Psalm xcv. 7). (Sanhedrin 98 a.) Here, too, Messiah's
sufferings may, perhaps, be regarded as undergone for the sake of
Israel. The fullest and most interesting passages of those dealing
with Messiah's sufferings and collected by S.B. (II. pp. 284–291)
come from the late Midrashic compilation known as the Pesikta
Rabbathi. Thus : ' Our teachers have said, There is no end to
the sufferings with which he (the Messiah) is afflicted in every generation according to the sins of each generation. Therefore God says
(Isaiah xlix. 8), In that hour I create thee anew, and will not afflict
thee any more ' (Pesikta R. 146 b). ' All the good which I will
do unto you I do through the merit (זכות) of the Messiah who
was kept back all those years. He is righteous and filled with
salvation (Zechariah ix. 9). That is the Messiah who recognizes

that God's judgment upon Israel is righteous, when they laugh at
him when he sits in the prison : therefore is he called just. And
why is he called filled with salvation ? Because he says, You
are all my children. Are ye not all only saved by the mercies of
God ? Afflicted and riding on an ass. That is the Messiah.
Why is he called afflicted ? Because he was afflicted all those
years in the prison, and the transgressors in Israel laughed at him.
And why riding upon an ass ? Because the transgressors have
no merit, but through his merit God protects them, and leads them
on a level way, and redeems them ' (Pesikta R. 159 b). ' In thy
light we shall see light. What is this light which the congregation
of Israel looks for ? That is the light of the Messiah, as it is said,
God saw the light and it was good. God looked at the Messiah
and his deeds before the world was created, and he hid the [primal
or archetypal] light for his Messiah and for his generation under
the throne of his glory. Then Satan said to God, Lord of the
world, for whom is this light which thou hast hidden under thy
throne of Glory ? God replied, For him who will put thee to shame.
Satan said, Show him to me. God said, Come and see him. When
Satan saw him, he was appalled, and he fell on his face, and he said,
Verily this is the Messiah who will cast me and all the Princes
(*i.e.* the angels) of the nations of the world into hell. In that same
hour, all the nations assembled together, and said to God, Who is
this into whose hands we are to fall, what is his name and his
excellence ? (טיבו). God said, It is Messiah, and his name is
Ephraim, the Messiah of my righteousness (Jer. xxxi. 9, 20). . . .
Then God began to make a bargain (מתנה) with the Messiah,
and said to him, The iniquities of these souls who are stored away
beside thine are destined in the future to bring thee under a yoke
of iron, and they will make thee as a calf whose eyes have become
dim, and they will strangle (משנקים) thy breath under the yoke,
and thy tongue will cleave to thy cheek. Dost thou accept this ?
(Is this thy will ?) The Messiah said, Will this anguish last many
years ? God said, Seven years have I decreed. If thy soul is grieved,
I will cast them out forthwith (*i.e.* he will annihilate all these pre-
existent souls). The Messiah replied, With rejoicing of heart and
soul I accept all this, but under the condition that not one (soul)
from Israel is lost. And not only the living shall be saved in my
day, but those too who are hidden in the dust, and not only they,

but also all the dead who have died from the days of Adam till now, and not only these, but even the abortions shall be saved in my day, and not only they, but also all whom thou hadst intended to create, but who were not created. On these conditions I am ready ' (Pesikta Rabbathi 161 a *fin.*, 161 b). (Are we to understand by the last sentence that the salvation which the Messiah is to bring about by his sufferings is not limited to Israel, but is universal ?) ' When the Son of David appears, they will bring beams of iron, and put them on his neck, till his frame is bowed down. And he will cry and weep, and his voice will ascend on high. He will say to God, How great are my spirit, my strength, my limbs ? Am I not flesh and blood ? Then God will reply, Ephraim, my righteous Messiah, long ago didst thou accept all this at the time of the creation. Now let thy pain be as my pain, for since the days when Nebuchadnezzar, the wicked (=, I suppose, Titus), burnt my Temple and caused my children to go into exile among the nations, by thy life, and by the life of my head, I have not ascended my throne. If thou believe it not, look upon the dew upon my head. (Canticles v. 2.) Then the Messiah will say, I am appeased ; it is enough for the slave to be as his master ' (Pesikta R. p. 162 a). ' In the time to come, in the month of Nisan, the Patriarchs will say, Ephraim, our righteous Messiah, though we are thy ancestors, thou art greater than we. For thou hast borne the sins of our children, and thou hast borne heavy punishments (מדות) such as neither the former nor the latter generations have endured, and thou becamest the laughter and the mocking of the nations for Israel's sake, and thou didst sit in darkness, and thine eyes saw no light. And thy skin shrank upon thy bones, and thy body withered like a tree, and thine eyes grew dark from fasting, and thy strength dried up like a potsherd, and all this befell thee because of the sins of our children. Is it thy will that thy children should enjoy the felicity, which God has destined to give them in abundance ? Perhaps, because of the pains which thou hast endured in overflowing measure for their sakes, and because thou hast lain fettered in prison, thy mind is not at rest because of them (אין דעתך נוחה מהם). Messiah will reply, Patriarchs, all that I have done, I have done only for your sakes and for your children, and for your honour and theirs, so that they may enjoy the felicity which God has destined to give them in abundance. Then they reply, May thy mind be appeased, for thou hast appeased (הנחת) the mind of thy Creator and our mind ' (Pesikta R. 163 a). It is probably true when S.B. say 'Aber nur Israels Sünde sühnt der Messias. Der Gedanke, dass der Messias die Sünde der Welt, also auch die der Nichtisraeliten, trägt (John i. 29), begegnet uns nirgends in der altrabbinischen Literatur.' [1] For though in one of the quotations from Pesikta R. some of the phrases sounded very universalistic, the prevailing idea was that expressed in a final passage from the Pesikta (not fully given here), where God says to the Messiah, ' Do not fear the nations who roar against thee like a lion, for they shall die by the breath of thy lips ' (Isaiah xi. 4). (Pesikta R. 163 a.) The conception of the Messiah's atoning pains, which in Isaiah liii. were intended for the nations (as I still believe), became limited to Israel. I should add that Moore does not think that the passages about the suffering Messiah in Pesikta R. must be regarded as in any respect the product of genuine Rabbinic thought. ' The work is late, and it is not certain that the Messianic homilies were originally a part of it. To take its testimony for authentic Rabbinic Judaism would be like taking that of a Carolingian author for primitive Christianity. Moreover, the passage in question is palpably an appropriation of Christian doctrine for a Jewish Messiah.' (The ' passage ' means, I take it, all the passages I have quoted from the Pesikta R.) (Moore, *Judaism*, I. p. 551.)

xxi. For the special purpose of this book I have little to say about any verse in this chapter. Faith has been dealt with before. But though really outside the plan of my book, I cannot refrain from quoting the curious parallel, if we can legitimately call it so, to 18–22, because of the strange story in which the ' parallel ' is contained. There was a Rabbi called R. Yose of Yodkart of whom, under certain special circumstances, another Rabbi said, ' How should a man who had no pity for his son or his daughter have any for me ? ' The Talmud then proceeds to relate how he wished for the death of both his son and his daughter, and how that wish (as I understand the tale) was immediately granted. The story about the son is as follows : ' One day R. Yose of Yodkart had

---

[1] ' The Messiah atones for Israel's sin only. That the Messiah carries the sin of the whole world, including, therefore, the sin of the Gentiles, is an idea which we nowhere meet with in the old Rabbinic literature.'

employed some labourers in the field. It became dark before R. Yose brought them something to eat. The labourers therefore complained to R. Yose's son that they were hungry. A fig-tree happened to be in the neighbourhood, so the son of R. Yose turned to that tree saying, Fig-tree, fig-tree! bring forth thy fruit, in order that the labourers of my father may eat. The tree immediately brought forth fruit, and the labourers ate. In the meantime his father (R. Yose) arrived and, addressing the labourers, said, Do not bear me a grudge, the reason I came late is because I was occupied by a matter of charity, and it is only now that I was able to come. They replied : May the Merciful satisfy thy hunger as thy son has satisfied ours. Said R. Yose, What do you mean by that ? They told him what had happened, whereupon R. Yose said, My son ! Thou hast troubled thy Creator to make the fig-tree yield fruit before its time, so mayest thou be gathered in before thy time' (Taanith 24 a ; Dr. Malter's translation, pp. 177 *fin.*, 178).

xxii. 2. The parallels to this parable are so curious that one at least ought perhaps to be given here : more will be found in S.B. In Sabbath 153 a (*cp.* Ecclesiastes R. on ix. 8 *fin.*) we read : ' R. Eliezer said, Repent a day before your death. His disciples asked him, Does a man know on what day he will die ? He replied, All the more let him repent to-day ; perhaps he will die to-morrow ; then he will pass all his days in repentance. R. Yochanan b. Zakkai told a parable. A king invited his servants to a banquet, but did not fix for them a time. The clever ones among them adorned themselves and sat at the entrance of the palace ; for they said, Can anything be wanting in the king's house ? (*i.e.* He has heaps of stores and food, so the banquet might begin quite soon). The foolish ones went on to their work, for they said, How can there be a banquet without preparation ? Suddenly the king asked for his servants. The clever ones came before him adorned, the foolish ones entered all dirty as they were. The king rejoiced over the clever ones : he was angry with the foolish ones, and said, They who adorned themselves for the banquet, let them sit and eat and drink. The others can stand and look on. R. Meir's son-in-law said in R. Meir's name : Then the dirty ones would look like serving-men : rather (the king must have said), Let all sit

down, but let the clean servants eat and drink, while the dirty ones
shall hunger and thirst.'

14. I need not add here anything to what has been said in earlier
passages (*e.g.* p. 207) about Rabbinic particularism and universalism,
and how they compare with the teaching of Jesus. On the whole,
the gloomy pessimism of xxii. 14, or of vii. 13, 14, seems to me less
characteristic of the Rabbis than of Jesus—if indeed these utterances
reflect his real opinion. Somehow, I find it less objectionable if a
teacher, in the heat of his enmity with the ' nations,' sends them
to perdition, than if another teacher in cold blood, and as a portion
of his regular teaching, declares that the large majority of the human
race are doomed to ruin and hell.

21. The ' parallels ' given to this famous verse in S.B. are not
in point. I wonder that they do not quote the well-known utterance
of Samuel, the third-century Rabbi, ' *Dina de-malchuta dina*,'
' the Law of the (gentile) kingdom (or authority) *is* the Law,' *i.e.*
is obligatory upon Jews, for it became so regularly accepted. On
the whole, it would seem to mean something on the same lines as
the saying of Jesus. Obey the authority, when religion is not at
stake. A passage quoted by Moore is very interesting. Enlarging on
the verse in Ecclesiastes (viii. 2) about ' keeping the King's commands,' a Rabbinic author remarks : ' God said to Israel, I adjure
you that if the government imposes on you harsh decrees, you shall
not rebel against it, whatever it decrees. But if it decrees that you
shall nullify the Law and the commandments and the Sabbath, do
not listen to it, but say to it, I will keep the king's command in
everything necessary to you, [but not further, for] it then is not
[merely] stopping you from the commandments, but making you
deny (שתכפרו) God.' The example of Hananiah and his friends
must be followed (Dan. ii. 13-18), who said to Nebuchadnezzar,
' Whatever you impose on us, levy of produce (וארנוניות) or tolls
(מסין) or poll tax (גולגליות), we will obey you, but to deny God we
will not obey you ' (Tanchuma B., *Noah*, xv. 20 a ; Moore II. p. 116).

23-33. S.B. say that the words of Jesus in 30 would have been
opposed to the current views of his age. (' Diese Worte dürften
den landläufigen Anschauungen zur Zeit Jesu durchaus wider-

sprochen haben.') They base this opinion on two grounds. (1) Direct evidence from the Rabbinic literature that in the life of the resurrection people *would* ' marry and be given in marriage ' and would beget and bear children. But the evidence, as they have to admit, is very dubious, and may only refer to the life of the Messianic era. (2) There is a familiar passage from Berachoth 17 a, according to which Rab (who died about A.D. 250) said, ' In the world to come there is no eating and drinking, or procreation and child-bearing, or trade and business, or enmity and strife, but the righteous sit with crowns on their head and enjoy the radiance of the Shechinah.' This passage, however, S.B. interpret to refer to the intermediate state between death and the resurrection, and not to the life *after* resurrection. In the intermediate state the soul lives without the body. That this is so is proved, they think, by a passage from the small tractate Kalla Rabathi. But even if this be correct, there would seem to be other passages, some of them quoted by S.B. themselves, in which non-marrying and non-procreation are referred to, and in which the term ' the world to come ' seems used quite generally, and not to refer specifically to the intermediate state. It is more probable, Mr. Loewe thinks, that, both in Jesus's time as in Rab's time, there was a grosser popular view according to which the life of the resurrection would be thoroughly material, and assimilated, except for its duration and joy, to our own, and another more refined view which is represented by the sayings of Jesus and of Rab. (So far as eating and drinking are concerned, *cp.* Moore I. p. 405. The Rabbis constantly quote Psalm l. 12, 13 for the purpose of showing that, as Moore says, ' there is in heaven no eating or drinking.' ' If Moses, while he was on the sacred mountain for forty days, neither ate nor drank, how much less is there eating and drinking before God ? That is what the words in Psalm l. 12 imply ' (Pesikta 57 b).)

34–40. In this important section there are several different points in regard to which parallels (or contrasts) can be sought. (1) We may ask how far was the Deuteronomic command to love God made much of, and spoken much about, in the Rabbinic literature and by the Rabbis. (2) Similarly, we may ask the same question as regards the love of our neighbour. Was Leviticus xix. 18 made much of, and much spoken about, by the Rabbis ? (3) We may ask whether there are parallels to this bringing together of the two commands to love God and to love man in Rabbinic literature. (4) We may ask whether 'neighbour' to Jesus meant something different from, and wider than, what it meant to any Rabbi. And, lastly (5), we can ask whether there are any good parallels in Rabbinic literature to dividing up the commandments into greater and lesser, or of distinguishing any two, or any one, as the greatest of all.

As regards (1) it may safely be asserted that love towards God was deeply felt by the Rabbis. It cannot be denied that the impression left upon the impartial reader of Rabbinic literature is that the Rabbis had a passionate devotion to their divine Master. In this matter they are certainly not wanting, and they have nothing to learn from Jesus or from anybody else. Nor should we lay too much stress upon the mere number of times in which love to God is actually *spoken* of. The Jesus of the Synoptic Gospels never speaks of love to God except in this single passage (we might add Luke xi. 42). Yet we should, I think, all allow that the general impression of his teaching is that love to God formed an integral part of it, and that he laid great stress upon that love. Nevertheless, except in this one passage, and then only in this quotation from Deuteronomy, he never directly inculcates such love. Yet even if we do not bear this caution much in mind, the Rabbis would have nothing to fear. Here, at least, there can be no contrast made between that attitude of man towards God which Jesus thought best and highest and the attitude which the Rabbis thought best and highest. In both cases it was 'love.' To serve God from love was the purest and best form of service. So definitely declare the Rabbis. The best and most beloved Pharisee is he who serves God from love. (Jer. Berachoth ix. § 7, 14 b.) It is usually maintained that Abraham served God from love, Job from fear, but it is also sometimes allowed that Job also served him from love, and in more than one interesting passage fear and love are intermixed. Thus it is said that there is a fear which is based on love. R. Meir said, In both Job's and Abraham's case it is said that they feared God, and in both cases they feared through love. Yet R. Simeon b. Eleazar held that he who serves from love is greater than he who serves from fear. In all these cases the fanciful proofs from Scripture are, to our taste, much inferior to the statements themselves. They are so verbal and strained. But these proofs are in accordance with the custom of the Rabbis. For instance, in Exodus xx. 6, God is said to show mercy *la' alafim* (plural) to the thousands of those who love him, whereas in Deut. vii. 9 God is said to show mercy to those who love him and keep his commandments, *l'elef dor*, to the thousandth generation. Those who keep his commandments are supposed to be equivalent to those who fear him, and the singular in *l'elef dor* is contrasted with the plural in *la' alafim*. The combination of fear and love is also taught in the famous saying which we find both in Jer. Sotah v. 7, 20 c, and in Jer. Berachoth ix. § 7, 14 b. (S.B. ii. 112.) It has already been quoted on p. 228: 'Act from love, for if thou wouldst hate, know that thou shouldest love, and he who loves, does not hate; act from fear, for if thou wouldst despise, know that nobody who fears, despises.' The meaning seems to be clearer in the Sotah passage which is preceded by the two quotations about loving God (Deut. vi. 5) and fearing him (Deut. vi. 13). The love of God will prevent you from hating and despising any man. ' A man fears his neighbour, and if the latter worries him, he leaves him and goes away, but do thou act from love, for there is no fear where there is love, and no love where there is fear, except in our relation to God' (Sifre 73 a). (This translation, though involving an unparalleled use of the Hebrew word *middah*, is followed by S.B. and Moore, ii. p. 99, and Dr. Büchler informs me that he believes it to be correct. No other rendering makes sense.) ' Love God with all thy heart, *i.e.* with both thy inclinations (both the *Yetzers*); with all thy heart, *i.e.* thy heart must be undivided (in its devotion to God); with all thy soul (= life); even if he take away thy life, as it is said, For thy sake are we killed all the day. With all thy soul: to thy last breath.' Then, punning on the sound of the word ' *Me'od,*' it is said : ' With whatever measure he metes out to thee, good or evil, must thou love him ' (Sifre 73 a, already used on Matt. x. 28 and on the Sermon on the Mount, p. 31). These phrases are repeated with variations again and again. They are even found in the legal Mishnah (Berachoth ix. 5). ' You must bless God (like Job) for the bad as well as for the good,' and then follows what has just been quoted about loving him with both the *Yetzers*. You must bless him even if he takes your life. You must bless him with all your substance, and with whatever measure he metes out to you. Over and over again are these passages, and such as these, repeated. So too do we find the story of Akiba's martyrdom repeated. Famous is the saying, ' Do not learn Torah for the sake of becoming rich or to be called Rabbi, or to acquire a reward : whatever you do, let it only be from love (*i.e.* of God) ' (Sifre 80 a *ad init.*). The disinterestedness of love is realized. Thus (Sukkah 49 b *fin.*) we find this : ' The Torah [that is practised and studied] for its own sake (*lishmah*) is a law of love ; the law [that is practised and studied] not for its own sake is a law without love.' The finest thing about the love of God which I have read is, perhaps, a passage in the Midrash to the Psalms, end of Psalm ix. (46 a). (S.B. do not seem to have it.) The heading to Psalm ix. in R.V. reads, ' To the Chief Musician : set to *Muth-labben.*' What is *Muth-labben* ? Punning on the words, the Midrash says : ' Perhaps it means " concerning the death of the righteous," the sons of the living God, who gave their souls to death for the Unity of the Name. Yet are they not like to dead people, but to sick people, as Solomon says, I am sick of love. (Canticles v. 8.) What does sick mean here ? Not sickness of head or of bowels, but sickness from love of God. And not mere sickness, but even *al mut*, unto death, as it says, They love thee *almuth* (Canticles i. 3), They love thee unto death, and as it says, For thy sake are we killed all the day (Psalm xliv. 23). There is no nation in the world, who, if God said, Go down into the sea, would go down into the sea, except Israel, which gives its life for its God. David said, Up to how far does the son love the Father ? So far that he gives his life for the father's honour. So Shadrach, Meshach, and Abednego were ready to give their lives, not on condition of being saved, but with the intention of being burnt, and why ? Because love is stronger than death. See how far the son loves the Father.' I have already quoted most of this passage in another connection (p. 232).

We may then legitimately say that the student of Rabbinic literature has nothing to learn from the Gospels about the love of God. Here Jesus has nothing new to teach. As regards the love of man, or the love of one's neighbour (question 2), and the meaning of the word neighbour (question 4), see notes on Matthew v. 43. Then as to question 3. Here the matter is complicated. Dr. Abrahams says : ' It does not seem that in any extant Rabbinic text, outside the Testaments of the Twelve Patriarchs, the *Shema* and the love of one's neighbour are associated ' (*Studies* I. p. 28). (In the Testaments an association occurs in Isaachar v. 2, vii. 5 ;

Dan. v. 3.) But as we find the combination in the Didache, and
as the Didache is predominantly Jewish, there seems a good deal of
force in Kohler's arguments that the combination was well known
even as far back as the age of Jesus, and that in a lost Jewish manual
for the instruction of proselytes, we should have found it even as
we find it in the Didache. (*Cp.* Kohler in his articles "Didache" and
"Didascalia" in *J.E.*, and also in his article on "Die Nächstenliebe
im Judentum" in *Festschrift zu H. Cohens siebzigsten Geburtstage*
(*Judaica*) 1912, and also Klein (G.), *Der älteste Christliche Katechis-
mus und die Jüdische Propaganda-Literatur*, 1909.) The question
is not susceptible of proof, and is not of very much importance.
It is certain that there would have been nothing surprising to a
Jewish ear in the collocation. Even Luke, who is not by any means
a wholly unprejudiced historian as regards Jews and Pharisees,
has no objection to the collocation being made, not by Jesus, but
by the Rabbi. He would not have allowed this had he thought that
the collocation was a new and original feature in the teaching of
Jesus. (*Cp.* my note *ad loc.*)

Lastly, comes the question of distinguishing between more
important and less important commands, and of reducing the many
commands of the Law to a few fundamental ones. What S.B. say
in these matters should be supplemented by Dr. Abrahams' chapter
on the 'greatest command' in *Studies*, I. pp. 18–29, by Kohler's
essay, and by the other authorities quoted or alluded to by Abrahams. S.B. are not, in this particular point, adequate by themselves.
The Rabbis, we may say, were familiar with the distinction between
ceremonial and moral commands, and *on the whole* they regarded
the 'moral' as more important and more fundamental than the
'ceremonial.' In this respect they would, to a considerable extent,
have agreed with Jesus. Yet they would not entirely have agreed
with him. Nor was it possible to do so, for men who, like them,
took the Law as it stands as the perfect gift of God, and regarded
the obligation to fulfil it in its entirety as binding upon every
Israelite. Moreover, we must remember that to them the fulfilment of the Law was a privilege and an honour; a joy as well
as a duty. Again, on certain ritual ordinances they laid, for
various reasons, not all of which we can fully appreciate and
understand, the most tremendous stress. Again, there was
some tendency to distinguish 'heavy' and 'light' commands

according to certain punishments or threats which happen to be attached to their infraction in the Codes. Nevertheless, on the whole, the ' heavy ' commands are the moral commands. The ' heaviest ' (apart from circumcision) are commands such as the prohibition of unchastity, idolatry or murder, the honouring of parents, the Sanctification of the Name. The distinction between ' light ' and ' heavy ' commands was well known, and is constantly mentioned and discussed. The ' heavy ' commands are usually the moral commands. Another line of difference, however, between light and heavy was ease and difficulty of fulfilment. This difference would to some extent coalesce with the difference between moral and ceremonial, but not entirely. Circumcision, for instance, was not regarded as easy of fulfilment, as it involved a certain risk to life. Nor was it considered that the lightest commands were rewarded least and the heaviest most. There were two strands in the Rabbinic teaching. One was frankly eudaemonistic : it did not say : ' Act thus for the sake of the reward,' but it did stress the reward. The other strain was opposed to this first one, urging that all fulfilment of the law should be from love, or for its own sake, or from sheer obedience. (All these three tend to run together and coalesce.) But when reward was spoken of, it was noted that, so far as the rewards of fulfilment took place upon earth, the Law did not differentiate much between one law and another. In a famous passage in Kiddushin (39 b) it is specially noted that the reward assigned to one of the most important of all commands (honouring of parents) and to the lightest of all commands (Deut. xxii. 7) is precisely the same. (See above, p. 37.) R. Jacob argues that the reward always refers to the life to come. (He quotes a case where in one and the same act both commands were fulfilled, and the son, so far from prolonging his days upon earth, died on the spot.)

Though the commands could be divided into light and heavy, and though the practical good sense, and the right religious feeling, of the Rabbis made them realize well the supereminent position of such negative commands as idolatry, murder, unchastity, and such positive commands as the Sanctification of the Name and the veneration of parents, yet the obligation of obedience to every command was equally binding. There were, as we have seen, nonmoral commands on which they laid tremendous stress, such as circumcision, or the Sabbath, and, again, there were moral commands over and above those that have been mentioned on which they felt no less deeply. Slander, for example, and putting another man to open shame, were held to be terrible sins ; and as regards positive commands, there is the famous and constantly quoted passage in the Mishnah of Peah (i. 1) as to the special place of charity (doing of loving deeds), making peace between man and man, and (once more) the reverence of parents, while the study of the Law is said to be as important as all of them together. Not only were all the commandments equally binding, but for the observance of each command there would be a reward. There is, as I have said, in Rabbinic teaching a complete blending and mingling together of the two points of view. On the one hand you are to act from love, for the law's own sake, *lishmah* ; on the other hand you may, and even ought to, remember that to every fulfilment God will assign its reward, whether in this world or the next. The state-ments made on the subject of reward are by no means consistent : they range from a denial of any reward in *this* world to an assertion that even the lightest command has its reward in *both* worlds. The sentence in Aboth (ii. 1), ' Be heedful of a light precept as of a grave one, for thou knowest not the grant of reward for each precept ' is well known. It was often quoted. Hence it was suggested that in the Pentateuch God had deliberately not assigned definite rewards to particular commands so that men might not be only assiduous to fulfil those commands to which the biggest rewards were attached. (About all this see Abrahams' essay in *Studies*, especially pp. 26, 27.) The Rabbis are perfectly frank and naïve in the whole matter, but if they are sincere about reward, they are no less sincere in their insistence on ' all for love,' ' all for its own sake,' ' all *lishmah*.' They are, in truth, always sincere, simple, and in undress. One Rabbi declared that the law of fringes weighed as heavily as all the other commandments. This was said sincerely, and yet, doubt-less, half playfully. It was said sincerely, because the Rabbi felt that by looking upon the fringes a man might be helped to remember all his other duties to God and do them. (' Sight leads to remem-brance, remembrance to doing.' *Cp.* the words in Numbers xv. 39, 40.) [1] On the other hand, only a few sentences later (Menachoth

---

[1] In Midrash Psalms on xc. (18) R. Hezekiah remarks that in Numbers xv. 39 the singular (Him) is used, not the plural (them, *i.e.* fringes). ' When they shall be to you for fringes, then you shall see Him (אתו) and remember His commands.'

43 b and 44 a), we are told 'there is no light command in the Law for which there is no reward in this world; the reward in the next world cannot be measured' (we know it not). The fringes law is then cited as an instance of such a light law, and its reward in this world is illustrated by a strange and touching story, illustrative of how a Rabbi could be both discerning and broad-minded. (It is a story which ends with a happy marriage between a repentant Jew and a repentant Gentile, who became a proselyte to Judaism.) [1]

Thus we are always brought back, it seems to me, to the same conclusion. The Pentateuch was both an inspiration and a bondage. The Rabbis took *all* its greatness and absorbed it. They took also *some* of its weakness and absorbed it. For by the terms of their faith they could not distinguish between one verse and another. All was the utterance, and every command embodied the will and purpose, of the perfect God, perfect in wisdom, perfect in righteousness, perfect in lovingkindness. Yet the Rabbis struggle (unconsciously) in their chains and against their limitations, for all these distinctions between light and heavy commands, all this insistence on 'for its own sake,' 'all for love,' all this special stress on 'moral' commands such as chastity and love of neighbour and so on, are extra-Pentateuchal; they are read *into* the text, and are not to be found *in* the text. They are rather due to the Prophets than to the Law, and may most properly be assigned to the credit of the Rabbis themselves. Jesus was less fettered than they were : the Law meant to him much less than it meant to them ; he was much less saturated with it than they : the Prophets were dearer to him than the Law, even though, theoretically, he (like Paul) held that the whole Law was God-given and inspired.

The Rabbis were also able—and it speaks volumes for their high moral sense, when one remembers their chains—to reduce the many commandments to a few fundamental ones. We have first of all Hillel's famous saying, ' What is hateful to you, do not to thy neighbour. This is the whole Law ; the rest is commentary,' concerning which something has been said on Matt. v. 43. In the Aboth R. Nathan it is called the Principle, or Substance, of the Law. The word *Kelal* is also used by Akiba and Ben Azzai in their

---

[1] The story is also found in Sifre 35 b, and is given in Midrash Sifre on Numbers translated by the Rev. P. P. Levertoff (S.P.C.K., 1926), pp. 111, 112.

famous aphorisms. As Dr. Abrahams says, they meant by *Kelal*
'a general or basic command from which all the other commands
could be deduced. They were not discriminating between the importance or unimportance of laws so much as between their fundamental or derivative character' (*Studies*, I. p. 24). 'R. Akiba said
that "Thou shalt love thy neighbour as thyself" was the great
(or chief, or greatest) general principle in the Law; Ben Azzai
said, "*This is the book of the generations of man*" is a greater
principle than the other.' Dr. Abrahams says, 'There is no difference between these Tannaim on the question itself: love of one's
fellow-man is fundamental, but while Akiba derives the conclusion
from Leviticus xix. 18, Ben Azzai points back to the story of the
Creation, to *the book of the generations of man*, as the basis of the
solidarity of the human race, and the obligation that accrues to
every man to love his fellow. Akiba himself elsewhere traces the
same duty to another phrase in the Genesis story (Mishnah Aboth
iii. 18, in Taylor III. 21): "Beloved is man in that he was created
in the image of God" (Genesis ix. 6; *cf.* the quotation from Genesis
Rabbah above). As Taylor remarks on this last passage in the
Mishnah (*Sayings of the Jewish Fathers*, ed. 2, p. 56): "Man is
beloved by God in whose image or likeness he was created; and
he should be beloved by his fellow-men as a consequence of this
love towards God himself"' (*Studies*, I. p. 20). Of this passage,
too, more has been said in the note on Matt. v. 43. S.B. also quote
Bar Kappara, who said, 'Which is the little sentence (or the very
small section) on which all the main matters (principles, or divisions)
of the Law depend? It is (Prov. iii. 6): In all thy ways acknowledge him, and he will direct (or make level) thy paths (Berachoth
63 a).' Here it may be noticed that the verb used corresponds exactly
with the verb in Matt. xxii. 40. In the middle of the third century
R. Simlai told how David, Isaiah, Micah, Amos, and Habakkuk
reduced the commandments of the Law from 613 to eleven, six,
three, two, and one. Dr. Abrahams translates the passage as follows:
'Six hundred and thirteen precepts were imparted to Moses, three
hundred and sixty-five negative (in correspondence with the days
of the solar year) and two hundred and forty-eight positive (in
correspondence with the number of a man's limbs). David came
and established them (lit. *made them stand, based them*, הֶעֱמִידָן)
as eleven, as it is written (Ps. xv.): Lord, who shall sojourn in

thy tent, who shall dwell in thy holy mountain ? (i.) He that walketh uprightly, and (ii.) worketh righteousness, and (iii.) speaketh the truth in his heart. (iv.) He that back-biteth not with his tongue, (v.) nor doeth evil to his neighbour, (vi.) nor taketh up a reproach against another ; (vii.) in whose eyes a reprobate is despised, (viii.) but who honoureth them that fear the Lord. (ix.) He that sweareth to his own hurt, and changeth not; (x.) he that putteth not out his money to usury, (xi.) nor taketh a bribe against the innocent. He that doeth these things shall never be moved. Thus David reduced the Law to *eleven* principles. Then Isaiah came and established them as *six* (xxxiii. 15): (i.) He that walketh in righteousness and (ii.) speaketh uprightly ; (iii.) he that despiseth the gain of deceits, (iv.) that shaketh his hands from holding of bribes, (v.) that stoppeth his ears from hearing of blood, and (vi.) shutteth his eyes from looking upon evil. Then came Micah and established them as *three* (Micah vi. 8) : What doth the Lord require of thee but (i.) to do justice, (ii.) to love mercy, and (iii.) to walk humbly with thy God ? Once more Isaiah established them as *two* (Is. lvi. 1): Thus saith the Lord: (i.) Keep ye judgment, and (ii.) do righteousness. Then came Amos and established them as *one* (Amos v. 4) : Thus saith the Lord, Seek ye me, and ye shall live, or (as R. Nachman b. Isaac preferred) : Habakkuk came and made the whole Law stand on one fundamental idea (Habakkuk ii. 4) : The righteous man liveth by his faith ' (*Studies*, I. 23). In the parallel in Tanchuma B. x., *Shofetim*, 16 b, Amos is said to have ' established ' them as two —' seek me (1) and live (2) '—while Habakkuk reduced them to one. For other variants and many interesting remarks and notes see Bacher, *Agada der palästinenischen Amoräer*, Vol. I. pp. 557–559. The attempt of S.B. III. p. 543 to prove that R. Simlai meant to disparage the value of Habakkuk's praise of faith must be regarded as a failure. Its polemical intention is fairly obvious. Rashi's remarks upon Rabbi Simlai's utterance cannot justly be used to substantiate S.B.'s opinion.

Thus, on the whole, we may say that the famous reply of Jesus (or of the scribe, as Luke has it) is in general accordance with Rabbinic opinion. It is not off the line, even though it may be added with Dr. Abrahams : ' We may suppose, however, that just as there were scruples in later ages (Chagigah 11 b), so not everyone in the age of Jesus was willing to admit these gradations.

. . . The questioner of Jesus desired an opinion as to whether Jesus did or did not share this fear of reducing the Law to fundamental rules' (p. 27). When all is said, however, it remains true that no simple, orthodox Rabbinic Jew of, say, the third century, if he had read or been told the Gospel story (without names !), would have protested, or thought that he was being told anything very novel or very extravagant.

xxiii. It would be outside the scope and purpose of this book to deal with the subject-matter of 1–36. It may, however, be mentioned that many of the sins which are attacked by Jesus in this section are also attacked by the Rabbis. It is obvious that some of these sins would be common to the ministers and clergymen and teachers of every age or religion. Among all such classes there would, for example, always be *some* persons who preach and do not practise. The Jewish objection to the attack in the section 1–36 is that the condemnation is not based on the exceptions, on the black sheep, but on the class as a whole, as if either *all* the Rabbis of the age of Jesus were hypocrites and vipers, or as if all Rabbis were *necessarily* hypocrites and vipers. That there were black sheep among the Rabbis of the first century would be freely conceded, and it is possible (though not certain) that the percentage of the black sheep was higher in the first century than afterwards. If it be once allowed (1) that it was unfair on the part of Jesus to tar all Rabbis, or all the Rabbis of his age, with the same brush, *or* (2) that he really did not do this, *or* (3) that he did not mean to do this, and that it is the fault of Matthew the ' editor,' the whole dispute would be at an end.

3. Both here and in some of the other verses S.B. have given the parallels very fairly. There are many Rabbinic sayings to the effect that ' he who learns, but does not do, had better never have been born.' ' He who learns, and does not do, will be more severely punished than he who neither learns nor does.' ' The interior of a Rabbi or of a disciple of the wise must correspond with his exterior ; he is no true disciple of the wise, or no true Rabbi, where the former does not agree with the latter.' And the doing must be *lishmah*, for the sake of the commands ; if not, it were better that such a disciple or Rabbi had never been born ' (Leviticus Rabba, *Bechuk-*

kothai, xxxv. 7 on xxvi. 3; Berachoth 17 a). One might add the passage from Yoma 72 b quoted on p. 118.

4. As to the heavy burdens there are, as S.B. show, some indications that the many Rabbinical additions or fences to the written Law were occasionally criticized adversely by the Rabbis themselves. One Rabbi said, ' Do not make the fence too high lest it fall and injure the plants ' (Gen. R., בראשית, xix. 3 on iii. 2). There is a very interesting passage which, with variants, occurs in both Talmuds as to certain Rabbinic ordinances. R. Joshua, who was always on the ' liberal ' side, compared the matter to pouring water into a jar which is full of oil; the oil runs over to waste. (Jer. Sabbath i. 3 c.) Or (as the Babylonian Talmud has it), as if, in a trough full of honey, you add pomegranates and nuts—the honey will exude. (Sabbath 153 b.) The sin of making the Law burdensome for others and evading it oneself is also alluded to by the Rabbis. Some of them specially say that they always took the severer line with themselves ; their decisions and interpretations were less rigorous for others than for themselves (*e.g.* Berachot 22 a ; Jer. Berachot i. 2, 3 a). And one of the many explanations given in the Gemara of the ' sly rogue ' mentioned in the Mishnah Sotah iii. 4 is the man who makes the Law easy for himself and hard for others (interprets on the easy side for himself, on the rigorous side for others). (Jer. Sotah iii. 3, 19 a ; Sotah 21 b.) All this doubtless shows that some of the sins of which Jesus here speaks were actual sins among actual bad Rabbis, but there is no good evidence that the percentage of bad Rabbis to the whole body of Rabbis was very high. A pretty story (S.B. II. p. 12) is told of R. Meir, who, against the view of other Rabbis of his day, allowed wine and oil to be mixed together on the Sabbath, and rubbed into or on to the sick. When *he* was ill, and his disciples wanted to do this, he would not allow it, and when his disciples demurred, and quoted his own ruling, he said : ' If I have ruled for others in the more easy way, I decide for myself in the harder way, for my colleagues did not agree with me in this my ruling' (Jer. Berachoth i. § 2, 3 a).

5. Here again the good Rabbis, the real representatives of Rabbinic Judaism, the typical products of legalism, took the same view as Jesus. S.B.'s quotations are fair, and could be added to.

It is rather stiff of S.B. to argue from these Rabbinic injunctions against some particular sin that therefore this sin must have been very prevalent, because otherwise these injunctions would not have been made. Were the injunctions of the Sermon on the Mount only made because of prevalent sins ? Surely ideals of morality are not stated and enjoined merely because of prevalent sins. But S.B. are pulled both ways. On the one hand, they are too honest not to give the Rabbinic injunctions which are closely parallel to the injunctions of Jesus ; on the other hand, as every passage attributed to Jesus must be authentic, and as every word in these passages must be perfect, and therefore justifiable and accurate, they are driven to show by every possible argument, good, bad, and indifferent, that all the charges against the Rabbis in xxiii. were entirely true and exact. We observe in S.B. a similar phenomenon to what we observe in the Rabbis. The written word is both an inspiration and a burden. With the Rabbis it is the Pentateuch ; with S.B. it is the text of the Gospels.

Already Hillel (Aboth i. 13) had said, ' He who makes a worldly use of the crown of the Torah shall waste away.' And *cp.* the passages about R. Tarphon and R. Zadok quoted on p. 225. In the enumeration of the seven kinds of Pharisees as given at the end of Jer. Berachoth, the first class is explained to be those who carry the commandments ' on the shoulder,' which is supposed to mean those who observe the commands in an ostentatious manner. Thus ostentatious piety is one of the inferior or spurious kinds of Pharisaism which the Talmud repudiates or condemns.

8. For this verse the passages in Nedarim 62 a and Sifre 80 a (*init.*) may also be used. Similar is the passage in Sifre 84 b, ' Perhaps you might say, I will learn Torah so that I may be called wise, or sit in the College, or gain long days in the world to come ; therefore it says, Thou shalt love the Lord your God ' (*i.e.* the learning must be only done from love).

11, 12. As to the ideas in these verses something has been said already in earlier notes. There can, I think, be little doubt that there was a considerable class consciousness among the Rabbis, a considerable pride in their profession, or rather a considerable pride in learning. This pride was quite consistent with individual

humility. Tremendous respect was paid to the Rabbi with acknowledged reputation and position. The story about Gamaliel, which
has already been quoted, is quite enough to prove this. To ' wait
on ' the older and more learned and full-fledged Rabbi was a duty
of the disciples. Did not R. Akiba say that he who does not wait
on the wise is worthy of death ? (Derech Eretz Zuta viii., שימש דלא
חכימיא קטלא חייב.) Yet the idea that ' he who is greatest among
you shall be your servant ' was, I think, a novel one. A society
in which the leaders should literally be servants is, however, very
difficult of realization, and, in spite of the words and injunctions
of Jesus, has seldom been realized. The abbot and the prior were
scarcely the mere servants of any monastery, and even the attempt
of St. Francis in this respect soon failed. Still, the ideal is a fine
one, and in the sense that the object or purpose of a leader is to
serve unselfishly those whom he leads, it can be, and has been,
fulfilled.

ὁ δὲ μείζων ὑμῶν ἔσται ὑμῶν διάκονος. Further reflection leads
me to believe that, in a somewhat different form and manner, the
Rabbis were also anxious that the community should come first,
and that its needs should be adequately looked after. They did
not say anything as notable and pregnant as ὃς ἂν θέλῃ ἐν ὑμῖν
εἶναι πρῶτος, ἔσται ὑμῶν δοῦλος, but they did, I think, feel that
the leaders of a community were under a grave responsibility to
serve it well, and that even sacred study should not, by any means,
invariably dispense a man from giving up part of his time to its
affairs.

To begin with, the whole community of Israel, which is reflected
in, or represented by, each distinct community in any separate
locality, was much more important (as they believed) in the eyes
of God than any individual Israelite. They never abandoned the
' collective ' point of view of the O.T., even though they had also
adopted and intensified the later individualism. The community
of Israel forms a sort of real, if mystical, personality. It is because
the community is known to, and beloved by, God that God knows
and loves each individual which composes it. (The quotations
which follow are all taken from Ziegler, *Die sittliche Welt des Judentums*, II. pp. 332–340.) ' The sacrifices of the community (ציבור)
are acceptable to God, and make atonement between Israel and
its Father in heaven ' (Tosefta Shekalim i. § 6, p. 174). ' Moses

said to God, I am one and Israel is six hundred thousand. Often have they sinned, and I have prayed for them, and thou hast forgiven them : thou hast had regard for the six hundred thousand, wilt thou not have regard to me ? God replied, The doom (גזרה) of a community cannot be compared with the doom of an individual ' (Tanchuma *Vaetchanan* 4 b). ' God does not reject the prayer of the multitude ' (רבים). (Sifre 51 a.) ' In an acceptable time ' (Ps. lxix. 14). ' When is that ? When the community prays.' (Berachoth 8 a.) ' Get thee down ' (Exodus xxxii. 7). ' What does this mean ? R. Eleazar said, God spake to Moses, Get you down from your greatness : I gave you greatness only because of Israel ; now that Israel has sinned, what art thou to me ? ' (Berachoth 32 a.)

Hence the Israelite's duty is to be one with the community ; never to live in isolation from it, to promote its unity, to share its joys and its sorrows, to serve it and help it according to his power. ' Israel will only then be redeemed when it forms one single band (אגדה) : when all are united, they will receive the presence of the Shechinah (Tanchuma B. iv., *Nitzabim* 25 a ; Tanchuma *Nitzabim* 25 b). Therefore, Hillel said, Separate not thyself from the community ' (Aboth ii. 5). So too Samuel said, ' Let not a man ever betake himself outside of the whole body ' (exclude himself from the community) (אל יוציא אדם את עצמו מן הכלל). (Berachoth 49 b *ad fin*.) ' The Rabbis teach : When Israel is in trouble, and one among them separates himself, the two angels of the Service who accompany a man, lay their hands on his head, and say, This man who has separated himself from the community, shall not see its consolation. And it is taught : If the community is in trouble, a man must not say, I will go to my house and eat and drink, and peace shall be with thee, O my soul. But a man must share in the trouble of the community, even as Moses did. He who shares in its troubles is worthy to see its consolation ' (Taanith 11 a). It is the Israelite's duty to occupy himself with, and to give time to, the affairs of the community. ' When R. Assi was dying, his nephew saw him weeping. He said, Why do you weep ? Is there any bit of the Law which you have not learnt ? Your disciples sit before you. Is there any deed of lovingkindness which you have not done ? And over and above all these qualities, you have kept yourself far from the judge's office, and you have not brought it over yourself to be appointed as an official for the needs of the community. He

replied, That is why I weep. Perhaps I shall have to give an account
(*i.e.* be condemned) because I was able to be a judge and did not
judge. A man who retires to his house, and says, What have I to
concern myself with the burden of the community, or with their
suits, why should I listen to their voice ; peace to thee, O my soul
—such a one destroys the world ' (Tanchuma *Mishpatim*, 91 a).
' He who sacrifices himself (מוסר עצמו) for Israel is worthy of
greatness and the Holy Spirit. (Numbers R. *Beha-alotecha*, xv. 20
on xi. 16.) R. Jeremiah said, He who occupies himself with the
affairs of the community is as one who studies the Law ' (Jer.
Berachoth iv. § 1, 8 d). ' R. Yochanan said that one may make
provision for (מפקחין פיקוח נפש ופיקוח רבים) saving of life and
for helping the community on the Sabbath, and one may go to the
synagogue to deal with the affairs of the many on the Sabbath,
and R. Jonathan said that one may visit theatres and circuses
and basilica on the Sabbath to deal with the affairs of the community.
For it says in Isaiah " thine own business "—that is forbidden,
business of heaven is allowed.' Thus the affairs of the community
are regarded as ' business of heaven ' (Sabbath 150 a). ' R. Judah
said, I once walked behind R. Akiba and R. Eleazar b. Azariah,
and the time came for saying the *Shema*, and it seemed to me that
they forbore (שנתיאשו) to say it because they were engaged on
affairs of the community ' (Tosefta Berachoth i. § 4, p. 1). For a
sin which a man has committed, and for which he deserves death
from the hand of God, what can he do so as to live ? If he is learned,
it is suggested that he study two pages of Bible and Talmud a
day, instead of one, and if he be not learned, let him become an
officer of the community or a superintendent of the poor. (Lev. R.,
קדושים, xxv. 1 *init.* on xix. 23.) And all work for the community,
all office-bearing, must be done for the sake of God (לשם שמים).
(Aboth ii. 2.) ' He who receives office (שררה) in order to profit
from it is like an adulterer, who gets his pleasure from a woman's
body ' (Pesikta R. 111 a). ' When leaders of the community are
found to be trustworthy, then they are worthy to pray for rain
and to be answered ' (Jer. Taanith i. § 4, 64 b). ' So long as a man
is only a simple Chaber, he is not bound to the community (he
need not concern himself with its affairs), and he is not punished
for its sins, but when he is appointed to a post and receives the
Talith of investiture, then he must not say, I am only concerned

with my own good, I am not bound to the community. On the contrary. All the burden of the community is upon him. If he sees a man doing wrong to his neighbour, or committing a sin, and he does not stop him, he shall be punished for his neglect ; the Holy Spirit says to him, You are responsible for your neighbour ; God says to him, You have entered the arena, and he who enters the arena must either be conquered or conquer. God says to him, You and I stand in the arena : either you conquer or I conquer you ' (Exodus R., *Jethro*, xxvii. 9 on xviii. 1). ' When the small obey the great, but the great do not carry the burden of the small, God will come to judgment ' (Ruth R. Introd. § 6 on i. 2). One of the three people about whom God weeps is the officer (פרנס) who is haughty (המתגאה) towards the community. (Chagigah 5 b.) ' God says, I am called holy, you are called holy ; if you have not all the qualities (המדות) which I have, you should not accept leadership (שררה). (Pesikta R. 111 a *ad fin.*) Moses said to God, when he asked God to pardon the people of Israel, If thou pardon them not, I should feel ashamed before my fathers, who would say, See the leader (פרנס) whom God has set over them ; he seeks greatness for himself ; he does not ask mercy for *them* ' (alluding to God's suggestion in Exodus xxxii. 10). (Berachoth 32 a.)

It would appear from these quotations as if the spirit which informs the great saying of Jesus, ' He who would be great among you, let him be your servant,' was not really alien or unknown to the Rabbis.

12. That humility is one of the greatest of the virtues was also taught by the Rabbis, and for the saying in 12 there are exact parallels—all variants of the general statement : ' him who humbles himself God will exalt, him who exalts himself God will humble ' (Erubin 13 b). Especially would he who exalts himself through the Law be abased and cast down, while he who abases himself for the sake of the Law shall be exalted. (Aboth R. Nathan xi. 23 b.) The whole passage of which S.B. give only this one sentence is worth quoting. ' Let not a man put a crown on his own head ; let others put it there. R. Akiba said, He who exalts himself because of the Law is like a dead body thrown on the road : every passer-by puts his hand to his nose and runs away. Ben Azzai said : If a man makes himself ugly for the Torah's sake, and eats dried dates, and

wears dirty clothes, and sits and watches at the doors of the wise, the passer-by calls him a fool, but at the end all the Torah will be with him.' (Cp. Berachoth 63 b with Levy's *Rabbinic Dictionary* under נבל, p. 327, col. 2.) 'He who walks with an erect carriage even a distance of four cubits is as though he pushed against the feet of the Shechinah' (Berachoth 43 b *fin.*). There are a number of familiar sayings about haughtiness in Sotah 4 b and 5 a. 'The haughty man (he in whom is נסות רוח) is as if he practised idolatry ; he is as if he denied God (כופר בעיקר); he is as if he committed every forbidden sexual act (כא על כל העריות). Let a man learn from the action of his Maker, who passed by all the tall mountains, and let his Shechinah rest on Mount Sinai, and he passed by all the beautiful trees, and let his Shechinah rest on a thorn bush. He who is haughty deserves to be hewn down like an idol. Over the haughty the Shechinah laments. God says : the haughty man and I cannot live together in the world. Him who is humble the Scripture regards as if he had offered all the offerings of the Law' (Sotah 5 b. Cp. Aboth v. 22). Among the forty-eight qualities by which the Torah is acquired, we find 'humility,' and 'claiming no merit for oneself,' but also 'waiting on the wise' and 'faith in the wise' (Aboth vi. 6). The utmost humility, on the one hand, but the utmost respect for superior knowledge, on the other, seem both of them to be Rabbinic ideals. I cannot forbear adding here a nice quotation which ought to have been given on the discussion about Learning and Doing. 'Rabbi Elazar said, what was the blessing which Moses said over the Law? It was: Blessed art thou, O Lord our God, who hast chosen this Law, and sanctified it, and hast pleasure in those who follow (literally, do) it. He did not say, In those who toil in it or in those who meditate on it, but in those who do it. A man may say, I have learnt neither wisdom nor the Law (*Torah*), what am I to do ? God replies, All wisdom and all *Torah* is one easy thing : every one who fears me and *does* the words of the Law (*Torah*), he has all wisdom and the whole *Torah* in his heart' (Deut. R. *Berachah* xi. 6).

13. The sin of hypocrisy is as much condemned by the Rabbis as by Jesus. The noun and the verb *chanufa* and *chanaf* can mean, however, both flattery as well as hypocrisy, and must sometimes be translated by the one and sometimes by the other. ' The hypocrite

brings God's wrath upon the world.' 'The hypocrite will fall into hell.' These, and other sentences of similar kind, come from Sotah 41 b. 'Four classes of men never receive the face of the Shechinah : mockers, hypocrites, liars, and slanderers' (Sotah 42 a). And so on. (*Cp.* Yoma 86 b, quoted on p. 119 *init.*)

15. The story of Jewish proselytism is of deep interest ; it has never been told with complete impartiality and accuracy and in adequate detail, but the plan of this book precludes my entering upon the fascinating subject here.

23, 26. The charge is one which doubtless was true for certain bad Rabbis of the first century. It is one which is familiar to us as levied against all institutional religions, which lay stress upon any outward forms. In all such religions, there will be formalists who stress the ' outward ' and neglect the ' inward.' To tithe cummin is, after all, easier than to show love. It is noteworthy that Jesus is made to say, ' though not to leave the others undone.' One wonders whether he would really have said that. Amos and Isaiah would not. But, then, they had not before them a written book which *ex hypothesi* was Mosaic, perfect and divine. The Law had come ' in between.' And Jesus would not, theoretically, have denied that the Law was Mosaic, perfect and divine, however much his true heart was with Amos and Hosea rather than with the ceremonial Law. The Rabbis could hardly be expected to take a line similar to that of Jesus. To them, even to the ' good ' Rabbis, though justice and love were of enormous and sovereign importance, yet tithing was a matter of very great importance too. One reason for this, Mr. Loewe holds, was that there was no legal sanction to enforce the payment of tithes, etc. ; this was a matter of honour. If a man evaded tax-paying, he was soon made to suffer, but if he evaded tithes, he did so with impunity, and others (priests, levites, or the poor) suffered. Hence this was an offence against honour, like cheating at cards. Thus the law of tithing was carried out with extraordinary scrupulosity, and the animus against the *Am ha-Aretz* and the dislike of eating with him were largely due to the suspicion under which he laboured of being inexact and care-less as regards the law of tithing. It may be remarked that S.B. state that tithing did not, however, extend to mint, though it did include ' anise and cummin.' As to the distinction between light and heavy, that has been spoken about before. The Rabbis would certainly have agreed that justice, fidelity, mercy, are all ' heavy ' commands, but they would not have allowed that tithing was ' light.'

xxiv. One can read in S.B. much interesting illustrative Rabbinic material in relation to this chapter, but for my purpose there is nothing in the chapter to which either parallel or contrast need be given.

xxv. 1. For the Rabbinic parallels to the parable of the Virgins see xxii. 2. (For a possibly truer explanation of the parable see Prof. Burkitt's article in *J.T.S.*, April 1929, pp. 267-270. He thinks that the fuller reading of verse one, now found in the old Latin version, viz. ' to meet the bridegroom *and the bride,*' is the original and right reading.)

14-30. The parable of the talents. S.B. do not give, and I have not found, a parable or teaching of precisely similar character in the Rabbinic literature, that is, if the parable means that ' the gifts and favours which God has given are to be used in his service ; they are, as it were, to be given back to God with increase ; they who so act will also themselves reap their reward.' The parable thus interpreted would not, however, be off the Rabbinic line. If it merely means that ' man's powers are to be used ; they are not to be neglected or allowed to rust ; inaction spells loss ; he who does not go forward, goes back,' then see xiii. 12.

Mr. Loewe has called my attention to a parable in Yalkut on Deut. vi. 4, § 837, folio 292 a. The story seems confused, and the text in disorder. There is a King who has two servants, one who fears and loves the King, one who only fears him. The King goes away, and apparently leaves his palace and estate to these two servants to deal with. The one who only fears the King does nothing, and the gardens and grounds become waste and desolate : the one who loves the King plants trees and flowers and fruits. When the King returns, he is pleased with the one servant and angry with the other. The point, however, of the parable is the difference of the reward of the servant who loves from the reward of the servant who only fears. He who loves God will enjoy both this world and the future world. Israel loves his Father who is in Heaven, and will inherit the world to come. The idolater has this world only.

21. The passage quoted by S.B. is rather nice. (Tanchuma *Shemoth* 61 b and Exodus Rabba ii., *Va-era* on iii. 1.) ' God does not give greatness to a man till he has proved him in a small matter : only then he promotes him to a great post. Two were proved and found faithful, and God promoted them to greatness. He tested David with the sheep . . . and God said, Thou wast found faithful with the sheep, I will give to thee *my* sheep that thou shouldst feed them. And so with Moses, who fed his father-in-law's sheep. To him God said the same ' (*cp.* on Matt. xviii. 12).

31–46. I am not interested in giving the various Rabbinic views about heaven and hell, or about the length and degree of punishment after death. The curious in such matters can now read the immense excursuses dealing with the subject in S.B. Vol. IV. The opinions of the Rabbis belong as much to the limbo of the past as the opinions of Jesus upon the same topics. The life after death is a hope, a yearning, a faith : its nature was disclosed neither to Jesus nor to the Rabbis. All that modern Jews are concerned with is in disbelieving any doctrine of ' eternal punishment ' or ' everlasting fire ' ; any doctrine of hell, or of after-death punishment, in fact, the purpose of which is not remedial and disciplinary ; ' Gehenna ' must lead to ' Paradise.' The views of Jesus about hell seem to have been no better and no worse than those of his contemporaries. There is no satisfactory evidence that he would have rejected, or that he did reject, the doctrine of eternal punishment any more than they did. The arguments which play with the words αἰώνιος seem to me very feeble. I feel pretty confident that eternal life meant to Jesus what it means to any unsophisticated man to-day : a life which goes on or endures for ever. So, too, eternal punishment meant a punishment which goes on or endures for ever.

On the other hand, that few *Israelites* were supposed to remain for ever in hell seems probable. Even of those who perished with Korah, the arch rebel, it is said in one place that they will return from hell. ' R. Judah b. Bathera said, They will have a share in the world to come : for what is lost will, at the last, be sought for.'

(A play upon, and a combination of, the two verses Numbers xvi. 33 and Psalms cxix. 176.) ' So too did Hannah pray for them, as it is said, The Lord casts down to Sheol (= Hell) and brings up again ' (Numbers R., *Korah*, xviii. 13). In general one may say that the Rabbinic views about the future life, about heaven and hell, about the last judgment, about temporary Gehennas and permanent Gehennas, about annihilation and endless ' punishment,' are very fluid. One can collect a mass of sayings and utterances from a heap of different Rabbis. There are few dogmatic and authoritative statements. The two chief dogmatic ones ought, perhaps, to be quoted here, well known and familiar as they are. The first is in Rosh ha-Shanah 16 b. On account of the importance of the passage, I have not translated it myself, but asked Mr. Loewe to do so for me, and he has added some footnotes. ' We have learnt in a Baraita (Tosefta Sanhedrin xiii. 3, p. 434) : The School of Shammai say, On the day of judgment there will be three classes, one consisting of the perfectly righteous, one of the perfectly wicked, and one of the intermediates. The first are straightway inscribed and sealed for perfect life, and the third are likewise straightway sealed for Gehinnom,[1] as it is said, And many of them that sleep in the dust of the earth shall awake, some to everlasting life and some to shame and everlasting contempt (Daniel xii. 2). The intermediate descend to Gehinnom and cry out, as it is said, And I will bring the third part through the fire and will refine them as silver is refined, and will try them as gold is tried : they shall call on my name, and I will hear them : I will say, It is my people : and they shall say, The Lord is my God (Zech. xiii. 9), and of them Hannah said, The Lord it is that slays and quickens; though he bring down to Sheol, he raises up (1 Sam. ii. 6). Beth Hillel taught: Abundant in lovingkindness (Ex. xxxiv. 6) means that he inclines towards the direction of lovingkindness. About them David said, I love the Lord because he has heard the voice of my supplications (Ps. cxvi. 1) : with reference to these intermediates also did David compose the whole section, I was brought low and he helped me (*ib.* 6). Those Jews and those Gentiles who sin with their bodies descend to Gehinnom and are judged there for twelve months. After twelve months their bodies are wasted

---

[1] I have left Gehinnom untranslated, because of its double sense of ' hell ' and ' purgatory.'

away, their breath (soul) is burnt; the wind scatters them
under the feet of the righteous, as it is said, And ye shall tread
down the wicked : for they shall be ashes under the soles of
your feet in the day that I shall do [this], says the Lord of Hosts
(Mal. iii. 21). But the *Minim*, the Informers,[1] the Atheists, who
repudiate the Law and deny the resurrection, and who separate
themselves from the ways of the congregation,[2] and who (for their
own purposes) cause panic in the land of the living, and who cause
the multitude to sin, *e.g.* Jeroboam, son of Nebat, and his fellows,
these descend to Gehinnom, and are judged there for generation
after generation, as it says, And they shall go forth, and look upon
the carcases of the men that have transgressed against me : for
their worm shall not die, neither shall their fire be quenched, and
they shall be an abhorring unto all flesh (Isaiah, last verse).
Gehinnom shall come to an end, but they shall not come to an end,
as it says And their beauty shall consume [3] the grave, from being
their dwelling [4] (Ps. xlix. 15). Why all this ? Because they put forth
their hand against the dwelling (of God), as it says לו מזבול לי (לו =
his, *i.e.* God's), his dwelling (not their dwelling). For *Zebhul*
is used of the sanctuary, as Solomon said, I have indeed built for
thee a dwelling (*Zebhul*, 1 Kings viii. 13). Of them Hannah says,
As for the Lord, his adversaries shall be broken into pieces
(1 Sam. ii. 10). R. Isaac b. Abin said, And their faces shall be
likened to the bottom of a pot. Raba said, These are some of
the fops of Mahoza [5] who are termed (nicknamed) hell's sons. Mar
said, Beth Hillel says, He is abundant in lovingkindness, *i.e.* He
inclines in the direction of lovingkindness. But [how do they
reconcile this with what follows when] it says, I will bring the third
part into the fire ? Well, that refers to the Israelites who sin
with their bodies. Israelites who sin with their bodies ! But
you just said that there was no "straightening" at all possible for

---

[1] Those who denounce to the (Roman) Government in time of persecution—
delatores.

[2] Rashi says that ' congregation ' is a wrong reading, as all the above-named
' separated themselves from the congregation ' : read ' Israel,' *i.e.* ' who abandon
Jewish life.'

[3] As the verb is being discussed, it looks as though the Talmud read לכַלּוֹת
(Piel of כלה), not לִבְלוֹת (*Kal* of בלה, or Piel) ; see *Oxford Lexicon, s.v.* בלה.

[4] I think the point lies in the מן, ' away from,' ' apart from,' their dwelling.

[5] A town on the Tigris of which the inhabitants were noted for luxury. *Lit.*
' the beautiful among the beautiful of Mahoza.'

these. (See Ecclesiastes i. 15, vii. 30.) [Yes], but that referred
to those whose sins were [far and away] more than their virtues;
here we are speaking of the intermediates (literally, those who
possess half merits and half sins) : even if these are in the category
of Israelites who sin with their bodies, they must inevitably be in
the category of, " And the third will I bring into the fire " (i.e. they
must ultimately be healed of sin). But even if they are not, then
"Abundant in lovingkindness " applies to them, and about them
David said, I loved the Lord, etc. (Ps. cxvi. ad init.). Raba
expounded this verse thus : What does I loved, etc., mean ?
The congregation of Israel said to God : Sovereign of the universe !
When am I beloved to Thee ? When thou hearest my supplications. It continues : Though I be made poor (brought low), yet
he will save me, that means, though I be poor in Mitzvoth, to
me is it fitting to be saved. Who are the Israelites who sin
with their bodies ? Rab says, The head that is not clad with
tefillin. Who are the Gentiles who sin with their bodies ? Raba
says, Those who sin with transgression [i.e. probably those who
commit incest]. Who are those who spread panic in the land of
the living ? Rab Chisda says this refers to the ἀρχισυνάγωγος (head
of the synagogue), who puts great fear into his congregation, but
not for the name of heaven. R. Judah says no man who does this
will see his son a scholar, as it says, Men do therefore fear him,
but he shall not see any that are wise of heart (Job xxxvii. 24).
Beth Hillel say, Abundant in lovingkindness, i.e. inclining towards
lovingkindness. How does God act ? R. Eliezer says, He treads
it (i.e. the pan of the virtues in the balance) down, as it says, He
will once again have mercy on us and tread down our sins
(Micah vii. 19). R. Yose b. Chanina said, He lifts up (the pan with
sins), as it says, He lifts up (pardons) sin and transgression. In
the school of Ishmael it was taught, He causes the sins to pass
away one by one from first to last : this is his attribute. Raba
says, But the sin itself is not wiped away, for if there are many
other sins, he reckons them with it (i.e. and then the man comes
under class three, i.e. he is perfectly wicked).[1] Raba said, Whoso-

---

[1] There are at least two ways of taking the difficult phrase מעביר ראשון ראשון.
According to Rashi it means ' he does not allow sin to accumulate,' i.e. he
pardons the first sin as it arises. The phrase can also be interpreted ' causing
sin after sin to pass away in due order.' It is so taken by Gaster in his translation

ever overlooks his attributes (*i.e.* does not stand upon his rights when others sin against him), all his sins are overlooked, as it says (Ex. xxxiv. 7), He forgives sin and overlooks transgression. For whom does he forgive sin ? For him who overlooks transgression (by others).'

The other passage is the even more familiar one in the Mishnah of Sanhedrin xi. 1, some of which has been quoted before on p. 245 : 'All Israel will have a share in the world to come. [The Biblical proof is Isaiah lx. 21, "They shall all be righteous."] The following have no share in the world to come. He who says the resurrection of the dead is not indicated in the Law, he who says the Law is not from heaven (*i.e.* divine), and the Epikouros. R. Akiba said : Also he who reads the alien books (ספרים חיצונים), and he who whispers over a wound, and says the words of Exodus xvi. 26 ; Abba Saul said, He too who pronounces the Divine Name (Yahweh) out loud. Three kings and four private persons have no share in the world to come. The three kings are Jeroboam, Ahab, and Manasseh. R. Judah said, Manasseh has a portion in the world to come. (2 Ch. xxxiii. 13.) The four private persons are Balaam, Doeg, Achitophel, and Gehazi.' It has been suggested that Balaam stands for Jesus. This is disputed. (For the whole passage *cp.* the interesting article in Hastings' *Encyclopaedia of Religion and Ethics*, 'Salvation, Jewish,' by the Rev. Morris Joseph, Vol. XI. pp. 142, 143.) It is pretty clear that Rabbis, when inveighing against particular offences (*e.g.* reading external, alien, heretical books, such as the Gospels), were wont to say, He who does so and so, will have no share in the life to come. Such statements must not be taken too seriously. Who the Epikouros is meant to be is doubtful. In the Gemara (99 b) two Rabbis say that he is a man who mocks at a disciple of the wise. Two others say it is one who mocks at his neighbour in the presence of a disciple of the wise. As an example of the mocking of the Rabbis and their disciples the words are given : ' What use are the Rabbis for us ?

---

of אל מלך יושב. (*Book of Prayer . . . according to the . . . Spanish and Portuguese Jews*, Atonement, Vol. I. p. 28, line 3 of English, London, 1904.) Davis and Adler (p. 89, *Service of the Synagogue*, Atonement, Vol. II., London, 1905) have ' causing them [the sins] to pass away one by one.' The phrase עון עצמו is also difficult and would suggest ' sin ' as opposed to ' punishment.' This would be the natural antithesis, but the context precludes it.

They study for themselves and learn for themselves ' : a rather pregnant and significant criticism.

On the whole, we may hold that the majority of Rabbis believed that far the greater number of hell's tenants would be the heathen, for (1) they were idolaters, and idolatry is sin, and (2) they were usually the enemies of Israel, and therefore the enemies of God. Nevertheless, we know that the famous R. Joshua taught that the ' righteous of all nations ' would inherit the life to come (Sanhedrin 105 a), and that this teaching gradually became the accepted doctrine of orthodox Judaism. Repentance was conceived as possible for a Gentile no less than for a Jew. It was a power or a grace against which no sin of any man, whether Jew or Gentile, was a bar. ' God says, My hands are stretched out towards the penitent : I reject no creature who gives me his heart in penitence. Therefore it says, Peace, peace to the far and to the near. To all who draw near to me, I draw near, and I heal them ' (Midrash Psalms on cxx. ad fin.). The word for ' creature ' is beriyyah, and it is fair to say that wherever the word beriyyah is used, the human being generally is meant, and not merely the Israelite. Perhaps the finest and most ' universalist ' passage in the Rabbinical literature is the following. It is made up of several older parallel passages, the existence of which increases its significance and import. The ninth verse of Psalm ix. runs : ' He shall rule the world with righteousness, and judge the peoples with uprightness.' The Midrash asks : ' What is, With uprightness ? R. Alexander says, With the uprightness in them. [This perhaps means either (1) according to the upright persons who have so far appeared among them, i.e. giving them the vicarious benefit of the righteousness of these particular persons, or (2) according to the righteousness which they possess, i.e. if any one of them has any good deed to show, or manifests any desire to repent.] (He judges them) through (the uprightness of) Rahab, Jethro, and Ruth. How ? God says to [a man who belongs to the] peoples of the world [i.e. to a heathen] : Why did you not draw nigh to me ? He answers, Because I was a thorough scoundrel, and I was ashamed. God replies, Were you worse than Rahab, who dwelt in the house upon the town wall, and she received robbers and practised immorality ? And did she not draw near to me, and did I not receive her, and did I not cause to descend from her prophets and righteous men ? Or were you worse than Jethro,

z

who was priest to an idol : and when he came nigh to me, did I not receive him, and cause to descend from him prophets and righteous men ? And when Ruth the Moabitess came to me, did I not receive her, and cause kings to be descended from her ? Again, R. Levi said, God judges the peoples with uprightness. He judges them by night, when they sleep [and cease from] their iniquities ; for by day they commit unchastity, and they rob and oppress : therefore God judges them by night when they are asleep—for then they cease from their sins—so that there may be for them a rising up in the world (to come). Why ? Because all are his creatures and the work of his hands. Where is the potter who seeks that his vessels should be broken ? Therefore he judges them in the night that they may stand firm in the world to come.' (Pesikta Rabbathi 167 b. *Cp.* Midrash Psalms on ix. 9, Jer. Rosh ha-Shanah 57 a and the Yalkut on Psalm ix. 9 ; Bacher, *Agada der palästinenischen Amoräer*, I. p. 198 ; II. p. 324.) One grand point in the utterances of Jesus in Matt. xxv. is their purely *ethical* tests for heaven and hell. In that respect they were far better than the tests of the later Church which included creed as much as deed, or made creed even more important than deed, and better than the tests of many of the Rabbis who sent the heathen to hell just because they were *not* Israel, or because they were Israel's foes. Yet the Synagogue became more purely ethical in its tests for *all* men sooner than the Church.

The valuable and interesting portion of the section consists in the noble verses 34–40. They are not made the less noble because of the fine parallels in the old Egyptian and other literatures. Some of these parallels are conveniently given in Klostermann, ed. 2, p. 205 *ad fin.* Because S.B. give no Rabbinic parallels, it must not be supposed that 34–40 are off the Jewish or Rabbinic line. That is not so. On the contrary. The sentiment is thoroughly Jewish, though the particular form in which it is cast remains peculiar to the Gospel. To begin with, the six good deeds described are all characteristic ' Rabbinic ' good deeds. All six are well-known features or examples of *Gemiluth Chesadim*, the doing of loving-kindnesses : (a) Feeding the hungry ; (b) giving drink to the thirsty ; (c) hospitality ; (d) clothing the naked ; (e) visiting the sick ; (f) visiting (and redeeming) the prisoners. But, in the second place, the passage may be compared with the Rabbinic doctrine of the

Imitation of God. As God is merciful, so should man be merciful, and so on. And this imitation of the divine attributes is the right imitation of God. In Dr. Abrahams' two essays, ' Man's forgiveness ' (*Studies*, I.), and in ' The Imitation of God ' (*Studies*, II.), all the salient passages are given. No one surely who looks at my book will not possess his book (it would be as if one bought a footstool, but did not possess a chair), and it seems rather absurd to quote them all over again. Thus : ' Rabbi Chama b. R. Chanina said : What means the Biblical command : Walk ye after the Lord your God ? (Deut. xiii. 4.) Is it possible for a man to walk after the Shechinah ? Is it not previously said : The Lord thy God is a consuming fire ? (Deut. iv. 24.) But the meaning is : Walk after the attributes of the Holy One. As he clothed the naked—Adam and Eve in the Garden (Genesis iii.)—so do thou clothe the naked ; as the Holy One visited the sick (appearing unto Abraham when he was ailing, Genesis xviii.), so do thou tend the sick ; as the Holy One comforted the mourners (consoling Isaac after the demise of his father, Genesis xxv.), so do thou comfort the mourners ; as the Holy One buried the dead (interring Moses in the valley, Deut. xxxiv.), so do thou bury the dead ' (Sotah 14 a. The passage has already been used on p. 105). ' As God is merciful and ,gracious, so be thou merciful and gracious ' (Sabbath 133 b, and often. *Cp.* on Matt. v. 45). Moreover, as the Gospel passage speaks of service rendered to the King-Messiah by service rendered to man, or rather to the Christian brotherhood, so the Rabbis speak of God receiving strength and satisfaction by men's righteousness. ' God is exalted when the Israelites observe justice.' ' When Israel does God's will, the Power (*i.e.* God's power) is strengthened ; when Israel disobeys, the Power is weakened ' (Deut. Rabba v., *Shofetim*, on xvi. 18, end ; Lamentations Rabba on i. 6). (*Studies*, II. pp. 180, 181. *Cp.* I. p. 154.) Whenever God sought to do the Israelites good, they changed their minds and sinned. So they kept on weakening God's power (מתישים כחו של מעלה). (Sifre 136 b *fin.*; Moore I. p. 472.) ' When Israel does God's will, they add power (כח) to the (divine) Might (גבורה) ' (Pesikta 166 b). Schechter says that the meaning is that Israel's sins ' prevent the channels of grace from flowing as freely and fully as was intended by God ' (*Some Aspects of Rabbinic Theology*, p. 239 *init.*). Remarkable is the saying, ' Happy is he who has caused *nachat ruach*, satisfaction, or quietness, of spirit to his

creator' (Berachoth 17 a, *Studies*, II. pp. 179, 182). 'God created
the world only in order that men should fear him : God has
nothing (cares for nothing) in the world except man's fear of him'
(Sabbath 31 b ; *Studies*, II. pp. 154, 182). It is clear that the
meaning is that the only service—even benefit !—you can render
God is by worshipping him and by imitating his attributes in
doing good to your fellowman. I would add one very fine passage
to those quoted by Dr. Abrahams from Midrash Psalms (c. xviii.
19, 243 b) : 'In the future world man will be asked : What was your
occupation ? If he reply, I fed the hungry, then they reply, That
is the gate of the Lord. He who feeds the hungry, let him enter.'
So with giving drink to the thirsty, clothing the naked, with
those who look after orphans, and with those, generally, who do
deeds of lovingkindness. All these are gates of the Lord, and
those who do such deeds shall enter within them. We may note
too the word 'man.' It is not, apparently, the Israelite only
who is asked the question ; it is 'man,' *i.e. every* man, be his race
and creed what they may.

xxvii. 60. The late legend about the entombment of R. Akiba
may conceivably have been partly made up as a sort of Jewish
makeweight to the entombment of Jesus. When Akiba had died,
the authorities did not allow his body to be buried ; it was brought
back into the prison, and a watch kept over it. Elijah went to
R. Joshua, and said that he (Elijah) was a priest, and that he
had come to tell him that Akiba was dead, and that his body
lay in the prison. The two went together to the prison, and they
found the gates open, and all the guards asleep. Elijah took up the
body of R. Akiba upon his shoulders. R. Joshua said, 'Did you not
tell me you were a priest ? Is not a priest forbidden to make himself
unclean with a corpse ? ' Elijah replied, 'Joshua, my son, God forbid' (חם ושלום), 'there is no question of uncleanness in the case of the
righteous or in the case of their disciples' (שאין טומאה בצדיקים אף לא
בתלמידיהם). So they journeyed the whole night together till they
came to Antipatris the reaper. There a cave opens itself before them,
in which they find a table, a chair, a bench, a bed, and a lamp. They
put Akiba's body on the bed, and go away. The lamp kindles itself,
and the cave closes. Elijah exclaims : 'Blessed (happy) are ye
righteous, and blessed are ye who toil in the Law, and happy are ye

who fear God. A place is kept and stored up and hidden for you in Eden for the time to come. Blessed art thou, Akiba, for whom a good dwelling has been found in the hour of thy death' (Midrash Proverbs on ix. 2, 31 a, b). The best part of the legend is the admirable saying : 'Uncleanness cannot touch the righteous'—a saying almost worthy to rank with Mark vii. 18.

LUKE

vi. The full notes in Matthew about the Sermon on the Mount include some references to the Lucan parallels and variants.

vii. 36–50. The beauty and nobility of the story, and especially of the famous verse 47, are undeniable. It is difficult to say how far the spirit of 47 and of the whole story are off the Rabbinic line or not. (For one thing, uncertainty still prevails whether the love is the result of the pardon or the cause of it, and this uncertainty increases the difficulty.) The Rabbis were not unwilling to believe in a sudden repentance. And the repentance might be caused by love. In a story, to which I have alluded in the section on Matt. xxii. 34–40, a harlot falls in love with a disciple of a Rabbi who was about to have immoral relations with her. She comes to the Rabbi, and asks to be received into Judaism. The Rabbi accepts her and bids her sin no more. The disciple and she are married and ' live happily ever after.' (Such, at least, we may assume to be the implied outcome of the story.) In two other stories we are told how one singular good action in a lifetime of undistinction, or even of sinful occupation, may suffice to make a man worthy to have his prayer for rain heard and answered by God. We may, I think, say that there is a certain distinction and distinctiveness about these two Talmudic stories and the Gospel story. Each one of them has a fragrance and a beauty of its own. The Gospel story cannot be said to be quite on, or quite off, the Rabbinic line, just as the first Rabbinic story (about the harlot) is not quite on, or quite off, the Gospel line. It is not in any way to detract from that Rabbinic story if we say that the Gospel story, from the beauty of its telling, from the genius which seems to breathe through it, from the nobility of the saying in 47, is more arresting than the Rabbinic story. Yet we may fitly rejoice that we have them both, and that we have both the Gospel manner and the Talmudic manner of suggesting that repentance and a sudden change of life are never impossible. What we do not get so markedly in the Rabbinic stories is the effect of the great personality upon the character and actions of others. The comparison of Jesus with Hillel is rather inept. If eccentric scholars like to argue that Jesus never existed, let them do so. There would seem to be almost more reason to believe that he never existed than that, though he did exist, he had not an exceptional personality, and was not possessed of a singular and, as some of the old Greeks might have said, a daimonic influence ; in short, that he was not a great religious genius.

The two stories about rain to which I referred in the previous paragraph run as follows. ' (In a time of drought) it was revealed to the Rabbis in a dream that a certain ass-driver should pray that rain might come. So they sent and fetched him. They asked him what his trade was, and he replied that he was an ass-driver. Then they said, Have you ever done any good deed in your life ? (Ass-drivers were not much thought of.) He answered, Once I hired my ass to a woman who began to weep on the road. I asked her why she wept, and she told me that her husband was in prison, and that she wished to sell her chastity to obtain his ransom. Then I sold my ass and gave her the price I received, and said to her, Take this, free thy husband and sin not. The Rabbis said to him, Worthy indeed art thou to pray for us and be answered.' Once, in similar circumstances, it was shown to the Rabbis in a dream that Pentekaka (*i.e.* the man of five sins) should pray for rain. ' Abbahu sent and fetched him. He asked him what his trade was. Pentekaka replied, Five sins does this man do daily ; I hire out harlots ; I deck the theatres ; I take the harlots' garments to the baths ; I clap and dance before them, and I beat the tympanum for their orgies. Abbahu said to him, Have you ever done one good deed ? He said, Once I was decking out the theatre when a woman came and wept behind one of the pillars. When I asked her why she was weeping, she told me that her husband was in prison, and that she was going to sell her honour to obtain his ransom. So I sold my bed and coverlet, and gave her the price, and said, Go, redeem thy husband and sin not. Abbahu said to him, Worthy art thou to pray and to be answered ' (Jer. Taanith i. § 4, 64 b ; S.B. II. p. 162).

ix. 55. 'He turned and rebuked them.' To these words we must add : 'And he said, Ye know not what manner of spirit ye are of. For the Son of Man did not come to destroy men's lives, but to save them.' And we must include also xix. 10: ' For the Son of man is come to seek and to save that which is lost.' I seem here to be opposed both to current Jewish and current Christian exposition. For, as against the latter, the spirit of these words (whether, as Harnack thinks, the addition to ix. 55 be genuine and authentic, or whether, as many scholars believe, it be not) seems to me in contradiction to fulminations such as ' vipers and children of hell,' or to ' depart into the everlasting fire.' As against the former, the words seem to me not only noble and beautiful, but, upon the whole, novel, and not completely to be paralleled, in letter or spirit, from Rabbinic sources. Ezekiel xxxiv. 16 is the source, but the words go beyond the source. Hillel said, ' Be of the disciples of Aaron, loving peace and pursuing peace, loving thy fellow-creatures, and drawing them near to the Torah' (Aboth i. 12). And we have heard Rabbinic sayings, such as, ' Be of those who are persecuted and not of the persecutors: be reviled and revile not.' Yet the words in Luke seem to me to go beyond even these. ' The *search* for the lost ' is a new feature. Nevertheless, I contend that it adds on to, but does not conflict with, Biblical and Rabbinic teaching at their purest and best. It extends the line ; it would not be fair to say that it is off the line, because that might be taken to mean that it is in antagonism to the line. It is an extension of the line, but goes in the same direction.

62. The saying in Aboth iii. 9, quoted by S.B., is a fair parallel, though not so appealing: ' He who is walking by the way and studying, and breaks off his study, and says, How fine is that tree, how fine is that field, him the Scripture regards as if he had forfeited his life.'

x. 29. With regard to the question of the range of the word for neighbour in Lev. xix. 18 *as interpreted* by the Rabbis, something has been said in the notes on Matt. v. 43. It is not unnatural that Christian scholars are so exceedingly sensitive about the parable of the Good Samaritan, and so exceedingly eager to deny any suggestion that the Rabbis ever possibly thought that neighbour could include the non-Jew. For as the injunction ' Thou shalt love thy neighbour as thyself ' is found in the O.T., and as Jesus quotes it as the ' heaviest ' or chief commandment of the Law, and as R. Akiba did the same, how can the immense superiority of the teaching of Jesus over the teaching of the Rabbis be secure, unless to Jesus ' neighbour ' definitely included non-Jews, while to the Rabbis it no less definitely excluded them ? And the *only* place in which it can be shown that to Jesus neighbour included the non-Jew is the parable of the Good Samaritan. Hence the contempt with which Halévy's suggestion about the original form of that parable has met with from Christian writers. Nevertheless, I am bound to admit that Dr. Abrahams (upon, as I think, insufficient grounds) has also rejected Halévy's hypothesis, so I will say no more about it in this place.

If Jesus had really wanted to explain his views that ' neighbour ' should be held to include the non-Jew, several curious things emerge. (1) Why is there no record of his having done so in Mark and Matthew ? Both in Mark xii. 28–34 and in Matt. xxii. 34–40, as well as in the Sermon on the Mount, such an explanation would have been very much to the point. (2) Again, why does the story fit the question so badly ? ' Who is my neighbour ? ' asks the Scribe. The answer given by the story should have been : ' Your neighbour is the man who needs your loving help, be he Jew or non-Jew.' Instead of which, the story answers the question, ' Whose neighbour am I ? ' The story must have existed, therefore, apart from the question, and the connection of 30–37 with 25–28 by means of 29 must be due to Luke. In other words, the story was not said for the first time by Jesus in answer to the question in 29. The question in 29 belongs to Luke ; not to Jesus. And the question in 36 is somewhat awkwardly worded. Loisy, who may be quite wrong about the ' intention symbolique ' of the whole story, is yet not unjustified when he says, ' La gaucherie de la combinaison saute aux yeux, et il suffit de rapprocher la question du docteur : " Qui est mon prochain ? " de celle de Jésus : " Lequel des trois a été prochain envers la victime des voleurs ? " pour en saisir l'artifice. On dit que Jésus, pour donner plus de force à son enseignement, s'abstient de réponse théorique et transporte la question de la charité sur le terrain pratique. Mais le fait est que la question est plutôt maladroitement renversée : le docteur demandait à savoir qui était son prochain, et Jésus lui apprend qu'un Samaritain charitable peut être le prochain d'un autre homme, qu'il faut agir comme le Samaritain pour être le prochain d'autrui' (Loisy, *Luc*, p. 310).

Nevertheless, taking the text as it stands, we may go so far as to say that Luke intends us to turn the parable round, as it were, and to apply it to the first question. As, to the Samaritan, neighbour meant ' the man who needed my help, even though he is a Jew ' (it is another, though often unnoticed, difficulty about the story in its present connection that it does not say, ' A Jew went down from J. to J.,' but merely, ' *a man* went down from J. to J.'), so, to the Jew, a neighbour must be he who needs his (the Jew's) help, even though he be a Samaritan.

How far, then, are there parallels to such teaching in the Rabbinic literature ? Dr. Abrahams has a very valuable essay on the Good Samaritan in *Studies*, II. 33–40. He says :

(1) ' The appearance of the Samaritan among the personages of the parable is explicable, not only on general grounds, but also as a device of moral art. To castigate one's own community, it is sometimes effective to praise those outside it. We have a very early instance of it in the Talmud ; the traditions of it are many ; it clearly emanates from an age when the Temple still stood. The hero of the story is Dama, son of Netinah. (*Cp*. p. 251.) He was a non-Jew, an idolater, dwelling in Askelon; evidently a man of means, and a πατὴρ βουλῆς. To what limits should a son go in honouring his father ? asked the Rabbi. Go forth and see what a certain idolater of Askelon did, is the answer. On one occasion he was silent and respectful when his mother publicly insulted him, and on another occasion refused to disturb his father, who lay asleep with his head on the key of the box containing the gem which the agents of the Sanhedrin wished to purchase for the High Priest's vestment. Though a very high price was offered, he refused to disturb his father, and the sale was not effected. In this way a heathen was put forward as the model of love and reverence towards parents. This is a Pharisaic parallel to the choice of a Samaritan in the Lucan parable ' (p. 36). He further (2) calls attention to two stories in the Rabbinic literature in which Jews act the part of the Samaritan.

(*a*) ' Bar Kappara walked by the shore of the lake at Cesarea. He saw a ship sink, and a proconsul (?) came out naked. When he saw him, he went up to him and gave him two *selaim*. Then he took him to his house, and gave him food and drink and three more *selaim,*|for he said, A great man like you must need them. After many days some Jews were imprisoned (*i.e.* on the instigation of the proconsul). They said, who shall go and plead for us ? One said to the other, Bar Kappara is much thought of by the Government. He said to them, But do you know that the Government does nothing for nothing ? They said to him, Here are 500 *denarii*. Go and appease (the Government) for us. He took them and went to the Government. When the proconsul saw him, he got up and greeted him, and said to him, Why have you troubled to come hither ? He said, To ask you to have pity on those Jews. He said, Do you know that a government does not do anything for nothing ? He said, I have 500 *denarii* ; take them and be appeased. He said, Let those 500 *denarii* be kept by you in pledge for the five *selaim*, and let your people be saved because of the food and drink which you gave me, and go home in peace and honour. To him the saying in Ecclesiastes xi. 1 may be applied ' (Ecclesiastes R. on xi. 1).

(*b*) Then there is the story or legend of Elazar ben Shammua, constructed upon similar lines to those of the former story. He too walks by the shore of the sea ; he sees a ship sink ; one man only emerges naked. The man meets some Jews, who are going up to Jerusalem for a festival. He says that he (a Roman) is of the descendants of ' Esau, your brother,' and he asks for some raiment to cover his nakedness. But these merciless Jews reply : ' May it happen to all thy people as to you ! ' Then he sees R. Elazar. He says, ' I see you are an old and honourable man, who knows well what is due to a fellow-creature, and esteems the honour of his fellow-men (את חכים ביקרי דברייתא—a characteristic Rabbinic virtue). Give me raiment to cover my nakedness.' R. Elazar takes off one of his seven garments and gives it to him, and then he takes him home, gives him food and drink, and 200 *denarii*, and shows him much honour. We are then' told that after some time the rescued Roman is made Emperor. He then issues an order that all Jews in that district are to be killed. R. Elazar, as in the previous story, is sent to court to ask for pardon, with the needful bribe of 4000 *denarii*. When the Emperor sees him, he greets him, and so on, as in the other story. When R. Elazar tells him why he has come, he says, Is there anything false in your Law ? No, says

R. Elazar. Then the Emperor quotes, (1) The Ammonite and Moabite shall not be received into the congregation of the Lord because they gave you no bread and water, (2) You shall not abhor an Edomite because he is your brother. 'Am I not a descendant of Esau, your brother? And yet you showed me no lovingkindness. They who transgress the Law are worthy of death. Then R. Elazar said, Though they are guilty, forgive them and have compassion. The Emperor replied, You know that this Government does not do anything for nothing. The Rabbi said, I have four thousand *denarii*; take them, and have pity. The Emperor replied, These four thousand *denarii* are given back to you because of the two hundred *denarii* which you gave to me, and the district shall be spared because of the food and drink which you bestowed on me. And go into my treasury, and take seven garments for the garment with which you clothed me, and return in peace to your nation which I have forgiven for your sake' (*ib.*).

The stories of Abba Tachna (*Studies*, I. p. 110) and of Nahum of Gimzu (*Studies*, II. p. 39) would be of great service in our connection if the leper in the one case, and the poor man in the other, were non-Jews. But this is not indicated in the stories. (Ecclesiastes Rabba on ix. 7, Taanith 21 a.) Yet it is interesting that both in these stories, as in the parable of the Good Samaritan, no stress is laid as to whether the man in trouble is a Jew or a non-Jew, though one would have surmised that it would have added greatly to their 'point' if, in the Rabbinic stories, it had been specially noted that the sufferers were non-Jews, and in the Gospel story it had been specially emphasized that he was a Jew. And that a Rabbinic story *could* speak of Jewish help rendered to a suffering Gentile we have just seen. Hence we are led to infer that the point of the original story of the Good Samaritan (whether the Samaritan be an original feature or no), like the point of the Rabbinic stories, was to urge the sovereign virtue of lovingkindness. It was not told to illustrate and elucidate the question, 'Who is my neighbour?'; it was not even told to urge that Jews ought to succour men of alien race, but it was told and constructed simply to teach quite generally the beauty and duty of succouring charity. It was, therefore, in all probability, Luke, and not Jesus, who used the story for the question which he himself devised. The retort of the scribe, if my hypothesis be correct, would not be historic. Again, it may be asked why *should* the scribe, wishing to show that he was, and had been, righteous, ask, ' Who is my neighbour ? ' Does he suppose that the reply of Jesus is insufficient because he has not explained what the range of neighbour is ? Certainly, if the scribe wanted δικαιῶσαι ἑαυτόν to show that he was rigʜteous, the question is as inept and unnatural as possible. This is one reason the more to believe that, so far as the addition from 29 is concerned, we are not listening to a conversation which actually and historically ever took place.

38–42. S.B. are perfectly correct when they say that the ' one thing,' of which, according to the Rabbis, there is ' need,' would be the study of the Law, and the quotations they give, which could easily be multiplied, are quite in point, not least R. Meir's saying (Aboth iv. 12) : ' Lessen thy toil for worldly goods, and be busy in the Torah : be humble of spirit before all men ; if thou neglectest the Torah, many causes for neglecting it will present themselves to thee, but if thou labourest in the Torah, he has abundant recompense to give thee.'

xii. 15. As to the moral dangers of money, see on Matt. xix. 23. The warning in 15 and the parable of 16–21 are on, and not off, the Rabbinic line. ' Love of money and hatred caused the destruction of the second Temple ' (T. Menachoth xiii. 22, p. 534).

48. We may compare a passage in Yebamoth 121 b quoted by Büchler, *Sins*, p. 195, n. 1. There was a pious pit-digger called Nechunyah. His daughter fell into a pit, but was rescued. R. Chanina b. Dora foretold her rescue, for he said, Would it be possible that a child of this pious man would suffer in respect of the very occupation of her father ? Nevertheless, said R. Abba, his son died of thirst. To this R. Chanina could only reply that God deals very strictly with those near to him (הקדוש ב״ה מדקדק עם סביבין כחוט השערה). The proof is a fanciful interpretation of Psalms l. 3 and lxxxix. 8. See also Büchler, *Sins*, p. 336, n. 4. The errors of the learned are regarded by God as wilful sins ; the wilful sins of the *Amme ha-Aretz* as errors. (Baba Mezia 33 b.) The reference to Lev. R., אמור, xxvii. 1 on xxii. 27, and the usual painful doctrine about the few sins of the righteous being strictly punished in this

world that they may have a fine time in the world to come, etc.,
should not be introduced here.   At least, I hope not.   The idea of
Baba Mezia and perhaps of Yebamoth is that God demands a higher
standard of the more highly endowed.   We may also utilize a
passage in Taanith 8 a : ' R. Yochanan said : He who conducts himself righteously here below is judged strictly in the heaven above '
(Dr. Malter's rendering).

xiii. 1–5.   I have alluded in my Commentary to the great use
which most Christian scholars are wont to make of this section as
also of John ix. 2.   They want to make this passage, like the passage
in John, prove that Jesus deliberately taught that from suffering
no inference must be made of precedent sin.   But ' the point of the
passage is not that the men who suffered were not guilty, but that they
were not *specially* guilty.   Why these men should have been chosen
out as example and warning, Jesus does not say.   The difficulty did
not occur to him.   Jesus does not criticize or deny the prevailing
doctrine of the time that suffering denoted guilt ' (my Commentary,
II. p. 500).   I might add that in John also any inference as to the
general views of the author on the general subject of suffering and
sin are no less illegitimate.   For all that Jesus says (or is made to
say) in that passage is that the blindness of the man in question
was *specially arranged* in order that Jesus might work a miracle of
healing. *In his particular case* neither the man himself nor his parents
had sinned.   But there is no indication whatever that in *other* cases
blindness or any other suffering may not be due to sin.   Moreover,
in the story of the paralytic in Mark, sin and suffering are united
together without dissent.   In fact, the point of Mark ii. 9 depends
entirely upon the idea that the man, being a paralytic, is also,
and for that very reason, a sinner.   Therefore, it is rash to argue
that Jesus was opposed to the ' Jewish ' doctrine of the connection
between suffering and sin.   On the other hand, there is equally
no doubt that that doctrine was pushed by the Rabbis to pre-
posterous and objectionable lengths.   There were, indeed, voices
raised against that fatal view of R. Ammi, ' no death without sin,
and no chastisements (or sufferings, *yissurin*) without iniquity.'
There was the sage utterance of R. Yannai (the only saying recorded
of him, and yet one that does him infinite credit, Bacher, *Agada
der Tannaiten*, Vol. II. p. 385), that it is not in our capacity to ex-

plain the sufferings of the righteous or the prosperity of the wicked. (Aboth iv. 19.) But, on the whole, the prevailing teaching, in spite of the happy theory of the chastisements of love, was, I fear, more in accordance with Ammi than with Yannai. The theory would perhaps have been less painful if the Rabbis had not gone on to assign certain punishments to certain offences, and also to connect with the theory the doctrine of measure for measure and tit for tat. One cannot read a section like Sabbath 32 a–33 b without justified reprobation. Here again we find the unfortunate result of knowing the Bible all too well, of regarding every word as inspired, perfect and accurate, and of playing exegetical and homiletic tricks with its sentences and phrases. The Rabbis kept on studying the Torah, but while they often studied it for good, they also often studied it for inutility. S.B. correctly state : ' Mehrfach hat man die Strafleiden für die einzelnen Sünden auf Grund von Schriftworten festzustellen versucht ; dabei hat dann die Neigung zum Statutarischen der Versuchung nicht widerstehen können, das, was in der Schrift *einmal* als Strafe für eine bestimmte Verfehlung erscheint, sofort als regelmässige Folge dieser Sünde hinzustellen. Nach dem Grundsatz " Mass gegen Mass " wuchs natürlich mit der Grösse der Sünde die Schwere der Strafe. Die grössten Katastrophen, die über den einzelnen oder die Gesammtheit hereinbrechen können, haben deshalb stets die schwersten Tatsünden zur Voraussetzung ; als solche gelten Götzendienst, Unzucht, Blutvergiessen, Raub, Rechtsbeugung und grundloser Hass. So gewann man ein förmlicher Strafverzeichnis für die einzelnen Sünden. Man wusste nicht bloss, welches Unheil auf eine bestimmte Sünde folgte, sondern konnte nun auch umgekehrt aus dem Unglück eines Menschen auf die Art seiner Versündigung schliessen. Das Leiden wurde zur Erkennungsmarke der Schuld ' (II. p. 193).[1] It may be said that such a passage as Sabbath 32 a–33 b

---

[1] 'The Rabbis often attempted to fix the punishments of different sins by means of various verses in the Bible. In doing this their legalistic tendency could not resist the temptation, if the Bible had incidentally mentioned that a certain punishment had once followed a certain sin, of declaring this punishment to be the regular result of this sin. Moreover, according to the fundamental principle of measure for measure, the severity of the punishment increased with the gravity of the sin. Thus the greatest catastrophes which can fall upon a community or an individual are always supposed to be the consequences of the heaviest sins : as such are reckoned, idolatry, sexual license, murder, robbery, unjust judgments and causeless hate.' (It may, at least, be noted that all these

must not be taken too seriously. The Rabbis were engaged in a sort of exegetical game. But what a painful game this would be ! For instance, one sentence runs, ' Because of the iniquity of robbery (גזל) locusts come, and famine, and men eat the flesh of their sons and daughters.' The Biblical verses quoted are Amos iv. 1 and 9 ; Joel i. 4. Doubtless there is some ingenuity in the proof. But if the writer or speaker did not really believe what he said or wrote, how objectionable the jest. Nor is there any clear sign that these utterances *were* made in jest. Compare the long and perfectly solemn statements—no less objectionable than those in Sabbath 32 a–33 b—in Aboth v. 11, 12. ' Seven kinds of punishments come into the world for seven important transgressions ' (Singer's *Prayer Book*, p. 200 *ad fin.*). There is no indication that the statements are not seriously meant. It seems almost impossible for us to understand the inner working of minds which brought out such grotesque opinions. Again, the sayings in Sabbath 32, 33 start from a dictum in the Mishnah, which, as I have often had occasion to observe, is still allowed to disgrace the *Authorized Daily Prayer Book* (p. 121). There is no hint that the saying is not most seriously meant. ' For three transgressions women die in childbirth ; because they have been negligent in regard to their periods of separation, in respect to the consecration of the first cake of the dough, and in the lighting of the Sabbath lamp.' How could men come to imagine such absurdities, and solemnly to write them down ? It seems inconceivable to us to-day ; yet when we reflect on all the absurdities and abominations which have been spoken, written, and (worst of all) done, in the name of religion, one must not judge the Rabbis too harshly. I feel about the Gospel teaching that, though there are things in it which I dislike and disbelieve, such as Matt. xxv. 41, 46, yet, somehow, there is never anything which is *absurd* : there are objectionable sayings, but not *ludicrously* objectionable sayings, such as the sayings in Aboth v. 11, 12, and Sabbath 32, 33. S.B. give many more instances which I do not care to repeat (II. pp. 194–197). It has been a disadvantage to Judaism to have for generations, as its second sacred book—for I suppose the Talmud

---

heaviest sins are *moral*.) ' In this way a regular catalogue of punishments was obtained for all the different sins. It was not only laid down what calamity would follow a particular sin, but from the misfortune which befell a man his particular sin could be inferred. Sufferings became the mark for the recognition of guilt.'

must be more or less so regarded—one which is so long and so composite, so unedited, as it were, and unexpurgated, so full of ' high and low,' so completely in ' undress,' as I have often called it, so naïvely and simply compiled. It has been an advantage to Christianity that its primary sacred book is so short, and so far as the Gospel portion of it is concerned, so carefully written with the direct object of edification.

xiv. 7–11. *Cp.* Matt. xviii. 4, xxiii. 6. All derives from Proverbs xxv. 7. The Rabbinic parallels are exact enough. Leviticus R., ויקרא, i. 5 on i. 1. ' R. Simeon b. Azzai said : Stay a few seats lower down than the seat which is your due, and wait till it is said to you, Come further up. For it is better that it should be said to you, Come up, than that it should be said to you, Go down. As Hillel said, My humiliation is my exaltation, and my exaltation my humiliation.' (For Hillel's saying *cp.* Bacher, *Agada der Tannaiten,* I. p. 5 *fin.*, note 6, 2nd ed. The meaning is that, quite generally, he who abases himself shall be exalted, and *vice versa.* Humility wins recognition from men and from God. Luke xiv. 11 means exactly the same. In Erubin 13 b, already quoted on xxiii. 12, we have it definitely stated : ' Him who abases himself God exalts, and *vice versa.* Him who seeks greatness, greatness flees, and *vice versa.*')

13. S.B. justly quote the pretty passage in Aboth R. Nathan (vii. 17 a) commenting on Aboth I. 5. ' Let your house be open ; let the poor be members of your household.' ' Let a man's house be open to the North and to the South and to the East and to the West, even like Job, who made four doors to his house that the poor might not be troubled to go round the house (to the front door). Members of your household : that is, let the poor relate what they have eaten and drunk in your house, as happened with Job. For when two poor men met, one said, Whence came you ? And the other said, Whither go you ? The answers were, From and to the house of Job. When the great suffering came upon Job, he said, Lord of the world, have I not fed the hungry and clothed the naked ? But God said, So far you have not reached to the half of the measure of Abraham, for you sat in your house, and when wayfarers came unto you, you gave wheaten bread to him

2 A

whose wont it was to eat wheaten bread, and meat to him whose
wont it was to eat meat, and wine to him whose wont it was to
drink wine. But Abraham did not so ; he went out and wandered
about, and when he found wayfarers, he brought them to his house,
and he gave wheaten bread to him whose wont it was *not* to eat
wheaten bread, and so with meat and wine. And not only this,
but he built large palaces on the roads, and put food and drink
within them, and all came and ate and drank and blessed God.
Therefore quiet, or appeasement, of spirit was granted to him,
and all that the mouth of man can ask for was found in his house.'
' When R. Huna dined (Taanith 20 b, foot), he opened the door
and said, He who wishes, let him come and eat.' ' Rabban Simeon
ben Gamaliel said : This was a custom in Jerusalem ; a towel
was spread on the top of the doorway ; all the time that the towel
was spread, guests could enter ; when the towel was removed,
guests were not allowed to enter ' (Tosefta Berachoth iv. § 8, p. 10.
Dr. A. Lukyn Williams' translation. But we must translate, instead
of ' guests,' ' wayfarers ' or ' passers by,' showing the range of the
hospitality in those olden days.)

The words in 12, 'and thou hast thy recompense,' and in 14,
' for they cannot recompense thee : but thou shalt have thy recom-
pence at the resurrection of the righteous,' are noteworthy. They
seem to depend upon the notion, for which there are endless parallels
in the Rabbinic literature, that the less recompense a man receives
for his good deeds upon earth, the more will he receive in the life
of the world to come, and that this future recompense is far more
worth having than any recompense on earth. But they also depend
upon the quite different idea (for which, too, there are Rabbinic
parallels) that, so far as our deeds upon earth are concerned, we
are to act *lishmah,* for the deed's own sake, and not for the hope
of reward.

25–35. I wonder what an absolutely impartial, and yet entirely
sympathetic, scholar would say about this and similar passages—
one learned in both Christian and Rabbinic literature ; sympathetic
both to the Christian and to the Rabbinic religion, though, perhaps,
belonging to neither. Is it both great and new ; is it both great
and off the Rabbinic line ? On the whole, I think that we must
say that it is, (1) if dangerous, yet also great, and (2) that it *is* off

the Rabbinic line. Yet by saying this it must *not* be imagined that
the Rabbinic line is a poor line. Deliberate, voluntary, and complete
renunciation is not put forward as an ideal by the Rabbis, except
in so far as they do demand that *every* sacrifice must be made for
the sanctification of God's holy name, if such sacrifice become
requisite through persecution. The abandonment of family life
lies outside any Rabbinic ideal, for the love of father and mother
and wife and children is itself a part of the highest possible ideal.
To sacrifice life for the sake of the Sanctification of the Name and
for the sake of the divine Unity was right, and the number of
Jewish martyrs is legion ; but the idea of going forth into the
world, and of renouncing all ties and bonds and possessions in order
to benefit society, or to propagate Judaism, or for some special
cause, seems to lie outside the Rabbinic range or line. But a passage
like Luke xiv. 25-35 does suggest such an ideal, and it has doubtless
stimulated and heartened those who, in one way or another, have
sought to make of the ideal a reality. (*Cp.* what I have said in
Vol. II. pp. 517, 518.)

xv. 1, 2. (*Cp.* Matt. ix. 11.) S.B. quote the remark in Mechilta
57 b on Exodus xviii. 1. ' The wise say, Let not a man associate
with sinners even to bring them near to the Torah.'

For the whole section 1-10 *cp.* Matt. xviii. 12-14.

8. The illustration about coins is used in Canticles R. i. § 1, 9, on
i. 1. ' If a man loses a coin in his house, he kindles many lights, and
seeks till he finds it. If for something which affords only an hour's
life in this world, a man kindles many lights, and searches till he
finds it, how much shouldst thou dig as for hidden treasure after
the words of the Law, which gives life both in this world and in the
next.' I see nothing unworthy in this illustration. To search for
knowledge and truth and religious illumination (and this is what
Torah meant to the old Rabbis) is a legitimate quest and worthy
of the utmost sacrifice. Fiebig's sneer, ' Das rabbinische Gleichnis
redet von der Tora, Jesus von dem Menschen, dem Sünder, der
Ethik ! ' is unjustified and unnecessary. Both illustrations are
right and seemly, but one cannot fitly compare one with the other.
You cannot say, *e.g.*, that a martyr for truth and knowledge is on
a lower plane than a martyr for goodness.

11–32. For the exquisite parable of the Prodigal Son the best parallel is that quoted by S.B. from Deut. R. ii. 24 (ואתחנן, on iv. 30 ; Wuensche, p. 32). 'A king's son fell into evil courses. The king sent his tutor to him with the message, Repent, my son (or "come to thyself," as in verse 16). But the son sent to his father to say, How can I (literally, with what face can I) return (or repent) ? I am ashamed (to come) before thee. Then the father sent to him to say, Can a son be ashamed to return to his father ? If you return, do you not return to your father ? So God sent Jeremiah to the Israelites who had sinned against him. He said to Jeremiah : Tell my sons to return (repent). They replied, How can we (with what face can we) return to God ? Then God said to them : My sons, if you return, is it not to your Father that you return ? ' The verb is always the same, namely, חזר, which means return, repent, come to yourselves, come back to God. Fiebig tries to minimize the obvious closeness of the parallel by saying that the son in the Midrash is Israel, whereas in Luke Jesus is thinking of any individual, not of the people as a whole. But could we possibly argue that the Rabbis did not feel that God was a loving father to the individual Israelite as well as to the people as a whole ? Surely not.

Sevenster, indeed (pp. 176–181), seeks to make a sharp distinction on both counts. God was not a loving Father to the individual Israelite as a human being, but, at best, only to the individual Israelite as a member of the community. So far as every Jew was concerned, this is really a distinction without a difference ; whether the mediation is one way or the other, in either case the pitying and forgiving love of God was, I fancy, strongly felt by each individual Israelite in his own individual life. As to the use of the term 'Father,' Sevenster might perhaps have read his Moore to greater advantage, though he makes one or two good hits. Again, Sevenster tries to show that God is longsuffering and indulgent in Rabbinical literature, but he does not forgive so perfectly or with such joy as in the Gospel. I doubt this. Sevenster does not know his Rabbinical literature, I think, quite *familiarly* enough. The numerous passages about God's reaction towards the first signs of man's repentance show how the land lies. ' If man moves an inch, God moves an ell to meet him.' The word ' joy ' may not occur in such passages, but the feeling or the conception is the same.

Sevenster naturally wants to make the difference between Jesus'
teaching and that of the Rabbis as wide as he *honestly* can, and
his honesty is to be highly commended, even if his conclusions may
not *always* be sound, or always capable of resisting the massive
learning of Abrahams and Moore. His whole book is well worth
reading and study.

xvi. 1–11. Money is not necessarily unrighteous, according to
the Rabbis. All depends on the use to which it is put. S.B. give
instances where the 'Mammon' of covetousness, wickedness,
falsity, etc., is used, but also one instance where the Mammon of
Falsity is contrasted with the Mammon of Truth (or perhaps of
Honesty as contrasted with Dishonesty). But the distinction was
meant literally, not as in Luke xvi. 11, where the true Mammon
is not money, but spiritual gifts or the felicity of the Kingdom. (See
the Commentary.) On the other hand, that ' you cannot serve God
and money ' is not by any means off the Rabbinic line. In spite
of their aversion to poverty, the Rabbis held no less strongly that
the actual *service* of money—avarice, covetousness, or even making
the acquisition of money for its own sake as the one purpose of
existence—was inconsistent with the service of the Torah and of
God. The quotations already made on Matt. xix. 23 are enough
to prove that, and yet others could be adduced.

19–31. I do not propose to give parallels from the Rabbinic
literature to the Gospel conceptions about Hell and Heaven. What
we may call the archaeology of the future life is not specially interesting or of living value, for Jesus and the Gospel compilers and the
Rabbis and the compilers of the Talmud were all equally ignorant
of it. Their views, moreover, have all a marked family likeness
to one another, and a marked divergence from our own.

24. A story, told twice in the Palestinian or Jerusalem
Talmud, and given in S.B., illustrates this verse. It is worth
quoting, because of its perfectly ingenuous exemplification of the
common Rabbinic view that not only are the prosperity of the
wicked on earth and the calamities of the righteous compensated
for by their different fortunes in the hereafter, but that a trifling
sin, or a few minor sins, of the righteous are punished on

earth, and one good deed or a few good deeds of the wicked
are rewarded on earth, in order that the way may be quite
clear for complete beatitude and complete misery in the life
to come. The doctrine of retribution—a weak point in Rabbinic
theology — is carried to a painful extreme. ' Two pious men
(or, in the variant, two disciples of the wise or two Rabbis)
lived in Ashkelon. They ate and drank together, and occupied
themselves with the Torah. One died, and no one accompanied
his body to the grave. Then the tax collector Mayan (or his
son) died, and the whole town followed his body. The living
pious man said : Woe, nothing evil happens to the wicked.
He saw a vision in a dream. A voice said, Despise (תיבזי) not
the sons of your Lord ; the one had committed one sin [and so by
his unaccompanied burial his iniquity is atoned for, or he has
received his punishment] ; the other had performed one good deed
[and so by his grand funeral he has received his reward]. What
sin had the one committed ? Far be it that he had ever committed
a [serious] sin. But once he put on the *Tefillin* for the head before
the *Tefillin* for the hand. And what good deed had the other performed ? Far be it that he had ever done a [really fine] deed.
But once he had arranged a meal for the Bouleutai [the municipal
councillors] of the city, and they did not come. And he said, Let
the poor eat it that it be not wasted. Others say, He once went
through the market-place, and he dropped a loaf, and a poor man
picked it up, and he said nothing so as not make him blush for shame.
After some days the pious man saw in a dream his companion walking
in the Garden (Paradise) under trees and by wells of water ; and
he saw the tax-collector, and his tongue sought to drink at the brink
of a river ; he tried to reach the water, but he could not ' (Jer.
Sanhedrin vi. § 9, 23 c ; Jer. Chagigah ii. § 2, 77 d). Again, there is
the story in Ruth R. iii. § 3 (*ad init.*) on i. 17, of the two robbers, one
of whom, on seeing the punishment of his companion, had repented,
and when he died (or was executed ?), went to heaven with the
company of the righteous, while the other went to hell. When he
complained, and also offered to repent, he was told it was too late.
' He who does not prepare for the Sabbath on Friday, what shall he
have to eat upon the Sabbath ? '

30. The presupposition of this verse is that it is of the most

urgent importance that the brothers should repent while yet living upon earth, because there will be no power or opportunity to repent in hell. This would seem to have been the prevailing opinion of the Rabbis also. *Cp.* the story just cited from Ruth R. S.B. say that it was the older view, but that when the fires of Gehenna were conceived as a purgatory for the great mass of Israelites (the 'in-betweens,' *cp.* the passage from Rosh ha-Shanah 16 b translated on Matt. xxv. 31–46), then repentance after death naturally came to be regarded as the indispensable condition of the redemption of the wicked from hell (whether it were the ' intermediate ' hell after death, or the ' ultimate ' hell after the last judgment). (II. p. 233.) I do not myself think that this statement is entirely accurate. The fires of Gehenna purify in themselves ; that is stated ; but I do not find it stated that they do not begin to exercise their purgatorial effect until or before there is repentance. This may be implied or assumed. It does not appear to be definitely stated. S.B. (Vol. IV. p. 1044 *fin.*) explain how, from the beginning of the second century A.D., even the intermediate Gehenna was also regarded as (for many) a purgatory (*i.e.* a purifying and atoning place and period of punishment). And they add : ' Voraussetzung bleibt natürlich, dass die Sühnkraft des zwischenzeitlichen Gehinnoms unterstützt wird durch die Bussfertigkeit des Gerichteten selbst ' (*cp.* p. 1047 *fin.*).[1] But only two instances are quoted of this penitence in hell. In the first the divergent opinions of two Rabbis as to the possibility or impossibility of repentance in Gehenna are reconciled by the particularistic explanation that the Gentile sinners cannot (or may not) repent in hell, whereas the Israelite sinners can and may. (Erubin 19 a.) The other passage says that the rebellious sinner against God is thrown into Gehenna, but that, if he repents, he is cast forth from it, even as an arrow is shot forth from the bow. (Tanchuma 27 b.) The same redeeming effect is produced by the prayers, and even the almsgiving, of the living, but to deal with the rise and development of this curious doctrine among the Rabbis would be outside the purview of this note. Mr. Loewe writes : ' It is characteristic of the Rabbis that these divergent opinions about repentance after death continued to flourish side by side. The Rabbis did not mind these inconsistencies. They thought of

---

[1] ' It is, of course, presupposed that the atoning power of the intermediate Purgatory will be supported by the repentance of the condemned person.'

one thing at a time, regardless of consequences. They felt the danger of letting people think that one could repent with ease after death, and thus continue to lead a sinful life upon earth ; so they preached the doctrine that after death there could be, and there was, no room or opportunity for repentance ; yet, on the other hand, they were no pessimists, and they were reluctant to put any limit to repentance or forgiveness and to the grace and goodness of God. Hence they *also* taught the doctrine that repentance *was* possible *after* death. The one doctrine was in flagrant contradiction to the other ; but they did not notice, or did not mind, the contradiction. Both doctrines were useful or even necessary, and so both doctrines were used and taught.'

xvii. 3.   To their great credit S.B. are almost always ready to quote the good parallels, and the quotation which they give here from Numbers Rabba, *Chukkath*, xix. 23 on xxi. 7 is not only pretty, but perfectly characteristic and on the Rabbinic line.   In the story of the serpents (Numbers xxi. 6) the plural is used in verse 6, but in verse 7 the people say, ' We have sinned, for we spoke against the Lord and against thee : pray unto the Lord that he take away the serpent (singular) from us.'   So the Midrash asks, Why the singular ?   There was only one serpent, after all, and Moses nevertheless prayed to God.   Why ?   That he did so shows you the humility of Moses, who did not hesitate to seek mercy for them, and it shows you the power of repentance.   Directly they said, We have sinned, he was reconciled to them : for the forgiver (the offended or wronged man) must not be cruel (*achzari*—the vice of hardness, cruelty, unforgivingness was especially censured by the Rabbis).   So with Abraham and Abimelech, and with Job and his friends.   So, if a man has wronged his neighbour, and he says, I have sinned, the other is called a sinner if he does not forgive him. This is proved from I Samuel xii. 23.

7–10.   A most noble and notable passage.   But because it is so, there is no need uncritically to vilipend the Rabbis.   The passage is great enough not to require any extra light by way of contrast and foil.   What I say on verse 7 (II. p. 543) is, I think, justified. S.B. quote Aboth ii. 9, how R. Yochanan ben Zakkai was wont to say, ' If thou hast learnt much Torah, ascribe not any merit to

thyself, for thereunto wast thou created.' But the passage from
the Liturgy (*P.B.* p. 7) should also have been quoted. 'Not
because of our righteous acts do we lay our supplications before
thee, but because of thine abundant mercies. What are we?
What is our piety? What our righteousness?' And so on. The
prayer must, I imagine, be early Rabbinic because it is alluded
to in Yoma 87 b. It depends on Daniel ix. 18, a very familiar
verse to the Rabbis, and inadequately translated in A.V. and
R.V. It should not run, 'We do not present our supplications
before thee *for* our righteousnesses, but *for* thy great mercies';
but it should run, 'We do not present our supplications
before thee *because of* our righteous deeds, but *because of* thy
great mercies.' Dr. Abrahams most justly says : 'In this passage we have the true Rabbinic spirit on the subject of "grace"
and "works." The Rabbis held that reward and punishment were
meted out in some sort of accordance with a man's righteousnes
and sin. But nothing that man, with his small powers and finite
opportunities, can do constitutes a *claim* on the favour of the
Almighty and the Infinite. In the final resort all that men receive
from the divine hand is an act of grace. Hence : *Not because of*
(*i.e.* relying on) *our righteous acts do we lay our supplications before
thee, but because of* (or relying on) *thine abundant mercies*' (*Annotated Prayer Book*, p. xxi). It is natural that whereas Christian
theologians do not mind that the Rabbis sang the excellences of
repentance, they are sensitive about claims and grace. One can
easily see why ! Nevertheless, the facts are as Dr. Abrahams has
stated them. On Deut. iii. 23, where Moses supplicated the Lord,
the Midrash (Deut. R. ii. *init.*) observes : 'R. Yochanan said, Hence
you can learn that a creature has nothing near his Creator (= a man
has no claim on his Creator). (שאין לבריה כלום אצל בוראו.) Moses,
the greatest of the Prophets, did not come to God except with
the language of supplication. God says, He who has something
in my hand (*i.e.* who offers to me some good deed), with him
I deal with the measure of mercy, but to him who has nothing
I am gracious with a free gift.' In Mid. Psalms iv. (1) verse 1,
20 b, we find, 'The congregation of Israel prays before God and
says : It is for thee, O God, to justify me ; if there is no merit
in me, act towards me in charity.' (The passage depends upon
the various meanings of *Zedek* and *Zedakah*, justify, righteous-

ness, and charity.) (*Cp.* also on iv. (7), verse 1, 23 a, nearly the same saying, and on xvii. (13), 67 b.) ' With whom may we compare David ? With one who had a wound on his hand. He goes to the doctor. The doctor says : I can't heal you, your wound is (too) big and the fee you offer is (too) small. He replies, I pray you, take all I have, and the rest supply from what you yourself possess, and have compassion with me. So said David : Healing comes from thee : because the wound is big, give me a big plaster ' (Mid. Psalms li. (3) 141 a). So throughout the short comments on Ps. xliv. (1), verse 1, 134 b : ' Not for their works were Israelites redeemed from Egypt, but so that God might make himself an eternal name and because of his favour (or grace).' Midrash Psalms xliv. (2), verse 26, 135 a, 'Rise up,' etc., and 'redeem us,' etc., ' If we have any good works, help ; and if we have no good works, help for thy name's sake.' Very similar are passages in Midrash Psalms xxii. (18), verse 3, 95 a, and lxxi. (2), verse 2, 162 a, top. Again, on lxxii. (1) 162 b, we read : ' If we have good deeds, he gives us from what is ours ; if we have not, he acts with charity and lovingkindness to us from what is his.' On Psalm cxix. (55), verse 123, 250 b, foot: ' Perhaps thou hast pleasure in our good works ? Merit of good works we have not : act towards us in lovingkindness. The men of old whom thou didst redeem, thou didst not redeem through their works : but thou didst act in loving-kindness towards them and didst redeem them. So do thou with us.' On Ps. cxli. (1), verse 1, 264 b, ' Hasten to me.' ' David said, As I hasten to do thy word so hasten thou to me. To what is the matter like ? To a man who has a suit before a lord. He sees that all the others have advocates to plead for them. He called to the lord and said, All have their advocates ; I have none : there is no one to plead for me. Be thou my advocate and my judge. So David said, Some trust in their fair and upright deeds; and some in the works of their fathers ; but I trust in thee. Although I have no good works, yet because I call upon thee, do thou answer me.' ' R. Elazar pointed out a contradiction between : With thee, O Lord, is grace (lovingkindness), and thou requitest each man according to his work. Solution : At first, the latter ; at the end, the former ' (Rosh ha-Shanah 17 b). On Exodus xv. 13 the Mechilta (42 b) says : ' Thou wroughtest *chesed* (love, grace, loving-kindness) for us, for no works were in our hand : the world from the

beginning was only built on *chesed.*' On Genesis xxiv. 12 the Midrash Rabba, חיי שרה, lx. 2, remarks : ' R. Isaac said, All need
grace (*chesed*), for even Abraham, for whose sake grace prevails
in the world, himself needed grace.' (This is the correct translation, as noted by Rabbi J. Fuerst in Wuensche, p. 530, correcting
the translation on p. 282.) Highly curious is a passage in Sifre.
Here it says that David and Moses could by their own good
deeds have annulled Israel's sins (היו יכולים לתלות את העברות).
Nevertheless, they only asked God to grant forgiveness to Israel by
his grace (freely, חנם). If they acted thus, how much more should
those who are not even one of their disciples ask forgiveness from
God by grace alone. (Sifre 70 b.) ' God is under no obligation to
his creatures at all; he gives gratuitously' (איני חייב לבריה כלום
אלא חנם אני נותן להם). This is adduced from Exodus xxxiii. 19.
(Tanchuma B. *Vaetchannan* xi. 5 a.)

These quotations are not from S.B., but from my own reading.
I add an interesting passage in Büchler, *Sins*, pp. 165–169, with
its valuable quotation from Semachoth viii. ' R. Akiba says,
The king (God) has four sons; one, when smitten, keeps silence
(and suffers); the second, when smitten, kicks ; the third, when
smitten, prays, and the fourth, when smitten, says to his father,
Smite me ! Abraham, when smitten, keeps silence ; when God
said to him, Gen. xxii. 2, " Take now thy son, thine only son, whom
thou lovest, even Isaac . . . and offer him there for a burnt-offering,"
he could have said to God, Yesterday Thou didst tell me, Gen. xxi.
12, " for in Isaac shall seed be called to thee," and yet it says,
Gen. xxii. 3, " And Abraham rose early in the morning," etc.
Job, when smitten, kicks, as it says, Job x. 2, " I will say unto God,
Do not condemn me ; make me know wherefore Thou contendest
with me." Hezekiah, when smitten, beseeches (God), as it says,
2 Reg. xx. 2, " and he prayed unto the Lord," etc. ; some say that
also Hezekiah, while smitten, kicks later on ; was it for him to
say, 2 Reg. xx. 3, Is. xxviii. 3, " and I have done that which is
good in Thy sight " ? David said to his Father, Smite me, as it
says, Psalm li. 4, " Wash me thoroughly from mine iniquity, and
cleanse me from my sin." This full statement of R. Akiba is in
itself of great value for the question of the love and the fear of God,
as it embodies his view of the various attitudes of Jews to visitations sent by God. As it appears, the least satisfactory of the three

relatively irreprehensible positions was taken up by king Hezekiah, as he prayed to God to free him from his mortal illness and to withdraw His decree to terminate his life. That assumption seems to be supported by the fact that another opinion placed Hezekiah's prayer, on account of its reference to his merits, on the same low level as Job's offensive reproaches. But, in any case, such a depreciative or even disparaging estimate appears to be harsh and strange, considering that God accepted the king's prayer and actually prolonged his life by fifteen years. The unnamed author of the strict view stigmatizes as בעט (cp. Deut. xxxii. 15), "kicking," Hezekiah's reference to his merits, as also his argument against the decree of God to terminate his life. The very strong word testifies to the scholar's reprobation of the king's attitude in pointing to his obedience to God, though it extended to his walking before God throughout the whole of his life. This judgment of the teacher definitely and cogently refutes the familiar assumption by the commentators of the New Testament of the Rabbis' bookkeeping of their meritorious and their sinful actions, and of their presentation of the balance to God in their calamity and suffering. As to the attitudes of the other two pious men, R. Akiba mentions first Abraham's silent submission to God's contradictory and inscrutable demand, and the Patriarch's unhesitating execution of God's will without even a word of reference to His earlier assurance of Israel's great future, and his immediate setting about sacrificing his son. And even such wordless obedience was not regarded by R. Akiba as an attitude of the highest religious standard, though in his list he mentioned it first. David's attitude was the purest and the highest in its religious and moral value, as he not only submitted without any complaint or question to the visitation inflicted by God, but even asked Him for further chastisements in order that he might obtain forgiveness of his sins.' The variant in Midrash Psalms xxvi. 1, 108 b, is also worth looking at. Dr. Büchler adds in a footnote, p. 168, n. 1, a passage from Sifre 70 b : ' Israel had two good leaders, Moses and David ; when they were punished for their sins, they could have referred to their good deeds (lit. connected the punishments with their merits), but they asked for the free consideration of God without any reference to their merits : how much more should the very smallest of their disciples ask for the consideration of God without any reference to his merits.' I am not sure that, as Dr.

Büchler explains the quotation, we to-day should not put Abraham above David. But, perhaps, Dr. Büchler is a little unjust to David. He did not, perhaps, say : ' Smite me,' in order to obtain forgiveness, but in order to get free from sin ; this is a distinction with some difference. I am not clear that Dr. Büchler has got the book-keeping business quite clearly. I have never seen it in the form in which he puts it. The usual charge is twofold. (1) That a balance may be drawn between a man's good and bad actions. If the good is a bit more than the bad, the man is virtuous or absolved ; if the other way, he is bad and guilty. (2) That sometimes God's rewards are represented as the results of man's merits. As to the first charge, this somewhat too arithmetical and mechanical view of goodness and badness does actually occur. As to the second, it can hardly be denied that there are a number of passages about *Zechuth* (merit), some of which are, distinctly, unpleasant enough. But the merit never seems to be regarded as a *claim*. God acts upon *Zechuth* according to as his own will, and as often as not the *Zechuth* is not the merit of the man to whom God vouchsafes mercy or happiness, but the merit of others. The individual Rabbi does not appear to consider that he can *demand* from God a recompense for his piety and ' good works.' The recompense is doubtless the *partial result* of the goodness. How could it rightly be otherwise ? But the recompense is out of proportion to the goodness, partly because God's heavenly rewards are out of all proportion to man's finite and limited goodness, partly because ' there is no man that sinneth not,' and grace is ever required and must always come into play. On the other hand, the thought of Luke xvi. 10, especially if we omit the word ἀχρεῖοι, is, I think, original—the thought, I mean, that ' whatever good a man does, he cannot do *more* than he *owes* to God, for to God he owes all that he is capable of doing.' I do not find exact parallels for this idea. And I also think that, as I have said in the Commentary (p. 543) ' the tilt against exaggerations and perversions of the doctrine of tit for tat is a prominent and characteristic feature of the teaching of Jesus. What we receive from God is grace and goodness, and not reward. There is no doubt that the *excessive* emphasis and elaboration of the doctrine of retribution was one of the weak spots in Rabbinic Judaism.'

I might mention here the emphasis laid by the Rabbis upon man receiving the chastisements and visitations of God with humility

and resignation. One must neither ' kick ' nor criticize. That was
Job's fault, for which many Rabbis blamed him. He kicked and
criticized and spoke rashly and even blasphemously. (See Büchler,
Sins, p. 173, n. 3, p. 175, etc.) 'R. Eliezer b. Jacob said, Thou shalt
not criticize the chastisements ; so David said, My heart is not
haughty, I have not criticized (הרהרתי) my creator.' (Büchler,
Sins, p. 173, n. 3, p. 174, 181. Midrash Tannaim, p. 111, on
Deut. xviii. 13.) So in Sifre 132 b, 'We must not criticize God's
ways even in the slightest degree' (p. 182). There must be no
complaints. 'R. Simon said, He who says in his prayer to God,
"Thy mercies reach the nest of a bird," implies thereby, "but me
Thy mercies have not reached," and complains by that of God's
ways' (Berachoth Mishnah v. 3 ; Jer. Berachoth v. 9 c ; Büchler,
p. 183). (This is a nobler explanation of the problematic words
about the bird's nest, and a quite different one from the more usual
explanations, for which see Cohen's *Berachoth*, p. 225.)

In the excursus on the parable of the Labourers in the Vineyard
(Vol. IV. pp. 488, 489) S.B. give certain passages, of which the
tendency, like the tendency of the saying of R. Yochanan ben Zakkai
(Aboth ii. 9) quoted above, is to imply that every Israelite is under a
moral compulsion to study and practise the Law. They were redeemed from Egypt on that condition, which applies to all their
generations. Though the words of the Law are not to be regarded
as a debt (חובה), no one is free to dispense with them. (Menachoth
99 b.) The Israelite is created for the service of (or to labour in)
the Law. (לעמל תורה. The phrase is a sort of semi-jest based
upon Job v. 7, 'Man is born unto trouble,' the word for ' trouble '
being also capable of signifying 'labour' or 'toil.') (Sanhedrin
99 b, top.) 'I am the Lord thy God who brought you out of the
land of Egypt on the condition (על תנאי) that you should receive
the yoke of the commandments : he who acknowledges the yoke of
the commandments acknowledges the coming out of Egypt : he
who rejects (כופר ב') the yoke of the commandments rejects the
coming out of Egypt.' 'To be your God.' 'Even against your will'
(בעל כורחכם). (Sifra on Lev. xi. 45, 57 b.) These last two words
are extremely strong. (*Cp.* on Lev. xix. 36, 91 b.) 'I brought
you out of the land of Egypt on condition that you should surrender
(שתמסרו) yourselves to sanctify my name' (do. on Lev. xxii. 33,
99 d). On Lev. xxv. 38 it is said, 'I brought you out of the land of

Egypt on the condition that you should accept the law against usury, for every one who acknowledges the law against usury acknowledges the coming out of Egypt, and he who denies the law of usury is as if he denied the Exodus from Egypt ' (Sifra 109 c). ' Why is the Exodus from Egypt mentioned in connection with every single commandment ? The matter can be compared to a king, the son of whose friend was taken prisoner. The king ransomed him, not as son, but as slave, so that if he should at any time disobey the king, the latter could say, You are my slave. So when he came back, the king said, Put on my sandals for me, take my clothes to the bath house. Then the man protested. The king took out the bill of sale, and said, You are my slave. So when God redeemed the children of Abraham his friend, he redeemed them, not as children, but as slaves, so that if he imposed upon them decrees and they obey not, he could say, Ye are my slaves. When they went into the desert, he began to order them some light and some heavy commands, Sabbath and incest commands, *e.g.*, and fringes and phylacteries. They began to protest. Then God said, Ye are my slaves. On this condition (על מנה) I redeemed you, that I should decree and you should fulfil ' (Sifre 35 a). Nevertheless, God's slaves are unlike man's slaves. God's ways are not like those of ' flesh and blood.' For a man acquires slaves that these may look after and sustain *him*, but God acquires slaves that he may look after and sustain *them* (זן ומפרנס אותם). (Sifre 77 a.)

Here in these passages we have another Rabbinic conception clearly expressed. The Law is a sign or expression of God's grace and love. The Israelites may well be proud of their immense privilege in having their wonderful Law to study and to fulfil. It is, and it should be, their boast and their exceeding great joy. But it is also their duty. They cannot get out of it. They cannot escape from it. It pursues them. They cannot say (as the very next passage in the Sifre distinctly states), We will give up the rewards and therefore we will escape the punishments : we will neither fulfil the Law nor ask for a reward (לא עושים ולא נוטלים שכר). That is impossible. They are God's slaves, and cannot escape his rule and his Law. They cannot say, We will be like the nations. Even against their will God will be their king. In every possible way the Rabbis incite to the observance of the Law. It is duty, privilege, joy : its fulfilment is an end in itself, and will procure reward in time and eternity. Its service is, moreover, inevitable. As the fish cannot breathe out of water, so will God not allow Israel to live without the Law.

xvii. 21.   It is interesting that S.B. make no comment upon this most famous verse. All obviously depends upon the meaning of the preposition ἐντός. (*Cp.* ii. pp. 546–549.) If it stands for 'among,' there is nothing here to be said one way or the other ; if it, however, means 'within,' and the first of my three main interpretations be the correct one, then I think it would have to be said that there is no clear Rabbinic parallel to a conception of the Kingdom as 'a spiritual principle, which works unseen and regeneratively in the hearts of men.'

I might add here that I omit any reference to the Rabbinic parallels or contrasts to 'with observation' (xvii. 20). The subject does not seem to have any living interest for us to-day.

xviii. 1.   'Pray without ceasing.'   S.B. seem in error when they say that this injunction is off the Rabbinic line. The Rabbis looked at the matter all round ; they saw the danger of too casual and frequent prayer. Prayer to them needed preparation ; one has to get into the right *Stimmung*. Therefore to pray the statutory three times a day was, from one point of view, enough. Moreover, one must not weary and worry God. Yet, from another point of view, the saying of R. Yochanan, 'Would that a man could pray the whole day long, for no prayer does harm,' is also, one feels, not off the line, even though it may have no exact parallel. (Jer. Berachoth i. § 1, 2 b; i. § 5, 3 b, etc.) The passages in Jer. Berachoth ix. § 1, 13 b, are really quite analogous ; *e.g.* 'A man has a defender (patron) ; if he worries him too much, the patron says, I will forget him, he worries me. But God is not so ; however much you worry him, he receives you.' (The worrying is through prayer.) So too Midrash Psalms iv. (3), verse 1, 20 b, and lv. (6), verse 23, 147 a.   Such passages are quite characteristic. *Cp.* pp. 122, 148.

9–12.   That this passage with its charming 'parable' justly illustrates one of the dangers of Rabbinic legalism, or, if you will, of the Rabbinic religion, cannot be doubted.   Objection can only be raised when the parable is said to illustrate, not the dangers and perversions of the Rabbinic religion, but the Rabbinic religion itself—as if the Pharisee of the parable were the average Pharisee and the average Rabbi produced by Rabbinic legalism, and worse still, as if this odious Pharisee represented not the perversion, but the type and even the ideal—as if he was the very man whom the Rabbis would wish to be and were. I feel convinced that this is false. As regards the two Rabbinic quotations given in Vol. II. pp. 556, 557 of my Commentary, I still believe that my remarks are accurate. Nor, I think, is the man who said the first quotation necessarily a self-satisfied prig, a self-righteous boaster. It may be true that the frame of mind which prompted the utterance, ' there but for the grace of God goes Richard Baxter,' is the higher, but, after all, what the Rabbi means is that by the grace of God he *has* been preserved from wasting his time and sinning and ending (according to the narrow views of his age) in hell. Well, if God did, for some inscrutable reason, so preserve him, may he not legitimately and genuinely, and yet humbly, thank God for his preservation ? I do not see that he is *necessarily* a self-satisfied prig any more than Dorcas was in the novel. (Vol. II. p. 557.) The caricature of the Dorcas type is a self-righteous prig no less than the caricature of the grateful Rabbi. But the Rabbi, no less than Dorcas, *can* be quite simple and genuine, the one in his gratitude, the other in her piety. What is justified criticism of perversions and caricatures is foolish and unhistoric if sweepingly applied to the normal and the ideal.

Perhaps I had better give ' the two Rabbinic quotations ' (Berachoth 28 b). The first runs : ' I give thanks before thee, O Lord my God, that thou hast set my portion with those who sit in the House of Study and not with those who sit at street corners ; for I and they rise early—I to words of Torah, but they to vain matters ; I and they labour, but I labour and receive a reward, whereas they labour and receive no reward ; I and they hasten—I to the life of the world to come, but they to the pit of destruction.' (For ' those who sit at street corners ' the Jerusalem Talmud reads ' those who frequent theatres and circuses.') The second runs : ' It was a favourite saying of the Rabbis of Yabneh : I am a creature (of God) and my neighbour is also his creature ; my work is in the city and his in the field ; I rise early to my work and he rises early

2 B

to his. As he cannot excel in my work, so I cannot excel in his work. But perhaps thou sayest, I do great things and he small things. We have learnt that (it matters not whether) a man does much or little, if only he directs his heart to Heaven' (Berachoth 17 a).

9. Hillel's saying, 'Trust not in thyself till the day of thy death' (Aboth ii. 5) was not exceptional. The general Rabbinic line was that a man should not be too confident or too despairing about his chances of 'salvation.' The Rabbis are often attacked both ways. Luke xviii. 9 and the quotation given in my Commentary, Vol. II. p. 556 *fin.*, prove their self-righteousness. The famous story of R. Yochanan b. Zakkai's death-bed, quoted on x. 28 (Berachoth 28 b), proves their despairingness and want of confidence—their lack of regenerative and justifying faith. I do not see how you can have it both ways. I notice that S.B. (Vol. II. p. 240) have no other good illustration to give except the passage quoted in my Commentary on p. 556 *fin.*, for the quotations from Erubin 21 b cannot be so regarded. 'Raba quoted Canticles xii. 11, 12, and said, The congregation of Israel speaks to God : Do not judge me as one judges dwellers in cities, among whom are found thefts and adulteries and perjuries. I will show thee disciples of the wise who occupy themselves with the Law in the midst of distress ; and I will show thee children of Esau, to whom thou hast given good in profusion, and yet they have denied thee.' 'Let us go up early to the vineyards. These are the houses of prayer and study : these are they who know the written word (the Scriptures) ; these are they who know the Mishnah ; these are they who know the Talmud.' 'There will I give thee my love. I will show thee my glory and my greatness, the renown of my sons and my daughters.' Israel's praise of itself is very different from individual self-righteousness. It is not fair to identify, or to infer, the one from the other.

14. S.B. consider, and, perhaps justly, that δεδικαιωμένος here means simply 'forgiven.' They go on to say that the Rabbis would have expressed the strongest disapprobation, and have been in the most emphatic disagreement, with Jesus in his verdict upon the tax-collector, because those who have dealt unjustly with their fellow-men cannot be forgiven till they have made restitution. There were legal statements to the effect that the repentance of

such men is difficult, who, like tax-collectors, do not know precisely whom, or all whom, they have injured. (It is assumed that every tax-collector was of necessity an oppressor : he farmed the taxes, and had to get as much as he could out of the unfortunate tax-payers.) ' He who robs the public (the many) must restore to the many. Worse is stealing from the many than stealing from an individual, for he who steals from an individual can appease him, and return the theft; the former cannot' (Tosefta Baba Kamma x. 14, p. 367, foot. Then follows a famous decision : ' He who steals from a non-Jew is bound to restore the theft to the non-Jew. Worse is stealing from a non-Jew than stealing from a Jew, because of the Profanation of the Name '). ' Hard is the repentance of the *Gabbaim* (Tax-collectors) and of the Tax-farmers ; they return (what they have wrongfully acquired) to those they know, and from the rest the needs of the community are defrayed ' (T. Baba Mezia viii. 26, p. 390). Later on, apparently, there was only a formal return, so as to fulfil the obligation towards God (לצאת ידי שמים), but the money was ultimately given back to the tax-collectors. As to the needs of the community, the making of cisterns and wells is suggested as a suitable means for the employment of the money (Baba Kamma 94 b). But such sayings (S.B. p. 248) are mainly legal. I am convinced that a repentant tax-collector, who gave up his job, would have been regarded by the Rabbis as a *good* penitent, and it would have been held that God would forgive him. I do not suppose that this, my view, could be rigorously proved and demonstrated by quotations. It is a question of feeling. He who has read much Rabbinic literature, and is impartial, will, I think, agree with me. Nor is there much self-righteousness in Erubin 21 b. Raba, quoting Canticles vii. 13, said, ' Israel says to God, Lord of the world, I have ordained more injunctions upon myself than those which thou hast ordained for me, and I have observed them.' The Pharisee of the story *did* mean that he had observed and done more than the Law required, and he was filled with self-satisfaction and self-righteousness thereat. But I do not think that the naïve saying of Raba can be so interpreted. The more laws and ordinances, the more beauty and glory and splendour and happiness, but not the more self-righteousness ; the more love to God, but not the more self-satisfaction. That Raba's saying is an allegorical interpretation of Canticles vii. 13 helps to prove my case. ' O my beloved.' That is God, and the speaker is Israel.

xix. 10. Here in this noble verse we have once more an original utterance of the greatest importance and significance. The Rabbis spoke much of the imitation of God. But I do not find that they bade man imitate God in regard to that one of his activities which God describes in Ezekiel xxxiv. 16, the verse upon which Luke xix. 10 is obviously based. And of what immense consequence this verse and its parallels have been ! Here Jesus goes far beyond his original mission and utterance in Mark i. 15 ; he himself will seek to help the sinner to repent ; he himself, by loving deeds and loving sympathy, will seek to save the lost. That is something both great and new. (τὸ ἀπολωλὸς ζητήσω are the words of the LXX in Ezekiel xxxiv. 16.)

xxi. 1–4. For this beautiful section the parallels (given by S.B. on Mark xii. 43, Vol. II. p. 46 *init.*) have been here used already in the course of the long supplementary note to the Sermon on the Mount, pp. 188, 189.

xxiii. 34. ' Father, forgive them, for they know not what they do.' I have spoken about these noble and beautiful words in the Commentary. Whether they are spurious or genuine does not, in one sense, much matter. Nor does it greatly matter if, being genuine, they refer, as Harnack argues, exclusively to the Roman soldiers. For the point is that they are now, and have practically always been, a portion of the Gospel story. They are a feature of the picture. It is true that Christendom has paid small heed to them. It has much more frequently and habitually given heed to the Gospel creation of the Jews thirsting for the blood of Jesus than the Gospel creation (if it be one) of Jesus forgiving those who sent him to his doom. Nevertheless, there stand the words, and ninety-nine readers out of every hundred would take them to apply to all the enemies of Jesus, whether Jewish or Roman, and not merely to the Roman soldiers. Hence, if ideals are to be matched with ideals, it is open for Christian scholars to say to Jewish scholars, what corresponding picture have you to set beside this picture of Jesus forgiving his enemies at the last hour ? What corresponding

picture, taken from the martyrologies of the Rabbinic literature ?
And I am bound to reply that, so far as I know, there is none.
Well, then, may it not justly be said that the words constitute a
religious advance, or that they constitute a religious gem without
which the religious literature of the world would be the poorer ?
No doubt if the words are authentic, and if, being authentic, Harnack is wrong as to their limitation, their beauty, their power and
their effect are all the greater ; but even if they are not genuine,
or if, being genuine, Harnack is right—even so they still remain
an utterance of deep significance. Nor can we say that they have
wholly failed or wholly been wasted. From time to time there
have been examples in history—was not Nurse Cavell a most
splendid instance ?—when the words have borne fruit and been
fulfilled in deed. And the world is still going on. They may be
fulfilled again.

43. It may be interesting to quote the Talmudic story in
which a Roman executioner is promised by a martyred Rabbi
that he shall receive the beatitudes of the life to come. It occurs
in Abodah Zarah 17 b–18 b. The story is told in two divisions, and
clearly is partly legendary and partly historical. I shall have to
make some omissions. ' When R. Elazar b. Perata I. and R.
Chanina b. Teradion were arrested, Elazar said to Chanina, Happy
are you that you have been arrested on one count, whereas I have
been arrested on five. Chanina answered, Happy are you, who
will be set free ; woe is me, who will not be delivered. You occupied
yourself with the study of the Law, and with deeds of charity,
whereas I occupied myself with the study of the Law only. Chanina
said this according to the teaching of R. Huna, who declared, He
who occupies himself with the study of the Law only is as if he had
no God.' I here make a long omission. ' They brought out R.
Chanina and asked him, Why did you occupy yourself with the
study of the Law ? He answered, Because God commanded me
to do so. They then sentenced him to be burnt alive, his wife to
be decapitated, and his daughter to be put in a brothel.' Then the
Talmud, as happens so frequently, falls a victim to its inveterate
desire to find a reason in human sin for human suffering ; I omit
the reasons which are given for all three sufferers. The story is
then resumed with a fresh introduction. ' When R. Yose b. Kisma

was ill, R. Chanina b. Teradion went to visit him. Yose said to him, Brother, do you not know that God has given dominion to this nation (*i.e.* Rome); that it has destroyed his house, burnt his sanctuary, slaughtered his saints, and that it still is established ? And I hear that you still occupy yourself with the study of the Law, and carry a scroll of the Law in your bosom. Chanina said, Heaven will have mercy upon me. Yose replied, I say sensible words to you, and you answer, Heaven will have mercy upon me! I shall be surprised if they do not burn you and your scroll with fire. Then Chanina said, What will be my lot as regards the life of the world to come ? Yose said, Have you anything to show ? ' Once more we note the old doctrine in another form. What good deed have you done to merit the guerdon of the blessedness of the life to come ? ' Chanina said, Purim money got mixed up with alms money, and I gave it all to the poor.' This apparently means that he supplied and put back the Purim distribution money from his own pocket. ' Then Yose said, In that case, may my portion be like unto your portion, and may my lot be as yours. After a few days R. Yose died, and all the great ones of Rome (the Roman authorities in Palestine) attended his funeral, and they mourned for him with a great mourning. When they returned, they met Chanina occupying himself with the study of the Law, holding assemblies in public, and carrying a scroll in his bosom. Then they took him, and wrapped the scroll round him, heaped bundles of willow wood about him, and set fire to them. Then they took woolly bits of cloth, soaked them in water, and laid them on his heart that he might not die quickly. Then his daughter said, Father, that I should have to see you thus ! He replied, if I were to be burnt alone, it would have been hard for me, but now that the Scroll of the Law is being burnt with me, He who will avenge His own humiliation in the burning of the Scroll will also avenge my humiliation. His disciples said to him, What do you see ? He replied, The leaves of the Scroll are being burnt and the letters are flying (up to heaven).' The idea is that the divine word has an indestructible existence of its own, independent of the material to which it is temporarily attached. ' Then they said to him, Open your mouth that the fire may enter into it.' (The object was that his tortures should be shortened.) ' He replied, It is better that He who gave me my soul should take it rather than that (I should break the rule) Let no man do himself an injury (or let no man do violence to himself).' Here the marked difference between Judaism and Stoicism becomes apparent. ' Then the executioner said to him, Master, if I increase the flame, and remove the bits of woolly cloth from your heart, will you bring me into the life of the world to come ? Chanina replied, Yes, I will. He said, Swear it to me. Then Chanina swore it. At once the executioner increased the flame, and removed the bits of woolly cloth from his heart, and his soul departed quickly. Then the executioner himself leaped into the fire (and was burnt). Then a heavenly voice was heard to say, R. Chanina b. Teradion and the Executioner are appointed for the life of the world to come. And Rabbi wept and said, Some attain their world (to come) in an hour, and some win it (only) in many years.'

APPENDIX I

ON FAITH

By H. LOEWE

ON re-reading my own remarks on Matt. viii. 10, one or two further points occur to me.

Something new in Jesus' conception of faith. Is it something new, after all ? Is it not perhaps something very old and even superseded ? This strikes me after looking up in succession all the passages on faith indicated on pages 201, 205. The impression left on one's mind is surely not that one is faced with a new theological development, but that one is right back again in Israel before the discovery of the Law. The counterparts to these passages are the episodes in the lives of Elijah and Elishah, *e.g.* Naaman, the Shunamite, the widow's cruse, etc. In such incidents the keystone is faith— faith pure and simple ; these incidents might be put in one book, together with the story of the centurion and other Gospel stories, and the whole would make continuous reading. Religion had advanced beyond this point. The Rabbis did not need so much to exhort their hearers to have faith as to act on the consequences of possessing faith, to live morally, to repent, to observe the Law, to sanctify the Name, etc. Hence it would appear as though the stressing of faith were relaxed. But this is only on the surface. Faith was presupposed ; what they wished to inculcate was the practical application of the belief. Possibly we have but a linguistic or homiletic difference ; essentially the preaching of Jesus was that of the Rabbis, but the method differed.

Was it the same ? One must always remember that Jesus was a free-lance, he had no responsibility. I am always saying this because it seems to me to intrude everywhere. He was in a position to pick and choose, to select a particular topic and ignore others, not out of indifference necessarily, but because other teachers were concerned with them. The difference is that between the rector of a parish, to whom the work of the church is the primary consideration, and the itinerant Salvationist. The rector must urge parents to observe the Mitzvoth, *e.g.* to baptize their children, to be regular in church attendance, to support charities, and to take part in all the duties of a member of a congregation. The Salvationist can confine himself to popular preaching on the Atonement, ' the blood of Jesus washes away sins,' ' only believe in the Cross, and you will be saved.' But does the rector believe in faith any the less because he is apparently the more interested in fasting communion or the colour of vestments ?

Again, what do we know of the preaching of the Rabbis to their Gentile audiences ? The Gospels tell us what Jesus said to Jews and to Gentiles, and we know that in speaking to Jews he ' fulfilled ' the Law. We have not much evidence about the things which Jews said to Gentiles in the diaspora. We can form an idea by taking Jonah's message to Nineveh as a sample, and by remembering various sayings about proselytes ; various sayings, because of the good as well as of the bad sayings. And the bad sayings about proselytes are exactly parallel to Jesus' bad sayings about Jews (*e.g.* Matt. viii. 11–12). Every preacher loses heart now and then, especially when he thinks his hearers are irreclaimable. (Incidentally one notices a difference between Jeremiah and Jesus in this regard.)

I think that of the various Gospel passages about faith, some refer to Gentiles or rough Galileans, and when Jesus said to them, ' have faith,' he meant ' for the moment believe (in God and me) : the next stage will come.' He was awaiting some further development—either the End, or else an organization of these converts into communities, by himself, his followers, or the Rabbis, in which case institutionalized religion would follow and further demands would be made. I cannot think that at this stage of history he wanted empty faith alone, without some disciplinary effect on life.

Another thing. Why did the faith-cures of Jesus arouse opposition ? Was it because Jesus laid more stress on faith than the Rabbis did, or was it because he advocated a different kind of faith ? I think it was the latter, if we may assume that what applied to his followers applied to him. As an instance, *cf.* Eccles. Rabba on x. 5, the well-known story of Ben Pandira, discussed by Travers Herford in his *Christianity in Midrash and Talmud*, p. 108 : ' The son of R. Joshua b. Levi had an obstruction in his throat, so they fetched one of the disciples of Ben Pandira (*i.e.* a Christian) to remove it. R. Joshua asked, " What did you say over him ? " " He said such and such a verse after such and such a verse." Joshua replied, " It would have been better that he had been buried rather than thou hadst said this verse over him." ' [The text is not quite clear : (*a*) Joshua may have said, ' What did he (the Christian) say

over you ? ' (b) I think Wuensche (p. 136) is wrong in rendering
' It would have been better for you (the Christian) to have been
buried.' I am sure that this refers to the patient. Joshua b.
Levi taught at Lyd in 260 c.e.]

Now, it is possible that Joshua b. Levi's motive was simply an
objection to Christian healing. But this is most unlikely, because
Joshua was notoriously friendly with Jewish Christians. Nor can
it be argued that, however friendly he may have been, he would
have objected to cures being effected in the name of Jesus, just as
we modern Jews, however friendly we may be to Christianity,
deprecate Jews going to certain Mission hospitals, where they are
invited to hear Christological prayers before receiving treatment.
This cannot have been the case, because then it would have said,
' he recited a verse from the Evangelion,' or 'he invoked the name
of Ben Pandira.' But the term *Pasuk* can refer only to the O.T.
scripture. The opposition cannot then have been that sometimes
found in the mediaeval Church towards the employment of Jewish
doctors. I think the objection was to the use of scriptural verses :
it was done, but it was deprecated. M'Neil (in his comment on
Exodus xv. 26, *Westminster Comm.*, ' None of the diseases which
I have put on the Egyptians will I put on thee, for I am the Lord
who heals thee ') says that the Jews used this verse as a charm.
That is a half-truth. What he should have said is that the use of
this verse as a charm was strongly repudiated by Jewish teachers.
According to Mishnah Sanhedrin xi. 1, he who does so has no share
in the world to come. Joshua, like many Rabbis, felt that it was
an unworthy faith that awaited a direct answer to prayer, and that
the recital of verses for curing came under this category. Other
Rabbis, who, like Jesus, dealt with cruder folk, took the opposite,
simpler view.

It seems to me that faith in sickness or stress was differently
interpreted by the Rabbis. I have already spoken about the
element of miracles and on the stress of faith in Jesus over and
above faith in God. I think that these elements were due not to
the novelty of Jesus' teaching about faith, but to their primitive-
ness, due, possibly, to their being addressed to an audience less
advanced theologically than the audience of Rabbis teaching in
Judaea, from whom something more than mere passive acceptance
of the belief in God was to be expected. Jesus' view was ' unless
you become as little children ' ; it was a kindergarten teaching,
needed for a kindergarten class. The Rabbis did not wish this to
be given to those who had grown older, and had passed to a higher
stage.

APPENDIX II

ON 'ACTING CLEVERLY'

(S.B. Vol. IV. pp. 14 foll.)

By H. LOEWE

ACCORDING to S.B. the outlook of the Jew is hopeless. Judaism lacks an adequate soteriology because the whole Rabbinic scheme of salvation collapsed, and this downfall was due to the deliberate subordination of the ethical element in religion to the dictates of private gain. By legalistic manipulations the interpretation of the Law was wrested from the true and made to conform to financial exigencies. This result was achieved by slavish adherence to the letter as opposed to the spirit : literalism was exerted to the fullest extent so as to make observance of the Law a paying proposition. Hence the Law ceased to be an effective instrument of salvation. Judaism became pure materialism. As a proof of this severe indictment five instances of duplicity are cited, viz. :

I. *Ma'aser Sheni* iv. 4: The evasion of the payment of the extra fifth enjoined on the owner who redeemed his own second tithe.
II. *Sabbath* xvi. 3: The illegitimate rescuing of food from a fire on a Sabbath.
III. *Temurah* v. 1: Substitution practised in case of first-born of animals in defiance of the Law.
IV. *Nazir* ii. 5: Fraduluent arrangement on the part of the two Nazarites by means of which they were enabled to defray each other's ritual expenses instead of each paying for a stranger.
V. *Tos. Bezah* iii. 2: Trickery in the rescue of an animal from a pit on the Sabbath day.

Let it be granted for the moment that everyone of these instances is to be accepted at its face value, as assessed by S.B., and that no word in mitigation is possible. Is the conclusion justifiable ? Are the facts that a certain number of apparently shady practices existed, or that some Rabbis enunciated principles that are said to be in flat contradiction to elementary ethics, sufficient to condemn the complete Rabbinic system ? If one were to ransack the speeches or writings of every ecclesiastical, patristic, or apostolic authority, if one were to make an *ad hoc* selection from Jesus' own words, would S.B. deem Christianity to be judged fairly by such an arbitrary, fragmentary, and unrepresentative pot - pourri ? Surely not. S.B. certainly may not be accused of unfair citation. For the defence they give far more evidence than for the prosecution. This is the curious fault of their reasoning. They are scrupulously careful to state their opponent's case. In the course of argument they put in all the favourable testimony, but in summing up they almost entirely ignore it. They are guilty, not of suppression but of misdirection. The key to the puzzle is easy to find. They are fair enough in setting out the facts, but they have reached their conclusion before coming into court. Firmly convinced in advance of their conclusion, they are logically compelled to regard all evidence as negligible that seems to run counter to that conclusion. It is extraordinary that they do not see that much of their adverse section *e* is answered by their own favourable section *f*. They set out, with no qualifying clause or reservation, four important principles designed by the Rabbis to prevent legalism from overstepping the proper bounds : four principles of great force and frequent occurrence (in one case they use the words ' eine grosse Reihe von Aussprüchen,' p. 15) should surely suffice to outweigh the instances of evasive action which they quoted as their thesis. Yet it is amazing to note S.B.'s conclusion that all these safeguards were superficial and unsuccessful ; they had no practical effect, and might as well not have been there at all. ' Jene Kautelen gleichen Schmuck u. Zierstücken, die man äusserlich am nomistischen Lehrgebäude angebracht hat ; sie hätten auch fehlen können ; die nomistische Soteriologie wäre von ihrem Fortfall unberührt geblieben.'

Let it be conceded for the sake of argument that the interpretation is true and that, further, S.B.'s reasoning is correct, *i.e.* that owing to these legalisms, and in spite of the ineffectual *Kautelen*, the whole system of Rabbinic soteriology crashed. The question immediately arises, what kept the Jews going ? If their soteriology crashed somewhere about A.D. 37, under the onslaught of Jesus, how is it that it lives to-day ? S.B. would surely make no claim that to-day and during the last 1900 years the Jew is and has been, man for man, morally worse than the Christian, and bereft of a hope of salvation ? No one in the face of history or common experience would make such an assertion ; S.B. are too learned and too fair-minded to do so. Where, then, has the Jew learnt

his morality, his love of truth and charity and virtue ? That there
has been the slightest borrowing from Christianity cannot for an
instant be imagined. Captive Greece may indeed take captive her
rude conqueror, but the persecuted do not learn mercy and justice
from their persecutors. What could Judaism have learnt from
Christianity during the Arian or Iconoclastic controversies, during
the suppression of heresy by the sword ? What Gospel rays could
have lit up the Ghetto ? What influence could Rome or Constanti-
nople have exercised on the heart of the Jew ? If to-day the words
honesty, righteousness, charity, and the like have a meaning for
the Jew the cause is no external one. Judaism has, in fact, been
self-sufficing. *Ex nihilo nihil fit* ; the Rabbinic system could not
have crashed, else how could we ' who cleave unto the Lord be alive
all of us this day ? '

That there has been progress and development in Judaism goes
without saying, but from a dead root there can be no growth. A
religion as unsound radically as S.B. suggest could not even have
survived, much less have progressed. Two common errors—one
Jewish, one Christian—are to be noted in connection with progress
in Judaism. On the one hand certain Jewish scholars seem to deny
progress as a force. They assume that as Judaism is to-day, so it
was 2000 years ago. If so, we are no better than our fathers and,
like Elijah, we should ask to die. These scholars believe that
Judaism arose on Sinai fixed and immutable for all time, but such
a conception is pagan and un-Jewish. Athene so sprang from the
head of Zeus, but the Torah is ever growing. Life without progress
is not worth living for a man. But if we believe in progress and
do not merely pay lip service to it as a fine ideal—for others—we
must be prepared to pay the price, *i.e.* to write down our assets if
need be. Some great names never lose their lustre : others may
now be valued as pioneers, whose achievements, valuable in their
time, have been surpassed by those of their followers. Others again
may have to be abandoned entirely : their point of view is no
longer our own ; we have advanced beyond it. We must be prepared to say in a new sense, ' our fathers erred and are no more.'
That there are Jewish scholars who, out of mistaken piety, deem
this selective process unjustifiable, is perfectly true. But they do
not realize that they cannot combine adherence to progress with
an inflexible resolve to justify every Rabbi who has ever lived.
The point is surely not worth labouring, but it must be mentioned
because of our present argument. On July 20–24, 1263, Moses b.
Nahman was engaged at Barcelona in vindicating, in the presence
of the king, the soteriology of Judaism against the attacks of
Pablo Christiani, who urged, much as S.B. do to-day, that the

system had crashed and that nothing remained for the Jew but baptism. A most noteworthy point about this highly interesting disputation was that when confronted with Pablo's list of Talmudic monstrosities Nahmanides boldly threw overboard and abandoned the whole Haggadah, declaring that fables were no theology and that the private opinion of any individual Rabbi lacked corporate authority. Although it is more than doubtful whether some of our present-day friends would follow Nahmanides, his example is good enough for many orthodox Jews. Nahmanides is in this respect a surer guide. In the seven centuries that intervene between us and Nahmanides we have learnt even to go farther. We may pass from Haggadah into the field of Halakhah. We need have no scruples, if necessary, in casting overboard all the five cases so diligently gathered by S.B. We are quite content to say, ' Well, yes, they are unpleasant cases in the highest degree, but not one Jew in a thousand has heard of them, not one in ten thousand moulds his life on them, what then do they amount to ? '

But if there are Jews who ignore progress, so also, in another direction, do S.B. They forget that Judaism has advanced, and they compare unlikes. They contrast primitive Judaism with one out of two norms, neither of which is a fair one. They involuntarily compare Mishnaic Judaism with Modern Christianity, expecting from Sepphoris the same canons, the same advance, and the same experience as the best academic and theological circles can show to-day. Or they compare the actual life of the Jew in Temple days with the theoretical utterances of Jesus. Now this will not do. You can match Trypho against Justin Martyr, Judah the Prince or Rab and Samuel against Jerome or Eusebius, but you cannot fairly expect every single Amora or Tanna to be the spiritual equal of Wesley or Henry Martyn, though in a very large number of cases the comparison would reveal equality. You can measure best with best and average with average, but not best with average, or the trial is unreal. Again, the Sermon on the Mount marks the highest level reached only by Jesus himself and is not to be regarded as representative of average Christianity. To measure the standards upheld in such ethical but purely theoretical declarations with those prevalent in everyday Jewish life contemporary with Jesus is uncritical. Instead, one must look to the primitive Church. Weighed against Paul's converts in Romans i., for example, the average Jewish congregation would emerge with credit. One cannot fail to be astonished that when Paul or James reproach their Churches for grave moral lapses, the obvious conclusion does not seem to occur to them. The Jew could fling the *Tu quoque* at Paul. ' Through the Law came sin to us, you say. But has your Christi-

anity brought your converts to a higher life ?   You lash your
Churches for shameless immorality such as never disgraced the
Synagogue ; in your attacks on the Law have you been able to find
things as bad with us ? '   What, then, has your breach with the Law
achieved save Bolshevik lawlessness ?   S.B. in this excursus on the
Bergpredigt seek, by raking up five doubtful practices on the part
of the Jews, to make the greatness of Jesus stand out more clearly.
They could have found with greater ease a series of far more striking
contrasts by turning over the epistles of the New Testament.

But this does not imply a wholesale condemnation of the primitive Church : nor does it claim, correspondingly, a complete white-
washing of the ancient Synagogue.   All that is demanded is a
recognition of the unfairness of comparing the best of one with the
worst of another, with pitting 1928 against A.D. 1, with picking this
and ignoring that, and with deeming the part to be greater than
the whole.   No Jew judges Christianity by the sale of indulgences,
by the Inquisition, by the not uncommon assumption that promises
made to a heathen need not be kept.[1]   What are these compared with
S.B.'s five points ?   And if Christianity can legitimately be allowed
to slough her skin for these big things, may not Judaism have a
similar privilege for the smaller ones ?

If like be paralleled with like, Judaism need have no fear.   But
if we were to follow S.B. we could take their five points and give
them measure for measure from the mediaeval Church.   What
would be the good ?   Such a travesty would no more be Christianity
than are their five points a faithful summary of Rabbinic soteriology
and its consequences.[2]

Let us now consider the five points.   It will be noted that they
belong to practical life and not to abstract ethics.   It is quite true

---

[1] *E.g.* of Richard I. and Saladin, or the Portuguese in India.

[2] As these lines are being written, the columns of *The Jewish Guardian* (Jan. 4,
1929, and previous issue) contain an illuminating example of this argument, in
the shape of an attempt by a Christian clergyman to justify the forcible baptism
of the infant Edgar Mortara and his abduction from his parents by the Church.
Now the fact that is of importance for us to note to-day is that, when this tragedy
occurred in 1858, the voice of enlightened Christendom was joined to that of out-
raged Jewry in loud, if ineffective, protest.   But Jews to-day have long forgotten
the Pope's action and have long hoped that no Christian, still less no Christian
clergyman, would ever be found to justify it.   In spite of the letters of the Rev.
A. F. Day they cannot believe that any Christians are influenced by the Mortara
case, or would tolerate its repetition.   This is the correct line to take, and Jews
have a right to expect a similar attitude from S.B.   One can always resurrect evil :
the point is, is it dead and bereft of power, or does it still serve as a model ?   One
could make Christianity responsible for the Mortara case only if the incident were
paralleled by others, approved and still possessed of influence on Christians after
an interval of seventy years.   By the same reasoning S.B.'s five points may be
left to repose in their far older tomb.

that Judaism takes cognizance of every sphere of life and that distinctions are hard to maintain between that which is sacred and that which is secular. But in the case of First Fruits, Tithes, etc., the process is rather reversed. In England tithes are regarded as an essentially ecclesiastical matter, because tithes go to the parson. But to the Jew the payment of tithes and all the other agricultural imposts corresponded roughly to the modern payment of Income Tax. It will be remembered that the Rabbis who discussed the methods by which the sums to be paid might be reduced were not concerned with the saving of their own pockets. How many Rabbis owned estates ? They were rather in the position of Inspectors of Taxes, who, well disposed towards their clients, pointed out how a lower assessment might be obtained by filling out the rebate clauses on the return. No doubt, in cases of bad harvests or domestic misfortunes some of the Rabbis remained adamant : others viewed the tithe-payer's difficulties with pity and suggested a lightening of his burden. To fulfil the letter of the Law is not necessarily the same as defrauding the revenue. This is more descriptive of the situation than a picture of a voluntary charitable contribution, grudgingly devoted and deceitfully curtailed.

But once again let us concede S.B.'s point; let us suppose that these are five cases of lenience designed to save the Jew's pocket at the expense of his conscience. If these are to be the norm by which we judge whether Rabbinic soteriology has crashed, well and good. It is notorious that the vast majority of the tithe and Sabbath regulations were not lenient. They were, on the contrary, stringent at the expense of the pocket. What then ? Well, if five lenient cases make the system crash, surely, by the same reasoning, the hundreds of stringent cases should uphold that system ! One cannot have it both ways. S.B. (IV. Part 2, p. 675) express their astonishment that *Orlah* should have survived the Temple, when neither the need for this ordinance nor the means of enforcing its execution remained, yet the people carried it out freely and loyally. Or again, we need go no farther than the Gospels. S.B. condemn the Pharisees and their system for laxity, Jesus condemns them for their severity. S.B. blame them for not exacting *Ma'aser Sheni*, Jesus for tithing rue and cummin. Which is right ?

It has already been remarked that the Rabbis did not stand to gain : they were, if we apply the canon of Lucius Cassius, disinterested parties. One need not now go into the cases where a Rabbi was *Mahmīr* (inclined to rigid decisions) for himself but *Mēqīl* (lenient) towards others. Mr. Montefiore has done so on p. 323. Besides, it is not quite clear who, according to S.B., are the villains here, the Rabbis or the people. But in the first instance which

2 c

they quote, the saving of the pocket is the least direct of all. This instance deals with *Ma'aser Sheni*, which they correctly describe as a *Zwangssparkasse* (p. 668). The yeoman was in duty bound to save up for a holiday to Jerusalem. If he could not conveniently take his tithes in kind, owing to the distance, he had to convert them into cash, adding a fifth to the value. But the fifth simply meant in the end a fifth better time for him, not for somebody else; it was a bookkeeping transaction. If the whole tendency of the *Ma'aser Sheni* regulations were legitimized cheating, why are so many of the other regulations strict? Thus the adjacent paragraph tells us that if *Ma'aser Sheni* be transferred from one place to another, and if the market rates vary in the two places, the assessment is to be that of the place of origin, not necessarily by the cheaper or by the dearer.

The regulations differ, some being lenient, others rigid. Lenience often appears because, as the Gemara goes on to say, *Berakhah* is associated with this tithe, 'when the Lord thy God shall have blessed thee in all thy handiwork.' This is to be a joyous holiday, not a strict duty. Hence the opinion that in the injunction 'if a man redeem HIS *Ma'aser* he must add a fifth to it,' 'his' refers to his own and not to another's. If you think this out, there is nothing very far-fetched in it. The underlying principle of *Berakhah* appears in other connections with regard to this *Ma'aser*, e.g. it must not be pledged (אין ממשכנין מפני שכתוב בו ברכה). (See מראה הפנים *in loc.*) This *Ma'aser* is to do what several well-disposed ladies and gentlemen have done at Oxford and Cambridge: it is to provide a Gaudy or College Feast, a good time. In the first part of M.S. iv. 4 we see that the beneficiaries of the legal fiction are, not the householder, but his friends or adult sons. The practice must not apply to young children or to Gentile slaves (מפני שירן כידו), because they are as he, and so he would benefit, for it would in any case be up to him to give them a good time and foot the bill. The result of the ערמה or 'klüglich handeln' is that A's friend B or A's adult son C gets a better holiday. This point is not brought out by S.B., who leave it to be inferred that it is always A who scores.

A, however, does score in the second case. A great deal is made of the question of *Berakhah*: the idea of the *Ma'aser* is enjoyment. Is then the householder to be at a disadvantage? There are two principles involved: (1) that of the fifth, (2) that of 'enjoyment.' Which is the more important? This is the point at issue. Various views prevail. But the object of (1) was to secure (2), *i.e.* to prevent the 'Gaudy money' from being used at home by the owner, not to provide a tax for the Temple. The conclusion would seem to be that in certain districts modifications—evasions if you like—

grew up as local practice; these some teachers condoned and approved, others condemned. Probably these divergences represent local variations of custom and are older than the interpretation of passages adduced for their sanction. In *Maʿaser Sheni*, as in other tithes and imposts, we find varieties of conformity. As S.B.—who never fail to give both sides—note (p. 641), the people were often over-generous, adding gold and silver baskets : they liked the pilgrimages, where they were welcomed with flutes and gaiety. S.B. might have made more of the שמחה של מצוה; it is one of the *Kautelen* which they have overlooked. The taxes were not an intolerable yoke. The *Haberim* were meticulous in paying their dues, the *Am ha-Aretz* often were niggardly. Some people made extra gifts, just as, to revert to income tax, the Chancellor of the Exchequer sometimes receives gifts from patriotic citizens, *Haberim*, while others follow the lead of the *Am ha-Aretz*. Human nature does not change; one cannot expect a universal level of conscientiousness; but one does not condemn the fiscal system of Great Britain or the honesty of Britons because people assess themselves to their best advantage and because a few take refuge in dishonest evasions and unworthy subterfuges.

Finally, before quitting the parallel of the income tax, it is well to recall that for the collection of the Jewish dues no sanction of force was available,[1] and it is doubtful whether history can show many similar cases of regular voluntary effort. Voluntary effort under stress of a calamity, a war, a sudden charitable impulse, we know often enough. But this was something different. This was constant and general. A kindred example is furnished by Cicero in his *Pro Flacco*, which tells of the funds sent by the diaspora for the Temple : the total amount astonished the Romans. When Jews were, year in year out, paying their religious taxes in this way, the puny instances of evasion count for little in comparison. To condemn the Rabbinic soteriology on their account would be as futile as to condemn Christology because of the trouser buttons which are, now and then, found in collection-bags.

With regard to the two cases in which the Sabbath is concerned little need be said. No. V. (the animal in the pit) is dealt with by Mr. Montefiore in *Synoptic Gospels* on Matthew xii. 11, and Israel Abrahams' *Studies*, I. 135.

No. II. concerns an emergency, and exceptional situations demand exceptional treatment. Bartinora's commentary may be noted. He points out that the men originally came forward not as hired labourers but as neighbours. The goods being legally

---

[1] *Aboth* v. 11–15 is scarcely to be understood if tithes could be recovered by civil process.

ownerless (*hefqer*), they were entitled to keep what they rescued from the fire, but they did not feel disposed to profit by another's misfortunes—since the owner was bound to renounce his title—and so, after Sabbath, they ' reckoned ' with the owner so that suitable accommodation might be reached.

The Rabbis were bound to keep midway between two extremes. The Commandments were to be observed, but they were given ' that a man live by them.' One does not decree on the community more than the community can reasonably bear. The Law is for all time, but the Law is progressive. The accommodation of the Law to changed circumstances demanded much sincerity, much learning, and much tact. Here and there they may have erred, but the bulk of their work has stood the test of time ; we must not overrate the failures. The legal fiction is easy to attack, but it has its good side. It serves to preserve the memory of a principle. *In fictione juris semper subsistit aequitas*, said Blackstone.[1] No system of law can do without it. Peppercorn rent is no immoral procedure, but a useful device of the leaseholding system. When the Duke of Wellington presents the reigning sovereign with a pennant every year in return for his tenure of his Scottish estate, the token is no evasion of proper rent, it is an historical memorial. That the legal fiction may lead to abuse will not be denied. Hard cases make good law in English and in Jewish jurisprudence. S.B. could have found stronger, though later, examples to adduce (*e.g.* selling the *Ḥameç* on Passover). But routine reduces nearly every legal form to mechanical observance. The institution of bail is one of the fundamental institutions of English justice, yet it is possible to describe the practice in the terms of Mr. Pickwick, who, it will be remembered, denounced the sureties as persons ready to perjure themselves before the judges of the land at half a crown a crime.

Enough has been written on the question of legal fictions by Schechter in the Appendix to Mr. Montefiore's *Hibbert Lectures*, and in the *Jew. Ency.*, *s.v.* (1) *Nomism*, (2) *Antinomianism*, (3) *Abrogation*, and (4) *Accommodation*. It has been pointed out over and over again that the legal fiction is not always bad, not all-pervading, and not permanent. Only one other point suggests itself. What was the alternative ? What did Jesus propose ? For him it was easy enough to denounce. He had no responsibility ; he was not called upon to be constructive ; he was in opposition. But what would he have done had he been in power ? We have seen the stoutest opponents of the Government, the boldest and most uncompromising Radicals become docile and conventional when office falls to their lot. The Keir Hardies and the John Burns become changed indeed

---

[1] For this view and the opposite see *Ency. Brit.*, ed. eleven, Vol. x. p. 319.

when they have to act and not merely to speak. The followers of Jesus in their turn were called upon to construct a practical policy. When faced with similar difficulties they also have had to make concessions. Canon law has its legal fictions, not only in the Vatican but in every Church which is a branch of institutionalized religion. History repeats itself regularly. Wesley was to the Anglican Church what Jesus was to the State religion of his age. But Wesleyanism triumphant has had to evolve its own legal system, and no doubt if one were to examine it with care a few anomalies and *Klüglich-keiten* might be revealed that are not in keeping with its founder's intentions. If not, why the successive offshoots from the Wesleyan Church ?

But in all these cases broad views must prevail. The test is not the legal fiction, not the institution, but the effect of the soteriology on life. Judged by this test and not by a few carefully selected details, irrelevant because they are unrepresentative and abnormal because of their rarity, the Rabbinic and the Christian systems, widely different but each appealing to millions of human souls, may be declared not to have crashed but to be fulfilling their God-ordained purpose.

APPENDIX III

ON REPENTANCE [1]

THE Rabbinic doctrine of Repentance is naturally based upon the Old Testament. Upon the varying conceptions of God and of his relation to man found in the Hebrew Bible the unsystematic and inconsistent religion of the Rabbis was reared. What we roughly call the Priestly and the Prophetic elements of the Old Testament both reappear in the Talmudic religion in a more or less successful harmony.

Repentance in the Old Testament is essentially a religious conception, and is constantly and closely connected with eschatological ideas of the Judgment and of the Messianic Age. To a considerable extent it preserves this character in the Rabbinical literature. It may be well to state here that I shall make no reference to any passage or theories concerning repentance which may be gathered from the apocryphal, apocalyptic, or pseudepigraphic writings. These sources are now easily accessible and fairly well known. It is, however, very noticeable, first, that nothing of great importance about repentance can be obtained from this quarter. The total amount of material is very small, and its quality on the whole is poor. Secondly, whereas the mixture of Hellenism with Judaism sometimes improved and spiritualized a given doctrine or created interesting novelties and developments, the reverse is the case with the subject of repentance. Sirach is better on repentance than the Wisdom of Solomon. The whole doctrine is genuinely and purely Hebraic, and Hellenism does not improve it. On the contrary, it tends to dry it up. Philo has little to say about repentance, and what he does say is of small account. In the New Testament the doctrine of Repentance is of importance in the Synoptics and in Acts, it is hardly touched upon in the epistles of St. Paul, and is wholly absent from the Fourth Gospel. Repentance is an emphatically Hebraic conception, and its full development is a genuine and specific excellence of Rabbinical and post-Rabbinical Judaism.[2]

[1] Reprinted from *The Jewish Quarterly Review*, Vol. XVI., Jan. 1904, pp. 211 *seq.*
[2] *Cf.* a striking note of F. Delitzsch in his Hebrew translation of the Epistle to the Romans. He alludes to a passage in the Pesikta Kahana 163 b (which I shall

There is no Hebrew noun in the Bible which exactly corresponds with our noun 'repentance.' [1] The verb נחם seems to mean 'to be sorry, to feel pain or regret,' and thus closely corresponds to the root-meaning of our word 'repentance.' It is, however, mainly used in reference to God. Of human regret, or repentance, it only occurs some six or seven times.[2] It does not appear to have acquired the particular connotation which was wanted. The root which was ultimately adopted, and of which only the verb is used in this sense in the Old Testament, had at once a more distinctly religious and also a more definitely practical significance. This verb is *shub*, which we usually translate by 'turn' or 'return.' It never quite obtained a technical meaning. It is used either of turning from evil or of turning to God. Its untechnical character is shown by the fact that it is also occasionally used to signify a turning away from God and rectitude. The noun *Teshubah*, which in the Talmudical literature is even more distinctly a precise theological term than repentance with us, is in the Old Testament only found in a non-religious sense. At what period *Teshubah* was first used to mean repentance, or at any rate 'a turning away from sin and a turning towards God,' cannot be exactly ascertained. I believe that, so far, the word has not been found in the Hebrew original of Sirach. We are therefore unable to trace it back beyond the Mishnah and the Eighteen Benedictions. But the best scholars are more and more coming to believe that a considerable number of these Benedictions are pre-Christian, and reach back to the Maccabaean era. In that case a famous and familiar prayer would be the earliest use of the word *Teshubah* in its new meaning of repentance which we are able to adduce. Let me quote this prayer at once, for so much of the Rabbinic doctrine of Repentance is contained in it : ' Cause us to return, O our Father, unto thy Law ; draw us near, O our King, unto thy service, and bring us back in perfect repentance unto thy presence. Blessed art thou, O Lord, who delightest in repentance.'

---

subsequently quote), and says it is one, ' wo der Unterschied der jüdischen und christlichen Anschauung in die Augen springt. Nach jener lässt sich Gott versöhnen durch Busse, nach dieser ist er versöhnt durch das Mittlerwerk Christi, und wird dem Einzelnen versöhnt, wenn dieser bussfertig und gläubig sich auf das der ganzen Menschheit geltende Mittlerwerk gründet. Die neutestamentliche Heilsordnung Gottes lautet auch wie *jer. Maccoth* ii. 6, f. 31 d. יעשה תשובה ויתכפר לו, aber die Busse ist nicht das Shünende selbst, sondern nur der Weg zur Versöhnung ' (*Paulus des Apostels Brief an die Römer . . . in das Hebräische übersetzt von Franz Delitzsch*, 1870, p. 81).

[1] נחם in Hosea xiii. 14 is doubtful. If the text is correct, it means rather pity ' than ' repentance.'

[2] See Exod. xiii. 17 ; Num. xxiii. 19 ; Judges xxi. 6 ; 1 Sam. xv. 29 ; Job xlii. 6 ; Jer. viii. 6, xxxi. 19.

The opening phrase ' Cause us to return ' is Biblical. For the verb *shub* is used not merely in the active, but also in the causative sense, and this usage is of great importance. Few sentences from Scripture are more familiar to Jewish ears than the verse in Lamentations : ' Turn thou us unto thee, O Lord, and we shall be turned ; renew our days as of old.'

It may be noted that *shub*, though more frequently connected with Israel and the community, is also applied to individuals. It is constantly followed by the ideas of pardon and restoration, and the annulment of intended punishment. It is a prophetic word, and rather religious than ethical. Apostasy from God can be healed by *shub*. Amos already employs the term, and the latest prophets do not neglect it. It is congenial to the prophetic element in the Book of Deuteronomy and to writers of the Deuteronomic school. Some of its instances acquired an intenser meaning, and are used again and again as texts by the Rabbinical fathers. Thus, to mention but two or three, we have the appeal of Hosea, ' O Israel, return unto the Lord thy God ; take with you words, and turn to the Lord,' quoted, played upon, and developed an innumerable number of times. The same may be said of the summons, ' Return thou backsliding Israel,' in Jeremiah, or of Ezekiel's chapter about the wicked man who turns from his evil way and is forgiven. The divine readiness to receive the penitent, of which we shall hear so much, is often illustrated by Zechariah and Malachi's exhortation, ' Return unto me, and I will return unto you, saith the Lord.' And where *shub* is used in quite a different signification and does not mean repentance at all, the Rabbis often interpret it in the familiar sense, with results which are sometimes almost amusing in their strange and strained ingenuity.

The prophetic doctrine of Repentance in the Old Testament is crossed by the priestly and sacrificial ideas of atonement, purification, and forgiveness, which also obtained an enormous hold upon the minds and hearts of the Jewish people. The mixture produced by the two different strains of teaching was never wholly brought into harmony by the Rabbis, though the prophetic element is largely predominant, and gives ethical colour and tone to the priestly conceptions. But theoretic consistency was never achieved.

The priestly ideas to which I refer centre in the institutions of the sin-offering and of the Day of Atonement. Of these the sin-offering became of diminishing importance. Even before the destruction of the Temple, it is clear that the ethical substitutes for the sin-offering, which afterwards became all-prevailing, had begun their beneficial influence. A large number of persons were unable to come up to Jerusalem to offer the statutory sacrifices. Moreover, even in the Pentateuch itself, the sin-offering and the guilt-offering are usually associated with involuntary offences ; they are not supposed to be applicable or efficacious in the case of serious moral transgressions deliberately committed. Nevertheless, traces occur in the Rabbinical literature of a less ethical conception of the sacrificial system. Thus we find it stated several times that no man in Jerusalem was burdened, or passed the night, with a consciousness of sin. For the morning sacrifice atoned for the sins of the night and the evening sacrifice for those of the day.[1] Or, again, it is said, ' As a man goes down to the brook dirty, and comes up clean, so a man went up to the sanctuary with sins, and came forth without them.'[2] But, on the whole, the exaltation of the sacrifices is used rather to emphasize the necessity for their ethical substitutes— prayer, charity, and repentance—now that the possibility of sacrifices had passed away. For he who truly repents ' is regarded by God as if he had gone to Jerusalem, rebuilt the altar and offered all the sacrifices of the law.'[3] It became a definite doctrine of the Rabbis that the substitutes for sacrifice are more potent than sacrifice.[4]

Far more important, however, than all other sacrifices, whether of the individual or of the community, were the ordinances of the Day of Atonement. Moreover, the Day of Atonement, though in the Pentateuchal legislation its essence and efficacy consisted in rites and sacrifices, which ceased when the Temple was destroyed, maintained and even increased its significance and solemnity after the sacrifices and the rites had disappeared. The persistence of the Day of Atonement's atoning efficacy independently of the Temple produced momentous effects in the Jewish religion, and was operative both for good and for evil.

It is impossible and needless to enter here upon a discussion of the objects and limitations of the Day of Atonement ordinance as laid down in the sixteenth chapter of Leviticus. We must, however, note first that the atoning power of the Day seems to reside in the rites performed by the priest, including the sacrifices and the scapegoat; and, secondly, that, in spite of certain qualifying implications elsewhere, the atonement was apparently efficacious for every kind of transgression. The words are, ' on that day shall he make an atonement for you to cleanse you, that ye may be clean from *all* your sins before the Lord.' Yet clearly, before the Temple was destroyed, a double process had set in. In the first place, the Day

---

[1] Numbers R. xxi. 21 (on xxviii. 3) ; Pesikta 55 b, 61 b.
[2] Midrash Psalms on v. § 1, 26 a.
[3] Leviticus Rabba vii. § 2, etc.
[4] Numbers Rabba xiii. § 18.

itself, with its fasting and confession, had acquired a solemn significance and value over and above the sacrifices and the scapegoat
and the blood. Secondly, the Day became spiritualized. A deeper
view of sin and of repentance grew up, a nobler conception of forgiveness and atonement. The local synagogues in every village and
town aided both these developments. Hence the Day of Atonement
survived the fall of the Temple, and its holy importance was even
increased by that tragic event. On the one hand, it afforded room
for a certain growth of superstition and formalism ; on the other
hand, it supplied opportunity for lofty thoughts and high endeavour.
Sometimes the two strains or tendencies are oddly fused together.
Fasting and prayer, repentance and ' good works,' ritualism independent of sacrifice and high doctrine transcending it, enabled the
people and their teachers to overcome the shock of the Temple's
loss, and to fashion a religion far superior to that of the priests.[1]

Yet Judaism could hardly have survived the days of Titus and
of Hadrian had it not been that by that time the doctrine of a future
life was ingrained into the hearts of all. As Gunkel has well said,
that dogma marks an epoch and a dividing line. On the one side
is the Judaism which precedes it, on the other the Judaism which
comes after. The famous story of the son who, at the request of
his father, climbs a tree, fetches the eggs, and lets the parent bird
go free—thereby fulfilling two Pentateuchal commands by a single
act—and who then falls down and is killed, shows the measure of
the change. For, according to the story, the promise of the fifth
commandment was not made void by the son's fall, but, on the
contrary, was confirmed. For the promise of ' length of days ' was
realized in the life to come.[2] Our own immediate subject is also
changed, like all other religious conceptions, by the doctrine of the
resurrection. For repentance becomes not only connected with the
redemption of Israel in the Messianic age, but also with the lot of
each individual Israelite at the last judgment, and in the world to
come. The solemnity of life, and the tremendous issues with which
right and wrong are charged, were vastly increased.

According to a familiar passage in the Mishnah, further elaborated
in the Talmud, the world receives its yearly judgment in the penitential season between New Year and the Day of Atonement. I
cannot go into the origin or even the details of this curious conception. It is sufficient to notice that this strange idea undoubtedly
exercised a very considerable influence upon religion and upon
action. The Talmud states that three books are opened on New
Year's Day : the righteous are inscribed for life, the wicked for

---

[1] *Cp.* throughout the informing and interesting articles on Atonement and the
Day of Atonement in the *Jewish Encyclopedia*.   [2] Kiddushin 39 b.

death, while the ' intermediate ' remain in suspense till the Day of Atonement. By good works and repentance they can make the swaying balance incline in their favour. Moreover, even the wicked—this seems the general idea—can cause the inscribed decree to be cancelled. Such is the power of repentance.[1] These odd conceptions had effects for good and evil. They produced a certain amount of formal charity, and of ' good works ' in the bad sense of the word, in the interval between New Year and the Day of Atonement. They produced some mere outward repentance and formalism, both then and upon the Day of Atonement itself. The notion that God was especially near to man, anxious and eager to pardon during the penitential season, was not entirely healthy. But, on the other hand, as repentance meant reparation and change of life, it is certain that many a quarrel was made up, many an injury made good, many a sin abandoned, many a good action accomplished. A real and lasting reformation of character was sometimes initiated, together with a deepening of the desire of the soul for closer communion with God.

The same double result was and still is the consequence of the Day of Atonement. For our present purpose we must note that the prevailing view, even when the juridical effect of the Day of Atonement is under discussion, is that while for some sins repentance is inadequate to secure immediate forgiveness, there is no sin for which the Day of Atonement without repentance can achieve the divine pardon. The famous Mishnah in Yoma (viii. 8) runs as follows : ' Death and the Day of Atonement atone together with repentance ; repentance atones for light sins, whether of omission or commission ; for heavy sins repentance holds the matter in suspense, till the Day of Atonement comes and atones.' [2] Here there is no atonement without repentance, but the Day of Atonement is required to complete the efficacy of the repentance. In another passage, however (Mishnah Shebuoth i. 6), the scapegoat is stated to atone for all sins, and no mention is made of repentance. The words are ' Other sins mentioned in the Law [besides the pollution of the sanctuary], whether light or grave, voluntary or involuntary . . . are atoned for by the scapegoat.' But this Mishnah, though supported by R. Judah the Prince, is contradicted by a subsequent R. Judah, and other authorities are also quoted to the effect that the atoning efficacy of the scapegoat only applies to those who have repented of their sins.[3] In the Jerusalem Talmud another suggestion is made, namely, that the Day of Atonement

---

[1] *Cp., e.g.*, Rosh ha-Shanah 17 b ; Yebamoth 105 a ; Pesikta Kahana 163 a.
[2] *Cp.* Yoma 85 b.
[3] Shebuoth 12 b–13 b. *Cp.* also Commentaries on Mishnah Shebuoth i. 6 (I.A.).

brings pardon even without repentance for sins of omission, whereas for sins of commission (always regarded as more serious by the Talmudists) repentance is an indispensable condition.[1] Rabbi Ishmael taught that there were four classes of atonement, and repentance was necessary for them all. ' If a man transgress a *negative* commandment, and repent, he is forgiven at once ; if he transgress a *positive* commandment, and repent, repentance holds the matter in suspense, till the Day of Atonement comes and atones. If he sin in matters involving the penalty of being " cut off from his people," or death at the hand of the Sanhedrin, repentance and the Day of Atonement hold the matter in suspense, and sufferings complete the atonement. But if he has profaned the divine name, repentance cannot hold the matter in suspense, the Day of Atonement cannot atone, and sufferings cannot complete the atonement, but they all together can (only) hold the matter in suspense, and death completes the atonement.'[2] Maimonides, in his codification of the Talmudic Law, says that the scapegoat, without repentance, atoned only for slight transgressions ; but I have not found a similar formula in the Talmuds.[3] In any case Maimonides makes a sharp distinction between the scapegoat and the Day of Atonement itself, and he proceeds to observe that, since the destruction of the Temple, ' There is nothing left us but repentance, which, however, atones for all transgressions.' And undoubtedly this is the prevailing Rabbinic view. Without repentance, no rites and no Day of Atonement can atone ; with repentance, no sin can separate between man and God.[4]

---

[1] Jer. Yoma viii. 6 (Schwab, v. p. 255).

[2] Yoma 86 a ; Aboth R. Nathan, chap. 29, 44 b. The same passage occurs with slight variants in Mechilta on Exod. xx. 7, p. 39 a (ed. Friedmann), and also in Tosefta Yoma v. (iv.) 8, p. 190. Further discussion upon the precise power of repentance to effect by itself expiation and forgiveness is found in Yoma 85 b *fin.* and 86 a *init.* As negative commands are more important than positive commands (*i.e.* sins of commission are worse than sins of omission), it is asked : Why does the Mishnah say that Repentance atones both for light sins of commission and *omission* ? For if it atones for sins of commission, *a fortiori* it atones for sins of omission. R. Judah then suggests that the sins of commission meant are not such sins of commission as consist in the transgression of a negative command *pur et simple*, but only those sins of commission which consist in the transgression of such negative commands *as depend upon a positive command.* (I suppose, *e.g.*, that the transgression of Exodus xxxv. 3 would be a sin of commission, consisting in the transgression of a negative command depending upon the positive command of Exodus xx. 8.)

[3] It may be, as suggested by a commentator (השם בליון) on the last words of Jer. Yoma viii. 6, that Maimonides derived his view from that passage, which is indeed somewhat corrupt in the editions (I.A.).

[4] *Cp.* Tosefta Yoma v. (iv.) 9, p. 190: ' Sin-offering and guilt-offering and death and the Day of Atonement do not expiate without repentance,' though R. Judah argues that the day of death is equivalent to repentance.

It may be desirable to quote a few passages in order to show the combination of lower and higher thought which sometimes occurs as regards the penitential season and the Day of Atonement. It may more accurately be said that these passages show, not so much a fusion or combination of higher and lower thought, as a desire to adjust the purer conceptions of repentance to the letter of the Priestly Law. For the Talmudists oscillated, as it were, unconsciously between two opposing doctrines. On the one hand, repentance and goodness are superior to sacrifice, and therefore the existing means of atonement are superior to the old sacrificial system ; on the other hand, the sacrificial system, like every other part of the Law, is perfect and divine, its loss a punishment and a deprivation, its return certain and desirable.

Thus, for instance, the famous words, ' Seek the Lord while he may be found, call ye upon him while he is near,' were interpreted to mean, ' Seek him specially between New Year and the Day of Atonement when he dwells among you.' During that short season the inscribed decree, not yet sealed till the Kippur day, was still susceptible of revocation and annulment. But these reflections are modified by others. It is asserted that to a *community* God is near at *all* times, and in other passages the whole conception of finality at the Day of Atonement is practically abandoned.[1] More than once we meet with the following : ' On the eve of the New Year the great (? pious) ones of a given generation fast, and God remits them a third of their sins ; from New Year to Atonement individuals fast, and God remits them a third of their sins ; on the Atonement Day all fast, and God says : What is done is done ; from this time a new reckoning begins.' [2] Elsewhere, too, the seeming importance of fasting is insisted on. Thus we read, ' When the Temple existed, a man brought a sacrifice, and it made atonement for him ; now that the Temple is no more, our soul is raised to thee in fasting, and thou reckonest the affliction of our souls as a perfect sacrifice, and we have nothing to which to cling but thy mercy.' [3] Or, again, a Rabbi says, ' May the diminution of my fat and blood be regarded as if I had offered them upon the altar.' [4] But one must not suppose that any but superstitious and foolish persons, who exist in all religious communities, believed that the fast, however imperative, was of avail without repentance and change of life. The familiar saying about the Ninevites marks the true Rabbinic position,[5] ' My brethren, it is not said of the Ninevites

---

[1] Pesikta Kahana 156 b ; Rosh ha-Shanah 16 a, b ; Yebamoth 105 a, etc.
[2] Ecclesiastes Rabba on ix. 7 ; Leviticus Rabba xxx. § 7, on xxiii. 40.
[3] Midrash Psalms on Ps. xxv. (3).
[4] Berachoth 17 a.
[5] Mishnah Taanith ii. 1, and 15 a, 16 a.

that God saw their sackcloth and their fasting, but that God saw their *works*, that they turned from their evil way.' 'Be not like fools,' say the teachers, 'who, when they sin, bring a sacrifice, but do not repent. They know not the difference between good and evil, and yet venture to make an offering to God.'[1] Several other passages could be quoted of similar import.

In other ways, too, the universality of the Day of Atonement's efficacy was curtailed. The same Mishnah in Yoma (viii. 9) goes on to say: 'If a man says, I will sin and repent, I will sin and repent, he is not allowed to repent. If a man says, I will sin, and the Day of Atonement will atone, for him the Day will bring no forgiveness. For sins between man and God the Day of Atonement brings forgiveness, for sins between man and man the Day brings no forgiveness until he is reconciled with his neighbour.' The first two of these clauses indicate the anxiety of the Rabbis to prevent the Atonement Day from degenerating into sheer superstition, and thus doing more harm than good. Hence the importance of the doctrine that for certain sins, or for certain attitudes of mind, repentance is impossible, or, as they put it, prevented. It may be convenient to indicate the views of the Rabbinic fathers upon the divine element in repentance, both in the way of aiding and of impeding its accomplishment.

There is no doubt that the Rabbis were strong believers in the freedom of the will. It is a man's own fault if he sins; under normal circumstances he can be good if he chooses. Ordinarily, moreover, it is never too late to mend. It may indeed be argued that, like Ezekiel, they taught a somewhat too atomistic kind of ethical psychology, as if a man could at his own will jump from virtue to vice or from vice to virtue. The dictum that God judges a man according to his present moral constitution is constantly repeated.[2] Yet the other side of the question is also not neglected, and it would be false to think that the Rabbis did not believe in divine help towards the achievement of rectitude or in the struggle for repentance. A famous passage in Yoma, often quoted elsewhere, though Maimonides misinterprets it in the interests of his own combative theology, is quite conclusive upon this point. 'For him who would pollute himself, the doors are open; he who would purify himself, is helped.' The simile which follows strengthens and explains the adage. 'It is like with the seller of naphtha and balsam; if a man buys naphtha, the seller says, Measure it yourself; if he buys balsam, the other says: Wait and I will help you measure, that we may both be perfumed.' 'Our father and king,' runs the familiar supplication, 'bring us back in perfect repentance unto thy pre-

---

[1] Berachoth 23 a.   [2] *Cp.*, *e.g.*, Genesis Rabba liii. § 14.

sence.'[1] 'It is never too late to mend,' like most proverbs, represents one side of a complex truth. And so the Rabbis have no consistent theory, but give expression to the various facts of life as they crop up or occur to them.

Thus we read in a quaint passage of the Midrash, the environment of which it would be a shame to cut off, ' It says in Canticles : His mouth (lit. palate) is most sweet. That is God. As it says in Amos : Seek me and live. Is there a sweeter palate than this ? It says in Ezekiel : I have no pleasure in the death of the wicked. Is there a sweeter mouth than this ? If a man has all his life been a complete sinner, and at the end becomes completely righteous, he will no longer stumble against wickedness, and God will account his former sins as merits, for it says : Myrrh, aloes, and cassia are all thy sins [here by a slight change of vowels the Midrash changes the *garments* of the original (Ps. xlv.) into *sins* !]. Thus his sins against God are as myrrh and aloes at the season of his contrition.'[2]

The Talmudists admit the possibility of death-bed repentances, and there are some good stories and striking adages on the subject. Thus, when R. Meir urges his teacher Elisha b. Abuya to repent of his apostasy, the sinner replies, ' Up till when will they receive me ? ' and the answer is, ' Till the very hour of death.' ' God leaves the chance of repentance open even in the very moment of his judgment.' Of a Rabbi whose sin of unchastity was notorious, the story is told that in the very hour and passion of his sin a fervour of repentance befalls him. He rushes forth and calls on the hills, and on heaven and earth, and on sun and moon and stars to implore for him compassion from God ; but they reply, each quoting a verse of scripture, that they have enough to do in asking compassion for themselves. Then he cries and laments till his soul leaves him, and a heavenly voice is heard to say that R. Eliezer b. Durdaya is destined for the world to come. Thus repentance and death atone for the most grievous sin. The remark with which R. Judah the Prince receives the story is a frequent one in the Talmud, ' Many can gain the world to come only after years and years, while another gains it in an hour.' And on this occasion the same Rabbi adds the quaint expression, ' Not enough that the penitent are received, they are even called Rabbi ! '[3]

Still, though the general tone of the Rabbis is joyful and en-

---

[1] Yoma 38 b, 39 a ; Singer's *Prayer Book*, p. 56.

[2] Numbers Rabba x. § 1. *Cp.* Jer. Peah i. 1, 16 b (Schwab, II. p. 20); Exodus Rabba xxxi. § 1 ; Kiddushin 40 b.

[3] Ruth R. vi. § 4 ; Tanchuma B. xi., תזריע, 20 a (Bacher, *Agada der paläst. Amoräer*, II. p. 360, n. 4); Abodah Zarah 17 a, 18 a. *Cp.* Genesis Rabba lxv. § 22.

couraging, God being represented as being eager to induce the sinner to repent up till the very last possible moment, they are not unaware that the evil inclination, the sinful tendency, at first weak as a spider's web, may become, through repeated sins, as strong as a cart-rope. At first a guest, it is at last the master of the house. The doctrine of habit is not unknown to them. Thus they say, ' If a man has the chance to sin once or twice and he resists, he will not sin again.' ' If you do not commit a sin three times, God will keep you from committing it for ever.' Sin hardens man's heart. ' If a man pollutes himself a little, they pollute him much ; if a man sanctifies himself a little, they sanctify him much.' [1] Frequently the sentence occurs, ' If a man has committed the same sin twice, it seems to him to be permitted.' [2] And the warning is uttered, ' A man is forgiven for his first offence and for his second and third, but not for the fourth.' In one place among the five kinds of sinners for whom there is no forgiveness figure those ' who sin in order to repent, and those who repent much and always sin afresh.' [3] In another passage we read, ' He who says I will sin and repent, is forgiven three times and then no more.' These quaint phrases, with their seemingly absurd precision, are all half-playfully deduced in odd and far-fetched ways from Biblical sentences or words ; they must not be taken literally, but in their spirit.

More serious is the doctrine that for some sins repentance is impossible. Over and over again we have the saying, ' For him who sins and causes others to sin no repentance is allowed or possible.' [4] The hardening of Pharaoh's heart is explained and justified on the theory that after giving several chances of repentance to a man, God shuts his heart against repentance, so that he may punish him for his sins.[5] ' He who is wholly given up to sin, is unable to repent, and there is no forgiveness to him for ever.' [6] The idea that he who causes the many to sin will not be allowed to repent is partly due to the common Talmudic doctrine that the worst sin is making others sin, just as the highest goodness is helping others to be good. But it is also partly to be accounted for by the very practical conception of repentance entertained by the Rabbis. The usual critics of the Rabbinic religion may say that this practical conception of repentance is a mark of legalism. That the Rabbinic equivalent of the verb ' repent ' is to ' do repentance ' has actually been used as an argument to show that Rabbinic repentance is a mere outward

[1] Yoma 38 b, 39 a: ' They pollute him ' is almost equivalent to ' He is polluted.'

[2] Yoma 86 b, etc. [3] Yoma 85 b; Aboth R. Nathan xxxix. 58 b and xl. 60 b.

[4] Aboth v. 26; Sanhedrin 107 b; Yoma 87 a.

[5] Exodus Rabba xi. §§ 1 and 3.

[6] Midrash Psalms on Ps. i. fin.

rite, an *opus operatum*.[1] The criticism is groundless and unjust, but it is true that to the Rabbis the essence of repentance lay in such a thorough change of mind that it issues in change of life and change of conduct. To repent from the fear of God is better than to repent through chastisement or suffering, and to repent from love is better than to repent from fear.[2] The true penitent is he who has the opportunity to do the same sin again, in the same environment, and who does it not.[3] To repent in old age of the sins of manhood or youth is of no great merit or avail.[4] It is, moreover, of the essence of repentance that the injury done to his neighbour should be repaired by the sinner, and the pardon of that neighbour obtained. This is the meaning of the Mishnah, that the sins of a man against his neighbour cannot be forgiven before satisfaction has been rendered and reconciliation secured. Although, from one point of view, nothing can be worse than idolatry or apostasy, yet the Talmudists also lay down the maxim that as he who is good towards heaven and towards his fellow-men is a good ' Zadik,' and he who is good towards heaven and bad towards his fellow-men is a *not good* ' Zadik,' so he who is wicked against heaven and wicked against his fellow-men is a bad sinner, while he, who is wicked against heaven, but not wicked against his fellow-men, is a *not bad* sinner.[5]

In accordance with this view the Talmudic prescriptions about practical repentance are very pressing and precise. So far as an injury could be undone, it was essential to cancel it as a condition of reconciliation with God. Reparation is a test of sincerity. Thus we find in Yoma : ' R. Isaac said : If a man affronts his neighbour, though only in words, he must appease him. If he can be appeased by a gift of money, spare it not if thou hast it, but if not, get friends to appease him. R. Chisda said : Thou must ask his pardon before three friends, and must ask it three times, and, says R. Yose b. Chanina, not more. R. Joseph b. Habish said : If the man thou hast wronged has died, thou must take ten persons with thee to his grave and say, I have sinned against the Lord and against this man whom I wronged.' The story is told that one Rabbi went to the house of another offended Rabbi on the eve of thirteen successive Days of Atonement to ask his forgiveness. Even though the wronger has made complete reparation in kind, says the Mishnah (Baba Kamma viii. 7), his deed is not forgiven till he has asked pardon from the

---

[1] *Cp.* my article on ' Rabbinic Judaism and the Epistles of St. Paul,' *J.Q.R.*, Jan. 1901, p. 202 ; Weber, *Jüdische Theologie*, 2nd ed. (1897), p. 261, and the note on p. 409.

[2] Yoma 86 a.   [3] Yoma 86 b.

[4] This seems the meaning of the saying in Abodah Zarah 19 a ; but *cp.* also, for the other side, the graceful passage, Sukkah 53 a.   [5] Kiddushin 40 a.

wronged. Why it is said that pardon need not be asked more than
three times depends partly upon an odd interpretation of a Biblical
verse, and partly upon the idea that if a man has been three times
publicly besought by another to forgive him and still refuses, then
the sin reverts to him and leaves the original offender. The refuser
is called cruel (*Achzari*) and is false to the character of the true
Israelite. The adages occur : ' If a man yields his rights, his sins
are forgiven.' ' God forgives him who forgives his neighbour.'
' So long as we are merciful, God is merciful to us ; if we are not
merciful to others, God is not merciful to us.' [1] And it is from the
practical point of view, though rather oddly exaggerated, that complete repentance is considered as impossible or difficult to those
persons who, from the very nature of their sin, cannot make a
complete restitution. Thus he who makes others sin is unable to
undo his wrong, for he cannot know or reach all those whom he has
influenced for evil. This seems to be the real reason of his inability
to become a perfect penitent, rather than the fantastic explanation
in Yoma that it would never do for *him* to be in heaven and his
deluded disciples in hell. So we are told that it is difficult for shepherds and tax-collectors to repent, the idea being that they do not
know the actual persons whom they have wronged, and thus cannot
make complete restitution. [2] We must, however, take these utterances with a grain of salt. From what is said about repentance
elsewhere, it would seem impossible to believe that the Rabbis
actually meant that a shepherd, even though he had fed his flock
upon various meadows whose owners were unknown to him, or if
he had forgotten to whom they belonged, or the particular spots
where he had pastured his sheep, would not be forgiven by God if
his repentance were sincere. Perhaps their meaning is rather that
wrongs committed against indefinite persons are not merely less
easy to repair, but more usually persisted in and less frequently
regretted and abandoned.

However this may be, it is certain that the real stress of the
Rabbis was laid upon the sincerity of repentance. That is why they
talk so often about the question of repeated sins and repeated con-
fessions. [3] If a repentance does not produce a change of heart and

---

[1] Yoma 87 a, b ; Jer. Yoma viii. 8 ; Baba Mezia 115 a ; Rosh ha-Shanah
17 a ; Jer. Baba Kamma viii. 8, 6 c (Schwab, x. p. 67) ; Tosefta Baba Kamma
ix. 30 ; Yoma 23 a ; Megillah 28 a.

[2] Baba Kamma 94 b, and Wuensche's explanatory note, ii. 2, p. 42.   In
Maimonides' section on Repentance, chap. iv., the list of such persons is considerably extended.

[3] *Cp.* the many discussions as to whether old or repeated sins are or are not
to be confessed again upon successive Days of Atonement.   *Cp.* Yoma 86 b ;
Exodus R. lii. § 2 ; Mid. Psalms xxxii. (2) ; Jer. Yoma viii. 9 (Schwab, v.
p. 257).

deed, what can it be worth ? Thus they say that it is useless to
confess with the mouth till the heart overflows with repentance.
Quoting as usual the Hosean bidding, ' Take with you words,' the
Pesikta remarks : ' God says to the Israelites I do not exact of you
sacrifices or sin-offerings, but that you appease me with prayer
and supplication and the collection of the heart.[1] " Take words,"
yet not mere empty words, but confession and prayer and tears.'
Familiar and frequent is the saying : ' If a man has an unclean thing
in his hands, he may wash them in all the seas of the world, and he
will never be clean. If he throw it away, a little water will quite
suffice.'[2]

The Rabbis were far from confining the need or utility of
repentance to the penitential season from New Year to the Day
of Atonement. Very common with them is the saying, ' Repent
one day before thy death.' When his disciples said to R. Eliezer,
' Does then a man know when he will die ? ' he answered : ' The
more necessary that he repent to-day. Then if he die to-morrow,
all his days will have been passed in penitence, as it says : Let thy
garments be always white.'[3]

For repentance is the great mediatorial bond between God and
man. It entered into the divine plan from the beginning. Hence
the frequent doctrine that repentance was one of the seven things
created before the world. ' God,' it says in one passage, ' marked
out the whole world, and it could not stand till he created repentance.'[4] It seems that, at first, the tradition ran that *six* things were
created before the world. To these R. Ahaba added repentance,
and his addition became so popular and was so much quoted that the
six things were enlarged to seven, of which repentance is always
one.[5] Though we meet the view that God exacts requital (for the
insistence on his eagerness to meet the sinner half-way led some,
perchance, to think that he was all too easy-going in his compassion
and forgiveness), yet the fundamental notion is that, as God chose
to create man frail and liable to sin, the only thing for God to do was
to aid him to repentance and to be ever ready to forgive him. In
one passage in the Midrash, Abraham is made to say to God : ' Thou

---

[1] The Rabbinic כונה can hardly be better rendered into English than by
the word ' collection ' (*cp.* German *Sammlung*). It seems a pity that Dr. Murray
has no later quotation than 1868.

[2] Midrash Psalms on Ps. xlv. § 4 ; Pesikta Rabbati, 198 b (ed. Friedmann) ;
Lamentations Rabba on iii. 40, 41.

[3] Aboth ii. 15 ; Sabbath 153 a ; Mid. Psalms on Ps. xc. (16) ; Ecclesiastes
Rabba on ix. 8.

[4] Pirke R. Eliezer, chap. iii.

[5] Genesis Rabba i. § 4 ; Nedarim 39 a, etc., etc. *Cp.* Bacher, *Agada der
paläst. Amoräer*, II. 510, III. 656, and his excellent notes. In the note (4) on III.
656, for Berachoth 54 a read Pesachim 54 a.

canst not lay hold of the cord at both ends at once.   If thou desirest strict justice, the world cannot endure ; if thou desirest the preservation of the world, strict justice cannot endure.' [1]

Repentance, therefore, is a constant necessity.   It is often compared with the sea, which is always accessible.   Men can bathe in it at every hour.   So the gates of repentance are ever wide open for all who wish to enter.[2]   God is represented as willing and even anxious to welcome the penitent.   Sentences like the following are usual : ' God says, My hands are stretched out towards the penitent : I thrust none back who gives me his heart in repentance.'   ' God's hand is stretched out under the wings of the heavenly chariot to snatch the penitent from the grasp of justice.'   ' He holds no creature for unworthy, but opens the door to all at every hour : he who would enter can enter.'   ' Open for me,' says God, ' a gateway of repentance as big as a needle's eye, and I will open for you gates wide enough for horses and chariots.'   ' If your sins are as high as heaven, even unto the seventh heaven, and even to the throne of glory, and you repent, I will receive you.' [3]

God is constantly represented as pleading with the Israelites to prove to them that repentance is within their power.   If Israel says, ' We are poor, we have no offerings to make,' God replies, ' I need only words.'   If they say, ' We know nothing ' [for by ' words ' the Midrash means the words of the Law], God says, ' Then weep and pray before me, and I will accept your prayer.' Or, again : ' The Israelites say, Lord, if we repent, will you accept our repentance ?   And God replies, I have accepted the repentance of Cain and Ahab and Jeconiah and Manasseh, and shall I not accept yours ? '   Or God and the Israelites are compared to a king and to the king's son who had gone from his father a journey of 100 days ; when he was urged to return to his father, he said, I cannot. Then his father sent to say, ' Return as far as you can, and I will come to you the rest of the way.' [4]   God loves the penitent.   Thus it is said : ' As a man joins the two feet of a bed, or as a man puts two boards together,' so God brings the repentant near to him.[5] Several times we meet with the saying that what is rejected in the sacrificial beasts is acceptable in man, that is, the bruised and contrite heart.   Or, again : ' Broken vessels are a disgrace for a man to use, but God loves the broken heart.'   ' Him who repents of his sin, God honours : he gives him a name of endearment.   So

[1] Leviticus R. x. § 1.

[2] Lamentations R. on iii. 43 ; Mid. Psalms on Ps. lxv. (4) ; Deut. R. ii. § 12.

[3] Exodus R. xii. § 4 ; Pesachim 119 a ; Mid. Psalms on Ps. cxx. (7) ; Canticles R. v. § 1, 2, on v. 2 ; Pesikta R. 185 a.

[4] Exodus R. xxxviii. § 4 ; Pesikta K. 160 a seq. ; Pesikta R. 184 b.

[5] Leviticus R. iii. § 3.

the sons of Korah after they repented were called Lilies (an allusion
to Psalm xlv. 1), and David was called the Servant of God.'[1] A
familiar prayer opens with the words : ' Thou givest a hand to
transgressors, and thy right hand is stretched out to receive the
penitent.'[2] God is ready to cancel decrees of punishment and
doom because of repentance. ' Three things,' it says in the Midrash,
' can cancel evil decrees, namely, prayer, almsgiving, and repentance.'
To these three great specifics some would add change of name,
good works, exile and fasting. In the Talmud four things are
mentioned as possessed of the power of annulling the decree of
judgment : ' almsgiving, prayer, change of name, and change of
action (in repentance).'[3] The collocations are odd, and not without
their dangers. Almsgiving and good works, regarded as preserva-
tives from evil, open the door to superstitious formalism and to a
degradation of charity. I pointed out before how the fantastic
idea was adopted that God judged the world between New Year
and the Day of Atonement. The fancy took root, and it largely
pervades the Jewish Liturgy. Thus in the *Prayer Book for the
Day of Atonement*, according to the German and Polish ritual,
there is a prayer to which great importance is attached and which
goes into the strangest details. These are, however, largely taken
from the Talmud. On the New Year we are told it is inscribed,
and on Atonement it is sealed, who are to live and who are to die,
and of those doomed to death, who are to die young and who old,
who by sword and who by famine, who by pestilence and who by
fire, and so on. But it is added, ' repentance, prayer, and almsgiving cancel the evil decree.' It would be interesting if a future
historian of the Jews could enquire into the religious and ethical
results of these conceptions for evil and for good.

In the Talmud an almost comic turn is given to the doctrine
of God's desire to forgive by the remark, based upon a queer interpretation of 2 Sam. xxiii. 1–3, that if God rules over man, the
righteous rule over him, because ' if God ordains a decree, the
righteous cancel it.' A strange prayer to himself is put into God's
mouth : ' May it be my will that my mercy overcomes my anger,
so that I may deal with my creatures according to the attribute of
mercy and not according to strict justice.'[4] Thus God begs his
children to repent while he is standing upon the attribute of mercy,
for if he be on the attribute of justice, he will not know how to
proceed.[5]

[1] Leviticus R. vii. § 2 ; Mid. Psalms on Ps. xviii. (3).
[2] Singer's *Prayer Book*, pp. 61 and 267.
[3] Genesis R. xliv. § 12 ; Leviticus R. x. § 5 ; Rosh ha-Shanah, 16 b ; Aboth
iv. 15.
[4] Moed Katon, 16 b ; Berachoth 7 a.   [5] Pesikta R. 182 b.

As an illustration of Midrashic inconsistency, which one has to interpret according to its prevailing sentiment, I may quote the following passages, which in one form or another occur again and again: 'Why is the plural used in the expression אֶרֶךְ אַפִּים? Because God is long-suffering both towards the righteous and the wicked. He is long-suffering towards the righteous in that he requites them in this world for the few sins which they have committed, so that they may receive their full reward in the world to come. He is long-suffering to the wicked in that he gives them ease in this world, and thus requites them for the few good deeds which they have done, in order to exact the full penalty of their sins in the world to come.' Another Rabbi said : ' The plural indicates that God is long-suffering before he exacts requital, and he is long-suffering (*i.e.* gentle or slow) while he exacts it.' R. Chanina said (and his saying is often quoted as a sort of corrective to a too easy-going conception of God) : ' He who says that God is long-suffering—that he leaves sin unpunished—may he suffer for his folly. God is long-suffering, but he exacts his due.' R. Levi said : ' His long-suffering consists in removing his wrath afar. It is like a king who had two cruel legions. The king said : If they are with me in the city, directly the inhabitants annoy me, they will fall upon them, and kill them : therefore I will send them away, and when the citizens anger me, during the time that I send for my troops and they arrive, the citizens may come and appease me. So God says : Wrath and anger are two angels of destruction, I will send them far away ; when the Israelites anger me, before the angels arrive, the Israelites may repent, and I shall receive their repentance.' R. Isaac says : ' God shuts the door behind the angels of wrath. Before he opens the door, his mercy is at hand.' [1]

God is not ashamed to state that he breaks his laws and leaves them unfulfilled in order that the Israelites may repent. Thus : ' God told Jeremiah : Bid the Israelites repent. They replied : How can we repent ? Have we not made God angry by our sins ? Then God bade Jeremiah say : Though I declared I would destroy the sinner who should do what you have done, have I done so ? No, for I am merciful, and I keep not anger for ever. . . . It is before your Father in heaven that you come.' [2] ' Beloved is repentance before God, for he cancels his own words for its sake. For it says in the Law, If a man take a wife and find something un-

---

[1] Pesikta K. 161 b. *Cp.* Buber's remarks in notes 93 *seq.* on this page ; the translation given above follows the Pesikta as corrected by the Jerusalem Talmud (I.A.) ; Jer. Taanith ii. 1, 65 b (Schwab, VI. p. 155) ; Baba Kamma 50 a, etc., etc. (Bacher, *Agada der paläst. Amoräer*, I. p. 8) ; *cp.* also Sanhedrin 111 a.

[2] Pesikta K. 165 a.

seemly in her, he shall write her a bill of divorcement and send her away, and if she become another man's wife and he divorce her or die, then her former husband may not take her again to be his wife, after she is defiled, for that is an abomination before the Lord. But God does not act thus. Even though the Israelites have forsaken him (their husband) and served other gods, God says (Jer. iii. 1), Repent, draw near to me, and I will receive you.'[1] Whatever arguments the Israelites adduce to show the hopelessness of repentance, God or his prophet is ready to cap them. Thus Jeremiah bade them repent, and said, Where are your fathers who sinned? They replied, Where are your prophets who did *not* sin? Then both quote Zechariah (for chronology does not exist for the Rabbis), and Jeremiah wins the day. Again he bids them repent, and they say, If a master sell his slave, or a man divorce his wife, what have they any more to do with each other? Then through his prophet God replies : ' Where is the bill of your mother's divorcement? Or to whom have I sold you? Only sin separates you from me. Therefore return.' ' Nebuchadnezzar,' says Resh-Lakish, ' was called God's servant to meet this very argument, for if a servant acquires property, to whom does that property belong?'[2] Israel, though acquired by Nebuchadnezzar the servant, still belonged to the servant's Master.

The Rabbis are fond of illustrating God's readiness to accept the penitent by pointing out the difference between God's ways and man's ways. The following are examples : ' If one man has offended another, it is uncertain if he will let himself be appeased at all, and even so, if he will be satisfied with mere words, but God only demands words, and is even grateful to receive them.'[3] ' If a man has put his neighbour openly to shame, and wants to be reconciled to him, the neighbour says, You put me to open shame and want a private reconciliation ! Fetch the people before whom you spoke ill of me, and I will be reconciled. God is not so ; a man reviles and blasphemes him in the open street, and God says, Repent in secret, and I will receive you.' ' If a man commits a crime, he is inscribed for ever in the books of the government, but if a man sin against God and repent, God washes away the entry of his sin.' ' To an earthly king a man goes full and returns empty ; to God he goes empty and returns full.' ' Man writes an accusation against his fellow, and (only) withdraws it for much money : God writes an accusation, and withdraws it for mere words (*i.e.* repentance, Hosea xiv. 2).' ' Man leaps suddenly upon his enemy to do him evil, but God warned Pharaoh before each plague that he might

---

[1] Pesikta R. 184 a ; Yoma 86 b.
[2] Sanhedrin 105 a.   [3] Yoma 86 b.

repent.' ' A man can shoot an arrow a few furlongs, but repentance reaches to the throne of glory.' [1]

The Rabbinic doctrine is perhaps best summed up in a familiar passage from the Pesikta : [2] ' Who is like God, a teacher of sinners that they may repent ? They asked Wisdom, What shall be the punishment of the sinner ? Wisdom answered : Evil pursues sinners. (Prov. xiii. 21.) They asked Prophecy. It replied : The soul that sins shall die. (Ezek. xviii. 4.) They asked the Law. It replied : Let him bring a sacrifice. (Lev. i. 4.) They asked God, and he replied : Let him repent and obtain his atonement. My children, what do I ask of you ? Seek me and live.'

Scattered throughout the Rabbinical literature are innumerable sayings in praise of repentance and its results. We find a number of them in Yoma. ' Great is repentance for it brings healing upon the world.' ' Great is repentance for it reaches to the throne of glory.' ' Great is repentance for it brings redemption to Israel.' The question is discussed whether the Messiah's coming is dependent upon Israel's repentance. One distinguished Rabbi said, ' The period of the redemption depends solely upon repentance and good works.' Then two others dispute as to whether Israel will be redeemed even without repentance, and the question is not decided with certainty. Elsewhere we read that ' The Messiah will come at his appointed day, whether the Israelites repent or no, but if they made complete repentance, God would send him even before his time.' Another Rabbi, with fine exaggeration, declares that ' If the Israelites repented for a single day, the redemption would ensue.' And God is made to say, ' It depends upon yourselves. As the lily blooms and her heart is turned upward, in that very hour I will bring the Redeemer.' [3]

Thus, ' as a garment which is dirty can be washed and made clean, so the Israelites, though sinful, can by repentance make themselves clean before God.' [4] It is disputed whether the penitent or the righteous who have not sinned occupy the higher place, but the general view is that where the penitent stand the righteous stand not.[5] ' Better,' said R. Jacob, ' is one hour of repentance and good deeds in this world than the whole life of the world to come ; yet better is one hour of blissfulness of spirit in the world to come than the whole life of this world.' [6]

[1] Yoma 86 b ; Pesikta K. 163 b ; Sifre, 50 b ; Pesikta R. 183 a, 185 a ; Exodus R. ix. § 9 ; Pesikta K. 163 a.
[2] Pesikta K. 158 b ; Jer. Makkoth ii. 6, 31 d (Schwab, XI. p. 89).
[3] Yoma 86 a and 86 b ; Sanhedrin 97 b ; Exodus R. xxv. 12 ; Pesikta K. 163 b ; Canticles Rabba v. § 1, on v. 2 ; Mid. Psalms on Ps. xlv. (3).
[4] Exodus R. xxiii. § 10.
[5] Berachoth 34 b ; Sanhedrin 99 a.   [6] Aboth iv. 24.

We have seen that the Rabbis distinguished between a repentance of fear and a repentance of love ; and also that the sincerity of repentance was mainly proved by its results. Occasionally we find sentences which speak of that element of repentance which we sometime call contrition. Thus they quote and use Joel's adage, ' Rend your hearts and not your garments.' They speak of self-humiliation within the heart which is better than a thousand lashes upon the back. The mere sense of shame is sufficient, says one, to secure forgiveness. Another declares that ' He who sacrifices his evil desire and confesses his sin is regarded as if he had honoured God in this world and in the world to come.' So, too, he who humbles his spirit is regarded as if he had offered all the sacrifices of the law ; while he who sins and is sorry is at once forgiven.[1] It is in accordance with the Rabbis' high estimate of repentance that it is formally declared to be a serious sin to remind a penitent of his former misdeeds.[2]

[I omit here the paragraphs in the original article dealing with the possibility of repentance after death, because the substance of them has been already given in other connections.]

The reader will have noticed the strange use of Bible texts in many of the quotations from the Rabbinic literature. It would be an interesting point for a scholar to consider how far the various dicta, and even the various opinions, of the Rabbis were influenced by literal or strained interpretations of Biblical passages, or whether these interpretations were merely dragged in to substantiate an opinion which was already formed. In any case, the Biblical verses doubtless affected the manner in which the opinions were enunciated. A few of the more usual passages as regards repentance may now be pointed out.

The favourite quotation, as I mentioned before, is doubtless the opening of the last chapter of Hosea : ' O Israel, return unto the Lord thy God, for thou hast stumbled by thine iniquity. Take with you words, and return unto the Lord ; say unto him, Take away all iniquity, and accept that which is good, so will we render as bullocks the offering of our lips.' In these verses the Rabbinic fathers found the full doctrine of repentance and confession. Here, too, they found the basis for their view that prayer, confession, and repentance are God's chosen substitutes for sacrifice and burnt-offering.

Next to this passage, they found, perhaps, the eighteenth chapter of Ezekiel most fruitful : ' Have I any pleasure in the death of the

---

[1] Berachoth 7 a, 12 b ; Sanhedrin 43 b ; Chagigah 5 a. The word used is מתחרט.

[2] Baba Mezia 58 b. *Cp.* Sirach viii. 5.

wicked, and not rather that he should turn from his way and live ? ' Jeremiah's exhortations, too, are quoted again and again : ' Return, O backsliding children. I am merciful. I will not keep anger for ever.' The Psalmist's ' broken and contrite heart ' is also much appealed to ; and the allusions are frequent to the verse, ' Blessed is he whose transgression is forgiven, whose sin is covered,' with its apparently contradictory sequence, ' Mine iniquity I have not hid,' and to the verse in Proverbs, ' He that covereth his transgressions shall not prosper, but whoso confesseth and forsaketh them shall obtain mercy.' The contradiction is prettily explained by one Rabbi on the assumption that the sin which is covered refers to sins against God, the sin which is openly confessed to sins against man.[1]

The foregoing quotations from Scripture were interpreted in their literal sense. I may now give two or three examples of un-natural or homiletic exegesis. We saw how ' Peace, peace to the far and to the near ' was used to assess the worth of the penitent. So, too, the verse of the Psalmist, 'A people which shall be created shall praise the Lord,' is explained to refer to sinners who repent and pray before God at New Year and the Day of Atonement, and who, because they change their deeds, are, as it were, created by God anew.[2]

It would take me too long and too far to mention the odd changes of vowels and letters which the Midrash sometimes indulges in to prove ·or illustrate its points, but reference must be made to two more Biblical texts which are constantly appealed to. The first is the enumeration of the divine attributes in Exodus xxxiv. or Numbers xiv. The Hebrew idiom of expressing emphasis by putting the infinite before the finite verb was possibly no longer familiar or intelligible to the Rabbis. At any rate, for homiletical reasons, they explain that the phrase, ונקה לא ינקה, must have a special meaning, for here, they say, it is distinctly stated that God will and that God will not acquit (the sinner). The explanation of the contradiction is that God will only acquit those who have repented of their sins.[3] The second passage to which I would refer is the third verse of the ninetieth Psalm : ' Thou turnest man to destruction ; then thou sayest, Return, ye children of men.' This is the invariable Biblical support for the Rabbinic doctrine that repentance was created before the world. Before, that is, God had formed the world, the divine voice had already proclaimed the necessity and the value of repentance. The first part of the verse is interpreted to mean,

---

[1] Yoma, 86 b; cf. Maimonides on Repentance, ii. 5.
[2] Midrash Psalms on Ps. cii. (3).
[3] Yoma 86 a; cf. Sifre 33 a.

Thou bringest man to contrition ; the second is the summons to repentance. Or again, ' Thou turnest man to destruction ' is supposed to signify ' Thou causest him to turn until he is crushed ' ; in other words, God accepts repentance up till the very moment of death. I may add that the verb *shub* is so associated in the Rabbinic mind with repentance, that, as in this interpretation of the ninetieth Psalm, they can hardly conceive it possible for it to mean anything else. A curious illustration of this tendency can be found in a verse from the Book of Kings, where it is stated of Josiah that there was no king like unto him who *turned* unto the Lord with all his heart. Hence one Rabbi infers that Josiah was a great penitent.[1]

Other Biblical heroes are connected by the Rabbis with the subject of repentance and with better reason than in the case of Josiah. Thus it is stated of Adam that God wanted him to repent, and opened the door thereto, but Adam was too proud to humble himself, and therefore he was driven from Paradise. Cain, on the other hand, did repent, and therefore at least half his punishment was remitted him. The Midrash tells how Adam, meeting Cain, asked how his case stood. Upon which Cain replies : I repented, and the matter is settled (I have been forgiven). Adam struck his face with amazement and said, I did not know that the power of repentance was so great. He at once composed and recited the ninety-second Psalm : ' It is good to confess (להודות) unto the Lord.' [2]

Of Abraham, on the other hand, we are told that he was appointed to lead the whole world to repentance. The meaning of this statement seems to be that Abraham is regarded as the great proselyte and proselyte-maker. He was therefore the first to lead men away from the falsehood and sin of idolatry into the purity and rectitude of monotheistic belief. Commenting upon the story of Abraham's vision in the night, the Midrash observes that Abraham was at first unable to drive the birds of prey from the carcass, but finally succeeded in doing so through repentance. Here the birds are regarded as a type of the persecutions from which the Israelites would have to suffer.[3]

The next Biblical character connected with repentance is Reuben. He repented of his part in the plot against Joseph, and God said to him : ' Not till now has a man sinned before me and repented,

---

[1] Sabbath 56 b.

[2] Tanchuma B. Bereshith, xxv. 10 a ; Numbers Rabba xiii. § 3 ; Genesis Rabba xxii. *ad fin.* ; Mid. Psalms on Ps. c. (2) ; Leviticus R. x. § 5. In the last place the Cain story is used as an illustration in the argument between R. Judah and R. Joshua b. Levi, of whom the former asserts that repentance does half and prayer does all, while the latter said that prayer does half and repentance does all.

[3] Genesis R. xxx. § 9, xliv. § 17.

therefore thy descendant shall be the first to summon the Israelites to repentance. Thou wouldst have brought back the beloved son to his father : thy descendant shall bring back the Israelites to their Father in heaven.'[1] This descendant was Hosea. It was the tribe of Reuben who encamped on the south side, for from the south come dew and rain, and Reuben is the typical penitent, and through the worth of repentance rain falls upon the earth. Judah is the type of the Law, and therefore Judah set forth first ; Reuben is the type of repentance, and therefore Reuben set forth second, for repentance is (only) second (in importance) to the Law. Elsewhere the large offering of the prince ' of the children of Reuben ' (Num. vii. 30–35) is said to be typical of, or to correspond with, Reuben's repentance when Joseph was sold, for repentance, it is characteristically added, is equivalent to all the sacrifices of the Law.[2]

In the same Midrash an eccentric remark is made about Balaam. The reason why he said to the angel ' I have sinned ' was because he knew that, if a man sins and confesses, the angels have no power to hurt him.[3] The subject of repentance is also referred to in connection with the golden calf, but I have noticed nothing worth quotation, except perhaps the odd idea of R. Joshua b. Levi that the Israelites only made the calf, just as David only committed the sin with Bathsheba and Uriah, in order to encourage sinners to become penitents and to return to God. Thus, if an individual sin, one can say, ' Even as David repented, so do thou repent ' ; and if a community sin, one can say, ' Even as Israel repented, so do you repent.'[4] Elsewhere also David is regarded as an example for penitents and sinners. It was he who said to God, ' Thou art a great God, and my sins are great. It beseems the great God to pardon great sins.' ' Let everyone who has sinned look at David ; for it is said, Behold, for a witness to the peoples I have appointed him.' ' David said to God, If thou receivest me, then sinners will submit to thee, and they will look at me, and I shall be a witness that thou receivest the penitent.' Playing upon and mispunctuating a verse in Samuel (2 Sam. xxiii. 1), a Rabbi says of David that he set up ' the yoke of repentance.'[5]

In many passages Jehoiachin or Coniah is pointed to as a salient example of the power of repentance in cancelling the divine oath

---

[1] The *first* penitent is variously named by different Rabbis as Cain, Abraham, Reuben, etc.

[2] Genesis R. lxxxiv. § 19 ; Numbers R. ii. § 10, iii. § 12 (on Num. iii. 38), xiii. § 18 ; Pesikta K. 159 b.

[3] Numbers R. xx. § 15.

[4] Exodus R. i. § 36 ; Numbers R. xx. § 20 ; Sanhedrin 7 a ; Abodah Zarah 4 b.

[5] Levit. R. v. 8 *ad fin.* ; Mid. Psalms on Ps. xl. (2), li. (3) ; Abodah Zarah 5 a ; Moed Katon 16 b.

and decree. For Jeremiah said, ' As I live, saith the Lord, write ye this man childless,' whereas in Chronicles we are told of his sons.[1]

But the penitent whose story is most frequently quoted, and who is most often used to point the moral, is Manasseh. Manasseh was the worst of all the kings of Judah, and yet he repented, and his repentance was accepted. For when the wicked king was carried to Babylon, bound in fetters and chains, and thrown, according to the legend, into a fiery furnace, he called upon all the gods of the world to whom he had sacrificed, and none made answer. ' Then he called upon God, and said, Lord, I have called upon all the gods of the world, and now I have realized that they are things of nought. Thou art the God of gods : if thou dost not hearken to me, I shall think that thou and they are as one. Then the angels arose, and stopped up all the windows of heaven, and they said, Wilt thou, O Lord, accept the repentance of a man who set up an idol in the very Temple itself ? But God replied, If I accept him not in his repentance, I shut the door upon all penitents. Wherefore God bored a hole under the throne of his glory, and received Manasseh's prayer.' Elsewhere it is said, ' If a man comes and says, God does not receive the penitent, then Manasseh will bear witness that there was no worse man in the world than he, and yet in the hour of his repentance God received him.' In a famous section of Mishnah Sanhedrin it is stated that Manasseh is one of three kings who have no share in the world to come. But R. Judah said that Manasseh has his portion in the world to come, while R. Yochanan averred that ' to deny such a portion to Manasseh is to make the hands of all penitents be slack.'[2]

As the Jews have been often said to be very ready to criticize themselves, while objecting to criticism from others, so we find some shrewd sayings about their history in connection with our particular subject. Thus we are told that Pharaoh's pursuit had a greater effect upon the Israelites than a hundred fast days and endless prayers. For in their fear they looked up to God and repented of their sins. And frequently it is said that sufferings or chastisements have been the means of Israel's repentance. On the other hand, as we have already seen, God is represented as the loving Father of Israel who hates to punish and longs to save. Rabbi Meir said, 'Israel is God's son who has been driven away by his pride and sinfulness from his Father's house (i.e. Palestine) ; but the son will repent and be restored.'[3] Sometimes, but much more

---

[1] Levit. R. x. § 5 ; Pesikta K. 163 a *fin.*

[2] Numbers Rabba xiv. § 1 ; Ruth R. v. § 6 ; Deut. R. ii. § 20 ; Pesikta K. 162 a ; Sanhedrin 90 a, 103 a ; Jer. Sanhedrin x. 28 c (Schwab xi. p. 50), etc.

[3] Bacher, *Agada der Tannaiten,* ii. p. 35 ; cf. Jer. Taanith 63 d, 64 a (Schwab vi. 142–144).

rarely, and only in contrast to the nations, Israel is depicted as specially susceptible to the gracious goodness of God. Only once or twice have I noticed a desire to extol the Rabbi or the student of the law. Thus we find it said that if you have seen a Rabbi commit a sin at night time, you may be sure that he has repented of it by the following day. And Akiba declared that as vessels of gold and crystal when broken can be mended, so for the student of the Law, (moral) repair is still possible. But in another place the very same thing is said of man generally : ' Let not a man say, Because I have sinned, no repair is possible for me,' but let him trust in God and repent, and God will receive him.' [1] Nebuchadnezzar told his general that the God of the Jews receives the penitent; therefore, 'when they are conquered, give them no opportunity to pray, lest they repent and their God have pity upon them.'

There are parts of the Day of Atonement liturgy which suggest an attitude of gloom and apprehension. But from the Mishnah onward—and we must remember that the words of the Mishnah are older than the completed code—the prevailing religious attitude of the Jew is hopeful. His God is a God of mercy, and though to sin is human, no less human is repentance, and the most essential attribute of God is forgiveness. The Talmud itself calls attention to this characteristically Jewish point of view. ' It is the custom,' it observes, ' among men when they appear before a court of justice to put on black clothes, and to let the beard grow long because of the uncertainty of the issue. Israelites do not act so : on the day when the judgment opens (the New Year), they are clad in white, and shave their beards, they eat and drink and rejoice in the conviction that God will do wonders for them.' [2] True repentance will turn voluntary sins into involuntary errors, and the strain of involuntary errors the Day of Atonement will wash away.[3] The Mishnah declares in the most solemn manner that every Israelite, with certain specified exceptions, will have a share in the world to come. But when we turn from the Rabbinic to the apocalyptic literature a different temper seems to prevail. There, if confidence exists, it is rather an arid pride of race than the justified hope of those who believe in a merciful God and in the efficacy and possibility of repentance. And when this unethical confidence is wanting, we find an anxiety and a mistrust utterly removed from, and unfamiliar to, the true Rabbinic religion. In the Fourth Book of Ezra, which is not so many years anterior to the Mishnah, the teaching is

---

[1] Berachoth 19 a ; Chagigah 15 a ; Mid. Psalms on Ps. xl. (3). The word translated by ' repair ' is תקנה.

[2] Jer. Rosh ha-Shanah i. 2, 57 b (Schwab VI. p. 65).

[3] Yoma 36 b, 86 b.

that many are 'lost' and few are 'saved.' Instead of cheerful hope, there prevails a spirit of gloom and despair. The author of the Epistle to the Romans would seem to have been filled with such a spirit before his conversion, or at any rate to regard it as a logically justified condition of mind for those who do not yet believe in the atoning death and resurrection of Christ, or for those who rejected these newer doctrines and clung to the older teachings of the Law and of the Prophets. Whence comes this strange difference of belief and of attitude between the apocalyptic and the Rabbinic literature, between the Fourth Book of Ezra and St. Paul on the one hand, and the Mishnah upon the other? Does this difference partly account for the fact that the apocalyptic and pseudepigraphic writings have not survived in Hebrew, and that the Rabbis seem to have regarded them as off the true line of tradition and as heretical? The complete solution of this puzzle is still to seek.

Meanwhile, the Rabbinic cheerfulness has remained a characteristic of Judaism till the present day, and the doctrine of Repentance is one of its causes. Though Rabbinic and mediaeval Jews were in one sense particularist, in another sense they were universalist. The theory of repentance helped them to keep clear of the gloomy doctrines of election and reprobation. The Fourth Gospel knows nothing of repentance, because it divides the world into children of light and children of darkness. From such teachings legal Judaism kept free. And this is partly owed to its doctrine of Repentance. Not unwisely, then, did the Rabbinic doctors declare, 'There is nothing greater than repentance; repentance is second to the Law.' [1]

[There are many good extra passages in Moore's chapters on Repentance (I. pp. 507–534), a few of which I should like to add on here. Israel and God dispute who should begin the process of repentance. A Biblical verse says, 'Turn thou us and we shall be turned'; therefore God should begin. But another verse says, 'Turn unto me, and I will turn unto you.' 'So let us turn together simultaneously' (שנינו כאחד). (Lam. R. on v. 21; Midrash Psalms lxxxv. $\frac{3}{2}$) 'God says to Israel, Repent in the Ten Days between New Year and the Day of Atonement, and I will justify (מזכה) you on the Day of Atonement, and create you a new creature' (Pesikta R. 169 a). 'If a man repents and goes back to his sins, that is no repentance. If one goes down to take a bath of purification, holding some unclean reptile in his hand, he gets no purification. He must cast away what he has in his hand; after that he can take his bath and be purified' (Pesikta R. 182 b; cp. Sirach xxxi. 30, 31).

Perhaps I may conclude this Appendix on repentance by a

[1] Deut. R. ii. § 24 *init.*; Numbers R. ii. § 10.

literal translation of the long and interesting passage in the Jerusalem Talmud, about the famous apostate R. Elisha b. Abuya, with which Mr. Loewe has been good enough to supply me (Jer. Chagigah 77 b–77 c).

R. Yudah bar Pazzi, in the name of R. Yose, son of Yudah, says : Three expounded [1] their Torah before their teacher, R. Joshua before R. Yochanan b. Zakkai, R. Akiba before R. Joshua, Hananyah b. Hakhinai before R. Akiba [sc. with success]. Henceforward their mind was not clear.[2] Four entered Paradise : [3] one glanced [4] and died : one glanced and was struck ; [5] one glanced and cut down the young plants : one entered and left in safety. Ben 'Azzai glanced and was struck. To him applies the verse ' Is it honey that thou hast found ? Then eat as much as will satisfy thee ' [i.e. not to excess]. (Prov. xxv. 16.) Ben Zoma glanced and died. To him applies the verse ' Precious in the sight of the Lord is death to his saints ' (Ps. cxi. 15).[6] Acher cut the plants.[7] Who was Acher (the ' other ') ? This was Elisha b. Abuyah, who slew the growing children [8] of the Law. They say that whenever he saw a pupil making progress in the Torah he ' slew ' him.[9] Further, when he entered a lecture-room and saw students sitting before their masters,

---

[1] הרצו, רצה, Hif. also=expound, recount. K. ha-E. (=the commentary Korban ha-Edah by David ben Naphtali Hirsch); ' Expounded the " chariot " (Ezekiel i.) before their teacher,' i.e. engaged in mystic or metaphysical studies.

[2] I take this to mean that these three alone stood the strain to which imitators succumbed. I take this view because we know that Akiba, for example, did not come to a bad end. The ' their ' in דעתן (' their mind ') is used loosely. K. ha-E., ' Their mind was not clear to comprehend things in their proper sense '; the Pene Mosheh (by Moses Margalioth ben Simeon), ' to lecture on the " chariot " ' ; neither commentator says ' whose mind ' is in question. [The phrase might also mean : ' Three, and only three, ever ventured to lecture in the presence of their teachers, and afterwards their minds were never at ease (by reason of their presumption).']

[3] Kor. ha-E. : ' Went up to heaven by means of the Name : but they did not ascend physically, only it seemed to them as though they did.' So also Pene Mosheh. פרדס is the well-known mnemonic for four methods of exegesis : Peshaṭ (plain sense), Remez (hint), Derash (Midrash), and Ṣod (esoteric meaning).

[4] At the Shechinah.

[5] Kor. ha-E. : ' His mind was affected.'

[6] Kor. ha-E. : ' Hard was his death before God since he died young, but his death was none the less inevitable, for " man cannot see Me and live." '

[7] Kor. ha-E. : ' He scoffed and perverted just as one who enters a park and picks the flowers.'

[8] רְבֵי adolescent. Kor. ha-E. takes this as רַבֵּי, ' the great ones of the Torah.' Pene Mosheh : ' When he saw lads growing up and being reared in the Torah, he slew them.' I think this is right. Elisha, like Socrates, was accused of corrupting the young.

[9] Kor. ha-E. : ' By enchantments or the Name,' i.e. he upset his faith and his reason.

he would say, 'For what purpose are they here?'[1] [In the end they will fail in their studies, and] this one's craft will be that of the builder, that one will be a carpenter, this one a hunter, that one a tailor. When they, [the disciples], heard this, [*i.e.* that they would fail in the Torah], they abandoned him, [their master or the Torah], and went away [to the crafts that had been predicted]. To Elisha applies the verse 'Suffer not thy mouth to cause thy flesh to sin' (Eccles. v. 5), 'because he corrupted the handiwork of that man.'[2] Now, in the time of persecution, the persecutors used to load burdens on the Jews [to make them violate the Sabbath], and the Jews hit upon the device of putting one burden upon two [bearers],[3] because of the ordinance 'If two jointly carry one load.' Then Acher advised the persecutors to load each Jew separately [in order to defeat their scheme], and this was done. Then the Jews conceived the plan of unloading in Karmillith[4] so as not to transfer the object from the private demesne to the public jurisdiction. Then Acher advised the persecutors to load the Jews with glass dishes,[5] and they did so.

R. Akiba entered and left in safety: to him applies the verse 'Draw me, we will run after thee' (Cant. i. 4).[6]

R. Meir was once sitting and lecturing in the Tiberias Academy, when Elisha, his [former] master passed by him, riding on a horse on the Sabbath. They came and told Meir that his master was without. So Meir interrupted his discourse and went out to him.[7]

---

[1] Lit. 'What are these sitting, doing, here? This man's work is that of a builder.' Pene M.: 'This one is obviously better fitted to be a . . .'

[2] Pene M.: 'He refers to himself, for by such speech he destroyed his own handiwork, as it was originally before he fell on evil courses.' Kor. ha-E.: 'For by the words of his mouth he was causing the young to sin, and it appears that these were his own children ("thine own flesh"): or else it is used generally, all Israel being brothers; the former view is preferable.'

[3] So that neither party should be doing a complete act, and so, the burden being lighter for each, the prohibition against bearing burdens would technically not have been infringed.

[4] The act of carrying involves a transfer from place to place, *e.g.* from private demesne to public jurisdiction. *Karmillith* is 'a marked-off plot in a public thoroughfare or an area which cannot be classified either as private or public' (Jastrow). The Jews sought to evade the persecutors by breaking their journey in Karmillith, unloading, exchanging burdens, and then reloading and ending at the appointed spot, thus avoiding a complete transfer in one act. The whole transaction is clearly rhetorical and unreal, and the story is artificial.

[5] Which would involve care and time in reloading, and thus the plan of the Jews would be impracticable.

[6] Kor. ha-E.: 'For he "glanced" with discretion because he did not go up on high until he completely grasped the true purport of what he saw below. As though it said "Draw me on, O my mind," for I have now understood all that is needful, all that I have already seen, therefore now "let me run after thee," and so "the King has brought me to his chambers." '

[7] Kor. ha-E.: To learn Torah from him.

Elisha asked Meir, ' What have you been expounding to-day ? '
Meir answered, ' Now the Lord blessed the latter days (lit. end) of
Job more than his beginning' (Job. xlii. 12). Elisha said, ' And how
did you open your lesson ? '[1] He replied, ' Also the Lord gave Job
twice as much as he had before (*ib.* 10), for he doubled all his wealth.'
Elisha said, ' Woe to those who are deceased and who find not :[2]
Akiba thy master was not wont thus to expound it. He used to say,
" God blessed the latter end of Job more than his beginning,"
through the merit of the fulfilled commandments and good deeds
which he did in the beginning.'[3] Then he asked Meir, ' On what did
you lecture afterwards ? ' Meir replied, ' On Eccles. vii. 8, " Better
the end of a thing than the beginning." ' He said, ' And how did
you take it ? ' Meir replied, ' It is like the case of a man who had
children in his youth, but they died : then in his old age again he
had children who flourished,[4] so we see that " better is the end than
the beginning " : or again, it is like a man who did business in his
youth and lost his money, but again, in his old age, he did business and gained, so " better, etc." : or it is like a man who learnt
Torah in his youth but forgot it, and then learnt again in his old
age, when it endured, so " better, etc." ' Elisha replied, ' Woe to
those who perish and find not ' : ' Akiba thy master used not to
teach thus, but rather, " Good is the end of a thing from the
beginning,[5] when it has been good from the beginning, and in my

---

[1] פתח, ' to open,' is the usual word for selecting text A as a peg for a discourse on text B. I think the meaning is ' What was your complementary verse ? '
The answer is verse 10, as stated by Meir in his reply. But this is not the view of
the commentators. Kor. ha-E. says ' Opened,' *i.e.* expounded ; *cf.* פתח in Exodus
xxviii. 11 *et al.* in the sense of *incising, engraving, cutting deep into a thing.* The
meaning is ' What deep, hidden truth did you derive ? ' The commentator in the
Krot. ed. has ' What exposition of it did you give ? '

[2] Levy and Jastrow take מורדין (*i.e.* pass away) intransitively, and this is the
usual meaning of the proverb. I think the context requires a transitive meaning,
and, after all, the Afel conjunction is here used, ' Woe to those who lose (*sc.* truth)
and find it not.' I do not think that משכחין can=משתכחין (so Kor. ha-E.), and
=' are no more found.'

[3] I take it that Akiba disapproved of Job's attitude, but deemed him ' saved'
because of his former goodness. Meir seems to have thought Job right all along
and to have explained the ' reward ' as material compensation. According to
Akiba, Elisha might similarly hope for salvation, but according to Meir he could not.

[4] ובוקנותו נתקיימו, ' and in his old age they were established, endured.'
Krot. ed. has ובוקנותו ונקרימו, a misprint, I think. קרם means to encrust,
e.g. in Ezekiel's vision of dry bones, ' I will draw skin over them, וקרמתי '; but
ונקרימו is an impossible form—mixed *hifil* and *nifal.*

[5] Pene Mosheh : ' If in the beginning his thought was directed to the good and
for the name of heaven (*sc.* then the end would be good also : this is deduced
from מן, *from* the beginning=in consequence of the beginning), and not like the
action of Abuyah, Elisha's father, which was as follows : '

case [1] there was such an instance. Abuyah my father was one of the great men of Jerusalem, and on the day when he celebrated my circumcision, he invited all the great ones of Jerusalem and put them in one house, and he put R. Eliezer and R. Joshua in another house. After they, [*i.e.* the former party], had eaten and drunk, they began to clap hands and dance." Said Eliezer to Joshua, "While these folk are busy in their fashion, let us busy ourselves in ours." So they sat and studied Torah. From plain Torah they came on to the Prophets, thence to the Hagiographa. Fire came down from heaven and played round them. Abuyah said to them, "Gentlemen, why have you come here to burn my house down on me?" They said, "God forbid, we have merely been sitting and rehearsing the words of the Law: from the Law we proceeded to the Prophets and thence to the Hagiographa, and the words were rejoicing as they did when they were given on Sinai, and fire licked them as it licked them on Sinai, for the fundamental essence of their giving on Sinai lay in their being given in fire, [*i.e.* in being divinely inspired], as it says 'And the mountain burnt in fire to the very heart of heaven'" (Deut. iv. 11). Said Abuyah to them, "Gentlemen, since the strength of the Torah is so great, if this my son be preserved for me, for the Torah will I separate him; [2] but since his motive was not pure (לשם שמים), therefore it was not fulfilled."' [3] Elisha said to Meir, 'And on what did you lecture afterwards?' Meir replied, 'On "gold and crystal cannot equal it"' (Job. xxviii. 17). Elisha said, 'And how did you expound it?' [4] He said, 'Words of Torah are precious (hard) to acquire as gold and easy to destroy as crystal: if they are broken, can one again make them into a vessel as they were? So also a scholar who has forgotten his learning, can he again relearn as at the outset?' Elisha said, 'Meir, that is enough: here ends the limit of the Sabbath (journey).' Meir said, 'And how do you know?' Elisha answered, 'From the steps of my horse, which I have been counting (*sc.* subconsciously).'

Kor. ha-E.: 'If the original intention was good and לשם שמים, but not if it was otherwise. Then only would the end be better than the beginning: and he brings a proof from Elisha.'

It appears to me that in this second case Elisha decides bitterly that Akiba is against him while Meir is for him, not as in the instance from Job, when Akiba's interpretation would leave Elisha an opportunity of repentance.

[1] So according to the Petrikov ed. which has וּבִי. Krot. ed. has וכי, 'and thus.'

[2] I think this is the best way: not 'If this my son be preserved for the Torah, I will make him a Pharisee.'

[3] Lit. 'It was not fulfilled in that man, *i.e.* in him' (Abuyah). In that case the subject of נתקיימה is כוונתו, his intention. The sentence could also be 'therefore it (the Torah) did not abide in me (Elisha).'

[4] See note 1, p. 418.

Meir said, ' And with all this wisdom that is in thee thou wilt not
return ? ' [1] He replied, ' I cannot.' ' Why not ? ' ' Because once
I was passing by the place of the Sanctuary. I was riding my horse
on the Day of Atonement which fell on a Sabbath, and I heard a
heavenly voice issue from the Sanctuary and say, " Return, O my
children, save Elisha ben Abuyah who knoweth my strength but
rebelleth against me." ' Now how did all this (atheism) come upon
him ? [2] Once he was sitting and learning in the valley of Genne-
sareth, when he saw a man climb a palm tree and take a dam with
the young birds. He came down from the tree in safety. On the
morrow Elisha saw another man climb the palm, take the young
and release the dam. As the man descended, a serpent stung him
fatally. Elisha said, ' It is written, Thou shalt certainly let the dam
go (Deut. xxii. 7), . . . that it be well (" good ") with thee and that thou
prolong thy days ' : where was the ' goodness ' [3] of the one ? Where
was the ' prolonging of days ' of the other ? Now Elisha was not
aware of the fact that long before him R. Jacob had explained this
verse thus : ' that it be well with thee,' i.e. in the world to come
where all is well, and ' that thou mayest prolong days,' i.e. in the
future existence which is long beyond measure. Others say that
[he became an agnostic] when he saw the tongue of R. Judah the
baker [4] lying in the dog's mouth, dripping with blood. He said, ' Is
this Torah and this its reward ? Is this indeed that tongue that
used to give forth words of Torah in their proper sense ? Is this the
tongue that laboured in the Torah all his (Judah's) days ? It is
clear that there is no reward and no resurrection.' Others again
say that when his mother was pregnant with him, she used to pass
by certain heathen houses, [5] and she smelt the smell of a certain
heretic, and this smell penetrated [6] to her body, like the virus of an
annulated snake (ἔχιδνα).

---

[1] Wisdom here means, I should think, instinctive aptitude for the Law. Although
you profess to be an agnostic, automatically you take note of the Law.

[2] Pene Mosheh : How did he make up his mind to follow evil courses ?
Kor. ha-E. : How did he come to go astray ? For had some doubt not arisen
in his heart he would never, in view of his great learning, have turned from the true
way.

[3] טובתו corresponding to ייטב לך, ' that it be well with thee,' i.e. morally,
not materially.

[4] On this martyr see Midrash, Shocher Ṭob, on Ps. ix. 13, with Buber's note
in loc.

[5] Not temples, I think, but atheist meetings, whence she derived certain sub-
versive ideas, here metaphorically called ריח, smell. Levy, s.v. פעפע, does take
this to refer to temples. He takes ריח literally, as incense. So does Kor. ha-E.,
which has תקרובת, i.e. offerings.

[6] פעפע, i.e. to shatter, cleave, or penetrate.

Later on Elisha fell ill and they came and told Meir, ' Behold,
thy master lies sick.' Meir went to visit him and found him ill and
said, ' Wilt thou not return ? ' Elisha answered, ' And [1] are [death-
bed] penitents accepted ? ' [2] Said Meir, ' Is it not written " Thou
bringest man back at the point of crushing " (Ps. xc. 3) and sayest,
Return, ye sons of men ? Till crushing, till the soul is crushed out,
God (lit. they) receives them.' At that moment Elisha wept and
passed away. R. Meir rejoiced, thinking that it was in penitence that
Elisha died. After they had buried Elisha, fire came down from
heaven and burnt his grave. They came and told Meir, ' Behold,
thy master's grave is burnt.' He went out, wishing to visit [3]
him, and he found the grave burnt. What did he do ? He took his
(Meir's) wrapper (*Tallith*) and spread it over him, saying [4] ' Spend
the night here ' (Ruth iii. 13). ' Spend the night here,' [5] *i.e.* in this
world which is to be compared with night : ' And it shall be in the
morning,' this is the world to come, which is all morning. ' If *he*
will redeem thee, it is good, let *him* redeem,' this *he* is the Holy One,
Blessed be He, who is ' good,' as it is said ' Good is the Lord to all
(even to sinners like Elisha), and his tender mercies are over all his
works (including Acher).' (Ps. cxlv. 9.) ' And if *He* is unwilling to
redeem thee, then will I redeem thee, as the Lord liveth.' Then the
fire was quenched.

They asked R. Meir : ' If they say to thee in that (*i.e.* the next)
world, " Whom dost thou wish to visit,[6] thy father or thy master ? " '
Meir answered, ' I would draw near to my master first and afterwards to my father.' They said, ' And will they listen to thee ? ' [7]

---

[1] אִין, if, verily, whether ; = הֵן, not אֵין.

[2] Krot. ed. Margin : ' Can a man be received as a penitent at a time when it is
no longer in his power to sin ? '

[3] מבקרתיה as above, when Elisha was sick. But I suspect the reading should
be מקברתיה, ' seeking to bury him,' *i.e.* replace the grave. בקר is the usual
word for visiting the sick, hardly of visiting a grave. If the text is right, it might
imply that Meir wished to visit Elisha in his burnt grave and win him to penitence
since he had not repented on his death-bed, as Meir had deemed. But the following narrative is against this, and, I think, supports מקברתיה.

[4] Kor. ha-E. : Meir took his own *Tallith* and spread it over the grave, knowing
that fire would not touch his garments, as happened in the case of the saint in
tractate Sabbath.

[5] Kor. ha-E. : As long as R. Meir lives, let him stay in Gehenna.

[6] בקר means more than merely ' visit,' it implies ' serve,' ' help.' Notice that
Meir's reply is מיקרב, ' to draw near to,' not מיבקר, ' to visit.' I suspect it
should be קרב in each case.

[7] Kor. ha-E. : ' Will they agree to thy rescuing a stranger from Gehenna
through thy *Zechuth* ? ' We have learnt ' A son may give *Zechuth* to his father,
but not a disciple to his master.'

He rejoined, 'Have we not so learned : One rescues the case ($\theta\acute{\eta}\kappa\eta$) of the scroll [1] together with the scroll ; the case of the phylacteries with the phylacteries ?   So one rescues Elisha, Acher (though he be) by the *Zechuth* of his Torah.'

Later his (Elisha's) daughters came to ask (lit. take) charity from Rabbi Judah the Prince, who decreed [a refusal, saying] (Ps. cix. 12), ' Let there be none to extend mercy to him, neither let there be any to extend favour to his fatherless children.' They said, ' Rabbi, regard not his deeds, regard his Torah.'   Then Rabbi Judah wept and decreed that Elisha's daughters should be supported.   He said, ' If this man, who laboured in the Torah, though not for the name of heaven, could produce [2] such [a scholar as R. Meir], from one who labours in the Torah for its own sake (*lishmah*), how much more will great scholars arise ? ']

---

[1] Kor. ha-E. : Because it is a sacred utensil.

[2] Lit. see what he has produced !

INDEX I

RABBINIC PASSAGES CITED AND REFERRED TO

Editions of Rabbinic Books frequently Quoted, and Method of Quotation

The Babylonian Talmud is quoted in the usual way by Tractate and folio; *e.g.* Kiddushin 39 b. No ' B ' or ' Bab ' is prefixed.

The Jerusalem Talmud is quoted by page and column of the Krotoschin edition of 1866. Chapter, and usually also paragraph, are added; *e.g.* Jer. Berachoth i. 5, 3 c.

The Mishnah is quoted by chapter and section; *e.g.* Sotah iv. 3.

The Tosefta is quoted according to chapter, section, and page of Zuckermandel's edition (1880), *e.g.* T. Baba Mezia iii. 25, p. 378.

(1) Aboth R. Nathan, ed. Schechter, 1887. Quoted by chapter and page; *e.g.* xv. 30 a. (Where the second version is not specially indicated, the first version is referred to.)

(2) Mechilta, ed. Friedmann, Vienna, 1870. Quoted by folio only; *e.g.* Mechilta 47 a.

(3) Midrash Mishle, ed. Buber, 1893. Quoted as Mid. Proverbs by verse and folio; *e.g.* Mid. Proverbs xxv. 21, 49 b.

(4) Pesikta Kahana, ed. Buber, Lyck, 1868. Quoted as ' Pesikta K.' or as ' Pesikta ' by folio only; *e.g.* Pesikta, 59 b.

(5) Pesikta Rabbathi, ed. Friedmann, Vienna, 1880. Quoted as Pesikta R., by folio only; *e.g.* Pesikta R., 132 b.

(6) Midrash Rabba, ed. Romm (3 vols.), Wilna, 1878: Genesis-Deuteronomy Rabba, quoted by (1) name of weekly portion (except where it is the first in the book, (2) division (*parashah*) and section (if there is one), and often also by (3) chapter and verse referred to; *e.g.* Genesis Rabba, Vayera, lv. 3, on xxii. 1. Canticles, Ruth, Lamentations, Ecclesiastes and Esther Rabba, quoted by (1) division (*parashah*) and section, and (2) chapter and verse referred to; *e.g.* Canticles R. i. 7 on i. 1, or merely by chapter and verse referred to, *e.g.* Ruth R. on ii. 3.

(7) Midrash Samuel, ed. Buber, Wilna, 1925. Quoted by division (*parashah*) and folio; *e.g.* Mid. Samuel xix. 29 b.

(8) Sifra, ed. Weiss and Schlossberg, Vienna, 1862. Quoted by folio and column. The chapter and verse of Leviticus referred to are usually added; *e.g.* Sifra 86 c on Leviticus xix. 1.

(9) Sifre, ed. Friedmann, Vienna 1864.   Quoted by folio only; *e.g.* Sifre 84 b.

(10) Tana d'be Eliahu (Seder Eliahu Rabba and Seder Eliahu Zuta), ed. Fried-mann, Vienna, 1902. Quoted thus; *e.g.* Tana Eliyahu (Seder Rabba or Seder Zuta), chapter vii. (vi.), p. 36.

(11) Tanchuma, ed. Vienna, 1863.   Quoted by folio; *e.g.* Tanchuma 57 a.

(12) Tanchuma, ed. Buber, Wilna, 1885.   Quoted (as Tanchuma B.) by name of division (*parashah*), chapter, and folio; *e.g.* Tanchuma B. *Bereshith* xxv. 10 a.

(13) Midrash Tannaim to Deuteronomy, ed. Hoffmann, Berlin, 1908–1909. Quoted by page only; *e.g.* Mid. Tannaim, p. 49.

(14) Midrash Tehillim (Shocher Tob), ed. Buber, Wilna, 1891. Quoted usually by number of Psalm, verse, section, and page; *e.g.* Mid. Psalms xviii. 32, § 26, 77 b, or xviii. § 26 on verse 32, 77 b.

(15) Yalkut (Shimeoni), ed. Warsaw, 1876.   Quoted by paragraph and Biblical passage referred to; *e.g.* Yalkut, § 467 on Leviticus ii. 1.

My references correspond generally with those of S.B., except in Mechilta and Sifra and Yalkut, where I have used different editions. In Midrash Rabba the editions used by me and them also differ, but in Genesis-Deuteronomy the *parashahs* correspond, and in all cases the Biblical references prevent any difficulty arising.

The three Appendices to my book begin on p. 377. The Rabbinic quotations from the Appendices are referred to less fully in the Index than those from the body of the book.

ABODAH ZARAH

	PAGE
2 a *fin.*-3 b	81
4 a	81, 166
4 b	412
17 a	399
17 b-18 b	373
18 a	399
19 a	188, 401
20 b	8
22 b	164
26 b	71
64 a	284

JER. ABODAH ZARAH

ii. 8, 41 d	146

M. ABODAH ZARAH

ii. 1, 26 a	70

ABOTH

i. 5	353
i. 6	145
i. 12 . . .	28, 73, 344

ABOTH (*Contd.*)—

	PAGE
i. 13	252, 324
i. 17	155
i. 18	151
ii. 1	38, 318
ii. 2	143, 327
ii. 5 . .	145, 171, 326, 370
ii. 6	9
ii. 9	360, 366
ii. 10	151
ii. 11	151
ii. 15	151, 403
iii. 6	240
iii. 7	267
iii. 9	344
iii. 11	155
iii. 14	9
iii. 15	166, 246
iii. 18	114, 320
iii. 19, 20	176
iii. 21, 22	155
iv. 1	278
iv. 2	37
iv. 3	74

ABOTH (*Contd.*)—

	PAGE
iv. 5	225, 298
iv. 7	. 225
iv. 11	. 277
iv. 12	143, 349
iv. 15	. 405
iv. 19	. 351
iv. 20	. 110
iv. 24	. 408
iv. 29	. 176
v. 11	. 352
v. 12	. 352
v. 22	7, 329
v. 23	. 126
v. 25	. 37
v. 26	. 400
vi. 4	. 282
vi. 6 , . . .	141, 329
vi. 8	. 276
vi. 9	. 139

ABOTH R. NATHAN

iv. 11 a	. 242
vii. 17 a	. 353
vii. 17 b	. 17
viii. 18 b	. 223
viii. 19 a	. 223
xi. 23 b	. 328
xii. 24 b	. 30
xii. 26 b	. 90
xv. 30 a	. 151
xvi. 31 b	151, 164
xvi. 32 b	10, 87
xx. 35 b	. 240
xxii. 37 b	. 156
xxiv. 39 a	. 156
xxix. 44 a	. 265
xxix. 44 b	. 396
xxxi. 46 a	. 256
xxxii. (2nd version) 36 a .	. 234
xxxix. 58 b	245, 400
xl. 60 b	. 400
xli. 65 b	. 159
xli. 67 a	96, 229

ARACHIN

15 b	10, 33
16 b	146, 266

BABA BATRA

8 a	. 255
9 b	. 112
10 b . . .	26, 33, 75, 112
15 b	. 146

BABA BATRA (*Contd.*)—

	PAGE
16 a	182, 230
21 a	. 100
60 b	. 146
75 a	. 39
91 b	. 230

JER. BABA BATRA

ii. 14, 13 c	. 67

BABA KAMMA

50 a	. 406
50 b	. 109
80 a	. 167
92 a	. 53
93 a	32, 96
94 b	371, 402
113 a	. 67
113 b	. 67

JER. BABA KAMMA

viii. 8, 6 c	. 402

M. BABA KAMMA

viii. 7, 92 a . . .	. 54
viii. 7	. 401
ix. *fin.*, 110 a . . .	. 40

T. BABA KAMMA

vii. 8, p. 358 . . .	. 67
ix. 29, p. 365 *fin.* .	. 97
ix. 29, p. 366 . .	. 135
ix. 30, p. 366 . .	. 402
x. 14, p. 367, foot .	. 371
x. 15, p. 368 . .	. 67
x. 18, p. 368 . .	. 40

BABA MEZIA

24 b	. 191
30 b	. 191
32 a	. 91
32 b	. 91
33 b	. 349
49 a	49, 50
58 b . . .	39, 192, 409
59 a	39, 45
59 b	146, 247
83 b-85 a . . .	. 304
85 a	48, 270
85 b	. 258
88 a *fin.* . . .	. 191
107 a	. 24
107 b	. 146

BABA MEZIA (*Contd.*)—

	PAGE
114 b	70
115 a	402

M. BABA MEZIA

iv. 2	50

T. BABA MEZIA

ii. 26, p. 375	93
viii. 26, p. 390	371

BECHOROTH

8 b	36
29 a	225

BERACHOTH

4 a	173
4 b	208
5 a	32, 35
6 a	116, 185
6 b	116
7 a	96, 405, 409
7 b	116
8 a	326
9 b	144
10 a	97
10 b	226
12 a	253
12 b	409
13 a	186
13 b	186
14 a	142
16 a	117
16 b	134, 137
17 a	54, 110, 134, 181, 185, 188, 298, 312, 323, 340, 370, 397
19 a	414
21 a	122
22 a	323
23 a	398
24 b	186
28 b	172, 228, 259, 369, 370
29 a	125, 172
29 b	128, 137, 148
30 b	183
31 a	148, 253
32 a	302, 326, 328
32 b	121, 124, 148, 149
33 b	120, 165, 192, 230
34 b	187, 217, 257, 260, 408
35 b	143
40 a	253

BERACHOTH (*Contd.*)—

	PAGE
43 b *fin.*	329
47 b	7
49 a	185
49 b *ad fin.*	326
54 b *fin.*	121
55 b	95
58 a	53, 230
58 b	226
60 b	24, 133
61 a	120
61 b	282
62 b	53
63 a	320
63 b	233, 329
64 a	26, 171, 236

JER. BERACHOTH

i. 1, 2 b	368
i. 1, 4 b	110
i. 2, 3 a	323
i. 5, 3 b	368
i. 8, 3 c	46
ii. 5, 5 a	117
iv. 1, 7 a	186
iv. 1, 7 b *ad fin.*	121
iv. 1, 8 d	124, 327
iv. 2, 7 d	90, 136, 181
iv. 3, 8 a	148
iv. 4, 8 b	117, 125
v. 1, 8 d	117
v. 3, 9 c	366
ix. 1, 13 a	147
ix. 1, 13 b	368
ix. 3, 13 d	167
ix. 7, 14 b	313, 314

M. BERACHOTH

ii. 1	186
iv. 2	259
iv. 4	117, 148
v. 1	124, 186
v. 3	366
ix. 5	31, 314

T. BERACHOTH

i. 4, p. 1	327
ii. 7, p. 4 *init.*	117
iii. 4, p. 6.	186
iii. 7, p. 6.	120
iii. 18, p. 8	186
iv. 8, p. 10	354

BEZAH

	PAGE
9 a	119
32 b	276

T. BEZAH

iii. 2	380

CHAGIGAH

5 a	112, 409
5 b	328
11 b	321
15 a	414

JER. CHAGIGAH

i. 7, 76 c	157, 159
ii. 2, 77 d	358
ii. 77 b-77 c . . .	416

CHULLIN

7 b	229
92 a	10, 84
94 a	67

DERECH ERETZ ZUTA

i.	46
iv.	225
viii.	325

ERUBIN

13 b	328, 353
19 a	359
21 b	370, 371
41 b	220, 276
65 a	187
95 b fin.-96 a init. . .	184

GITTIN

7 a	96
32 b	93
61 a	92
62 a	92
70 a	278
90 b	47

M. GITTIN

v. 9	92

HORAYOTH

10 a ad fin. . . .	299

KALLA

	PAGE
Col. 1 fin. (ed. : Vienna, 1868) .	41

M. KERITOTH

vi. 3	168

T. KERITOTH

iv. 4, p. 566	168

KETHUBOTH

8 b	304
50 a	57
67 b . . . 41, 57, 112, 259
77 b	166
103 b	169
111 a	173
111 b	6, 236

KIDDUSHIN

30 b	182
31 a	251
31 b	250, 305
32 a	250
32 b . . .	192, 299
36 a	114
39 b . . . 145, 317, 394
40 a . . 42, 185, 232, 401
40 b . 21, 158, 159, 176, 399
41 a	45
69 b	253
70 a . . . 146, 217
70 b	146
81 b fin. . . .	217
82 a	277
82 b	141

JER. KIDDUSHIN

i. 61 b . . .	37, 249
i. 61 d	178
iv. 12, 66 d fin. . .	138

M. KIDDUSHIN

iv. 14	141, 277

JER. KILAIM

ix. 4, 32 b . . .	273, 303

MA'ASER SHENI

iv. 4	380

MAKKOTH

		PAGE
5 b .	. . . . .	48
10 b	. . . .	20

JER. MAKKOTH

| ii. 6, 31 d . | . . . | 391, 408 |

MEGILLAH

10 b	. . .	106, 214, 262
13 a	. . . .	213, 258
14 a	. . . .	200
16 a	. . . .	94
17 b	. . . .	221
18 a	. . . .	120
20 a	. . . .	187
28 a	. .	90, 135, 402
61 a	. . . .	120

JER. MEGILLAH

| iii. 2, 74 a | . . . | 102 |

M. MEGILLAH

| ii. 1 . | . . . . | 185 |

MENACHOTH

43 b	. . . .	26
43 b, 44 a .	. .	318 fin.
65 a	. . . .	39
99 b	. .	158, 188, 366
100 a	. . .	99
110 a ad init.	. .	126
110 a	. . .	188, 242

T. MENACHOTH

| xiii. 22, p. 534 . | . . | 349 |

MOED KATON

| 16 b | . . . | 405, 412 |
| 28 a | . . . | 301 |

NAZIR

| 19 a | . . . . | 138 |
| 23 b | . . . . | 188 |

M. NAZIR

| ii. 5 . | . . . | 380 |

NEDARIM

| 10 a | . . . | 168 |
| 20 b | . . . | 43 |

NEDARIM (Contd.)—

		PAGE
22 a	. . . .	38
22 b	. . . .	38
25 a	. . . .	213
38 a	. . . .	277
39 a	. . . .	403
41 a	. . .	6, 221
62 a	.	188, 190, 225, 324
64 b	. . . .	276
81 a	. . . .	270

JER. NEDARIM

| i. 1, 41 b . | . . . . | 138 |

T. NEDARIM

| i. 1, p. 276 | . . . | 168 |

M. NEGAIM

| ii. 1 . | . . . . | 304 |

NIDDAH

13 a	. . . .	46
13 b init. .	. . .	42
70 b	. . .	106, 264

JER. PEAH

i. 1, 15 b .	. . .	57, 139
i. 1, 15 c .	. .	84, 249, 251
i. 1, 15 d .	. . .	33, 159
i. 1, 16 b .	. .	42, 175, 399

M. PEAH

| i. 1 . | . . . | 158, 318 |

PESACHIM

49 a ad fin.	. . .	11
49 b	. . .	7
50 a	. . .	33, 257
66 b	. . .	38
87 b	. . .	211
113 b	. .	98, 99, 101
119 a	. . .	404

ROSH HA-SHANAH

16 a	. . .	397
16 b	.	333, 359, 397, 405
16 b-17 a .	. .	179
17 a .	. .	135, 402
28 a .	. .	184

JER. ROSH HA-SHANAH

| i. 2, 57 b . | . . | 414 |
| ii. 6, 58 b . | . . | 122 |

M. Rosh ha-Shanah

	PAGE
iii. 8	125, 126

T. Rosh ha-Shanah

iii. 6 *fin.* p. 212	184

Sabbath

10 a	121
11 a	45
13 b	31
25 b	278
31 a	150
31 b, top	156
31 b	340
32 a-33 b	351
33 a	5, 280
33 b	301
55 a	166, 272
55 b	273
56 b	411
87 a	269
88 b	32, 53, 98
89 b	302
92 a	277
104 a and *par.* . . .	20
107 b	229
116 a	48
118 b	169
119 b	270
127 a	145
128 b	244
133 b	339
150 a	327
151 a	278
151 b	23, 135
152 b	24
153 a	310, 403
153 b	323

Jer. Sabbath

i. 3 b *ad fin.*	171
i. 3 c	323

M. Sabbath

ii. 6	280
xvi. 3	380

T. Sabbath

xiii. 5, p. 129	99

Sanhedrin

6 b	28
7 a	96, 412

Sanhedrin (*Contd.*)—

	PAGE
11 a	43
18 a	146
19 a	146
24 a	6
37 a	96
39 b . . 106, 108, 214, 262	
43 b	409
55 a	259
72 a	53
74 a	232
74 b	232
75 a	41
88 b	8
90 a . . . 145, 247, 413	
92 a	6
96 a	270
97 b	408
98 a	306
98 b	306
99 a 260, 408	
99 b . . 188, 222, 336, 366	
100 a 23, 34	
100 b	144
101 a	167
103 a	413
105 a . 76, 96, 148, 210, 337, 407	
106 b 26, 183	
107 b	400
111 a 108, 406	

Jer. Sanhedrin

vi. 9, 23 c	358
x. 28 c	413
xi. 30 b	78

M. Sanhedrin

ii. 1	304
iii. 2	49
iv. 5	67, 256
vi. 5	264
xi.	245
xi. 1 . . . . 336, 379	
xi. 6, end	106

T. Sanhedrin

xiii. 2, p. 434 . . .	75, 210
xiii. 3, p. 434 . . .	333

Semachoth

iii. *fin.*	169
viii.	363

JER. SHEBIITH

	PAGE
iv. 2, 35 b	225
ix. 1, 38 d . . .	229

SHEBUOTH

12 b-13 b	395
18 b	139
36 a	49

JER. SHEBUOTH

| vi. 6, 37 a . . . | 49 |

M. SHEBUOTH

| i. 6 . . . . . | 395 |

T. SHEBUOTH

| iii. 6, p. 450 . . . | 82 |

M. SHEKALIM

| v. 6 . . . . . | 112 |

T. SHEKALIM

| i. 6, p. 174 . . . | 325 |

SOTAH

2 a	230
4 b	8, 329
5 a . . .	8, 148, 329
5 b	8, 329
12 a	283
14 a . 105, 299, 302, 339
21 b	323
22 a	7
30 b	228
31 a	190
41 b . . .	118, 330
42 a	330
42 b	118
48 b . . .	142, 205

JER. SOTAH

| i. 4, 16 d . . . . | 28 |
| iii. 3, 19 a . . | 323 |
| v. 7, 20 c . . 190, 228, 314 |

M. SOTAH

iii. 4	323
iv. 5	228
v. 5	228
ix. 15 . . .	9, 125

SUKKAH

	PAGE
20 a	304
45 b	167
49 b . . 190, 241, 315
52 b	181
53 a . . . 168, 401

JER. SUKKAH

| v. 3, 55 b . . . . | 168 |

M. SUKKAH

| v. 4 . . . . . | 168 |

T. SUKKAH

| iv. 2, p. 198 . . . | 168 |

TAANITH

2 a	148
7 a	108, 183
7 b	97
8 a	30, 350
10 b	300
11 a . . .	138, 326
15 a	397
16 a	397
20 a fin. . . .	39
20 b . . .	284, 354
21 a . . .	144, 348
21 b . . .	113, 238
22 a	237
23 b	129
24 a . . .	283, 310
24 b	275
25 a	187
25 b . . .	53

JER. TAANITH

i. 63 d, 64 a . . .	413
i. 4, 64 b . . .	327, 343
ii. 1, 65 a . . .	146
ii. 1, 65 b . . .	406
iii. 7, 66 d . . .	168
iv. 4, 66 c . . .	133
iv. 7, 68 c . . .	24

M. TAANITH

| ii. 1 . . . . | 397 |

TAMID

| 28 a . . . . | 265 |
| 32 a . . . . | 234 |

TEMURAH

					PAGE
15 b	.	.	.	.	167

M. TEMURAH

v. 1	.	.	.	.	.	380

JER. TERUMOTH

viii. 10, 46 b	.	.	.	224

YEBAMOTH

5 b	.	.	.	.	.	230
37 b	.	.	.	.	44
63 a	.	.	.	.	45
63 b	.	.	.	.	269
103 b	.	.	.	.	164
105 a	.	.	.	395, 397
121 b	.	.	.	.	349

YOMA

9 a	.	.	.	.	.	89
9 b	.	.	.	.	.	99
18 b	.	.	.	.	44
23 a	.	.	.	53, 97, 402
29 a	.	.	.	41, 42, 121
35 b	.	.	.	.	281
36 b	.	.	.	.	414
38 b	.	.	20, 21, 399, 400
39 a	.	.	21, 399, 400
69 b	.	.	.	.	79
72 b	.	.	118, 183, 323
77 a fin.	.	.	.	.	247
85 b	.	.	395, 396, 400
86 a	.	35, 245, 396, 401, 408, 410
86 b	.	119, 245, 330, 400, 401, 402,
		407, 408, 410, 414
87 a	.	.	267, 400, 402
87 b	.	.	267, 361, 402

JER. YOMA

viii. 6	.	.	.	.	396
viii. 8	.	.	.	.	402
viii. 9	.	.	.	.	402

M. YOMA

viii. 8	.	.	.	.	395
viii. 9	.	.	40, 126, 398

T. YOMA

v. (iv.) 8, p. 190	.	.	396
v. (iv.) 9, p. 190	.	.	396

GENESIS RABBA

					PAGE
i. 4 on i. 1	.	.	.	.	403
ix. 11 on ii. 1	.	.	.	.	145
xix. 3 on iii. 2	.	.	.	323
xx. 9 on iii. 17	.	.	.	229
xxii. 6 on iv. 6	.	.	.	180
xxii. 13 ad fin. on iv. 16	.	411
xxiv. 7 ad fin. on v. 1	.	74
xxvii. 1 on vi. 6	.	.	181

Noah

xxx. 9 on vi. 9	.	.	.	411
xxxiii. 3 on viii. 1	.	108, 209
xxxiv. 10 on viii. 21	.	.	181
xxxv. 1 on ix. 8	.	.	269
xxxv. 2 on ix. 8	.	.	167
xxxvii. ad fin. on x. 26	.	259
xxxviii. 3 on xi. 1	.	.	95

Lekh Lekha

xliv. 5 on xv. 1	.	.	.	302
xliv. 12 on xv. 5	.	.	405
xliv. 17 on xv. 17	.	.	411
xlv. 7 on xvi. 9	.	.	53

Va-yera

xlix. 6 and 9 on xviii. 25	.	78
liii. 14 on xxi. 14	.	.	398
lv. 3 on xxii. 1	.	.	106

Chaye Sarah

lx. 2 ad init. on xxiv. 12	.	179, 363
lxii. 2 on xxv. 8	.	169, 176

Toledoth

lxv. 22 on xxvii. 23	.	.	399

Va-yishlach

lxxvi. 2 on xxxii. 7	.	.	173
lxxix. 6 on xxxiii. 18	.	229

Va-yesheb

lxxxiv. 19 on xxxvii. 29	.	412
lxxxvi. 6 on xxxix. 2	.	259

Mik-ketz

xcii. init. 1 on xliii. 14	.	220

Va-yiggash

xciii. 11 ad fin. on xlv. 9	.	176

Va-yechi

xcvi. 5 on xlvii. 29	.	.	273
xcvi. 5 fin. on xlvii. 29	.	303

EXODUS RABBA

i. 36	.	.	.	.	412

Va-yera

		PAGE
ii. on iii. 1	. . .	259, 332
ix. 9	. . . .	408

Bo

xi. 1 and 3	. . .	400
xii. 4	. . . .	404

Beshallach

xxi. on xiv. 15	. . .	148
xxii. on xiv. 31	. . .	148
xxiii. 5 on xv. 1	. .	205
xxiii. 10	. . . .	408
xxiii. on xv. 2	. . .	238
xxv. 12	. . . .	408
xxvi. on xvii. 8	. . .	105

Jethro

xxvii. 9 on xviii. 1	. .	328

Mishpatim

xxx. 13 on xxii. 1	. .	153
xxxi. 1	. . . .	399
xxxi. *ad init.* on xxii. 25	.	269
xxxi. on xxii. 25	. .	276
xxxi. 3 on xxii. 25	. .	277
xxxi. 5 on xxii. 25	. .	278

Terumah

xxxv. 4	. . . .	301

Te-tzaveh

xxxviii. 4	. . . .	404

Ki Tissa

xli. on xxxi. 1, 2	. .	189
xlii. 9 on xxxii. 7 *ad fin.*	.	233

Pekude

lii. 2	. . . .	402
lii. 3	. . . .	279

LEVITICUS RABBA

i. 5 on i. 1	. . .	353
ii. 12 *fin.* on ii. 2	. .	242
iii. 3 on ii. 1	. . .	404
iii. 5 on ii. 1 *fin.*	. .	188
v. 8 *ad fin.* on iv. 3	.	84, 412

Tsau

vii. 2 on vi. 1	. .	393, 405
ix. 3 on vii. 11	. .	29
ix. 9 on vii. 12	. .	28
x. 1 *ad init.* on viii. 1, 2	.	303
x. 1 on viii. 1, 2	. .	404
x. 5 on viii. 1, 2	.	405, 411, 413

Metzora

		PAGE
xviii. 1 *fin.* on xv. 1	. .	24
xix. 2 on xv. 25	. .	49

Achare Moth

xx. 12 *ad fin.* on xvi. 1	.	301
xxiii. 9 on xviii. 3	. .	41
xxiii. 12 on xviii. 3	. .	41
xxiii. 13 *fin.* on xviii. 3	.	26

Kedoshim

xxv. 1 *init.* on xix. 23	.	327

Emor

xxvi. 7 on xxi. 1	. .	247
xxvii. 1 on xxii. 27	. .	349
xxvii. 5 on xxii. 27	. .	33
xxviii. 1 *ad init.* on xxiii. 10	.	257
xxix. 2 on xxiii. 24	. .	204
xxx. 7 on xxiii. 40	. .	397
xxxi. 9 on xxiv. 2	. .	253

Behar

xxxiv. 1 on xxv. 39	. .	58
xxxiv. 8 on xxv. 39	.	189, 235
xxxiv. 14 on xxv. 39	. .	150

Be-chuk-kothai

xxxv. 7 on xxvi. 3	.	118, 322
xxxvii. 2 on xxvii. 2	. .	283

NUMBERS RABBA

i. 7 on i. 3	. . .	225
ii. 3 on ii. 2	. . .	271
ii. 10 on ii. 3	. .	412, 415
iii. 12 on iii. 38	. . .	412

Naso

viii. 1, 2 on v. 6	. .	212
viii. 2 on v. 6	. . .	84
x. 1 on vi. 2	. . .	399
xiii. 3 on vii. 12	. .	411
xiii. 18 on vii. 30	.	393, 412
xiv. 1 on vii. 48	. .	413

Be-haa-lotekha

xv. 20 on xi. 16	. .	327

Shelach Lecha

xvii. 6 on xv. 39	. .	46

Korah

xviii. 13 on xvi. 32	. .	333

Chukkath

xix. 1 on xix. 2	. .	243
xix. 23 on xxi. 7	. .	360

Balak

	PAGE
xx. 12 on xxii. 20-22 . . .	264
xx. 15 on xxii. 31 . . .	412
xx. 20 on xxiii. 15 . . .	412

Phineas

xxi. 21 on xxviii. 3 . . .	393

DEUTERONOMY RABBA

i. on i. 1	257

Va-et-chan-nan

ii. 1 on iii. 23	190
ii. *init.* on iii. 23 . . .	361
ii. on iv. 30	356
ii. 12	404
ii. 20	413
ii. 24 *init.*	415

Shofetim

v. on xvi. 18	242
v. on xvi. 18, near end .	69, 339

Ki Tetze

vi. 1 on xxii. 6	288

Berachah

xi. 6 on xxxiii. 1 . . .	329

CANTICLES RABBA

i. § 1, 8 on i. 1 . . .	252
i. § 1, 9 on i. 1 . . .	355
i. § 3, 2 on i. 3 . . .	35
i. § 14, 3 on i. 14 . . .	302
i. § 15, 2 on i. 15 . . .	233
i. § 15, 4 on i. 15 . . .	35
ii. § 4 on ii. 4 . . .	271
ii. § 16, 1 on ii. 16 .	69, 233
v. § 1, 2 on v. 2 . . .	404
v. § 1, 2 on v. 2 . . .	408
vi. § 1 *init.* on vi. 1 .	69, 233
vi. § 11, 1 on vi. 11 . .	253
viii. § 7, 1 on viii. 7 . .	254
viii. § 12, 2 on viii. 13 .	187

RUTH RABBA

Intro., near end, § 1 on i. 1.	69
Intro., § 6 on i. 2 . .	328
iii. § 3 on i. 17 . . .	358
v. § 6	413
v. § 6 on ii. 14 . . .	305
vi. § 4	399
vii. § 6 on iii. 18 . .	49

ECCLESIASTES RABBA

	PAGE
On i. 8 *fin.*	273
On iv. 1	118
On iv. 6 *fin.*	189
On iv. 13	164
On viii. 1	243
On viii. 4	106
On ix. 7	348, 397
On ix. 8 . . .	310, 403
On ix. 10	153, 257
On ix. 15 . .	130, 164, 165
On x. 5	378
On x. 11	34
On xi. 1 . . .	90, 92, 347

LAMENTATIONS RABBA

Intro., § 10, p. 349 . . .	149
On i. 6 . . .	271, 339
On ii. 1	169
On iii. 40, 41	403
On iii. 43	404
On iii. 43, 44	149
On iv. 1	224
On v. 21	415

ESTHER RABBA

Parashah i. § 17 on i. 3 . .	119

MIDRASH SAMUEL

xix. 29 b	305

MIDRASH PSALMS

i. (15) on verse 1, 7 b .	239
i. *fin.* 12 b . . .	400
ii. (7) on verse 5, 14 a .	70
iv. (1) on verse 1, 20 b .	362
iv. (1) on verse 2, 20 b .	179
iv. (3) on verse 2, 21 b .	147, 148
iv. (3) on verse 1, 20 b .	368
iv. (3) on verse 2, 22 a .	149
iv. (7) on verse 1, 23 a .	362
iv. (9) on verse 5, 23 b .	117
v. (1) 26 a . . .	393
v. (3) on verse 1, 26 a .	280
vii. (3) on verse 1 *ad fin.*, 32 b .	94
viii. (4) on verse 3, 38 b .	301
ix. (2) on verse 1, 40 b .	243
ix. (3) on verse 1, 41 a, foot .	290
ix. *fin.* 46 a . . .	233
x. (7) *ad fin.* on verse 16, 49 a .	148
xi. (6) on verse 7, 51 a .	25, 257
xvi. (11) on verse 10, 62 a .	33
xvii. (8) on verse 12, 66 b .	158 *fin.*
xvii. (13) on verse 14, 67 b	179

2 F

MIDRASH PSALMS (*Contd.*)—

PAGE

xviii. (3) 405
xviii. (11) on verse 7, 71 a . . 233
xxii. (3) on verse 1, 91 a . . 108
xxii. (18) on verse 3, 95 a . . 362
xxv. (3) 397
xxvi. (2) on verse 1, 108 b . . 364
xxvi. (3) on verses 2-4, 109 a . 296
xxviii. (2) on verse 1, 115 a . 233
xxx. (4) on verse 1, 118 a . . 70
xxxi. (8) on verse 24, 120 b . 204
xxxi. (9) on verse 24, 121 a . 189
xxxii. (2) 121 b . . . 402
xxxiv. (2) on verse 23, 124 a . 182
xl. (1) on verse 1, 129 a . . 203
xl. (2) 129 a 412
xl. (3) 129 b 414
xli. (8) on verse 10, 131 a . . 95
xliv. (1) on verse 1, 134 b . . 362
xliv. (2) on verse 26, 135 a . . 362
xlv. (3) 135 b 408
xlv. (4) 135 b 403
li. (2) on verse 3, 141 a . 362, 412
lv. (6) on verse, 23, 147 a . . 368
lvi. (1) on verse 1, 147 b . . 53
lxv. (2) on verse 3, 156 b . . 148
lxv. (4) 157 a 404
lxviii. (8) on verse 14, 159 a . 233
lxxi. (2) on verse 2, 162 a . . 362
lxxii. (1) on verse 1, 162 b . . 362
lxxxv. (4) 186 b 415
lxxxvi. (1) on verse 1, 186 b . 33
xc. (10) on verse 1, 196 a . . 267
xc. (16) 197 a 403
xc. (18) on verse 16, 197 b . . 318
xciv. (1) on verse 1, 209 a . . 106
xcix. (3) on verse 4, 212 a . . 93
c. (2) 212 b 411
cii. (3) 216 a 410
ciii. (12) on verse 9, 218 b . . 107
civ. (27) on verse 35, 224 b 97, 263
cxviii. (17) on verse 19, 243 b . 340
cxix. (7) on verse 11, 246 b . 182
cxix. (41) on verse 97, 249 b . 240
cxix. (55) on verse 123, 250 b 179, 362
cxx. (7) on verse 7, 253 a . 337, 404
cxli. (1) on verse 1, 264 b . . 362
cxli. (1) on verse 1, 265 b . . 179
cxlvi. (7) on verse 8, 268 b . . 84
cxlvi. (8) on verse 9, 268 b . . 212

MIDRASH PROVERBS

31 a, b on ix. 2 341
38 b on xiv. 34 75

MIDRASH PROVERBS (*Contd.*)—

PAGE

42 b on xvii. 1 76
49 b on xxv. 21, 22 . . . 94

MECHILTA

1 b 78
2 a 302
23 b 140
27 a 69
29 a 119
29 b 203
30 a 203
34 b 214, 262
37 a . . . 69, 105, 238
37 b 35
38 a 208
38 b, 39 a 78
39 a 396
41 b 147
42 b 362
45 b 119
46 a 158
46 a, b 252
47 b 132, 140
52 b 147
57 b 355
59 a . . . 108, 208, 235
59 b *fin.* 191
62 a 77
63 b 219
66 a 49
68 a 106
68 b 128
70 a 251
72 b 31
74 a 27, 126
80 b *init.* 65
88 b 66
96 a 58
99 a 91
99 b 91
104 a *init.* 244
Mishpatim xviii. ed. Horowitz
    and Rabin, p. 311 . . . 212

MECHILTA OF R. SIMEON

III 41

MIDRASH TADSHE

29 209

MIDRASH TANNAIM

P. 71 114
P. 82 58
P. 111 (on Deut. xviii. 13) . . 366

Pesikta Kahana

	PAGE
12 b	75
27 a	90
40 b	192, 243
55 b	393
57 b	312
60 b	242
61 b	164, 393
87 a	234
88 b	229
102 b	36
117 a	280
125 b	303
139 a fin.	16
156 a fin.	75, 78
156 b	397
158 b	117, 408
159 b	412
160 a seq.	404
161 a	148
161 b	108, 406
162 a	413
163 a	395, 408
163 a fin.	413
163 b	40, 390, 408
165 a	406
166 b	339
178 b	283
179 b	25
180 a	257
200 a	78

Pesikta Rabbathi

	PAGE
2 a	26
53 b	75
36 b	75
42 b	253
59 a	143
111 a	327
111 a ad fin.	328
112 b	49
112 b, 113 a	48
124 b	41
132 b	114
146 b	306
152 a	229
159 b	307
161 a fin., 161 b	308
162 a	308
163 a	309
165 a	135
167 b	338
169 a	415

Pesikta Rabbathi—(Contd.)—

	PAGE
182 b	405, 415
183 a	408
184 a	407
184 b	404
185 a	404, 408
185 b, 186 a	177
195 a fin.-b	108
198 b	403

Pesikta Zutarta

On Num. viii. seq.	90

Pirke R. Eliezer

iii.	403
xxv.	277
xxxiv.	48

Sifra

28 a on Lev. v. 23-25	40
57 b on Lev. xi. 45	366
85 d on Lev. xviii. 4	156
86 a on Lev. xviii. 4	194
86 b on Lev. xviii. 5	130
86 c on Lev. xix. 2	36, 111
89 b on Lev. xix. 18	66, 89
91 b on Lev. xix. 36	366
92 a on Lev. xx. 10	66
93 d on Lev. xx. 26	127, 193
99 d on Lev. xxii. 33	130, 366
109 b on Lev. xxv. 35	59
109 c on Lev. xxv. 38	367
110 c ad fin. on Lev. xxvi. 3	118
112 c fin. on Lev. xxvi. 46	126

Sifre

12 b	28, 264
13 a	28
22 b	68
27 a	12
28 b	120
32 a	213
33 a	82, 410
35 a	112, 367
35 b	319
37 a	81, 263
39 b (last line)	278
48 b	302
50 b	408
51 a	326
54 a	243
59 b fin.	41
64 a	265

SIFRE (*Contd.*)—

				PAGE
65 b	.	.	.	. 265
68 b	.	.	.	67, 300
70 b	.	.	.	363, 364
71 b	.	.	.	. 149
73 a	.	.	.	190, 191, 228
73 a, b	.	.	.	. 31
73 b	.	.	.	191, 228
77 a	.	.	.	236, 367
78 b	.	.	.	209, 274
79 a	.	.	.	. 158
79 b	.	.	.	158, 159
80 a *init.*	.	.	228, 315, 324
80 a	.	.	.	. 118
82 b	.	.	.	. 182
83 a	.	.	.	. 257
84 a	.	.	.	. 37
84 b	.	125, 159, 298, 324
85 a	.	.	105, 213, 258
86 a	.	.	.	. 152
93 b *ad fin.*	.	.	.	23
95 b	.	.	.	. 139
97 b	.	.	.	. 66
98 a *fin.*, b *init.*	.	.	.	57
108 a	.	.	.	. 66
108 b	.	.	.	. 89
115 a	.	.	.	. 93
121 b	.	.	.	. 66
131 b *ad fin.*	.	.	.	298
132 a *fin.*	.	.	.	. 125
132 b	.	.	.	130, 366
133 a	.	.	.	. 114
136 b	.	.	.	. 339
137 a	.	.	.	. 114
138 b	.	.	.	. 151
139 a	.	.	.	. 263
140 a *ad fin.*	.	.	.	301
140 b	.	.	.	. 185
142 b	.	.	.	. 77
144 a	.	.	.	. 36

TANA ELIYAHU

Seder Rabba

			PAGE
Chap. xv. p. 81 .	.	.	. 84
Chap. xvii. p. 88	.	.	. 84
Chap. xix. p. 111	.	.	. 128
Chap. xxvi. p. 140	.	.	. 65
Chap. xxviii. p. 149	.	.	. 128

Seder Zuta

			PAGE
Chap. vii. p. 184	.	.	. 84

TANCHUMA

				PAGE
Vaetchanan 4 b .	.	.	. 326
Bereshith 4 b	.	.	. 180
Ki Tetze 19 b	.	.	. 290
Vayera 24 a, foot	.	.	. 264
Vayera 27 b	.	.	. 359
Chaye Sarah 28 b *init.*	.	.	186
Toledoth 33 a	.	.	. 172
Shemoth 61 b	.	.	. 332
Va'era 68 b	.	.	. 37
Mishpatim 91 a .	.	.	93, 327
Ki Tissa 110 a .	.	.	. 286
Ki Tissa 119 a .	.	.	. 226
Pekude 127 a	.	.	. 230
Vayikra 136 a .	.	.	. 48
Shemini 149 b .	.	.	. 194
Emor 171 b	.	.	. 175
Naso 197 a *ad fin.*	.	.	. 187
Ki Tabo 24 b	.	.	. 7
Nitzabim 25 b	.	.	. 326

TANCHUMA B

				PAGE
Bereshith xxv. 10 a	.	.	. 411
Bereshith xxxvii. 13 a .	.	.	78
Noah iv. 15 b	.	.	. 181
Noah xv. 20 a	.	.	. 311
Noah xxviii. 28 b	.	.	. 78
Vayera ix. 46 a .	.	.	. 78
Vayera xxx. 52 a	.	.	. 135
Vayera xxxviii. 54 b .	.	.	212
Chaye Sarah vi. 60 a .	.	.	256
Toledoth xiv. 67 b	.	.	. 149
Va'era xi. 13 b .	.	.	. 79
Mishpatim i. 40 b	.	.	. 93
Ki Tissa xvi. 58 b	.	.	. 179
Shemini x. 14 b	.	.	. 75
Tazria viii. 18 a, b	.	.	. 230
Tazria xi. 20 a .	.	.	. 399
Mattoth i. 79 a .	.	.	. 49
Vaetchanan xi. 5 a	.	.	. 363
Shofetim x. 16 b	.	.	. 321
Tabo iv. 24 a .	.	.	. 33
Nitzabim iv. 25 a	.	.	. 326
Ve-zot-ha-Berachah iii. 28 a .	.	.	78

YALKUT

			PAGE
§ 447 on Lev. ii. 1	.	.	. 189
§ 766 on Num. xxiii. 9	.	.	. 256
§ 837 on Deut. vi. 4 .	.	.	331
§ 961, end, on Prov. xxiv. 17	.	93

INDEX II

SUBJECTS DEALT WITH

Adultery. *See* Marital relations

Almsgiving. *See* Charitable deeds

Amme ha-Aretz, 3-15, 239, 255, 270.
  Authors cited on Abrahams, 9;
  Elbogen, 6; Moore, 13 *seq.*; S.B.,
  4, 5, 6 f., 9, 10. *See also* Learning;
  Sinners

Anger, 38 f.

Anxiety for the future, 140 f.

Asceticism, 138; Moore cited on, 138 f.

Beatitudes, 1 *seq.*; Rabbinic religion
  contrasted with, 1 f.; Windisch
  cited on, 34 f. *See also* Rabbinic
  religion

Charitable deeds and almsgiving, 56
  seq., 112 f., 223, 258, 275, 338 f.,
  348. *See also* God, imitation of;
  Hospitality; Riches

'Chastisements of love,' 31 f., 220;
  uncomplaining acceptance of, 365 f.
  See also Martyrdom; Sin, its connection with physical suffering

Children, 258, 270 f.

Discipleship, 218, 237; requirements of,
  225 f.

Divorce, Rabbinic laws concerning, 48

Doxology, 134 f.; Aptowitzer on, 135

'Dying to live,' 234

Enemies, love of, 59 *seq.*; Christian
  criticism of supposed Jewish teaching on, 59 *seq.*; O.T. teaching on,
  63 f.; praying for, 96 *seq.* Authors
  cited on, Eisler, 64 f.; Güdemann,
  86; Kittel, 91 *seq.*; Windisch,
  103 f.; Haas, 104. *See also* Ger;
  Gentiles; Hatred; Jesus, originality of; Mankind, love of; Particularism

Externalism, 21 f., 330. *See also*
  Legalism

Faith, 201 *seq.*, 217; teachings of
  Rabbis and Jesus contrasted, 203

'Faith and works,' 154 f. *See also*
  Law, study of

Faithfulness in small things, 332

Family ties. *See* Parents; Renunciation

Fasting. *See* Asceticism

'Father (Our),' 113 f.; Jewish liturgical use of, 125 f.; '(my),' 128;
  Lukyn Williams on, 129

Fig tree, Rabbinic parallel to story of,
  309 f.

Forgiveness, God's. *See* God

Forgiveness, man's, 40, 96 *seq.*, 133,
  267 f., 360, 373 *seq.*; Sevenster on,
  136

Freedom of the will, 165 f., 180, 271

Gentiles, Rabbinic laws concerning, 42,
  65 *seq.*, 371; relations of Jews with,
  66 f., 93; repentance among, 78,
  337 *seq. See also* Enemies, love of;
  Ger; Neighbour, love of; Particularism; Salvation

Ger, meaning of, 59

God, fear and love of, 190 f., 214, 228 f.,
  298, 312 *seq.*; nearness of, 147. *See
  also* Martyrdom; Sanctification of
  the Name. Forgiveness and mercy
  of, 108 f., 268, 286, 335 f.; his
  attitude towards destruction of the
  wicked, 262 *seq.*; Sevenster on,
  356 f. *See also* Merit; Reward;
  Salvation. Imitation of, 104 *seq.*,
  339 f. Authors cited on, Abrahams,
  105, 109, 339; Windisch, 109 f.
  See also Charitable deeds. Provi-

dential care of, 229 f. ; probable meaning of 'to see God,' 25. Authors cited on, Klostermann, 25 ; S.B., 25 f. Grace of : See Forgiveness and mercy (above) ; Merit ; Reward ; Tit for tat. *See also* Rabbinic religion (contrasted with Christianity)

Golden Rule, the, 150 f. ; Kittel cited on, 151

Goodness, redemptive power of outstanding acts of, 343 ; perseverance in, 344

Greetings, 110

Hatred, 88 *seq.*, 97 f., 265 f. Authors cited on, Abrahams, 90, 100 f. ; Travers Herford, 88. *See also* Enemies, love of ; Reproof

Hell. *See* Particularism ; Repentance ; Salvation

Heretical books, 99

Holiness, 110 f., 139. Authors cited on, Abrahams, 110, 111 ; Kohler, 111

Hospitality, 17, 353 f.

Humility, 5 *seq.*, 17, 255, 258, 266, 328 f., 369 ; S.B. cited on, 5

Hypocrisy, 118 f., 329 f. *See also* Law ; Legalism

Ideal, Rabbis' sense of the, 170 f.

Ideal life, 141, 224

Idolatry, 213

Injuries, Rabbinic laws concerning, 54. *See also* Forgiveness ; Hatred

Intention and deed, 41 f. Authors cited on, Abrahams, Moore and Sevenster, 41 ; Kittel, 42

Jesus, ' inwardness ' of teaching of, 21, 26 ; originality of, 47, 52, 85, 102 f., 221 f., 254 f., 299, 325, 344, 365, 372 ; absoluteness of teaching of, 230 f. ; criticism of his attacks on the Rabbis, 38, 322, 323, 330, 369. S.B. cited on, 323 f. *See also* Rabbinic religion

Judaism, universalism of (orthodox), 210 f. (liberal), 214

' Judge not,' 145

Justice. *See* Reward ; Tit for tat

Kawwanah, Rabbinic conception of, 183 *seq.*

Kingdom (or Kingship) of God, 131 f., 253, 368 ; in the Jewish liturgy, 131 f. ; Schechter cited on, 132

Law (or Laws), divine gift of the, 14 f., 76 *seq.* ; Rabbinic appreciation of the, 37, 254 ; distinctions in precepts of the (' small ' and ' great '), 37 f., 316 f. (' moral ' and ' ceremonial '), 240 *seq.*, 316 *seq.* ; dietary, 254 f. ; disinterested love of the, 314 f. ; sufficiency of for all needs, 142 ; possibility of complete fulfilment of the, 166 *seq.*, 271 *seq.* ; joy of fulfilling the, 198, 239 f., 316 ; legitimate pleasure sanctified by the, 16 ; supreme importance of study of the, 155 *seq.*, 349, 356, 366 ; necessity of blind obedience to certain, 193, 243 ; rewards for fulfilment of the, 289, 317 ; bondage of the, 319 ; fundamental precepts of the, 319 *seq.* ; Abrahams cited on, 321 f. ; exceeding the letter of the, 191, 282 ; Rabbis' gratuitous teaching of the, 225 ; civil law in conflict with Rabbinic, 311 ; attitude of Jesus and Rabbis to the, 160 f., 195. Authors cited on, Fridrichsen, 162 ; S.B., 198 f. Attitude of Paul and Rabbis to the, 174. *See also Amme ha-Aretz* ; Hypocrisy ; *Lishmah* ; Merit ; Old Testament ; Rabbinic religion ; Reward ; Superstition

Learning, 235 *seq.*, 324 f. ; antithesis between doing and, 154 *seq.*, 322 ; God's part in acquisition of, 252. *See also* ' Faith and works ' ; Humility ; Law, study of the ; Riches

Legalism, 21, 145, 169, 174, 368 f. ; S.B. cited on, 161 *seq.*, 178, 196 *seq. See also* Law ; Old Testament ; Rabbinic religion

Life of the resurrection, marriage in, 311 f.

' Light of the world,' 35 ; Abrahams cited on, 36

Lishmah, Rabbinic conception of, 188 *seq.*, 266, 296, 298, 318. *See also* Law, disinterested love of the

Liturgy, test passages in Jewish, 99 ; Abrahams cited on, 99. *See also*

Kingdom of God; Prayers, some Rabbinic; Rabbinic religion
'Lost,' search for the, 221 f.

Mankind, love of, 71 *seq.*; Travers Herford cited on, 73
Marital relations, 43; Kittel cited on, 42 f. *See also* Unchastity
Martyrdom, 31 *seq.*, 231 *seq.* Authors cited on, Moore, 31; S.B., 33. *See also* Renunciation; Sanctification of the Name
Merit, 295 *seq.*, 361 *seq.*; Marmorstein cited on, 295; vicarious element in, 297; ethical and religious results of Rabbinic doctrine of, 297 f.; Abrahams cited on, 361. *See also* Reward
Messiah, Rabbinic conceptions of the, 305 *seq.*; particularist element in, 308 f.; Moore cited on, 309; banquet parables concerning the, 310 f.
Miracles, 205 f., 247 *seq. See also* Fig tree
Monotheism, Jewish, 84
Mustard seed, metaphorical use of, 253

Nationalism, 261 f.
Neighbour, love of, 59 *seq.*, 312 f.; difficulties in parable of Good Samaritan regarding, 344 *seq.*; Abrahams cited on, 346 *seq. See also* Ger; Mankind, love of; Particularism

Oaths, 48 f. *See also* Truthfulness
Old Testament, attitude of Jesus and Rabbis to, 262; effect on Rabbinic teaching of, 294, 351 *seq.*; S.B. cited on, 351. *See also* Law, bondage of the

Parables, Rabbinic use of, 252
Parents, love and honour of, 230 f., 249 *seq.*
Particularism, 42, 63 *seq.*, 107 *seq.*, 207 *seq.*, 308 f., 337 *seq.* Authors cited on, Coulton, 84; Moore, 76 f. *See also* Enemies, love of; Gentiles; Neighbour, love of; Proselytes; Salvation
Peace, 27 *seq.*, 240; S.B. cited on, 27
Piety, ostentatious, 115, 324. *See also* Prayer
Prayer (or Prayers), lengthy, 115 *seq.*, 368. Authors cited on, Abrahams, 115; Oman, 115. Laws concerning

Jewish statutory, 117, 185 f.; non-statutory, 123; communal element in, 128; personal affairs secondary in importance to, 142 *seq.*; efficacy of, 147; nearness to God in, 147; need of *Kawwanah* in, 185 f.; some Rabbinic prayers, 54, 136, 140, 170, 172, 181 f., 221, 275, 352, 361
Precedence in heaven, 257
Profanation of the Name. *See* Sanctification of the Name
Prophets, Rabbis' attitude towards. *See* Law, dietary
Proselytes, 211 *seq.*
Pure in heart, 23 f.; Klostermann cited on, 23 f.
Purity, connection between bodily and spiritual, 220

Rabbinic religion, contrasted with Christianity, discussion of views of Fridrichsen, 162; S.B., 161 *seq.*, 190 *seq.*; Sevenster, 356 f.; Windisch, 160 f.; double strain in, 183; effect of fall of Jerusalem on, 198 f., 210; Burkitt on, 198; Jewish liturgy the true index of, 170. *See also* Beatitudes; Law; Old Testament
Rea, meaning of, 60 f.; 65
Remnant, doctrine of the, 216
Renunciation, 354 f.
Repentance, 245, 260 *seq.*, 342, 356, 390; Fiebig cited on, 355; after death, 359; for stealing, 371. *See also* Gentiles; God, forgiveness of; Particularism; Salvation; Sin
Reproof, 264 *seq.*; S.B. cited on, 264 f.
'Resist not evil,' Jesus' and Rabbis' teaching contrasted, 49 *seq.*; Windisch cited on, 55 f. *See also* Tit for tat
Retribution. *See* Reward; Salvation
Reward and punishment, 34, 294 *seq.*; Rabbinic stories of unequal, 286 f. Authors cited on, Curtis, 298; S.B., 291; Maimonides' theory of, 291 *seq. See also* Merit; Riches (and Poverty); Salvation; Tit for tat
Riches (and Poverty), 139, 140, 274 *seq.*, 284; regarded as reward or punishment, 277 *seq.*; as a trust, 281; knowledge superior to, 278; pros-

perity hereafter compensating for lack of, 278, 354 ; love of the Law requiring sacrifice of, 283 ; moral dangers of, 349, 357 ; teaching of Jesus and Rabbis summed up, 284 f. *See also* Charitable deeds and almsgiving

Righteous, God's higher standard for the, 349 f.

Righteousness, man's yearning for, 17 *seq.* Authors cited on, Loisy, 23; S.B., 19. Deeds the test of, 153 *seq.* ; God's part in human striving for, 20 f. *See also* ' Faith and works,' Learning and doing

' Rock,' Rabbinic use of metaphor of, 255 f.

Sabbath, observance of the, 240 f., 243 f.

Salvation, 82 *seq.*, 108 f., 151 f., 212 *seq.*, 229, 261 *seq.*, 311, 332 *seq.* ; Guttmann cited on, 82 f. ; double strain in Rabbinic teaching on, 86 f., 213 ; Windisch cited on, 153 ; Rabbis' uncertainty of personal, 173 f., 370 ; S.B. cited on, 172, 173 ; tests for, 336 *seq.* *See also* Particularism ; Repentance ; Sin, unatonable

Sanctification of the Name, 35 f., 67, 129 f., 231 *seq.*, 317 ; Moore cited on, 35. *See also* Martyrdom ; Renunciation ; Repentance for stealing

Self - righteousness.   *See* Humility ; Piety

Sermon on the Mount, Windisch cited on, 160

Service (of others), Jesus' teaching on lowly, 299, 325 f. ; nearest Rabbinic parallels to, 259, 299 f. ; (of the community of Israel), Rabbinic teaching on, 325 *seq.*

Shame, putting a man to open, 246, 259, 266, 318

Shechinah, presence of, 267, 277

Signs and wonders. *See* Miracles

Sin, human responsibility for, 18, 180 *seq.*, 200 ; ' original,' 24 ; S.B. cited on, 163 f. ; connection of physical suffering with, 5 f., 169, 219 f., 221, 279 f., 350 *seq.* ; S.B. cited on, 351 ; punishment for, 219, 261 *seq.*, 279 f. ; power to forgive, 221 ; unatonable, 244 *seq.*, 334,

336 ; causing others to, 259. *See also Yetzer ha-Ra* ; Salvation ; Suffering, vicarious

Single-mindedness, 140 ; Abrahams cited on, 140

Sinners, attitude of Jesus and Rabbis towards, 221 *seq.*, 342 f., 356, 372. *See also Amme ha-Aretz*

Slander, 33 f. ; S.B. cited on, 33 f.

Soul, value of each human, 256

Stories and anecdotes :

I

Aaron, anecdotes about, 29 f.

Abraham, anecdotes about, 353 f.

Ass-driver who sold his ass and gave the money to a woman, 343

Ass-drivers who hated each other, the two, 93

Canals of nourishment for the hair, stories about, 230

Chasid who kept a goat, 167

Chasid who was over-confident of his virtue, 171 f.

Children, anecdotes about, 270

Cities that perished, 48

Disciple who repented and the harlot who became a proselyte, 342

Equal (or unequal) pay for equal (or unequal) work, stories about, 287 *seq.*

God, Moses, and the big treasure store, 179 f.

God, Moses, and the community of Israel, anecdotes about, 326

God, the Attribute of Justice, the righteous, and the wicked, 271 f.

God, the nations, and the reward for fulfilling the Law, 79 *seq.*

God, Satan, and the Messiah, 306 *seq.*

God's demand for sureties from Israel that the Law would be kept, 301

God's remonstrance to the heathen who do not draw near to him, 337 f.

Good works superior to learning, anecdotes about, 153, 156 f.

Haman, Mordecai, and the horse, 94

Holy Spirit listening to the reading of the Shema, 187

Israel, anecdotes about duty towards community of, 326

Job, anecdotes about, 353

Stories and anecdotes (*Contd.*)—
King and the strange stag in his flock, 211 f.
King who gave a banquet to his servants, 310
King and his two servants who served him through love and fear, 331
King who redeemed his friend's son as a slave, 367
King's son who fell into evil ways, 356
Korah's story of the poor widow's difficulties under the Law, 239
Law, anecdotes about the giving of the, 76 f.
Man who gave money to his divorced wife, 150
Marriages, anecdotes about one-day, 44 f.
Miracles that happened because of (*a*) the man who lent tools to dig graves, (*b*) the woman who lent her oven, 238
Moses and the kid that ran away, 260
Pious man and the tax-collector, and their fate hereafter, 358
Pious pit-digger whose son died of thirst, 349
Precepts of the Law reduced from 613 to 1, 320 f.
Rabbis and their burial clothes, 273
Rabbis and their methods of praying, 121 *seq.*
Rabbis who had completely fulfilled the Law, 166
Rain, anecdotes about, 273 f.
Robbers who died and their different fates hereafter, 358
Shechinah and the criminal going to execution, 264
Woman and the denars lost in the dough, 48 f.
Woman who offered a handful of meal, 188 f.

II

Abba the Bleeder, deeds of, 113
Abba the Bleeder, his cushions and the scholars, 113
Abbahu and his son who neglected study for good works, 159
Acha b. Abba's discussion with R. Chisda about women, 217
Akiba's entombment, 340 f.

Stories and anecdotes (*Contd.*)—
Akiba's martyrdom, 32
Akiba's story of God and the four sons, 363
Assi's death-bed repentance for his shortcomings towards the community, 326 f.
Baba b. Buta and his daily offering for doubtful sins, 168
Bar Kappara who gave relief to the proconsul, 346 f.
Ben Azzai's reason for not marrying, 269
Berokah of Chuza, Elijah, the jailer, and the merry-makers, 237
Chanin ha-Nechba who was asked by children to pray for rain, 129
Chanina who refused to forgive Rab, 267 f.
Chanina whose prayer cured the son of Gamaliel, 217
Chanina's martyrdom and the executioner who repented, 373 f.
Chanina's rebuke to the man who prayed, 120
Chisda, Ulla, and the rich man's ruined house, 226 f.
Chiya b. Abba's grief and its atoning power, 304
Dama b. Netina and the jewel, 251, 346
Elazar b. Charsom who renounced riches to study the Law, 280 f.
Elazar b. Perata and Chanina b. Teradion who were arrested, 373
Elazar ben Shammua who helped a Roman who became Emperor, 347
Elazar who gave all he had to charity, 283
Elazar's advice to Mar Ukba about those who annoyed him, 96
Elazar's self-inflicted sufferings for conscience' sake, 303
Eliezer and the disciples who shortened, or lengthened, their prayers, 119 f.
Eliezer who tried to prove himself right by miracles, 247 f.
Gamaliel who waited on the wise men at his banquet, 235 f.
Gamaliel's rebuke to Rabbis whom he appointed as leaders, 299
Hillel, the proselyte, and the Golden Rule, 150

Stories and anecdotes (*Contd.*)—
Hillel's adventure on the roof in the snow, 280
Huna who bought vegetables and threw them away, 284
Huna who would not reprove Chiya to his face, 266
Jonah and his method of giving alms, 58
Jonathan who was fed in a famine, 255
Joshua b. Levi and Ula who was in hiding, 224
Joshua b. Levi, Elijah, and the Messiah, 306
Joshua b. Chananya and the boy whom he rescued, 223 f.
Joshua, the heretic, and the cock, 96
Judah the Prince and the man who ate garlic, 44
Judah the Prince's callousness to the calf, 303
Judah the Prince's toothache miraculously cured, 303
Meir and the woman to whom he gave a bill of divorcement, 44
Meir and the woman who spat in his eyes, 28
Meir, Beruria, and the wicked neighbours, 97, 263
Meir's easier ruling for others than for himself, 323
Monobaz and the distribution of his treasure to the poor, 139
Pentekaka who sold his bed and gave the proceeds to a woman, 343
Raba and the poor man, 40 f.
Raba's method of announcing his illness, 95
Simeon b. Chalafta who received a jewel by miracle and restored it, 279
Simeon b. Yochai and the snarer of birds, 229
Simeon who offered a valley of gold coins to his disciples, 279
Simon b. Elazar and the ugly man whom he insulted, 39
Tarphon, Akiba, and the discussion about learning and doing, 158

Stories and anecdotes (*Contd.*)—
Tarphon who ate figs and was beaten, 225
Tarphon's care for his mother, 249
Yannai and the ignorant man who was a peacemaker, 29
Yannai and the tree which leant over the road, 146
Yochanan and Ilfa who sat under a wall, 144
Yochanan and the man whom he called *Rayka*, 39
Yochanan b. Zakkai on his death-bed, 227 f.
Yochanan who sold his land to study the Law, 254, 283
Yose b. Kisma's refusal of wealth, 139
Yose's reply to Valeria, 269
Yose of Yodkart and the fig tree which bore fruit prematurely, 310
Zadok's dream in the ruined temple, 128
Zera and the wicked neighbours who repented, 96

Suffering, vicarious, 300 *seq.* *See also* Messiah
Superstition, Rabbis' attitude to, 192, 204, 242, 247 f. *See also* Miracles

Tit for tat (measure for measure), doctrine of, 51, 144 f., 286 *seq.*; Klostermann cited on, 51; its bearing on doctrine of eternal punishment, 286. *See also* 'Resist not evil'; Sin, its connection with physical suffering
Tithing, law of, 330
Truthfulness, unqualified, 50. *See also* Oaths

Unchastity, 40 *seq.*, 66. *See also* Marital relations; Intention and deed; Unclean acts
Unclean acts, punishment for, 46
Universalism. *See* Gentiles; Kingdom of God; Particularism

Women, attitude of Jesus and Rabbis to, 47 f., 217 f.

Yetzer ha-Ra, 20, 24, 88, 93, 164 *seq.*, 180 *seq.* *See also* Sin